Economics Essays

Springer
Berlin
Heidelberg
New York
Barcelona
Hong Kong
London
Milan
Paris
Singapore
Tokyo

Gérard Debreu · Wilhelm Neuefeind
Walter Trockel
Editors

Economics Essays

A Festschrift for
WERNER HILDENBRAND

With 33 Figures
and 12 Tables

Springer

Prof. Dr. Gérard Debreu
University of California
549 Evans Hall # 3880
Berkeley CA 94720-3880
USA

Prof. Dr. Wilhelm Neuefeind
Washington University in St. Louis
Department of Economics
Box 1208
St. Louis, MO 63130
USA

Prof. Dr. Walter Trockel
Universität Bielefeld
Institut für Mathematische Wirtschaftsforschung (IMW)
Postfach 100131
33501 Bielefeld
Germany

ISBN 3-540-41882-2 Springer-Verlag Berlin Heidelberg New York

Library of Congress Cataloging-in-Publication Data applied for
Die Deutsche Bibliothek – CIP-Einheitsaufnahme
Economics Essays: A Festschrift for Werner Hildenbrand / Gérard Debreu ... ed. – Berlin; Heidelberg; New York; Barcelona; Hong Kong; London; Milan; Paris; Singapore; Tokyo: Springer, 2001
ISBN 3-540-41882-2

Springer-Verlag Berlin Heidelberg New York
a member of BertelsmannSpringer Science+Business Media GmbH
http://www.springer.de

Hardcover-Design: Erich Kirchner, Heidelberg

SPIN 10834663 42/2202-5 4 3 2 1 0 – Printed on acid-free paper

Preface

Back in the good old days on the fourth floor of the Altbau of Bonn's Juridicum, Werner Hildenbrand put an end to a debate about a festschrift in honor of an economist on the occasion of his turning 60 with a laconic: "Much too early." Remembering his position five years ago, we did not dare to think about one for him. But now he has turned 65. If consulted, he would most likely still answer: "Much too early." However, he has to take his official retirement, and we believe that this is the right moment for such an endeavor. No doubt Werner Hildenbrand will not really retire. As professor emeritus, free from the constraints of a rigid teaching schedule and the burden of committee meetings, he will be able to indulge his passions. We expect him to pursue, with undiminished enthusiasm, his research, travel, golfing, the arts, and culinary pleasures – escaping real retirement.

He will leave a tremendous void at the university even if he will stay on and continue his scholarly pursuits in Bonn. He made the University of Bonn Germany's leading institution for economic theory. Without him, the university would not have been able to keep two *Sonderforschungsbereiche* in economics for so long. They provided the means to attract a large number of distinguished researchers from around the world to work or give seminars in and spread the word about Bonn. All contributors to this volume spent time in Bonn. He loved to work in the department: he turned down several prestigious offers from other institutions in Germany and abroad, preferring to stay in Bonn.

Yet the influence of Werner Hildenbrand's work, scholarly and otherwise, reaches far beyond Bonn. The depth and breadth of his scholarly work are impressive, and his influence on Economics and economists through his activities at CORE, in Paris, Florence, Strasbourg, Berkeley, and Stanford, among other places, had a significant impact on the profession. He was the founding editor of *The Journal of Mathematical Economics*, offering scholars the opportunity to publish theoretical results which other journals might have considered technically too demanding. Without his work, *Mathematical Economics* would not have become what it is today. He made it a regular and respected topic at the famous *Mathematical Research Institute* in Oberwolfach. He co-founded the enormously successful *European Doctoral Program*, focussed on theoretical economics, and sponsored and organized the BOWOs, the important Bonn Workshops on Economic Theory. In the Theoretische Ausschuss of the Verein für Socialpolitik, whose staid members had long focussed on topics no longer central to economics, he opened the door for modern economic theory.

Not surprisingly, Werner Hildenbrand was often honored: He received the prestigious Leibniz, Max Planck, and von Humboldt-Gay Lussac prizes and presented the Walras-Bowley, Marshall, Schumpeter, and Thünen Lectures.

An early Fellow of the Econometric Society, he was elected into its Council several times. He was the Program Chairman for its 4th World Congress. He is a member of several academies and an honorary member of the American Economic Association. He was asked to serve on the editorial boards of highly ranked journals.
His influence is perpetuated through his former doctoral students, who now work in a wide array of areas, including Economic Theory, Game Theory, Industrial Organization, Public Finance, Financial Economics, Experimental Economics, and Applied Econometrics – many as professors throughout the world. As an advisor and friend he shaped both their scholarly views and their professional careers.
Many other people have reason to honor Werner Hildenbrand, reason to be grateful to him. Those of us who contributed to the creation of this *festschrift*, want to take this occasion to thank him. Some have benefited as his students, some influenced his scholarly interests and development and were influenced in turn, and some have collaborated with him or do so still.
The editors would like to thank the authors, Ms. Adelheid Baker in Bielefeld, Ms. Karen Rensing in St. Louis, the Zentrum für interdisziplinäre Forschung (*ZiF*) at the University of Bielefeld for its hospitality to W.N. during the project *Making Choices* in 1999/2000, and, in particular, Washington University in St. Louis, where the lion's share of the editorial work was done.

Werner, as described by Gérard in his *Introduction*, there has been a radical change in your scholarly work. You have been innovative and thought provoking while remaining consistent – a feat few ever achieve. We hope you carry on just that way.

Ad multos annos, Werner!

January 2001

Wilhelm Neuefeind *Saint Louis, Missouri*
Walter Trockel *Bielefeld*

Contents

Introduction

Gérard Debreu

University of California

Werner Hildenbrand is two economists.

The first was one of the more sophisticated mathematical economists of 1974, the time when his book, *Core and Equilibria of a Large Economy*, appeared. In this role, in the context of General Equilibrium Analysis, he published, sometimes with co-authors, altogether more than thirty theoretical articles on measure spaces of economic agents, or on mathematical questions directly related to them.

The second is an econometrician of great originality who contributed to raise the field in which he was working to its highest levels, shunning any statement about the economy that cannot be supported, in the strictest manner, by empirical evidence. In this capacity he published about as many articles as in the first (according to a 1998 bibliography), several of them with other authors.

The metamorphosis from one incarnation to the next was reported in the first five paragraphs of the Preface of his *Market Demand* (1994). Some of the circumstances in which this critical change occurred are the source of vivid memories. On the eve of a few days vacation, I asked him to stay in the house that was then my residence in Northern California. He was not there when I returned, but he had left, in the living room, a piece of paper that told, concisely, of the unexpected results he had obtained, and that he published shortly in *Econometrica*, 1983. In this article, he proved the following theorem, where the common demand function $f(p,w)$ of all agents is assumed to satisfy the weak axiom of revealed preference (for all pairs (p^1,w^1) and (p^2,w^2), $p^2.f(p^1,w^1) \leq w^2$ implies $p^1.f(p^2,w^2) \geq w^1$). If the distribution of individual total expenditure w has a non-increasing density ρ, then the market demand function $F(p)(= \int f(p,w)\rho(w)dw)$ is monotone, i.e., for any two price-vectors p and q, $(q-p).(F(q)-F(p)) \leq 0$. (In particular, if all prices but one, the hth, remain fixed, $(q^h - p^h)\left(F(q^h) - F(p^h)\right) \leq 0$ and all partial demand curves are non-increasing.)

In this paper, on page 998 he also notes "that aggregating individual demand over a large group of individuals can lead to properties of the market demand function F which, in general, individual demand functions do not possess." This formulation prefigures the full research program that he carried out later, and that he describes as follows in the Preface of his book *Market Demand* (1994) "to analyze which new properties are *created* by the aggregation procedure. I want to defend in this book the thesis that "sufficient heterogeneity" of a large population of households leads to useful properties of the mean demand of the population."

His scientific career is divided, most naturally, in two main periods.

From his birth, on May 25, 1936, to the end of his formal studies in 1964 in Heidelberg, Germany, under Professors Köthe and Krickeberg, twenty-eight years elapsed. Of these he lived the last eight years (1956-64) in Heidelberg (where he was, in succession, Teaching Assistant (1958-61), Research Assistant (1962-4), Lecturer (1964-6), Project Leader (1965-9)), with the exception of one year (1961-2), when he was a Research Fellow at the University of Bonn, Germany, where he later became a Professor in 1969.

After the first world congress of the Econometric Society in Rome, Italy, in 1965, when we met for the first time, he spent a brief period (1965-6), lecturing in Statistics in Karlsruhe, Germany, and then began, over the next 20 years, a long series of visits to Berkeley, California (Assistant Professor in 1966-7; Associate Professor in 1967-8; Professor in 1969-70, in 1973-4, and in 1985-6). In particular, in 1966-70, he was in Berkeley almost three years out of four, as well as a visiting Professor of Economics at Stanford University, California, for six months in 1970. He seemed to have become a permanent resident of the San Francisco Bay Area. In the mean time, he was Research Professor at the University of Louvain,Belgium (1968-76), and Professor of Economics at the University of Bonn from 1969 to this day. He was also a visitor at the European University Institute in Florence, Italy; at the University of California in San Diego, California; at the University Louis Pasteur in Strasbourg, France; at the Chaire Européenne du Collège de France, Paris, France, in 1993-4.

Among the honors that he received, only a small international minority will be noted. He was the Walras-Bowley lecturer at the meeting of the Econometric Society in Montreal, Canada, in 1979; the Marshall lecturer at the meeting of the European Economic Association in Bologna, Italy, in 1988; an Honorary member of the American Economic Association in 1995; the Schumpeter lecturer at the meeting of the European Economic Association in Toulouse, France, in 1997. In this second period, he published, in addition to the two books already mentioned, *Lineare ökonomische Modelle*, 1975 (with K. Hildenbrand), and *Introduction to Equilibrium Analysis*, 1976 (with A. Kirman), which became *Equilibrium Analysis*, 1988 (with A. Kirman). When teaching a graduate introductory course in mathematical economics, one is invited to prepare a list of books that auditors are advised to read in connection with the instruction. For many years, the book by Hildenbrand and Kirman headed that list. To the credit of his energy, and of the authority he had acquired in the profession, he, also, edited *Advances in Economic Theory*, 1982, and *Advances in Econometrics*, 1982; *Contributions to Mathematical Economics*, 1986 (with A. Mas-Colell), and *Handbook of Mathematical Economics*, vol. IV, 1991 (with H. Sonnenschein). Finally, he created in 1974, (and was, for eleven years, the editor of) the *Journal of Mathematical Economics.* Thereby he powerfully helped the development of mathematical economics. During his editorship, the first volumes of JME, and, often, each one of the issues in these volumes, contained articles making significant, occasionally far-reaching, progress in economic theory.

In the work on GE analysis that he did first (1965-73), his main mathematical tool is measure theory, to which he devotes, in the first part of his *Core and Equilibria of a Large Economy*, forty pages (half of the number of pages he allocates to pure mathematics in Part I, the mathematical introduction). That part became a major source of references on measure theory for economists.

Central for Werner Hildenbrand's study is a concept due to Aumann (1964 and 1966). A measure space of economic agents is mathematically a set A of elements, each one of them representing an agent $a \in A$; a σ-algebra $\mathcal{A}$ of subsets of A, the coalitions ($\mathcal{A}$ is closed under complementation and countable unions); a countably additive counting measure $\nu : \mathcal{A} \to [0,1]$, where, denoting by N a set of integers, $\nu(\bigcup_{i \in N} A_i) = \sum_{i \in N} \nu(A_i)$, provided that the sets A_i $(i \in N)$ are mutually disjoint.

The measure ν in $(A, \mathcal{A}, \nu)$, mathematically, is a probability (with a different interpretation). This brought Werner Hildenbrand back to the beginning of his mathematical career when he taught probability theory. In his work, the results concerning that theory cover a wide range from Analytic Sets to the article of Yosida and Hewitt (1952). Especially important among them is the theorem of Lyapunov (1940). In its statement, one needs the concept of an atom for a real measure μ. The set F in $\mathcal{A}$ is an *atom* if $[\mu(F) > 0$, and $E \in \mathcal{A}$ and $E \subset F]$ implies [either $\mu(E) = \mu(F)$, or $\mu(E) = 0]$. Lyapunov's theorem asserts that if ν_i $(i = 1, \ldots, m)$ are atomless measures on $(A, \mathcal{A})$, then the set of points in $\mathbb{R}^m$ with coordinates $\nu_1(E), \cdots, \nu_m(E)$ for every E in $\mathcal{A}$, is convex and closed.

This theorem is the mathematical basis for one of the most significant discoveries of economic theory in the past fifty years (a discovery gradually made by M. Farrell, *JPE*, 1959; J. Rothenberg, *JPE*, 1960; and, above all, Aumann, *Econometrica*, 1964), that assuming the measure ν in $(A, \mathcal{A}, \nu)$ is atomless dispenses one from assuming convexity of preferences for individual agents.

The fundamental result of Lyapunov was introduced in economic theory by Vind, *International Economic Review*, 1964. A form can be given, without appealing to measure theory, in the following fashion (Shapley-Folkman theorem quoted, and extended by Starr, *Econometrica*, 1969). Let there be a sequence of compact, non-empty subsets of $\mathbb{R}^l$, bounded in a ball centered at the origin with radius b; let $\mathcal{F}$ be a finite subfamily of that sequence; and let $\sharp\mathcal{F}$ be the number of elements of $\mathcal{F}$. Then the mean of this finite subfamily, when $\sharp\mathcal{F}$ is arbitrarily large, becomes convex in the following sense. The non-convexity $\delta(X)$ of a subset X of $\mathbb{R}^l$ can be measured, in a precise way, by the maximum of the distance from a point x in coX to X, where coX denotes the convex hull of $X : \delta(X) = \max_{x \in coX} d(x, X)$. In the latter equality, $d(x, X) = \min_{y \in X} d(x, y)$, where $d(x, y)$ is defined as a distance between two points x and y of $\mathbb{R}^l$. Thus, a compact set X is convex if, and only if, $\delta(X) = 0$. Apply this definition of non-convexity to the set $X_{\mathcal{F}} = \frac{1}{\sharp\mathcal{F}} \sum_{S \in \mathcal{F}} S$. One has $\delta(X_{\mathcal{F}}) \leq c/\sharp\mathcal{F}$, where c is a constant depending only on the bound b, and on the dimension l of the space $\mathbb{R}^l$. In particular, $\lim_{\sharp\mathcal{F} \to \infty} \delta(X_{\mathcal{F}}) = 0$.

But, even though a mathematical economist may write a great deal, it usually remains impossible to make, from his works, a reliable conjecture about his personality, because, in particular, formalized expression has deprived an author of his literary style for several decades. This makes the reader unable to guess, for example, that one of the main traits of Werner Hildenbrand's character is his straightforwardness that goes far beyond what is common in human discourse. The fact that his response is so direct sometimes seems excessive, it may, however, be the origin of steadfast friendships.

The Rationale for Measurability*

Robert J. Aumann

Department of Mathematics and Center for Rationality and Interactive Decision Theory, The Hebrew University of Jerusalem

Measure spaces — specifically non-atomic ones — have been used to model large economies for nearly four decades. With his many research and expository contributions to the subject, and the many students whom he inspired with his enthusiasm and intellectual drive, Werner Hildenbrand deserves much of the credit for this development. In this brief note we explore the conceptual underpinnings of the measure-space model.

An economy is modelled as a set A — the set of *agents* — together with a family $\mathcal{A}$ of subsets of A, called *measurable* sets, on which the various measures that characterize the economy are defined. The family $\mathcal{A}$ is taken to be a σ-field, i.e., closed under complementation and countable unions. For definiteness, take A to be the closed unit interval $[0, 1]$. If $\mathcal{A}$ is too large — if there are too many measurable sets — then it becomes difficult to define measures. For example, if *all* subsets of A are measurable, then under the continuum hypothesis, the only measures are the purely atomic ones — those that assign positive measure to some denumerable subset of A, and 0 to its complement.[1] If we want to allow non-atomic measures like Lebesgue measure, which assigns to each interval the length of that interval, we must restrict the field $\mathcal{A}$ of measurable sets. This can be done, e.g., by taking $\mathcal{A}$ to be the *Borel* field, defined as the smallest σ-field that contains all intervals.

This motivation for measurability is mathematical — it explains why taking all sets as measurable will not allow us to construct the models that we wish to construct. But the conceptual meaning of measurability remains somewhat of a puzzle. In the continuum (non-atomic) model of an economy, individual traders presumably correspond to single points. In thinking of sets of traders (or coalitions), there seems to be no good reason to forbid *any* set from forming, including a set that is not Borel measurable or indeed not Lebesgue measurable. Yet in defining, say, the core of a nonatomic economy, we restrict the "coalitions" to be Borel (or Lebesgue) measurable sets. To be sure, we would have *mathematical* difficulties if we would not do so. But what is the *conceptual* justification of this restriction?

To answer this question, we must rethink the notion of continuum economy. A continuum economy is a model; obviously no real economy actually

* Research support from the National Science Foundation under Grant SBR 97 30205 is gratefully acknowledged.

[1] See, e.g., Sierpinski,(1956), Proposition C_{53}.

has a continuum of agents. Individual agents in the real economy may be modelled by individual points[2] in the continuum. But that does *not* necessarily mean that coalitions in the real economy — which may indeed consist of arbitrary sets of real agents — are necessarily modellable by arbitrary subsets of the continuum.

For example, any coalition in the real economy has a total endowment; at given prices p, it has a total demand. These quantities are essential in specifying and analyzing the economy. Therefore coalitions should be modelled as sets for which these quantities can be defined. These quantities are *measures.* Thus coalitions must be modelled as *measurable* sets.

Differently put: The notion of an infinite set depends on the context and the application. In the economic context, the finite sets that arise are endowed with economically significant measures. Therefore, their analogues in the nonatomic model must also be endowed with measures. And so, they *must* be measurable.

We must not let ourselves get carried away by words, and in particular by the word "set." Unlike finite sets, infinite sets are abstractions. During the century and a half since Cantor, mathematicians have become used to a particular intuitive notion of "set;" even so, this notion has had to be modified and refined several times. At this time a particular notion, defined by a particular axiomatization (ZFC), has become widely accepted. But still it is by no means the only one; there are many variations, even within set theory. For example, one may or may not add the continuum hypothesis to the axioms; one may or may not remove the axiom of choice; and if one does remove it, one may or may not replace it by the axiom of determinateness. These variations are only a few out of many, and all of them profoundly affect the intuitive notion of "set."

Moreover, all these variations deal with only one aspect of sets: their cardinality. Finite sets have other aspects as well. For example, when discussing subsets S of a finite set A, the proportion $|S|/|A|$ — how much of A is in S — is often of interest. Though this sounds closely related to cardinality, Cantorian set theory has no way of generalizing it to infinite sets. In applications such as ours, there may well be various parameters — "weights" — associated with the points in a finite set (like the endowment of an agent); the "total weight" of a finite set then becomes relevant. Again, Cantorian set theory is unable to handle this in the infinite case. Other applications may involve other attributes of finite sets, and then the appropriate infinite generalization should be able to deal with *them.*

In brief, the Cantorian notion of set is just one way of thinking of (infinite) sets; there are other ways. There is no unique "right" way, and the most appropriate way in any given context depends on that context — on the application being discussed.

---

[2] An alternative is to think of individuals as "infinitesimal sets;" see Aumann and Shapley (1974), Section 29, pp. 176-178.

In the economic application being discussed here, large finite sets S of agents are modelled by infinite sets. Such an S constitutes a certain proportion of the set A of all agents, and it has a certain total endowment vector, which is important when defining, say, the core (as well as the Shapley value and other economic concepts). So in the non-atomic model, S must be modelled in a way that allows one to associate quantities like total endowment with it. Such quantities are *measures.* That is, S must be *measurable.*

What we're suggesting is that for our purposes — in our application — *all* "sets" should be thought of as measurable. The generalization of the concept of a finite set that is appropriate for our purposes is not just any set (in the Cantorian sense), but a measurable set. Large finite coalitions do have a total endowment; so if we wish to model such coalitions when we go to the non-atomic model, we must restrict ourselves to measurable sets. If it isn't measurable, we shouldn't think of it as a set at all.

Actually, the idea that "all sets are Borel" is not all that revolutionary. For a set to be Borel means that it is constructible in a specified way from intervals. Some kind of constructibility is implicit also in ZFC, otherwise one runs into the classic set-theoretic paradoxes.

But that is not the viewpoint we espouse here. Rather, it is that the notion of "set" (finite or infinite) that is appropriate to the economic application is a *measurable* set, not just a set in the sense of Cantor's set theory.

References

1. Aumann, R. J., and L. S. Shapley, *Values of Non-Atomic Games,* Princeton University Press, 1974.
2. Sierpinski,W., *Hypothèse du Continu,* Chelsea, 1956.

Inferior Goods, Giffen Goods, and Shochu*

Shmuel Baruch[1] and Yakar Kannai[2]

[1] School of Business, University of Utah, UT 84112, USA
[2] Department of Mathematics, The Weizmann Institute of Science, Rehovot, Israel

Abstract. According to a well-known result by W. Hildenbrand [6], if all consumers possess the same demand function and the density of the expenditure distribution is decreasing, than the average income effect term is non-negative even if inferior goods are present, so that the aggregate demand must be monotone. We show that if the expenditure density is uni-modal and a certain relation between the income density and individual demand is satisfied, than the average income effect term is negative and Giffen goods are not ruled out. We show that the lowest-grade rice-based Japanese spirit (shochu) satisfies this condition. The data suggest that this commodity might be a Giffen good.

1 Introduction

Consider an individual facing a price vector $\mathbf{p} \in R^n$ and having budget I. Denote his demand for the j-th commodity by $f_j(\mathbf{p}, I)$. Recall that the j-th commodity is said to be *inferior* (at $(\mathbf{p}, I)$) if $\frac{\partial f_j(\mathbf{p},I)}{\partial I} < 0$ and *Giffen* if $\frac{\partial f_j(\mathbf{p},I)}{\partial p_j} \geq 0$. (If a good is not inferior then it is said to be *normal*. A good which is normal at all income levels cannot be Giffen — see section 2.) It is well known ([8],[9]) that no simple condition rules out Giffen goods. It is also known that inferior goods exist in abundance (at least when incomes are sufficiently high). What is somewhat puzzling is the almost non-existence of Giffen goods for aggregate market demand ("Such goods are more frequent in exam questions than in real life" ([2], p. 8)).

The first breakthrough came in [6], where it was shown that if all consumers in the economy have the same demand function $\mathbf{f}(\mathbf{p}, I)$ and if the expenditure distribution density $\rho(I)$ is decreasing, then the "law of demand" holds, i.e., the price differential of demand is a strictly negative-definite matrix. In particular, there are no Giffen goods. Actually it is proved that the average income effect term $\int f_j(\mathbf{p}, I)\frac{\partial f_j(\mathbf{p},I)}{\partial I}\rho(I)dI$ is non-negative (note that our sign convention differs from that of [6]). Underlying this result is the observation that for a sufficiently low income, every good is normal. Thus, if

* This research was partly supported by a MINERVA foundation (Germany) grant. We are indebted to the participants of seminars at the University of Bonn, University of Minnesota, University of Bielefeld, and Central Economic Mathematical Institute (Moscow), for helpful suggestions.

there are enough poor people in the economy that have not reached their saturation points, market demand function behaves as if goods were normal.

In the next section we show that if the expenditure distribution is unimodal and the degree in which the good fails to be normal is related appropriately to the distribution then the average income effect term is negative. (This happens if the commodity is so inferior that most poor households have reached their saturation points.) Thus we exhibit a case where at least a necessary condition for the Giffen effect is satisfied. In the search for possible candidates for Giffen goods, we came across the Japanese alcoholic beverage Shochu. This is a very low grade of "spirit" distilled from rice, and as the cheapest of all alcoholic beverages is consumed mainly by the poor. Based on data in [1] we could show that not only is shochu an inferior good, but it seems to satisfy (if we are willing to make some assumptions) the condition for a negative average mean income effect term. It appears that shochu may be a candidate for a Giffen good. The description and analysis of the data is presented in section 3.

Many reasons were suggested in the literature for the difficulty of observing a Giffen good. A stability argument put forward in [3] shows that only rarely could a Giffen good be observed. Moreover, enough dispersity of preference relations (or of demand functions) effectively rule out the Giffen effect (see [4] for an early result). Since we use time series we are forced to use only a relatively short time interval. In a longer interval many characteristics would change and the effect will no longer be discernible. In particular we make the assumption (clearly wrong in the long run) that the demand for shochu does not change much over time or with expenditure.

The situation considered here (partial equilibrium) differs from that studied in [10] (general equilibrium—endogenous I). The role of I is played by the budget allotted by the household for total living expenditures. We believe that to assume that there is no contemporaneous relation between prices and income is a reasonable assumption in a society where the disposable income of most households is primarily predetermined (by wages etc.). Therefore, we follow the approach taken in Hildebrand [6] and others and assume that at a given point is time, prices do not effect incomes.

2 Mean income effect terms

Recall the Slutsky relation: Let the demand $f_i(\mathbf{p}, I)$ (for the i-th commodity) be a continuously differentiable function of $(\mathbf{p}, I) \in R^{n+1}_{++}$. Then the substitution matrix $S = \{s_{ij}\}_{i,j=1}^n$ defined by

$$s_{ij} = \frac{\partial f_i(\mathbf{p}, I)}{\partial p_j} + f_j(\mathbf{p}, I)\frac{\partial f_i(\mathbf{p}, I)}{\partial I} . \qquad (1)$$

is symmetric, negative semidefinite, and negative definite on the orthogonal complement of $\mathbf{p}$. In particular $s_{i,i} < 0$. The term $f_j(\mathbf{p}, I)\frac{\partial f_i(\mathbf{p},I)}{\partial I}$ represents the *income* effect. For our purposes it is convenient to rewrite (1) as

$$\frac{\partial f_i(\mathbf{p}, I)}{\partial p_j} = s_{ij} - f_j(\mathbf{p}, I)\frac{\partial f_i(\mathbf{p}, I)}{\partial I} . \tag{2}$$

Setting $i = j$ in (2) we see that a good may be Giffen only if it is inferior somewhere. From now on we consider only (except in Remark 2) diagonal terms ($i = j$ — own price derivatives) and drop the subindices for goods and prices. Suppose that our economy consists of a continuum of consumers who differ only by the amount I they set aside for expenditure (but they all have the same demand function f). Let $\rho(I)$ denote the density of the distribution of I (so that $\int \rho(I)dI = 1$). Then the (mean) market demand is given by $\int f(p, I)\rho(I)dI$. A necessary condition for the market demand to exhibit a Giffen behavior (i.e., that $\frac{\partial \int f(p,I)\rho(I)dI}{\partial p}$ be non-negative) is that the mean income effect term, $\int f(p, I)\frac{\partial f(p,I)}{\partial I}\rho(I)dI$, is strictly negative. Hildenbrand [6] noted that if the density $\rho(I)$ is a decreasing function of I then this term is non-negative (even if the commodity is inferior for certain values of I).

We now see what may happen if the distribution is uni-modal. We assume that the following holds:

(**UM**) : The density of the expenditure distribution is a C^1 function supported on a compact interval $[0, R]$ with a unique maximum at $x = a \in (0, R)$.

It follows that for every $y \in (0, \rho(a))$ the exist numbers b^l_y and b^r_y such that $b^l_y < a < b^r_y < R$ and $\rho(b^l_y) = \rho(b^r_y) = y$. Moreover, the numbers b^l_y and b^r_y are uniquely determined and depend continuously on y. We relate the inferior character of the commodity (with respect to the individual demand function $f(p, I)$ at a given price $p \in P$ where P is an open set of price vectors) to the expenditure distribution by assuming the following:

(**ID**) : For all $y \in (0, \rho(a))$ and $p \in P$, $f(p, b^l_y) > f(p, b^r_y)$.

A demand function and a density satisfying (**UM**) and (**ID**) (for a certain fixed p) are illustrated in Fig. 1.

We may now state the main result of this section.

Theorem 1 *If the assumptions (***UM***) and (***ID***) hold, and all individuals have the same demand function f, then the mean income effect term is negative for each $p \in P$, i.e.,*

$$\int f(p, I)\frac{\partial f(p, I)}{\partial I}\rho(I)dI < 0 . \tag{3}$$

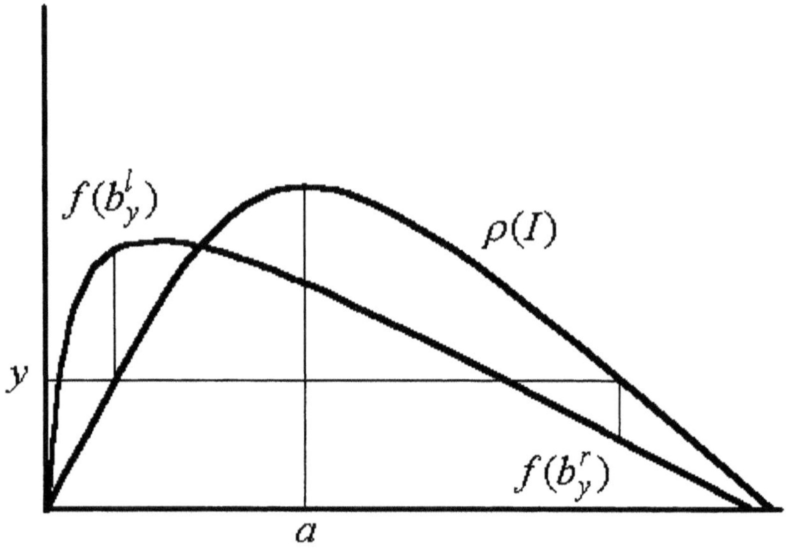

Fig. 1. Illustration of (**UM**) and (**ID**)

Proof: Integrating by parts, we see that

$$\int f(p,I)\frac{\partial f(p,I)}{\partial I}\rho(I)dI = \frac{f(p,I)^2}{2}\rho(I)\Big|_{I=0}^{I=R} - \int \frac{f(p,I)^2}{2}\rho'(I)dI \ . \tag{4}$$

By assumption, $\frac{f(p,I)^2}{2}\rho(I) = 0$ at $I = 0$ and $I = R$. Hence the mean income effect term is equal to

$$-\int_0^a \frac{f(p,I)^2}{2}\rho'(I)dI - \int_a^R \frac{f(p,I)^2}{2}\rho'(I)dI \ . \tag{5}$$

We now introduce the new integration variable $y = \rho(I)$ on each of the intervals $(0, a)$ and (a, R) (thus $I = b_y^l$ or $I = b_y^r$), and noting that $\rho(I)$ is increasing on $(0, a)$ and decreasing on (a, R), we find that

$$\int f(p,I)\frac{\partial f(p,I)}{\partial I}\rho(I)dI = -\int_0^{\rho(a)} \frac{f(p,b_y^l)^2}{2}dy + \int_0^{\rho(a)} \frac{f(p,b_y^r)^2}{2}dy < 0, \tag{6}$$

where the last inequality follows from (**ID**). QED

Remark 1: We could replace the assumption that ρ is compactly supported by a suitable decay condition on the product $f(p,I)^2\rho(I)$. Similarly, it is possible to replace $(0, R)$ by another interval (contained in the non-negative half line) and the assumptions about the vanishing of f and ρ at the ends of the interval could be relaxed.

Remark 2: Recall that the (Jacobian) matrix of price derivatives $D\mathbf{f}(\mathbf{p})$ is negative semi-definite if for every vector $\mathbf{v} \in R^n$

$$\sum_{i,j=1}^{n} \frac{\partial f_i(\mathbf{p}, I)}{\partial p_j} v_i v_j \leq 0 \,. \tag{7}$$

(The left hand side may be interpreted as the own price derivative of a *package* of commodities—compare [7], p.172.) The corresponding mean income effect term is $\int \sum_{i,j=1}^{n} f_j(\mathbf{p}, I) \frac{\partial f_i(\mathbf{p},I)}{\partial I} v_i v_j \rho(I) dI$. This term is positive if $\mathbf{v}$ is proportional to $\mathbf{p}$. If $\mathbf{v} \neq \mathbf{p}$ we may generalize Theorem 1 to obtain negative mean income effect terms if for all $y \in (0, \rho(a))$, $\sum_i^n f_j(\mathbf{p},, b_y^l) v_j > \sum_i^n f_j(\mathbf{p},, b_y^r) v_j$ ((**ID**) holds for the package). The proof follows that of Theorem 1.

3 Shochu

The following rice-based alcoholic beverages are listed in [1] (ordered according to increasing price): shochu, second grade sake, first grade sake, and special grade sake. Shochu (distilled alcohol) is consumed more by the poor than by the rich. On the other hand, special grade sake is by far a rich person beverage. This is illustrated by Table 1, where the total expenditure for alcoholic beverages and the consumption of shochu and of special grade sake are listed (for the year 1987).

Table 1. Inferiority of Shochu

Income quintile	Living expenditure (Thousand Yen)	Alcoholic beverage expenditure (Yen)	Shochu consumption (100 ml.)	sp. gr. Sake consumption (100 ml.)
1	2113	37,822	6,910	311
2	2760	46,837	5,894	637
3	3164	51,155	5,242	415
4	3779	54,755	5,478	674
5	5040	60,003	3,946	1022

It is possible (in analogy to the classical story about potatoes) that as the price of shochu goes up, poor people who want to drink the same amount of

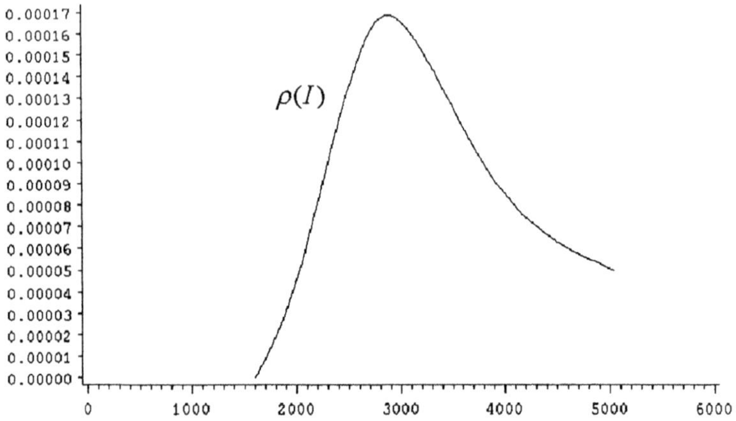

Fig. 2. Density of Living Expenditures (in Thousand Yen)

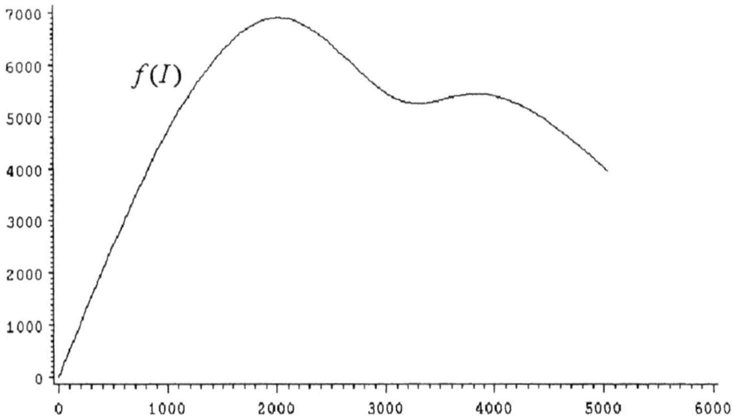

Fig. 3. The Engel Curve: The Horizontal Axis Shows Total Annual Living Expenditure in Thousand Yen; The Vertical Axis Shows Quantity of Shochu Consumed (in 100 ml.)

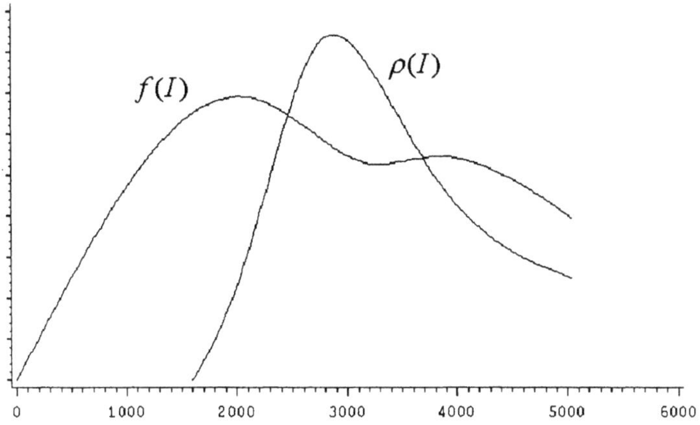

Fig. 4. Combined Engel Curve and Density of Living Expenditures

alcohol (perhaps due to an addiction), have to give up the more expensive alcoholic drinks, and therefore consume more shochu.

As a first step we would like to estimate the mean income effect term for shochu, or at least to determine its sign. To this end, time-series data are not appropriate, and we have to use cross-sectional data. Since the published data do not provide us with finer cross-sectional data, we use Table (1) to estimate the distribution of Income and the Engel curve (consumption as a function of income or of living expenditure) under the assumption that all individuals possess the same demand function. See figures 2 and 3 respectively. Since the conditions of the Theorem in section 2 are invariant under rescaling of the vertical axis, we provide in Figure 4 a draw of both of the curves after rescaling the vertical axis. It clearly appears that Condition (**ID**) holds and hence the mean income effect term is negative.

We now turn to examine the movements of prices and quantities consumed of shochu and special grade sake. We had data for special grade sake for the period January 1987 through March 1989. While we had data for other beverages for more extended periods, we decided to analyze shochu for the same period. When using time series one has to verify that there are no appreciable changes in the structure of the economy (such as population shifts, changes in cost of living, and so on). During the later part of 1989 (due to the illness and then the death of the emperor?) we could observe some changes. On the other hand, the period chosen is characterized by stability.

We estimate demand for a beverage by regressing the logarithms of quantities consumed on the log of the prices. We use a dummy variable dec equal to 1 if the month is December (during that month there is a large increase in alcohol consumption). To identify demand we used the one month lagged prime interest rate — it is unlikely that this variable influences demand, but it probably does have an effect on supply, and thus may be used as an identifying variable. Lagged interest (int(-1)) and dec are used as instruments (exogenous) variables as we apply a three-stage estimation method for the demand-and-supply model ([5],[11]). For the demand equation we also add an autoregressive term AR(1), and iterate 3sls ([11]).

The results are summarized in the following tables (numbers in brackets are the p values – the levels of significance – of the regression coefficients):

Table 2. First Stage

Dependent Variable	Dec	interest(-1)	R^2	DW
shochu price	-.024 (.04)	-.03 (.001)	.40	1.40
sp. gr. sake price	.058 (.005)	-.045 (.004)	.25	1.64

Table 3. Demand

Dependent Variable	Dec	own price	R^2	AR(1)	DW
shochu consumption	.62 (.000)	8.81 (.004)	.21	.59 (.02)	1.27
sp. gr. sake consumption	2.56 (.000)	-6.11 (.03)	.70	-.44 (.001)	1.96

It appears from Table 2 that the lagged interest rate may indeed be utilized as an identifying variable. The differing signs of the own price elasticities for shochu and special grade sake Table 3 suggest that while special grade sake is clearly a normal commodity, shochu may be a Giffen good. (We note that for first and second grade sake the elasticities are not statistically significant, but second grade had a positive price elasticity whereas first grade has a negative one.)

References

1. Annual report on the family income and expenditure survey (1987-1989), Statistics Bureau, Management and Coordination Agency, Japan.
2. Cassels, J.W.S. (1981) Economics for mathematicians. Cambridge University Press, Cambridge, UK.
3. Dougan W. R. (1982) Giffen Good and Law of Demand. J. Political Econ. **90**, 8009-8015.

4. Grandmont J.M. (1987) Distributions of preferences and the "law of demand". Econometrica **55**, 155–161.
5. Gujarati, D.N. (1995) Basic econometrics. 3rd ed. McGraw-Hill, New York.
6. Hildenbrand, W. (1983) On the "law of demand". Econometrica **51**, 997–1019.
7. Hurwicz L., Jordan J., Kannai Y. (1987) On the demand generated by a smooth concavifiable preference ordering. J. Math. Econ. **16**, 169–189.
8. Kannai, Y. (1989) A characterization of monotone individual demand functions. J. Math. Econ. **18**, 87–94.
9. Mityuschin, L.G., Polterovich, V.M. (1978) Criteria for monotonicity of demand functions (in Russian), Ekonomiki i Mathematicheskii Metody bf 14, 122–128.
10. Nachbar, J.H. (1998) The last word on Giffen goods? Econ. Theory **11**, 403–412.
11. Pindyck R.S., Rubinfeld D.L. (1991) Econometric models and economic forecasts. 3rd ed. McGraw-Hill, New York.

Information and Efficiency in Coordination Games: Recent Experimental Results

Siegfried K. Berninghaus and Karl-Martin Ehrhart

Institute of Statistics and Mathematical Economics
University of Karlsruhe

Abstract. Previous experimental results of repeated coordination games show that subjects often end up in "poor" equilibria. Strategic uncertainty about the opponents' moves induces players to select poor, but secure, equilibria. In our paper, we investigate how public information on previous moves of opponents may be used to reduce strategic uncertainty and, therefore, favor coordination on superior equilibria.

1 Introduction

Interest in coordination games arose in the eighties when theoretical results were confronted with experimental evidence. Simple, symmetric normal form coordination games are characterized by multiple equilibria which can even be Pareto-ranked. From a theoretical viewpoint, the problem of strategy choice in such games can be solved by the payoff-dominance principle which requires that completely rational players choose the strategy resulting in the highest payoff level (Pareto-dominant equilibrium).[1] In a series of stimulating papers, however, van Huyck et al. and Cooper et al. report on experimental results which are in sharp contrast to the Pareto-dominance principle [1], [2], [3], [4], [5]. In simple symmetric 2×2 games with two symmetric Nash equilibria in pure strategies, randomly paired subjects often prefer the strategy which results in the Pareto-inferior equilibrium if it appears to be more "secure" against coordination failures.

Why do players in experimental coordination games perform so poorly? This problem has been addressed in many articles on such games published during the past decade. The main intention of these articles was to isolate particular determinants of equilibrium selection in coordination games. For example, in a variant of the basic coordination problem, some players were allowed the option of receiving a sure outcome (*outside option*) instead of playing the coordination game [4]. This creates a two-stage game in which the power of *forward induction* can be explored. If the outside option is sufficiently high such that it dominates the payoff from some of the strategies in the coordination game, it can be observed that in plays in which the outside

[1] The problem of strategy choice is more serious when the Nash equilibria cannot be ranked at all.

option was not taken players seemed to have eliminated the payoff-dominated equilibrium strategies from consideration and, therefore, often coordinated on Pareto-superior equilibria. Beside the effects of outside options, many more determinants for equilibrium selection in coordination games have been found by varying the experimental design. By interpreting these results appropriately, we obtain a better insight into how poor equilibrium outcomes or even coordination failures in repeated coordination games can be avoided. We will give a short survey on the most important equilibrium selection mechanisms in coordination games in section 4 below.

In most experiments in *repeated coordination games*, payoff functions presented to the subjects in the form of payoff tables were common knowledge. However, the opponents' strategy choices in previous periods were not publicly announced. In this paper, we focus on symmetric coordination games of the *weakest link type*. A strategy followed by a single player in a given period can be interpreted as his *effort level* allocated to a joint production process whose production output is determined by the minimum effort player [6]. As far as we know, in all experiments in weakest link games conducted so far, only the previous period **minimum effort level of a group** has been publicly announced to the groups' participants in each period. Needless to say, this is a very restrictive assumption. In real life, coordination problems players often have better information than their group's minimum effort level. They may have at least a rough idea of the **distribution** of their opponents' previous strategy choices.

It is the main purpose of our paper to study the effects of less restrictive information assumptions on successful coordination. More precisely, we consider three treatments of experiments in which subjects are told in each period either the previous a) group minimum effort (treatment I), b) distribution of the players' strategy choices (treatment II), or c) each player's individual strategy choice (treatment III). It turns out that the willingness to coordinate on Pareto-superior equilibria and the degree of information about the opponents' strategy choice is positively correlated. In our experiments, players show a strong tendency to choose the Pareto-dominant strategy in treatments II and III, while in treatment I they again perform poorly.

Our paper is organized as follows: In section 2 we discuss the basics of coordination games and its economic relevance. In particular, weakest link games are introduced in full detail. Section 3 contains the description of our experiments and the results. By subdividing the subjects participating in the experiments into those who actually chose the group's minimum in the previous period and those who chose an effort level above the group's minimum, a satisfactory explanation for different coordination behavior in the different treatments will be given. Our results show that the role of information as a coordination device in weakest link type games has been underestimated so far. Finally, in section 4, we give a brief overview of further determinants of strategy choice in repeated coordination games.

2 The basics of coordination games

2.1 The strategic problem

In our paper, coordination games are defined as symmetric normal form games with multiple Nash-equilibria in pure strategies which can be Pareto-ranked. In such games we typically face a serious *equilibrium selection problem*. As a simple starting point, let us consider the following 2×2 coordination game (introduced by Cooper et al. [4]) which is characterized by the payoff table below.

Table 1. CG-game

	X	Y
X	(800, 800)	(800, 0)
Y	(0, 800)	(1000, 1000)

In this simple 2×2 game (called CG-game) pure strategies are elements of the strategy set $\Sigma = \{X, Y\}$. There are two pure strategy Nash equilibria (X, X) and (Y, Y). The equilibrium in which both players choose Y, obviously Pareto-dominates the equilibrium (X, X). Arguments for Pareto-domination as an equilibrium selection criterion imply that the (Y, Y) outcome should be observed in the playing of this game. However, playing the Pareto-dominant equilibrium (Y, Y) might be risky. For example, if player 2 (the column player) has a significant doubt that player 1 will choose Y, he might only get 1000 payoff units. By symmetry, the same reasoning is valid for player 1 (row player). If both players doubt that the other will choose Y, they might decide to play it safe and select the more secure strategy X. By choosing X, each player receives 800 payoff units independently of the opponent's strategy choice.

Harsanyi and Selten have formulated the concept of *risk dominance* to capture precisely the idea of relative riskiness of two strategies in two-person games [7]. In our simple 2×2 coordination game, we argue that a player may not know which strategy his opponent will select. Without any knowledge about the opponents' strategy choice, it is plausible to assume that she will choose X or Y with equal probability. Then, the expected payoff of the row player is equal to

$$\text{for} \quad X : 800, \qquad \text{for} \quad Y : 500.$$

Strategy X should be selected since it has higher expected payoff. This coincides with Harsanyi's and Selten's risk dominance criterion for symmetric 2×2 games, which also recommends choosing strategy X in the CG-game.[2] While Pareto-dominance arguments will certainly convince completely rational players to play the (Y, Y) equilibrium, there is enough empirical evidence from laboratory experiments to suggest that subjects prefer to play the less risky equilibrium in repeated coordination games. When the Pareto-dominant and the risk-dominant equilibrium do not coincide, we run into a serious welfare problem. Many experimental economists have felt challenged by this result and have tried to modify the experimental design of coordination games in order to induce players to select Pareto-better equilibria. In section 4, we survey some recent developments in this field.

2.2 The weakest link game

In our paper, we will focus on equilibrium selection in *weakest link games* which are more complex than the CG-game. A weakest link game can be described as a symmetric n-person game with a finite strategy set Σ and payoff function

$$H(\sigma_i, \sigma_{-i}) = a \min\{\sigma_1, \dots, \sigma_n\} - b\sigma_i + c, \tag{1}$$

where $\sigma_i \in \Sigma$ denotes the strategy choice of player i and $\sigma_{-i} = (\sigma_1, \dots, \sigma_{i-1}, \sigma_{i+1}, \dots, \sigma_n)$ denotes the strategy choice of $i's$ opponents. Furthermore, we require $a > b > 0$. Parameter $c \geq 0$ is not essential for the theoretical results of weakest link games, it only serves to keep the absolute payoff levels above zero, which is crucial for conducting the experiments. According to Bryant, one can interpret the weakest link game describing a joint production process in which each firm contributes a particular input level $\sigma_i \in \Sigma$ [6]. Production is characterized by a Leontieff production function, and part of the output is supposed to be shared equally between the firms. After subtracting production costs $b\sigma_i$, the payoff of the game $H(\sigma_i, \sigma_{-i}) = a \min\{\sigma_i, \sigma_{-i}\} - b\sigma_i$ may be interpreted as firm $i's$ profit.

In experiments, the strategy set Σ is restricted to a finite subset of integers $\{1, 2, \dots, \bar{\sigma}\}$. From definition (1) and inequality $a > b > 0$ we immediately obtain the following results for weakest link games.

Fact 1 *The game has $\bar{\sigma}$ symmetric Nash equilibria in pure strategies, which can be Pareto-ranked. There are no other equilibria in pure strategies for this game.*

[2] In more precise terms, consider a symmetric 2×2 coordination game with payoff table

	X	Y
X	(a, a)	(b, c)
Y	(c, b)	(d, d)

(X, X) is called risk-dominant if the inequality $(a - c) > (d - b)$ holds; this is true of the CG-game, as can be easily checked.

Fact 2 *In the unique Pareto-dominant equilibrium, all n players choose the maximum feasible action $\bar{\sigma}$.*

If players cannot explicitly coordinate their strategy choices either by pre-play communication or another mechanism, they face a nontrivial coordination problem. All feasible strategies are potential Nash-equilibrium outcomes. However, the Nash concept does not prescribe the outcome of this coordination game. Moreover, standard equilibrium refinements do not reduce the set of equilibria.

In all experiments which we consider here, the one-shot weakest link game is *repeated a finite number of times*. Obviously, the set of Nash equilibria and subgame perfect equilibria for this finitely repeated weakest link game includes all of the Nash equilibria from the one-shot game. This can be summarized as follows:

Fact 3 *A sequence of (pure) strategy configurations in the $T-$fold repetition of the weakest link game $\{\sigma^t\}_{t=1}^T$ constitutes a Nash-equilibrium of the repeated game if for each $t = 1, \ldots, T$ σ^t is a Nash-equilibrium of the one-shot weakest link game.*

Although finite repetitions of the weakest link game generate many new equilibrium outcomes for the repeated game (payoff criterion: average period payoffs),[3] we neglect the "repeated game aspect" here. Experimental evidence on coordination games shows that subjects, in general, behave myopically. The purpose of finite repetitions of coordination games in experiments is to allow for learning about the future strategy choice of others and thus to resolve strategic uncertainty in the one-shot game rather than isolate sophisticated repeated game strategies. Although there are more equilibrium outcomes in the repeated game than in the one-shot game, the lower and upper bound on the equilibrium payoffs are the same. Playing the worst (best) equilibrium of the one-shot game $(1, \ldots, 1)$ $((\bar{\sigma}, \ldots, \bar{\sigma}))$ in all periods of the repeated game constitutes the worst (best) equilibrium of the repeated game.

---

[3] As a simple example, we consider a 2-person weakest link game with $a \geq 2b$ which is repeated once. A subgame perfect equilibrium of the repeated game can be described, for example, as follows:

> In period 1: Player 1 chooses effort level equal to x and player 2 equal to y with $x, y \in \{1, \ldots, \bar{\sigma}\}$,
>
> In period 2: Both players choose effort level equal to $\bar{\sigma}$ if player 1 chose x and player 2 chose y in the previous period. Otherwise, both select the minimum effort level equal to 1.

3 Conducting the experiments

3.1 Experimental design

In our experiments, subjects were confronted with a weakest link game satisfying the following assumptions: $\Sigma = \{1, 2, \ldots, 9\}$, a = 0.30 [DM], b = 0.15 [DM] and c = 1.50 [DM]. Payoffs were shown to the subjects in numerical payoff tables which were common knowledge. This corresponds exactly to the experimental design of Berninghaus and Ehrhart [9].

We ran our experiments in computerized form, with 24 groups of subjects in 12 sessions. In each session exactly two groups were involved. For each group there were 10 repetitions of the stage game. Subjects knew the number of their group members and the number of repetitions in advance. However, they did not know the group members personally. In each period, subjects could choose one of the effort levels from the set $\{1, \ldots, 9\}$. The treatments differed with respect to the public information given to subjects in the group.

- In **treatment I**, each subject of a group was only informed of the group's *minimum effort level* in the previous period.
- In **treatment II**, each subject was informed of the *distribution of effort levels* in the group prevailing in the previous period.
- In **treatment III**, each subject was informed of the *individual effort level* chosen by each player in the group in the previous period.[4]

Moreover, in each period information about previous choices and previous individual per period payoff was available for each player (on the computer screen by request). Treatments differed with respect to the strength of information about the other players' strategy choices. In treatment III, we assumed *perfect information*, while in treatment I, an extremely "low degree of information" was available.[5] Our experimental design was motivated as follows. The information given in treatment I might be misleading. Suppose all players wanted to coordinate on the Pareto-dominant equilibrium, but they were not convinced that all group members had the same intention or that all group members understood the basic strategic problem in weakest link games. In this case, we expected players to be encouraged to continue with high effort levels for a while, provided most of the group members actually chose high effort levels in the previous periods. However, suppose a player knew only his group's minimum effort level,[6] which turned out to be rather low in actual experiments; he might be discouraged from choosing high

[4] Note that in this treatment each member of a group could be identified by a natural number. Still, the group members did not know each other personally.

[5] Notice, however, this is not equivalent to *no information* about the other group members' strategy choices.

[6] This information assumption has been made in most experimental investigations of the weakest link game (for example [1]).

effort values for the following periods even if most players actually tried out high effort levels in the past. To put it in more abstract terms, knowing only the minimum of a sample distribution provides almost no information about the *support* of this distribution. Confronted with this uncertainty, risk-averse subjects should tend to choose low effort levels, as actually turned to be the case in our experiments of treatment I.

Eight experiments were run in each treatment. Sixty-four persons (8 groups with 8 subjects each) participated in each treatment, so that a total of 192 subjects participated in all treatments. Each subject was paid his individual payoff accumulated during the course of the play. The average earning of a subject was equal to DM 18.68. The minimum payment was equal to DM 5.70 and the maximum payment equal to DM 28.50.[7] The average earning in treatment I was equal to DM 15.97, while in treatment II and treatment III, subjects earned significantly more (DM 19.46 and DM 20.60).

3.2 Experimental results

Our aggregate experimental results are presented in tables 2 and 3.[8]

Table 2. Number of groups which reached effort level 1 and/or 9

treatment	minimum = 1 chosen at least once	maximum = 9 chosen at least once
I	6	1
II	6	2
III	5	4

Table 3. Average minimum effort and average effort level

treatment	average minimum	average effort level	first round average effort
I	2.79	5.27	7.89
II	5.25	7.58	7.88
III	5.73	7.75	7.78

[7] The maximum payment was reached by an atypical group in treatment I which, in contrast to the remaining groups, invariably coordinated on the Pareto-dominant equilibrium right from the start.

[8] We have taken the results of this section from [8].

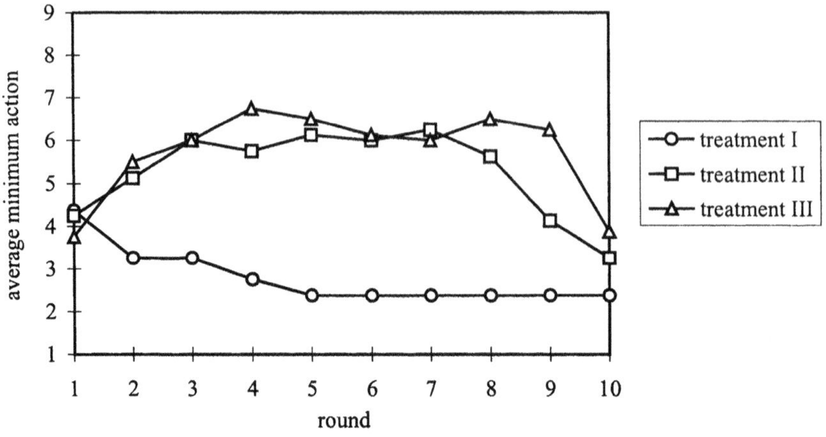

Fig. 1. Average minimum effort level

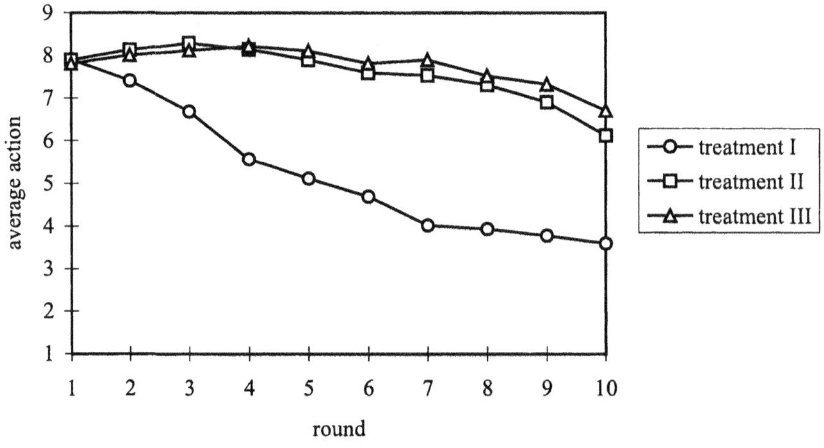

Fig. 2. Average effort level

Tables 2 and 3 report on average values (over all iterations and over the groups in each treatment). In order to show the evolution of effort levels during the course of the game, we present the time paths of the average effort levels and average minimum effort levels in figures 1 and 2.

Our experimental results can be briefly characterized as follows:

1. Subjects in treatment I behaved very similarly to subjects in treatment A in the experiments of van Huyck et al. [1]. Starting from a relatively high average effort level in the first period, the average minimum effort level soon declined. Looking at the groups' behavior in treatment I, we observe that 6 groups reached the minimum effort level 1, while two groups had the lowest minimum effort level over all periods, equaling 4 and 9.[9]
2. Groups in treatments II and III behaved significantly different from groups in treatment I.[10]
3. According to table 2, in treatment II, two groups reached the Pareto-dominant equilibrium, while in treatment III, four groups were successful in reaching the Pareto-dominant equilibrium. The average minimum effort and the average effort level were not significantly different. Moreover, groups in both treatments behaved similarly. After a few periods, players tended to coordinate on a good equilibrium. In approaching the final round, the players' average effort level tended to decrease, which seemed to show a kind of "endgame effect" for coordination games. To summarize, subjects seemed to react similarly to the information given in treatments II and III, although the two scenarios differed considerably with respect to their information content. In treatment III, each player could be identified with his choice, while in treatment II an individual player could not be identified.
4. Pairwise comparison of average first period effort did not show significant differences between the treatments.[11] This seems to be a "stable" result since it has been be observed in many (weakest link game) coordination experiments with varying design.

The first and last points deserve further comments. To start with point 4: The same observation concerning first period effort levels has been made in many actual experiments on weakest link games irrespective of the particular design. It seems to be almost an experimental regularity that subjects' behavior in the first period is independent of the treatment under consideration.

On point 1: In treatment I, we replicated the experiments by van Huyck et al. [1]. Subjects in our experiments behaved almost exactly as subjects in their experiments, which strengthens our belief that this pattern of behavior is a "stable" regularity in repeated weakest link games. It is one of the main

[9] Notice that players in one group showed unusual behavior (see f.n. 7). All players in this group start with maximum effort level equal to 9 and keep this level during the course of the play.

[10] Pairwise comparison of average effort levels between treatments I-II, I-III, and II-III via U-test shows *p-values* of 0.012, 0.019, and 0.287. Sample size: one sample unit per group, 8 observations per treatment.

[11] Pairwise comparison of initial average effort levels between treatments I-II, I-III, and II-III via U-test resulted in *p-values* of 0.493, 0.319, and 0.339. Sample size: one sample unit per player, 64 observations per treatment.

results of our paper that this regularity in behavior crucially depends on the information assumption made in treatment I.

3.3 Searching for an explanation

Our experimental data show that most groups did not play the Pareto-dominant equilibrium at all, or they reached it only after some iterations and played it for some rounds. However, differences in behavior can be observed among treatments I, II, and III. We want to isolate the driving forces behind these results.

First, we focus on strategy switching by the players. We analyze the individual data of our experiments with respect to the *average number of strategy changes* per player per round.[12]

Table 4. Percentage of strategy changes

treatment	# of groups	percentage of strategy changes from one round to the next		
		all players	minimum players	non-minimum players
I	7	42.7	30.1	55.3
II	8	37.5	62.2	34.5
III	8	28.3	66.6	23.8

Column 3 in table 4 presents the results for all players, while column 4 (5) only the decisions of those players who were minimum players (non-mininum players) in the previous period. It is remarkable to note how average strategy changes differ over treatments. We see a clear tendency of better informed players to be less active. However, the picture changes drastically when we separate the players of each group into those who were minimum players and those who were non-minimum players in the previous round. Minimum players were more active when they were better informed, while non-minimum players showed the opposite pattern of behavior.[13] The results in table 4 are

[12] In computing the numerical values in the tables below we set up the following conventions: 1) We neglect strategy switches of players in groups which played the Pareto-dominant equilibrium in the previous period. Thus, we do not consider the data of the unique group in treatment I in which all subjects played the Pareto-dominant equilibrium in all rounds. 2) We are only interested in whether a player switches his strategy ("favourable event") or not ("unfavourable event"), irrespective of the quantitative increase or decrease of his effort level.

[13] Pairwise comparison of percentage of strategy changes between treatments I-II, I-III, and II-III by U-test shows *p-values* of 0.009, 0.017, and 0.380 for minimum players, and 0.014, 0.002, and 0.164 for non-minimum players. Comparison of the results for all players in a group exhibits only a significant difference between

based on groups as sample units.[14]

In the previous analysis we were interested in how actively subjects adapt their strategies from one period to the next. To explain the difference in behavior, it would be even more important to know the *direction* of strategy changes. Therefore, we now differentiate between players who reduce their effort level from one period to the next ("<"), keep their effort level constant ("=") or increase their effort level (">"). We compare the treatments pairwise by applying the Mann-Whitney U-test. Significant values of the U-statistic and p-values are written in bold numbers (5% level of significance, two-sided U-test, one sample unit per group).

Table 5. Percentage of directional strategy changes (all players)

treatment	# of groups	<	=	>
I	7	30.2	57.3	12.5
II	8	20.3	62.5	17.8
III	8	13.9	71.7	14.4

comparison	# of groups	U (p-value)	U (p-value)	U (p-value)
I-II	7, 8	**8 (0.010)**	22.5 (0.287)	14 (0.060)
I-III	7, 8	**0.5 (0.000)**	**9.5 (0.017)**	21.5 (0.249)
II-III	8, 8	19.5 (0.107)	21.5 (0.152)	22.5 (0.178)

In table 5, we analyze the behavior of all players. Without differentiating between minimum and non-minimum players, we see a clear tendency of better informed players to be more cautious in reducing their effort level and more conservative in sticking to the previous period effort level. The frequency of increasing effort levels is not significantly different between the treatments. We do obtain the following significant differences, however: In treatment I, the frequency of reduced effort levels is significantly higher than in treatments II and III. The frequency of unchanged effort levels is significantly higher in treatment III than treatment I.

Results are different when we consider only those subjects who already selected the group's minimum effort level in the previous period (table 6). We note that less informed players (treatment I) tend to stick more strongly

treatment I and III at a 5% level of significance. Sample size: one sample unit per group, 8 observations per treatment.

[14] When we analyze our data with respect to single strategy changes as sample units, we also observe significant differences between treatment II and treatment III. All players and non-minimum players are significantly more active in treatment II than treatment III.

Table 6. Percentage of directional strategy changes (minimum players)

treatment	# of groups	<	=	>
I	7	0.3	69.9	29.7
II	8	3.5	37.8	58.8
III	8	10.0	33.4	56.6
comparison	# of groups	U (p-value)	U (p-value)	U (p-value)
I-II	7, 8	20 (0.198)	**7.5 (0.009)**	**8.5 (0.012)**
I-III	7, 8	20 (0.198)	**9.5 (0.017)**	**12 (0.036)**
II-III	8, 8	27.5 (0.337)	28.5 (0.380)	30 (0.439)

to the minimum effort level in the following period compared with better informed players. As a complementary result, better informed minimum players (treatments II and III) are more willing to increase their effort level in the next round.

Table 7. Percentage of directional strategy changes (non-minimum players)

treatment	# of groups	<	=	>
I	7	52.8	44.7	2.5
II	8	25.9	65.5	8.5
III	8	14.0	76.2	6.8
comparison	# of groups	U (p-value)	U (p-value)	U (p-value)
I-II	7, 8	**0.5 (0.000)**	**9 (0.014)**	**12 (0.036)**
I-III	7, 8	**3 (0.001)**	**4 (0.002)**	14 (0.060)
II-III	8, 8	22.5 (0.178)	22(0.164)	26 (0.287)

In Table 7, we consider only those players who did not select the group's minimum effort level. We see that less informed players tend to decrease their effort level with significantly greater probability than better informed players, who exhibit a greater tendency to maintain their previous period effort level.

Summarizing the data in the previous tables, we see that *learning direction theory* (see, e.g. [10]) may help to explain the difference in our results in treatment I versus treatments II and III. Learning direction theory roughly says that a player who fails to hit a given "target" will move to the left if he missed the target from the right and vice versa. Analogously, a minimum player may show a tendency to increase his efforts while a non-minimum player at least does not increase his effort level. We see from our experimental results that players in treatment I who already selected the minimum effort level in a given period have a significantly lower tendency to increase the effort level than players in treatments II and III. This may be explained by the fact that subjects in treatments II and III are better informed about the distribution of actually chosen effort levels. They know how many players did not choose the minimum effort level and, therefore, may be willing to coordinate on better equilibria. The same argument can be applied to the better informed non-minimum players, who tend to stick to their previously chosen effort level, compared to players in treatment I, who prefer to decrease their effort level in order to approach the previous period's minimum.

Both experimental regularities (concerning the minimum and the non-minimum players) seem to produce significantly different behavior between the groups in treatment I, on the one side, and the groups in treatment II and III, on the other. Although no significant differences were found in behavior between treatments II and III, clear tendencies could be identified. In treatment III, more groups reached the Pareto-dominant equilibrium than in treatment II. Subjects in treatment III were less active than subjects in treatment II. A close look at the individual data shows that subjects in treatment III seem to "signal" their behavior to opponents by keeping their effort level constant for a while. Such a behavior makes sense when each player can be identified by her strategy choice, as is actually assumed in treatment III. By sticking to the same, (relatively) high effort level, players may encourage their group's members either to experiment with higher effort levels or at least not to drop their effort level to the minimum. This may be an explanation for the fact that subjects in treatment II performed "more poorly" than subjects in treatment III. When subjects only know the distribution of effort levels in their respective group, as assumed in treatment II, players can at most recognize that there is a particular percentage of players who want to coordinate on relatively high effort levels. Since the same percentage level may be generated by different subjects switching their strategies from one period to the next in a particular way, it is more difficult for a single player to build up a reputation for being a benevolent player who wants to coordinate on Pareto-superior equilibria. In order to draw more definitive conclusions, which are moreover better empirically supported, we need to conduct further experiments with larger sample sizes.

4 Further determinants of equilibrium selection

Since the publication of the results of van Huyck et al. and Cooper et al., much experimental research has been devoted to isolating further determinants in equilibrium selection in coordination games and, particularly, in weakest link games.

Number of players: According to van Huyck et al. [1], the *number of players* participating in a weakest link game is crucial for equilibrium selection. Van Huyck et al. ran experiments varying the number of players, restricting the strategy space of the weakest link game to the set of integers between 1 and 7. In their basic treatment, they chose $a = 0.20$ [\$], $b = 0.10$ [\$], and $c = 0.00$ [\$]. There were between 14 and 16 persons involved in the baseline treatment, and play was repeated 10 times. After each period, subjects were told the minimum action chosen by the other players. No other information was disclosed.

The most important finding by van Huyck et al. is that the Pareto-dominant Nash equilibrium is never observed in the basic treatment. Although some players start with an action level equal to 7, over time play tends to converge to the secure Nash equilibrium in which the lowest effort level is chosen.

In another treatment, the number of players participating in the coordination game was reduced to 2. Then the results changed dramatically. When two players were paired, play converged to the Pareto-dominant Nash equilibrium for 12 out of 14 subjects. These results show that the *number of players* participating in a weakest link game is an important determinant for equilibrium selection.

Preplay communication: In another paper, Cooper et al. present experimental evidence on nonbinding preplay communication [5]. The coordination game with preplay communication is a two-stage game. In the first stage, players in a 2×2 coordination game communicate by sending messages. In the second stage, players choose their actions. Since the players' payoffs are independent of the messages sent, it is a "cheap talk game." Even in a cheap talk game, messages may influence actual play by affecting the beliefs which players hold about the action choice of their opponent players. Messages are restricted to lie in the set of strategies available to the players. Two alternative communication structures are investigated. In the *one-way communication setting*, only one player sends a nonbinding message of his intention to play a certain strategy. In the *two-way communication setting*, both players send messages to each other simultaneously.

Each player participates in a sequence of 2×2 coordination games whose payoff table is shown in table 1 with different anonymous players within his cohort. One person is designated the row player and the other the column player. Pairings are done by the computer. A player does not know the history of decisions made by any other players in the cohort. The experiments were organized as follows: Each cohort participated in two separate sessions. In session I, all players participated in ten 2×2 coordination games characterized by table 1. Session I consisted of 11 periods. Players alternated between row and column players. Session I was supposed to provide players with experience in experimental procedures. In session II all players participated in twenty additional 2×2 games such that each subject played twice against each opponent both row and column player. This session consisted of 22 periods. In session II, the communication structure between the players was varied.

With no communication, the secure Nash equilibrium was observed in 160 plays, while the Pareto-dominant equilibrium could never be observed. The coordination problem was completely resolved in the two-way communication treatment. The Pareto-dominant Nash equilibrium was observed in 150 plays (out of the total number of 165). The Pareto-inferior equilibrium was never selected by the players. The results in the one-way communication were different from either of the other two treatments. There were significantly more plays of the Pareto-dominant outcome than in the no-communication treatment and significantly more plays of the Pareto-inferior outcome, compared to the two-way communication treatment.

Outside options: In two stimulating papers, Cooper et al. analyze the impact of *outside options* on coordination failure [5], [11]. In their experimental design, each player participated in a sequence of one-shot games with different anonymous players, where the payoff table of the baseline two-person game is given by table 1. No player knew the history of decisions made by any other player in his cohort. Results of these experiments were compared with results from another treatment which differed only in that the baseline 2×2 coordination game was extended to a two-stage game in which the row player could choose an outside option at the first stage and terminate the game. Otherwise, the players reached the second stage and simultaneously chose an action in the 2×2 coordination game with payoff table 1. In one of the treatments, the outside option was fixed at 900. That is, the row player was permitted to choose to play the simple 2×2 coordination game or receive 900. Since the row player should reject the outside option only if he expects to earn more playing the game, the column player according to the principle of *forward induction*, should be certain that the row player will not choose action 1 since that cannot result in a higher payoff than 900. Experiments were organized in 2 sessions in exactly the same way as described in the previous paragraph (preplay communication).

In the treatment without the outside option, the Pareto-dominant Nash equilibrium was never observed, while 97% of play was at the Pareto-inferior Nash equilibrium. The results changed dramatically when the game was played with a prior stage in which the row player had the choice of a relevant outside option. Here, 77% of outcomes were at the Pareto-dominant equilibrium. Only 2% settled at the Pareto-inferior equilibrium, and 21% disequilibrium action pairs were observed, while disequilibrium in the treatment without outside option was quite rare. The outside option itself was selected almost 40% of the time.

Credible assignments: Instead of preplay communication to solve the coordination problem, one might expect that some individual –an arbitrator or mediator– with the ability to make common information assignments to all players of the game has the same effect on equilibrium selection. In a paper by van Huyck et al., the existence of an arbitrator is postulated who can make common information assignments [12]. However, these assignments are not assumed to be binding on the players. An arbiter may influence the outcome of a game since he has the ability to focus players' expectations on a specific equilibrium which might help to solve the equilibrium selection problem. We do not want to go into the details of the experimental design of van Huyck et al., but focus on one treatment in their paper (called "game B") instead. Game B is a two-person game characterized by the following payoff table:

Table 8. Payoff table of "game B"

	X	Y	Z
X	(9, 9)	(0, 0)	(0, 0)
Y	(0, 0)	(5, 5)	(0, 0)
Z	(0, 0)	(0, 0)	(1, 1)

Since the arbitrator's assignment could conflict with payoff dominance, it is not clear that the outcome of this game will satisfy the mutually best response property if an arbitrator assigns (Z, Z).

The participants in the experiment were randomly paired such that a row player participant played with a given column player participant once during the experiment. That is, subjects were confronted with an anonymous opponent in each period. An experiment lasted 12 periods. In the first 3 periods, no preplay communication of any kind was allowed. In the remaining periods, an arbitrator assigned an equilibrium point to the subjects before they played game B. Without an arbitrator, Pareto-dominance accurately predicts the outcome of game B. Subjects never implemented either of the inefficient Nash equilibria. Nevertheless, subjects were influenced by the arbitrator's assignment. An assignment to the Pareto-inferior equilibrium (Y, Y) was credible to 25% of the players. More subjects defected to the Pareto-dominant action when the arbitrator assigned the equilibrium action pair (Z, Z). To summarize, in game B the action pairs (Y, Y) and (Z, Z) are strict equilibrium points, but they are not very credible assignments.[15]

Optimization premium: In a recent article, Battalio et al. elaborate on an interesting observation which may help to better understand the phenomenon

[15] This result is in sharp contrast to a treatment called "game A" in [13], in which a *pure symmetric coordination game* is investigated. In such games, the symmetric Nash equilibria can no longer be ranked since they induce equal payoff. The introduction of an arbitrator, however, helped the players to focus expectations on a specific equilibrium.

of equilibrium selection in coordination games [14]. The authors consider three symmetric 2×2 coordination games which differ with respect to the *optimization premium*, which is the difference between the payoff of the best response to an opponent's strategy and the inferior response. Let us consider for illustration a symmetric coordination game with payoff matrix

$$A = \begin{pmatrix} a & b \\ c & d \end{pmatrix}.$$

A coordination game is characterized by the inequalities $a > c$ and $d > b$. Let $\pi(X, k)$ denote the expected payoff to a player who plays action X and expects his opponent player to play action X with probability k. And $\pi(Y, k)$ is defined similarly for action Y. Then, the optimization premium is a function $\rho : [0, 1] \longrightarrow I\!R$ given by

$$\rho(k) := \pi(X, k) - \pi(Y, k) = \delta(k - k^*),$$

where $\delta := (a - c + d - b)$ is called the optimization premium parameter and $k^* := \frac{d-b}{a-c+d-b}$ is the unique Nash equilibrium in strictly mixed strategies. Battalio et al. consider three coordination games in which action pair (Y, Y) is the risk-dominant and (X, X) is the Pareto-dominant equilibrium. According to the definition of risk dominance, the inequality $(a - c) < (d - b)$ holds, which implies $k^* > \frac{1}{2}$. For $k < k^*$ the best response action is Y, for $k > k^*$ it is action X. The games considered differ with respect to the value of parameter δ, which determines the value of the optimization premium. In particular, for games 1, 2, and 3, it is assumed that $\delta_1 = 50$, $\delta_2 = 25$, and $\delta_3 = 15$. In game 1, for example, playing other than the best response to action X (action Y) results in a pecuniary loss equal to 10 (40), which adds up to 50.

Battalio et al. hypothesize that subjects' behavior will more likely converge to the Pareto-dominant equilibrium, the smaller the optimization premium is. In their experiments, players in a cohort[16] play one of the three games 75 times. A random matching protocol to pair subjects within a cohort is utilized. Subjects are informed that they are randomly paired with an anonymous opponent. They cannot use common information about previous outcomes to coordinate on an equilibrium. The experimental evidence supports the conjecture of Battalio et al. In period 1 behavior, there was a strong tendency to play the Pareto-dominant strategy. After 75 periods, the results changed drastically. Only 5% of subjects chose the Pareto-dominant action in game 1, while 44% chose the Pareto-dominant action in game 3, which is characterized by the smallest optimization premium of all three games. And 25% of subjects in game 2 chose the Pareto-dominant action. Given convergence, the cohorts playing game 3 converged to the Pareto-dominant equilibrium more often, while the cohorts playing game 2 mostly converged to the risk-dominant equilibrium and chorts playing game 1 converged exclusively to the risk-dominant equilibrium.

[16] Each cohort had 8 participants.

Time horizon: Berninghaus and Ehrhart analyze the impact of the number of repetitions of a weakest link game on coordination failure [9]. The baseline game is a weakest link game with $a = 0.20$ [DM/minute], $b = 0.10$ [DM/minute] and $c = 1.00$ [DM/minute].[17] The strategy space is restricted to the set of natural numbers between 1 to 9. The number of participants of the baseline game is equal to 8. The experiments were run with 18 groups (consisting of 8 subjects each). For 6 groups there were 10 repetitions of the baseline game (treatment A). For another 6 groups there were 30 repetitions (treatment B) and, finally, for the remaining 6 groups there were 90 repetitions (treatment C). Regardless of the treatment, each experiment lasted exactly 15 min (900 s). The treatments differed only with respect to the length d of the period. In treatment A, d is equal to 90s, in treatment B, it is equal to 30s, and in treatment C, it is equal to 10s.[18] In each period, the only information given to all subjects is the minimum effort level of the group in the previous period. Moreover, the subjects know the payoff of the baseline game.

Among the groups in treatment A, subjects tended to choose low action values (average 3.91), while in treatment C, subjects tended to choose high action values (average 7.48). The average action level of subjects in treatment B was equal to 5.84. By considering the time path of action averages in each group separately, we discovered that in treatment B half of the groups tended to low action values while the other half tended to high action values. The results were much clearer for treatments A and C, in which most groups in treatment A coordinated on low actions values, while most groups in treatment C coordinated on high action values. The results of Berninghaus and Ehrhart show that the total number of repetitions of a baseline coordination game is another important determinant of equilibrium selection. One can hypothesize that players are more patient and tolerant in seeking coordination on the Pareto-dominant equilibrium when they expect more repetitions yet to come. Subjects in the experiments seem to be willing to sacrifice payoff at the outset when the sacrifice has a long payout period.

Berninghaus and Ehrhart interpret the experimental results with a *learning direction* approach. The *learning direction* theory is a qualitative learning theory which can be illustrated by a simple example of an archer trying to

[17] These experiments were conducted in "almost continuous" time. Players' payoffs per period were accumulated (integrated) over the respective period. Since the period length varied from treatment to treatment (see the explanations below), the parameters a, b, and c also varied over treatments. For a more detailed exposition, see [9].

[18] This particular design was chosen for the following reasons: Suppose the period length was the same for all treatments, and that it was equal to 90s as in treatment A. Then players in treatment C (90 periods) would have to play the game for more than 2 h (135 min), while playing the baseline game in treatment A would last only 15 min. Obviously, it would make no sense to compare the experimental results of the two treatments.

hit a tree with his arrows. When he misses the tree, he corrects his posture. If the arrow passed to the right of the tree, he turns to the left, and if it passed to the left of the tree, he turns to the right. Translated into our weakest link game scenario, players may feel frustrated when a symmetric equilibrium has not been chosen in the previous period. Therefore, one would expect that players who chose too high or too low an action value will change their decision in the next period in the same way as the bowman in the example. In fact, by analyzing the experimental data, one observes that the minimum players in a group almost never reduced their action level and players above the group's minimum increased their action level only very rarely. Furthermore, the frequency of minimum players raising their action value in the next period did not differ significantly between treatments. This was not true for non-minimum players, who showed a different behavior between the treatments. In a treatment with more iterations, one could observe a significantly lower frequency of reducing the action level than in a treatment with fewer iterations. Non-minimum players in treatment A reduced their action level more often than non-minimum players in treatment C. Players in treatment C exhibited a higher degree of tolerance to miscoordination and, therefore, had a higher chance of coordinating on the Pareto-dominant equilibrium. It is interesting to note that a learning direction argument also seems to explain our experimental results in this paper, as was shown in section 3.3.

Up to now, we have exclusively considered determinants of equilibrium selection in weakest link games. We complete our brief survey of empirically relevant equilibrium selection principles in coordination games by dealing with so-called *guessing games.* These are also coordination games with multiple Pareto-rankable Nash equilibria. In these games, players have to select one of the numbers out of a finite set of natural numbers. In the experimental guessing games addressed below, subjects had to select a number between 1 and 7. The payoff of an individual player is supposed to be decreasing in terms of the difference between a player's strategy choice and the median choice of his opponents. When players cannot engage in preplay communication, they face an *average opinion problem.*[19] Although this type of game has the same formal structure as the coordination games dealt with in this paper,[20] experimental results show that subjects in experiments seem to employ different principles of behavior in guessing games (e.g. [2]). In most instances, players coordinated on the numbers 4 and 5, which are neither the secure nor the Pareto-dominant equilibrium.

In an interesting paper, van Huyck et al. analyze **auctions** as another equilibrium selection mechanism [13]. When the right to participate in the

19 Keynes provides an excellent exposition of these games in beauty contests and stock markets [15].

20 The only Nash equilibria are the symmetric equilibria in which players coordinate on the same number. When all players choose 7, it is the Pareto-dominant equilibrium.

guessing game is sold by auction, the resulting price of this right reflects an average forecast of the outcome of the coordination game. Players may use price P of the right to participate in the game to reduce strategic uncertainty by eliminating outcomes that do not pay at least P. This is based on "forward induction" considerations in that it involves drawing an inference about future play in a subgame which is based on information about the actions leading up to the subgame. Van Huyck at al. report that the outcome in the guessing game changed dramatically when players had to purchase the right to participate via an auction.[21] The behavior of subjects always converged to the Pareto-dominant outcome.

Cachon and Camerer describe another selection criterion for guessing games, called **loss avoidance principle** [16]. According to this principle, players do not pick strategies that result in certain losses for themselves, provided other strategies are available. They choose only strategies likely to result in a gain. The loss avoidance principle is the game theoretic counterpart to findings that show the different perception of gains and losses in individual decision making under uncertainty [17].[22] Game theoretic loss avoidance is more general than the findings in individual decision making since it postulates that players also expect their opponents to avoid losses. To illustrate how loss avoidance works in van Huyck's guessing game, subjects had to pay a fixed, commonly known entrance fee, which is equivalent to subtracting a fixed amount from all payoffs. The value of the fee was chosen such that the selection of the lower numbers resulted in a certain loss. In experiments in the guessing game, it turned out that subjects coordinated only on numbers that did not result in certain losses. Roughly speaking, by increasing the entrance fee, one can induce the players to coordinate on Pareto-superior equilibria, which shows that loss avoidance is in fact an effective mechanism for selecting "better" equilibria among a set of Pareto-rankable Nash equilibria.

References

1. Van Huyck, J., R.C. Battalio, and R.O. Beil (1990) Tacit coordination games, strategic uncertainty and coordination failure. American Economic Review **80**, 234–248
2. Van Huyck, J., R.C. Battalio, and R.O. Beil (1991) Strategic uncertainty, equilibrium selection, and coordination failure in average opinion games. Quarterly Journal of Economics **106**, 895–910

[21] The auction works as follows: Eighteen subjects bid for nine rights to participate in the guessing game. The initial price is less than payoff of the worst equilibrium. Every 5 seconds, the price is raised by increment until only nine subjects remain. These subjects then proceed to play the guessing game.

[22] People seem to dislike losses more than they like equal-sized gains. Therefore, they are often willing to take risks to avoid losses, while they avoid risks that can yield equal-sized gains.

3. Cooper, R.W., D.V. De Jong, R. Forsythe, and T.W. Ross (1990) Selection criteria in coordination games. American Economic Review **80**, 218–233
4. Cooper, R.W., D.V. De Jong, R. Forsythe, and T.W. Ross (1992) Forward induction in coordination games. Economics Letters **40**, 167–172
5. Cooper, R.W., D.V. De Jong, R. Forsythe, and T.W. Ross (1992) Communication in coordination games. Quarterly Journal of Economics **107**, 739–771
6. Bryant, J., (1983) A simple rational expectations Keynes-type model. Quarterly Journal of Economics **97**, 525–529
7. Harsanyi, J.C. and R. Selten (1988) A General Theory of Equilibrium Selection in Games. The MIT Press, Cambridge, Massachusetts
8. Berninghaus, S.K. and K.-M. Ehrhart (2000) Coordination and information: Recent experimental results. Institute of Statistics and Mathematical Economics, University of Karlsruhe, mimeo
9. Berninghaus, S.K. and K.-M. Ehrhart (1998) Time horizon and equilibrium selection in tacit coordination games: Experimental results. Journal of Economic Behavior and Organization **37**, 231–248
10. Selten, R. and R. Stoecker (1986) End behavior in sequences of finite prisoner's dilemma supergames: A learning theory approach. Journal of Economic Behavior and Organization **7**, 47–70
11. Cooper, R.W., D.V. De Jong, R. Forsythe, and T.W. Ross (1993) Forward induction in the Battle-of-the-Sexes Games. American Economic Review **83**, 1303–1316
12. Van Huyck, J., A.B. Gillette, and R.C. Battalio (1992) Credible assignments in coordination games. Games and Economic Behavior **4**, 606–626
13. Van Huyck, J., R.C. Battalio, and R.O. Beil (1993) Asset markets as an equilibrium selection mechanism: Coordination failure, game form auctions, and tacit communication. Games and Economic Behavior **5**, 485–504
14. Battalio, R., L. Samuelson, and J. van Huyck (1999) Optimization incentives and coordination failure in laboratory stag hunt games. mimeo
15. Keynes, J.M. (1936) The general theory of interest, employment, and money. McMillan, London
16. Cachon, G. and C. Camerer (1996) Loss avoidance and forward induction in experimental coordination games. Quarterly Journal of Economics **111**, 165–194
17. Tversky, A., and D. Kahneman (1991) Loss aversion in riskless choice: A reference-dependent model. Quarterly Journal of Economics **106**, 1039–1061

Market Innovation and Entrepreneurship: A Knightian View

Truman F. Bewley

Cowles Foundation, Yale University

Abstract. Stimulated by Frank Knight's book, *Risk, Uncertainty and Profit*, I present a theory of innovation based on what I term Knightian decision theory. The theory includes a concept of uncertainty aversion, a behavioral property manifested by reluctance to undertake new unevaluatable risks. The aversion is compounded when people are obliged to cooperate in undertaking risks. The theory leads to the conclusion that innovation in business is the natural domain of individual investors with unusually low levels of uncertainty aversion. In addition, it should be difficult to innovate new markets for insurance of unevaluatable risks, for the success of a new market requires that many people overcome their aversion to uncertainty and enter the market.

1 Introduction

I use what I call Knightian decision theory to express formally Frank Knight's (1921) ideas on uncertainty, insurance, and entrepreneurship. This formulation of his ideas has interesting implications.

Knight distinguished between risk and uncertainty, and I will maintain his distinction throughout what follows. A gamble is risky if the probabilities of outcomes are known. Otherwise, the gamble is uncertain. Knight claimed that uncertain gambles cannot be insured and that the role of the entrepreneur is to initiate uncertain investments. Investments involving only risk can be readily marketed and therefore do not require a special person to undertake them. These ideas cannot be reconciled with Bayesian decision theory, but they do make sense in the framework of Knightian decision theory.

Formal expression of Knight's ideas yields theoretical insights that may have some empirical validity. For instance, the explanation of why it is difficult to insure uncertain gambles gives a new explanation of why markets are incomplete; one that complements the usual arguments involving moral hazard, adverse selection, and transactions costs. Although these explanations are convincing in many cases, they seem inadequate in others where the Knightian explanation could apply. Examples are markets for distant future delivery of standardized commodities and markets for unemployment insurance. Another insight has to do with betting. Everyday experience indicates that probability assessments of some events vary widely among individuals. Such differences of opinion help explain some economic phenomena. If decision makers are Bayesian, however, any two people with different opinions about an observable event could gain *ex ante* by exchanging a bet on the event. Since such bets seldom occur, it is natural to conclude that the differences of opinion are due to differences of information, since no bets would be made if differences of opinion were due solely to difference of information (Geanakoplos and Sebenius (1983)). It is not always reasonable to assume that people with different opinion have different information, and Knightian decision theory explains how people could have different opinions based on the same information and yet not want to exchange bets. Differences of opinion, which seem natural in the Knightian framework, provide easy explanations of two puzzles in finance, the lack of diversification of individual investment portfolios and the fact that closed end mutual funds often sell at a discount. A Knightian argument also resolves the Ellsberg paradox.

According to the Knightian characterization, the entrepreneur is someone with unusual opinions or an unusually low level of uncertainty aversion. If this description is valid, pooling and diversification of entrepreneurial risks discourage entrepreneurship. This conclusion is the opposite of the one that would be drawn if risk aversion were the principal inhibitor of entrepreneurship. The Knightian description also makes it possible to visualize a world in which waves of innovation occur naturally. Entrepreneurship, through innovation, creates knowledge that in turn reduces the uncertainty about the prospects of other possible innovations. Since uncertainty discourages innovation, reduction of uncertainty stimulates new innovations, which, whether successful or not, create new knowledge, and the process can feed on itself indefinitely.

This paper is written in the spirit of experimentation with ideas. I do not claim that Knightian decision theory gives a good approximation of reality. This decision theory is certainly a fallible guide to human behavior, because it does not differ from the expected utility hypothesis in the case of choice among risky alternatives, and experimental work reveals many divergences from the predictions of that hypothesis (Schoemaker (1982)). It is probably too much to expect any theory of rationality to give correct predictions in all cases for all individuals, since human behavior is so erratic. All that is required is a theory of behavior that is roughly correct most of the time. The expected utility hypothesis is certainly not the only reasonable theory of rational choice under uncertainty, and many economic phenomena are difficult to explain using the hypothesis. It seems worthwhile, therefore, to try out other definitions of rationality in the hope of finding one that yields simple economic models giving a better fit to reality than the ones we now have.

The experiment presented here should not be seen as an interpretation Knight's work, but rather as an attempt to develop ideas suggested by it. LeRoy and Singell (1987) have argued that by uncertainty Knight meant "situations in which insurance markets collapse because of moral hazard or adverse selection." They may be right. Knight's work is too informal to permit precise interpretation.

2 Outline of Knightian decision theory

I describe briefly the main ideas of the Knightian decision theory. They are developed more fully in Bewley (1986). I modify the usual axiomatic basis of Bayesian decision theory by eliminating the assumption that preferences over lotteries are complete and by adding an inertia hypothesis.

When the completeness assumption is dropped, preferences retain the same representation as in the Bayesian theory, except that the single subjective probability distribution is replaced by a family of distributions denoted by Π. One lottery is preferred to another if and only if it has higher expected utility according to all distributions in Π. Formally, if S is a state space with measurable subsets $\mathcal{S}$ and if $x : S \to (-\infty, \infty)$ and $y : S \to (-\infty, \infty)$ are lotteries measurable with respect to $\mathcal{S}$, then x is preferred to y if and only if

$$\int u(x(s), s)\pi(ds) > \int u(y(s), s)\pi(ds),$$

for all π in Π, where $u(z, s)$ is the utility of payoff z in state s and each π is a probability measure on $\mathcal{S}$. The multiplicity of subjective distributions, π, expresses ignorance of the true distribution. It is assumed that if the probability of an event is known, then its subjective probability equals the known probability, for all π in Π. The theory, therefore, does not contradict that of von Neumann and Morgenstern. New information is incorporated by conditioning and applying Bayes rule to each of the distributions in Π, so that learning is treated in the Knightian theory just as it is treated in the Bayesian theory. If a sequence of observations identifies asymptotically the true stochastic mechanism governing the environment, then as observations accumulate the set of subjective distribution, Π, shrinks down to the single true distribution and uncertainty disappears asymptotically.

In the Knightian theory, it is not correct to say that a lottery x is revealed to be preferred to y if x is chosen when y is available. Because preferences are incomplete, it is only possible to say that y is revealed not to be preferred to x.

The inertia assumption says, roughly, that x is revealed to be preferred to y if x is chosen when y is available and y is the *status quo*. In decision theoretic language, the *status quo* is defined to be planned behavior specified by a full contingent program defined for a whole decision tree. The inertia assumption is that the *status quo* is abandoned only when new alternatives become available that are preferred to it, and the new alternative adopted must be preferred to the *status quo*. The *status quo* is in the decision maker's head and so has the same logical standing as a preference ordering.

It is not obvious how to relate the inertia assumption to observed behavior. Inertia is defined in terms of a program for a decision tree, and yet people clearly do not formulate such programs unless they have been trained to do so and then only when solving certain specific problems. Even if we assume that a person acts as if he followed a full contingent program for a decision tree, we do not know precisely how the tree and program are formulated, and this is the information that is required to apply the inertia assumption. This ambiguity is the chief theoretical weakness of Knightian decision theory. It arises, because the inertia assumption applies to those circumstances where the decision tree model makes the least sense as a model of actual behavior. It is probably best to think of the *status quo* as routines or rules used for guiding behavior in typical situations.

The inertia assumption and the multiplicity of subjective distributions make it possible to define a notion of uncertainty aversion. A decision maker with a large set of subjective distributions is reluctant to abandon the *status quo* and so can be said to be averse to uncertainty. Uncertainty aversion is distinct from risk aversion and does not involve aversion to uncertainty itself but only to movement away from the *status quo*.

A Knightian decision maker acts just like a Bayesian one, except when choosing between the *status quo* and new alternatives. That is, he chooses a program that is optimal with respect to one of his or her subjective distributions. This assertion follows from the natural assumption that a Knightian decision maker adopts a program that is undominated in the sense that no other program is preferred to it. If the decision maker can choose among programs randomly, then it follows from Minkowski's separation theorem that an undominated program is optimal with respect to some distribution $\bar{\pi}$ in Π. I refer to $\bar{\pi}$ as the decision maker's opinion. It is revealed by the decision maker's choice of program. It is, however, not determined by a preference ordering. Knightian decision theory has nothing to say about the selection of opinion, which remains unaltered as an unconditional probability distribution as long as the decision maker sticks with the *status quo* program. New information, however, does affect the opinion through conditioning.

If the decision maker abandons the *status quo* in favor of a new opportunity, then the opinion may change, as the following example illustrates. The example is portrayed in Figure 1. There are two states, a and b. The variables x_a and x_b are the utility payoffs in states a and b, respectively. The original choice set is OAB. The *status quo* is C. The open cone bounded by the lines cC and Cc' is assumed to be the set of points preferred to C. The original opinion is $\pi = (\pi_a, \pi_b)$. The new alternative is D and the new choice set is $OADB$. The point D is the optimal point in $OADB$ according to the opinion π, but D is not preferred to C. By the inertia assumption, a point such as C', preferred to C, will be chosen. The new opinion is, therefore, the probability vector π', perpendicular to the line DB.

New alternatives to the *status quo* may be presented as a surprise by the external environment or may be things the decision maker dreams up himself. Knightian decision theory is not intended to model the entire thinking

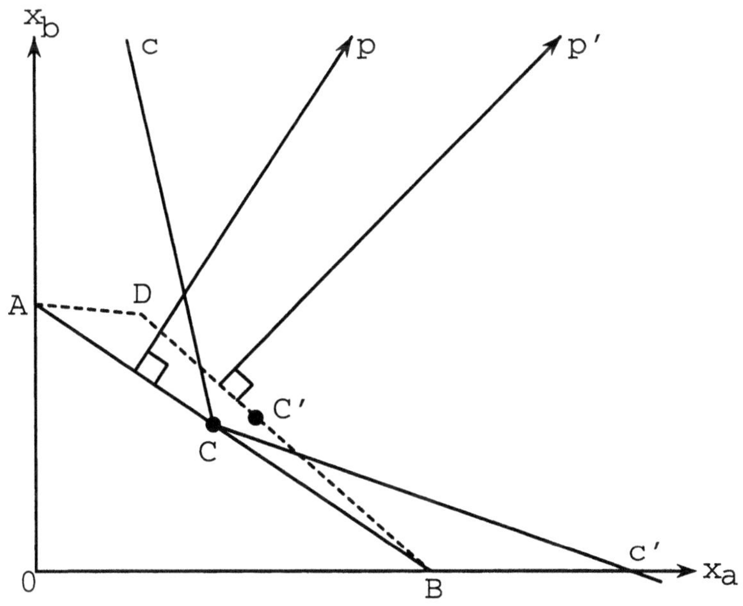

Figure 1

process of the decision maker. If decision maker were to be viewed as boundedly rational, then he or she might at some time perceive new opportunities that had previously been present but had gone unnoticed. Knightian decision theory, however, does not require that the decision maker be boundedly rational. Preference incompleteness does not imply irrationality nor any bound on computational capacity.

3 The absence of betting

Knightian decision theory yields an explanation of the infrequency of betting on events of unknown probability. The explanation may be grasped by imagining two individuals, 1 and 2, who may exchange a bet on event A of unknown probability. Suppose the individuals each attach an interval of probabilities to the event, the interval being $[\underline{\pi}_n, \bar{\pi}_n]$, for individual n, for $n = 1$ and 2. Consider a bet according to which individual 1 receives b dollars if A occurs and pays one dollar if A does not occur. Think of the bet as small, so that risk aversion may be ignored, and suppose that the event does not affect the personal fortunes of the individuals, so that the value of money to them does not depend on the occurrence of A. Next, assume that for both individuals, the possibility of making a bet on A comes as a surprise or is not part of their habits; their *status quo* programs do not cover the possibility of making such a bet. Then, individual 1 makes the bet if and only if $b\pi - (1-\pi) > 0$, which is the same as $\pi > (1+b)^{-1}$, for all π in $[\underline{\pi}_1, \bar{\pi}_1]$. Similarly, individual 2 makes the bet if and only if $-b\pi + (1-\pi) > 0$, which is the same as $\pi < (1+b)^{-1}$, for all $\pi \in [\underline{\pi}_2, \bar{\pi}_2]$. Thus, the bet would be acceptable to both individuals only if $\bar{\pi}_2 < (1+b)^{-1} < \underline{\pi}_1$. In other words, a bet at some odds would be acceptable to both if and only if the intervals $[\underline{\pi}_1, \bar{\pi}_1]$ and $[\underline{\pi}_2, \bar{\pi}_2]$ do not overlap. If the intervals overlapped, no betting would occur.

Even if the intervals did overlap, the opinions of the individuals could differ, the opinion of each being an arbitrary point in his or her own probability interval. The opinions would rationalize the decisions covered by the *status quo* program. Thus, the individuals might express widely differing views on the likely outcome of some political situation and yet not be willing to exchange a bet on the outcome.

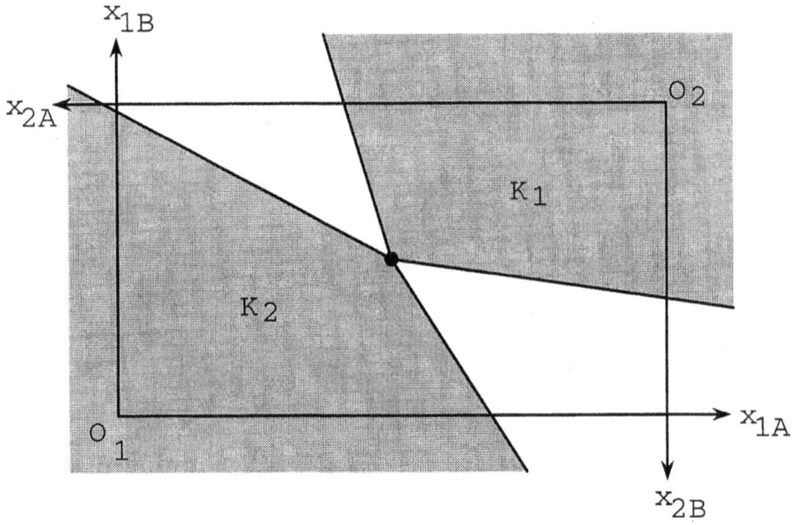

Figure 2

The geometry of the argument may be seen in the Edgeworth box diagram in Figure 2. The horizontal axes are the payoffs in the event A. The vertical axes are the payoffs in the complementary event, B, and the cone K_n, for $n = 1$ or 2, is defined by the formula

$$K_n = \{(x_A, x_B) | \pi x_A + (1-\pi)x_B \geq w_n, \text{ for all } \pi \in [\underline{\pi}_n, \bar{\pi}_n]\}.$$

where w_n is the initial wealth of individual n. Betting occurs if and only if $K_1 \cap K_2 \neq \emptyset$, which occurs if and only if $[\underline{\pi}_1, \bar{\pi}_1] \cap [\underline{\pi}_2, \bar{\pi}_2] = \emptyset$.

The argument is easily generalized to the case of many events and individuals. Let $\mathcal{A}$ be a finite collection of events in a state space, S. The events in $\mathcal{A}$ need not be disjoint and need not cover S. Let the set of subjective probability distributions of individual n over S be Π_n and let $\Pi_n^{\mathcal{A}} = \{(\sum_{\hat{A} \in \mathcal{A}} \pi(\hat{A}))^{-1}(\pi(A))_{A \in \mathcal{A}} | \pi \in \Pi_n\}$. A system of bets on events in $\mathcal{A}$ is a set of functions $x_n : \mathcal{A} \to (-\infty, \infty)$, for $n = 1, 2, ..., N$, such that $\sum_{n=1}^N x_n = 0$. Define the system to be acceptable if $x_n \neq 0$, for some n, and, for all n, either $x_n = 0$ or $\sum_{A \in \mathcal{A}} \pi(A) x_n(A) > 0$, for all $\pi \in \Pi_n^{\mathcal{A}}$. Betting occurs on the events in $\mathcal{A}$, if and only if there is an acceptable system of bets.

3.1. Proposition *There is an acceptable system of bets if and only if* $\bigcap_{n=1}^N \Pi_n^{\mathcal{A}} = \emptyset$.

Proof Let $R^{\mathcal{A}}$ be the set of functions $x : \mathcal{A} \to (-\infty, \infty)$. For each individual n, let $K_n = \{x \in R^{\mathcal{A}} | \sum_{A \in \mathcal{A}} \pi(A) x(A) > 0$, for all $\pi \in \Pi_n^{\mathcal{A}}\}$. Let $K = \{x \in \times_{n=1}^N (K_n \cup \{0\}) | \sum_{n=1}^N x_n = 0\}$. There is an acceptable system if and only if $K \neq \{0\}$. It is sufficient to show that $K = \{0\}$, if and only if $\bigcap_{n=1}^N \Pi_n^{\mathcal{A}} \neq \emptyset$. Clearly, if $\bigcap_{n=1}^N \Pi_n^{\mathcal{A}} \neq \emptyset$, then $K = \{0\}$. Let $X = \sum_{n=1}^N (K_n \cup \{0\})$. If $K = \{0\}$, then $X \cap R_-^{\mathcal{A}} = \{0\}$, where $R_-^{\mathcal{A}} = \{x \in R^{\mathcal{A}} | x(A) \leq 0$, for all $A\}$. Since each of the sets K_n is convex, the set X is convex. Let $\pi \in R^{\mathcal{A}}$ separate X from $R^{\mathcal{A}}$. Normalize π so that $\sum_{A \in \mathcal{A}} \pi(A) = 1$. Then, $\pi \in \bigcap_{n=1}^N \Pi_n^{\mathcal{A}}$, so that $\bigcap_{n=1}^N \Pi_n^{\mathcal{A}} \neq \emptyset$. □

If the events in $\mathcal{A}$ are uncertain and disjoint and if individuals are uncertainty averse, then the no betting condition, $\bigcap_{n=1}^N \Pi_n^{\mathcal{A}} \neq \emptyset$, is plausible, for each set $\Pi_n^{\mathcal{A}}$ is of full dimension in the convex set $\{(\sum_{\hat{A} \in \mathcal{A}} \pi(\hat{A}))^{-1}(\pi(A))_{A \in \mathcal{A}}$ $| \pi$ is a probability distribution $X\}$.

It might well be asked why an explanation for the absence of betting is needed when gambling is so common. Gambling at known odds, as in casinos, seems bizarre from the standpoint of both the Bayesian and Knightian decision theories. Because the house takes a share, the expected value of gains from such gambling is negative. It is natural to conclude that rational gamblers are risk lovers or love the excitement of gambling. In some gambling, such as horse racing, the probability of winning is unknown, so that gamblers can legitimately imagine that their bets have positive expected value, though the house or track takes a share of the bets. From the Knightian viewpoint, such betting is simply part of the *status quo*, and individuals bet because their opinions differ. From the Bayesian point of view, it is necessary to assume that the bettors have different prior distributions over the horses's prospects. If they had the same priors and different information, then no betting should occur.

Proposition 3.1 should be thought of as expressing resistance to innovation in betting. It is meant to answer the common argument that individuals in contact who have the same information should have the same subjective distributions over observed events, for if they did not, they would exchange bets, and such betting is not common. Proposition 3.1 is not contradicted by the existence of institutionalized betting, though it does not explain how such betting got started.

4 The Ellsberg paradox

The argument of the previous section gives an explanation of the Ellsberg paradox (Ellsberg (1961, 1963)). He observed experimentally that people prefer a lottery giving a dollar with probability one half to a lottery giving a dollar with completely unknown odds. According to both the Knightian and Bayesian points of view, the first lottery is worth fifty cents (or slightly less if allowance is made for risk aversion). If a Bayesian applies the principle of insufficient reason to the second lottery, then it is also worth fifty cents to him - hence the paradox.

In the Knightian framework, the paradox disappears if it is assumed that betting at known odds is covered by the *status quo* program, whereas the bet at unknown odds is not. It is easy to imagine that betting at known odds is covered by the *status quo*, for a simple rule determines the optimal choice — maximize expected utility. With these assumptions about the *status quo*, the choice of lottery with known odds does not reveal a preference for that lottery, because it could indicate that the individual had difficulty comparing the two lotteries and found the lottery with known odds familiar.

It would be interesting to reverse the Ellsberg experiment so as to make the lottery with unknown odds the *status quo*, though it is difficult to imagine how to be sure do so. The experimenter could give the lottery to the subject or make him select it by offering the choice between it and, say, five cents. Possession of the lottery might make it part of the *status quo*.

5 A simple treatment of insurance

An easy generalization of the results of Section 3 provides an explanation of the absence of markets for the insurance of uncertain events. Let the set of states, S, be finite. For each s in S, let $u_n(x,s)$ be the utility of individual n for money held in state s, where $n = 1, \ldots., N$. Assume that, for all n and s, $u_n(x,s)$, is increasing, concave, and differentiable as a function of x. Let w_{ns} be the monetary endowment of individual n in state s and assume that w_{ns} is positive, for all n and s. Let Π_n be trader n's set of subjective probability distributions over S and let $\mathcal{A}$ be a collection of subsets of S of unknown probability. An $\mathcal{A}$-trade for individual n is a function $x : \mathcal{A} \to (-\infty, \infty)$ such that $(w_n + x)(s) \geq 0$, for all s in $\bigcup_{A \in \mathcal{A}} A$, where $(w_n + x) : S \to (-\infty, \infty)$

is defined by the formula $(w_n + x)(s) = w_n(s) + \sum\{x(A)|A \in \mathcal{A}\}$. An $\mathcal{A}$-reallocation is a vector $x = (x_1, ..., x_N)$, where $x_n$is an $\mathcal{A}$-trade for individual n. The $\mathcal{A}$-reallocation, x, is feasible if $\sum_{n=1}^{N} x_n(A) = 0$, for all $A \in \mathcal{A}$. Assume that the *status quo* program of each individual does not cover trade in contracts contingent on events in $\mathcal{A}$. Then, trade in such contracts will occur only if there exists an acceptable $\mathcal{A}$-reallocation, x, where $x = (x_1, ..., x_N)$ is acceptable if, for all n, either $x_n = 0$ or $\sum_{s \in S} \pi(s)[u_n((x_n + w_n)(s), s) - u_n(w_n(s), s)] > 0$, for all π in Π_n. Let $\lambda_{ns} = (d/dx)u(w_n(s), s)$, for all s and n, and define $\Pi_n^{\mathcal{A},\lambda}$ by the formula

$$\Pi_n^{\mathcal{A},\lambda} = \left\{ \left. \left(\left(\sum_{\hat{A} \in \mathcal{A}} \sum_{s \in \hat{A}} \pi(s)\lambda_{ns} \right)^{-1} \left(\sum_{s \in A} \pi(s)\lambda_{ns} \right) \right)_{A \in \mathcal{A}} \right| \pi \in \Pi_n \right\}.$$

Proposition 3.1 generalizes to the following.

5.1. Proposition There exists an acceptable feasible $\mathcal{A}$-reallocation if and only if $\bigcap_{n=1}^{N} \Pi_n^{\mathcal{A},\lambda} = \emptyset$.

The geometric intuition behind this proposition may be seen in the Edgeworth box diagram of Figure 3, for the case of two states, a and b, and with $\mathcal{A} = \{a\} \cup \{b\}$. The sets K_n are defined by the formula $K_n = \{(y_a, y_b)|\pi(a) u_n(y_a, a) + \pi(b)u_n(y_b, b)$, for all $\pi \in \Pi_n\}$, for $n = 1$ and 2. If the conditions of the proposition hold, then there would be no trade if markets for insurance of events in A were introduced, so that the market innovation would fail.

6 Insurance with Gilboa–Schmeidler preferences

Gilboa and Schmeidler (1989) give an axiomatic characterization of a class of preferences having a form of uncertainty aversion related to but distinct from that of Knightian decision theory. Their class of preferences explains the rarity of betting on uncertain events and explains the Ellsberg paradox, but does not explain the difficulty of insuring uncertain events. In fact, their class of preference makes insurance even more likely than does the usual Bayesian or Savage class of preferences.

Using the notation of the previous section, a Gilboa–Schmeidler utility function, defined on vectors $x : S \to [0, \infty)$of money holdings, is of the form

$$U(x) = \min \left\{ \sum_{s \in S} \pi(s)u(x(s), s)|\pi \in \Pi \right\}.$$

The utility functions show aversion to uncertainty, if Π contains more than one point. Because the preference ordering represented by U is complete, an inertia assumption is not needed in order to define uncertainty aversion.

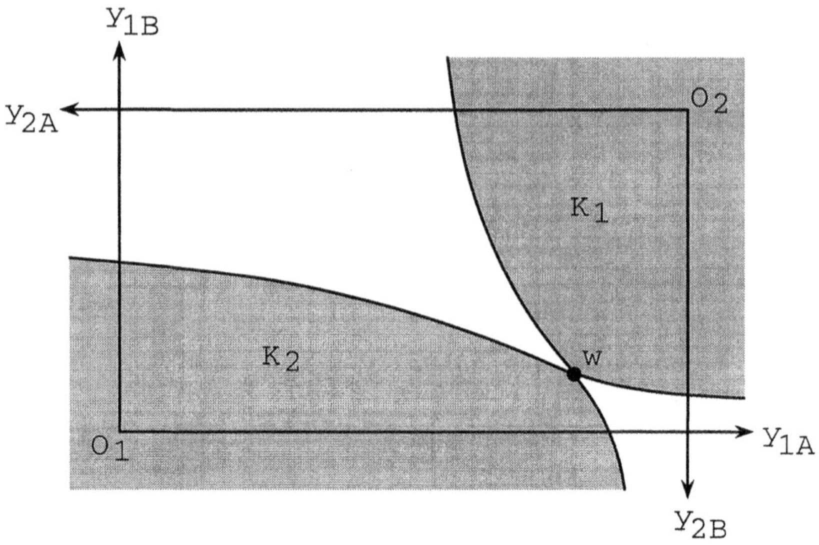

Figure 3

Roughly speaking, an uncertainty averse individual with Gilboa–Schmeidler preferences wants to equate the level of utility in different states, whereas individuals with Bayesian or Savage preferences wish to equate the marginal utilities of money in different states. The desire of people with Gilboa–Schmeidler preferences to trade in insurance increases with their aversion to uncertainty. This remark is illustrated in Figure 4, which is an Edgeworth box diagram with the same notation as Figure 3. The shaded region is the set of mutually advantageous trade.

7 Asset trading and diversity of opinion

One of the puzzles of finance is why individual investors hold undiversified portfolios of securities (Blume and Friend (1978), Chapter 2). If investors' expectations are rational, then diversification reduces risk without sacrificing expected return. Common explanations of the puzzle are transactions costs, investor ignorance of alternative investments, and ignorance of the advantages of diversification. Variation of opinion makes possible an additional explanation; investors buy those few securities that they believe have the highest returns. Lack of diversification may be interpreted as indirect evidence of the existence of variation in opinion. Harrison and Kreps (1978) have developed a stock market model with diverse investor opinion, and in their model it is clear that individual portfolios can be concentrated in a few stocks.

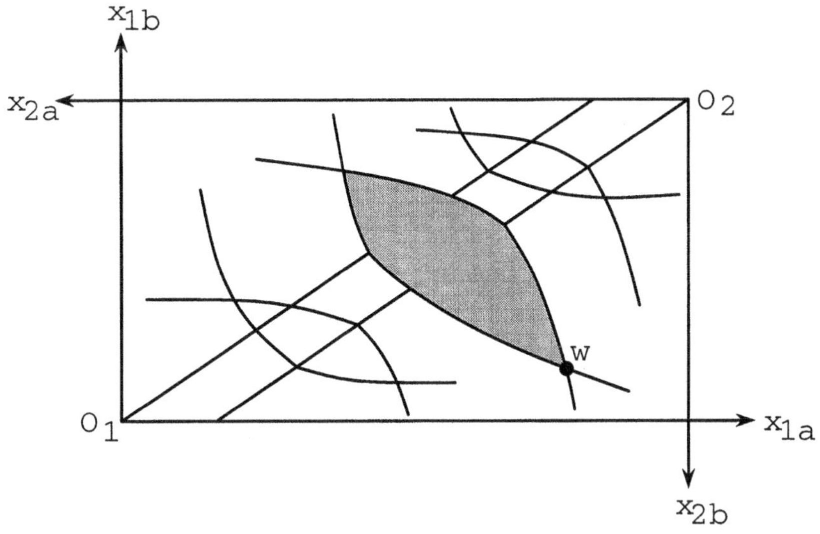

Figure 4

Another puzzle from finance is that closed end mutual funds often sell at a discount from the total value of their investments. Part of the puzzle is why arbitrage operations don't eliminate the discount, though perhaps margin requirements discourage the short sales needed for such operations. The puzzle addressed here is why the discount arises at all.

Like the lack of diversification, the discount can be interpreted as evidence of variation in investor opinion. If the assets of the fund were sold separately, each would be bought by the investor who valued it most. Selling the assets jointly obliges buyers to accept what they value little along with what they value highly.

In order to see this point more clearly, consider a simple two-period model with K assets and N investors. Let the price of each asset in period one be one and let R_k be the random value of asset k plus its dividend in period two. The interest rate is r and the proportion of the fund's assets invested in asset k is y_k. The expectation operator for investor n is denoted by E_n. The value in period 1 of one share of the fund to investor n is $(1+r)^{-1}\sum_{k=1}^{K} y_k E_n R_k$, so that the price of one share is $(1+r)^{-1}\max_n[\sum_{k=1}^{K} y_k E_n R_k]$. If the assets of the fund were sold separately, the value would be $(1+r)^{-1}\sum_{k=1}^{K} y_k \max_n[E_n R_k]$, which exceeds $(1+r)^{-1}\max_n[\sum_{k=1}^{K} y_k E_n R_k]$, if the numbers $E_n R_k$ vary as n varies.[1]

[1] Dow and Werlang (1988) have investigated the implications of Gilboa–Schmeidler preferences for securities trading. Such preferences imply inertia with respect to

8 The entrepreneur

Frank Knight described entrepreneurs as people who undertake investments with unevaluatable and therefore uninsurable risks. This intuition makes good sense in the Knightian framework. It is easy to imagine that if the risks of a new enterprise were evaluatable, then markets would be organized for contingent claims on those risks. The entrepreneur would then become the agent of a large group of claim holders, investors, or insurance companies. He or she would not need to bear the risk, because it could be marketed. If the risks of a new enterprise were difficult to evaluate, then by what has been said in Section 5, it might be difficult to spread the risk through insurance markets or to groups of investors. In Knightian language, the initial investors would have to be people who were unusual in their willingness to undertake the risk. If the enterprise were something new and unexpected, then the inertia assumption would imply that the initial investors would have to be people with low aversion to uncertainty and with subjective probabilities that favored the enterprise. If the enterprise were not a new idea, then the inertia assumption would not apply and the theory would lead to the conclusion that the initial investors are people with opinions that favor the enterprise.

The two characterizations just given of the entrepreneur may give some insight into the innovation process. For instance, they imply that more innovation will occur if the decision to innovate is dispersed among many individuals than if it is concentrated in the hands of a few. Similarly, a new enterprise would be less likely to be undertaken if a group of investors all had to agree to undertake it than if any one in the group could do so. Hence, large organizations might be more conservative than individuals acting independently.

I turn now to a more formal model. Let Γ be a set of dated events and let Π be a set of subjective probability distributions on the state space, S, underlying Γ. The set Γ is built up from S as follows. There are T time periods, and for each period t, with $1 \leq t \leq T$, there is a partition, $\mathcal{S}_t$, of S into events occurring at time t. The partition $\mathcal{S}_{t+1}$ refines S_t, for all $t < T$, and $\mathcal{S}_1 = \{S\}$. The dated event tree, Γ, is defined to be $\{(t, A) | 1 \leq t \leq T \text{ and } A \in \mathcal{S}_1\}$. If π is in Π, let π_Γ be the probability on Γ defined by $\pi_\Gamma(G) = T^{-1} \sum_{(t,A) \in G} \pi(A)$. A potential enterprise is defined by a function $y : \Gamma \to R$, where $y(t, A)$ is the monetary net return from the enterprise in dated event $(t, A) \in \Gamma$. Consider a potential entrepreneur with subjective probability distributions Π and with Knightian preferences. For simplicity, assume that interest rates are zero and that the entrepreneur is risk neutral and attaches the same utility to money in all dated events. Then, the value to the entrepreneur of an enterprise with return vector y according to π in Π is $\pi_\Gamma \cdot y = \sum_{(t,A) \in \Gamma} \pi_\Gamma(t, A) y(t, A)$.

---

the position of holding none of an asset. Dow and Werlang mention that Gilboa–Schmeidler preferences could explain lack of portfolio diversification.

Assume that the potential entrepreneur has not previously been aware of the possibility of an enterprise with return vector, y, so that the inertia assumption applies to the decision to undertake y. Assume also that the only alternative use of funds is to hold money. Then, the enterprise is undertaken if and only if $\pi_{\Gamma} \cdot y > 0$, for all $\pi \in \Pi$. Therefore, the enterprise is more likely to be undertaken the smaller is Π, i.e., the less uncertainty averse the investor is. If the enterprise has long been under consideration by the individual, then he undertakes it only if it is profitable according to his or her opinion $\bar{\pi} \in \Pi$.

If it is believed that risk aversion seriously inhibits the undertaking of new enterprises, then their creation should be encouraged by diversification and the spreading of risks. That is, the most daring innovators should be large organizations that pool the funds of many people to invest in many new businesses. According to the Knightian theory, however, both diversification and risk sharing discourage entrepreneurship.

Consider, first of all, the effects of diversification. Let there be K possible new enterprises, having return vectors $y_k : \Gamma \rightarrow R$, for $k = 1, ..., K$. Suppose, on the one hand, that the investor has long been familiar with the enterprises, so that they are evaluated according to a fixed opinion, $\bar{\pi} \in \Pi$. Then, even if risk averse, he or she might well prefer to concentrate investments in those few enterprises k, for which $\bar{\pi}_{\Gamma} \cdot y_k$ was highest. Suppose, on the other hand, that the investor has just become aware of the possibility of investing in the K new enterprises. He or she is not willing to invest in enterprise k, unless $\min\{\pi_{\Gamma} \cdot y_k | \pi \in \Pi\} > 0$. It is quite possible that $\min\{\pi_{\Gamma} \cdot y_k | \pi \in \Pi\} > 0$, for a particular value of k, yet $\min\{\pi_{\Gamma} \cdot \sum_{j=1}^{K} y_j | \pi \in \Pi\} < 0$, so that the investor could be willing to invest in one particular enterprise, but not willing to share equally in all of them. For this reason, diversification could tend to discourage investment in new businesses.

Diversity of opinion also makes it difficult to share unevaluatable risk. Suppose there are N investors who must decide whether to invest in a new enterprise represented by $y : \Gamma \rightarrow R$. Let Π_n be the set of subjective probabilities of investor n, for $n = 1, ..., N$, and assume the investors must decide by majority vote. Suppose, first of all, that the inertia assumption does not apply and let $\bar{\pi}_n \in \Pi_n$ be the opinion of investor n, for all n. Then, the investment will be undertaken only if $\bar{\pi}_{n\Gamma} \cdot y > 0$, for a majority of n. If the investors act independently and each can finance the investment alone, then the enterprise is undertaken if $\max_n \bar{\pi}_{n\Gamma} y > 0$, a condition that is more likely to be satisfied than the previous condition. Suppose now that the inertia assumption applies. If the investors act separately, the enterprise is undertaken if $\min\{\pi_{\Gamma} \cdot y | \pi \in \Pi_n\} > 0$, for some n. If they are to act together, this inequality must apply for a majority of n. Thus, cooperation lessens the likelihood of innovation.

Any cooperation by a group can lead to a strong form of collective uncertainty aversion, discussed in the literature on shareholder control (Drèze (1985)). Suppose N individuals must act by unanimous decision and suppose that none of the individuals are uncertainty averse. Then, unless the group finds a way to compromise, one action is chosen over another, only if it yields greater expected return according to everyone's subjective distributions. This requirement makes the group uncertainty averse, unless all individuals have the same subjective distribution.

In conclusion, Knightian decision theory leads to the idea that innovation and the foundation of new enterprises are the natural domain of unusual individual investors acting alone or nearly alone, because the risks associated with a new enterprise are difficult to evaluate. As an enterprise becomes established and develops a history, its prospects probably become easier to evaluate and so attract the interest of a larger number of investors.[2]

9 Non-optimality of dispersed innovation

Though innovation may be encouraged by investor independence, lack of coordination among investors can cause economic inefficiency, as the following example illustrates. The inefficiency results from diversity of opinion and the inability of investors to sell profits forward on markets for contingent claims.

Example: There are two periods, two types of people, two people of each type, and two states in period 2, s_v and s_w. People of type 1 live only in period 2. People of type 2 live in both periods. Production transforms labor of period 1 into consumption goods in period 2. Consumption occurs in period 2. There are four types of consumption good. Each person of type 1 is endowed with one unit of good 1. Each person of type 2 has one unit of labor and can produce any of goods 2, 3, and 4 in any relative quantities at the rate of one unit of good per unit of labor. The utility function of a person of type 2 is $u(x_1, x_2, x_3, x_4) = x_1$, where x_k is the quantity of good k consumed. The utility functions of all people of type 1 are equal to $v(x_1, x_2, x_3, x_4) = x_1 + x_2 + \frac{3}{2}x_3$ in state s_v and equal to $w(x_1, x_2, x_3, x_4) = x_1 + x_2 + \frac{3}{2}x_4$ in state s_w. In period 1, people of type 2 do not know the true state, but they learn it in period 2. The set of subjective probability distributions of people of type 2 is

$$\Pi = \left\{(\pi(s_v), \pi(s_w)) | \pi(s_v) + \pi(s_w) = 1 \text{ and } \tfrac{1}{4} \leq \pi(s_v) \leq \tfrac{3}{4}\right\}.$$

In period 2, commodities are traded in a competitive equilibrium. The unit of account in period 2 is good 1. The prices of goods 2, 3, and 4 are, respectively, 1, 3/2, and 0 in state s_v and 1, 0, and 3/2 in state s_w. People of type 2 know in period 1 that these will be the period 2 prices as a function of the state. Give the name V to one of the people of type 2 and the name W

[2] The theory of entrepreneurship just presented differs from that of Schumpeter. He did not envision the entrepreneur as an investor, but as a leader of men (Schumpeter (1939), pp. 102–104).

to the other and let the opinion of V be $(\pi(s_v), \pi(s_w)) = (3/4, 1/4)$ and that of W be $(\pi(s_v), \pi(s_w)) = (1/4, 3/4)$. In equilibrium, V produces only good 3 and W produces only good 4, people of type 1 have utility 1 in both states, V has utility 3/2 in state s_v and 0 in state s_w, and W has utility 0 in state s_v and 3/2 in state s_w.

This outcome is not Pareto optimal. Suppose that both V and W produced only good 2, that in state s_v person W gives one unit of good 2 to person V and that in state s_w person V gives one unit of good 2 to person W. Then, person V would have utility 2 in state s_v and 0 in state s_w and person W would have utility 0 in state s_v and 2 in state s_w. People of type 1 would continue to have utility 1 in both states. The new outcome clearly Pareto dominates the equilibrium in both states.

10 The information externality of innovation

As is well-known from the literature on patent rights, innovation creates knowledge and so gives rise to an externality. It is possible to see, in a Knightian model, how this externality could cause one innovation to stimulate others and so lead to the waves of innovation that Schumpeter claimed to observe ((1939), p. 100). The knowledge created by one innovation can reduce the uncertainty associated with other possible innovations and so make them more attractive to investors. The knowledge also stimulates innovations by indicating which new ones are most likely to succeed.

There are at least two sorts of knowledge created by innovation. One has to do with new concepts or ideas, and the other has to do with experimental verification. The conception of new ideas has to do with bounded rationality and so has no place in the Knightian framework. The process of experimental verification can, however, be expressed in Knightian terms in the same way that it can be expressed in the Bayesian framework. As was pointed out in section 2, an individual uses information to update by conditioning his or her subjective distributions. Information reduces uncertainty by confining the set of subjective distributions to a smaller region around the true distribution.

The following example illustrates how, in a Knightian model, the informational externality can cause innovations to stimulate each other in an endless chain. The example also shows how a person with an odd opinion can initiate such a chain.

Example: Consider an overlapping generations model where people live two periods. Each person is endowed with one unit of labor in the first period of life that may be used to produce a consumption good for the succeeding period. The production technology is linear, with production at the rate of one unit of consumption good per unit of labor. All consumption occurs in the second period of life.

There are countably many types of consumption goods. One is indexed by the number 1, and the others are indexed by all possible finite sequences of symbols a and b. Let C denote the set of all such finite sequences and let $X = \{x : \{1\} \cup C \to [0, \infty) | x(c) \neq 0$, for at most finitely many values of $c\}$. X is the consumption set of every consumer.

There are two types of people, types 1 and 2. Type 1 people can produce only good 1. Those of type 2 can produce any good. There are 100 people of type 2 and 2^t of type 1 in period t. In each period, exchange is determined by competitive equilibrium.

The utility function of a person of type 2 is $v : X \to [0, \infty)$, where $v(x) = x_1$. People of type 2 do not know the utility of a person of type 1. The set of possible types of utility functions is $\{1\} \cup S$, where $S = \{(s_1, s_2, \ldots) | s_n = a$ or b, for all $n\}$. The utility function corresponding to the symbol 1 is v. The utility function corresponding to s in S is $v_s : X \to [0, \infty)$, defined by the formula

$$v_s(x) = x_1 + \sum_{n=1}^{\infty} \left[\left(\frac{10}{9}\right)^n x_{s_1, \ldots, s_n} + \left(\frac{10}{9}\right)^{n-1} x_{s_1, \ldots, s_{n-1}, s_n^*} \right],$$

where $s_n^* = a$, if $s_n = b$, and $s_n^* = b$, if $s_n = a$. Give S the usual Borel σ-field generated by the product of the discreet topologies on $\{a, b\}$. Each person of type 2 has the set of subjective distributions

$$\begin{aligned} \Pi = \{\pi | \pi & \text{ is a probability distribution on } \{1\} \cup S \text{ such that } \tfrac{1}{14} \leq \pi(1) \leq \tfrac{3}{14} \\ & \text{and } \tfrac{1}{4} \leq \pi[s_{n+1} = b | S \text{ and } (s_1, \ldots, s_n) = (\bar{s}_1, \ldots, \bar{s}_n)] \leq \tfrac{3}{4}, \\ & \text{for all } n = 1, 2, \ldots \text{ and for all } (\bar{s}_1, \ldots, \bar{s}_n)\}, \end{aligned}$$

where $\pi[\cdot|\cdot]$is the conditional distribution generated by π. The true utility function of a person of type 1 is $u = v_{\hat{b}}$, where $\hat{b} = (b, b, \ldots) \in S$.

Suppose that until period 1 all people of type 2 have been producing the good of type 1, so that they have no information about the utility function of people of type 1. Suppose that the inertia assumption does not apply to the production decisions of people of type 2. Suppose that in period 1, an unusual young person of type 2 has the opinion that the true state lies in S with probability 13/14 and that if the state is in S, it satisfies $s_1 = a$ with probability 3/4. If this person produces good a, he or she can expect to gain

$$\frac{13}{14}\left(\frac{10}{9}\left(\frac{3}{4}\right) + \frac{1}{4}\right) = \frac{13}{14}\left(\frac{13}{12}\right) > 1.$$

The gain in utility from producing good 1 is 1. Therefore, he or she produces good a. Once that good is produced, it will be known in period 2 that the true state is in S and that $s_1 = b$. It is easy to calculate that in each period t thereafter, people of type 2 know that $s_1 = \cdots = s_{t-1} = b$ and each person of type 2, regardless of opinion, produces either $(c_1, \ldots, c_t) = (b, \ldots, b, a)$ or $(c_1, \ldots, c_t) = (b, \ldots, b, b)$, thus revealing in period t that $s_t = b$.

The above example works equally well if it is assumed that the inertia assumption applies to all innovations. In that case, the initiator of the chain of innovations would have to be a person with an unusually low aversion to uncertainty.

The existence of the informational externality is a well-known argument for subsidizing innovation. The need for such subsidization is reduced by diversity of opinion. That diversity may even lead to excessive experimentation, as was shown in Section 9. In the Knightian framework, the optimal size of the subsidy can be estimated only very imprecisely, since key quantities are imponderables.

11 Conclusion

Knightian decision theory may give insight into the process of innovation in business. Uncertainty and uncertainty aversion make innovation difficult and impede sharing of innovation risk through insurance markets. According to the theory, single individuals with little aversion to uncertainty are most likely to initiate new products, production processes, or forms of business. Entrepreneurs would tend to hinder each other's initiatives, if they acted as a group. Not only would they have to overcome each others' aversion to uncertainty, but their opinions would have to be in near agreement for them to cooperate. If they did cooperate, diversity of opinion among them would lead to something resembling a collective aversion to uncertainty.

References

1. Bewley, Truman (1986), "Knightian Decision Theory: Part 1," Cowles Foundation Discussion Paper No. 807.
2. Blume, Marshall E. and Irwin Friend (1978), *The Changing Role of the Individual Investor.* New York: Wiley.
3. Dow, James and Sergio Ribiero da Costa Werlang (1988), "Uncertainty Aversion and Optimal Choice of Portfolio," CARESS Working Paper No. 88–04, University of Pennsylvania.
4. Drèze, Jacques (1985), "(Uncertainty and) The Firm in General Equilibrium Theory," *Economic Journal*, supplement to Volume 95, pp. 1–20.
5. Ellsberg, Daniel (1961), "Risk, Ambiguity, and the Savage Axioms," *Quarterly Journal of Economics*, 75, 643–449.
6. Ellsberg, Daniel (1963), "Reply," *Quarterly Journal of Economics*, 77, 336–347.
7. Geanakoplos, John and James K. Sebenius (1983), "Don't Bet on It: Contingent Agreements and Asymmetric Information," *Journal of the American Statistical Association*, 78, 424–426.
8. Gilboa, Itzhak and David Schmeidler (1989), "Maxmin Expected Utility with a Non-unique Prior," *Journal of Mathematicsl Economics*, 18, 141–153.
9. Harrison, J. Michael and David Kreps (1978), "Speculative Investor Behavior in a Stock Market with Heterogeneous Expectations," *Quarterly Journal of Economics*, 92, 323–326.
10. Knight, Frank (1921), *Risk, Uncertainty, and Profit.* Boston and New York: Houghton–Mifflin.

11. LeRoy, Stephen F. and Larry D. Singell, Jr. (1987), "Knight on Risk and Uncertainty," *Journal of Political Economy*, 95, 394–406.
12. Schumpeter, Joseph (1939), *Business Cycles*, Vol. 1. New York and London: McGraw–Hill.
13. Schoemaker, Paul (1982), "The Expected Utility Model: Its Variants, Purposes, Evidence and Limitations," *Journal of Economic Literature*, 20, 529–563.

Objectives of an Imperfectly Competitive Firm: A Surplus Approach.*

Egbert Dierker[1], Hildegard Dierker[1], and Birgit Grodal[2]

[1] Institut für Wirtschaftswissenschaften, Universität Wien, Hohenstaufengasse 9, A-1010 Wien, Austria
[2] Centre of Industrial Economics and Økonomisk Institut, Københavns Universitet, Studiestræde 6, DK-1455 København, Denmark

Abstract. We consider a firm acting strategically on behalf of its shareholders. The price normalization problem arising in general equilibrium models of imperfect competition can be overcome by using the concept of real wealth maximization. This concept is based on shareholders' aggregate demand and does not involve any utility comparisons. We explore the efficiency properties of real wealth maxima for the group of shareholders. A strategy is called S-efficient (S stands for shareholders) if there is no other strategy such that shareholders' new total demand can be redistributed in a way that all shareholders will be better off. Our main result states that the set of real wealth maximizing strategies coincides with the set of S-efficient strategies provided that shareholders' social surplus is concave. Thus, even if a firm does not know the preferences of its shareholders it can achieve S-efficiency by selecting a real wealth maximizing strategy.

1 Introduction

In this paper we consider a simple model of a firm acting strategically on behalf of its shareholders. The firm influences relative prices in the economy either by its production decision or directly as a price setter. We assume that the firm is owned by a large number (ideally, a continuum) of small shareholders who take prices and wealth as given when choosing their consumption plans. The wealth of a consumer consists of the value of his initial endowment and his profit share. If a firm is engaged in imperfect competition, the strategy choice not only affects the wealth of its shareholders, but also the prices shareholders face as consumers on the market. Since demand patterns and shareholdings differ across individuals, different shareholders would like their firm to pursue different objectives. A similar problem is encountered in economies with incomplete markets, where shareholders disagree because of their idiosyncratic insurance needs. Thus, in the case of imperfect competi-

* E. and H. Dierker would like to thank the Centre of Industrial Economics and the Institute of Economics, University of Copenhagen, for their hospitality. Financial support from both institutions is gratefully acknowledged.

tion as well as incomplete markets, a social choice problem arises for which there is no obvious solution [see, in particular, Arrow (1983), p. 2].[1]

In the literature, this social choice problem is often assumed away. In the field of industrial organization, it is nearly always taken for granted that shareholders only consume and own goods whose prices do not depend on the actions of their firm. Similarly, in the finance literature dealing with incomplete markets, the firm is often assumed to disregard the fact that the choice of its production plan influences the insurance possibilities of its shareholders ("market value maximization").

In many models of imperfect competition firms are assumed to maximize profits. However, it is well known from the literature that this objective is ill-defined unless particular, strong assumptions are made, see for example Gabszewicz and Vial (1972) and H. Dierker and Grodal (1986). Since the price level remains undetermined, profits are normalized by using one of the commodities as numéraire or, more generally, by applying some price normalization rule. But different price normalizations entail profit functions which are, in general, not related to each other by monotone transformations. Hence, maximization of profits in different normalizations amounts to firms pursuing different objectives.

To overcome the price normalization problem, E. Dierker and Grodal (1999) propose the concept of real wealth maximization. Given the strategies of all other firms, the strategy $\hat{\sigma}$ maximizes shareholders' real wealth if it is undominated in the following sense: There does not exist another strategy σ' such that the aggregate demand of all shareholders at $\hat{\sigma}$ is in the interior of their aggregate budget set at σ'.

Real wealth maximization is based on profits and the composition of the aggregate demand of the firm's shareholders. Moreover, it is independent of any a priori chosen price normalization. If real wealth maximization is applied, shareholders' aggregate demand endogenously yields a yardstick to compare profits. If $\hat{\sigma}$ is a real wealth maximum and $\hat{D}$ is shareholders' total demand at $\hat{\sigma}$, then shareholders' wealth never suffices to buy more than $\hat{D}$.

In an important contribution to the theory of incomplete markets, Drèze (1974) defines the goal of a firm by using Pareto comparisons accompanied by redistribution. Given the production decisions of all other firms, a production decision of the firm under consideration leads to an allocation of goods among its shareholders. In general, these allocations will not be Pareto comparable. Therefore, Drèze proposes the following test that a production decision has to pass: It must be impossible to choose another production plan together with a redistribution scheme for the group of shareholders such that all shareholders will be better off if they keep their portfolio fixed. Clearly, since markets are incomplete, the redistribution is only allowed to involve the good available to the group of shareholders at the present date $t = 0$.

[1] Headnote to Arrow (1950) in Arrow (1983). We are grateful to M. Hellwig for drawing our attention to this headnote.

We will now formulate the analogue of the Drèze criterion for the case of imperfect competition. Consider a specific firm and assume that the strategies of all other firms are given. The strategy σ of the firm gives rise to a price system which, together with the profits $\Pi(\sigma)$, determines the budget set of each shareholder. Thus, each strategy σ induces an allocation of goods among the shareholders of the firm under consideration. As in the case of incomplete markets, these allocations will, in general, not be Pareto ranked. We say that strategy σ' of a firm dominates strategy σ if the aggregate demand of the shareholders of this firm at σ' can be redistributed in such a way that every shareholder will be better off. In analogy to the Drèze criterion, we propose the following test that a strategy $\bar{\sigma}$ has to pass: There is no strategy σ' that dominates $\bar{\sigma}$. An undominated strategy is called S-efficient (S stands for shareholders).

It is important to clarify the role that redistribution plays in our setting. We want to emphasize that no redistribution ever takes place among the shareholders.[2] Redistribution only arises in the form of the following thought experiment. Suppose there is an omniscient hypothetical planner who can freely redistribute goods among shareholders. If the firm chooses a certain strategy σ, the hypothetical planner checks whether there exists another strategy σ' such that he can achieve a Pareto improvement for the shareholders by redistributing their aggregate demand at σ' among them. If he can, the strategy σ is discarded. If he cannot, σ can be implemented. Clearly, to implement σ, the planner is not needed. Therefore, the assumption of an omniscient planner who possesses the power to perform any lump sum redistribution presents no restriction here since it is used only to single out certain allocations, which can be obtained without any help of a planner.[3]

The Drèze criterion is based on Pareto comparisons and cannot be stated without reference to preferences. To make Pareto comparisons the firm is supposed to know the distribution of shareholders' preferences. By contrast, a firm maximizing shareholders' real wealth only needs to know their aggregate demand function. Obviously, these informational requirements are much less demanding, and the question arises as to how both concepts are related to each other.

In order to analyze how real wealth maxima and S-efficient allocations are related, a particular type of imperfect competition must be stipulated. We opt for a framework in which firms set prices and we study the behavior of

[2] This point has caused a certain amount of confusion in the literature on general equilibrium theory with incomplete markets. In our view, the usual definition of the set of feasible allocations is inappropriate since redistribution at time $t = 0$ is allowed to take place in the traditional definition of a feasible allocation.

[3] Drèze's characterization of the objective of a firm is intimately related to Shapley's extension of the value to NTU games. In both cases, the solution concept involves a tool that is not available to the agents. This hypothetical tool is used to formulate the following postulate: The outcome should be such that no improvement would be possible even if the tool were available.

a firm under the assumption that the prices of its competitors are given. For this purpose, it suffices to focus on an economy with two commodities and a price setting monopolist who produces good 1 using good 0, the numéraire, as input. The strategy P of the firm is the decision to offer one unit of the product in exchange for P units of the numéraire.

We will show that any S-efficient strategy maximizes shareholders' real wealth if the firm's profit function is concave. Since real wealth maximization is defined without reference to utility functions, the more interesting question is whether a real wealth maximizing strategy is S-efficient.

To address this question, we first assume that shareholders have quasilinear preferences. In this case, shareholders' preferences can be aggregated into a single preference relation, for which shareholders' social surplus is a utility representation. Therefore, S-efficiency amounts to maximizing the utility of the representative owner, that is to surplus maximization. Moreover, a surplus maximizing strategy maximizes real wealth [cf. Section 5]. Thus, if there is a unique real wealth maximizing strategy it must be S-efficient.

In order to formulate conditions ensuring a unique real wealth maximum, we introduce the notion of a shareholder's marginal willingness to pay for an increase of the strategy P. The sum of these marginal willingnesses vanishes if and only if real wealth is maximized. Thus, if the sum of the marginal willingnesses is strictly decreasing, there is only one real wealth maximum. It turns out that this monotonicity property is equivalent to the strict concavity of the surplus function. Hence, if shareholders' utilities are quasilinear, strict concavity of the surplus function implies that real wealth maximization entails a unique outcome, which is S-efficient.

If we give up the quasilinear framework, some of these statements carry over and others are lost or need to be modified. In the quasilinear setting, the existence of an S-efficient outcome is obvious. However, S-efficiency may be unobtainable in more general cases. We present an example in which there are several real wealth maxima, but all of them dominated. The nonexistence of an S-efficient outcome relies on the fact that the wealth of a shareholder is given by a fixed assignment of initial endowments and profit shares. Thus, nonexistence is due to a conflict between efficiency and distribution. The incompatibility of efficiency with a given distribution was first shown by Guesnerie (1975) in the context of nonconvex production sets.

A natural way to ensure existence of S-efficient outcomes and the S-efficiency of real wealth maxima is to generalize the insight obtained from the quasilinear case. Let $\hat{P}$ maximize real wealth and define shareholders' compensated social surplus associated with $\hat{P}$ as the difference between the aggregate wealth they obtain at some strategy P and the expenditures needed to keep them on the utility levels they have at $\hat{P}$. If this social surplus function is concave, then $\hat{P}$ is S-efficient. To obtain uniqueness of a real wealth maximum we use strict concavity of shareholders' uncompensated surplus function.

Therefore, concavity of surplus functions plays a crucial role in the quasilinear as well as the general case. Hence, we show the invariance of this property with respect to the choice of economically meaningful linear structures on strategies and on wealth.

The paper is organized as follows: Section 2 introduces the model. In Section 3 and Section 4, real wealth maximization and S-efficiency are defined, respectively. In Section 5, we analyze the connection between social surplus maximization, real wealth maximization, and S-efficiency in the quasilinear setting. Section 6 is devoted to the invariance of the concavity of the profit and the surplus functions with respect to meaningful normalization rules. Section 7 presents the example. In Section 8, it is shown that real wealth maximization and S-efficiency are identical goals if shareholders' compensated social surplus is concave. Section 9 concludes the paper.

2 Model and basic notation

It suffices to consider an economy with two commodities and one price setting monopolist who produces good 1 using good 0, the numéraire, as input. The analysis will be essentially the same as that of a price setting firm in an oligopolistic market if the prices of its competitors are given. For simplicity's sake, we assume that the firm has fixed unit costs $c > 0$. The strategy P is the commitment to deliver one unit of the product in exchange for P units of the numéraire. If commodity 0 serves as numéraire, we use the subscript N. For instance, profits obtained at prices $(1, P)$ are denoted $\Pi_N(P)$.

The consumers are denoted by $I = \{1, \cdots, m\}$. Consumer $i \in I$ has shares $\vartheta^i \geq 0$ in the firm. We assume that the firm has a large set $\mathfrak{I} = \{i \in I \mid \vartheta^i > 0\}$ of shareholders and that all consumers, owners as well as nonowners, take their budget sets as given. Suppose, for simplicity's sake, that the consumption set of every consumer equals $\mathbb{R}^2_+$ and that no consumer has initial endowments of the product, that is, consumer i has the initial endowment $e^i = (e^i_0, 0)$ where $e^i_0 > 0$.

Since Pareto comparisons are made, we assume that every consumer i has a C^1 demand function d^i that is generated by a strictly convex, monotone preference relation $\succ^i$, which can be represented by the C^2 utility function U^i. Moreover, whenever convenient, expenditure functions are assumed to be C^2 in prices. The demand function d^i is homogeneous of degree 0 and satisfies the budget identity $(1, P)d^i(1, P, W^i_N) = W^i_N$. The wealth of consumer i at prices $(1, P)$ is described by the function $W^i_N(P) = e^i_0 + \vartheta^i \Pi_N(P)$ and $W_N(P) = \sum_{i \in \mathfrak{I}} W^i_N(P)$ denotes the aggregate wealth of the shareholders.

We assume throughout that profit expectations are correct, that is, the demand based on consumers' wealth expectations generates precisely the expected profits if the monopolist satisfies the demand for its product. That is to say, profits fulfill the equation $\Pi_N(P) = (P - c)d_1(P)$, where $d_1(P) = \sum_{i=1}^m d^i_1(1, P, W^i_N(P))$ is the total demand of all consumers for good 1 if prices are $(1, P)$ and profits are $\Pi_N(P)$. We assume that Π_N is a continuous function. Let $D^i(P) = d^i(1, P, W_N^i(P))$ denote shareholder i's demand corresponding to strategy P. Shareholders' aggregate demand is $D(P) = \sum_{i \in \mathcal{I}} D^i(P)$. Let P_{max} be the smallest P at which Π_N attains its maximum. Clearly, no shareholder wishes the firm to charge a price above P_{max}. Therefore, we consider only strategies in $\mathcal{P} = [c, P_{max}]$. We assume that $W_N(P) > 0$ for all $P \in \mathcal{P}$. Moreover, the demand of the nonowners for the firm's product is assumed to be positive if $P = c$.

Since we only analyze commodity assignments to the group $\mathcal{I}$ of shareholders, we call such assignments allocations for short. For every strategy $P \in \mathcal{P}$, there exists exactly one allocation, namely the allocation $(D^i(P))_{i \in \mathcal{I}}$. An allocation is attainable iff it can be implemented by a strategy choice of the firm.

Definition *The allocation $(x^i)_{i \in \mathcal{I}}$ is* attainable *iff there exists $P \in \mathcal{P}$ such that $x^i = D^i(P)$ for all $i \in \mathcal{I}$.*

Observe that no sidepayments occur in the definition of an attainable allocation. As we have already mentioned, all agents, shareholders as well as nonshareholders, buy the firm's product at market prices. Thus, consumers are treated as anonymous. Nobody knows which characteristics any other, particular consumer possesses. This fact is in accordance with the Walrasian tradition. Walras equilibria depend only on the distribution of agents' characteristics. In the present framework no additional information is assumed. Therefore, sidepayments cannot be made.

3 Real wealth maximization

Each strategy P defines the budget line

$$BL(P) = \{(x_0, x_1) \in \mathbb{R}^2 \mid x_0 + Px_1 = W_N(P)\} \tag{1}$$

and the corresponding budget set

$$AB(P) = \{(x_0, x_1) \in \mathbb{R}^2_+ \mid (1, P)(x_0, x_1) \leq W_N(P)\}$$

of the group of owners. Their aggregate budget set is $AB = \bigcup_{P \in \mathcal{P}} AB(P)$. Note that AB is compact since $\mathcal{P}$ is compact and W_N is continuous. Since $\mathbb{R}^2_+ \setminus AB(P)$ is convex for every P and $AB = \mathbb{R}^2_+ \setminus \bigcap_{P \in \mathcal{P}} (\mathbb{R}^2_+ \setminus AB(P))$, the aggregate budget set is the complement of a convex set. The North-East boundary of AB is called the *aggregate budget curve ABC*. More precisely,

$$ABC = \{x \in AB \mid \nexists\, z \gg 0 \text{ such that } x + z \in AB\}.$$

We define the objective of the monopolist without making a priori assumptions on the demand behavior of the shareholders. Consider two different strategies P_1, P_2 and the corresponding aggregate budget sets $AB(P_1)$

and $AB(P_2)$. First, we look at the extreme case, in which $AB(P_1)$ is strictly contained in $AB(P_2)$. Let $x \geq 0, x \neq 0$, be any commodity bundle. Clearly, the number of units of the bundle x which the shareholders can afford if the firm chooses strategy P_2 is strictly larger than the number of units they can buy if the firm chooses strategy P_1. Whatever bundle the firm uses to evaluate the real wealth of the shareholders, their aggregate wealth is larger at P_2 than at P_1. We assume that a real wealth maximizing firm choosing between P_1 and P_2 will select P_2, although it may very well be that some shareholders, due to distributional effects, prefer strategy P_1 to P_2.

In general, the budget sets corresponding to different strategies of the firm will not be ordered by inclusion. Hence, the ordering of budget sets according to the number of units of the bundle x which can be bought out of shareholders' aggregate wealth depends on the choice of the reference bundle x. However, when the firm considers a strategy P, it is assumed to know the composition $x(P) = D(P)/\|D(P)\|$ of shareholders' aggregate demand at P. In our opinion, it is natural for the firm to use $x(P)$ as the reference bundle.

Note that shareholders do in general not agree on the strategy choice of their firm. Shareholder i wants the firm to maximize $U^i(D^i(P))$. Since shareholders differ with regard to shares, endowments, and preferences, they want the firm to pursue different goals. As a consequence, there will typically be a continuum of strategies that cannot be Pareto ranked. Pareto comparisons of attainable states cannot provide us with a useful definition of the goal of the firm.

The same holds true for profit maximization unless very strong assumptions are made. The maximization of profits Π_N measured in terms of the numéraire is justified only if shareholders neither own nor consume the firm's product. Moreover, different ways to normalize prices and measure profits lead to different profit functions and hence different maxima. If there is no clear, a priori specified connection between some commodity basket used to define profits and the shareholders' desires, the maximization of a profit function cannot be used as an objective of the firm acting on behalf of its shareholders. In E. Dierker and Grodal (1999), the following relation is used to introduce an objective of the firm:

Definition *Shareholders' real wealth at $P_1 \in \mathcal{P}$ can be increased by strategy $P_2 \in \mathcal{P}$, in symbols $P_1 \prec_{rw} P_2$, iff $(1, P_2)D(P_1) < W_N(P_2)$.*

The objective of the firm is to choose a strategy $\hat{P}$ such that there is no other strategy P which increases shareholders' real wealth. That is to say, there is no other strategy P such that the aggregate demand $D(\hat{P})$ lies below the budget line $BL(P)$. If such a strategy P existed, the group of shareholders could buy more units of the bundle $D(\hat{P})$ if the firm chose strategy P instead of $\hat{P}$.

Definition *Strategy* $\hat{P} \in \mathcal{P}$ maximizes shareholders' real wealth *if there is no strategy* $P \in \mathcal{P}$ *such that* $(1, P)D(\hat{P}) < W_N(P)$, *that is to say, if* $D(\hat{P}) \in ABC$.

Strategies maximizing shareholders' real wealth need not exist since the relation $\prec_{rw}$ need neither be acyclic nor convex. E. Dierker and Grodal (1998) state conditions on the aggregate demand function ensuring that $\prec_{rw}$ is acyclic. Also, they show the convexity of $\prec_{rw}$ if the profit function is concave. In either case, a real wealth maximum exists.

Observe that real wealth maximization reduces to profit maximization in the case of perfect competition with complete markets. Moreover, it generalizes the standard approach in industrial organization, in which it is (implicitly) assumed that shareholders only own and consume the numéraire commodity.

The first order condition for real wealth maximization states that shareholders' marginal wealth equals their aggregate demand for the product.[4] Since we assume the value of the initial endowment, which takes the form $(e_0^i, 0)$, to be independent of P, we know that marginal wealth equals marginal profits.

Remark 1 *If* Π_N *is* C^1 *and if* $\hat{P}$ *maximizes shareholders' real wealth, then*

$$W_N'(\hat{P}) = \Pi_N'(\hat{P}) = D_1(\hat{P}) \ .$$

In the remainder of this section, we present two alternative formulations of the first order condition for real wealth maximization. The first will be used to establish the uniqueness of a real wealth maximum and is based on the concept of shareholder i's *indirect utility function* $u^i : \mathcal{P} \times \mathbb{R}_+ \to \mathbb{R}$ which is defined as

$$u^i(P, \tau) = U^i(d^i(1, P, W_N^i(P) + \tau)) \, .$$

Agent i obtains the utility $u^i(P, \tau)$ if the relative price P is chosen and if i gets τ units of the bundle $(1, 0)$ as sidepayment. His marginal willingness to pay for an infinitesimal change in the relative price P of the firm's product is defined by

$$MW^i(P) = \frac{\partial_P u^i(P, 0)}{\partial_\tau u^i(P, 0)} \, .$$

Remark 2 *Let* $\bar{P} \in \operatorname{int} \mathcal{P}$. *Then* $\bar{P}$ *satisfies the first order condition for real wealth maximization iff* $\sum_{i \in \mathcal{I}} MW^i(\bar{P}) = 0$.

Proof. By differentiation of u^i we obtain

$$\begin{aligned} \partial_P u^i(P, 0) &= \partial_P \tilde{v}^i(1, P, W_N^i(P)) \\ &\quad + \partial_W \tilde{v}^i(1, P, W_N^i(P)) \cdot \partial_P (W_N^i(P)), \end{aligned}$$

[4] For a proof, see E. Dierker and Grodal (1998).

where $\tilde{v}^i$ is shareholder i's ordinary indirect utility function. Using Roy's identity we get

$$MW^i(P) = -D_1^i(P) + \vartheta^i \Pi_N'(P) .$$

By summation,

$$\sum_{i \in \mathcal{I}} MW^i(P) = \Pi_N'(P) - D_1(P) = W_N'(P) - D_1(P) .$$

Then $\bar{P}$ satisfies the first order condition for real wealth maximization iff $\sum_{i \in \mathcal{I}} MW^i(\bar{P}) = 0$. □

Furthermore, it is worth noting that the first order condition for real wealth maximization characterizes the envelope of the family of aggregate budget lines. To each strategy $P \in \mathcal{P}$ there corresponds the budget line

$$L_P = \{(x_0, x_1, P) \in \mathbb{R}^2 \times \mathcal{P} \mid (1, P) \cdot (x_0, x_1) - W_N(P) = 0\} .$$

The difference between L_P and $BL(P)$ as defined in (1) is that L_P is embedded in $\mathbb{R}^2 \times \mathcal{P}$, whereas $BL(P) \subset \mathbb{R}^2$. The 1-parameter family of budget lines $\{L_P\}_{P \in \mathcal{P}}$ forms a smooth 2-dimensional manifold denoted $\mathcal{L}$ since the derivative of the mapping $(x_0, x_1, P) \mapsto x_0 + Px_1 - W_N(P)$ does not vanish. Now, project $\mathcal{L}$ into the commodity space $\mathbb{R}^2$. The *envelope* of the family of budget lines is defined as the set of critical values of the projection of $\mathcal{L}$ into the commodity space $\mathbb{R}^2$. It is characterized by the condition $\partial_P(x_0 + Px_1 - W_N(P)) = 0$, that is to say $W_N'(P) = x_1$, together with the budget equation. Thus, the envelope is given by

$$Env = \{(x_0, x_1) \in \mathbb{R}^2 \mid \exists P \in \mathcal{P} \text{ with } x_0 + Px_1 = W_N(P) \text{ and } W_N'(P) = x_1\}.$$

Remark 3 *Strategy $\bar{P} \in \mathcal{P}$ satisfies the first order condition $W_N'(\bar{P}) = \Pi_N'(\bar{P}) = D_1(\bar{P})$ for real wealth maximization iff $D(\bar{P})$ lies in Env.*

4 S-efficiency

S-efficiency refers to Pareto comparisons among the shareholders of a firm. The firm wants to extract wealth from the nonowners. However, if the firm raises its price for that purpose, then the shareholders themselves also have to pay more since they must buy the firm's product at market prices.

If the firm chooses P, then the group of shareholders obtains the profit $\Pi_N(P)$ as well as the commodity bundle $D(P)$. Note that the way the profit is raised cannot be separated from the way it is spent since the choice of strategy P determines both the profit income and the consumption of every shareholder. The definition of S-efficiency must take this link into account.

The concept of S-efficiency is based on the following thought experiment: Suppose $\bar{P}$ has been chosen and is compared with the alternative P. Clearly, if P is implemented, the group of shareholders receives the bundle $D(P)$, and the profit $\Pi_N(P)$ contains the part $(P-c)D_1(P)$ derived from this bundle. In order to keep this relation intact, $D(P)$ is kept fixed in the thought experiment. Assume that the group of shareholders could, after having obtained $D(P)$, redistribute this bundle in order to compensate the losers of the move from $\bar{P}$ to P. They would then certainly not move from the original strategy $\bar{P}$ to the alternative P if they could not even obtain a Pareto improvement for themselves in this hypothetical situation.

We are now going to define S-efficiency in a more formal way.

Definition *The strategy $P_1 \in \mathcal{P}$ is* dominated *by the strategy $P_2 \in \mathcal{P}$ iff there exist bundles $(x^i)_{i\in\mathcal{I}}$ such that $\sum_{i\in\mathcal{I}} x^i = D(P_2)$ and $D^i(P_1) \prec^i x^i$ for all $i \in \mathcal{I}$.*

A strategy $\bar{P}$ is undominated if there is no $P \in \mathcal{P}$ such that $D(P)$ can be distributed among the shareholders in a way which leaves them better off than at $\bar{P}$. An undominated strategy $\bar{P}$ and the corresponding allocation $(D^i(\bar{P}))_{i\in\mathcal{I}}$ are called S-efficient.

Definition *Strategy $\bar{P}$ and the corresponding allocation $(D^i(\bar{P}))_{i\in\mathcal{I}}$ are* S-efficient *iff there does not exist a strategy $P \in \mathcal{P}$ dominating $\bar{P}$.*

We derive the first order condition for S-efficiency.

Proposition 1 *Let the profit function Π_N be C^1 and assume that the allocation $(D^i(\bar{P}))_{i\in\mathcal{I}}$ is S-efficient. Then strategy $\bar{P}$ satisfies the first order condition*

$$(1,\bar{P}) \cdot (D_0'(\bar{P}), D_1'(\bar{P})) = 0\,.$$

This condition is equivalent to the first order condition for real wealth maximization, i.e. $D_1(\bar{P}) = W_N'(\bar{P})$.

Proof. Since Π_N is C^1, shareholders' aggregate demand D is C^1. Let $\bar{P} \in \mathcal{P}$ and assume that the allocation $(D^i(\bar{P}))_{i\in\mathcal{I}}$ is S-efficient. Assume by way of contradiction that $(1,\bar{P})\cdot(D_0'(\bar{P}), D_1'(\bar{P})) \neq 0$. Without loss of generality let $(1,\bar{P})\cdot(D_0'(\bar{P}), D_1'(\bar{P})) > 0$. (If this expression is negative, consider strategies $P < \bar{P}$.) Then $(1,\bar{P})(D(P) - D(\bar{P})) > 0$ for $P > \bar{P}$ and $|P-\bar{P}|$ sufficiently small. Since all preferences are strictly convex and the utility functions are C^2, there exists $\varepsilon > 0$ such that for any shareholder i the following condition holds. If $u \in \mathbb{R}^2$, $\|u\| < \varepsilon$, $(1,\bar{P})\cdot u > 0$, and $D^i(\bar{P}) + u \in \mathbb{R}^2_+$, then $D^i(\bar{P}) + u \succ^i D^i(\bar{P})$ [see, e.g., Magill and Quinzii (1996), p. 359]. Since D is continuous, there exists $\delta > 0$ such that $\|D(P) - D(\bar{P})\| < \epsilon$ for $|P-\bar{P}| < \delta$. Now let $u^i = \vartheta^i(D(P) - D(\bar{P}))$. For $|P-\bar{P}|$ sufficiently small we obtain $D^i(\bar{P}) + \vartheta^i(D(P) - D(\bar{P})) \succ^i D^i(\bar{P})$ for all shareholders i. However, as $\sum_{i\in\mathcal{I}}(D^i(\bar{P}) + \vartheta^i(D(P) - D(\bar{P}))) = D(P)$, this contradicts the fact that $(D^i(\bar{P}))_{i\in\mathcal{I}}$ is S-efficient. Hence, $(1,\bar{P})\cdot(D_0'(\bar{P}), D_1'(\bar{P})) = 0$.

To ascertain that the first order condition for S-efficiency coincides with the first order condition for real wealth maximization, we differentiate the budget equation $(1,P) \cdot D(P) = W_N(P)$ and obtain $(1,P) \cdot (D_0'(P), D_1'(P)) + D_1(P) = W_N'(P)$. Hence, $(1,P) \cdot (D_0'(P), D_1'(P)) = 0$ iff $D_1(P) = W_N'(P)$. □

On the assumption that the profit function Π_N is concave, E. Dierker and Grodal (1998), Theorem 3, show that a real wealth maximum is obtained whenever the first order condition for real wealth maximization is satisfied. Thus, Proposition 1 implies the following:

Proposition 2 *Let D and Π_N be C^1 and Π_N be concave. Assume that the strategy $\hat{P}$ is S-efficient. Then strategy $\hat{P}$ maximizes shareholders' real wealth.*

5 S-efficiency and uniqueness of real wealth maxima: The quasilinear case

To explore the conditions under which the converse of Proposition 2 holds, it is illuminating to investigate the case in which all shareholders have quasilinear utility functions U^i. This setting has the following major advantage: Although shareholders may differ radically in their individual assessments of the strategy of their firm, their preferences can be aggregated into a single one for the following reason. Consider any two utility profiles of the shareholders and add their individually preferred sets. Then one of the aggregate preferred sets must be contained in the other. In other words, Scitovsky curves do not intersect each other due to the absence of income effects that affect the demand for the product. Therefore, the Scitovsky curves describe the preferences of a single consumer. Let U^{Rep} denote a utility function of this consumer. Let S_1 and S_2 be two aggregate preferred sets corresponding to the utility levels U_1 and U_2, respectively. Then $U_2 > U_1$ iff $S_2 \subset \text{int}\, S_1$.[5] Clearly, if income effects are permitted, additional phenomena enter the picture. They will be analyzed in the following sections.

For the maximization of the utility of the representative owner, there is a clear economic interpretation. Since shareholders have quasilinear utilities, their consumer surplus is unambiguously defined and their social surplus can be written as $S_N(P) = \Pi_N(P) + \int_P^\infty D_1(p)dp$. Assume that $S_N(P_1) < S_N(P_2)$ and let U_1 and U_2 be the associated utility levels, respectively. Let E_N^{Rep} denote the expenditure function of the representative owner. Then $\Pi_N(P_1) < \Pi_N(P_2) + \int_{P_2}^{P_1} D_1(p)dp = \Pi_N(P_2) + (E_N^{Rep}(P_1, U_2) - E_N^{Rep}(P_2, U_2))$. Denoting shareholders' aggregate initial endowment by $(e_0, 0)$, we have $e_0 + \Pi_N(P_1) = E_N^{Rep}(P_1, U_1)$ and $e_0 + \Pi_N(P_2) = E_N^{Rep}(P_2, U_2)$. As a consequence, the above inequality becomes $E_N^{Rep}(P_1, U_1) < E_N^{Rep}(P_2, U_2) + (E_N^{Rep}(P_1, U_2) - E_N^{Rep}(P_2, U_2)) = E_N^{Rep}(P_1, U_2)$, and we conclude that $U_1 < U_2$. This argument shows that surplus maximization amounts to maximizing the utility of

[5] This refers to the interior relative to $\mathbb{R}_+^2$.

the representative owner. In particular, a surplus maximum must be undominated.

The first order condition for surplus maximization, $\Pi'_N(P) = D_1(P)$, coincides with the first order condition for real wealth maximization. Moreover, the real wealth shareholders obtain at P_1 can be increased by choice of P_2, in symbols $P_1 \prec_{rw} P_2$, iff $(1, P_2)D(P_1) < W_N(P_2)$. Therefore, $P_1 \prec_{rw} P_2$ implies $U_1 < U_2$. Note, however, that the relation $\prec_{rw}$ is not complete. It may be that the surplus maximum is unique, but that additional real wealth maxima exist at the same time.

Remark 4 *Assume that shareholders' utility functions are quasilinear. Then surplus maximization and the maximization of the representative owner's utility coincide. Furthermore, $P_1 \prec_{rw} P_2$ implies $U_1 < U_2$. In particular, a unique real wealth maximum is a surplus maximum and, therefore, undominated.*

Thus, the question arises as to the conditions entailing the uniqueness of a real wealth maximum. Obviously, if P equals unit costs c, profits vanish. Since the demand of the nonowners is positive at $P = c$ by assumption, an infinitesimal price increase raises shareholders' wealth, and the sum of the marginal willingnesses $MW^i(c)$ is positive. Similarly, if $P = P_{max}$, no shareholder's marginal willingness MW^i will be positive, and every shareholder who consumes a positive amount of the product would benefit from a lower price. Thus, $\sum_{i \in \mathcal{I}} MW^i(P_{max})$ is negative. Naturally, a unique real wealth maximum results if one assumes that $\sum_{i \in \mathcal{I}} MW^i(P)$ is strictly decreasing in the interval $\mathcal{P} = [c, P_{max}]$.

The present quasilinear setting provides an ideal framework for the interpretation of this monotonicity assumption. As laid out below, the marginal willingness $MW^i(P)$ can easily be integrated with respect to P, and the result is closely connected to i's share of the social surplus.

Given $\tilde{P}$, let $T^i : \mathcal{P} \to \mathbb{R}$ describe the compensation shareholder i needs in order to stay at the utility level $\tilde{U}^i$, that is, $T^i(P)$ is uniquely defined by the equation $u^i(P, T^i(P)) = \tilde{U}^i = u^i(\tilde{P}, 0)$. Clearly, if P is raised infinitesimally, $dT^i(P)/dP$ has to be given to i in order to keep him at the utility level $\tilde{U}^i$. That is to say, i's marginal willingness is given by $MW^i(P) = -dT^i(P)/dP$. The assumption that $\sum_{i \in \mathcal{I}} MW^i(P)$ is strictly decreasing can then be restated as follows: The aggregate compensation $T(P) = \sum_{i \in \mathcal{I}} T^i(P)$ needed to keep every shareholder i on the utility level $\tilde{U}^i$ is a strictly convex function of P. One can think of $T(P)$ as the amount of shareholders' social surplus that can be liberated if the firm moves from P to $\tilde{P}$. In this case, shareholder i's share of the social surplus increases by $T^i(P)$.

The monotonicity assumption entailing the uniqueness and S-efficiency of a real wealth maximum can be rephrased as follows. We assume that Π_N is concave. Then the domain $C^i = \{(P, \tau) \in \mathcal{P} \times \mathbb{R} \mid W^i_N(P) + \tau \geq 0\}$ of the indirect utility function u^i is convex for every $i \in \mathcal{I}$. The *aggregate preferred set* associated with the surplus maximizing strategy $\tilde{P}$, and the resulting utility profile $(\tilde{U}^i)_{i\in\mathcal{I}}$ is

$$\tilde{A} = \{(P, \sum_{i\in\mathcal{I}} \tau^i) \in \mathcal{P} \times \mathbb{R} \mid (P, \tau^i) \in C^i \text{ and } u^i(P, \tau^i) \geq \tilde{U}^i \text{ for each } i \in \mathcal{I}\}.$$

Note that $\tilde{A}$ is the epigraph $\{(P, \tau) \in \mathcal{P} \times \mathbb{R} \mid \tau \geq T(P)\}$ of the aggregate compensation function T and that $\tilde{A}$ is strictly convex iff T is strictly convex.[6] As argued above, this is the case iff $\sum_{i\in\mathcal{I}} MW^i(P)$ is strictly decreasing.

The results are summarized in the following proposition.

Proposition 3 *Assume that the utility functions U^i of the shareholders $i \in \mathcal{I}$ are quasilinear and assume that the profit function Π_N is concave. Let $\tilde{P}$ denote a surplus maximizing strategy and $(\tilde{U}^i)_{i\in\mathcal{I}}$ the associated utility profile of the shareholders. Then the following conditions are equivalent:*

i) *The sum $\sum_{i\in\mathcal{I}} MW^i(P)$ of the marginal willingnesses to increase P is strictly decreasing for $P \in \mathcal{P} = [c, P_{max}]$.*
ii) *The total compensation $T = \sum_{i\in\mathcal{I}} T^i : \mathcal{P} \to \mathbb{R}$ needed to keep every shareholder on the utility level $\tilde{U}^i$ is a strictly convex function.*
iii) *The aggregate preferred set $\tilde{A} \subset \mathcal{P} \times \mathbb{R}$ is strictly convex.*

Each of these conditions implies the uniqueness and S-efficiency of a real wealth maximum. Moreover, maximization of real wealth and maximization of shareholders' social surplus coincide in this case.

6 Linear structures on strategies and wealth

In Proposition 2 the profit function Π_N is assumed to be concave. Moreover, in Proposition 3 S-efficiency and uniqueness of a real wealth maximum are derived from an assumption either requiring a certain convexity property directly [see conditions ii) and iii)], or stipulating the monotonicity of $\sum_{i\in\mathcal{I}} MW^i(P)$. However, whenever we speak about the concavity or convexity of some set or function, we need an underlying linear structure. In the present case, we need linear structures on the sets of strategies and wealth, respectively.

In order to introduce such linear structures, we have expressed prices and wealth in units of commodity 0. Instead of using a particular good as numéraire, one could have taken any commodity bundle $x = (x_0, x_1)$, $x_0 > 0$. This leads to the question of whether Propositions 2 and 3 and other statements are invariant with respect to the choice of bundle x. In this section, we show that the concavity of the profit function, the convexity of the aggregate

[6] More precisely, the lower boundary of $\tilde{A}$ is strictly convex, i.e., $\tilde{A}$ is the intersection of a strictly convex set with $\mathcal{P} \times \mathbb{R}$.

preferred set $\tilde{A}$, and related items are invariant with respect to the choice of bundle x.[7]

Prices normalized with respect to x are denoted (π_0, π_1), that is, (π_0, π_1) satisfies $\pi_0 x_0 + \pi_1 x_1 = 1$. Thus, π_1 denotes the output price in terms of bundle x and the corresponding input price is $\pi_0 = (1 - \pi_1 x_1)/x_0$. If bundle x is used to measure wealth, then W_x denotes the maximal number of units of bundle x affordable at prices (π_0, π_1).

Consider any $A_N \subset \mathbb{R}_+ \times \mathbb{R}$. As before, the subscript N indicates that we use good 0 as numéraire. The first component of $(P, W_N) \in A_N$ corresponds to the price system $(1, P)$, the second measures the wealth in terms of the bundle $(1, 0)$. Now replace $(1, 0)$ by an alternative bundle $x = (x_0, x_1)$, $x_0 > 0$. Then $\mathbb{R}_+ \times \mathbb{R}$, and hence A_N, are transformed as follows:

$$(P, W_N) \mapsto t_x(P, W_N) = \left(\frac{1}{x_0 + P x_1}\right)(P, W_N).$$

The price system corresponding to $(1, P)$ in the x-normalization is given by $(1/(x_0 + P x_1), P/(x_0 + P x_1))$. Hence, the first coordinate of $t_x(P, W_N)$ equals $\pi_1 = P/(x_0 + P x_1)$. Moreover, the wealth W_N is the number of units of the bundle $(1, 0)$ which can be bought at the price system $(1, P)$. At the price system (π_0, π_1) the corresponding wealth is $(W_N, 0)(\pi_0, \pi_1) = \pi_0 W_N$. The number of units of the bundle x, given the wealth $\pi_0 W_N$, is $W_x = W_N \pi_0/(\pi_0 x_0 + \pi_1 x_1) = W_N/(x_0 + P x_1)$. Thus, the second coordinate of $t_x(P, W_N)$ is $W_N/(x_0 + P x_1)$.

Proposition 4 *If prices are normalized with respect to an arbitrary consumption bundle $x \in \mathbb{R}^2_+ \setminus \{0\}$, then the set $A_x = t_x(A_N)$ is convex iff A_N is convex.*

Proof. Consider any points (P, W_N) and (P', W'_N) in A_N. A simple calculation shows that, for any $\delta \in [0, 1]$,

$$t_x(\delta(P, W_N) + (1 - \delta)(P', W'_N)) = \lambda t_x(P, W_N) + (1 - \lambda) t_x(P', W'_N),$$

where $\lambda = \delta(x_0 + P x_1)/(x_0 + (\delta P + (1 - \delta)P')x_1))$. Note that λ, when considered as a function of $\delta \in [0, 1]$, is bijective. Hence, A_x is convex iff A_N is convex. □

Proposition 4 entails that the concavity of the profit function, the expenditure function, or the surplus function does not depend on which commodity bundle is used to normalize prices and measure wealth. This is due to the following fact: If the set below the graph of one of these functions is convex if the N-normalization is used, its image under the mapping t_x is convex.

We use the profit function to illustrate the invariance. Let Π_x denote profits as a function of the output price if bundle x has been used to normalize

[7] This follows from observations in E. Dierker and Grodal (1999). Here we shall present a shorter and more direct argument.

prices and measure wealth. We want to show that the profit function Π_x is concave for any bundle x iff Π_N is concave.

With the price system (π_0, π_1), the firm obtains the profit $\Pi_N(\pi_1/\pi_0)$ in terms of good 0, which corresponds to the value $(\pi_0, \pi_1)(\Pi_N(\pi_1/\pi_0), 0)$. This profit enables the shareholders to buy $\Pi_x(\pi_1) = \pi_0 \Pi_N(\pi_1/\pi_0)$ units of bundle x. Substitution yields

$$\Pi_x(\pi_1) = \frac{1 - \pi_1 x_1}{x_0} \, \Pi_N\Big(\frac{\pi_1}{(1 - \pi_1 x_1)/x_0}\Big),$$

where π_1 lies in the range of the transformed prices with $\pi_1 < 1/x_1$. Hence, we obtain $t_x(P, \Pi_N(P)) = (\pi_1, \Pi_x(\pi_1))$ for all $P \in \mathbb{R}_+$. Clearly, Π_x is concave iff $\{\pi_1, r) \mid r \leq \Pi_x(\pi_1)\}$ is convex. Note that, in the above argument, Π_x can be replaced by expenditure or surplus as a function of the output price.

Remark 5 *Assume that only normalization rules that have an economic interpretation are used. That is to say, there is a commodity bundle $x \geq 0, x \neq 0$, such that $px = 1$ for all prices under consideration. Wealth is expressed in units of the same bundle x. In that case, the concavity of the profit, expenditure or surplus function does not depend on the normalization rule used. As a consequence, the results in this paper are independent of the choice of the normalization rule.*

7 Nonexistence of S-efficient strategies

In the quasilinear case, there can be several real wealth maxima. They need not all be undominated. However, there is always at least one S-efficient real wealth maximum, namely the maximum of shareholders' social surplus.

Now we will consider a framework in which no representative owner exists. In our example there is no undominated attainable allocation. There are two real wealth maxima, but each of them dominates the other.

The example is constructed as follows: The aggregate demand function g of all nonowners is taken as being linear. The group of owners of the firm can "almost" be represented by one agent. In fact, there are two owners of the firm, a large one with a CES utility function and a small one with a quasilinear utility function. The weights are calibrated such that the two real wealth maxima yield approximately the same utility for the large CES owner.

In the example, the profit function Π_N of the firm is not concave. In order to show that the absence of an S-efficient allocation does not depend on the nonconcavity of the profit function, we also consider the concavification $\tilde{\Pi}_N$ of the profit function and note that the phenomenon persists.

There is one firm with constant unit costs $c = 1$. The demand function of the nonowners is given by

$$g(1, P) = 1000 - P.$$

There are two (types of) owners with initial endowments, $e^1 = (1000, 0)$ and $e^2 = (542, 0)$. They have the following CES and quasilinear utility functions, respectively.

$$U^1(x_0, x_1) = x_0^{\frac{10}{11}} + (21x_1)^{\frac{10}{11}}$$
$$U^2(x_0, x_1) = x_0 + 144x_1^{\frac{1}{2}} .$$

The (large) CES shareholder owns the fraction 0.999 of the firm and the (small) quasilinear shareholder the fraction 0.001.

A simple computation yields that the profit function is given by

$$\Pi_N(P) = (P-1)\frac{1000 - P + \frac{72^2}{P^2} + \frac{21^{10} \cdot 10^3}{P(21^{10}+P^{10})}}{1 - (P-1)\frac{21^{10} \cdot 0.999}{P(21^{10}+P^{10})}} .$$

The demand functions of the first and second owner are

$$D^1(P) = \left(\frac{P^{10}(10^3 + 0.999 \cdot \Pi_N(P))}{21^{10} + P^{10}}, \frac{21^{10}(10^3 + 0.999 \cdot \Pi_N(P))}{P(21^{10} + P^{10})}\right)$$
$$D^2(P) = \left(542 + 0.001 \cdot \Pi_N(P) - \frac{72^2}{P}, \frac{72^2}{P^2}\right) ,$$

respectively. Shareholders' total demand is $D(P) = D^1(P) + D^2(P)$.

A calculation yields that there are three strategies which satisfy the first order condition $\Pi_N'(P) = D_1(P)$ for real wealth maximization, namely

$$P_A \approx 12.94, \qquad P_B \approx 500.48, \qquad P_C \approx 26.45 .$$

However, as the profit function Π_N is not concave, the first order condition is not sufficient. A direct investigation shows that the two strategies $P_A \approx 12.94$ and $P_B \approx 500.48$ are real wealth maximizing strategies, whereas P_C is not. For instance, $D(P_C)$ lies in the interior of the budget set $AB(P_B)$ associated with P_B.

The aggregate budget curve ABC has a kink since the profit function does not coincide with its concavification $\tilde{\Pi}_N$ [cf. E. Dierker and Grodal (1999), Section 3]. However, the profit function Π_N and its concavification $\tilde{\Pi}_N$ coincide at P_A and P_B. Thus, real wealth is also maximized at P_A and P_B if $\tilde{\Pi}_N$ rather than Π_N is used.

We want to investigate whether the strategies $P_A \approx 12.94$ and $P_B \approx 500.48$ are dominated, more precisely, whether either of the real wealth maximizing strategies is dominated by the other one. First, we calculate the utility levels of the two owners when the firm chooses strategy P_B and obtain

$$U^1(D^1(P_B)) \approx 80840.74 \qquad \text{and} \qquad U^2(D^2(P_B)) \approx 801.87 .$$

In order to show that the strategy P_A dominates strategy P_B, we calculate the aggregate demand at P_A and get $D(P_A) \approx (1496.08, 11828.65)$. Now we let $x^2 = (0.2, 31)$ and $x^1 = D(P_A) - x^2$ and obtain the corresponding utility levels of the owners

$$U^1(x^1) \approx 80872.80 \qquad \text{and} \qquad U^2(x^2) \approx 801.96\,.$$

Hence, we have distributed the aggregate demand at P_A such that both owners are better off, that is, P_A dominates P_B.

Similarly, the utility levels at strategy P_A are

$$U^1(D^1(P_A)) \approx 80734.10 \qquad \text{and} \qquad U^2(D^2(P_A)) \approx 1095.69$$

and the aggregate demand at strategy P_B is $D(P_B) \approx (251042.23, 0.021)$. Now we let $x^2 = (1095.70, 0)$ and $x^1 = D(P_B) - x^2$ and obtain the utility levels

$$U^1(x^1) \approx 80748.83 \qquad \text{and} \qquad U^2(x^2) = 1095.70\,.$$

We see that the strategy P_B dominates P_A. Thus, in the example, neither of the real wealth maximizing strategies leads to an S-efficient allocation. Moreover, each of the two real wealth maximizing strategies dominates the other.

Remark 6 *In the example, no attainable allocation is S-efficient.*

Proof. According to Proposition 1, the first order condition $\Pi_N'(P) = D_1(P)$ for real wealth maximization holds at any S-efficient allocation. The only strategies satisfying this condition are P_A, P_B, and P_C. Since P_A dominates P_B and vice versa, the only remaining candidate is P_C. However, the utility levels obtained at P_C are $U^1(D^1(P_C)) \approx 11282.17$ and $U^2(D^2(P_C)) \approx 765.40$. Both owners prefer the bundles they obtain at P_A and at P_B. Thus, the strategy P_C is dominated by P_A and by P_B. □

One could conjecture that the nonexistence of S-efficient allocations is due to the fact that the profit function is not concave. We will show that this conjecture is false.

Consider the concavification $\tilde{\Pi}_N$ of the profit function and define the demand function $\tilde{g}$ for the nonowners in such a way that $\tilde{g}$ generates the profit function $\tilde{\Pi}_N$, i.e. $\tilde{g}(P) = (\tilde{\Pi}_N - (P-1)\tilde{D}_1(P))/(P-1)$, where $\tilde{D}_1$ is the aggregate demand of the shareholders when they obtain profit $\tilde{\Pi}_N$. It turns out that $\tilde{\Pi}_N$ is obtained by replacing the graph of Π_N by a straight line in the interval given approximately by $[13.96, 397.14]$. Outside of this interval $\tilde{\Pi}_N$ coincides with Π_N.

First, note that P_A lies to the left of the interval and P_B lies to the right. P_A and P_B are real wealth maximizing strategies in the economy with the concavified profit function $\tilde{\Pi}_N$. As before, P_A dominates P_B and vice versa. Second, if Π_N is replaced by its concavification $\tilde{\Pi}_N$, then P_C is turned into a real wealth maximum. We know that P_C satisfies the first order condition for real wealth maximization without maximizing real wealth. Thus, according to Remark 3, $D(P_C)$ lies in Env, but not in ABC. Clearly, shareholders' aggregate demand function D also changes if the profit function is concavified, and the critical point P_C moves to the nearby point $\tilde{P}_C \approx 29.19$, which lies in the envelope after concavification. Since $\tilde{\Pi}_N$ is concave, $\tilde{P}_C$ must maximize real wealth [see the end of Section 4].

Since $\tilde{\Pi}$ is linear (i.e. barely concave) on a segment around $\tilde{P}_C$, it is not surprising that $\tilde{P}_C$ is dominated by points very close to $\tilde{P}_C$. Here we suppress these calculations and show that, more interestingly, $\tilde{P}_C$ is dominated by both other real wealth maxima, P_A and P_B. The utility levels of the two owners at $\tilde{P}_C$ are

$$U^1(\tilde{D}^1(\tilde{P}_C)) \approx 55116.89 \qquad \text{and} \qquad U^2(\tilde{D}^2(\tilde{P}_C)) \approx 882.36\,.$$

In order to show that P_A dominates $\tilde{P}_C$, we distribute the aggregate demand $\tilde{D}(P_A) = D(P_A) \approx (1496.08, 11828.65)$ as follows: We set $x^2 = (0, 40)$ and $x^1 = D(P_A) - x^2$ and obtain the utility levels

$$U^1(x^1) \approx 80817.34 \qquad \text{and} \qquad U^2(x^2) \approx 910.74\,.$$

Hence, we have distributed the aggregate demand at P_A such that both owners are better off than they were at P_A, that is, P_A dominates $\tilde{P}_C$.

Similarly, to show that P_B dominates $\tilde{P}_C$, we distribute the aggregate demand $\tilde{D}(P_B) = D(P_B) \approx (251042.23, 0.021)$ in the following way: We set $x^2 = (1000, 0)$ and $x^1 = D(P_A) - x^2$ and get utility levels

$$U^1(x^1) \approx 80776.92 \qquad \text{and} \qquad U^2(x^2) = 1000\,.$$

In the concavified economy, the profit function is, of course, not strictly concave. However, by continuity we can easily obtain the same conclusions in an economy with a strictly concave profit function.

Proposition 5 *There are robust examples with concave profit functions in which every real wealth maximum is dominated by another real wealth maximum. As a consequence, no S-efficient strategy exists.*

8 Equivalence of real wealth maximization and S-efficiency

The analysis of the representative agent model in Section 5 provides an insight that is absent from the traditional models of general equilibrium theory and industrial organization. Clearly, the particular structure of representative consumer models also presents a risk. In his paper "On the "Law of Demand"", Werner Hildenbrand (1983), p. 998, points out: "There is a *qualitative difference* in market and individual demand functions. This observation shows that the concept of a "representative consumer," which is often used in the literature, does not really simplify the analysis; on the contrary, it might be misleading." Representative consumer models have often been misused. However, we are going to argue that, with a sufficient degree of precaution, the study of representative agent models helps improve general equilibrium theory with imperfect competition.

To illustrate this point, we come back to the discussion of Proposition 3 in terms of surplus maximization or, alternatively, in terms of the utility of the representative owner. There, shareholders' social surplus takes the form

$$S_N(P) = \Pi_N(P) + \sum_{i \in \mathfrak{I}} \int_P^\infty D_1^i(p)dp = \Pi_N(P) - E_N^{Rep}(P) + const\,, \qquad (2)$$

that is, it encompasses not only the profits accruing to the representative owner but also his expenditures E_N^{Rep} (which are independent of the utility level in the present case). By contrast, in the usual G.E. or I.O. models, expenditures do not appear in the definition of the goal of a firm. Indeed, the models present special cases in which consumer surplus vanishes. Clearly, if it vanishes, it can be neglected. However, because the fact that it only vanishes in degenerate cases has been ignored, the price normalization problem has arisen.

If the goal of the firm is based on shareholders' social surplus rather than on profits, it is natural to impose the concavity assumption on $S_N(P)$ rather than on the profit function $\Pi_N(P)$.[8] Clearly, S_N can be concave only if Π_N is concave since the expenditure function E_N^{Rep} is concave in P. Remember that i's compensation function T^i is implicitly defined by $u^i(P, T^i(P)) = \tilde{U}^i = u^i(\tilde{P}, 0)$, where the tilde indicates the surplus maximum. Thus, if i possesses $W_N^i(P) + T^i(P)$, he can just reach $\tilde{U}^i$. Therefore, the aggregate compensation $T(P) = \sum_{i \in \mathfrak{I}} T^i(P)$ is given by $e_0 + \Pi_N(P) + T(P) = E_N^{Rep}(P)$. Setting *const* in (2) equal to e_0, we get $S_N(P) = -T(P)$ and $S_N(\tilde{P}) = 0$. Hence, the aggregate compensation function always equals $T(P) = S_N(\tilde{P}) - S_N(P)$. Obviously, T is strictly convex iff the social surplus S_N is strictly concave. Therefore, Proposition 3 can also be interpreted as follows:

Remark 7 *In the quasilinear setting S-efficiency and uniqueness of a real wealth maximum are obtained if shareholders' social surplus S_N is a strictly concave function of the strategy P.*

---

[8] As pointed out in Section 5, S_N is a utility function of the representative owner and individual utility functions are ordinal concepts. However, the concavity of S_N plays an important role in the present context. The representative owner differs from an ordinary consumer in the following sense: It is often appropriate to break down his utility function into a sum of such functions. Here they consist of the profit shares and the consumer surpluses which the individual shareholders receive [cf. (2)].

If one leaves the quasilinear framework, the situation becomes more complex. First, the conditions for S-efficiency and uniqueness of a real wealth maximum no longer coincide (see below). Second, according to Remark 6, S-efficient strategies may not exist. However, it turns out that the concavity of an appropriately defined social surplus function yields S-efficiency of a real wealth maximizing strategy. Hence S-efficient strategies exist.

Now we focus on the relationship between real wealth maximization and S-efficiency. In the light of surplus theory, one is led to proceed as follows [see Luenberger (1995), chapter 6, sections 7 and 8]: Consider any strategy $\check{P}$, and let $\check{U} = (\check{U}^i)_{i \in \mathcal{I}}$ be the associated utility profile of the shareholders. Given $\check{P}$, define shareholders' compensated social surplus as

$$S_N(P, \check{U}) = W_N(P) - \sum_{i \in \mathcal{I}} E_N^i(P, \check{U}^i),$$

where $E_N^i(P, \check{U}^i)$ denotes i's expenditures in terms of the input good 0. We say that $\check{P}$ maximizes social surplus if $\check{P}$ maximizes $S_N(\cdot, \check{U})$.

Let $\hat{P}$ be any real wealth maximizing strategy and $S_N(\cdot, \hat{U})$ the associated social surplus function. The argument for S-efficiency of $\hat{P}$ relies on the inequality $S_N(\cdot, \hat{U}) = W_N(\cdot) - \sum_{i \in \mathcal{I}} E_N^i(\cdot, \hat{U}^i) \leq S_N(\hat{P}, \hat{U}) = 0$, which follows from the concavity of $S_N(\cdot, \hat{U})$.

Theorem *Assume that Π_N is C^1. Consider any strategy $\hat{P} \in \mathcal{P}$ and let $\hat{U}^i = U^i(D^i(\hat{P}))$ and $\hat{U} = (\hat{U}^i)_{i \in \mathcal{I}}$. Assume that shareholders' compensated social surplus $S_N(\cdot, \hat{U})$ is concave. Then $\hat{P}$ is S-efficient if and only if $\hat{P}$ maximizes shareholders' real wealth.*

Proof. Since $S_N(\cdot, \hat{U})$ is concave, Π_N is concave and Proposition 2 applies. Thus, it suffices to prove that $\hat{P}$ is S-efficient if it satisfies the first order condition for real wealth maximization. In this case, $\partial_P S_N(\hat{P}, \hat{U}) = W_N'(\hat{P}) - \sum_{i \in \mathcal{I}} \partial_P E_N^i(\hat{P}, \hat{U}^i) = D_1(\hat{P}) - \sum_{i \in \mathcal{I}} h_1^i(\hat{P}, \hat{U}^i) = 0$, where h_1^i denotes shareholder i's Hicksian demand for good 1. Hence, the concave function $S_N(\cdot, \hat{U})$ attains its maximum at $\hat{P}$. Hence, $S_N(P, \hat{U}) \leq S_N(\hat{P}, \hat{U})$ for all $P \in \mathcal{P}$.

Now let $V = \{x \in \mathbb{R}_+^2 \mid x = \sum_{i \in \mathcal{I}} x^i, U^i(x^i) > \hat{U}^i \text{ for all } i \in \mathcal{I}\}$ and consider any $x \in V$. For all $P \in \mathcal{P}$ we have $(1, P)x \geq \sum_{i \in \mathcal{I}} E_N^i(P, \hat{U}^i) \geq W_N(P)$. Indeed, $(1, P)x > W_N(P)$ for all $P \in \mathcal{P}$ since preferences are monotone and continuous. Hence, $x \notin AB(P)$ for all $P \in \mathcal{P}$ and, consequently, $x \notin AB$. Therefore, $V \cap AB = \emptyset$. Since $D(P) \in AB$ for all $P \in \mathcal{P}$, we get $D(P) \notin V$ for all $P \in \mathcal{P}$. Hence, $\hat{P}$ is S-efficient. □

Remark 8

1) *Under the assumptions of the Theorem, real wealth maximization and S-efficiency both coincide with compensated surplus maximization.*
2) *S-efficiency of a real wealth maximum is also achieved under the weaker condition that $S_N(\cdot, \hat{U})$ has a unique maximizer and a positive (negative) derivative to the left (right) of the maximizer.*

The latter condition coincides with strict pseudoconcavity. However, pseudoconcavity is not invariant with respect to the choice of the bundle used to normalize prices. In the Theorem, concavity of $S_N(\cdot, \hat{U})$ is assumed in order to employ an invariant assumption yielding the full equivalence of the solution concepts. An S-efficient strategy maximizes real wealth under the weaker assumption that Π_N is concave.

Remember that strategy $\hat{P}$ is S-efficient if there is no strategy P such that shareholders' aggregate demand $D(P)$ can be redistributed in a way that all shareholders will be better off. The proof of the Theorem shows the following stronger property of the real wealth maximizing strategy: There is no other strategy such that shareholders' new wealth can be redistributed in a way that all shareholders can buy a preferred bundle on the market.

The Theorem is based on the assumption that shareholders' compensated social surplus $S_N(\cdot, \hat{U})$ is concave. As in the quasilinear case, concavity of $S_N(\cdot, \hat{U})$ is equivalent to convexity of the aggregate preferred set $\hat{A}$ corresponding to $\hat{U}$ and equivalent to convexity of the sum of the compensation functions $T^i(\cdot, \hat{U}^i) : \mathcal{P} \to \mathbb{R}$ defined by the condition $u^i(P, T^i(P, \hat{U}^i)) = \hat{U}^i = u^i(\hat{P}, 0)$.

In the quasilinear case, strict concavity of shareholders' social surplus implies uniqueness and S-efficiency of a real wealth maximum. Clearly, strict concavity of $S_N(\cdot, \hat{U})$ does not imply uniqueness if income effects are permitted. Therefore, we consider shareholders' uncompensated surplus

$$S_N^{unc}(P) = \Pi_N(P) + \int_P^\infty D_1(p)dp\,.$$

Remark 9 *If S_N^{unc} is strictly concave and C^1, the real wealth maximum is uniquely determined.*

Remark 9 holds since $dS_N^{unc}(P)/dP = \sum_{i\in\mathcal{I}} MW^i(P)$ is strictly decreasing and any real wealth maximum $\hat{P}$ has to satisfy $\sum_{i\in\mathcal{I}} MW^i(\hat{P}) = 0$ [cf. Remark 2]. Note that the conclusion also holds under the weaker assumption of strict pseudoconcavity.

There is no clear connection between concavity of the compensated surplus function $S_N(\cdot, \hat{U})$ used in the Theorem and concavity of the uncompensated surplus function S_N^{unc}. By differentiation it is easily seen that for any P and corresponding utility profile $U_P = (U^i(D^i(P)))_{i\in\mathcal{I}}$ we have

$$\tfrac{\partial^2}{\partial P^2} S_N^{unc}(P) = \tfrac{\partial^2}{\partial P^2} S_N(P, U_P) + \tag{3}$$
$$\textstyle\sum_{i\in\mathcal{I}} \tfrac{\partial}{\partial W} d_1^i(1, P, W_N^i(P)) \cdot (d_1^i(1, P, W_N^i(P)) - \vartheta^i \Pi_N'(P))\,. \tag{4}$$

In the absence of income effects term (4) vanishes. However, in general it can have any sign.

9 Conclusion

The price normalization problem arising in general equilibrium models of imperfect competition can be overcome in two different ways. First, the objective of a firm can be described as maximization of shareholders' real wealth. This concept is based on the aggregate demand of the shareholders and does not rely on utility considerations. Second, in the spirit of Drèze's concept of the goal of a perfectly competitive firm in a setting with incomplete markets, we say that strategy P_1 of a firm is dominated by P_2 if shareholders' total demand $D(P_2)$ can be redistributed in such a way that all shareholders will be better off than at P_1. An undominated strategy is called S-efficient. In this paper, we have investigated the relationship between the two goals, real wealth maximization and S-efficiency.

First, we observe that the first order conditions for the two objectives coincide. Second, if the profit function is concave, an S-efficient strategy maximizes real wealth since the first order condition is sufficient for real wealth maximization.

S-efficiency of real wealth maxima is first explored in the setting of quasilinear preferences. In this case, shareholders' social surplus is unambiguously defined. We show that strict concavity of the social surplus function entails the coincidence of both solution concepts. Moreover, they coincide with surplus maximization. Furthermore, strict concavity of the surplus function implies uniqueness.

The quasilinear case exhibits properties that do not carry over smoothly to the general case. If utilities are quasilinear, there always exists an S-efficient strategy. By means of an example, we show that there are economies without quasilinear preferences in which each real wealth maximum is dominated by another and no S-efficient outcome exists.

In the general case, shareholders' social surplus also plays a decisive role. Since there are various nonequivalent versions of the notion of consumer surplus we describe our procedure. Each real wealth maximum determines a reference utility profile $\hat{U}$. Compensated social surplus $S_N(\cdot, \hat{U})$ is defined as the difference between the wealth generated and the wealth shareholders need in order to retain their respective utility levels. Our central result can be summarized as follows: If shareholders' compensated social surplus is concave for every real wealth maximum, both solution concepts coincide. Moreover, if $S_N(\cdot, \hat{U})$ and, hence, Π_N are concave the existence of undominated strategies can be shown.

In the quasilinear case, strict concavity of the social surplus function implies uniqueness of a real wealth maximum. Clearly, the surplus function $S_N(\cdot, \hat{U})$ is a welfare oriented concept based on compensated demand. Therefore, it is not an appropriate tool to establish the uniqueness of a real wealth maximum if income effects are permitted. However, if $S_N(\cdot, \hat{U})$ is replaced by the uncompensated surplus function $S_N^{unc}(P) = \Pi_N(P) + \int_P^\infty D_1(p)dp$, strict (pseudo)concavity of this surplus function implies that there cannot be multiple real wealth maxima.

Our arguments rely on concavity of the social surplus function. Since profit maximization is ill-defined due to the price normalization problem, we show that our results are independent of which commodity bundle is used to normalize prices and measure wealth.

The paper shows that surplus theory provides a useful tool to unify different concepts of the objective of a firm acting in the interest of its shareholders.

References

1. Arrow, K. : A Difficulty in the Concept of Social Welfare, Journal of Political Economy 58, 328-346 (1950)
2. Arrow, K. : Collected Papers of Kenneth Arrow. Social Choice and Justice. Cambridge: The Bellknap Press of Harvard University Press (1983)
3. Dierker, E., B. Grodal : Modelling Policy Issues in a World of Imperfect Competition, Scandinavian Journal of Economics 100, 153-179 (1998)
4. Dierker, E., B. Grodal : The Price Normalization Problem in Imperfect Competition and the Objective of the Firm, Economic Theory 14, 257-284 (1999)
5. Dierker, H., B. Grodal : Non-Existence of Cournot-Walras Equilibrium in a General Equilibrium Model with Two Oligopolists, in W. Hildenbrand and A. Mas-Colell eds., Contributions to Mathematical Economics, North Holland, 167-185 (1986)
6. Drèze, J.H. , Investment under Private Ownership: Optimality, Equilibrium and Stability, in Allocation Under Uncertainty; Equilibrium and Optimality, J.H. Drèze ed., New York: Wiley, 129-165 (1974)
7. Gabszewicz, J., J.P. Vial : Oligopoly "à la Cournot" in a General Equilibrium Analysis, Journal of Economic Theory 4, 381-400 (1972)
8. Guesnerie, R. : Pareto Optimality in Non-convex Economies, Econometrica 43, 1-31 (1975)
9. Hildenbrand, W. : On the "Law of Demand", Econometrica 51, 997-1019 (1983)
10. Luenberger, D. : Microeconomic Theory, New York: McGraw-Hill (1995)
11. Magill, M., M. Quinzii : Theory of Incomplete Markets, Cambridge, London: MIT Press (1996)

Monetary Equilibria*

Jacques H. Drèze and Heracles M. Polemarchakis

CORE, Université Catholique de Louvain, Belgium

Abstract. The introduction of banks that issue money and supply balances and pay out their profits as dividends is the natural modification of the model of general competitive equilibrium that encompasses monetary economies with an operative transactions technology. Monetary policy sets nominal rates of interest and accommodates the demand for balances; alternatively, it sets the supply of balances and rates of interest adjust for money markets to clear. Competitive equilibria exist. Under uncertainty, monetary policy fails to determine the distribution of the rate of inflation or the allocation of resources at equilibrium. If, in addition to rates of interest, monetary policy sets the prices of contingent loans subject to no-arbitrage constraints, or targets the distribution of the terminal level of prices, it lifts the multiplicity.

1 Introduction and preview

The almost universal prevalence of monetary exchange and the central place of monetary policy in macroeconomic analysis provide clear incentives to extend the canonical general equilibrium model of Arrow-Debreu-McKenzie (1954) to a monetary economy. The concern dates back to Walras (1902); it was revived by Patinkin (1965) and led to a number of contemporary formulations.

This paper develops a formulation that retains the generality of the canonical model under the simplest possible extension that captures the essentials of monetary exchange.

The formulation proceeds from the following premises:

1. Non-interest-bearing fiat money is dominated by interest-bearing nominal assets as a store of value; the demand for money accordingly results from its role in facilitating transactions: "money buys goods."
2. Fiat money is created at no cost by banks that lend it to individuals and firms at nominal non-negative interest rates.
3. Banks keep balanced accounts, so that outstanding money is the counterpart of assets, claims on individuals and firms; it is "inside money."
4. Banks are owned; profits, equal to interest earned on assets, accrue to shareholders.

* We wish to thank Gaetano Bloise, Gaël Giraud, Andrés Neumeyer and Paolo Siconolfi for helpful comments. An earlier draft was circulated in 1998.

Premise (1) assigns a central role to modeling the transactions technology that underlies the demand for money. Some, notably Ostroy and Starr (1974) or, more recently, Kyotaki and Wright (1989), have looked upstream of market institutions, in order to explain why most transactions take the form of exchanges of goods for money. It is sufficient to take this commonplace observation as a factual starting point. Premise (2) is a simplification that neglects the operating costs of banks; it is a useful first approximation. Taking into account operating costs could lead to models of competitive money supply, not introduced here. Premise (3) rules out "outside money," the focus of much monetary theory; it obviates the artificial conundrum, pointed out by Hahn (1965), that money could not maintain a positive price at equilibrium. It allows for a finite horizon, and it does not invoke overlapping generations, temporary equilibrium, or infinitely lived individuals. Still, the results extend without qualitative modification to infinite horizons, in Bloise, Drèze and Polemarchakis (2000). Importantly, premise (4) preserves Walras' law; failure to adopt that premise has led authors like Dubey and Geanakoplos (1992, 2000) to different conclusions on the multiplicity of equilibria.

The formulation proceeds from the following modeling options:

1. Time is divided into a finite number of "periods," of arbitrary length. Within a period, prices of commodities and rates of interest are constant, but interest accounting on monetary transactions is continuous, with no compounding within the period; for accounting purposes, values are expressed as of the beginning of the period. Analytically, periods are "dates" or points in time.
2. Uncertainty is described, following the canonical model and Debreu (1960), by an event-tree.
   In an abstract economy, an analytically convenient if artificial construct, the event-tree is only implicit.
3. The government is not a separate agent. Thus, a central bank is also owned by individuals.
4. There are no initial positions in monetary claims or assets; individuals have no initial holdings of balances or nominal claims.
5. In line with commodities, money at distinct date events defines distinct moneys, yielding distinct transaction services. There can be multiple currency areas, though the interpretation is not spelled out formally.

To anticipate, the following properties hold at equilibrium:

1. In a single-currency-area economy that extends over $t = 1, \ldots, T$ periods of time under certainty, once nominal rates of interest are set, there remains 1 degree of nominal multiplicity, corresponding to the overall or, alternatively, the initial or terminal level of prices; nominal interest rates have real effects.
2. In a single-currency-area economy that extends over T periods of time under uncertainty, with an event-tree that consists of N nodes s_t, of

which S are terminal: $N - T + 1 \geq S \geq 1$, if the N rates of interest, r_{s_t}, are set, there remain an additional S degrees of nominal multiplicity; one simple statement is that the S terminal price levels could be selected arbitrarily, without affecting the allocation of resources at equilibrium; an alternative statement is that monetary policy can control expected inflation, but not variability of inflation.

3. In an economy, not formally studied here, with H currencies, that extends over an event-tree with N nodes, of which S are terminal, if HN rates of interest, r_{h,s_t}, are set, there remain HS degrees of multiplicity, H — fold the number that characterizes a single currency area; exchange rates could be selected arbitrarily, without affecting the allocation of resources at equilibrium; yet, uncovered interest parity and purchasing power parity for commodities that are perfect substitutes in consumption or production hold throughout.

The paper is organised as follows. Section 2 describes a monetary economy, and defines an associated abstract economy. Equilibria in the abstract economy are the subject of section 3, which is self-contained. Section 4 addresses multiplicity of equilibria in the monetary economy and gives an example. Section 5 concludes.

2 A monetary economy

2.1 The transactions demand for money

The transactions demand for money is usually derived either from constraints on admissible transactions, or from optimizing behaviour in the face of transactions costs. The first approach is exemplified by the "cash-in-advance constraint" introduced by Clower (1967), which specifies that purchases cannot exceed cash balances held at the beginning of the period. If p are prices, z net trades, z_+ net purchases, z_- net sales,[1] $\hat{m}$ are initial money balances and m are terminal money balances, the cash-in-advance story unfolds as follows.

An individual acquires cash balances $\hat{m}^i \geq 0$ by borrowing initially from the bank in exchange for bonds at the rate of interest r, according to the constraint

$$b^i + \hat{m}^i = 0.$$

Subsequently he purchases commodities according to the constraint

$$pz_+^i - \hat{m}^i \leq 0.$$

He accumulates end-of-period balances through receipts from the sale of commodities according to the constraint

$$-pz_-^i + m^i = 0.$$

[1] For a scalar, $z_+ = \max\{z, 0\}$ and $z_- = -\max\{-z, 0\}$; for a vector, $z_+ = (\ldots, z_{k+} \ldots)$ and $z_- = (\ldots, z_{k-} \ldots)$.

At the end of the period, or at the beginning of a subsequent, fictitious period that serves for accounting purposes, the individual settles his debt according to the constraint

$$-(1+r)b^i - m^i \leq v^i,$$

where v^i is the dividend income of the individual. The budget constraints reduce to the single, over-all budget constraint in beginning-of-period values

$$pz^i + \hat{r}m^i \leq \tilde{v}^i,$$

where

$$\hat{r} = \frac{r}{1+r}, \quad \tilde{v}^i = \frac{v^i}{1+r},$$

while the cash-in-advance constraint takes the alternative, equivalent form

$$pz_- \leq m.$$

In order to consider the cash-in-advance constraint, one introduces the exchange set correspondence, here defined by

$$\Phi(p) = \mathcal{Z} \cap \{(z,m) : pz_- \leq m\},$$

where $\mathcal{Z}$ is the net trade set, the translation of the consumption set by the endowment of an individual.

Similar reasoning leads to the production set correspondence defined, under a simple cash-in-advance constraint, by

$$\Psi(p) = \mathcal{Y} \cap \{(y,n) : py_+ \leq -n\},$$

where y is the production plan, y_+ are net outputs, $-n \geq 0$ is money balances (an input) and $\mathcal{Y}$ the production set of a firm.

The obvious limitation of the cash-in-advance technology is the arbitrary period for which purchases require initial balances.

The second approach avoids this limitation, by allowing multiple cash withdrawals or transactions within a period, or cash holdings carried across periods. It is exemplified by the inventory model of Baumol (1952) and Tobin (1956), where money demand results from an optimal tradeoff between the opportunity (interest) cost of holding cash balances and the cost of multiple transactions.

For illustration purposes, expenditures flow at a constant rate within a single period, and receipts are concentrated at its end. Optimal cash withdrawals are then of equal size and equally spaced. Each withdrawal is the counterpart of a loan from the bank, to be reimbursed with interest at the end of the period. A simple calculation shows that, with τ withdrawals, the interest charge is $r\overline{m} = rpz_+((1+\tau)/2\tau)$, with $\overline{m}$ the average amount owed to the bank over the period. Still for illustration, the cost of each transaction is one unit of leisure time, and $u(z,t)$ represents the preferences of the individual, with $t = \bar{t} - \tau$ leisure time net of transactions. The exchange set correspondence is

$$\Phi(p) = \mathcal{Z} \cap \left\{(z, m) : 2\overline{m}(\bar{t} - t) = pz_+(1 + (\bar{t} - t))\right\},$$

and the budget constraint is

$$pz + r\overline{m} \leq v,$$

where $v \geq 0$ is dividend income.

The first order condition for optimization, ignoring the integer constraint on τ, is

$$\tau = \left(\frac{\lambda r p z_+}{2\frac{\partial u}{\partial t}}\right)^{\frac{1}{2}},$$

where λ is the Lagrange multiplier of the budget constraint. The cost of a transaction in terms of income, the marginal rate of substitution between leisure and income, is $(1/\lambda)(\partial u/\partial t)$, whereas pz_+ measures total spending; this is precisely the Baumol-Tobin formula.

Many model optimization under transaction costs by introducing "money in the utility function." — typically in the form of real balances. In the illustration of the Baumol -Tobin formula, one could substitute the transactions constraint in the utility function and write

$$u(z, \overline{m}, p) = u(z, \bar{t} - \frac{pz_+}{2\overline{m} - pz_+});$$

nevertheless, p and $\overline{m}$ would not enter utility in the form of real balances. More importantly, the resulting formulation would be in the nature of a reduced form. Such a formulation is not in the spirit of the canonical model, which distinguishes clearly subjective preferences from objective opportunities.

It could be argued that "liquidity," as measured by real balances, is desirable in itself, as provision for unforeseen outlays. This is the precautionary demand for money. In the canonical model, uncertainty is modeled through alternative states of the environment. Opportunities for outlays contingent on future states are naturally captured by the exchange set correspondence. Liquidity refers to access to a broader set of consumption plans, which is beneficial utility-wise. It would be improper to count these benefits twice.

On these grounds, here, balances, prices and rates of interest do not enter as arguments of preferences , though they did in earlier presentations — Drèze and Polemarchakis (1999, 2000). As asserted there, all results remain valid under that alternative formulation, which remains consistent when it corresponds to a properly defined reduced form.

In order to accomodate a variety of specifications for the transactions technology, we rely on the abstract correspondences Ψ (firms) and Φ (individuals). And we prove existence of equilibria for an abstract economy, under general assumptions in the tradition of the canonical model.

It is in the nature of the transactions technology that the exchange set correspondence defines liquidity requirements in terms of spot prices, separately for each money, k; for example, money at a particular date-event, $s_t = k$, or money in a currency area, k. The relevant constraints are of the form $(z_k, m_k) \in \Phi_k(p_k)$, where the vectors z_k and p_k are restrictions of z and p to the commodities that money k buys, distinct from the commodities associated with $k' \neq k$. One then writes $\Phi(p) = \times_k \Phi_k(p_k)$ and states that the economy has a product structure. If, in addition, the exchange sets Φ_k are homogeneous of degree 0 in (p_k, m_k), one states that the economy is (0-)homogeneous. Homogeneity means that the transactions technology is scale-invariant (free of "money illusion"). Similar definitions apply to the production-set correspondences of firms. Homogeneity is relevant to the transition from the abstract economy to specific applications.

2.2 Exchange sets and budget constraints

To define a monetary economy extending over time under uncertainty, the following notation and definitions are introduced.

Dates are $t \in \mathcal{T} = \{1, \ldots, T\}$. States of the world are $s \in \mathcal{S} = \{1, \ldots, S\}$. The resolution of uncertainty is described by $(\mathcal{S}_t : t \in \mathcal{T})$, an increasing sequence of partitions of the set of states of the world. Events at a date are $s_t \in \mathcal{S}_t = \{1, \ldots, S_t\}$. For a date-event, s_t, and a date $\hat{t} < t$, the predecessor of s_t at $\hat{t}$ is $s_{\hat{t}}(s_t)$, the date-event $s_{\hat{t}} \in \mathcal{S}_{\hat{t}}$, such that $s_t \subset s_{\hat{t}}$; for $\hat{t} > t$, the set of successors of s_t at $\hat{t}$ is the set $\mathcal{S}_{\hat{t}}(s_t)$, of date-events $s_{\hat{t}} \in \mathcal{S}_{\hat{t}}$, such that $s_{\hat{t}} \subset s_t$. No uncertainty is resolved prior to date 1: $\mathcal{S}_1 = \{\mathcal{S}\}$ and $s_1 = 1$, while all uncertainty is resolved by date $T : \mathcal{S}_T = \{\{s\} : s \in \mathcal{S}\}$. The set of date-events is $\mathcal{N} = \cup_{t \in \mathcal{T}} \mathcal{S}_t$, with cardinality N. It is sometimes convenient to augment the set of dates to $\mathcal{T}^* = \{1, \ldots, T, \ T+1\}$. Events at date $T+1$ coincide with events at date $T : \mathcal{S}_{T+1} = \mathcal{S}_T$. The augmented set of date-events is $\mathcal{N}^* = \cup_{t \in \mathcal{T}^*} \mathcal{S}_t$, with cardinality $N + S$.

Commodities are $l \in \mathcal{L} = \{1, \ldots, L\}$. A bundle of commodities at a date-event, s_t, is [2] $x_{s_t} = (x_{l,s_t} : l \in \mathcal{L})'$; across date-events, a bundle of commodities is $x = (x_t : t \in \mathcal{T})$. Prices of commodities at a date-event, s_t, are $p_{s_t} = (p_{l,s_t} : l \in \mathcal{L})$; across date-events, prices of commodities are $p = (p_t : t \in \mathcal{T})$.

Elementary securities and bonds of one date maturity effect transfers of revenue. The elementary security with payoff one unit of revenue at a date-event, s_{t+1}, is traded at the date-event $s_t(s_{t+1})$. At a date-event, s_t, elementary securities are [3] $s_{t+1} \in \mathcal{S}_{t+1}(s_t)$, and a portfolio of elementary

[2] For a finite, non-empty set, $\mathcal{K}$, a variable, x, which takes different values, x_k, for $k \in \mathcal{K}$, and for $\mathcal{K}' \subset \mathcal{K}$, a non-empty subset, $x_{\mathcal{K}'} = \{x_k : k \in \mathcal{K}'\}$; when there is no ambiguity, $x = x_{\mathcal{K}}$. Also, "$'$" denotes the transpose.

[3] It is pedantic to use an index for elementary securities different from the date-event at which they pay off.

securities is $(\eta_{s_{t+1}} : s_{t+1} \in \mathcal{S}_{t+1}(s_t))'$. Prices of assets at a date-event, s_t, are $(q_{s_{t+1}} : s_{t+1} \in \mathcal{S}_{t+1}(s_t))$. The bond traded at a date-event, s_t, yields interest r_{s_t} at every date event $s_{t+1} \in \mathcal{S}_{t+1}(s_t)$; and $\hat{r}_{s_t} = r_{s_t}(1 + r_{s_t})^{-1}$. At a date-event, s_t, holdings of bonds are b_{s_t}.

A firm is described by the production set correspondence that assigns to prices of commodities, prices of elementary securities and rates of interest, (p, q, r), production plans, bundles of commodities and balances, (y, n), across date-events.

An individual is described by the exchange set correspondence that assigns to prices of commodities, prices of elementary securities and rates of interest, (p, q, r), net trades of commodities and balances, (z, m), across date-events; the utility function defined over net trades of commodities, z, across date-events; and shares in firms and banks.

A monetary economy is defined here for a simple cash-in-advance technology; the extension to other transactions technologies is the subject of remark 2 below. The simple formulation embodies the following conventions.

1. Firms are allowed to distribute negative dividends to raise equity capital; accordingly, they do not trade securities; a simple dividend policy, spelled out below, calls for distributing at the beginning of each period the economic profit of the period.
2. Individuals trade elementary securities against cash at the beginning of each period, before trading in commodities; they trade with the bank, they borrow or lend, for the net amount required to meet the cash-in-advance constraint.
3. Interest accounting does not distinguish the end of a period from the beginning of the next one; the distinction remains essential, however, for information about states and for prices or rates of interest.

At the beginning of period t, at node s_t, an individual collects dividends $v^i_{s_t}$ (detailed below) and the proceeds of earlier investment $\eta^i_{s_t}$; he inherits terminal balances $m^i_{s_{t-1}(s_t)}$ and a debt to the bank $b^i_{s_{t-1}(s_t)}(1+r_{s_{t-1}(s_t)})$; and he acquires or sells elementary securities at a net cost $\sum_{s_{t+1}\in\mathcal{S}_{t+1}(s_t)} q_{s_{t+1}}\eta^i_{s_{t+1}}$. In order to settle these transactions and to have cash for commodity purchases, he exchanges with the bank bonds $b^i_{s_t}$ for initial balances $\hat{m}^i_{s_t}$, according to the constraint

$$-b^i_{s_t} = \hat{m}^i_{s_t} \geq p_{s_t} z^i_{s_t+} + \textstyle\sum_{s_{t+1}\in\mathcal{S}_{t+1}(s_t)} q_{s_{t+1}}\eta^i_{s_{t+1}} - \eta^i_{s_t} - v^i_{s_t}$$
$$-b^i_{s_{t-1}(s_t)}(1 + r_{s_{t-1}(s_t)}) - m^i_{s_{t-1}}.$$

He then accumulates cash balances through receipts for sales of commodities according to the constraint

$$p_{s_t} z^i_{s_t-} \;\leq\; m^i_{s_t}.$$

He enters period $t+1$ with holdings of elementary securities $\eta_{s_{t+1}}$, cash balances $m^i_{s_t}$ and debt to the bank $b^i_{s_t}(1+r_{s_t})$.

The individual maximizes his utility function subject to the budget constraints

$$p_1 z_1 + \sum_{s_2 \in S_2} q_{s_2}\eta_{s_2} + m_1 + b_1 = v^i_1,$$

$$p_{s_t} z_{s_t} + \sum_{s_{t+1} \in S_{t+1}(s_t)} q_{s_{t+1}}\eta_{s_{t+1}} + m_{s_t} + b_{s_t} = \eta_{s_t} + m_{s_{t-1}(s_t)} + (1 + r_{s_{t-1}(s_t)})b_{s_{t-1}(s_t)} + v^i_{s_t},$$

$$p_{s_T} z_{s_T} + m_{s_T} + b_{s_T} = \eta_{s_T} + m_{s_{T-1}(s_T)} + (1 + r_{s_{T-1}(s_T)})b_{s_{T-1}(s_T)} + v^i_{s_T},$$

$$0 = m_{s_T} + (1 + r_{s_T})b_{s_T}.$$

No-arbitrage in the market for bonds and elementary securities requires that

$$\frac{1}{1+r_{s_t}} = \sum_{s_{t+1} \in S_{t+1}(s_t)} q_{s_{t+1}}.$$

Under this condition, uniform holdings of elementary securities are perfect substitutes for bank loans, and individual demands are indeterminate. A simple way to lift the indeterminacy is the impose, at each s_t,

$$m^i_{s_t} + b^i_{s_t}(1 + r_{s_t}) \; = \; 0.$$

This implements transfers across periods through holdings of elementary securities, while bank loans provide within-period liquidity. Under this harmless convention, the budget constraints simplify to the "semi-reduced" form

$$p_1 z_1 + \sum_{s_2 \in S_2} q_{s_2}\eta_{s_2} + \hat{r}_1 m_1 \; = \; v^i_1,$$

$$p_{s_t} z_{s_t} + \sum_{s_{t+1} \in S_{t+1}(s_t)} q_{s_{t+1}}\eta_{s_{t+1}} + \hat{r}_{s_t} m_{s_t} \; = \; \eta_{s_t} + v^i_{s_t},$$

$$p_{s_T} z_{s_T} + \hat{r}_{s_T} m_{s_T} \; = \; \eta_{s_T} + v^i_{s_T}.$$

A firm, j, chooses a production plan of commodities and balances (y^j, n^j). At the beginning of period t, node s_t, it exchanges with the bank bonds $b^j_{s_t}$ for initial balances $\hat{n}^j_{s_t} \leq 0$ in the amount needed to pay for inputs y_{j-} and to issue dividends $v^j_{s_t}$, namely

$$b^j_{s_t} \; = \; -\hat{n}^j_{s_t} \; = \; p_{s_t} y^j_{s_{t-}} + v^j_{s_t}.$$

It then accumulates cash balances through receipts for sales of outputs,

$$-n^j_{s_t} \; = \; p_{s_t} y^j_{s_{t+}}$$

and uses these terminal balances to repay its debt to the bank:

$$b^j_{s_t}(1 + r_{s_t}) + n^j_{s_t} \;=\; 0.$$

This defines implicitly the dividends (the dividend policy) as

$$v^j_{s_t} \;=\; p_{s_t} y^j_{s_t} + \hat{r}_{s_t} n^j_{s_t}.$$

The bank initially issues balances $\hat{M}_{s_t}$, as demanded by individuals and firms in exchange for bonds. It earns interest $r_{s_t}\hat{M}_{s_t}$ which it pays out as dividends – thereby bringing the total quantity of money to $(1 + r_{s_t})\hat{M}_{s_t} = M_{s_t}$. The dividends may indifferently be expressed as $r_{s_t}\hat{M}_{s_t}$ or $\hat{r}_{s_t} M_{s_t}$.

The dividend income of individual i is

$$v^i_{s_t} \;=\; \sum_{j\in J} \theta^{ij} v^j_{s_t} + \theta^{i,J+1} v^{J+1}_{s_t} \;=\; \sum_{j\in J} \theta^{ij}(p_{s_t} y^j_{s_t} + \hat{r}_{s_t} n^j_{s_t}) + \theta^{i,J+1}\hat{r}_{s_t} M_{s_t}.$$

It is homogeneous of degree 1 in $(p_{s_t}, \cdots, n^j_{s_t}, \cdots, M_{s_t})$.

2.3 Consolidation and abstraction

The profit maximisation problem of a firm, j, calls for maximising the present value of profits. Prices of elementary securities define cumulative prices of elementary securities

$$\tilde{q}_{s_t} \;=\; 1 \times q_{s_2(s_t)} \times \cdots \times q_{s_{t-1}(s_t)} \times q_{s_t}.$$

The present value of firm j's profits (dividends) is

$$\tilde{v}^j \;=\; \sum_{s_t\in\mathcal{N}} \tilde{q}_{s_t}(p_{s_t} y^j_{s_t} + \hat{r}_{s_t} n^j_{s_t}) \;=\; \sum_{s_t\in\mathcal{N}} \tilde{q}_{s_t} v^j_{s_t}$$

which it maximises subject to the cash-in-advance constraints

$$-n^j_{s_t} \;=\; p_{s_t} y^j_{s_t+}.$$

The problem can also be stated in terms of present-value prices and balances

$$\tilde{p}_{s_t} \;=\; \tilde{q}_{s_t} p_{s_t}, \quad \tilde{n}^j_{s_t} \;=\; \tilde{q}_{s_t} n^j_{s_t};$$

the firm maximises

$$\tilde{p} y^j + \hat{r}\tilde{n}_j,$$

subject to

$$-\tilde{n}^j_{s_t} = \tilde{p}_{s_t} y^j_{s_t+}, \; s_t \in \mathcal{N}.$$

The equivalence of the two formulations follows from the homogeneity of the cash-in-advance constraints in (p, n).

Similarly, the budget constraints of an individual, i, can be consolidated into the single present-value constraint

$$\sum_{s_t \in \mathcal{N}} \tilde{q}_{s_t} \{p_{s_t} z_{s_t} + \sum_{s_{t+1} \in S_{t+1}(s_t)} q_{s_{t+1}} \eta_{s_{t+1}} + \hat{r}_{s_t} m_{s_t}\} = \sum_{s_t \in \mathcal{N}} \tilde{q}_{s_t} (\eta_{s_t} + v^i_{s_t})$$

or equivalently (after cancelling the η-terms)

$$\sum_{s_t \in \mathcal{N}} \{\tilde{p}_{s_t} z_{s_t} + \hat{r}_{s_t} \tilde{m}_{s_t}\} = \sum_{j \in J} \theta^{ij} \tilde{v}^j + \theta^{i,J+1} \tilde{v}^{J+1} := \tilde{v}^i,$$

where $\tilde{m}_{s_t} := \tilde{q}_{s_t} m_{s_t}$ and $\tilde{v}^{J+1} = \sum_{s_t \in \mathcal{N}} \tilde{q}_{s_t} \hat{r}_{s_t} M_{s_t}$. In vector notation,

$$\tilde{p}z + \hat{r}\tilde{m} = \tilde{v}^i.$$

Individual i maximises utility $u^i(z)$ subject to this consolidated budget constraint and to the cash-in-advance constraints

$$\tilde{m}_{s_t} = \tilde{p}_{s_t} z_{s_t -}, s_t \in \mathcal{N},$$

the homogeneity of which (in p, m) establishes the equivalence of the original and consolidated formulations.

The consolidated formulation eliminates explicit reference to the financial assets η and their prices q, to the bonds b, and to the nominal spot prices p. In particular, the price information guiding individual choices is reduced from the vector (p, q, r) of dimension $NL + (S-1) + N$ (taking no-arbitrage conditions into account), to the vector $(\tilde{p}, r)$ of dimension $NL + N$. This reduction is at the root of the multiplicity property stated in section 4, where we spell out in more detail the links between the two formulations. In general (beyond the simple cash-in-advance specification adopted here), their equivalence rests on the homogeneity property defined in section 2.1.

The full price information (p, q, r) is required to guide the portfolio choices of individuals. Also, in a monetary economy, spot price levels (inflation rates) matter. Yet, it is analytically convenient to study existence and other characteristics of equilibria for an abstract model, suceptible of interpretations encompassing a variety of applications – as defined for instance by alternative transactions technologies. The consolidated economy defined in terms of present-value prices and balances serves that purpose. It is studied in the next section.

Although artificial as a representation of an economy extending over time under uncertainty, the abstract economy describes directly an economy extending over a single period under certainty (spot prices are present-value prices, a.s.o.). In an economy extending over T periods of time under certainty, with present-value prices $\tilde{p}_t = \tilde{q}_t p_t$, the no-arbitrage conditions imply

$q_t = (1 + r_{t-1})^{-1}$, all t. Once the nominal rates of interest are given, the cumulative prices $\tilde{q}_t$ are also given, and the translation of spot prices into present-value prices is immediate. The original and abstract economies are identical, under homogeneity.

Remark 1. The cash-in-advance economy described above specifies payment of the dividends of the firms and of the bank, for each node s_t, *before* individuals acquire the cash balances needed there for commodity purchases. As a consequence, terminal balances of individuals are defined by the simple expression $m^i_{s_t} = p_{s_t} z^i_{s_t -}$, and this expression summarises neatly the implications of the cash-in-advance technology. In particular, homogeneity in (p, m^i) of the exchange set correspondence is immediately verified: $(z_k, m_k) \in \Phi^i_k(p_k)$ iff $(z_k, \lambda m_k) \in \Phi^i_k(\lambda p_k)$. When paid after the acquisition of cash balances for the purchases of commodities, the dividends appear under terminal balances, now defined by

$$m^i_{s_t} = p_{s_t} z_{s_t -} + v^i_{s_t} = p_{s_t} z_{s_t -} + \sum_{j \in J} \theta^{ij} (p_{s_t} y^j_{s_t} + \hat{r}_{s_t} n^j_{s_t}) + \theta^{i, J+1} \hat{r}_{s_t} M_{s_t}.$$

This expression is homogeneous in $(p_{s_t}, m^i_{s_t}, (n^j_{s_t})_{j \in J}, M_{s_t})$. But the exchange set correspondence is now be defined by

$$\Phi^i(p, (y^j, n^j)_{j \in J}, M) = \times_{s_t \in \mathcal{N}} \Phi^i_{s_t}(p_{s_t}, (y^j_{s_t}, n^j_{s_t})_{j \in J}, M_{s_t}).$$

That extension is not introduced explicitly in the definition of the abstract economy, to avoid ancillary complication. See however remark 3 below.

Remark 2. For simplicity, the description above of a monetary economy has been confined to the cash-in-advance transactions technology. The extension to more general technologies, including in particular inventory models à la Baumol-Tobin, is easy to outline. At the beginning of period t, at node s_t, an individual, i, still collects dividends $v^i_{s_t}$ and proceeds of earlier investment $\eta^i_{s_t}$; he inherits terminal balances $m^i_{s_{t-1}(s_t)}$ and a debt to the bank, provisionally denoted $d^i_{s_{t-1}(s_t)}$; and he acquires elementary securities at a net cost $\sum_{s_{t+1} \in S_{t+1}(s_t)} q_{s_{t+1}} \eta_{s_{t+1}}$. He then exchanges with the bank bonds $b^{i0}_{s_t}$ for initial balances $\hat{m}^i_{s_t}$ according to the constraint

$$-b^{i0}_{s_t} = \hat{m}^i_{s_t} \geq \max\{0, \sum_{s_{t+1} \in S_{t+1}(s_t)} q_{s_{t+1}} \eta^i_{s_{t+1}} - \eta^i_{s_t} - v^i_{s_t} - m^i_{s_{t-1}(s_t)} - d^i_{s_{t-1}(s_t)}\}.$$

Next, net trades $z^i_{s_t}$ and new financial transactions, say $b^{i\nu}_{s_t}, \nu = 1, 2, \cdots$, occur. The timing of net trades, the timing, nature and number of new financial transactions result from individual optimisation constrained by the exchange correspondence. The amount of cash on hand rises (falls) additively with negative (positive) components of $p_{s_t} z^i_{s_t}$ and $b^{i\nu}_{s_t}$ – without ever becoming negative. Terminal balances are

$$m^i_{s_t} = -p_{s_t} z^i_{s_t} - \sum_{\nu \geq 0} b^{i\nu}_{s_t} := -p_{s_t} z^i_{s_t} - b^i_{s_t},$$

where $b^i_{s_t}$ is the terminal level of the principal due ($b^i_{s_t} < 0$) or owned ($b^i_{s_t} > 0$) as a consequence of all transactions with the bank within period t. The interest associated with $b^i_{s_t}$ is $r_{s_t} \bar{b}^i_{s_t}$, where $\bar{b}^i_{s_t}$ is the average debt to the bank over the period, as implicitly defined by the sequence of transactions. Thus, the terminal debt to the bank is $d^i_{s_t} = b^i_{s_t} + r_{s_t} \bar{b}^i_{s_t}$. It replaces the term $b^i_{s_t}(1+r_{s_t})$ appearing in the previous subsection. In the illustration of section 2.1, $b^i_{s_t} = p_{s_t} z_{s_{t+}}$ and $\bar{b}_{s_t} = p_{s_t} z_{s_{t+}}((1+\tau)/2\tau)$. This simple dissociation of the principal of the debt from the interest liability should permit reconciliation of our abstract formulation with a variety of specifications of the transactions technology.

3 An abstract economy

3.1 Notation and definitions

Commodities are $l \in \mathcal{L} = \{1, \ldots, L\}$, a finite, non-empty set. A bundle of commodities is $z = (z_l : l \in \mathcal{L})'$. Prices of commodities are [4] $p = (p_l : l \in \mathcal{L}) > 0$.

Media of exchange, moneys, are $k \in \mathcal{K} = \{1, \ldots, K\}$, a finite, non-empty set. Balances are $m = (m_k : k \in \mathcal{K})'$. Rates of interest are $r = (r_k : k \in \mathcal{K}) \geq 0$.

At prices of commodities and rates of interest (p, r), the value of a bundle of commodities and balances (z, m) is

$$(p, r)(z, m) = pz + rm.$$

Agents in the economy are monetary authorities, banks, $k \in \mathcal{K} = \{1, \ldots, K\}$, firms, $j \in \mathcal{J} = \{1, \ldots, J\}$, and individuals, $i \in \mathcal{I} = \{1, \ldots, I\}$, finite, non-empty sets.

Associated with the monetary authority k, there is the medium of exchange, k, whose supply, $M^k \geq 0$, is under its control. Across monetary authorities, the supply of balances is $M = (M^k : k \in \mathcal{K})'$.

A currency, k, serves as a medium of exchange for commodities $\mathcal{L}_k \subset \mathcal{L}$. For $k \neq \tilde{k}$, distinct currencies, $\mathcal{L}_k \cap \mathcal{L}_{\tilde{k}} = \emptyset$: commodities for which different currencies serve as media of exchange are distinct; for a bundle of commodities, z, and for a currency, k, the projection to components $k \in \mathcal{L}_k$, is z_k; similarly, for prices, p_k is the projection to components $k \in \mathcal{L}_k$.

[4] "$\gg$," "$>$," "$\geq$" and "$\ll$," "$<$," "$\leq$" are vector inequalities.

A firm is described by the production set correspondence, Ψ^j, that assigns to prices of commodities a subset, $\Psi^j(p)$, of bundles of commodities and non-positive balances: for $(y, n) \in \Psi^j(p)$, the production plan of commodities is y, while balances, an input, are $n \leq 0$.

An individual is described by the triple, (Φ^i, u^i, θ^i), of an exchange set correspondence, an ordinal utility function and shares in banks and firms. The exchange set correspondence, Φ^i, assigns to prices of commodities a subset, $\Phi^i(p)$, of bundles of commodities and non-negative balances: for $(z, m) \in \Phi^j(p)$, the net trade or exchange of commodities is z while balances are $m \geq 0$. The utility function has domain the net-trade set, which includes $\Phi^i(p)$ for each p. Shares in firms and banks are $\theta^i = (\theta^{i,\mathcal{J}}, \theta^{i,\mathcal{K}}) = (\theta^{i,j} : j \in \mathcal{J}, \theta^{i,J+k} : k \in \mathcal{K})$.

Across firms, the production set correspondence is $\Psi^{\mathcal{J}} = \times_{j \in \mathcal{J}} \Psi^j$; across individuals, the exchange set correspondence is $\Phi^{\mathcal{I}} = \times_{i \in \mathcal{I}} \Phi^i$.

The allocation correspondence, A, assigns to prices of commodities and rates of interest a subset $A(p, r) \subset \Psi^{\mathcal{J}}(p, r) \times \Phi^{\mathcal{I}}(p, r)$ of allocations, $a = ((y, n)^j : j \in \mathcal{J}, (z, m)^i : i \in \mathcal{I})$, production plans and balances for firms and net trades and balances for individuals. At an allocation, the aggregate excess demand for commodities is $z^a = \sum_{i \in \mathcal{I}} z^i - \sum_{j \in \mathcal{J}} y^j$; the allocation is *feasible* if $z^a = 0$. If the supply of balances is M, the aggregate excess demand for balances is $m^a = \sum_{i \in \mathcal{I}} m^i - \sum_{j \in \mathcal{J}} n^j - M$; the allocation is feasible for supply of balances M if it is feasible and, in addition, $m^a = 0$.

The autarkic allocation is $a^0(p, r)$, with $(y, n)^j = 0$, for every firm and $(z, m)^j = 0$, for every individual.

An allocation, $a \in A(p, r)$, is weakly Pareto superior to an allocation, $\hat{a} \in A(\hat{p}, \hat{r})$, if $u^i(z^i) \geq u^i(\hat{z}^i)$ for every individual; it is Pareto superior if the preference is strict: $u^i(z^i) > u^i(\hat{z}^i)$, for some individual.

A feasible allocation, $a \in \mathbf{A}(p, r)$, is *Pareto optimal* if there do not exist prices of commodities and rates of interest, $(\hat{p}, \hat{r})$ and a feasible allocation, $\hat{a} \in \mathbf{A}(\hat{p}, \hat{r})$, that is Pareto superior; it is weakly Pareto optimal if no feasible allocation is strictly Pareto superior. The allocation is Pareto optimal at prices of commodities and rates of interest (p, r) if there do not exist a feasible allocation, $\hat{a} \in \mathbf{A}(p, r)$, that is Pareto superior. Similarly, for supply of balances M.

3.2 Assumptions

Standard assumptions extend to an economy in which money serves as a medium of exchange.

Assumption 1 *The production set correspondence is closed and convex valued, and it allows for no-production:* $(0, 0) \in \Psi^j(p)$.

Assumption 2 *The production set correspondence is continuous.*

Assumption 3 *If* $-\hat{n}_{\hat{k}} \geq p_{\hat{k}} y_{\hat{k}+}$, *and* $\hat{n} = (\ldots, \hat{n}_k, \ldots)$, *with* $\hat{n}_k = n_k$, *for* $k \neq \hat{k}$, *then* $(y, n) \in \Psi^j(p) \Rightarrow (y, \hat{n}) \in \Psi^j(p)$.

The firm attains satiation in balances in a medium of exchange if they exceed the revenue from sales.

The aggregate production set correspondence is $\Psi^a = \sum_{j \in \mathcal{J}} \Psi^j$.

Assumption 4 *The aggregate production set correspondence does not allow for free lunches in the production of commodities:* $(y, n) \in \Psi^a(p) \Rightarrow y \not> 0$, *neither for reversibility in the production of commodities:* $(y, n) \in \Psi^a(p)$ *and* $(y, \hat{n}) \in -\Psi^a(p) \Rightarrow y = 0$.

Assumption 5 *The aggregate production set correspondence allows for the free disposal of commodities:* $(y, n) \in \Psi^a(p)$, *and* $\hat{y} \leq y$, *while* $p_l = 0$ *for* $\hat{y}_l < y_l$, *implies* $(\hat{y}, n) \in \Psi^a(p)$.

Assumption 6 *The exchange set correspondence is closed and convex valued, it is bounded from below: there exists* $\underline{\underline{z}}^i$, *such that* $(z, m) \in \Phi^i(p) \Rightarrow (z, m) \geq (\underline{\underline{z}}^i, 0)$, *and it allows for no - exchange:* $(0, 0) \in \Phi^i(p)$.

Assumption 7 *The exchange set correspondence is continuous.*

Assumption 8 *There exists* $\underline{z}^i \ll 0$, *such that* $(\underline{z}^i, \underline{m}) \in \Phi^i(p)$, *where* $\underline{m}_k = p_k \underline{z}_{k-}$. *The shares in banks and firms are non-negative:* $\theta^i = (\theta^{i,\mathcal{K}}, \theta^{i,\mathcal{J}}) \geq 0$.

For rates of interest $\mathbf{1}^K \geq r \geq 0$, no-exchange is not a minimum wealth point: $p\underline{z} + r\underline{m} = \sum_{k \in \mathcal{K}} (1 - r_k) p_k \underline{z}_k < 0$.

Assumption 9 *The utility function is quasi-concave: for every net trade, the set* $U^i(z) = \{\hat{z} : u^i(\hat{z}) \geq u^i(z)\}$ *is convex.*

Assumption 10 *The utility function is continuous.*

Assumption 11 *There is no local satiation in the net trades of commodities and balances: for every net trade and for every* [5] $\varepsilon > 0, U^i_\varepsilon(z) = \{\hat{z} : u^i(\hat{z}) > u^i(z),$ *and* $\|(\hat{z} - z)\| < \varepsilon\} \neq \emptyset$.

Assumption 12 *If* $\hat{m}_{\hat{k}} \geq p_{\hat{k}} z_{\hat{k}-}$, *and* $\hat{m} = (\ldots, \hat{m}_k, \ldots)$, *with* $\hat{m}_k = m_k$, *for* $k \neq \hat{k}$, *then* $(z, m) \in \Phi^i(p) \Rightarrow (z, \hat{m}) \in \Phi^i(p)$.

The individual attains satiation in balances in a medium of exchange if they exceed the revenue from sales.

Assumption 13 *Every firm and every bank is owned* [6] $: \sum_{i \in \mathcal{I}} \theta^i = \mathbf{1}^{J+K}$.

An economy that satisfies standard assumptions can, but need not be homogeneous in the prices of commodities and balances.

[5] "$\| \;\|$" denotes the Euclidean distance.

[6] $\mathbf{1}^N$ is the vector of 1's of dimension N; $\mathbf{1}^N_n$ is the n-th unit vector of dimension N.

3.3 Equilibria

At rates of interest r, the profit of a bank if it issues balances M^k is

$$v^k(r^k, M^k) = r^k M^k.$$

At prices of commodities and rates of interest (p, r), the profit of a firm if it chooses production plan of commodities and balances (y, n) is

$$v^j(y, n, p, r) = (p, r)(y, n).$$

The profit maximization problem of the firm is

$$\max v^j, \text{ s.t. } (y, n) \in \Psi^j(p).$$

The set of solutions to the profit maximization problem is $(y^j, n^j)(p, r)$, the production correspondence is (y^j, n^j), and the maximal profit of the firm is $\hat{v}^j(p, r) = (p, r)(y^j, n^j)(p, r)$; whenever $(y^j, n^j)(p, r) = \emptyset$, $v^j(p, r) = -\infty$.

At prices of commodities, rates of interest and supply of balances (p, r, M), the profit income of an individual is

$$\hat{v}^i(p, r, M) = \sum_{k \in \mathcal{K}} \theta^{i,k} v^k(r^k, M^k) + \sum_{j \in \mathcal{J}} \theta^{i,j} \hat{v}^j(p, r).$$

The utility maximization problem of the individual is

$$\max u^i, \text{ s.t. } (z, m) \in \Phi^i(p), \ (p, r)(z, m) \leq \hat{v}^i(p, r, M).$$

The set of solutions to the optimization problem of the individual is $(z^i, m^i)(p, r, M)$, and (z^i, m^i) is his exchange correspondence.

The aggregate excess demand correspondence is $(z^a, m^a) = \sum_{i \in \mathcal{I}}(z^i, m^i) - \sum_{j \in \mathcal{J}}(y^j, n^j) - (0, M)$.

Competitive equilibrium prices of commodities, rates of interest and supply of balances, (p^*, r^*, M^*), are such that $0 \in (z^a, m^a)(p^*, r^*, M^*)$. Competitive equilibrium prices of commodities and rates of interest, (p^*, r^*), are such that (p^*, r^*, M) are competitive equilibrium prices of commodities, rates of interest and supply of balances, for some supply of balances, M. For rates of interest r, competitive equilibrium prices of commodities, p^*, are such that (p^*, r) are competitive equilibrium prices of commodities and rates of interest. For supply of balances M, competitive equilibrium prices of commodities and rates of interest, (p^*, r^*) are such that (p^*, r^*, M) are competitive equilibrium prices of commodities, rates of interest, and supply of balances.

Associated with competitive equilibrium prices of commodities and rates of interest, (p^*, r^*), there is a feasible allocation $a(p^*, r^*)$.

Monetary authorities set rates of interest and accommodate the demand for balances; alternatively, monetary authorities set the supply of balances and rates of interest adjust to attain equilibrium.

Proposition 1. *For rates of interest $\mathbf{1}^K \geq r \geq 0$ and for any scalar $c > 0$, there exist competitive equilibrium prices of commodities, p^*, with $\sum_{l \in \mathcal{L}} p_l^* = c$.*

Proof Rates of interest are $r = (\ldots, r_k, \ldots) \geq 0$.

The set of prices of commodities is $\mathcal{P}_c = \left\{p > 0 : \sum_{l \in \mathcal{L}} p_l = c\right\}$.

There exists $b > 0$, such that, for prices of commodities and rates of interest $(p, r) \in \mathcal{P} \times \{r\}$, if $z^a \leq 0$, then, for every firm, $\|y^j\| < b$, and, for every individual, $\|z^i\| < b$.

The truncated optimization problem of a firm is the profit maximization problem subject to the constraints

$$\|y\| \leq b, \ -n \leq \mathbf{1}^K cb.$$

The set of solutions is $(y_b^j, n_b^j)(p, r)$, the production correspondence is (y_b^j, n_b^j), the maximal profit is $\hat{v}_b^j(p, r)$, and the profit function is $\hat{v}_b^j$.

The profit income of an individual is

$$v_b^i(p, r, M) = \sum_{k \in \mathcal{K}} \theta^{i,k} v^k(r^k, M^k) + \sum_{j \in \mathcal{J}} \theta^{i,j} \hat{v}_b^j(p, r).$$

The truncated optimization problem of the individual is the utility maximization problem with profit income $v_b^i(p, r, M)$ and subject to the constraints

$$\|z\| \leq b, \ m_k \leq \mathbf{1}^K cb.$$

The set of solutions is $(z_b^i, m_b^i)(p, r, M)$, and the modified exchange correspondence is (z_b^i, m_b^i).

If, at a solution to the truncated optimization problems of firms and individuals, for every firm $\|y^j\| < b$, and, for every individual, $\|z^i\| < b$, then, since the economy is convex, the truncation is not a binding constraint.

The aggregate, truncated excess demand correspondence is

$$(z_b^a, m_b^a) = \sum_{i \in \mathcal{I}} (z_b^i, m_b^i) - \sum_{j \in \mathcal{J}} (y_b^j, n_b^j) - (0, M).$$

The truncated set of balances is $\mathcal{M}_{c,b} = \left\{M \geq 0 : M \leq \mathbf{1}^K(cb(I + J))\right\}$.

The set of aggregate, truncated excess demand for commodities is $\mathcal{Z}_b^a = \{z : \|z\| \leq b(I + J)\}$.

For every firm, the truncated production correspondence is non - empty, compact, convex valued and upper hemi-continuous; the profit function is non-negative. For every individual, the truncated exchange correspondence is non-empty, compact, convex valued and upper hemi-continuous. The aggregate, truncated excess demand correspondence is non-empty, compact, convex valued and upper hemi-continuous; it satisfies $(p, r)(z_b^a, m_b^a) \leq 0$.

The correspondence $f = (f_1, f_2, f_3)$, with domain $\mathcal{P}_c \times \mathcal{Z}_b^a \times \mathcal{M}_{c,b}$ is defined by $f_1 = \arg\max\left\{p z_b^a : p \in \mathcal{P}_c\right\}$, $f_2 = z_b^a(p, r, M)$, and $f_3 = m_b^a(p, r, M)$.

There exists (p^*, z^{a*}, m^{a*}), a fixed point, and an associated allocation, $a(p^*, r) = ((y^{j*}, n^{j*}) : j \in \mathcal{J}, (z^{i*}, m^{i*}) : i \in \mathcal{I})$.

At the fixed point, $m^{a*} = 0$ and $p^* z^{a*} \leq 0$.

It follows that $z^{a*} \leq 0$, $p^* z^{a*} = 0$, and $m^{a*} = 0$.

For every firm, $(y^{j*}, n^{j*}) \in (y^j, n^j)(p^*, r)$, while $(z^{i*}, m^{j*}) \in (z^i, m^i)(p^*, r, M^*)$, for every individual.

In order to show that p^* are competitive equilibrium prices of commodities at rates of interest r, it remains to show that $z^{a*} = 0$; but, since $z_l^{a*} < 0 \Rightarrow p_l^* = 0$, the free disposal of commodities accommodates this. □

The restriction to rates of interest $0 \leq r_k \leq 1$, is natural: rates of interest in the abstract economy typically correspond to rates of interest $\hat{r}_k = r_k/(1+r_k) \leq 1$ in the underlying economy.

Corollary 1. *For supply of balances $\overline{M} \geq 0$, and for $\overline{c} > 0$, there exist competitive equilibrium prices of commodities and rates of interest, (p^*, r^*), with $\sum_{l \in \mathcal{L}} p_l^* = \overline{c}$.*

Remark 3. In a more general specification, the exchange set of an individual varies with rates of interest, the supply of balances by banks, and the production plans and holdings of balances by firms: one writes $\Phi^i(p, r, \ldots M^k, \ldots, y^j, n^j, \ldots)$. This allows for financial policies of firms and banks that modify the transactions constraints faced by individuals. Readers may verify that the proof as written covers the more general specification, with the single caution that the last statement in assumption 5 should be modified to read: "and it allows for no-exchange, when the profits of firms are non-negative:

$$(p, r)(y^j, n^j) \geq 0 \text{ for all } j \in J \text{ implies } (0, 0) \in \Phi^i(p, (y^j, n^j)_{j \in J}, M)."$$

The reasoning is similar to that applicable in the canonical model, to the effect that the budget correspondence is non-empty valued.

Remark 4. The abstract economy is a general model covering applications to various transactions technologies. In applications, the prices entering the definitions of the production and exchange set correspondences are typically spot nominal prices, distinct from the present-value prices entering the definitions of profits and of consolidated budget constraints – a distinction not present in the abstract economy. The transition from the abstract economy to economies with a specific transactions technology is well-defined whenever that technology has a homogeneous product structure, implying that the production and exchange set correspondences can be written indifferently in terms of spot, or in terms of present-value prices and balances.

The economy has a *product structure* if:

the production set correspondence of a firm is $\Psi^j = \mathcal{Y}^j \cap (\times_{k \in \mathcal{K}} \Psi^j_k)$, where $\mathcal{Y}^j$ is the production set, independent of the prices of commodities, while Ψ^j_k describes transactions constraints in commodities served by currency k;
the exchange set correspondence of an individual is $\Phi^i = \mathcal{Z}^i \cap (\times_{k \in \mathcal{K}} \Phi^i_k)$, where $\mathcal{Z}^i$ is the net trade set, independent of the prices of commodities, while Φ^i_k describes transactions constraints in commodities served by currency k.

The economy is (0-)*homogeneous* in prices of commodities and balances if it has a product structure and, for any scalar, $c > 0$, and any currency, k,

$$(y_k, n_k) \in \Psi^j_k(p_k) \Rightarrow (y_k, cn_k) \in \Psi^j_k(cp_k);$$
$$(z_k, m_k) \in \Phi^i_k(p_k) \Rightarrow (z_k, cm_k) \in \Phi^i(cp_k).$$

3.4 Characteristics of equilibria

Multiplicity The economy displays *multiplicity of degree* I if there exists an open set of competitive equilibrium prices of commodities, rates of interest and supplies of balances of dimension I.

Competitive equilibrium prices of commodities, rates of interest and supplies of balances (p^*, r^*, M^*) and (p^{**}, r^{**}, M^{**}) are *essentially distinct* if, for an allocation, $a(p^*, r^*)$, associated with (p^*, r^*, M^*), for any allocation, $a(p^{**}, r^{**})$, associated with (p^{**}, r^{**}, M^{**}), for some individual, $u^i(z^{i**}) \neq u^i(z^{i*})$.

The economy displays *real multiplicity of degree* R if there exists an open set of essentially distinct competitive equilibrium prices of commodities, rates of interest and supplies of balances of dimension R.

Competitive equilibrium prices of commodities, rates of interest and supplies of balances (p^*, r^*, M^*) and (p^{**}, r^{**}, M^{**}) are *equivalent* if, for any allocation, $a(p^*, r^*)$, associated with (p^*, r^*, M^*), there exists an allocation, $a(p^{**}, r^{**})$, associated with (p^{**}, r^{**}, M^{**}), such that, for every individual, $u^i(z^{i**}) = u^i(z^{i*})$.

The economy displays *nominal multiplicity of degree* N if there exists an open set of equivalent competitive equilibrium prices of commodities, rates of interest and supplies of balances of dimension N.

Corollary 2. *The economy displays* $K+1$ *degrees of multiplicity; if the economy is homogeneous, 1 degree of multiplicity is nominal.*

Further specification of the role of balances in the production correspondences of firms and and the exchange correspondences of individuals is required to identify degrees of real multiplicity. If individuals hold initial nominal positions, all $K+1$ degrees of multiplicity may be real.

Monetary equilibria The exchange set correspondence captures, among others, the role of balances in the exchange of commodities for an individual; the production set correspondence captures, among others, the role of balances in the exchange of commodities for a firm.

Competitive equilibrium prices of commodities, rates of interest and supply of balances, (p^*, r^*, M^*), are *monetary* if

$$r_k^* M_k^* \neq 0, \quad \text{for some } k \in \mathcal{K}.$$

Money is essential if, for some individual, if $(z, m) \in \Phi^i(p, r)$, then $m = 0 \Rightarrow pz_- = 0$; or, for some firm, if $(y, n) \in \Psi^j(p, r)$, then $n = 0 \Rightarrow py_+ = 0$.

This is the case when cash-in-advance constraints are operative.

Under assumptions implying that no production-no trade cannot be an equilibrium, if money is essential, every equilibrium is monetary.

Optimality An allocation associated with competitive equilibrium prices of commodities, rates of interest and supplies of balances (p^*, r^*, M^*) is optimal at prices of commodities and rates of interest (p^*, r^*), for supplies of balances M^*. This conditional optimality result is a straightforward extension of the classical welfare theorem for economies with preferences and technologies invariant with respect to prices or rates of interest. In light of the control of the supplies of balances or of the rates of interest by monetary authorities, this conditional notion of optimality is not appropriate.

A stronger characterization of optimality is not possible, as long as the dependence of transactions on prices and rates of interest remains unrestricted.

The production set correspondence is independent of the prices of commodities and rates of interest as long as the firm attains satiation in balances if $(y, \ldots, -p_k y_{k+}, \ldots) \in \Psi^j(p) \Rightarrow (y, \ldots, -\hat{p}_k y_{k+}, \ldots) \in \Psi^j(\hat{p})$.

The production set Ψ^j, is defined by $y \in \Psi^j \Leftrightarrow (y, \ldots, -p_k y_{k+}, \ldots) \in \Psi^j(p)$.

The exchange set correspondence is independent of the prices of commodities and rates of interest as long as the individual attains satiation in balances if $(z, \ldots, p_k z_{k-}, \ldots) \in \Phi^i(p) \Rightarrow (z, \ldots, \hat{p}_k z_{k-}, \cdots) \in \Phi^i(\hat{p})$.

The exchange set Φ^i, is defined by $z \in \Phi^i \Leftrightarrow (z, \cdots \hat{p}_k z_{k-}, \ldots) \in \Phi^i(p)$.

The economy is *separable* between the consumption or production of commodities and the exchange of commodities if the production set correspondences of firms and the exchange set correspondences of individuals are independent of the prices of commodities, as long as satiation in balances is attained.

A distribution of revenue is $d = (\tau^i : i \in \mathcal{I})$, such that $\sum_{i \in \mathcal{I}} \tau^i = 0$.

With a distribution of revenue, the budget constraint of an individual is

$$pz + rm = \hat{v}^i(p, r, M) + \tau^i.$$

Corollary 3. *If the economy is separable, and $a(p^*, r^*)$ is a competitive equilibrium allocation, there exists a distribution of revenue, d^*, and an associated competitive equilibrium allocation $a(p^{**}, r^{**})$, with rates of interest $r^{**} = 0$, that is weakly Pareto superior. A competitive equilibrium allocation, $a(p^{**}, r^{**})$, associated with rates of interest $r^{**} = 0$, is Pareto optimal.*

Proof It suffices to show that there exists d^* such that, for each $i, p^{**}z^{i*} \leq p^{**}z^{i**} = v^{i**} + \tau^{i*}$. If $\tau^{i*} = p^{**}z^{i*} - v^{i**}$, then

$$\sum_{i \in I} \tau^{i*} = p^{**} \sum_{i \in I} z^{i*} - p^{**} \sum_{j \in J} y^{j**} \leq$$

$$p^{**} \sum_{i \in I} z^{i*} - p^{**} \sum_{j \in J} y^{j*} = 0. \qquad \square$$

This result establishes existence of a suitable distribution of revenue, but is of little help to a compute it, since it depends upon prices p^{**} that clear markets given the distribution. A weaker, but more operational result, is that, *starting from a realised* competitive equilibrium allocation $a(p^*, r^*)$, one can define *explicitly* a weakly Pareto-improving distribution d^*, namely $\tau^{i*} = \theta^{i,J+1} v^{J+1*} - rm^{i*} + \sum_{j \in J} \theta^{ij} rn^{j*}$.

It is optimal for individuals and firms to attain satiation in balances.

4 Time, uncertainty and multiplicity

4.1 Multiplicity

A simple cash-in-advance economy was defined in section 2 by:

(i) individuals, i, solving

$$\max_{z,m} u^i(z),$$

subject to

$$m_{s_t} = p_{s_t} z_{s_{t-1}}, \quad s_t \in \mathcal{N},$$

and the semi-reduced form constraints

$$p_1 z_1 + \sum_{s_2 \in S_2} q_{s_2} \eta_{s_2} + \hat{r}_1 m_1 = v_1^i,$$

$$p_{s_t} z_{s_t} + \sum_{s_{t+1} \in S_{t+1}(s_t)} q_{s_{t+1}} \eta_{s_{t+1}} + \hat{r}_{s_t} m_{s_t} = \eta_{s_t} + v_{s_t}^i,$$

$$p_{s_T} z_{s_T} + \hat{r}_{s_T} m_{s_T} = \eta_{s_T} + v_{s_T}^i;$$

(ii) firms, j, solving

$$\max_{y,n} \sum_{s_t \in \mathcal{N}} \tilde{q}_{s_t} (p_{s_t} y_{s_t} + \hat{r}_{s_t} n_{s_t}) = \sum_{s_t \in \mathcal{N}} \tilde{q}_{s_t} v_{s_t}^j$$

subject to

$$-n_{s_t} = p_{s_t} y_{s_{t+}}, s_t \in \mathcal{N};$$

(iii) the bank, announcing the interest rates r and distributing profits

$$v_{s_t}^{J+1} = \hat{r}_{s_t} M_{s_t}, s_t \in N.$$

Using the notation $\tilde{p}_{s_t} = \tilde{q}_{s_t} p_{s_t}, \tilde{m}_{s_t}^i = \tilde{q}_{s_t} m_{s_t}^i, \tilde{n}_{s_t}^j = \tilde{q}_{s_t} n_{s_t}^j, \tilde{M}_{s_t} = \tilde{q}_{s_t} M_{s_t}, \tilde{v}_{s_t}^i = \sum_{s_t \in N} \tilde{q}_{s_t} v_{s_t}^i, \tilde{v}_{s_t}^j = \sum_{s_t \in N} \tilde{q}_{s_t} v_{s_t}^j$ and $\tilde{v}^{J+1} = \sum_{s_t \in N} \tilde{q}_{s_t} v_{s_t}^{J+1}$, reducing the individual budget constraints to their present value consolidation yields the alternative formulation

(i') $\max_{z,\tilde{m}} u^i(z)$ subject to $\tilde{m}_{s_t} = \tilde{p}_{s_t} z_{s_{t-}}$ and $\tilde{p}z + \hat{r}\tilde{m} = \tilde{v}^i$;

(ii') $\max_{y,\tilde{n}} \tilde{p}y + \hat{r}\tilde{n} = \tilde{v}^j$ subject to $-\tilde{n}_{s_t} = \tilde{p}_{s_t} y_{s_{t+}}$;

(iii') $\tilde{v}^{J+1} = \hat{r}\tilde{M}$.

This alternative formulation fits the definition of an abstract economy. Hence, by proposition 1, there exist, for arbitrary $\hat{r} \geq 0$ and $c > 0$, competitive equilibrium prices $\tilde{p}^*$ (with $\tilde{p}^* 1^{NL} = c$) and an associated allocation $a(\tilde{p}^*, \hat{r}) = ((z^{i*}, \tilde{m}^{i*})_{i \in I}, (y^{j*}, \tilde{n}^{j*})_{j \in J}, \tilde{M}^*)$.

Actually, there exists a multiplicity of degree $S-1$ of competitive equlibria with $(p^*, \tilde{q}^*, r)$ such that $\tilde{q}_{s_t}^* p_{s_t}^* = \tilde{p}_{s_t}^*, s_t \in N$, and $(r/(1+r)) = \hat{r}$. The construction of the set of these equilibria, starting from some $(\tilde{p}^*, a(\tilde{p}^*, \hat{r}))$, is straight forward. It is convenient and more transparent to exhibit at once the multiplicity of degree S of equilibria obtained by varying as well the constant c in proposition 1. The construction then proceeds as follows.

1. Select arbitrarily positive constants $c_{s_T} > 0, s_T \in S_T$, and define the nominal spot price vector $p_{s_T}^* > 0$ by $p_{s_T}^* \tilde{q}_{s_T}^* = \tilde{p}_{s_T}^*$, with $\tilde{q}_{s_T}^* > 0$, such that $\sum_{l \in \mathcal{L}} p_{l s_T}^* = c_{s_T}$.
2. For each s_{T-1}, for each $s_T \in S_T(s_{T-1})$, define $q_{s_T}^*$ (the nominal spot price at s_{T-1} of elementary security s_T) by $q_{s_T}^* = \alpha_{s_T} \tilde{q}_{s_T}^*$, with $\alpha_{s_T} > 0$, such that $\sum_{s_T \in S_T(s_{T-1})} q_{s_T}^* = (1+r_{s_{T-1}})^{-1}$. Define $\tilde{q}_{s_{T-1}}^* = \tilde{q}_{s_T}^* / q_{s_T}^*$ (any $s_T \in S_T(s_{T-1})$, the ratio is unique) and $p_{s_{T-1}}^* = \tilde{p}_{s_{T-1}}^* / \tilde{q}_{s_{T-1}}^*$.
   This general step may be repeated backwards for each $s_{T-2}, s_{T-3}, \cdots$ down to s_1. This yields vectors $p^*, \tilde{q}^*, q^*$ such that, for each s_t, $\tilde{p}_{s_t}^* = \tilde{q}_{s_t}^* p_{s_t}^*$ and $\sum_{s_{t+1} \in S_{t+1}(s_t)} q_{s_{t+1}}^* = (1+r_{s_t})^{-1}$, where $\tilde{p}_{s_t}^*$ is a competitive equilibrium price vector of the abstract economy, for some normalising constant c (implicitly determined by the arbitrary constants c_{s_T}). From now on, the variables $(\tilde{m}^{i*}, \tilde{n}^{j*}, M^*)$ are taken congruent with that normalising constant.
3. For each $s_t \in N$, for each i, or j, define $m_{s_t}^{i*} = \tilde{m}_{s_t}^{i*} / \tilde{q}_{s_t}^*, n_{s_t}^{j*} = \tilde{n}_{s_t}^{j*} / \tilde{q}_{s_t}^*$; define $M_{s_t}^* = \tilde{M}_{s_t}^* / \tilde{q}_{s_t}^*$. By homogeneity (by inspection, in this

simple case), for each i, resp. j, $(z^{i*}, m^{i*}) \in \Phi^i(p^*)$ and $(y^{j*}, n^{j*}) \in \Psi^j(p^*)$. Also, define $v^{j*}_{s_t} = p^*_{s_t} y^{j*}_{s_t} + \hat{r}_{s_t} n^{j*}_{s_t}$, $v^{J+1*}_{s_t} = \hat{r}_{s_t} M_{s_t}$.

4. For each $s_T \in S_T$, for each i, define $\eta^{i*}_{s_T} - p^*_{s_T} z^{i*}_{s_T+} = \hat{r}_{s_T} m^*_{s_T} - v^{i*}_{s_T} = \hat{r}_{s_T} m^*_{s_T} - \sum_{j\in J} \theta^{ij}(p^*_{s_T} y^{j*}_{s_T} + \hat{r}_{s_T} n^{j*}_{s_T}) - \theta^{iJ+1} \hat{r}_{s_T} M^*_{s_T}$. Equilibrium on the commodity markets and the definition of $M^* = \sum_{i\in I} m^{i*} - \sum_{j\in J} n^{j*}$ imply $\sum_{i\in I} \eta^{i*}_{s_T} = 0$ (equilibrium on the market for elementary security s_T, as per Walras law).
5. For each $s_{T-1} \in S_{T-1}$, for each i, define $\eta^{i*}_{s_{T-1}} = p^*_{s_{T-1}} z^{i*}_{s_{T-1}} + \sum_{s_T \in S_T(s_{T-1})} q^*_{s_T} \eta^{i*}_{s_T} + (r_{s_T}/(1+r_{s_T})) m^{i*}_{s_{T-1}} - v^{i*}_{s_{T-1}}$. Again, $\sum_{i\in I} \eta^{i*}_{s_{T-1}} = 0$. This general step may be repeated backwards for each $s_{T-2}, s_{T-3}, \cdots$, down to s_1.

In short: since prices of elementary securities, q_{s_t}, can be set arbitrarily, subject to the arbitrage conditions, given non - negative rates of interest r_{s_t}, there exists a competitive equilibrium allocation with arbitrary values for q_{s_T}, the prices of elementary securities associated with terminal nodes or, equivalently, the level of prices, $\sum_{l\in\mathcal{L}} p_{l,s_T}$, at the terminal nodes.

Proposition 2. *In the economy that extends over finite time under uncertainty, if the economy is 0-homogeneous, then, for nominal rates of interest $r \geq 0$, there exist, for any scalars $c_{S_T} = (\ldots, c_{s_T}, \ldots) \gg 0$, competitive equilibrium contingent prices of commodities, $\tilde{p}^*$, and associated spot prices, p^*, with $\sum_{l\in\mathcal{L}} p^*_{l,s_T} = c_{s_T}$, for every state of the world s_T. The allocations of commodities associated with alternative scalars, c_{S_T} are equivalent.*

It thus takes more than standard monetary policy to control the variability of price levels across future events.

4.2 Example

A parametric economy illustrates the results.

Dates are $t = 1, 2$.

States of the world $s \in \mathcal{S}$, a finite set, realize at date 2; date-events are 1 and $s_2 \in \mathcal{S}_2 = \mathcal{S}$.

There is one commodity; a quantity of the commodity at a date event is z_1 or z_{s_2}. The prices of the commodities at a date-event are p_1 or p_{s_2}.

Elementary securities and bonds of one date maturity effect transfers of revenue between date 1 and the events at date 2. Holdings of the elementary security with payoff one unit of revenue at the date-event s_2, are η_{s_2}, and its price is q_{s_2}; rates of interest are r_1 and $r_{s_2}; \hat{r} = r(1+r)^{-1}$.

There is no production. Individuals are $i = 1, 2$.

Money serves as a medium of exchange at each date-event. Balances at a date-event are m_1 and m_{s_2}. The supply of balances is M_1 and M_{s_2}.

The preferences of individual 1 over net trades are described by the intertemporal von Neumann-Morgenstern utility function defined by $u^1(z_1, \ldots,$

$z_{s_2}, \ldots) = \ln(e_1 + z_1) + \delta \mathrm{E} \ln(z_{s_2})$, and of individual 2 by $u^2(z_1, \ldots, z_{s_2}, \ldots) = \ln(z_1) + \delta \mathrm{E} \ln(e_{s_2} + z_{s_2})$, where expectations are with respect to a strictly positive probability measure, $\pi = (\ldots, \pi_{s_2}, \ldots)$ over the set of states of the world or events at date 2. Equivalently, individuals 1 and 2 have logarithmic utility functions over consumption, and endowments e_1 and e_{s_2}, respectively. The share of individual 1 in the bank at each date-event is $\theta^1 \geq 0$, and that of individual 2 is $\theta^2 = 1 - \theta^1 \geq 0$.

A cash-in-advance constraint is operative at each date - event.

The sequence of budget constraints for an individual is

$$p_1 z_1 + \sum_{s_2} q_{s_2} \eta_{s_2} + \hat{r}_1 m_1 = v_1^i$$

$$p_{s_2} z_{s_2} + \hat{r}_{s_2} m_{s_2} = \eta_{s_2} + v_2^i.$$

Given their specialised endowments, agents trade as follows.

At date 1, individual 1 buys elementary securities in amounts $\eta^1_{s_2} > 0$, and pays for them with cash borrowed from the bank; individual 2 sells elementary securities in amounts $\eta^2_{s_2} < 0$, and uses the proceeds to buy the commodity from individual 1, who in turn uses the proceeds to settle his loan from the bank. The bank lends $\sum_{s_2} q_{s_2} \eta^1_{s_2}$ to individual 1 at a profit $v_1 = \hat{r}_1 \sum_{s_2} q_{s_2} \eta^1_{s_2}$ which it distributes.

At date 2, state s_2, individual 1 collects $\eta^1_{s_2}$ and uses the proceeds to buy an amount $z^1_{s_2}$ of the commodity from individual 2. Individual 2 borrows $\eta^2_{s_2}$ from the bank to honour his elementary security committment. He then sells an amount $z^2_{s_2}$ of the commodity and uses the proceeds to settle his loan from the bank. The bank lends $-\eta^2_{s_2}$ to individual 2 at a profit $v_{s_2} = -\hat{r}_{s_2} \eta^2_{s_2}$ which it distributes.

The banks sets the interest rates r_1 and r_{s_2}. In order to exhibit a readable analytical solution, we impose $r_{s_2} = r_2$ for all s_2 in $\mathcal{S}_2$. In line with proposition 2, we take the spot prices of the commodity at date 2, p_{s_2}, as given and solve for the prices of elementary securities q_{s_2}, for p_1, and for the trades in assets and commodities. We invite readers to consider the simpler formulae that obtain when $\hat{r}_1 = \hat{r}_2 = 0$, or when $\mathcal{S} = 1$ (certainty).

After endogenising the profit distribution, the equilibrium net trades are given by

$$-z_1^1 = z_1^2 = \sum_{s_2 \in \mathcal{S}_2} q_{s_2} \eta^1_{s_2} / p_1 (1 + \hat{r}_1 + \hat{r}_1 \theta^1)$$

$$z^1_{s_2} = -z^2_{s_2} = \eta^1_{s_2} (1 + 2\hat{r}_2) / p_{s_2} (1 + \hat{r}_2 + \hat{r}_2 \theta^2).$$

The solution for q_{s_2} is transparent. Define $(ep)^H = (\sum_{s_2 \in \mathcal{S}_2} \pi_{s_2} / e_{s_2} p_{s_2})^{-1}$, the harmonic mean of the (exogenous) value of period 2 endowments. Then:

$$q_{s_2} = \frac{\pi_{s_2}}{e_{s_2}p_{s_2}} \frac{(ep)^H}{1+r_1}.$$

As expected, q_{s_2} is homogeneous of degree -1 in p_{s_2}; the product $q_{s_2}p_{s_2}$ is determined by primitives. The solution for $\eta^1_{s_2}$ is unfortunately less transparent:

$$\eta^1_{s_2} = e_{s_2}p_{s_2}(1+\hat{r}_1)(1+\hat{r}_2+\hat{r}_2\theta^2)/\left\{\delta(1+2\hat{r}_1)+(1+\hat{r}_2)(1+\hat{r}_1+\hat{r}_1\theta^1)\right\}.$$

The distribution of bank profits is the source of the complication. Note however that $q_{s_2}\eta^1_{s_2}$ is constant across the states s_2, under our shortcut of setting $r_{s_2} = r_2$ across states. The solution for p_1 is disheartening, though it simplifies to $p_1 = (ep)^H/e_1$, when $r_1 = r_2 = 0$. In general

$$p_1 = \frac{(ep)^H}{e_1(1+2r_1)} \frac{(1+2\hat{r}_2)(1+\hat{r}_1+\hat{r}_1\theta^1)+\delta(1+\hat{r}_1)(1+\hat{r}_2+\hat{r}_2\theta^2)}{(1+\hat{r}_2)(1+\hat{r}_1+\hat{r}_1\theta^1)+\delta(1+2\hat{r}_1)(1+\hat{r}_2+\hat{r}_2\theta^2)}.$$

It is of interest to exhibit the ratio, across individuals, of the marginal rates of substitution (MRS's) between consumption at different date-events. For two states s_2, s_2', the MRS's of the two individuals are the same, and equal to $\frac{\eta^1_{s_2}p_{s_2'}}{\eta^1_{s_2'}p_{s_2}}$. On the other hand, the MRS's between consumption at s_1 and s_2 differ by a factor $(1+\hat{r}_1)$, reflecting the misallocation induced by the cash-in-advance constraint.

5 Conclusion

In economies with an operative transactions technology, and money that provides liquidity services, competitive equilibria exist; which assures the consistency of the specification.

Nevertheless, competitive equilibrium allocations are multiple; and they may be Pareto comparable. If monetary policy sets the rates of interest (either directly, or indirectly through the money supply), then under certainty all future rates of inflation are determined, but the overall price level remains indeterminate. Inflation rates are positively correlated with nominal interest rates, pointing to the limitations of equilibrium theory to study out of equilibrium situations, a frequent concern of monetary authorities. Under uncertainty, expected rates of inflation are determined, but the variability of inflation is indeterminate, even though markets for nominal securities are complete. This leaves room for alternative determinants of inflation paths, for instance: (i) a more comprehensive monetary policy, setting not only interest rates but also quantities of money, or exchange rates, or prices of elementary securities; (ii) a process of nominal price adjustments, driven by price-setting agents, nominal contracts a.s.o.; (iii) nominal constraints associated with initial positions (e.g. public debt), policy committments (e.g., pensions) or the like.

The multiplicity of equilibria delimits the scope of monetary policy and the degrees of freedom available to policy makers. The welfare implications of alternative choices of policy parameters demonstrate the real effects of monetary policy.

Wealth effects that reflect imperfect "Ricardian equivalence," and price rigidities or structural constraints on price adjustments also make for effective monetary policy.

Speculatively, nominal rigidities (price-level stickiness) might be the saving grace of monetary economies: they prevent price-level jumps, which otherwise could generate excessive inflation variability, unchecked by monetary policy. Downward rigidities at controlled rates of expected inflation place on upper bound on inflation variances.

The failure of monetary policy to determine the distribution of the rate of inflation parallels the results in Lucas and Stokey (1987), Sargent and Wallace (1975) or Woodford (1994).

An extension encompasses a market for assets which is incomplete.

References

1. Arrow, K. J. and G. Debreu (1954): Existence of an equilibrium for a competitive economy. Econometrica 22, 265-290.
2. Baumol, W. J. (1952): The transactions demand for cash: an inventory theoretic approach. Quarterly Journal of Economics 66, 545-556.
3. Bloise, G., J. H. Drèze and H. M. Polemarchakis (2000): Monetary equlibria over an infinite horizon. Draft in Progress, CORE, Université Catholi- que de Louvain.
4. Clower, R. (1967): A reconsideration of the microfoundations of monetary theory. Western Economic Journal 6, 1-8.
5. Debreu, G. (1960): Une économie de l'incertain. Economie Appliquée 13, 111-116.
6. Drèze, J.H. and H. M. Polemarchakis (1999): Money and monetary policy in general equilibrium. In: L.-A. Gérard-Varet, A. P. Kirman and M. Ruggiero (eds.): Economics, the Next Ten Years. Oxford University Press.
7. Drèze, J.H. and H. M. Polemarchakis (2000): Intertemporal general equilibrium and monetary theory. In: A. Leijonhufvud (ed.): Monetary Theory as a Basis for Monetary Policy. Macmillan.
8. Dubey, P. and J. D. Geanakoplos (1992): The value of money in a finite horizon economy: a role for banks. In: P. S. Dasgupta, D. Gale, O. D. Hart and E. Maskin (eds.): Economic Analysis of Markets and Games, Essays in Honor of Frank Hahn. M.I.T. Press, 407-444.
9. Dubey, P. and J. D. Geanakoplos (2000): Inside and outside money, gains to trade and IS-LM. Mimeo. Yale University.

10. Hahn, F. H. (1965): On some problems in proving the existence of an equilibrium in a monetary economy. In F. H. Hahn and F. P. R. Brechling (eds): The Theory of Interest Rates. Macmillan.
11. Kyotaki, N. and R. Wright (1989): On money as a medium of exchange. Journal of Political Economy 97, 927-954.
12. Lucas, R. E. and N. L. Stokey (1987): Money and rates of interest in a cash-in-advance economy. Econometrica 55, 491-513.
13. McKenzie, L.W. (1954): On equilibrium in Graham's model of world trade and other competitive systems. Econometrica 22, 147-161.
14. Ostroy, J. M. and R. M. Starr (1974): Money and the Decentralization of Exchange. Econometrica 42, 1093-1113.
15. Patinkin D. (1965; 2-nd edition): Money, Interest and Prices. Harper and Row.
16. Sargent, T. and N. Wallace (1975): Rational expectations, the optimal monetary instrument and the optimal money supply rule. Journal of Political Economy 83, 241-254.
17. Tobin, J. (1956): The interest-elasticity of transactions demand for cash. Review of Economics and Statistics 38, 241-247.
18. Walras, L. (1902; 4-th edition): Eléments d'Economie Politique Pure. F. Rouge.
19. Woodford, M. (1994): Monetary policy and price level determinacy in a cash-in advance economy. Economic Theory 4, 345-380.

Strategic Multilateral Exchange and Taxes

Jean J. Gabszewicz[1] and Lisa Grazzini*[2]

[1] CORE, Université Catholique de Louvain, Belgium
[2] CORE, Université Catholique de Louvain, Belgium, and Dipartimento di Scienze Economiche, Università di Firenze, Italy

Abstract. This contribution investigates the effectiveness and welfare implications of fiscal policies in a context of multilateral trade, when traders behave strategically. The present approach deals simultaneously with two aspects of fiscal policies: collecting resources for redistributive purposes and correcting distortions related to imperfectly competitive behaviour.

1 Introduction

Because it provides the most simple version of markets' interaction, the exchange model constitutes a natural starting point for exploring specific issues in general equilibrium theory. Professor Hildenbrand himself has not disregarded to use this model extensively in his elegant contributions to core theory; thus we hope he will forgive us to use it as well in our own contribution to the Festschrift prepared in his honour! This contribution investigates the effectiveness and welfare implications of fiscal policies in a context of multilateral trade, when traders behave strategically.

One of the objectives pursued when taxing economic agents is to collect resources for redistributive purposes. With imperfect competition, taxation can also serve the purpose of correcting distortions generated by the market mechanism. The present approach deals simultaneously with these two facets of fiscal policies, in an exchange economy in which some agents – the "inside agents" – participate to exchange while the remaining ones – the "outside agents"– are excluded from trade, simply because they do not own any initial resources: this constitutes a stylized formulation of more elaborate redistributive schemes. In the present context, the redistributive purpose of taxation consists accordingly in transferring to the outside agents initial resources levied on inside agents, in order to guarantee them some minimal survival resources. The first question we raise is whether these transfers can allow to reach a Pareto-optimal overall-allocation, providing preassigned utility levels to outside agents, and taking into account the fact that inside agents play a strategic market game when exchanging goods among them. Here the second

* The second author gratefully acknowledges a European Commission Trade and Mobility fellowship No ERBFMBICT971936.

facet of fiscal policy enters into the picture. Indeed, strategic behaviour generally affects trade in a way which destroys Pareto-efficiency, complicating thereby the possibility of reaching a Pareto-optimal outcome via transfers. Nevertheless, we show that there exist lump-sum taxes and transfers reaching a Pareto-optimal overall-allocation of goods among inside and outside agents, which simultaneously constitutes a Nash equilibrium outcome in the strategic market game played by the inside agents. This result is reminiscent of the second welfare theorem, but this time applies to strategic trade.

The significance of this result should however be tempered due to the well-known drawbacks of lump-sum taxes: informational requirements needed to make them effective and non-anonymity, since they can require to be personalized on the basis of the characteristics of each agent. It is thus natural to examine whether alternative methods of taxation could not be effective in reaching a Pareto-optimal outcome while avoiding the drawbacks we have just referred to. Leaving aside the informational problem of identifying these characteristics, we examine then whether non-anonymity can be somewhat relaxed by imposing taxes affecting each good in the same proportion, as it is in particular the case for commodity taxation, which bears on transactions, and as if it would be the case if taxes would bear on initial endowments with the same tax rate per good for all agents (endowment taxation). Using a simple example, we show that such fiscal policies are not sufficient tools to reach an overall Pareto-optimal allocation: trade distortions due to imperfect competition cannot be wiped out via such methods. Finally, we propose an alternative method combining anonymous endowment taxation and transfers among inside agents, proportional to the amount sent for exchange, and test it on our particular example. We show that this method is effective both in resorbing trade distortions due to strategic behaviour, and in providing an overall-allocation among inside and outside agents which is Pareto-optimal.

The above analysis uses a strategic market game formulation in order to describe the outcome resulting from strategic interaction among the inside agents in the exchange economy (Shapley (1976), Shapley and Shubik (1977), Gabszewicz and Michel (1997)). This formulation can be viewed as an extension of the Cournot oligopoly model into two directions: first, it is cast into a general equilibrium context and, second, *all* participants to exchange behave strategically using quantities as strategies. To the best of our knowledge, the only paper using strategic market games in order to explore fiscal policy measures in a context of market power is Gabszewicz and Grazzini (1999).[1] This paper concentrates on the second facet of fiscal policy measures referred above. Namely, it raises the question whether taxing strategic agents

[1] This analysis relies on the non-cooperative concept of Nash equilibrium, and should be distinguished from the cooperative framework used in other contexts in which taxation and strategic power have been analysed, like in Aumann and Kurz (1977).

could induce them to restore a competitive outcome while continuing to exert their market power. Through a series of examples of *bilateral oligopolies*, introduced in Cordella and Gabszewicz (1998) and Bloch and Ferrer (2000), we show that taxes combined with transfers proportional to the amounts of goods sent for exchange are sufficient instruments to resorb the distortions due to strategic behaviour and restore competitive exchange. The present contribution can be viewed as an extension of the latter paper since, beyond the problem of counterdistortionary measures, it also deals with the issue of redistributing resources not only among agents directly participating to exchange, but also in favor of some agents who are excluded from trade.

Two earlier contributions to the problem of taxing market power in a general equilibrium set-up are those of Myles (1989) and Guesnerie and Laffont (1978). Myles (1989) extends the theory of optimal commodity taxation to a general equilibrium model with imperfect competition. His analysis is focused on the Ramsey problem of choosing commodity tax rates to maximise welfare subject to a given level of public revenue when markets operate in a non competitive framework. Guesnerie and Laffont (1978) study optimal taxation when the objective of the government is to restore first best Pareto efficiency when this first best is destroyed by the non competitive behaviour of a monopolist. Although the issues analysed in the above contributions are close to our own subject, they differ from ours in several respects. First, their analysis is cast into a model inspired from Gabszewicz and Vial (1972), which constitutes a much more general set-up than the one considered here. This model involves a productive sector with firms behaving noncompetitively while consumers are price-takers. However, a difficulty arises with this formulation, because taxes and transfers are not invariant with respect to the normalization rule used to normalize prices, while this difficulty disappears in our approach. Furthermore, only some agents behave strategically: in particular, the Guesnerie-Laffont's paper considers only the case of a monopolistic agent.

The next section provides a general definition of a strategic market game and studies the possibility of reaching an overall Pareto-optimal allocation when the outcome of this game depends on lump-sum taxes on inside agents to be transferred to the outside agents. Sections 3, 4 and 5 are devoted to analyse the possibility of obtaining a similar result using more anonymous tax and transfer schemes, like commodity taxation (section 3), endowment taxation (section 4) and endowment taxation combined with incentive transfers (section 5). Section 6 provides a short conclusion.

2 Strategic market games and Pareto-optimality

In this section, we first define a general class of strategic market games as follows. Consider an exchange economy involving $n+m$ agents i, $i = 1, ..., n+m$, and l goods h, $h = 1, ..., l$. The initial ownership of these goods is fully concentrated in the hands of the first n agents, ω_i, $\omega_i \in R^l_+$, $\omega_i \neq 0$, denoting the *initial endowment* of agent i, $i = 1, ..., n$. By assumption, we set $\omega_i = 0$, for agents i, $i = n+1, ..., n+m$: only agents i, $i = 1, ..., n$, named hereafter the *inside agents*, participate to exchange and are accordingly the *players* in the strategic market game. Agents i, $i = n+1, ..., n+m$, are excluded from trade and we call them the *outside agents*. We denote by U_i, $i = 1, ..., n+m$, the *utility function* of agent i, representing his preference relation among the commodity bundles x, $x \in R^l_+$. Standard assumptions on U_i, -continuity, strict monotonicity and strict quasi-concavity-, are made from the outset. An *allocation* is a n-tuple of commodity bundles $(x_1, ..., x_i, ..., x_n)$ such that $\sum_{i=1}^n x_i = \sum_{i=1}^n \omega_i$. The strategy set S_i of agent i, $i = 1, ..., n$, is defined by $S_i = \{y \mid 0 \leq y \leq \omega_i\}$. Given an n-tuple of strategies $(y_1, ..., y_i, ..., y_n)$, a price vector $p(y_1, ..., y_i, ..., y_n) \in R^l_+$ obtains as a result of some price formation mechanism (an example is considered below). To this price vector is associated an allocation assigning the bundle $z_i(p(y_1, ..., y_i, ..., y_n))$ to player i, $i = 1, ..., n$, which specifies the commodity bundle he obtains at the vector of strategies $(y_1, ..., y_i, ..., y_n)$. The *payoffs* V_i of the strategic market game are defined as

$$V_i(y_1, ..., y_i, ..., y_n) = U_i(z_i(p(y_1, ..., y_i, ..., y_n))).$$

The particular vector of strategies $(y_1, ..., y_i, ..., y_n) = (0, ..., 0, ..., 0)$ corresponds to a situation in which no player sends any strictly positive amount of some commodity to the market for trade. In that case, no trade can occur and the utility level enjoyed by agent i at this vector of strategies is given by the utility level reached at his initial endowment, i.e.

$$V_i(0, ..., 0, ..., 0) = U_i(\omega_i). \tag{1}$$

Furthermore, when all players, but one, -say player i-, select as strategy the null vector, no trade can occur either, so that the utility level reached by player i cannot exceed in that case the level $U_i(\omega_i)$. Thus, we set, for all $i = 1, ..., n$, and all $y_i \neq 0$,

$$U_i(0, ..., y_i, ..., 0) \leq U_i(\omega_i). \tag{2}$$

A *strategic equilibrium* is a Nash equilibrium of the strategic market game we have just defined, namely, a n-tuple of strategies $(y_1^*, ..., y_i^*, ..., y_n^*)$, $y_i^* \in S_i$, such that, $\forall i = 1, ..., n$, $\forall y_i \in S_i$

$$U_i(z_i(p(y_i^*, y_{-i}^*))) \geq U_i(z_i(p(y_i, y_{-i}^*))),$$

with y_{-i}^* denoting the $(n-1)$-tuple of strategies y_k^*, $k \neq i$.

To illustrate the above definition of a strategic market game, we consider the price formation mechanism proposed by Gabszewicz and Michel (1997), which will be used below in the examples analysed in the following sections.[2] Let each agent i, $i = 1, ..., n$, choose a strategy $y_i \in S_i$ and consider a price vector p, $p \neq 0$. Given the choice y_i, the income of agent i (i.e. the value of resources sent to the market) is equal to $p \cdot y_i$, where $p \cdot y_i$ denotes the scalar product of p and y_i. If trader i, endowed with income $p \cdot y_i$, chooses to buy a commodity bundle x, he reaches a utility level equal to $U_i(\omega_i - y_i + x)$: $\omega_i - y_i$ is the bundle of goods still remaining available for consumption given the choice of strategy y_i, and x is the vector of purchases performed at the price system p. Accordingly, given p and y_i, the choice of x is dictated by the solution to the program

$$\operatorname*{Max}_{x} \quad U_i(\omega_i - y_i + x) \quad s.t. \quad p \cdot x \leq p \cdot y_i \quad and \quad x \geq 0.$$

Denote by $x_i(p, y_i)$ the solution to this problem: by monotonicity, continuity and strict quasi-concavity of U_i, this solution exists and is unique.

Let $p(y_1, ..., y_i, ..., y_n)$ be a price system which clears all markets in the exchange economy in which traders i, $i = 1, ..., n$, are endowed with initial holdings y_i, i.e. $p(y_1, ..., y_i, ..., y_n)$ solves

$$\sum_{i=1}^{n} x_i(p, y_i) = \sum_{i=1}^{n} y_i \tag{3}$$

(standard assumptions guarantee the existence of a price system $p(y_1, ..., y_i, ..., y_n)$ for any n-tuple of strategies $(y_1, ..., y_i, ..., y_n)$, $y_i \in S_i$, at which trade occurs; we shall *assume* that this price system is unique). The payoff V_i of the game is then defined by

$$V_i(y_1, ..., y_i, ..., y_n) = U_i(z_i(p(y_1, ..., y_i, ..., y_n))),$$

with $z_i(p(y_1, ..., y_i, ..., y_n)) = \omega_i - y_i + x_i(p(y_1, ..., y_i, ..., y_n))$. Furthermore, if all players i select the strategy $y_i = 0$, no exchange can occur and the price system $p(y_1, ..., y_i, ..., y_n)$ is not defined, so that all traders remain with their initial endowments and reach utility levels $V_i(0, ..., 0, ..., 0) = U_i(\omega_i)$. If one of these traders would deviate from 0 to some alternative strategy $y_i \neq 0$, while the remaining traders stick to the strategy 0, no trade can occur either, and the utility level of player i is given by $V_i(0, ..., y_i, ..., 0) = U_i(\omega_i - y_i) < U_i(\omega_i)$, where strict inequality follows from the monotonicity assumption. Accordingly, for the price mechanism we have just described, the payoffs V_i satisfy equations (1) and (2).

In the following we are interested in identifying tax and transfer schemes through which outside agents i, $i = n + 1, ..., n + m$, obtain a share of the

[2] Alternative mechanisms have been proposed in the literature on strategic market games; see, for example, Dubey and Shubik (1978), Amir, Sahi, Shubik and Yao (1990).

resources initially owned by inside agents who participate directly to the exchange process described in the above strategic market game. The redistributive purpose pursued with such schemes consists in providing agents, who are initially deprived from any resource, with some amount of the various commodities, thereby allowing them to survive, in spite of the fact that they are unable to participate directly to trade. Formally, we assume that these "survival" levels are represented by utility levels -say $\overline{U}_i$-, for the outside agents i, $i = n+1, .., n+m$. These utility levels constrain accordingly the set of transfers and corresponding taxes which can be used in order to meet these preassigned levels. In this spirit, we define utility levels $\overline{U}_i$, $i = n+1, .., n+m$, as *feasible* if there exists lump-sum taxes t_i, $t_i \in R^l_+$, and transfers s_i, $s_i \in R^l_+$, $i = n+1, .., n+m$, such that

$$(i)\ \ t_i \leq \omega_i, \quad i = 1, ..., n;$$

$$(ii)\ \ \textstyle\sum_{i=n+1}^{n+m} s_i = \sum_{i=1}^{n} t_i,$$

$$(iii)\ \ U_i(s_i) \geq \overline{U}_i, \quad i = n+1, ..., n+m.$$

Given taxes t_i, a *post-tax allocation* among inside agents is a n-tuple of commodity bundles $(x_1, ..., x_i, ..., x_n)$ such that

$$\sum_{i=1}^{n} x_i = \sum_{i=1}^{n} (\omega_i - t_i).$$

Now we are in a position to state the following

Proposition 1. *Given any preassigned feasible utility levels $\overline{U}_i$ for outside agents i, $i = n+1, ..., n+m$, there exist lump-sum taxes t_i on inside agents' endowments ω_i, $i = 1, ..., n$, and transfers s_i from inside agents to outside agents, such that*
(i) the overall-allocation of goods $(\omega_1 - t_1, ..., \omega_n - t_n; s_{n+1}, ..., s_{n+m})$ among inside and outside agents is Pareto-optimal, and outside agents obtain, at that overall-allocation, commodity bundles providing utility levels $\overline{U}_i$, $i = n+1, ..., n+m$;
(ii) the post-tax allocation $(\omega_1 - t_1, ..., \omega_n - t_n)$ among inside agents is the unique Nash equilibrium of the strategic market game in which the strategy sets of inside agents are defined by $S_i = \{y_i \mid 0 \leq y_i \leq \omega_i - t_i\}$.

Proof. In the exchange economy with $(n+m)$ agents made of the inside agents $i = 1, ..., n$ and the outside agents $i = n+1, ..., n+m$, a *$(n+m)$*-tuple of commodity bundles $(x^*_1, ..., x^*_n; x^*_{n+1}, ..., x^*_{n+m})$ is Pareto-optimal if it solves the problem

$$\max_{x_1,\ldots,x_{n+m}} \sum_{i=1}^{n+m} U_i(x_i) \qquad s.t.$$

$$(i) \quad \sum_{i=1}^{n+m} x_i = \sum_{i=1}^{n} \omega_i \tag{4}$$

$$(ii) \quad x_i \geq 0, \qquad i = 1, \ldots, n+m.$$

Furthermore, since the preassigned utility levels $\overline{U}_i$, $i = n+1, \ldots, n+m$, are feasible for lump-sum taxes t_i and transfers s_i, the *(n+m)*-tuple of commodity bundles $(x_1^*, \ldots, x_n^*; x_{n+1}^*, \ldots, x_{n+m}^*)$ can be chosen eventually in order to solve the problem

$$\max_{x_1,\ldots,x_{n+m}} \sum_{i=1}^{n} U_i(x_i) \qquad s.t.$$

$$(i) \quad \sum_{i=n+1}^{n+m} s_i = \sum_{i=1}^{n} t_i$$

$$(ii) \quad x_i = \omega_i - t_i \geq 0; \quad i = 1, \ldots, n; \tag{5}$$

$$(iii) \quad x_i = s_i \geq 0; \quad i = n+1, \ldots, n+m;$$

$$(iv) \quad U_i(x_i) = U_i(s_i) \geq \overline{U}_i, \qquad i = n+1, \ldots, n+m.$$

Since the function $\sum_{i=1}^{n} U_i(x_i)$ is continuous as a sum of continuous functions, and the set of vectors satisfying (i), (ii), (iii) and (iv) is non-empty and compact, there exists a *(n+m)*-tuple of commodity bundles $(x_1^*, , \ldots, x_n^*; x_{n+1}^*, \ldots, x_{n+m}^*) = (\omega_1 - t_1^*, \ldots, \omega_n - t_n^*; \; s_{n+1}^*, \ldots, s_{n+m}^*)$ which is a solution to problem (5).

Now consider the exchange economy consisting of the n inside traders with initial endowments $\omega_i - t_i^*$, $i = 1, \ldots, n$. The allocation $(\omega_1 - t_1^*, \ldots, \omega_n - t_n^*)$ of the resources $\sum_{i=1}^{n}(\omega_i - t_i^*)$ among inside agents is also Pareto-optimal in the subeconomy consisting of these inside agents. If some agent $i \in \{1, \ldots, n\}$ uses a strategy y_i which differs from the null vector, he reaches a utility level $V_i(y_i, y_{-i})$, with $y_{-i} = (0, \ldots, 0)$, smaller or equal to $V_i(0, \ldots, 0)$, in the subeconomy consisting of n inside agents (see (2)). Accordingly, no unilateral deviation from the allocation $(\omega_1 - t_1^*, \ldots, \omega_n - t_n^*)$ can increase the utility of an inside agent, so that $(\omega_1 - t_1^*, \ldots, \omega_n - t_n^*)$ is a Nash equilibrium in the strategic market game in which the set of strategies S_i of agent i is given by $S_i = \{y_i \mid 0 \leq y_i \leq \omega_i - t_i^*\}$, $i = 1, \ldots, n$.

Finally, the uniqueness of equilibrium follows from the fact that any alternative strategic equilibrium would generate an allocation which is Pareto dominated by the allocation $(\omega_1 - t_1^*, \ldots, \omega_n - t_n^*)$. Accordingly, at least one inside agent can deviate from the strategy he has selected at this alternative Nash equilibrium by playing the strategy 0, and obtain a higher payoff, a contradiction. □

Proposition 1 is simply a restatement of the second welfare theorem formulated for our particular setting with some agents excluded from trade and the remaining ones behaving strategically while, in the usual formulation of this theorem, the Pareto-optimal allocation is viewed as "sustained" by competitive prices. The proof of this proposition takes advantage of the fact that the initial allocation of an exchange economy always appears as the outcome of a Nash equilibrium in the associated market game (the so-called *trivial equilibrium*, see Dubey and Shubik (1978)).

The usual criticisms against lump-sum taxes and transfers needed to sustain a particular Pareto-optimal allocation as a competitive outcome, applies as well in our attempt to sustain such an allocation as a strategic equilibrium. In particular, these taxes and transfers need to be personalized since they vary across agents depending on the quantity of resources required to achieve the particular Pareto-optimal allocation. Thus, it is natural to wonder whether it is possible to design taxes which are not linked to individual characteristics, but rather to the commodities themselves, like in the case of commodity taxation. Such taxes appear as more *anonymous*, to the extent that they are imposed on all consumers in the same manner for the same good. In an exchange economy, one can think of two types of taxes satisfying this anonymity criterion. The first one consists in imposing a tax t^h on good h, to be collected on transactions concerning good h: this is *commodity taxation*. The second one consists in imposing a tax t^h on the hth–component of ω_i, independently of i, before transactions take place: this is *endowment taxation*. In the next two sections, we examine whether using such tax instruments could be sufficient to perform the job which we have just seen to be feasible with personalized lump-sum taxes and transfers.

3 Commodity taxation

In this section, we construct a particular example of an exchange economy and show that commodity taxation is not a sufficient instrument in order to realize a Pareto-optimal allocation when inside agents behave strategically. Consider an exchange economy with two goods, 1 and 2, and consisting of $n+1$ agents, namely n inside agents and one outside agent. The inside agents fall into two *types*, with $\frac{n}{2}$ agents of each type. All agents i, $i = 1, ..., n+1$, have the same utility function U, which is defined by

$$U(x^1, x^2) = x^1 x^2. \tag{6}$$

Initial endowments are defined by

$$\omega_i = (1, 0), \qquad i = 1, ..., \frac{n}{2} \tag{7}$$

$$\omega_i = (0, 1), \qquad i = \frac{n}{2} + 1, ..., n \tag{8}$$

and

$$\omega_i = (0,0), \qquad i = n+1. \tag{9}$$

To the exchange economy consisting of the n inside agents, we may associate a strategic market game Γ as follows. For all agents, the *strategy set* S_i consists of the $[0,1]$ - interval. For an agent $i \in \{1, ..., \frac{n}{2}\}$, we denote by q_i a strategy in $[0,1]$: q_i is to be interpreted as the quantity of good 1 that agent i sends to the market for trade. Similarly, b_i, $b_i \in [0,1]$, denotes a strategy of agent i, $i \in \{\frac{n}{2}+1, ..., n\}$. Given an n-tuple of strategies $(q,b) = (q_1, ..., q_{\frac{n}{2}}; b_{\frac{n}{2}+1}, ..., b_n)$, the resulting allocation of goods obtains as

$$(1 - q_i, pq_i)$$

for an agent i in $\{1, ..., \frac{n}{2}\}$, and

$$(\frac{b_i}{p}, 1 - b_i)$$

for an agent i in $\{\frac{n}{2}+1, ..., n\}$, with p denoting the price of good 1 expressed in units of good 2 (good 2 serves as numeraire). Using the price mechanism defined above by equation (3), this price follows from the equality of demand and supply of good 1, i.e. it satisfies the equation:

$$\sum_{k=\frac{n}{2}+1}^{n} b_k = p \sum_{k=1}^{\frac{n}{2}} q_k;$$

or

$$p = \frac{\sum_{k=\frac{n}{2}+1}^{n} b_k}{\sum_{k=1}^{\frac{n}{2}} q_k}.$$

Accordingly, given an n-tuple (q,b) of strategies, the *payoffs* in the strategic market game Γ obtain as

$$V_i(q,b) = U(1 - q_i, \frac{\sum_{k=\frac{n}{2}+1}^{n} b_k}{\sum_{k=1}^{\frac{n}{2}} q_k} q_i),$$

for $i = 1, ..., \frac{n}{2}$, and

$$V_i(q,b) = U(\frac{\sum_{k=1}^{\frac{n}{2}} q_k}{\sum_{k=\frac{n}{2}+1}^{n} b_k} b_i, 1 - b_i),$$

for $i = \frac{n}{2}+1, ..., n$.

At the vector of strategies $(\hat{q}, \hat{b})$ defined by

$$(\hat{q}, \hat{b}) = (0, \ldots, 0; 0, \ldots, 0),$$

payoffs are defined by

$$V_i(\hat{q},\hat{b}) = U(\omega_i) = 0, \qquad i = 1,...,n.$$

A *strategic equilibrium* is a n-tuple of strategies $(q_1^*,...,q_{\frac{n}{2}}^*; b_{\frac{n}{2}+1}^*,...,b_n^*)$ such that no trader has an advantage to deviate unilaterally from his choice. As noticed above, it is a general property of strategic market games that the vector of strategies $(\hat{q},\hat{b})$ where each trader bids and supplies nothing is always a strategic equilibrium (the so-called *trivial equilibrium*). As shown in Gabszewicz and Michel (1997) where this example is introduced, all traders of the same type must adopt the same strategy at equilibrium and, apart from the trivial one, *the vector of strategies* (q^*,b^*) *defined by*

$$(q^*,b^*) = \left(\frac{n-2}{2(n-1)}, \frac{n-2}{2(n-1)}\right) \tag{10}$$

is the only strategic equilibrium of the market game Γ.[3]

Now suppose that commodity taxes t^h, $h = 1,2$, are levied on transactions in order to provide the outside agent $n+1$ with some amount of the two goods and realize thereby a feasible utility level $\overline{U}$ for him. More specifically, suppose that, *when exchange takes place*, a per unit tax t^1, $0 < t^1 < 1$, is levied on the supply of good 1 and a per unit tax t^2, $0 < t^2 < 1$, is levied on the supply of good 2, giving rise to a total tax product equal to $t^1 \sum_{k=1}^{\frac{n}{2}} q_k$ units of good 1, and $t^2 \sum_{k=\frac{n}{2}+1}^{n} b_k$ units of good 2. Furthermore, suppose that, *after trade has occurred* at an n-tuple of strategies $(q_1,...,q_{\frac{n}{2}}; b_{\frac{n}{2}+1},...,b_n)$, the total product of the tax $t^1 \sum_{k=1}^{\frac{n}{2}} q_k$ in good 1 and $t^2 \sum_{k=\frac{n}{2}+1}^{n} b_k$ in good 2 is transferred to the outside agent $n+1$. Consequently, this commodity tax and transfer scheme generates a new strategic market game Γ' as follows. Given a commodity tax t^1, $0 < t^1 < 1$, and a commodity tax t^2, $0 < t^2 < 1$, the strategy set of inside agents i, $i = 1,...,n$, is the interval $[0,1]$. Furthermore, the initial endowments are still $\omega_i = (1,0)$, $i \in \{1,...,\frac{n}{2}\}$ and $\omega_i = (0,1)$, $i \in \{\frac{n}{2}+1,...,n\}$. However, the price $p(q_1,...,q_{\frac{n}{2}}; b_{\frac{n}{2}+1},...,b_n)$ now obtains as

$$p(q_1,...,q_{\frac{n}{2}}; b_{\frac{n}{2}+1},...,b_n) = \frac{(1-t^2)\sum_{k=\frac{n}{2}+1}^{n} b_k}{(1-t^1)\sum_{k=1}^{\frac{n}{2}} q_k},$$

and the resulting post-tax allocation of goods in the game Γ' is given by

$$x_i = \left(1 - q_i, \frac{(1-t^2)\sum_{k=\frac{n}{2}+1}^{n} b_k}{(1-t^1)\sum_{k=1}^{\frac{n}{2}} q_k} q_i(1-t^1)\right), \qquad i = 1,...,\frac{n}{2} \tag{11}$$

[3] It is easy to see that the strategic equilibrium converges to the unique competitive equilibrium of the exchange economy when $n \to \infty$. This simply reflects the fact that competition is restored when the number of traders increases without limit.

$$x_i = \left(\frac{(1-t^1)\sum_{k=1}^{\frac{n}{2}} q_k}{(1-t^2)\sum_{k=\frac{n}{2}+1}^{n} b_k} b_i(1-t^2), 1-b_i \right). \qquad i = \frac{n}{2}+1, ..., n \quad (12)$$

It gives rise to utility levels

$$V_i(q,b) = (1-q_i)\left(\frac{(1-t^2)\sum_{k=\frac{n}{2}+1}^{n} b_k}{\sum_{k=1}^{\frac{n}{2}} q_k} q_i \right), \qquad i = 1, ..., \frac{n}{2} \quad (13)$$

and

$$V_i(q,b) = \left(\frac{(1-t^1)\sum_{k=1}^{\frac{n}{2}} q_k}{\sum_{k=\frac{n}{2}+1}^{n} b_k} b_i \right)(1-b_i), \qquad i = \frac{n}{2}+1, ..., n. \quad (14)$$

In the following proposition, we show that the commodity taxes and transfers scheme defined above does not allow to obtain a Pareto-optimal overall-allocation, with the outside agent obtaining the preassigned utility level $\overline{U}$ at the outcome of the strategic market game Γ'.

Proposition 2. *Given any utility level $\overline{U}$ for the outside agent $n+1$, there do not exist commodity taxes t^h, $h = 1,2$ such that, when the product of these taxes is transferred to agent $n+1$, (i) the overall-allocation resulting from this transfer and from the strategic equilibrium of the game Γ' is Pareto-optimal and (ii) the utility of the outside agent after transfer is at least equal to $\overline{U}$.*

Proof. Suppose, contrary to proposition 2, that there exist commodity taxes t^h, $h = 1,2$, for which requirements *(i)* and *(ii)* are met. First, we show that, even with these taxes t^h, $h = 1,2$, the vector of strategies (q^*, b^*) of the game Γ, as obtained in (10), remains the unique interior Nash equilibrium of the strategic market game Γ'. The first order conditions which must be satisfied at an interior equilibrium are

$$\frac{\partial V_i}{\partial q_i} = (1-q_i)\left(\frac{\sum_{k=\frac{n}{2}+1}^{n} b_k \left(\sum_{k=1}^{\frac{n}{2}} q_k - q_i\right)}{\left(\sum_{k=1}^{\frac{n}{2}} q_k\right)^2} \right) - \frac{\sum_{k=\frac{n}{2}+1}^{n} b_k}{\sum_{k=1}^{\frac{n}{2}} q_k} q_i = 0, i = 1, ..., \tfrac{n}{2}$$

$$\frac{\partial V_i}{\partial b_i} = (1-b_i)\left(\frac{\sum_{k=1}^{\frac{n}{2}} q_k \left(\sum_{k=\frac{n}{2}+1}^{n} b_k - b_i\right)}{\left(\sum_{k=\frac{n}{2}+1}^{n} b_k\right)^2} \right) - \frac{\sum_{k=1}^{\frac{n}{2}} q_k}{\sum_{k=\frac{n}{2}+1}^{n} b_k} b_i = 0,$$

$$i = \tfrac{n}{2}+1, ..., n.$$

Using the fact that all traders of the same type must adopt the same strategy at equilibrium,[4] we may denote by q (resp. b) the supply of inside agents $i \in \{1, ..., \frac{n}{2}\}$ (resp. $i \in \{\frac{n}{2}+1, ..., n\}$) on the market. Using this property, the first order conditions which must be satisfied at an interior strategic equilibrium can be rewritten as

$$\frac{(n-2)(1-q)}{nq} - 1 = 0, \qquad i = 1, ..., \frac{n}{2} \quad (15)$$

[4] For a formal proof, see Gabszewicz and Grazzini (1999), Appendix, p.493.

$$\frac{(n-2)(1-b)}{nb} - 1 = 0, \qquad i = \frac{n}{2} + 1, ..., n, \tag{16}$$

so that the interior equilibrium is given by $(q^*, b^*) = \left(\frac{n-2}{2(n-1)}, \frac{n-2}{2(n-1)}\right)$ (simple calculations show that this vector of strategies is the unique interior equilibrium). Furthermore, notice that, at the strategic equilibrium, we have

$$p(q^*, b^*) = \frac{1-t^2}{1-t^1}. \tag{17}$$

Substituting the equilibrium values q^* and b^* into the payoffs V_i (see (13) and (14)), we obtain

$$V_i(q^*, b^*) = \frac{n(n-2)(1-t^2)}{4(n-1)^2}, \qquad i = 1, ..., \frac{n}{2} \tag{18}$$

and

$$V_i(q^*, b^*) = \frac{n(n-2)(1-t^1)}{4(n-1)^2}, \qquad i = \frac{n}{2} + 1, ..., n. \tag{19}$$

Any Pareto-optimal allocation, which would follow from commodity taxes t^1 and t^2 and provide agent $n+1$ with utility level $\overline{U}$, must solve the problem

$$\max_{t^1, t^2} \textstyle\sum_{i=1}^n V_i(q^*, b^*) \qquad s.t.$$

$$U(\tfrac{n}{2}t^1 q^*, \tfrac{n}{2}t^2 b^*) = \overline{U},$$

or

$$\max_{t^1,t^2} \tfrac{n}{2} \cdot \tfrac{n(n-2)(1-t^2)}{4(n-1)^2} + \tfrac{n}{2} \cdot \tfrac{n(n-2)(1-t^1)}{4(n-1)^2} \qquad s.t.$$

$$\left(t^1 \tfrac{n}{2} \tfrac{(n-2)}{2(n-1)}\right)\left(t^2 \tfrac{n}{2} \tfrac{(n-2)}{2(n-1)}\right) = \overline{U}. \tag{20}$$

Simple calculations show that the unique solution to this problem is $t^1 = t^2 = t^* = \frac{4(n-1)\sqrt{\overline{U}}}{n(n-2)}$. Substituting the value t^* into (11) and (12) reveals that the marginal rate of substitution between good 1 and good 2 is equal to $1 - \frac{2(1+2\sqrt{\overline{U}})}{n} + \frac{4\sqrt{\overline{U}}}{n^2}$ for the inside agents i, $i = 1, ..., \frac{n}{2}$; the rate equals $1/\left(1 - \frac{2(1+2\sqrt{\overline{U}})}{n} + \frac{4\sqrt{\overline{U}}}{n^2}\right)$ for the inside agents i, $i = \frac{n}{2} + 1, ..., n$; and the rate equals 1 for the outside agent $2n+1$. Consequently, these marginal rates of substitution vary across agents, so that the resulting overall-allocation cannot be Pareto-optimal, a contradiction to our initial assumption. □

Having reached this negative outcome, we examine in the next section whether endowment taxation cannot realize the objective which was unsuccessfully pursued with commodity taxation.

4 Endowment taxation

Consider now the following tax and transfer scheme. Firstly, *before exchange takes place*, taxes are introduced which consist in collecting, for each good, and each inside agent, a share t^h, $h = 1, 2$, of the amount of commodity h he owns initially: we call this tax scheme *endowment taxation*. Secondly, *after trade has occurred*, the product of these taxes is redistributed in favor of the outside agent who gets accordingly $\frac{n}{2}t^h$ of good $h = 1, 2$.

More specifically, consider again the same example of exchange economy as in section 3. The endowment tax and transfer scheme we have just considered generates a new strategic market game Γ'' as follows. Since, after taxation, traders are deprived from a share of their initial endowment, they start the game Γ'' with strategy sets S_i equal to the interval $\left[0, 1 - t^1\right]$ for agents $i = 1, ..., \frac{n}{2}$, and to the interval $\left[0, 1 - t^2\right]$ for $i = \frac{n}{2} + 1, ..., n$. Given any n-tuple of strategies $(q_1, ..., q_{\frac{n}{2}}; b_{\frac{n}{2}+1}, ..., b_n)$ the resulting price is

$$p(q_1, ..., q_{\frac{n}{2}}; b_{\frac{n}{2}+1}, ..., b_n) = \frac{\sum_{k=\frac{n}{2}+1}^{n} b_k}{\sum_{k=1}^{\frac{n}{2}} q_k},$$

giving rise to the post-tax allocation of goods

$$x_i = \left(1 - t^1 - q_i, \frac{\sum_{k=\frac{n}{2}+1}^{n} b_k}{\sum_{k=1}^{\frac{n}{2}} q_k} q_i\right), \qquad i = 1, ..., \frac{n}{2} \tag{21}$$

$$x_i = \left(\frac{\sum_{k=1}^{\frac{n}{2}} q_k}{\sum_{k=\frac{n}{2}+1}^{n} b_k} b_i, 1 - t^2 - b_i\right), \qquad i = \frac{n}{2} + 1, ..., n. \tag{22}$$

These outcomes generate utility levels

$$V_i(q, b) = (1 - t^1 - q_i)\left(\frac{\sum_{k=\frac{n}{2}+1}^{n} b_k}{\sum_{k=1}^{\frac{n}{2}} q_k} q_i\right), \qquad i = 1, ..., \frac{n}{2} \tag{23}$$

and

$$V_i(q, b) = \left(\frac{\sum_{k=1}^{\frac{n}{2}} q_k}{\sum_{k=\frac{n}{2}+1}^{n} b_k} b_i\right)(1 - t^2 - b_i), \qquad i = \frac{n}{2} + 1, ..., n. \tag{24}$$

In the following proposition, we show that the endowment tax and transfer scheme we consider above does not allow either to obtain a Pareto-optimal overall-allocation, with the outside agent obtaining the preassigned utility level $\overline{U}$, at the outcome of the strategic market game Γ''.

Proposition 3. *Given any utility level $\overline{U}$ for the outside agent $n + 1$, there do not exist endowment taxes t^h, $h = 1, 2$ such that, when the product of these taxes is transferred to agent $n+1$, (i) the overall-allocation resulting from this transfer and from the strategic equilibrium of the game Γ'' is Pareto-optimal and (ii) the utility of the outside agent after transfer is at least equal to $\overline{U}$.*

Proof. Suppose, contrary to proposition 3, that there exist endowment taxes t^h, $h = 1, 2$, for which requirements *(i)* and *(ii)* are met. First, we show that (q^*, b^*) defined by

$$(q^*, b^*) = \left(\frac{(1 - t^1)(n - 2)}{2(n - 1)}, \frac{(1 - t^2)(n - 2)}{2(n - 1)} \right), \tag{25}$$

is the unique interior strategic equilibrium of the market game Γ''. Using the fact that all traders of the same type must adopt the same strategy at equilibrium, we may denote by q (resp. b) the supply of inside agents $i \in \{1, ..., \frac{n}{2}\}$ (resp. $i \in \{\frac{n}{2} + 1, ..., n\}$) on the market. The first order conditions which must be satisfied at an interior equilibrium can then be written as

$$\frac{(1 - t^1 - q)(n - 2)}{nq} - 1 = 0, \qquad i = 1, ..., \frac{n}{2} \tag{26}$$

$$\frac{(1 - t^2 - b)(n - 2)}{nb} - 1 = 0, \qquad i = \frac{n}{2} + 1, ..., n. \tag{27}$$

Simple calculations show that the vector of strategies (q^*, b^*) in (25) is the unique interior equilibrium. Furthermore, notice that, at the strategic equilibrium, we have

$$p(q^*, b^*) = \frac{1 - t^2}{1 - t^1}. \tag{28}$$

Substituting the equilibrium values q^* and b^* into the payoffs V_i (see (23) and (24)), we obtain

$$V_i(q^*, b^*) = \frac{n(n - 2)(1 - t^1)(1 - t^2)}{4(n - 1)^2}, \qquad i = 1, ..., n. \tag{29}$$

Any Pareto-optimal allocation which would follow from endowment taxes t^1 and t^2 and provide agent $n + 1$ with utility level $\overline{U}$ must solve the problem

$$\max_{t^1, t^2} \sum_{i=1}^{n} V_i(q^*, b^*) \qquad s.t.$$

$$U(\tfrac{n}{2}t^1, \tfrac{n}{2}t^2) = \overline{U},$$

or

$$\max_{t^1, t^2} n \cdot \frac{n(n-2)(1-t^1)(1-t^2)}{4(n-1)^2} \qquad s.t.$$

$$\left(\tfrac{n}{2}t^1\right)\left(\tfrac{n}{2}t^2\right) = \overline{U}. \tag{30}$$

Simple calculations show that the unique solution to this problem is $t^1 = t^2 = t^* = \frac{2\sqrt{\overline{u}}}{n}$. Substituting the optimal value t^* into (21) and (22) reveals that the marginal rate of substitution between good 1 and good 2 is equal to $\frac{n-2}{n}$ for the inside agents i, $i = 1, ..., \frac{n}{2}$, to $\frac{n}{n-2}$ for the inside agents i, $i = \frac{n}{2}+1, ..., n$, and to 1 for the outside agent $2n+1$. Consequently, these marginal rates of substitution vary across agents, so that the resulting overall-allocation cannot be Pareto-optimal, a contradiction. □

The negative results shown in section 3 and 4 both follow from the same cause: the tax schemes proposed are not powerful enough to wipe out the distortions introduced by the strategic behaviour of inside agents. Optimal taxes corresponding to these schemes can only reach a "second best" because they are unable to manipulate sufficiently the game in order to neutralize the market power of inside agents.

In the next section, we propose a tax and transfer scheme relying, as in this section, on endowment taxation but combined with a more elaborate system of transfers: these will not only go from the inside agents to the outside one, but also take place among the inside agents themselves. As it will be shown, when applied to our example, this method will be proved to be a powerful instrument both as a counterdistortionary measure and as an efficient redistributive tool.

5 Endowment taxation and incentive transfers

In this section, we start by defining a tax and transfer scheme which is specific to the exchange economy we have considered in the two previous sections. The aim of this tax and transfer scheme is not only to insure a preassigned utility level to the outside agent, but also to resorb the distortion resulting from the strategic behaviour of inside agents. First, *before exchange takes place*, suppose that endowment taxes are levied, as in the preceding section, on the goods owned initially by inside agents. Furthermore, *after trade has occurred*, a share of the product of these taxes is redistributed among inside agents, while the remaining part is transferred to the outside one. More specifically, the share received by inside agents is redistributed among them *in a manner assigning to them a quantity of the good they do not own initially, which is proportional to the amount of the good they own initially and supply for exchange*. In other words, the transfer received by each inside agent, in units of the good which is not initially owned, increases as he raises the amount of the initially owned good he sends to the market. Furthermore, the transfer received by the outside agent is required to assign a commodity bundle providing him the utility level $\overline{U}$.

Clearly, the imposition of this tax and transfer scheme allows a manipulation of the market game Γ defined above. On the one hand, the strategy set of inside agents is no longer the unit interval $[0, 1]$, but an interval strictly included in it. On the other hand, transfers among inside agents of the share of the tax product they receive reshape their payoffs in the game since these transfers have now to be added to the outcomes already obtained from strategic exchange. In the following, we show that there exists a tax and transfer scheme which manipulates the game in such a way that the allocation corresponding to the interior strategic equilibrium of this game is a competitive allocation in the subeconomy consisting of the inside agents. Furthermore, the transfer obtained by the agent $n+1$ generates a utility level $\overline{U}$, and the overall-allocation is Pareto-optimal.

In the following, we suppose that $\overline{U} < \frac{n^2}{4}$.[5] Let a tax t^h, $t^h = t = \tau + \frac{2\sqrt{\overline{U}}}{n}$, be levied on both goods $h = 1, 2$. Furthermore, assume that, after trade has occurred at an n-tuple of strategies $(q_1, ..., q_{\frac{n}{2}}; b_{\frac{n}{2}+1}, ..., b_n)$, a share $\frac{\tau}{\frac{1}{2}-\tau-\frac{\sqrt{\overline{U}}}{n}}$, $0 < \tau < \frac{1}{4} - \frac{\sqrt{\overline{U}}}{2n}$, of the total tax product in good 1 (resp. good 2) is transferred to each agent $i \in \{\frac{n}{2}+1, ..., n\}$ (resp. $i \in \{1, ..., \frac{n}{2}\}$), while the remaining share of the tax product in each good ($\sqrt{\overline{U}}$) is redistributed to the outside agent. This tax and transfers scheme generates a new strategic market game Γ''' as follows. The strategy set of all agents is the interval $[0, 1-t]$. The post-tax allocation of the game Γ''' at a vector of strategies $(q_1, ..., q_{\frac{n}{2}}; b_{\frac{n}{2}+1}, ..., b_n)$ now obtain as

$$x_i = \left(1 - \tau - \frac{2\sqrt{\overline{U}}}{n} - q_i, \frac{\sum_{k=\frac{n}{2}+1}^{n} b_k}{\sum_{k=1}^{\frac{n}{2}} q_k} q_i + \frac{\tau}{\frac{1}{2} - \tau - \frac{\sqrt{\overline{U}}}{n}} q_i\right), \quad i = 1, ..., \frac{n}{2} \tag{31}$$

$$x_i = \left(\frac{\sum_{k=1}^{\frac{n}{2}} q_k}{\sum_{k=\frac{n}{2}+1}^{n} b_k} b_i + \frac{\tau}{\frac{1}{2} - \tau - \frac{\sqrt{\overline{U}}}{n}} b_i, 1 - \tau - \frac{2\sqrt{\overline{U}}}{n} - b_i\right), i = \frac{n}{2} + 1, ..., n \tag{32}$$

giving rise to utility levels

$$V_i(q,b) = (1 - \tau - \frac{2\sqrt{\overline{U}}}{n} - q_i)\left(\frac{\sum_{k=\frac{n}{2}+1}^{n} b_k}{\sum_{k=1}^{\frac{n}{2}} q_k} q_i + \frac{\tau}{\frac{1}{2} - \tau - \frac{\sqrt{\overline{U}}}{n}} q_i\right), i = 1, ..., \frac{n}{2} \tag{33}$$

and

$$V_i(q,b) = \left(\frac{\sum_{k=1}^{\frac{n}{2}} q_k}{\sum_{k=\frac{n}{2}+1}^{n} b_k} b_i + \frac{\tau b_i}{\frac{1}{2} - \tau - \frac{\sqrt{\overline{U}}}{n}}\right)(1 - \tau - \frac{2\sqrt{\overline{U}}}{n} - b_i), i = \frac{n}{2} + 1, ..., n. \tag{34}$$

Proposition 4. *Given a feasible preassigned utility level $\overline{U}$ for the outside agent $n+1$, there exists endowment taxes t^h, $h = 1, 2$, and incentive transfers of a share of the resulting tax product among inside agents such that, (i)*

[5] This assumption is equivalent to assume that the utility level $\overline{U}$ is feasible.

when the remaining share of this product is transferred to the outside agent, the overall-allocation resulting from this transfer and from the strategic equilibrium of the game Γ''' is Pareto-optimal and (ii) the utility of the outside agent at the commodity bundle obtained from the transfer is equal to $\overline{U}$.

Proof. First, take out, from the initial endowment of the inside agent i, an amount equal to $\frac{2\sqrt{\overline{U}}}{n}$ from the good he owns initially, and transfer it to the outside agent. Then the latter gets the bundle $(\sqrt{\overline{U}}, \sqrt{\overline{U}})$ and obtains accordingly a utility level equal to $\sqrt{\overline{U}} \cdot \sqrt{\overline{U}} = \overline{U}$. Furthermore, impose also, on each inside agent i's endowment a levy τ on the good he owns initially, with

$$\tau = \frac{n - 2\sqrt{\overline{U}}}{n(n+2)}. \tag{35}$$

Using the fact that all inside agents of the same type must adopt the same strategy at equilibrium, we denote by q (resp. b) the strategy inside agents $i \in \{1, ..., \frac{n}{2}\}$ (resp. $i \in \{\frac{n}{2} + 1, ..., n\}$) use at such an equilibrium. Using this property, the first order conditions which must be satisfied at an interior strategic equilibrium can be written as

$$(1 - \tau - \frac{2\sqrt{\overline{U}}}{n} - q)\left(\frac{n-2}{n}\frac{b}{q} + \frac{\tau}{\frac{1}{2} - \tau - \frac{\sqrt{\overline{U}}}{n}}\right) - \left(b + \frac{\tau}{\frac{1}{2} - \tau - \frac{\sqrt{\overline{U}}}{n}} q\right) = 0,$$

$$(1 - \tau - \frac{2\sqrt{\overline{U}}}{n} - b)\left(\frac{n-2}{n}\frac{q}{b} + \frac{\tau}{\frac{1}{2} - \tau - \frac{\sqrt{\overline{U}}}{n}}\right) - \left(q + \frac{\tau}{\frac{1}{2} - \tau - \frac{\sqrt{\overline{U}}}{n}} b\right) = 0,$$

with τ as defined in (35). The only solution of the above system is given by (q^*, b^*) with

$$q^* = b^* = \frac{n - 2\sqrt{\overline{U}}}{2(n+2)},$$

which is accordingly the unique interior Nash equilibrium of the game Γ'''. Furthermore, it is easily checked that the transfers among inside agents are feasible at equilibrium. Substituting these values into (31) and (32), we obtain

$$x_i^* = \left(\frac{1}{2} - \frac{\sqrt{\overline{U}}}{n}, \frac{1}{2} - \frac{\sqrt{\overline{U}}}{n}\right), \qquad i = 1, ..., n.$$

Accordingly, the common marginal rate of substitution between the two goods, at the post-tax allocation, is equal to one for all inside agents which is also the value of the marginal rate of substitution of the outside agent $n+1$ at the commodity bundle $(\sqrt{\overline{U}}, \sqrt{\overline{U}})$ he gets from the transfer. We conclude that the overall-allocation is Pareto-optimal. □

6 Concluding remarks

Arriving at the end of this paper, we are aware that it is certainly a rather difficult piece of work that the patient reader had to swallow. It is so because it combines the well-known intricacies encountered when analysing strategic multilateral trade, with the arcane mysteries of optimal taxation. Furthermore, our analysis is cast into the framework of exchange economies which, by their very nature, are never met in real life. This gives to our paper a flavour of abstraction which is not in line with current academic fashion. In spite of these drawbacks, we hope that reading our paper has provided its readers, and in particular Professor Hildenbrand himself, with some enjoyable time and stimulating ideas, inasmuch as they were sufficiently patient to tolerate us until its end!

References

1. Amir, R., Sahi, S., Shubik, M., Yao, S. (1990): A Strategic Market Game with Complete Markets. Journal of Economic Theory 51, 126–143
2. Aumann, R. J., Kurz, M. (1977): Power and Taxes. Econometrica 45, 1137–1161
3. Bloch, F., Ferrer, H. (2000): Strategic Complements and Substitutes in Bilateral Oligopolies. Economic Letters, forthcoming
4. Cordella, T., Gabszewicz, J. J. (1998): "Nice" Trivial Equilibria in Strategic Market Games. Games and Economic Behavior 22, 162–169
5. Dubey, P., Shubik, M. (1978): A Theory of Money and Financial Institutions. 28. The Non-cooperative Equilibria of a Closed Trading Economy with Market Supply and Bidding Strategies. Journal of Economic Theory 17, 1–20
6. Gabszewicz J. J., Grazzini L. (1999): Taxing Market Power. Journal of Public Economic Theory Vol. 1 (4), 475–497
7. Gabszewicz, J. J., Michel, P. (1997): Oligopoly Equilibrium in Exchange Economies. In: Eaton, B. C., and Harris, R. G. (Eds.): Trade, Technology and Economics. Essays in Honour of Richard G. Lipsey. Edward Elgar, Cheltenham, 217–240
8. Gabszewicz, J. J., Vial, J. P. (1972): Oligopoly "à la Cournot" in General Equilibrium Analysis. Journal of Economic Theory 4, 381–400
9. Guesnerie, R., Laffont, J. J. (1978): Taxing Price makers. Journal of Economic Theory 19, 423-455
10. Myles, G. D. (1989): Ramsey Tax Rules for Economies with Imperfect Competition. Journal of Public Economics 38, 95115
11. Shapley, L. (1976): Noncooperative General Exchange. In: Lin S. (Ed.): Theory and Measurement of Economic Externalities. Academic Press, New York, 155175
12. Shapley, L., Shubik, M. (1977): Trade Using One Commodity as a Means of Payment. Journal of Political Economy 85, 937-968

Walras Equilibrium with Coordination

Birgit Grodal and Karl Vind

Økonomisk Institut, Københavns Universitet, Studiestræde 6, DK-1455 København, Denmark

Abstract. We consider a pure exchange economy with private ownership in which consumers have interdependent preferences. Hence, consumers' preferences are defined on the states of the economy. In a Walras equilibrium for such an economy, it may, of course, be possible for two or more consumers to simultaneously change their net trades and thereby obtain a preferred state. We use the concept of coordination introduced by Vind (1983) to define an exogenously given coordination structure in the economy and define a new equilibrium concept, *Walras equilibrium with coordination.* In such an equilibrium individual consumers take prices and initial endowments as given, and consumers do not expect to be able to obtain a preferred state when they coordinate their choice of net trades. By using the existence theorem for an equilibrium in a social system with coordination, we set conditions for the existence of a Walras equilibrium with coordination.

1 Introduction

We consider a pure exchange economy with private ownership in which consumers have interdependent preferences. We assume that a state of the economy specifies the net trade of each consumer and that consumers' preferences are defined on the states of the economy. In a Walras equilibrium for such an economy, it may, of course, be possible for two or more consumers to simultaneously change their net trades and thereby obtain a preferred state. In order to allow consumers to coordinate their net trades, we use the concept of coordination introduced by Vind (1983) to define an exogenously given coordination structure in the economy and to define a new equilibrium concept, *Walras equilibrium with coordination.*

Coordination is specified by coordination functions for the consumers and an approval function. A coordination function for a consumer specifies for each state x of the economy and each alternative state y that state the consumer believes will be the outcome if in state x all consumers $c \in C$ change their net trades to $y(c)$. Clearly, a coordination function could specify that the consumer only coordinates with himself or, at the other extreme, that he coordinates with all other consumers. Typically, each consumer coordinates his net trade with a subset of the set of consumers. We do not assume that coordination is symmetric, that is, consumer c may coordinate with d without d coordinating with c. Moreover, two consumers may coordinate in some commodities and not in others.

In traditional economic theory a household is endowed with a vector of initial resources and a preference relation which is often assumed to be a total preorder. However, a household typically has several members. In our formalization of a household, each member will be endowed with his own initial resources and his own preference relation. Moreover, each member is described by a coordination function which may, for example, specify that he coordinates his net trade with the net trades of all the other members of the household. As we do not allow members of a household to transfer budgets, our approach leads to a household decision problem that is different from the one discussed in Browning and Chiappori (1998) and Gersbach and Haller (1999), for example.

Clearly, to define an equilibrium state, we also have to specify the set of consumers who has to approve a change from one state x to another state y. In the traditional Walras equilibrium, where a consumer (household with a single budget constraint) only considers his own change of net trade, the change should just be approved by the consumers who change their net trades; hence, as there is no coordination, it is enough to look at a deviation by a single consumer (household). In our formalization, we explicitly have to define the set of consumers who has to approve a change. This is done by enlarging the description of the economy with an approval function. For each state x and each alternative state y, this function specifies the set of consumers who has to approve a change from x to y. Note that, since consumers have different coordination functions, they expect different states to be the outcome of the change from x to y. In the household example the approval function might, for example, specify that the change has to be approved by all those consumers who are members of a household where at least one consumer has changed his net trade.

The market institution we study in this paper is a complete Walrasian market. Thus, all commodities have associated prices. We do not allow consumers to transfer budgets even if they coordinate with other consumers. Hence, a consumer has to choose a net trade with non-positive value at the prevailing prices. In a Walras equilibrium with coordination, consumers take prices and initial endowments as given, satisfy their budget constraint, and there is market clearing. Moreover, there does not exist an alternative state y such that each of the consumers who has to approve the change to y satisfies his budget constraint and prefers the state which he believes will be the outcome from the change to y.

By using the existence theorem for an equilibrium in a social system with coordination (Vind 1983 and Keiding 1985), we set conditions for the existence of a Walras equilibrium with coordination. Apart from the assumptions on the coordination functions and the approval function, the conditions correspond to those used for the existence of a Walras equilibrium in an economy with externalities by Shafer and Sonnenschein (1975). In particular, we do not assume that preferences are complete or transitive.

The concept of a Walras equilibrium with coordination and the existence result are interesting not only in terms of the most obvious interpretation, namely to analyze equilibria in an economy with externalities in consumption. It also turns out that Walras equilibrium with coordination in partitions is a useful tool for analyzing economies where consumers have several budget constraints[1]. By splitting each of the consumers into as many agents as he has budget constraints, we obtain a new economy in which each agent has only one budget constraint, but agents have interdependent preferences even if consumers have independent preferences. In order to reach an equivalence between the original maximization problem for a consumer and the maximization problems for the agents corresponding to him in the new economy, we assume that agents coming from the same consumer coordinate their actions. This tool is used in Grodal and Vind (1989) to study economies with a much richer set of market institutions.

In an economy where all consumers have independent preferences there is no need for coordination, and the definition of a Walras equilibrium with coordination reduces to the definition of a Walras equilibrium. Similarly, if each consumer only coordinates his choice of net trade with himself a Walras equilibrium with coordination is a usual Walras equilibrium. In general the set of Walras equilibria with coordination depends on the coordination functions as well as the approval function. Walras equilibria with coordination will not, in general, be Pareto optimal even if all consumers coordinate with all other consumers in all commodities. The reason is that, although the coordination functions allow consumers to coordinate their net trades, consumers have to satisfy their budget constraints individually.

In section 2, we define the economy. Section 3 contains the equilibrium definition. The existence theorem is presented in section 4. Section 5 contains some examples of coordination structures.

2 The economy

We consider a pure exchange economy

$$\mathcal{E} = \left(L, C, Y, (X_c, P_c, e_c)_{c \in C}, g\right)$$

where for all $c \in C$

(i) L is a finite set of commodities,
(ii) C is a finite set of consumers,
(iii) $Y = \mathbb{R}^{CL}$ is the state space of the economy,
(iv) $X_c \subset Y$ is the set of net trade states that are feasible for consumer c,
(v) $\mathcal{P}_c : X_c \to 2^{X_c}$ is the preference correspondence for consumer c,

[1] When markets are incomplete consumers have several budget constraints; see for example Duffie and Shafer (1985).

(vi) $e_c : Y \times Y \to Y$ is the coordination function for consumer c,
(vii) $g : Y \times Y \to 2^C$ is the approval function.

A state $x \in Y$ specifies the net trade $x(c) \in \mathbb{R}^L$ for each consumer $c \in C$. We use the notation $x(c, h)$ for consumer c's net trade in commodity $h \in L$. Apart from the coordination functions e_c, $c \in C$ and the approval function g, the description of the economy $\mathcal{E}$ is the standard one when consumers have interdependent preferences: Each consumer c is described by the states X_c which are feasible for him, and a preference correspondence $\mathcal{P}_c$ where $\mathcal{P}_c(x)$ are the states preferred by consumer c to the state x. The coordination function e_c specifies for each state $x \in Y$ and each alternative state $y \in Y$ the state $e_c(x, y)$ which consumer c expects to be the outcome when, in state x, the consumer d has chosen the net trade $y(d)$, $d \in C$. Moreover, we assume that there is an approval function $g : Y \times Y \to 2^C$. For each pair of states $x, y \in Y$, $g(x, y) \subset C$ gives the set of consumers who has to approve the change from x to y.

We will assume that the coordination functions satisfy the following assumption:

Assumption (Coordination Assumption) *For each consumer $c \in C$ the coordination function $e_c : Y \times Y \to Y$ satisfies*

(i) *For all* $(d, h) \in C \times L : e_c(x, y)(d, h) = \begin{cases} x(d, h) & \textit{for all } x, y \in Y \\ \textit{or} & \\ y(d, h) & \textit{for all } x, y \in Y \end{cases}$

(ii) $e_c(x, y)(c) = y(c)$ *for all* $x, y \in Y$

The assumption specifies the special coordination functions we use in this paper. The first part of the assumption states that consumer $c \in C$ expects states where consumer d's net trade in commodity h is d's old net trade in h for all states x and alternative states y, or it is d's new net trade in commodity h. We say that c coordinates his net trade with the net trade in commodity h of consumer d if $e_c(x, y)(d, h) = y(d, h)$ for all $x, y \in Y$. We say that c coordinates with consumer d if there exists a commodity h such that c coordinates his net trade with d's net trade in commodity h. The second part of the assumption states the natural condition that consumer c coordinates his net trade in all commodities with himself. It should be noted that we do not assume that the coordination relation is symmetric or transitive.

Assumption (Feasible Net Trade Assumption)

(A) *For all $c \in C$ the feasible set X_c and the coordination function e_c satisfy the following: for all $x \in \cap_{d \in C} X_d$ and $y \in Y$, $e_c(x, y) \in X_c \Rightarrow y \in X_c$.*

(B) *The feasible sets X_c, $c \in C$ and the coordination functions e_c, $c \in C$ satisfy the following: for all $x, y \in \cap_{c \in C} X_c$, $e_d(x, y) \in \cap_{c \in C} X_c$ for all $d \in C$.*

Assume that, if a consumer $c \in C$ coordinates with consumer d, he coordinates with d in all commodities $h \in L$. The feasible net trade assumption will then be satisfied if, for all $c \in C$, the feasible set X_c has the form $X_c = X'_c \times \prod_{d \neq c} \mathbb{R}^L$ for some $X'_c \subset \mathbb{R}^L$. That is, a state x is feasible for c iff c's net trade is in X'_c. The assumption is also satisfied in the following case: Let R_c be the set of consumers with whom c coordinates and assume that there exist individually feasible sets of net trades $X'_c \subset \mathbb{R}^L$ for $c \in C$ such that $X_c = \prod_{d \in R_c} X'_d \times \prod_{d \notin R_c} \mathbb{R}^L$. This last assumption says that a state is feasible for consumer c iff all the consumers with whom he coordinates have net trades in the individually feasible sets of net trades.

As mentioned above, the approval function $g : Y \times Y \to 2^C$ specifies the set of consumers who has to approve the change from state x to state y. An approval function g will naturally have the following property: $\{c \in C \mid x(c) \neq y(c)\} \subset g(x,y) \subset \{c \in C \mid e_c(x,y) \neq x\}$ for all $x, y \in Y$. This property amounts to the following: First, all consumers who actually change their net trade should approve the change. Moreover, only consumers who coordinate with a consumer who has changed his net trade are included in the set of consumers who has to approve the change. In the existence theorem in section 5, we assume that $g(x,y) = \{c \in C \mid e_c(x,y) \neq x\}$ for all $x, y \in Y$, that is, all consumers who coordinate with some consumer who changes his net trade have to approve the change.

3 Walras equilibrium with coordination

We shall use the following notation. Let $\mathbf{1}$ be the vector $(1, \cdots, 1) \in \mathbb{R}^{CL}$. Moreover, let $\Delta = \{p \in \mathbb{R}^L_+ \mid \sum_{h=1}^L p_h = 1\}$ be the non-negative price simplex in $\mathbb{R}^L$.

The definition of feasible states for our economy $\mathcal{E}$ is:

Definition (Feasible States) *A state $x \in Y$ is feasible for the economy $\mathcal{E}$ if*

(i) $x \in \cap_{c \in C} X_c$ *and*
(ii) $\sum_{c \in C} x(c) \leq 0$.

The set of feasible states is denoted $F(\mathcal{E}) \subset Y$.

Lemma *Assume that $\{x(c) \in \mathbb{R}^L \mid x \in X_c\}$ is bounded from below for each consumer $c \in C$. Then there exists $K > 0$ such that $F(\mathcal{E}) \subset int\widetilde{Y}$ where $\widetilde{Y} = \{x \in Y \mid -K\mathbf{1} \leq x \leq K\mathbf{1}\}$.*

Proof. By assumption $\cap_{c \in C} X_c$ is bounded below. As, moreover, $\sum_{c \in C} x(c) \leq 0$ for all $x \in F(\mathcal{E})$, it follows that $F(\mathcal{E})$ is bounded from above. □

Definition (Walras Equilibrium with Coordination) A Walras equilibrium with coordination *in the economy* $\mathcal{E}$ *is a pair* $(p, x) \in \Delta \times F(\mathcal{E})$ *consisting of a price and a feasible state such that*

(I) $px(c) \leq 0$ *for all* $c \in C$,
(II) *there does not exist* $y \in \mathbb{R}^{CL}$ *with* $y \neq x$, *such that for all* $c \in g(x, y)$, $py(c) \leq 0$ *and* $e_c(x, y) \in \mathcal{P}_c(x)$,
(III) $p_h \sum_{c \in C} x_h(c) = 0$ *for all* $h \in L$.

The equilibrium condition (I) states that all consumers take prices as given and choose a net trade with non-positive value at the given prices. Hence, no transfer of budget is allowed even if consumers coordinate their net trades. The equilibrium (II) condition states that there does not exist a non-empty set of consumers who can simultaneously change their net trades such that all consumers who have to approve the change expect to obtain a preferred state. The condition (III) states that the price of a commodity is zero if the aggregate net trade is negative.

Clearly, if the feasible states and the preferences of a consumer are independent (i.e., feasibility and the preferences of a consumer are defined by his own net trades), then for any coordination functions, a Walras equilibrium with coordination is exactly the same as a Walras equilibrium in the economy where the coordination functions have been disregarded.

4 The existence theorem

Before stating our existence theorem for the economy $\mathcal{E}$, we introduce the assumption of local non-satiation in $\mathcal{E}$.

Assumption (Local Non-Satiation) *For all* $x \in X$ *and for all* $c \in C$ *and all open neighborhoods* U *in* $\mathbb{R}^L$ *of* $x(c)$ *there exists* $x' \in U$ *such that letting the state* $y \in Y$ *be defined by* $y(d) = x(d)$ *for* $d \neq c$ *and* $y(c) = x'$ *then* $e_d(x, y) \in \mathcal{P}_d(x)$ *for all* d *with* $e_d(x, y) \neq x$. *If the assumption is satisfied for consumer* c, *we say that* c *is locally non-satiated.*

The condition states that consumer c can find a net trade x' locally such that he, as well as the consumers that coordinate with him, get a preferred state if c changes his action from $x(c)$ to x'. Clearly, the condition is satisfied if all consumers who coordinate with a given consumer are benevolent and each consumer has monotone preferences or just local non-satiation in his own consumption.

Theorem 1 (Equilibrium) *Let* $\mathcal{E}$ *be the economy as described above and assume*

(i) X_c *is closed, convex,* $0 \in \mathrm{int} X_c$, *and* $\{x(c) \in \mathbb{R}^L \mid x \in X_c\}$ *is bounded from below, for all* $c \in C$,

(ii) $\mathcal{P}_c$ *is irreflexive and has open graph and convex values, for all* $c \in C$,

(iii) *all consumers* $c \in C$ *are locally non-satiated,*

(iv) *the coordination assumption is satisfied,*

(v) *the feasible net trade assumption is satisfied,*

(vi) *for all* $c \in C$ *there exists* $(X^c, \mathcal{P}^c)$ *such that* $X_c \subset intX^c$ *and* $\mathcal{P}_c(x) = \mathcal{P}^c(x) \cap X_c$ *for all* $x \in X_c$, *and* $(X^c, \mathcal{P}^c)$ *satisfies* (i) *and* (ii),

(vii) $g(x, y) = \{c \in C \,|e_c(x, y) \neq x\}$ *for all* $x, y \in Y$.

Then there exists a Walras equilibrium with coordination in $\mathcal{E}$.

It is well known that the existence of a Walras equilibrium in an economy can be shown by converting the economy into a social system by adding an agent who sets prices, using an existence theorem for a Nash equilibrium in the social system, and finally showing that a Nash equilibrium in the social system is a Walras equilibrium in the original economy (see Arrow and Debreu 1954 for a proof). Our proof of the existence of a Walras equilibrium with coordination parallels this proof. However, we convert our economy with coordination into a social system with coordination as defined by Vind (1983) and use the existence theorem for an equilibrium in a social system with coordination by Keiding (1985). The definition of a social system with coordination and the equilibrium existence theorem are included in the Appendix.

Proof. First, we truncate the economy $\mathcal{E}$. By the lemma there exists a compact and convex set $\widetilde{Y} = \{x \in Y| - K\mathbf{1} \leq x \leq K\mathbf{1}\}$ with $K > 0$ such that $F(\mathcal{E}) \subset int\widetilde{X}$. Let $\widetilde{X}_c = X_c \cap \widetilde{Y}$ and let $\tilde{\mathcal{E}}$ be the corresponding truncated economy. Second, we define the social system with coordination $\Gamma = (A, (\mathcal{X}_a, \beta_a, \mathcal{P}_a, e_a)_{a \in A}, g)$ corresponding to the economy $\tilde{\mathcal{E}}$. The agents A are obtained by adding an agent $a = 0$ who sets prices, that is, $A = C \cup \{0\}$. The state space for Γ is $\mathcal{Y} = \mathbb{R}^L \times \mathbb{R}^{CL}$. The feasible states for agent $a \in C$ are defined by $\mathcal{X}_a = \mathbb{R}^L \times \widetilde{X}_a$ and for $a = 0$ by $\mathcal{X}_0 = \Delta \times \mathbb{R}^{CL}$. Let $\mathcal{X} = \cap_{a \in A} \mathcal{X}_a$. The constraint function $\beta_a : \mathcal{X} \to \mathcal{X}$ is defined by $\beta_a(p, x) = \{(q, y) \in \mathcal{X} \mid py(a) \leq 0\}$ for $a \in C$. For $a = 0$ we let $\beta_0(p, x) = \mathcal{X}$. For all agents $a \in C$ and all $((p, x)(q, y)) \in \mathcal{X} \times \mathcal{X}$ we let $e_a((p, x), (q, y)) = (p, e_a(x, y))$, that is, all consumers use their coordination functions from $\mathcal{E}$ and do not coordinate with the price maker[2]. Note that the definition of $\widetilde{Y}$ together with the assumption (v) imply that $e_a((p, x), (q, y)) \in \mathcal{X}$ for all $a \in C$. For $a = 0$ and all $((p, x)(q, y)) \in \mathcal{X} \times \mathcal{X}$ we let $e_0((p, x), (q, y)) = (q, x) \in \mathcal{X}$. That is, the price maker does not coordinate with any of the consumers. Similarly, the preferences of agent $a \in C$ are defined by $\mathcal{P}_a(p, x) = \{(q, y) \in \mathcal{X} \mid y \in \mathcal{P}_a(x)\}$ for all $(p, x) \in \mathcal{X}$. The preferences of the price setter are defined in the usual way by $\mathcal{P}_0(p, x) = \{(q, y) \in \mathcal{X} \mid q \cdot \sum_{c \in C} x(c) > p \cdot \sum_{c \in C} x(c)\}$. Finally,

[2] For notational simplicity, we use the same symbols for the coordination functions of the consumers and the approval function in Γ and in $\mathcal{E}$.

the approval function g in Γ is defined in the same way as in $\mathcal{E}$, that is, $g((p,x)(q,y)) = \{a \in A \mid e_a((p,x),(q,y)) \neq (p,x)\}$.

In order to obtain an equilibrium in our social system with coordination, we have to show that the assumptions of Theorem 2 in the Appendix are satisfied. By way of construction we have that $\widetilde{X} \subset \mathbb{R}^{L+CL}$ is non-empty, compact, and convex. Thus assumption (a) is satisfied. By definition, $\beta : \mathcal{X} \times \mathcal{X} \to \mathcal{X}$ is given by $\beta(p,x) = \cap_{a\in A}\beta_a(p,x) = \{(q,y) \in \mathcal{X} \mid p \cdot x(c) \leq 0 \text{ for all } c \in C\}$. Clearly, β has closed and convex values. By assumption (i) the values are non-empty. Also, the correspondence β is upper hemi continuous. To see that it is lower hemi continuous, consider $(p,x) \in \mathcal{X}$, $(q,y) \in \beta(p,x)$, and a sequence $(p^n, x^n) \in \mathcal{X}$ converging to (p,x). By assumption (i) and the construction of $\widetilde{Y}$, there exists $\underline{u} << 0 \in \widetilde{X}$. Hence, for all n we have $p^n\underline{u}(c) < 0$ for all $c \in C$. We now construct a sequence y^n converging to y with $(q,y^n) \in \cap_{c\in C}\beta_c(p,x)$ by letting $y^n = \lambda^n y + (1-\lambda^n)\underline{u}$ for suitably chosen weights $\lambda^n \in [0,1]$. Indeed, if $p^n \cdot y(c) \leq 0$ for all $c \in C$ let $\lambda^n = 1$, and if $p^n \cdot y(d) > 0$ for some $d \in C$ let λ^n be such that $\max_{c\in C} p^n(\lambda^n y(c) + (1-\lambda^n)\underline{u}) = 0$. Clearly, due to the convexity of $\cap_{c\in C}\widetilde{X}_c$, we have that $y^n \in \cap_{c\in C}\widetilde{X}_c$ and hence $(q,y^n) \in \cap_{c\in C}\beta_c(p,x)$. As $(q,y^n) \in \beta_0(p^n,x^n)$, we obtain $(q,y^n) \in \beta(p^n,x^n)$. Moreover, as p^n converges to p and $p \cdot y(c) \leq 0$ for all $c \in C$, we have λ^n converging to 1, and y^n converging to y, accordingly. Hence, the lower hemi continuity of β is obtained.

The condition (c) for all $a \in C$ follows directly from assumption (ii); and for $a = 0$ it is trivially satisfied by the definition of $\mathcal{P}_0$.

The condition (d) is fulfilled for all agents $c \in C$ by assumption (iv), and by the definition of e_0 for agent $a = 0$.

To show that (e) is satisfied for all agents, take any $(p,x) \in \mathcal{X}$. Consider first the agent $a = 0$ and any $(q,y) \in \mathcal{X}$. As $e_0((p,x)(q,y)) \in \beta_0((p,x))$ iff $q \in \Delta$ the condition (e) is satisfied for $a = 0$. Now consider $c \in C$ and $(q,y) \in \mathcal{X}$ such that $e_c((p,x)(q,y)) \in \beta_c(p,x)$. As $e_c((p,x)(q,y))(c) = y(c)$ by assumption (iv), we have $py(c) \leq 0$. Moreover, as $(q,y) \in \mathcal{X}$, we obtain $(q,y) \in \beta_c(p,x)$. Thus (e) is satisfied for all agents $a \in A$.

The condition (f') for agents $c \in C$ follows immediately from assumption (v) and our definition of $\mathcal{P}_c$. For the agent $a = 0$ let Δ^0 be any open set containing Δ and not containing 0. Clearly, the preferences of $a = 0$ can be extended to $\Delta^0 \times \mathbb{R}^{CL}$. Hence the condition (f') is satisfied.

The condition (g) is satisfied since we defined the coordination functions in Γ such that no consumer coordinates with $a = 0$ and the agent $a = 0$ does not coordinate with any consumer.

We conclude that there exists an equilibrium state $(p^*, x^*) \in \mathcal{X}$ for the social system Γ. Hence, we have

(1) $(p^*, x^*) \in \beta(p^*, x^*)$ and

(2) $\nexists (q,y) \in \mathcal{X}$ such that $e_a((p^*,x^*),(q,y)) \neq (p^*,x^*)$ for some a $\in A$, and $e_a((p^*,x^*),(q,y)) \in \mathcal{P}_a(p^*,x^*) \cap \beta_a(p^*,x^*)$ for a $\in g((p^*,x^*),(q,y))$.

We will now show that (p^*, x^*) is a Walras equilibrium with coordination in the original economy $\mathcal{E}$. Clearly, by the definition of $\mathcal{X}$ we have that $(p^*, x^*) \in \Delta \times \cap_{c\in C} X_c$. Hence, to show that $x^* \in F(\mathcal{E})$, we only need to show that $\sum_{c\in C} x^*(c) \le 0$. First, note that the definition of β and condition (i) yields $p^* \cdot x(c) \le 0$ for all $c \in C$ and hence $p^* \sum_{c\in C} x^*(c) \le 0$. Now assume that there exists $h \in L$ such that $\sum_{c\in C} x^*_h(c) > 0$. Define $q \in \Delta$ by $q_k = 0$ for $k \ne h$ and $q_h = 1$ and consider the state $(q, x^*) \in \mathcal{X}$. Clearly, $p^* \ne q$ as $p^* \sum_{c\in C} x^*(c) \le 0$ and $q \sum_{c\in C} x^*(c) > 0$. Moreover, $e_c((p^*, x^*), (q, x^*)) = (p^*, x^*)$ for all $c \in C$ and $e_0((p^*, x^*), (q, x^*)) = (q, x^*)$ and hence $g((p^*, x^*)(q, x^*)) = \{0\}$. As $((p^*, x^*), (q, x^*)) \in \mathcal{P}_0(p^*, x^*) \cap \beta_0(p^*, x^*)$, we have a contradiction to (2). Thus, $\sum_{c\in C} x^*(c) \le 0$ and hence $x^* \in F(\mathcal{E})$.

Clearly, condition (I) in the definition of a Walras equilibrium with coordination is also fulfilled by the definition of β_c, $c \in C$, and (1).

To prove that (II) is satisfied, assume, conversely, that there exists a state $y \in Y$ with $y \ne x^*$ such that $p^* \cdot y(c) \le 0$ and $e_c(x^*, y) \in X_c \cap \mathcal{P}_c(x^*)$ for all $c \in g(x^*, y)$. First, we prove that $y \in \cap_{c\in C} X_c$. Indeed, consider $c \in g(x^*, y)$. As $x^* \in \cap_{c\in C} X_c$ and $e_c(x^*, y) \in X_c$, assumption (v) yields $y \in X_c$. For $c \notin g(x^*, y)$ we have $e_c(x^*, y) = x^* \in X_c$ and hence, again by assumption (v), that $y \in X_c$. Hence $x \in \cap_{c\in C} X_c$. Moreover, as $x^* \in F(\mathcal{E}) \subset int\tilde{Y}$ and $\cap_{c\in C} X_c$ is convex, we obtain that $\lambda y + (1-\lambda)x^* \in \cap_{c\in C} \tilde{X}_c$ for $\lambda > 0$ sufficiently small, say, for $\lambda = \tilde{\lambda} > 0$. Let $y' = \tilde{\lambda} y + (1-\tilde{\lambda})x^*$. Then $(p^*, y') \in \mathcal{X}$. We will now show that the state (p^*, y') can be used to violate condition (2) above. Clearly, $e_a((p^*, x^*), (p^*, y')) \ne (p^*, x^*)$ for $a \in g(x^*, y)$. Moreover, $g((p^*, x^*), (p^*, y')) = g(x^*, y)$ as $0 \notin g((p^*, x^*), (p^*, y'))$. Consider $c \in g(x^*, y)$. As $p^* y'(c) \le 0$, we have $e_c((p^*, x^*), (p^*, y')) \in \beta_c(p^*, x^*)$. To show that $e_c((p^*, x^*), (p^*, y')) \in \mathcal{P}_c(p^*, x^*)$, note that assumption (iii) implies that (p^*, x^*) belongs to the boundary of $\mathcal{P}_c(p^*, x^*)$. Hence, the convexity of $\mathcal{P}_c(x^*)$ and X_c implies that $\tilde{\lambda} e_c((p^*, x^*), (p^*, y)) + (1-\tilde{\lambda})(p^*, x^*) \in \mathcal{P}_c(p^*, x^*)$. As $\tilde{\lambda} e_c((p^*, x^*), (p^*, y)) + (1-\tilde{\lambda})(p^*, x^*) = e_c((p^*, x^*), (p^*, y'))$, we have a violation of (2).

We will now show that $p^* \cdot \sum_{c\in C} x^*(c) = 0$. Assume that there exists a consumer $c \in C$ for which $p^* \cdot x^*(c) < 0$. Again, by assumption (iii) and $F(\mathcal{E}) \subset int\tilde{X}$, consumer c can find a net trade $y(c)$ with $p^* \cdot y(c) < 0$ such that when c is the only consumer who changes net trade, we obtain a state $(p^*, y) \in \mathcal{X}$ with $(p^*, y) \in \mathcal{P}_c(x^*, x^*) \cap \beta_c(p^*, x^*)$ for all $c \in g((p^*, x^*), (p^*, y))$. This contradicts the fact that (p^*, x^*) satisfies condition (2) above. Hence condition (III) in the definition of a Walras equilibrium with coordination is satisfied.

We have now shown that (p^*, x^*) is a Walras equilibrium with coordination in the economy $\mathcal{E}$. □

We have already commented on the assumptions (iii), (iv), and (vii) on the coordination functions and the approval function in Theorem 1. The assumptions (i) and (ii) are well known from the existence theorems for an ordinary Walras equilibrium. However, since we allow externalities in the feasible net trade sets, we assume that 0 is in the interior of the set of feasible net trade states X_c for all $c \in C$. In section 2 we discussed the feasible net trade assumption and gave two examples of sets X_c, $c \in C$ such that the assumption was satisfied. In both cases we obtain $0 \in intX_c$, for all $c \in C$, if 0 is in the interior of their individually feasible net trade sets X_c' for all $c \in C$. The assumption that $0 \in intX_c$ can, of course, be replaced by the assumption that $0 \in X_c$ by introducing the concept of a quasi Walras equilibrium with coordination and only proving the existence of such equilibria. The assumption (vi) states that the preferences of all consumers are well behaved on the boundary of their feasible net trade sets.

5 Special cases

In this section we consider some examples of coordination functions and approval functions. We assume that the coordination assumption is satisfied. Moreover, we assume that if a consumer $c \in C$ coordinates with a consumer $d \in C$ then he coordinates with d in all commodities $h \in L$. In this case an alternative way to describe the coordination function e_c is to specify a *coordination relation* R on $C \times C$, where $c R d$ iff c coordinates with d. By assumption R is reflexive. Let $R_c = \{d \in C \mid c R d\}$ be the consumers with whom c coordinates. Thus, $e_c(x, y) = ((y(d))_{d \in R_c}, (x(d))_{d \notin R_c})$.

We say that *coordination is symmetric* iff R is symmetric. Also, we say that *coordination is transitive* iff R is transitive. Given a coordination relation R, an approval function $g : Y \times Y \to Y$ can be generated in the following way. Consider for each $c \in C$ the set $R_c^{-1} = \{d \in C \mid d R c\}$. R_c^{-1} are all consumers d who coordinate their net trade with c. The approval function g used in Theorem 1 is given by $g(x, y) = \cup_{\{c \in C | x(c) \neq y(c)\}} R_c^{-1}$ for all $x, y \in Y$. Clearly, we could, in general, have defined an approval structure as a family $(B_c)_{c \in C}$ based on the interpretation that a state in which consumer c has changed his net trade has to be approved by consumers in B_c. Naturally, $c \in B_c$ for all c. Moreover, we assume $B_c \subset R_c^{-1}$ because only these consumers coordinate their net trade with c and are therefore informed about c's new net trade. Consequently, we define an *approval structure* as a family $(B_c)_{c \in C}$ with $\{c\} \subset B_c \subset R_c^{-1}$ for all $c \in C$. The approval function g corresponding to the approval structure $(B_c)_{c \in C}$ is defined by $g(x, y) = \cup_{\{c \in C | x(c) \neq y(c)\}} B_c$ for all $x, y \in Y$.

5.1 No coordination

No coordination means that the coordination is given by the coordination relation R where $c R d$ iff $c = d$. Thus, for any state x and alternative state y, consumer c believes that the state in which he is the only one who has changed his net trade from $x(c)$ to $y(c)$ will be the outcome. As $c \in B_c \subset R_c^{-1}$, the approval structure must be given by $B_c = \{c\}$. Clearly, condition (II) in the definition of a Walras equilibrium with coordination in this case states that there is no consumer c who can find a $y(c) \in \mathbb{R}^L$ with $py(c) \leq 0$ such that $((x(d))_{d \neq c}, y(c)) \in \mathcal{P}_c(x)$. Thus, if there is no coordination in $\mathcal{E}$, a Walras equilibrium with coordination is indeed a traditional Walras equilibrium.

5.2 Coordination in a partition

Remark 1 *Coordination according to the relation R is symmetric and transitive if and only if the family $(R_c)_{c \in C}$ is a partition of C.*

Coordination in a partition can be used to model the decision problem in an economy with households. Typically, a household consists of several consumers whose preferences are interdependent. Hence let us assume that the set of consumers is divided into households and that the coordination relation is given by coordination in the partition of households. We still have to specify the approval structure. Assume that the approval structure is the one considered in Theorem 1, i.e. $B_c = R_c^{-1} = R_c$ for all $c \in C$. Condition (I) in the definition of a Walras equilibrium with coordination in this economy states that each member of a household individually has to satisfy the budget constraint. Condition (II) states that there is no household whose members can find new net trades satisfying their budget constraints such that all members of the household prefer the state in which they obtain the new net trades. For example, it is impossible to improve the situation of the members of a household by their simultaneously stopping smoking or starting drinking. Note that the Walras equilibria with coordination in this economy are exactly the same as the ones in the economy where all members of a household have identical preferences given by the intersection of the preference correspondences of the household members. Indeed, when there is coordination in a partition, then $e_d(x, y) = e_c(x, y)$ for all d, c in the same element of the partition. Hence, condition II in the definition of a Walras equilibrium with coordination is satisfied iff there does not exist an element F in the partition and net trades $(y(c))_{c \in F}$ with the property that $py(c) \leq 0$ and $e_c(x, y) \in \cap_{d \in F} \mathcal{P}_d(x)$ for all $c \in F$.

Clearly, the equilibrium concept becomes weaker if a given approval structure is enlarged. The existence theorem in this paper assumes that $B_c = R_c^{-1} = R_c$, that is, the largest possible approval structure is assumed. However, it should be noted that if we had considered approval structures (B_c') such that $B_c' \subset B_c$, then there would not necessarily exist a Walras equilibrium with coordination. Consider, for example, an economy with two consumers $C = \{1, 2\}$ and two commodities, and the coordination relation $i\,R\,j$ for $i, j \in C$. Let $X_1 = X_2 = X = (\mathbb{R}_+^2 - \{\omega\}) \times (\mathbb{R}_+^2 - \{\omega\})$ for some $\omega \in \mathbb{R}_+^2$ and let the consumers preference correspondences be given by $u_i : X \to X$ with $grad_{x_j} u_i \neq 0$ for all $i, j \in C$. When the approval structure is $B_1 = \{1\}$

and $B_2 = \{2\}$, we can easily choose u_1 and u_2 such that the first order conditions for a Walras equilibrium with coordination are inconsistent.

5.3 Complete coordination

Complete coordination is the coordination relation R for which $c\,R\,d$ for all $c, d \in C$ and approval structure $B_c = C$ for all $c \in C$. Hence for all $c \in C$ the coordination function is given by $e_c(x, y) = y$, and the approval function is given by $g(x, y) = C$ for all $x, y \in Y$. Note, that even with complete coordination, Walras equilibria with coordination is not, in general, Pareto optimal. The reason is that consumers have individual budget constraints, and without independence some transfer of budgets might be advantageous for all agents.

5.4 Arbitrary coordination structures

Clearly, there are many interpretations where coordination structures that are not symmetric or transitive are natural. In a hierarchical structure, or when consumers choose sequentially, coordination is not symmetric. Moreover, assume that we have households and coordination within households, but that, in addition, consumers have partner relations with other consumers, creating further coordination for some consumers. In this case, we will typically have a situation in which coordination is not transitive.

In general there is no trivial connection between Walras equilibria in an economy and Walras equilibria with coordination when the description of the basic economy has been enlarged with a coordination relation R and an approval structure $(B_c)_{c \in C}$. Consider, however, the case where $B_c = \{c\}$ for all $c \in C$ and hence $g(x, y) = \{c \in C \mid x(c) \neq y(c)\}$. Clearly, here the set of equilibria with coordination is a subset (possibly empty) of the set of Walras equilibria. Coordination might, also enlarge the set of equilibria, though[3]. Consider again an economy with $C = \{1, 2\}$. Let $X_1 = (\mathbb{R}^L_+ - \{\omega_1\}) \times \mathbb{R}^L$ and $X_2 = (\mathbb{R}^L_+ - \{\omega_1\}) \times (\mathbb{R}^L_+ - \{\omega_2\})$ with $\omega_i \in \mathbb{R}^L_+$ for $i = 1, 2$. Let the consumers' preference correspondences be given by the utility functions $u_1 : X_1 \to \mathbb{R}$ with $u_1(x(1), x(2)) = v_1(x(1))$ for some strictly monotone function $v_1 : \mathbb{R}^L_+ - \{\omega_1\} \to \mathbb{R}$, and $u_2 : X_2 \to \mathbb{R}$ with $u_2(x(1), x(2)) = v_2(x(2)) - v_1(x(1))$ for some strictly monotone function $v_2 : \mathbb{R}^L_+ - \{\omega_2\} \to \mathbb{R}$. Assume that $R_1 = \{1\}$ and $R_2 = \{1, 2\}$ and that $B_c = R_c^{-1}$ for $c \in C$. Hence $B_1 = \{1, 2\}$ and $B_2 = \{2\}$. Clearly, in this example, the set of Walras equilibria is a subset of the Walras equilibria with coordination. However, the set of Walras equilibria with coordination is much larger than the set of Walras equilibria. We will show that $(p^*, x^*) \in \Delta \times Y$ is a Walras equilibrium with coordination if $x^*(2)$ is a maximal element for v_2 in $\{x \in \mathbb{R}^L_+ - \{\omega_2\} \mid p^* x \leq 0\}$ and

[3] It can easily be shown that, in general, this holds with the type of preferences used in the next example.

$x^*(1) = -x^*(2) \in \mathbb{R}^L_+ - \{\omega_1\}$. Clearly, x^* is feasible. Moreover, as v_2 is strictly monotone, we have $p^*x^*(2) = 0$ and hence $p^*x^*(1) = 0$. Thus, condition I is satisfied. Condition III is trivially satisfied as $x^*(1) + x^*(2) = 0$. Now assume that condition II is violated. Hence there exists $y \neq x^*$ such that $p^*y(c) \leq 0$ and $e_c(x^*, y) \in \mathcal{P}_c$ for $c \in g(x^*, y)$. First, assume that $y(2) = x^*(2)$. Hence $g(x^*, y) = B_1 = \{1, 2\}$. However, by definition of $x^*(2)$ we cannot have $e_1(x^*, y) \in \mathcal{P}_1(x^*)$ and $e_2(x^*, y) \in \mathcal{P}_2(x^*)$. Second, assume that $y(1) = x^*(1)$. Thus, $g(x^*, y) = B_2 = \{2\}$ and again the definition of $x^*(2)$ results in a contradiction. Last, consider the case where $y(1) \neq x^*(1)$ and $y(2) \neq x^*(2)$. Then, as $p^*y(1) \leq 0$, $p^*y(2) \leq 0$, and $g(x^*, y) = \{1, 2\}$, the definition of $x^*(2)$ again implies that it is impossible to have $e_1(x^*, y) = (y(1), x^*(2)) \in \mathcal{P}_1(x^*)$ and $e_2(x^*, y) = y \in \mathcal{P}_2(x^*)$. Again we have a contradiction. Hence, we conclude that (p^*, x^*) is a Walras equilibrium with coordination. Note, that if, in the example, we use the approval structure $B_c = \{c\}$ for $c \in C$, then the set of Walras equilibria with coordination is identical to the set of Walras equilibria.

Appendix: A social system with coordination

This section repeats concepts from Vind (1983) and repeats the existence theorem for an equilibrium in Vind (1983) with the assumptions in the improved version in Keiding (1985).

Definition (Social System with Coordination) *A social system with coordination is an indexed family*

$$\Gamma = \left(A, (\mathcal{X}_a, \beta_a, \mathcal{P}_a, e_a)_{a \in A}, g\right),$$

where

- *A is a finite set of agents,*
- *$\mathcal{X}_a \subset \mathbb{R}^\ell$ are the feasible states for agent a. The state space $\mathcal{X}$ of the system is defined as $\mathcal{X} = \cap_{a \in A} \mathcal{X}_a$,*
- *$\beta_a : \mathcal{X} \to 2^{\mathcal{X}}$ gives for each $x \in \mathcal{X}$, the set, $\beta_a(x)$, of states which are attainable for agent a. The correspondence $\beta : \mathcal{X} \to 2^{\mathcal{X}}$ is defined as $\beta(x) = \cap_{a \in A} \beta_a(x)$,*
- *$\mathcal{P}_a : \mathcal{X} \to 2^{\mathcal{X}}$ is the preference correspondence of agent $a \in A$,*
- *$e_a : \mathcal{X} \times \mathcal{X} \to \mathcal{X}$ is the coordination function of $a \in A$,*
- *$g : \mathcal{X} \times \mathcal{X} \to 2^A$ is the approval function.*

Definition (Equilibrium) *An equilibrium in the social system with coordination is a state $x^* \in \mathcal{X}$ such that*

(1) *$x^* \in \beta(x^*)$ and*
(2) *$\nexists y \in \mathcal{X}$ such that $e_a(x^*, y) \neq x^*$ for some $a \in A$, and $e_a(x^*, y) \in \mathcal{P}_a(x^*) \cap \beta_a(x)$ for $a \in g(x^*, y)$.*

Theorem 2 *Let* $\left(A, \mathcal{X}, (\beta_a, \mathcal{P}_a, e_a)_{a\in A}, g\right)$ *be a social system with coordination such that for all* $a \in A$ *and for all* $x \in \mathcal{X}$

(a) $\mathcal{X}$ *is a non-empty, convex, compact subset of* $\mathbb{R}^\ell$,
(b) β *is continuous with closed, convex and non-empty values,*
(c) $\mathcal{P}_a$ *has open graph, convex values and* $x \notin \mathcal{P}_a(x)$,
(d) e_a *is continuous,* $e_a(x, \cdot)$ *is affine, and* $e_a(x, x) = x$,
(e) $e_a(x, y) \in \beta_a(x) \Rightarrow y \in \beta_a(x)$,
(f') *there exists a convex and compact set* $\mathcal{X}^a$ *with* $\mathcal{X} \subset int\mathcal{X}^a$ *and a correspondence* $\mathcal{P}^a : \mathcal{X}^a \to \mathcal{X}^a$ *which is irreflexive with open graph and convex (possibly empty) values such that* $\mathcal{P}^a(x) = \mathcal{P}_a(x) \cap \mathcal{X}$ *for all* $x \in \mathcal{X}$,
(g) $g(x, y) = \{a \in A \,|\, e_a(x, y) \neq x\}$.

Then there exists an equilibrium in Γ.

Proof. See Corollary 1 in Keiding (1985)[4].

References

1. Arrow, K., G. Debreu: Existence of an Equilibrium for a Competitive Economy, Econometrica 22, 265-290 (1954)
2. Browning, M., P.A. Chiappori: Efficient Intra-Household Allocations: A General Characterization and Empirical Tests, Econometrica 66, 1241-1278 (1998)
3. Duffie, D., W. Shafer: Equilibrium in Incomplete Markets: I; A Basic Model of Generic Existence, Journal of Mathematical Economics 14, 285-300 (1985)
4. Gersbach, H., H. Haller: Intra-Household Bargaining Power and Equilibrium Consumption, Working Paper Virginia Tech 99-03, (1999)
5. Grodal, B., K. Vind: Equilibrium with Arbitrary Market Structures, University of Copenhagen, (1989)
6. Keiding, H.: On the Existence of Equilibrium in Social Systems with Coordination, Journal of Mathematical Economics 14, 105-111 (1985)
7. Shafer,W., H. Sonnenschein: Equilibrium in Abstract Economies without Ordered Preferences, Journal of Mathematical Economic 2, 345-348 (1975)
8. Vind, K.: Equilibrium with Coordination, Journal of Mathematical Economics 12, 275-285 (1983)

[4] The assumption that β has convex values has been forgotten in the statement of Corollary 1 in Keiding (1985).

On the Robustness of the Analysis of Expectational Coordination: From 3 to $n + 2$ goods

Roger Guesnerie

Delta, joint unit CNRS, EHESS, ENS, and Collège de France, Paris

Abstract. The paper analyses the robustness of the conclusions previously obtained, showing that, in a simple three-goods model, the success of "eductive" expectational coordination is related to low supply elasticity, high demand elasticity, and high marginal propensity to consume (or high elementary Keynesian multiplier). Similar generalized factors have analogous qualitative effects, although new factors (heteroneity of beliefs) appear. Also, the positive coordination effect of the income effect, through the Keynesian multiplier action, is now less powerful.

1 Introduction

This paper contributes to a research program that aims at assessing the Rational Expectations Hypothesis, an hypothesis that has taken over most fields of economic modelling since the pioneering article of Muth (1961). Some skepticism on the plausibility of a uniformly valid modelling tool for expectations motivates this program. Such feelings do not necessarily challenge the rationality hypothesis per se, but are at variance with the frequent assertion according to which "the rational expectations hypothesis is nothing else than the extension of the rationality hypothesis to expectations." Such an assertion had been more or less explicitly accepted, at least untill recently, by many users of the theory. On the contrary, it is assumed here, in line with a view that is more and more frequent among economic theorists and game theorists and reflected in the just alluded to research program (see Guesnerie (2000a) for an overview), that the satisfactory coordination of expectations that occurs when they are "rational" has to be explained rather than assumed[1], even if the individual rationality of agents is taken for granted.

The critical assessment of models and hypotheses, even if they are widely accepted and routinely used, is a key activity of modern economic theory.

[1] For example, it makes sense to adjoin the equilibrium with a process of formation of expectations. Once the expectations equilibrium is supplemented with some kind of "stability" criterion, whatever it may be, the validity of the rational expectations hypothesis is subject to verification. The success of this verification is likely to depend on the specific characteristics of the situation under scrutiny. The rational expectations hypothesis will then appear not to be equally reasonable for all situations.

The need and fruitfulness of such a critical effort has been taught to me by the best theorists and mathematical economists I had the chance to meet during the period of my economic education. Werner Hildenbrand was one of them: my interest in the just evoked program reflects to some extent an influence on my intellectual development that, I hope, he would not disavow. More specifically, the present paper aims at testing the robustness of ideas that have been obtained from simpler exploratory models. I am aware that the robustness tests implemented here have to be developed and completed. But I hope that the reader, especially one of them, will be convinced that an exploration research program may still avoid to fall into "Mickey Mouse economics!"

This paper examines a stylised model of short run equilibrium which is a multidimensional version of the model analysed in Guesnerie (2000b). It shares with the previous one its three basic features. First, firms take today simultaneous hiring decisions, depending on wages. Second, the profitability of these decisions depends upon tomorrow's prices and then indirectly on total income available to consumers. Third, attention is focused, along the lines of hypotheses just evoked and made fully explicit later, on the process of the formation of tomorrow's expectations that determine today's behaviour. The difference is that the economy consists of a finite number of sectors, instead of one in the previous paper.

The plan goes as follows:

- In section 2, entitled "Preliminaries," the solution to the expectational coordination problem provided by the Rational Expectations Hypothesis is briefly and critically reassessed. The "eductive" viewpoint taken in this paper is introduced from a simple and hopefully illustrative story.
- Section 3 presents the model, the equilibrium, and stability concepts.
- Section 4 und 5 give the main results of the paper and offer a brief discussion of its meaning and shortcomings.
- A Conclusion is finally offered.

2 Preliminaries

2.1 Justifying the Rational Expectations Hypothesis

The usual criteria of stability of expectations belong to three broad categories.

First, the Rational Expectations Hypothesis can be justified from the *uniqueness* of the corresponding equilibrium: a rational expectations equilibrium (REE) is an unavoidable "focal point" for the coordination of expectations whenever there is a unique such equilibrium. A contrario, the existence of multiple REE creates ambiguity on the conditions of coordination. Insistence on uniqueness qualifies Muth's original claim, without necessarily dismissing the rationality justification that underlies it. However, modern avatars of the rationality justification have made clear that rationality alone, could not sustain the rationality of expectations and have switched to considering whether it could derive from a much stronger assumption i.e the Common Knowledge of Rationality.

Common Knowledge of Rationality allows "understanding" or "educing" the actions taken by others, through a collective process of so-called *eductive* learning. Common Knowledge of Rationality may or may not imply the knowledge of equilibrium actions. The just sketched line of investigation has very close connections with the (old) game theoretical ideas that have been (recently) associated with the concepts of "rationalizable solutions," "subjectively correlated equilibrium" (but more on that later)[2].

A last category of justifications refers to processes of learning that are *evolutive* rather than eductive: boundedly rational agents use more or less "adhoc" learning rules that reconsider expectations once they turn out to be falsified; this process may lead to the asymptotic real time convergence of the system towards the REE.

In this paper, the validity of the rational expectations hypothesis is assessed from the Common Knowledge of Rationality viewpoint. Attention is however mainly concentrated on a necessary condition (associated with the idea of Iterative Expectational stability, IE-stability from now on[3]) for the convergence of the eductive learning process triggered by the Common Knowledge Hypothesis.

It should be stressed here that there are extremely close connections between this second and the third, evolutive viewpoint. In spite of the considerable differences of a priori motivations, the analysis of the consequences of Common Knowledge captures features of the situation that are also central to the convergence of evolutive learning processes.

Let us also note that our approach to the stability of expectations clearly departs from the logic of the uniqueness viewpoint, alluded to before, (in particular, because our argument is developed within a model that has a unique equilibrium). Still, it is not necessarily irrelevant to adepts of the latter viewpoint: in case of multiplicity, the type of argument used here can serve to design a selection device for equilibria.[4]

[2] The elimination of dominated strategies is discussed already in Luce-Raiffa (1957); the corresponding ideas have been further elaborated by Farqharson (1969), and Moulin (1979). Discussion stimulated by Bernheim (1984) and Pearce (1984), includes Tan-Werlang (1988), and Aumman (1987)

[3] à la De Canio (1978), Lucas (1978), and Evans (1985). See also, for criticisms of the foundations of the concept IE-stability, that are fully answered here, Calvo (1983).

[4] In a completely different perspective, the learning process that will be described, can also be viewed as an algorithm, which, in good cases, allows the computation of equilibrium. Within such an algorithm the questions raised by Hellwig (1993) in a similar setting, have an unambiguous, (although variable across models), answer.

2.2 The logic of the expectational analysis: an introductory example

Consider the following games: in Game 1, each of n players, in a closed room, writes down a number between zero and one hundred. The winner is the one whose number is closest to x times the average number announced by the others ($0 \leq x \leq 1$), in case of tie, the prize is shared. Let us now consider Game 2: the rule is similar, but for two aspects: the number to be announced is no longer bounded, the coefficient x is strictly greater than one. Both games have a unique Nash equilibrium, that consists of a joint announcement of zero by all players.[5] However, several arguments sugggest that the equilibrium is more credible for Game 1 than for Game 2. The first argument can be called "eductive:" in the first game, one notes that no player will play more than one hundred, so that the winning number cannot be above $100x$; but if each player realizes that, no one will announce more than $100x$, so that the winning number cannot be above $100x^2$; understanding that, nobody will announce more than $100x^2$, and so on. But if x is strictly smaller than one, the sequence $100x^n$ converges to zero, and the speed of convergence increases when x decreases. Formally, the argument uses the fact that agents are rational (it is why they do not play more than $100x$), the fact that they know that the others are rational (so that they do not play more than $100x^2$) and ultimately, when the argument goes on, it will use the full power of the Common Knowledge of Rationality hypothesis.[6] The conclusion of this analysis is that the Nash equilibrium of Game 1 has better justifications than the one of Game 2.[7] One can even add that the smaller is x, the more convincing the justification is.

In a sense, the ultimate purpose of the present research program to which this paper belongs, and which has been surveyed in Guesnerie (2000a) is to transpose to the economic situations under scrutiny, each one generating one "class of game" somewhat more complex than the above one, the types of considerations that have been sketched: in some cases, one will conclude that the situation under scrutiny leads to an equilibrium that looks like the equilibrium of Game 1, while in other cases the equilibrium displays instabilities

[5] This comes from the straigthforward remark that a Nash equilibrium announcement, y_1, y_2, ...,y_n, has to satisfy: $y_i = x(\sum_{j \neq i} y_j)/(n-1)$ and hence, by summation, $\sum y_i = x(\sum y_i)$.

[6] Another argument would consider the repetition of the game and the fact that boundedly rational agents will asssume, for example, that their partners write down, at step n, the winning number of step $n-1$; the repetition of the Game will bring outcomes that will come soon close to zero, and the sooner, the closer x is to zero. Naturally, both the eductive and the evolutive argument fail in Game 2: non equilibrium expectations are amplified either in a mental guessing process or in a real repetitive situation.

[7] Game 1 is one of the subjects of investigation of Nagel's 1989 thesis, see Nagel (1995). Her findings give much more substance to the brief assessment of the game presented here.

similar to those identified in Game 2. As above, at least in some cases, this basic classification will be refined by associating to the situation some number, analogous to the number x above, negatively correlated with the "credibility "of the equilibrium. The precise concepts used here, such as Strong Rationality, Local Strong Rationality, or Expectational Stability of the equilibrium are briefly recalled in next section.

3 Framework and equilibria

3.1 The basic framework

Let us now present the general framework in which the analysis of the present text takes place. We will then be in a position to describe the equilibrium equations that will also depend on the specific market clearing assumptions that will be adopted.

The production sector consists of n sectors indexed by $l = 1, ..., n$. In each sector, there are N_l firms (N_l large) that produce the same good. Firm il can hire at most one worker and produces α_i^l units of good l.

Without loss of generality we have $\alpha_i^l \geq \alpha_{i+1}^l$, i.e. firms are ranked in order of productivity. The total production of good l is denoted Q_l. When firm il hires workers at the (sure) wage w and sells its product (for sure) at price p_l, its supply – which is the Walrasian competitive supply – is denoted $S_i^l(p_l/w)$. Naturally, $S_i^l(p_l/w)$ equals α_i^l if $\alpha_i^l p_l \geq w$ and zero otherwise.

Note the individual decision making units described here are *independent decision-makers.*

One may however approximate the aggregate production function in sector l, by a monotonic and smooth[8] function that relates total production of good l, Q_l to total employment E_l: $Q_l = f_l(E_l)$ and that satisfies by definition $\sum_1^n \alpha_i^l = f_l(n)$ where n is the number of workers employed.

Total aggregate price-taking commodity supply, in sector l, $\sum_i S_i^l(p_l/w)$ is denoted $S_l(p_l/w)$.

The vector of aggregate supply is denoted $S(p/w)$.

The production sector having been defined, the basic structure of the model can be presented:

i) The model takes into account essentially two subperiods: this morning and this afternoon. In the morning, firms hire workers that are available on the labour market; in the afternoon, the goods produced with the labour hired in the morning will be sold on the goods market.

ii) Households are workers in the morning and buyers in the afternoon. Their purchasing power consists of the money holdings they carry from the

[8] With indivisibilities in labour, the aggregate production would be discontinuous. With divisible labour within firm i, the function is continuous but not everywhere differentiable.

day before and of the total available income (wages in the morning plus profit) they have earned. Their desired spending on goods depends on their prices and on available income; the savings behaviour implies a potential discrepancy between desired spending and the value of production: this is a key and classical feature of the three-goods models (see Barro-Grossman (1969) and Malinvaud (1977)), of which this model is a $(n+2)$–goods generalisation.

Making explicit the money holding behaviour, (and simultaneously the commodity demand behaviour) requires that we appeal to some kind of monetary theory that will hopefully remain simple. As we know, there is nothing like a simple and fully satisfactory monetary theory: one will have to compromise. One possibility, in the tradition of the three-goods model, is the introduction of money balances in the utility function. One might also, in a similar but maybe cleaner vein, adopt a variant of the cash-in-advance apparatus à la Lucas-Stokey (1988).[9]

Here, we will adopt a somewhat more general formulation, a special case of which will be made fully explicit.

The general formulation consists of describing demand on the goods markets from a partly unspecified demand function $Z_l(p, R, M_0)$, where p, R, and M_0, denote the (n-dimensional) price vector of goods, total income, and the total quantity of money, respectively. Also, all the derivatives with respect to R are supposed to be positive (no inferior goods).

Note that this formulation supposes that a single index of income, R, and money holdings M_0, is a sufficient statistics for determining demand and hence, that neither the distribution of income nor the distribution of money holdings matters. As we shall see, this does not necessarily imply that we have a "representative consumer;"[10] the assumption however rules out the additional coordination problems that occur when the just evoked distributional issues matter.

We shall assume:

Assumption (A1):
There exist functions $\alpha(\cdot)$ and $\alpha'(\cdot)$, with their values being smaller than 1, such that

[9] Also, the model could for example be viewed as an overlapping generations model in which each time period consist of one day: then, the young work during the morning and consume and save during the afternoon. The old who have worked, consumed, and saved on the previous day spend their money in the afternoon of the present day. The part of the income of the young that has not been consumed is held in money and, in equilibrium, equals the quantity of money previously held by the old.

Although this interpretation is consistent, it tells a story that is unlikely to make sense when the period length has to be viewed as short – much below half a life!

[10] In particular, the implicit model has a large number of consumers. Even when they are identical, the analysis would not view them as representative since differences of beliefs are always a priori considered.

i) $p \cdot (\partial Z/\partial R)(\cdot) = \alpha'(\cdot)$, and
ii) $p \cdot Z(\cdot) = \alpha(\cdot)R + M_0$.

The marginal (i) and the average (ii) propensity to consume (from current income) are smaller than one. ii) also expresses that previously saved money is used to consume.

We shall often assume for the local analysis of expectational coordination, that the following assumption also holds:

Assumption (A2):
$\alpha(\cdot) = \alpha'(\cdot) = \alpha$ being a constant.

The Appendix describes a fully specified prototype of the model, where money holdings are explained with a very crude signal story.[11] The advantage of this crude signal story is that the intertemporal equilibrium reduces to a sequence of "daily" equilibria: the intertemporal "eductive" problem, that we are going to analyse, coincides with the intra-day problem. In the more sophisticated version of the model, for example when money appears in the utility function, today's demand of money holdings depends on price expectations tomorrow. Rational expectations mean rational expectations within the day and rational expectations across days.

The inconvenience of the story is that the demand effects associated with a proportional increase of all commodity prices are too simplistic: they reduce to an income effect, ruling out important substitution effects between goods and money balances.[12]

3.2 Daily equilibria

The market clearing conditions can now be made explicit:

1) a market clearing price equalizes the supply of the firms and competitive demand of households.

2) the money wage in the morning is fixed at $\overline{w}$

Finally, we suppose that the morning labour supply is not responsive to prices and is fixed (later E_0)

We define accordingly for the considered day,[13] a fixed wage (Keynesian) equilibrium, in which agents have rational expectations in the morning.

---

[11] Note also that the explicit protoype model always fits assumption (A1). It also fits assumption (A2), whenever the two types of consuming agents have the same marginal propensity to save: $\{\partial D_{Cl}/\partial R\}(p, R) = \{\partial D_{Pl}/\partial R\}(p, R + M_0/(1-\alpha))$.In that case, the $\alpha(\cdot)$ of the general formulation is nothing else than the α of the special model.

[12] Note that such substitution effects are allowed to play a role in Guesnerie (2000b).

[13] I use here the word daily rather than temporary that migth be misleading: temporary equilibria are associated with exogenous expectations.

Definition 1. Given the total quantity of money M_0, a *"Daily" Rational Expectations (Keynesian) Fixed Wage Equilibrium* of this system will be associated with production levels $Q_l^\star$, prices $p_l^\star$, and national income $R^\star$ that will meet the following conditions:

i) $Z_l(p^*, R^*, M_0) = Q_l^*, \forall l = 1, ..., n,$
ii) $R^* = \sum_l p_l^* Q_l^*,$
iii) $S_l(p_l^*/\overline{w}) = Q_l^*,$
iv) $\sum_l f_l^{-1}(Q_l^*) < E_0.$

The conditions speak for themselves:

i) expresses market clearing on all the goods markets, and because of (A1)-(ii) implies market clearing on the money market.[14]

ii) says that total income, wage plus profit is equally attributed to consumers.

iii) is the production supply when the price vector is $(p^*, \overline{w})$, and

iv) says that total labour demand from the firms is smaller than labour supply.

Again, the modelling options are those of the so-called three-goods model, but adapted to the n-commodity context under consideration. The simplifying formulation of excess demand has already been discussed: its one-dimensional counterpart fits the formulation of Guesnerie (2000 b). The assumption of uniform labour rationing (implicitly made in condition ii)) seems reasonable for our purpose; the fact that total income is available in the afternoon, rather than wage income only, for example, reflects a standard although debatable modelling choice which, however, has only secondary effects on our analysis (see Guesnerie (2000b)) for a more comprehensive discussion).

3.3 Eductive coordination

The model has then, flexible prices, fixed wage and rational expectations. The first two assumptions are taken for granted, the third one is not. More precisely, the question under scrutiny here is whether the equilibrium is Strongly Rational in sense of Guesnerie (1992) (one could still say that it is the unique rationalizable equilibrium or that it is "dominant solvable"). The concept and

[14] In our specific model presented in the Appendix, equation (i) can be made explicit as condition

(i′) $(2\alpha-1)D_{Cl}(p^*, R^*)+(1-\alpha)D_{Pl}(p^*, R^*+M_0/(1-\alpha)) = Q_l^*, \forall l = 1, ..., n.$
The money market equilibrium can be discussed in a more explicit way: $\alpha\mu = \alpha(2-1/\alpha)$ agents consume today, from their today income, $(1-\alpha)$ agents consume today from their today income plus the money acquired yesterday ($M_0/(1-\alpha)$ per capita). (i′) plus (ii), together with the definition of D, and the fact that $\alpha(1-\mu) = 1-\alpha$, imply that $1-\alpha$ agents save their whole income R^*. This implies that the money market clears.

a number of its applications have been discussed elsewhere (see for example Guesnerie (2000a)). Roughly speaking, we wonder whether the assumption that morning decision-makers, i.e. the firms, have Common Knowledge (from now on CK) of the situation, triggers the conclusion that they have CK of the equilibrium. In other words, whether the iterative elimination of non best responses triggered by the CK assumption leads to the equilibrium situation: when the answer is positive, we say that the equilibrium is Strongly Rational. We however limit attention to the case where initial beliefs are restricted (at least hypothetically) by a local CK restriction; the corresponding concept is that of local Strong Rationality.

Let us sum up: our analysis a priori focuses attention on the relationship between the following assertions:

Assertion (B1):
In the morning:

- Profit maximising firms are Bayesian Rational.

- They know that the morning wage is fixed at $\overline{w}$, and that the market clearing prices tomorrow will be determined from total supply Q_l in all sectors, according to the following equations:
$Z_l(p, R, M_0) = Q_l$ for $l = 1, ..., n$, $R = \sum p_l Q_l$.

- These two facts are CK.

Assertion (B2):
The sequence $(Q_1, ..., Q_n)$ belongs to a compact, of non empty interior, neighbourhood of $(Q_1^*, ..., Q_n^*)$, the fixed wage Rational Expectations Equilibrium and this fact is (hypothetically)[15] CK.

Assertion (B3):
The fixed wage Rational Expectations Equilibrium $(Q_1^*, ..., Q_n^*)$ is CK.

The following definitions hold:

When (B1) $\Longrightarrow$(B3), the equilibrium is Strongly Rational.

When (B1) plus (B2) $\Longrightarrow$ (B3) (for some small neighbourhood), the Equilibrium is said Locally Strongly Rational.

In fact the paper mainly focuses on a weaker condition called Iterative Expectational Stability, which is necessary for Strong Rationality and that we shall explain below.

[15] this restriction is said to be hypothetical, unless it were implemented by some appropriate external policy (import or export calls for example). In fact, (B2) may be in a sense incompatible with (B3): this will occur whenever actions compatible with (B2) will trigger quantities outside of the considered neighbourhood. In a sense, Local Strong Rationality (LSR) only asserts that (B2) is a coherent sentence, at least for some non trivial neighbourhood. It would probably be logically more satisfactory, but plausibly less appealing, to introduce LSR in this way.

4 Necessary conditions for "eductive coordination": one result

4.1 Preliminaries

Let us remind that if the production of good k is denoted Q_k, then the market clearing equations for goods can be written:

$$Z_l(p_1, p_2, ..., p_n; \sum_k p_k Q_k; M_0) = Q_l$$

Differentating the above expression, we get: $\sum_k \{\partial Z_l/\partial p_k + Q_k \partial Z_l/\partial R\}$ $dp_k + (\sum_{k \neq l}\{p_k \partial Z_l/\partial R)\} dQ_k) = (1 - p_l \partial Z_l/\partial R) dQ_l$.

In vector notation:

$(\partial Z)\, dp = (I - A) dQ$

where (∂Z) is a matrix of pseudo-compensated[16] demand and where A is the matrix whose diagonal elements are of the form $(p_l \partial Z_l/\partial R)$ and off diagonal elements are of the form $(p_k \partial Z_l/\partial R)$ in the lth row, kth column.

Let us say a few words about the matrix A:

$$A = \begin{pmatrix} p_1 \partial Z_1/\partial R & p_k \partial Z_1/\partial R & .... & ..... \; p_n \partial Z_1/\partial R \\ .... & .... & .... & ..... \; .... \\ p_1 \partial Z_l/\partial R & p_k \partial Z_l/\partial R & p_l \partial Z_l/\partial R & ..... \; p_n \partial Z_l/\partial R \\ .... & .... & .... & ..... \; .... \\ p_1 \partial Z_n/\partial R & p_k \partial Z_n/\partial R & .... & ..... \; p_n \partial Z_n/\partial R \end{pmatrix}$$

A is of rank one: all its columns are proportional. Its image is one-dimensional, along the direction of the vector $\partial Z/\partial R$. Note that $p \cdot (\partial Z/\partial R) = \alpha'$ (resp. α), where α' (resp. α) is also the marginal (average) propensity to consume, so that α' (resp.α) is the eigenvalue associated with the eigenvector $\partial Z/\partial R$: Indeed, $\alpha' < 1$, or with assumption A2)[17], $\alpha < 1$, is the only non-zero eigenvalue, so that the matrix A is productive (no inferior goods). Also, its kernel is $(n-1)$-dimensional: $\{x | p \cdot x = 0\}$.[18]Now, let us come to the

[16] sum of the matrix of compensated like (indeed the matrix of compensated derivatives in the interpretation taken here, where demand conditional to the signal C comes from a continuum of identical consumers) derivatives associated with the demand triggered by the signal C, and of the Jacobian matrix associated with D_P, the demand trigerred, today, by the signal P, yesterday.

[17] i.e in the explicit formulation with identical income effects across consumers,

[18] Note that the transpose of A, A^t, is:

$$\begin{pmatrix} p_1 \partial Z_1/\partial R) & p_1 \partial Z_l/\partial R) & .... & .... \; p_1 \partial Z_n/\partial R) \\ .... & .... & .... & .... \; .... \\ p_l \partial Z_1/\partial R) & p_l \partial Z_k/\partial R) & p_l \partial Z_l/\partial R & .... \; p_l \partial Z_n/\partial R) \\ .... & .... & .... & .... \; .... \\ p_n \partial Z_1/\partial R) & p_n \partial Z_l/\partial R) & .... & .... \; p_n \partial Z_n/\partial R) \end{pmatrix}$$

It has proportional rows, an eigenvector p, with eigenvalue α (under the conditions stressed above) and the kernel: $\{x | (\partial Z/\partial R) \cdot x = 0\}$.

matrix $I - A$: $\partial Z / \partial R$ is an eigenvector associated with the eigenvalue $1 - \alpha$, and the space normal to p is an eigenspace with eigenvalue 1.

4.2 A basic insight

From now, unless we explicitly mention the contrary, we shall make assumptions (A1) and (A2). Note that nothing crucial depends on (A2) but it makes the reference to the specific model immediate. We can state:

Proposition 1. *The Fixed Wage Rational Expectations Equilibrium is Locally Strongly Rational only if it is Locally Iteratively Expectationally Stable. When (∂Z) is invertible, this latter fact is equivalent to: The eigenvalue of highest modulus of the matrix $(\partial S)(\partial Z)^{-1}(I - A)$, evaluated at equilibrium, is smaller than one.*

Proof. We first introduce informally the matrix $(\partial S)(\partial Z)^{-1}(I - A)$. A formal definition of Iterative Expectational Stability, as well as a proof of the fact that it is required for Local Strong Rationality, are given in Evans-Guesnerie (1993). For the first part of the Proposition, it has only to be shown that the present model can be encompassed in their setting, so that their Proposition 2 applies.

Here, we shall stick to an informal argument and definition, that makes however clear why the matrix $(\partial S)(\partial Z)^{-1}(I - A)$ matters.

Intuitively, Strong Rationality implies the following: If all agents, here firms, have beliefs over the production vector, associated with probability distributions the support of which is a small compact ball around the equilibrium productions, then it must intuitively be the case that, for Strong Rationality to hold, either local or global, the individual decisions triggered by such beliefs induce total production levels that remain close to the equilibrium quantities, or in the case under consideration, remain in the initial ball.

A fortiori, the above remark applies whenever the initial beliefs of the firms are degenerate, for example when they are identical and consist of point expectations, rather than of probability distributions: it is indeed what the concept of Iterative Expectational Stability expresses (see footnote 3).

Then, let us consider point expectations that differ from the equilibrium expectations by $dQ = (dQ_1, dQ_2, ..., dQ_n)$,

The corresponding belief triggers, according to the above market clearing equation and assuming that (∂Z) is invertible, a change in prices equaling to $dp = (\partial Z)^{-1}(I - A)dQ$. This price change induces a supply change $(\partial S)(\partial Z)^{-1}(I - A)dQ$.

For the evoked condition to hold, the associated linear mapping must be contracting: Hence the second part of the proposition is proven. □

The qualitative factors that are stressed here are the same as those appearing in the case of a single commodity treated in Guesnerie (2000b). Indeed, with one comodity, $(\partial S)(\partial Z)^{-1}(I - A)$ is nothing else, with straightforward notation, than $(s/z)(1 - \alpha)$, which is the expression found in the just quoted article.[19], i.e the ratio of the derivative of supply with respect to price and of the derivative of demand multiplied by the marginal propensity to save. Equivalently, what matters is the *ratio of supply elasticity and demand elasticity multiplied by the inverse of the elementary Keynesian multiplier.* Note that the one-dimensional formula: $(s/z)(1 - \alpha) < 1$, does not provide, strictly speaking comparative statics results.[20], unless we compare situations with constant elasticities of supply and demand and fixed propensity to consume. However, it stresses a useful and clear fact that will have a key role in any comparative statics exercise: everything equal, a larger propensity to consume, or a higher elementary Keynesian multiplier favours stability. The n-commodities analysis makes clear that the qualitative conclusions of the 1-commodity case have to be qualified.

i) As we said, in the $(n+2)-$goods case, the condition stressed here is a necessary and sufficient condition for Local Iterative Expectational Stability, but contrarily to what happens in the three-goods case, this condition is not equivalent to Local Strong Rationality.[21] In the general case, a necessary and sufficient condition for Local Strong Rationality would have to take into account additional restrictions associated with the heterogeneity of beliefs: however, the analysis of this dimension of expectational coordination would routinely proceed along the lines of Evans-Guesnerie (1993).

ii) Leaving in the shadow the heterogenity of beliefs, one has concluded that the qualitative features of the one-dimensional analysis of Iterative Expectational Stability have an n-dimensional close counterpart: the counterpart of the supply and demand derivatives are the supply and demand Jacobian matrices ∂S and ∂Z, the counterpart of the (marginal) propensity to save – or of the elementary Keynesian multiplier – is $I - A$, or $(I - A)^{-1}$. However, it is unclear to which extent the powerful effects on expectational coordination of a small propensity to save, or equivalently a high "elementary" Keynesian multiplier, generalize here.

[19] However, in the formulation of the standard three goods model, the marginal propensity to consume is allowed to differ from the average one, contrarily to what has been assumed here.

[20] It is interesting to compare the "eductive stability" of (equilibria of) different economies or, in the same economy, of exogenous changes or different policy choices.

[21] Note that the argument requires efficient labour rationing, an assumption that is not used here.

5 Further Inquiry

The role of the Keynesian effects, stressed in simple game theoretical models with strategic complementarities by Cooper and John (1989), has then been ascertained in the more complex context of the three-goods model, in which strategic complementarities are dominated by strategic substitutabilities. The question now raised is a robustness issue. Can we still clearly detect and ascertain, in the $(n+2)$-goods model, and within the same pre-comparative statics exercise performed in the three-goods case, a positive expectational coordination effect of the marginal propensity to consume?[22]

5.1 A necessary condition

We are first exhibiting a necessary condition tht provides a clearer link with the one-dimensional case.

Proposition 2. *For IE- Stability to hold, it is necessary that:* $(\frac{1}{1-\alpha})\,\|(\partial Z)\|_E \cdot \left\|(\partial S\,)^{-1}\right\|_E > 1$ *where* $\|\cdot\|_E$ *is the matrix norm induced by the Euclidean vector norm on a basis of* $I\!R^n$ *that consists of the vector* $(\partial Z/\partial R)$ *and of an orthogonal basis in the hyperplane normal to* p.

Proof. For IE-stability to hold, it is necessary that the modulus of the eigenvalue of highest modulus of the matrix $B = (\partial S)\,(\partial Z)^{-1}\,(I-A)$ be (strictly) smaller than 1.[23]. This implies that the modulus of all eigenvalues of $B^{-1} = (I-A)^{-1}\,(\partial Z)\,(\partial S)^{-1}$ is (strictly) higher than 1, and consequently that the norm of B^{-1}, for any matrix norm, is greater than 1. Formally: $\left\|(I-A)^{-1}\,(\partial Z)\,(\partial S)^{-1}\right\| > 1$.

But $\left\|(I-A)^{-1}\right\|\,\|(\partial Z)\|\,\left\|(\partial S\,)^{-1}\right\| \geq \left\|(I-A)^{-1}\,(\partial Z)\,(\partial S)^{-1}\right\|$. Also, since A is productive, we have $(I-A)^{-1} = I + A + A^2 + \ldots$ and $\left\|(I-A)^{-1}\right\| = \left\|I + A + A^2 + \ldots\right\|$ and $\|I\| + \|A\| + \left\|A^2\right\| + \ldots \|A^n\| + \ldots \geq \left\|I + A + A^2 + \ldots\right\|$, so that, necessarily, $(\|I\| + \|A\| + \left\|A^2\right\| + \ldots \|A^n\| + \ldots)\,\|(\partial Z)\|\,\left\|(\partial S\,)^{-1}\right\| > 1$.

Now take as matrix norm the norm induced by the Euclidean norm taken on the basis associated with the eigen space of A, that consists of the vector $\partial Z/\partial R$, and of any basis of the hyperplane orthogonal to p. With this matrix norm: $\|I\| = 1$ and $\|A\| = \alpha$.

Hence the conclusion. □

[22] In a sense, the mathematical question that is associated might be formulated as follows: Assume that, as we shall do later, the matrix A is parametrized by β, with $A_\beta = \beta A$. How does the modulus of the eigenvalue of highest modulus of $(\partial S)(\partial Z^{-1})(I - A_\beta)$ vary with β ?

[23] One says also that the *spectral radius* is smaller than one (see Horn-Johnson (1990)).

The necessary condition of the proposition is interesting, in particular because its one dimensional counterpart reduces to the necessary and sufficient condition of Guesnerie (2000b). Also, the role of the elementary Keynesian multiplier $\frac{1}{1-\alpha}$in triggering the above general necessary condition justifies comments similar to the qualitative comments made on the three-goods model.

5.2 Sufficient conditions

A first attempt at clarifying the sufficiency issue is presented now.

The basic norm inequality shows that a sufficient condition for IE Stability is $\|\partial S\| \left\|(\partial Z)^{-1}\right\| \|(I-A)\| < 1$.

We would provide a clearcut extension of the one-dimensional conclusion, if we could replace the inequality by $(s^{\max}/z^{\min})(1-\alpha) < 1$, where $s^{\max}, z^{\min}, \alpha$ are respectively the maximal supply derivative, the modulus of the eigenvalue of smallest modulus of ∂Z, and the propensity to consume.

Clearly, this cannot be exactly true: for any norm, it follows from Horn-Johnson (1990) that $\left\|(\partial Z)^{-1}\right\| \geq 1/z^{\min}$, but also, and more disturbingly, that $\|(I-A)\| \geq 1$.

However, one can still exploit the freedom in the choice of norms, ($\|.\|$ designated *any* a priori chosen matrix norm), together with the properties of A, in order to get some additional insights on the conditions of IE-Stability.

Note, for example, that the first assertion is equivalent to: $\|\partial S\| \left\|(\partial Z)^{-1}\right\| < 1/\left\|(I-A)\right\|$. This, together with $\|(I-A)\| \leq \|I\| + \|A)\|$, allows us to conclude that $\|\partial S\| \left\|(\partial Z)^{-1}\right\| < 1/(1+\|A\|)$ is a sufficient condition for IE-Stability (for any norm).

Now let us recall that the spectral norm $\|A\|_s$ of A is the absolute value of the eigenvalue with highest absolute value of A^tA (Horn-Johnson (1990)). In the following, $\|\cdot\|_e$ denotes the Euclidean vector norm.

Now, the symmetric matrix A^tA, consists of proportional rows, the l-th row being, with straigthforward notation: $\|\partial Z/\partial R)\|_e^2 p_l \, p^t$. It has a unique non-zero eigenvalue $\|\partial Z/\partial R)\|_e^2 \|p\|_e^2$, associated with the eigenvector p.

It follows that the spectral norm[24] of A is $\|p\|_e \|\partial Z/\partial R\|_e$. Writing $p \cdot \partial Z/\partial R = \|p\|_e \|\partial Z/\partial R\|_e (\cos\theta)$, it follows that the spectral norm of A is $\alpha/(\cos\theta)$ with θ being the angle between p and $\partial Z/\partial R$. Thus, we just proved the following

Statement A sufficient condition for IE-Stability, is:

$$\|\partial S\|_s \left\|(\partial Z)^{-1}\right\|_s < \cos\theta/(\alpha + \cos\theta),$$

with θ being the "angle" between *p and* $\partial Z/\partial R$.

---

[24] As a matrix norm, the spectral norm is higher than the modulus of the eigenvalue of highest modulus of A.

Unfortunately, the just obtained statement may not be that useful: a higher marginal propensity to consume does not seem to make, everything else equal, the sufficient condition easier to check, on the contrary![25]

The above analysis of sufficiency is disappointing for our purpose and suggests, to the least, that the role of the marginal propensity to save is now much more ambiguous.

Another teaching of the analysis is that, in order to fully elucidate the exact interplay of income and price effects in expectational coordination, we probably need:

- A more careful assessment of the properties of excess demand.
- A preliminary assessment of the product $(\partial Z)^{-1}(I - A)$ as a whole, as opposed to the previous separate assessment of (the norms of) the two matrices (∂Z) and $(I - A)$.

The full exploitation of these remarks is outside the scope of the present analysis. We shall however explore the case where excess demand meets the gross substitutability-like assumption that $-(\partial Z)^{-1}$ is a positive matrix. Hence $-(\partial S)(\partial Z)^{-1}$ is a positive matrix.

Let us define, as in footnote 22, $A_\beta = \beta A$, for positive β. This provides a parametrisation of the marginal propensity to consume which equals $\beta\alpha$ for the matrix A_β.

There is then a range of values of β, the interval $(0, \beta^{\max})$, for which $-B_\beta = -(\partial S)(\partial Z)^{-1}(I - A_\beta) = -(\partial S)(\partial Z)^{-1} + (\partial S)(\partial Z)^{-1} A_\beta$ is a positive matrix. With this in mind we show:

Proposition 3. *Under the gross substitutability-like assumption introduced above, if for some β_0, $(\partial S)(\partial Z)^{-1}(I - A_\beta)$ has a spectral radius smaller than one, then this spectral radius decreases in the range $\beta \in (\beta_0, \beta^{\max})$.*

Proof. We note, from Perron-Frobenius, that the eigenvalue of highest modulus is real and positive and smaller than one for $-B_{\beta_0}$. The fact that this eigenvalue decreases for $\beta > \beta_0$, reflects the fact that if $\beta \in (\beta_0, \beta^{\max})$, $-B_{\beta_0} > -B_\beta$. Then, when $\lim (-\lambda B_{\beta_0})^n, \lambda > 0$, tends to zero, there exists $\gamma > 1$, such that $\lim (-\gamma\lambda B_\beta)^n$ tends to zero. The conclusion follows from the fact that limit $A^n = 0$ is equivalent to the fact that the spectral radius of A is strictly smaller than one (Horn-Johnson (1990)). □

As emphasized previously, the result is not, strictly speaking, a comparative statics result: in a complex problem, when one changes β, one also changes (∂S) and (∂Z). However, it unambiguously stresses the positive effect of the "elementary Keynesian multiplier" on coordination, agreeing with the intuition drawn from the one-dimensional analysis: when β increases, the

[25] Also, the relationship between the type of norms adopted and the eigenvalue of highest modulus (for example, the spectral norm of (∂Z) and its spectral radius) is a priori unclear and cannor be fully elucidated in the absence of more specific assumptions on demand.

marginal propensity to consume (and the Keynesian multiplier) increases, and the decrease of the spectral radius indicates that expectational coordination is "improving."

6 Conclusion

This paper has attempted to check the robustness of the expectational analysis of a three good-type model by imbedding it in an n-dimensional context. It has confirmed the role and the qualitative effects of supply and demand derivatives in expectational coordination. However the stabilizing role of income effects is likely, "in general" to be less clearcut in the n-dimensional context considered here than what was suggested by the one dimensional analysis of the three goods model. The full clarification of the problem calls for additional work. Such work is likely to stress specificities of expectational coordination that relate with the specific forms of the global Excess demand function: it may then have at this stage closer connections with the work of Werner Hildenbrand on consumption.

Note, finally that related papers study expectational coordination along similar lines, in particular, Ghosal (1999) and Guesnerie and Hens (2000) focus attention on a two-period exchange economy, and provide complementary pieces for a more comprehensive theory of expectational coordination in standard general equilibrium models.

Appendix: A fully specified special case

The specific story that provides a fully explicit and parsimonious illustration of the general model,[26] is the following.

There is a continuum of agents of mass one. At each period, each agent receives a signal, either C, consume immediately, or P, postpone consumption to the next period. These signals are i.i.d. between agents and periods and the probability of C is μ. The signals are obeyed - for example an agent who receives C consumes today his available income - but an agent who has received P yesterday, consumes today, whatever signal he receives today. The process can be viewed as a two states Markov process ($\{C, P\}$) with the transition matrix

$$\begin{pmatrix} \mu & 1-\mu \\ 1 & 0 \end{pmatrix}$$

which has the ergodic distribution $(\alpha, 1-\alpha)$ with $1-\alpha+\alpha\mu = \alpha$, i.e. $\alpha = 1/(2-\mu)$.[27] Equivalently, $\mu = (2 - 1/\alpha)$ or $1 - \mu = 1/\alpha - 1$.

[26] For a similar story in a finance context, see Allen-Gale (1994).

[27] For example for $\mu = 0, \alpha = 1/2$, half of the agents consume today, because they have not consumed yesterday, half the agents postpone, because they obey their signal. With $\mu = 1, \alpha = 1$, all agents receive the C signal and consume.

In this crude version, the individual demand is necessarily of the form $D_S(p, R)$,[28] where p is the vector of goods prices (expressed in terms of money, the price of which is one) and R is the income available to the agent, and where S designates either C or P, (immediate consumption behaviour may be different from postponed consumption behaviour).

Under this assumption, aggregate demand in the afternoon is nothing else, (with obvious notation), than: $\int_C D_C(p, R)dR + \int_P D_P(p, R)dR$. The following analysis, however, is much simplified if we assume that demand does not depend on the income distribution. This occurs if for example all agents are a priori similar. Then, aggregate demand equals $\alpha D_C(p, R_C) + D_P(p, R_P)$ where R_C is the total income of an agent who has received the signal C, and R_P is the income of an agent who has received the signal P.

References

1. Allen F., and D. Gale, "Limited Market Participation and Volatility of Asset Prices," *American Economic Review,* 84, [1994], 933-955.
2. Aumann R., "Correlated Equilibrium as an Expression of Bayesian Rationality," *Econometrica*, 55, (1987) 1-18.
3. Barro R., H. Grossman, "A General Disequilibrium Model of Income and Employment," *American Economic Review*, 61,(1971), 82-93.
4. Bernheim B.D., "Rationalizable Strategic Behavior," *Econometrica*, 52, (1984), 1007-28.
5. Bryant J., "The paradox of Thrift, Liquidity Preferences and Animal Spirits," *Econometrica*, 55, (1987), 1231-37.
6. Calvo G.A., "Comments on Rational Expectations in Macroeconomic Models," in *Individual Forecasting and Aggregate Outcomes*, Frydman R. and Phelps E. eds., Cambridge University Press, (1983).
7. Cooper R., A. John, "Coordinating Coordination Failures in Keynesian Macroeconomics," *Quarterly Journal of Economics,* (1989), 242-264.
8. Drèze J., "Walras-Keynes Equilibria, coordination and macroeconomics" Discussion Paper(1996).
9. De Canio S.J., "Rational Expectations and Learning from Experience," *Quarterly Journal of Economics*, (1979), 93, 47-58.
10. Evans G.W., "Expectational Stability and the Multiple Equilibrium Problem in Linear Rational Expectations Models," *Quarterly Journal of Economics*, 100, (1985),1217-33.
11. Evans G.W., R.Guesnerie, "Rationalizability, Strong Rationality and Expectational Stability," *Games and Economic Behaviour,* 5, (1993), 632-646.
12. Farqharson R., *Theory of Voting*, New Haven: Yale University Press, (1969).
13. Ghosal S., "Eductive Stability in an Intertemporal Economy," University of Warwick, mimeo, (1999).

[28] The story can however be made more sophisticated, by supposing that the signal affects positively or negatively the rate of time preference between today and tomorrow: money holdings serve to adapt consumption to signals, and the aggregate demand function is more complex that previously.

14. Guesnerie R., "An Exploration of the Eductive Justifications of the Rational Expectations Hypothesis," *American Economic Review*, 82, (1992),1254-1278.
15. Guesnerie R., "Anchoring Economic Predictions in Common Knowledge," to appear *Econometrica*, 2000a.
16. Guesnerie R., " On Short run Expectational Coordination: Fixed versus flexible wages," to appear, *Quarterly Journal of Economics*, 2000b.
17. Guesnerie R., T. Hens, "Expectational Coordination in Sequential Exchange Economies," mimeo, (2000).
18. Hellwig M., "The Conceptual Structure of Macroeconomic Models: The Income Equation." Discussion Paper 1993, Basel.
19. Horn R., C. Johnson, (1990) "Matrix Analysis," Cambridge University Press.
20. Luce R., H. Raiffa, *Games and Decisions,* New York, Wiley, (1957).
21. Lucas R.E., Jr., "Asset Prices in an Exchange Economy," *Econometrica*, 46, (1978), 1429-45.
22. Malinvaud E., "The Theory of Unemployment Reconsidered," Basil Blackwell, (1977).
23. Milgrom P., J. Roberts, "Rationalizability, Learning and Equilibrium in Games with Strategic Complementarities," *Econometrica*, 58, (1990),1255-1277.
24. Moulin H., "Dominance Solvable Voting Schemes," *Econometrica*, 47, (1979), 1337-351.
25. Muth J., "Rational Expectations and the Theory of Price Movements," *Econometrica*, 29, (1961), 315-35.
26. Nagel R., "Unraveling in Guessing Games: An Experimental Study," *American Economic Review*, 85, (1995), 1313-1326.
27. Pearce D., "Rationalizable Strategic Behavior and the Problem of Perfection," *Econometrica*, 52, (1984), 1029-50.
28. Tan T., S.R. Costa da Werlang, "On Aumann's Notion of Common Knowledge, an Alternative Approach," *Journal of Economic Theory*, 45,(1988), 370-91.

Nonparametric Estimation of Additive Models with Homogeneous Components*

Wolfgang Härdle[1], Woocheol Kim[1], and Gautam Tripathi[2]

[1] Institut für Statistik und Ökonometrie, Humboldt-Universität zu Berlin
[2] Department of Economics, University of Wisconsin, Madison

Abstract. The importance of homogeneity as a restriction on functional forms has been well recognized in economic theory. Imposing additive separability is also popular since many economics models become easier to interpret and estimate when the explanatory variables are additively separable. In this paper we combine the two restrictions and propose a two-step nonparametric procedure for estimating additive models whose unknown component functions may be homogeneous of known degree. In the first step we obtain preliminary estimates of the components by imposing homogeneity on local linear fits. In the second step these pilot estimates are marginally integrated to produce estimators of the additive components which possess optimal rates of convergence. We derive the asymptotic theory of these two-step estimators and illustrate their use on data collected from livestock farms in Wisconsin.

1 Introduction

Nonparametric methods play a useful role in exploratory data analysis by producing consistent estimates of models without relying upon any particular parameterization of the underlying functional forms. Such methods are particularly useful in economics, since in most cases economic theory does not reveal the exact functional relationship between variables. What can be deduced from the theory is usually limited to qualitative or shape properties of the underlying functional forms. For example, although we do not know the exact functional form of a Marshallian demand function, economic theory tells us that these functions are homogeneous of degree zero in prices and income (see e.g. Hildenbrand (1994)). While associating particular functional forms with economic models can create a potential source of misspecification, it does seem reasonable to incorporate restrictions imposed by the theory into estimation procedures. Imposing a valid shape restriction on an estimator usually enhances its performance and leads to better inference.

The shape property we study in this paper is homogeneity. Homogeneous functions seem to be pervasive in economic analysis. For instance, apart from

* We thank Stefan Sperlich for providing us with the cleaned up data for the application in section 4, and Xenia Matschke for some useful comments. The authors also acknowledge support by the Deutsche Forschungsgemeinschaft via SFB 373 at Humboldt University, Berlin.

the demand function example described earlier, in microeconomic theory the cost minimizing behavior of competitive firms implies linear homogeneity of the cost function in input prices. The homogeneity restriction is strong and from an econometric point of view it delivers useful information for statistical inference. In particular, Tripathi and Kim (2000) showed that homogeneity can be exploited to increase the statistical accuracy of estimates. Compared with the usual nonparametric estimate of a conditional mean function which is obtained without imposing any prior restrictions, homogeneity of the regression surface permits a reduction in the dimension of the surface and so leads to a faster rate of convergence of the surface estimates. Despite this dimension reduction, Tripathi and Kim's approach suffers from the usual curse of dimensionality when the number of regressors is large. Moreover, the standard nonparametric regression model they study does not allow for the possibility of imposing homogeneity on a subset of the regressors. To overcome these limitations, in this paper we assume additive separability among the homogeneous and non-homogeneous components and extend the estimation of homogeneous functions to nonparametric additive models. Additive separability is frequently used to simplify structure and is basic to many economic models. See, for example, Deaton and Muellbauer (1980). In nonparametric regression the assumption of additive separability alleviates the deterioration in the attainable convergence rates in high dimensions – the well-known "curse of dimensionality" problem (Stone, 1985).

Our objective is to estimate a model with additively separable components when the functional forms of the components are unknown, although we do know that some of them are homogeneous of known degree. Specifically, we let

$$y_i = f_1(X_{1i}, .., X_{di}) + f_2(Z_{1i}, .., Z_{si}) + \varepsilon_i, \tag{1}$$

where at least one component function, say f_1, is homogeneous of known degree α_1; i.e. $f_1(\lambda x_1, .., \lambda x_d) = \lambda^{\alpha_1} f_1(x_1, .., x_d)$, $\forall(\lambda, x) \in R_{++} \times S_1$, where S_1 denotes the support of $(X_1, .., X_d)$ and α_1 is known. We follow a two-step procedure to estimate (1): In the first step we use a local linear approach, see Fan (1992), to impose homogeneity on estimates of f_1 and f_2. These preliminary estimates are consistent, although not rate-optimal. Therefore, in the second step we marginally integrate the preliminary estimates to obtain rate optimal estimators of f_1 and f_2.

As an example of (1) consider a case where the observed cost of production for a competitive firm is the sum of the variable and fixed costs. While standard microeconomic theory restricts the variable costs to be linearly homogeneous in input prices, we can assume the fixed cost to be an unknown function of some other covariates. Note that (1) allows f_2 to be homogeneous functions of known degree α_2, where α_2 may or may not be the same as α_1. This comes in handy if we wish to estimate the cost function of a firm producing two distinct products using different inputs. Although we do not pursue it in this paper, the approach used for estimating (1) can also be extended to handle a model with multiplicatively separable components and dependent data: According to the theory of option pricing, the option price Π_t is homogeneous in the price of the underlying asset S_t, and the exercise price K. See Ghysels et al (1998). Under multiplicative separability, a nonparametric model for the option price can be constructed as $\Pi_t = f_1(S_t, K) f_2(T-t, X_t) + \varepsilon_t$, where f_1 is linearly homogeneous, $T-t$ indexes "time to expiration," and X_t denotes some other variables such as S_{t-1} or volatility.

The paper is organized as follows. In section 2 we introduce the numeraire approach as a convenient tool for imposing homogeneity in local linear estimation, and describe our two-step estimation procedure. Section 3 has the main statistical results. In section 4 we apply our method to estimate an additively separable aggregate level production function for livestock production in Wisconsin. All proofs have been confined to the Appendix.

2 Estimation

2.1 Numeraire approach and marginal integration

For convenience of exposition we begin by assuming that both components in (1) are homogeneous. Throughout the paper we maintain the assumption that the degree of homogeneity is known. To impose homogeneity on our estimator we reparameterize (1) using a numeraire argument. We introduce the following notation; $U_i = (X_{1i}/X_{di}, .., X_{(d-1)i}/X_{di})$, $V_i = (Z_{1i}/Z_{si}, .., Z_{(s-1)i}/Z_{si})$, $\beta_1(U_i) = f_1(U_i, 1)$, and $\beta_2(V_i) = f_2(V_i, 1)$. From the homogeneity of f_1 it follows that $f_1(X_{1i}, .., X_{di}) = X_{di}^{\alpha_1} f_1(X_{1i}/X_{di}, .., X_{(d-1)i}/X_{di}, 1) = X_{di}^{\alpha_1} \cdot$ $\cdot \beta_1(U_i)$. Hence we can rewrite (1) as

$$Y_i = X_{di}^{\alpha_1} \beta_1(U_i) + Z_{si}^{\alpha_2} \beta_2(V_i) + \varepsilon_i. \tag{2}$$

Observe that additive models with only one homogeneous component can be treated as a special case of (2) by letting $Z_{si} = 1$ and $V_i = Z_i$. Therefore, w.l.o.g we can work with (2) as far as obtaining the statistical theory for estimating (1) is concerned. More importantly, when $\alpha_1 = \alpha_2 = 1$, (2) generalizes the varying-coefficient model of Hastie and Tibshrani (1993). In Chen and Tsay (1993), and Chen (1997), the coefficient functions were assumed to depend on a common covariate. However, the β_i's in (2) are allowed to be functions of different covariates. Thus studying (2) is of independent interest and allows us to deal with a larger class of varying-coefficient models. Henceforth, we focus on estimating (2).

The benefits from reparameterization are obvious. To obtain consistent estimates of f_1, one has only to estimate β_1 via $\widehat{f_1}(x) = x_d^{\alpha_1} \widehat{\beta}_1(u)$. The resulting estimator $x \mapsto \widehat{f_1}(x)$ is homogeneous of degree α_1 by construction. Furthermore, since β_1 has only $(d-1)$ arguments, homogeneity helps in enhancing the optimal rate of convergence to $n^{-2/(4+(d-1))}$ under twice differentiability. However, the reader should note that an optimal-rate estimator for β_1 cannot be obtained by a simple application of local linear regression to (2). To get a faster rate we use the "marginal integration" (MI) technique, which has been developed by Newey (1994), Tjøstheim and Auestadt (1994), and Linton and Nielsen (1995). To get some intuition behind MI consider (1) but without any homogeneity restriction on the components. Let $\widehat{f}(x,z)$ be a pilot nonparametric smoother for the conditional mean function – for instance, this could be the Nadaraya-Watson kernel smoother. An estimate of $f_1(x)$ can be obtained by integrating out z in $\widehat{f}(x,z)$. In other words, we can employ $\widehat{f}_1(x) = \int \widehat{f}(x,z)dP_Z$ or $\widehat{f}_1(x) = \frac{1}{n}\sum_{k=1}^{n} \widehat{f}(x, Z_k)$ to estimate $f_1(x)$ consistently up to some constant, where P_Z is a probability measure w.r.t Z. When f_1 is twice continuously differentiable, $\widehat{f}_1(x)$ converges at the optimal rate $n^{-2/(4+d)}$. See Linton and Nielsen (1995) or Linton and Härdle (1997). When applied to (2) this argument also shows that we can consistently estimate $f_1(x)$ at rate $n^{-2/(4+d)}$. However, the resulting estimate cannot be homogeneous. Moreover, the rate $n^{-2/(4+d)}$ is not optimal. It is slower than $n^{-2/(4+(d-1))}$, the attainable rate for (2). To obtain an estimator with the better rate we note that the first-step estimate $\widehat{\beta}_1(u)$ is effectively a function of (u, V_i). Hence, if we marginally integrate $\widehat{\beta}_1(u, V_i)$ w.r.t. V_i we will get the rate optimal estimate of β_1. We now make the preceding discussion rigorous.

2.2 Two-step procedure

Let $\widehat{\beta}_{j0}$ and $\widehat{\beta}_{jk}$ denote estimates of the level $\beta_j(\cdot)$ and the partial derivative of $\beta_j(\cdot)$ w.r.t. the kth component, respectively. Also, let $w = (u,v)$ and $\widehat{\beta}(w) = (\widehat{\beta}_{10}(w), \widehat{\beta}_{11}(w), ..., \widehat{\beta}_{1(d-1)}(w), \widehat{\beta}_{20}(w), \widehat{\beta}_{21}(w),...,\widehat{\beta}_{2(s-1)}(w))$. If $\beta(w) = (\beta_1(u), \beta_2(v))$ is differentiable at w we can locally approximate $\beta_j(\cdot)$ by a linear function. In the first step we estimate local linear fits for β_j and its partial derivatives as:

$$\widehat{\beta}(w) = \arg\min_b \frac{1}{n}\sum_{i=1}^{n} K_h(W_i - w)\{y_i - [b_{10} + \sum_{k=1}^{d-1} h_1 b_{1k}\left(\frac{U_{ki}-u_k}{h_1}\right)]X_{di}^{\alpha_1} \tag{3}$$

$$-[b_{20} + \sum_{k=1}^{s-1} h_2 b_{2k}\left(\frac{V_{ki}-v_k}{h_2}\right)]Z_{si}^{\alpha_2}\}^2.$$

Here $K_h(w) = K_{h_1}(u) K_{h_2}(v) = \frac{1}{h_1^{d-1}}\frac{1}{h_2^{s-1}}\prod_{l=1}^{d-1} K\left(\frac{u_l}{h_1}\right)\prod_{l=1}^{s-1} K\left(\frac{v_l}{h_2}\right)$, and K is a real valued function on R with compact support. Minimizing (3) w.r.t. the b_1's and b_2's yields

$$\widehat{\beta}(w) = Q^{-1}\left(\mathbf{M}(w)^T \mathbf{\Omega}(w)\mathbf{M}(w)\right)^{-1}(\mathbf{M}(w)^T\mathbf{\Omega}(w)\mathbf{y}), \tag{4}$$

where $Q = diag_{d+s}(1, h_1, ., h_1, 1, h_2, .., h_2)$, $\mathbf{y} = (y_1, ..., y_n)^T$, and $\mathbf{\Omega}(w) = diag_{1\le i\le n} K_h(W_i - w)$. The matrix $\mathbf{M}(w) = [\mathbf{M}_1(w)\ \mathbf{M}_2(w)]$ where

$$\mathbf{M}_1(w) = \begin{bmatrix} X_{d1}^{\alpha_1} & X_{d1}^{\alpha_1}(U_{11}-u_1)/h_1 & .. & X_{d1}^{\alpha_1}\left(U_{(d-1)1}-u_{(d-1)}\right)/h_1 \\ \vdots & \vdots & \vdots & \vdots \\ X_{dn}^{\alpha_1}, & X_{dn}^{\alpha_1}(U_{1n}-u_1)/h_1 & .. & X_{dn}^{\alpha_1}\left(U_{(d-1)n}-u_{(d-1)}\right)/h_1 \end{bmatrix}, \text{and}$$

$$\mathbf{M}_2(w) = \begin{bmatrix} Z_{s1}^{\alpha_2} & Z_{s1}^{\alpha_2}(V_{11}-v_1)/h_2 & .. & Z_{s1}^{\alpha_2}\left(V_{(s-1)1}-v_{(s-1)}\right)/h_2 \\ \vdots & \vdots & \vdots & \vdots \\ Z_{sn}^{\alpha_2} & Z_{sn}^{\alpha_2}(V_{1n}-v_1)/h_2 & .. & Z_{s1}^{\alpha_2}\left(V_{(s-1)n}-v_{(s-1)}\right)/h_2 \end{bmatrix}.$$

Note that when only one of the component functions, say f_1, is homogeneous the expressions given above can be simplified by plugging in $Z_{si} = 1$ and $V_{ki} = Z_{ki}$ for $k = 1,..,s$. Furthermore, the notation $\widehat{\beta}_{1k}(w)$ emphasizes the fact that the estimated value depends on both u and v, although $\widehat{\beta}_{1k}(w)$ itself is a consistent estimate of $\beta_{1k}(u)$. In particular, this shows that the rate of convergence of $\widehat{\beta}_{10}(w)$ is the same as that of a multivariate smoothing regression with covariates W. In the second step, to achieve the optimal rate of convergence for the first additive component, we marginally integrate the pilot estimates $\widehat{\beta}_{10}(u, V_i)$ over V_i; i.e. we obtain

$$\widehat{\beta}_{10}^*(u) = \frac{1}{n}\sum_{i=1}^{n}\widehat{\beta}_{10}(u, V_i) \tag{5}$$

where e_k is a (d+s)×1 column vector with the kth element being one and others zero. Similarly, $\widehat{\beta}_{20}^*(v) = \frac{1}{n}\sum_{i=1}^{n}\widehat{\beta}_{20}(U_i, v)$, and an estimate of the regression surface can be written as $\widehat{f}^*(x, z) = x_d^{\alpha_1}\widehat{\beta}_1^*(u) + z_s^{\alpha_2}\widehat{\beta}_2^*(v)$.

3 Asymptotic theory

The results in this section are derived under the following technical conditions:

A1. *$\{y_i, X_i, Z_i\}_{i=1}^n$ is iid with $E(\varepsilon|X,Z) = 0$ and $E(\varepsilon^2|X,Z) = \sigma^2(X,Z) < \infty$.*

A2. *The functions $f_1, f_2, \beta_1, \beta_2, \sigma$ and the densities (marginal and joint) p_X, p_Z, $p_{X,Z}$ are twice continuously differentiable with bounded partial derivatives.*

A3. *p_X, p_Z and $p_{X,Z}$ are bounded away from zero on their compact supports.*

A4. *The matrix $E\left(W^TW|X_d = x_d, Z_s = z_s\right)$ is of full rank and its inverse is element by element bounded in a neighborhood of (x_d, z_s).*

A5. *The kernel K is a compactly supported density such that $\int uK(u)\,du = 0$. Also, $|K(x_1) - K(x_2)| < c|x_1 - x_2|$ for all x_1 and x_2 in its support.*

A6. *$h_i \downarrow 0$ and $nh_i^{d+s-2} \uparrow \infty$ for $i \in \{1, 2\}$.*

A7. *$h_2^{(s-1)}/h_1^2 \to \infty$, $nh_1^{(d-1)}h_2^{2(s-1)}/\ln^2 n \to \infty$, $h_1 \to 0$, and $nh_1 \to \infty$.*

Most of the assumptions above are standard in the kernel estimation literature. The additional bandwidth condition in A7 allows us to use approximation Lemmas 4.2 and 4.3 of Yang, Härdle, and Nielsen (1999) in the proofs. Our first result is the asymptotic normality of the local linear fit given in (4). It is easy to see that (4) can be interpreted as a WLS estimate for a linear model. So let $W_{1i} = U_i$, $W_{2i} = V_i$, $U_i = (U_{1i}, .., U_{in})^T$, and $V_i = (V_{1i}, .., V_{in})^T$. Observe that we can write $\widehat{\beta}(w) = Q^{-1}S_n^{-1}t_n$, where $S_n = \begin{bmatrix} S_{11n}(w) & S'_{21n}(w) \\ S_{21n}(w) & S_{22n}(w) \end{bmatrix}$, $S_{ij} = \begin{bmatrix} s^{00}_{ijn}(w) & s^{01T}_{ijn}(w) \\ s^{01}_{ijn}(w) & s^{11}_{ijn}(w) \end{bmatrix}$ $i, j \in \{1, 2\}$, and

$$s^{lm}_{jkn}(w) = \frac{1}{n}\sum_{i=1}^{n} K_h(W_i - w)\left(\frac{W_{ji} - w_j}{h_j}\right)^l \left[\left(\frac{W_{ki} - w_k}{h_k}\right)^m\right]^T \times$$
$$X_{di}^{\alpha_1(2-j)} Z_{si}^{\alpha_2(j-1)} X_{di}^{\alpha_1(2-k)} Z_{si}^{\alpha_2(k-1)}$$

for $k, l \in \{0, 1\}$. Furthermore, $t_n = \begin{bmatrix} t_{1n}(w) \\ t_{2n}(w) \end{bmatrix}$ and $t_{jn} = \begin{bmatrix} t^0_{jn}(w) \\ t^1_{jn}(w) \end{bmatrix}$, where $t^l_{jn}(w) = \frac{1}{n}\sum_{i=1}^{n} K_h(W_i - w)\left(\frac{W_{ji} - w_j}{h_j}\right)^l X_{di}^{\alpha_1(2-j)} Z_{si}^{\alpha_2(j-1)} y_i$.

Since we are only interested in the level estimates, we can separate them out by premultiplying with $E^T = [e_1, e_{d+1}]^T$; $\widehat{\beta}_0(w) \equiv \left[\widehat{\beta}_{10}(w), \widehat{\beta}_{20}(w)\right]^T = E^T Q^{-1} S_n^{-1} t_n = E^T S_n^{-1} t_n$. Under A2 we can use Lemma 1 in the appendix to decompose the estimation errors as

$$\widehat{\beta}_0(w) - \beta_0(w) = BIAS_n + \widetilde{\tau}_n + o_p(h_1^2) + o_p(h_2^2), \tag{6}$$

where the bias term and the leading stochastic terms are given by

$$BIAS_n = E^T Q^{-1} S_n^{-1} B_n,\ B_n = [B_{1n}, B_{2n}]^T,\ B_{jn} = [B^0_{jn}, B^1_{jn}]^T,$$
$$B^l_{nj} = \frac{1}{n}\sum_{i=1}^{n} K_h(W_i - w)\left(\frac{W_{ji} - w_j}{h_j}\right)^l X_{di}^{\alpha_1(2-j)} Z_{si}^{\alpha_2(j-1)} \times$$
$$\sum_{k=1}^{2} \frac{h_j^2}{2} X_{di}^{\alpha_1(2-k)} Z_{si}^{\alpha_2(k-1)} \left[\left(\frac{W_{ki} - w_k}{h_j}\right)^T D^2\beta_k(w_k) \frac{W_{ki} - w_k}{h_k}\right]$$
$$\widetilde{\tau}_n = E^T Q^{-1} S_n^{-1}(w)\tau_n(w),$$
$$\tau_n = \begin{bmatrix} \tau_{1n}(w) \\ \tau_{2n}(w) \end{bmatrix},\ \tau_{jn}(w) = \begin{bmatrix} \tau^0_{jn}(w) \\ \tau^1_{jn}(w) \end{bmatrix},$$
$$\tau^l_{jn}(w) = \frac{1}{n}\sum_{i=1}^{n} K_h(W_i - w)\left(\frac{W_{ji} - w_j}{h_j}\right)^l X_{di}^{\alpha_1(2-j)} Z_{si}^{\alpha_2(j-1)} \varepsilon_i.$$

Henceforth, let $\mu_K^2 = \int K(u)u^2 du$ and $||K||_2^2 = \int K^2(r)dr$. Applying the result for the convergence of the bias term $BIAS_n$ (see Lemma 2 in appendix), and the asymptotic normality of the stochastic term $\widetilde{\tau}_n$ (see Lemma 3 in appendix), we obtain the following result. Let $\sigma_1^2(W, X_d, Z_s) = E_{|(W,X_d,Z_s)}(\varepsilon^2)$.

Theorem 1. *Under A1–A6,*

$$\sqrt{nh^{d+s-2}}\left[\widehat{\beta}_0(w) - \beta_0(w) - BIAS_\beta\right] \longrightarrow^{\mathcal{L}} N\left(0, \Sigma_\beta\right), \text{ where}$$

$$BIAS_\beta = \frac{h^2}{2}\mu_K^2 \begin{bmatrix} tr\left(D^2\beta_1(w_1)\right) + \frac{E(X_d^{\alpha_1}Z_s^{\alpha_2}|W=w)}{E(X_d^{2\alpha_1}|W=w)} tr\left(D^2\beta_2(w_2)\right) \\ tr\left(D^2\beta_2(w_2)\right) + \frac{E(X_d^{\alpha_1}Z_s^{\alpha_2}|W=w)}{E(Z_s^{2\alpha_2}|W=w)} tr\left(D^2\beta_1(w_1)\right) \end{bmatrix}, \text{ and}$$

$$\Sigma_\beta \equiv \frac{||K||_2^2}{p_W(w)} \begin{bmatrix} \frac{E(X_d^{2\alpha_1}\sigma_1^2(W,X_d,Z_s)|W=w)}{E^2(X_d^{2\alpha_1}|W=w)} & \frac{E(X_d^{\alpha_1}Z_s^{\alpha_2}\sigma_1^2(W,X_d,Z_s)|W=w)}{E(X_d^{2\alpha_1}|W=w)E(Z_s^{2\alpha_2}|W=w)} \\ \frac{E(X_d^{\alpha_1}Z_s^{\alpha_2}\sigma_1^2(W,X_d,Z_s)|W=w)}{E(X_d^{2\alpha_1}|W=w)E(Z_s^{2\alpha_2}|W=w)} & \frac{E(Z_s^{2\alpha_2}\sigma_1^2(W,X_d,Z_s)|W=w)}{E^2(Z_s^{2\alpha_2}|W=w)} \end{bmatrix}.$$

Large sample behavior of the estimated regression surface $\widehat{f}(x,z) = x_d^{\alpha_1}\widehat{\beta}_1(u) + z_s^{\alpha_2}\widehat{\beta}_2(v)$ is given by the following corollary.

Corollary 2. *Under the conditions of Theorem 1,*

$$\sqrt{nh^{d+s-2}}\left[\widehat{f}(x,z) - f(x,z) - BIAS_f\right] \longrightarrow^{\mathcal{L}} N\left(0,\ \Sigma_f\right),$$

where $BIAS_f = \frac{h^2}{2}\left[x_d^{\alpha_1}, z_s^{\alpha_2}\right]' BIAS$, *and*

$$\Sigma_f = p_W^{-1}(w)\,||K||_2^2\Big(\frac{x_d^{2\alpha_1}E(X_d^{2\alpha_1}\sigma_1^2(W,X_d,Z_s)|W=w)}{E^2(X_d^{2\alpha_1}|W=w)}$$
$$+2\frac{x_d^{\alpha_1}z_s^{\alpha_2}E(X_d^{\alpha_1}Z_s^{\alpha_2}\sigma_1^2(W,X_d,Z_s)|W=w)}{E(X_d^{2\alpha_1}|W=w)E(Z_s^{2\alpha_2}|W=w)} + \frac{z_s^{2\alpha_2}E(Z_s^{2\alpha_2}\sigma_1^2(W,X_d,Z_s)|W=w)}{E^2(Z_s^{2\alpha_2}|W=w)}\Big).$$

Note that the convergence rates in Theorem 1 and Corollary 2 are of the order $O_p(\sqrt{nh^{d+s-2}})$, which is to be expected by looking at the dimension of the kernel function employed in the smoothing. As in Fan (1992) the asymptotic bias takes a simple form. Namely, it depends only on the second derivatives of the functional form being estimated. However, the bias of $\widehat{\beta}_{10}(w)$ also depends on $D^2\beta_2(w_2)$. This is a natural extension of the result in Tripathi and Kim (1999) where the authors looked at the simpler model $Y_i = X_{di}^{\alpha_1}\beta_1(U_i) + \varepsilon_i$.

We now obtain the limiting distribution for the second step estimates in (5). Recalling the decomposition for the pilot estimates in (6), the estimation errors $\widehat{\beta}_1^*(u) - \beta_1(u)$ from the marginal integration procedure can be decomposed as $(1/n)\sum_{j=1}^n[\widehat{\beta}_{10}(u,V_j) - \beta_1(u)] = BIAS_n^*(u) + \widetilde{\tau}_n^*(u) + o_p(h_1^2) + o_p(h_2^2)$, where the bias term $BIAS_n^*(u) = \frac{1}{n}\sum_{j=1}^n e_1^T S_n^{-1}(u,V_j)B_n(u,V_j)$, and the stochastic term $\widetilde{\tau}_n^*(u) = \frac{1}{n}\sum_{j=1}^n e_1^T S_n^{-1}(u,V_j)\tau_n(u,V_j)$. The following result is proved in the appendix. Let $\sigma_2^2(W, X_d) = E_{|(W,X_d)}(\varepsilon^2)$.

Theorem 3. *Under A1-A5 and A7 it follows that:*

(i) $\sqrt{nh_1^{d-1}}\left[\widehat{\beta}_1^*(u) - \beta_1(u) - BIAS_{\beta_1}^*(u)\right] \longrightarrow^{\mathcal{L}} N\left(0,\ \Sigma_{\beta_1}^*\right),$

where $BIAS^*_{\beta_1}(u)$
$= \mu_K^2 \left[\frac{h_1^2}{2} tr\left(D^2\beta_1(u)\right) + \frac{h_2^2}{2} \int p_V(v) \frac{E(X_d^{\alpha_1} Z_s^{\alpha_2} | W=u,v)}{E(X_d^{2\alpha_1} | W=u,v)} tr\left(D^2\beta_2(v)\right) dv \right],$
$\Sigma^*_{\beta_1} = ||K||_2^2 \int \frac{p_V^2(s_2)}{p_W(u,s_2)} \frac{E(X_d^{2\alpha_1}\sigma_2^2(W,X_d)|W=(u,s_2))}{E^2(X_d^{2\alpha_1}|W=(u,s_2))} ds_2.$
(ii) $\sqrt{nh_1^{d-1}} \left[\widehat{f}_1^*(x) - f_1(x) - BIAS^*_{f_1}(x) \right] \longrightarrow^{\mathcal{L}} N\left(0,\ \Sigma^*_{f_1}\right),$
where $BIAS^*_{f_1}(x) = x_d^{\alpha_1} BIAS^*(u)$, *and* $\Sigma^*_{f_1} = x_d^{2\alpha_1} \Sigma^*_{\beta_1}$.

Theorem 3 shows that the marginally integrated pilot estimate achieves its optimal rate of convergence. A similar result holds for $\widehat{\beta}_2^*(v)$, but with a different rate $\sqrt{nh_2^{s-1}}$. If we choose a smaller bandwidth in the nuisance direction so that $h_2^2/h_1^2 \to 0$, the bias term in Theorem 3 simplifies to $BIAS^*(u) = \frac{h_1^2}{2}\mu_K^2 tr\left(D^2\beta_1(u)\right)$. Moreover, if the error term is homoscedastic, the asymptotic variance reduces to $||K||_2^{2(d-1)}\sigma_\varepsilon^2 \int \frac{p_V^2(s_2)}{p_W(u,s_2)} ds_2$. Thus, for this special case, our results coincide with the results obtained from marginal integration for unrestricted additive models. We end this section with a corollary to Theorem 4. This shows the asymptotic normality of our two-step procedure for the special case $Z_s^{\alpha_2} = 1$ and $V_{ki} = Z_{ki}$ for $k = 1,.., s$; i.e. when only the first component is homogeneous.

Corollary 4. *Under the conditions of Theorem 3,*

$$(i)\sqrt{nh_1^{d-1}} \left[\widehat{f}_1^*(x) - f_1(x) - BIAS^*_{f_1}(x) \right] \longrightarrow^{\mathcal{L}}$$
$$N\left(0,\ ||K||_2^{2(d-1)} x_d^{2\alpha_1} \int \frac{p_Z^2(z)}{p_{U,Z}(u,z)} \frac{E_{|(U=u,Z=z)}(X_d^{2\alpha_1}\sigma_2^2(U,X_d,Z))}{E^2_{|(U=u,Z=z)}(X_d^{2\alpha_1})} dz\right),$$

where

$$BIAS^*_{f_1}(u) = \mu_K^2 x_d^{\alpha_1} \times$$
$$\left[\frac{h_1^2}{2} tr\left(D^2\beta_1(u)\right) + \frac{h_2^2}{2} \int p_Z(z) \frac{E_{|(U=u,Z=z)}(X_d^{\alpha_1})}{E_{|(U=u,Z=z)}(X_d^{2\alpha_1})} tr\left(D^2\beta_2(z)\right) dz \right],$$

$$(ii)\ \sqrt{nh_2^s} \left[\widehat{f}_2^*(z) - f_2(z) - BIAS^*_{f_2}(z) \right] \longrightarrow^{\mathcal{L}}$$
$$N\left(0, ||K||_2^{2s} \int \frac{p_U^2(u)}{p_{U,Z}(u,z)} E_{|(U=u,Z=z)}\left(\sigma_2^2(U,Z,X_d)\right) du\right),$$

where

$$BIAS_{f_2}^*(u)$$
$$= \mu_K^2 \left[\frac{h_2^2}{2} tr\left(D^2\beta_2(z)\right) + \frac{h_1^2}{2} \int p_U(u)\, E_{|(U=u,Z=z)}\left(X_d^{\alpha_1}\right) tr\left(D^2\beta_1(u)\right) du \right].$$

4 Application

4.1 Setup

In this section we estimate an additively separable aggregate level production function for livestock production in Wisconsin. The data used was collected in 1987 by the Farm Credit Service of Saint Paul, Minnesota, by sampling more than 1000 farms in Wisconsin. However, we only use a subset of the original data after deleting: (*i*) farms with incomplete records, (*ii*) farms which were considered to be outliers, (*iii*) non livestock producing farms, and (*iv*) farms with at least one factor input set to zero. This leaves us with 250 observations. More details about this data set may be found in Chavas and Aliber (1993), Severance-Lossin (1994), and Severance-Lossin and Sperlich (1997). The output variable is livestock (y), while the inputs are family labor (l_1), miscellaneous inputs (e.g repairs, rent, custom hiring, supplies, insurance, gas, oil and utilities) (l_2), intermediate (i.e. with useful life of one to ten years) assets (l_3), hired labor (l_4), and animal inputs (e.g purchased feed, breeding, and veterinary services) (l_5). Since all variables are measured in dollars, what we actually have is cost and revenue data. However, assuming that the law of one price holds throughout Wisconsin, these dollar values are directly proportional to the quantities of the input factors and the output. In particular, under this assumption we can treat $(l_1, \ldots, l_5) = \tilde{l}$ measured in dollars as legitimate factors of production.

We specify the production function $f(\tilde{l})$ as being the conditional expectation of $y|\tilde{l}$. Therefore, the following canonical regression model holds:

$$y = f(\tilde{l}) + \varepsilon. \tag{7}$$

We will refer to (7) as the "unrestricted" model. Before taking a nonparametric approach, let us carry out a purely parametric analysis by assuming that f has the popular Cobb-Douglas form; i.e. $f(\tilde{l}) = A l_1^{\beta_1} l_2^{\beta_2} l_3^{\beta_3} l_4^{\beta_4} l_5^{\beta_5}$. Estimating the resulting linear model by OLS, we get $\widehat{\log y} = 1.886(0.289) + 0.063(0.020) log l_1 + 0.289(0.025) log l_2 + 0.305(0.034) log l_3 + 0.031(0.007) log l_4 + 0.277(0.023) log l_5, R^2 = 0.900$. At 1% level we failed to reject the hypothesis that $\sum_{i=1}^{5} \beta_i = 1$; i.e. we cannot reject the hypothesis of constant returns to scale under a Cobb-Douglas specification. Although this linear fit seems to be quite good, the results are susceptible to potential misspecification in the functional form for f. Additionally, since some factors of production may be "fixed", it seems reasonable to impose linear homogeneity only on those factors which are "variable."

We now relax the functional form assumption and add some structure to (7) by additively separating f into two components: f_1, which operates on the fixed factors of production; and f_2, which uses the variable factors of production. It still remains to decide which components of $\tilde{l}$ should be treated as fixed (resp. variable). Since family labor supply is quite inelastic, it seems reasonable to think of l_1 as a fixed factor. On the other hand while it may also seem reasonable to treat miscellaneous inputs and intermediate assets as fixed factors at the farm level, recall that we are interested in estimating the aggregate level production function. At the industry level these factors may well be variable. For example, at the industry level, we would expect the larger farms to employ more of the intermediate assets than the smaller farms. A simple, albeit non rigorous, way to check whether factor l_i is fixed or variable is to plot l_i/y against y. If l_i is fixed then ceteris paribus we expect the ratio l_i/y to decline with increasing y. After scaling the data so that the sample variance is one, in Figure 1 we display the estimated Nadaraya-Watson regression curves of l_i/y against y for $i = 1, \ldots, 5$. From this figure we can see that l_1/y (corresponding to family labor) is the only ratio that seems to decline with y. Therefore, we treat l_1 as the fixed (and $l_2, \ldots, l_5$ as the variable) factors at the aggregate level. So let $\tilde{l} = (\tilde{x}, \tilde{z})$, where $\tilde{x} = (l_1)$ is the vector of fixed factors and $\tilde{z} = (l_2, l_3, l_4, l_5)$ the vector of variable factors. Imposing additive separability on f in terms of $\tilde{x}$ and $\tilde{z}$, we can write $y = f_1(\tilde{x}) + f_2(\tilde{z}) + \varepsilon$. Finally, as we are treating $\tilde{z}$ as the vector of variable inputs, let us also assume that f_2 is homogeneous of degree $r = 1$. Therefore, we have that

$$y = f_1(x_1) + z_4 f_2(\frac{z_1}{z_4}, \frac{z_2}{z_4}, \frac{z_3}{z_4}, 1) + \varepsilon. \tag{8}$$

Henceforth, we will call (8) the "restricted" model. The reader should keep in mind that the restrictions of additive separability and linear homogeneity, although seemingly reasonable in our context, are merely modeling assumptions which we take as given. Furthermore, although the specification in (8) is weaker than the componentwise additive separability used in Severance-Lossin and Sperlich (1997), it does impose a strong restriction on the marginal product of family labor; namely, that it is independent of other inputs. To ensure that these restrictions allow sensible inference, we have to statistically test whether the data support the specification given in (8). However, this testing is beyond the scope of the present paper and is left for future research. For the present we confine ourselves to estimating the production relationship described by (8).

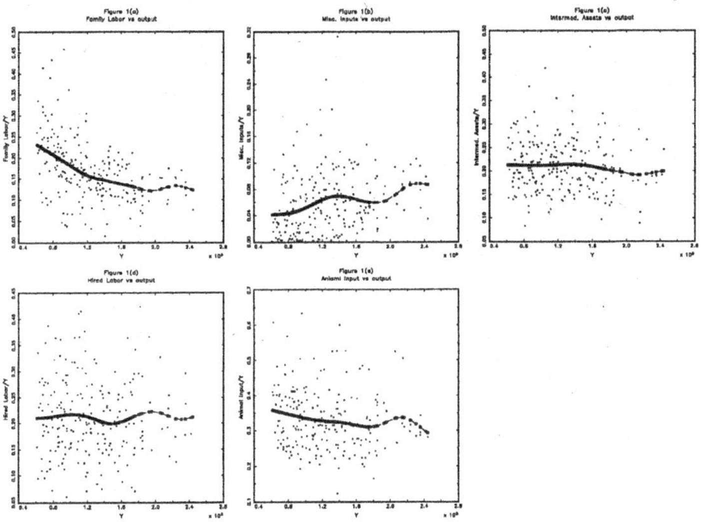

Fig. 1. Scatter plots of Input/Output Ratios and NW estimates (a)Familiy Labor (b)Misc. Inputs (c)Intermed. Asset (d)Hired Labor (e)Animal Input

4.2 Results

Although we can certainly estimate f_1, f_2, and f, due to the high dimensionality of the arguments of f_2 and f we cannot display their estimates as three dimensional surface plots. However, estimates of f_1 can certainly be displayed. In Figure 3(a) we plot the estimated f_1 versus the scaled x_1 (family labor). The same graph also displays the estimated marginal product of family labor $(df_1(x_1)/dx_1)$ against x_1. Another useful feature of a production function that economists find interesting is the elasticity of scale $e(\tilde{x}, \tilde{z})$. As defined in Varian (1992, Page 16), the elasticity of scale measures the percent increase in output due to an increase in the scale of operations (i.e. a one percent increase in all inputs). Using Euler's theorem for homogeneous functions, it is straightforward to show that: $e(\tilde{x}, \tilde{z}) = \frac{\tilde{x}'\nabla_{\tilde{x}} f_1(\tilde{x}, \tilde{z}) + r f_2(\tilde{z})}{f_1(\tilde{x}) + f_2(\tilde{z})}$ for the restricted model, while it is $\frac{\tilde{x}'\nabla_{\tilde{x}} f(\tilde{x}, \tilde{z}) + \tilde{z}'\nabla_{\tilde{z}} f(\tilde{x}, \tilde{z})}{f(\tilde{x}, \tilde{z})}$ for the unrestricted model. The presence of r in the above expression is merely for the sake of generality in case f_2 is homogeneous of degree r. For the present, since we are assuming that f_2 is linearly homogeneous, we can set $r = 1$. In Figures 2(a) and 2(b) we plot the estimated scale elasticities against the output y for the restricted and unrestricted models. Figures 2(c), 2(d), and 3(b) display the histograms of the output and family labor. These histograms show where the data is concentrated, which allows us to identify the range over which the obtained nonparametric estimates are valid.

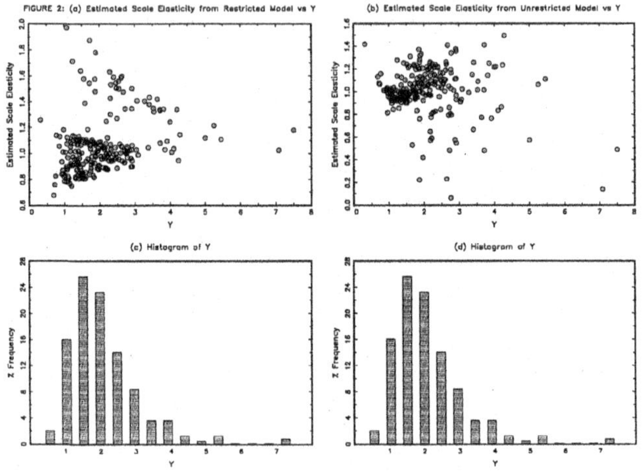

Fig. 2. Estimated Elasticities of Scale:(a)Restricted (b) Unrestricted

The procedure described in the paper was implemented in GAUSS. The data was first scaled by the sample standard deviation to have unit sample variance. A Gaussian kernel was then used to estimate f, f_1, and f_2 at each of the 250 observations. Using these estimates we calculated $e(\tilde{x}_i, \tilde{z}_i)$ for $i = 1, \ldots, 250$. Forgoing a (possibly) complicated data driven approach, the bandwidths used in the estimation procedure were simply fixed at $h_1 = n^{-\frac{1}{4+d}}, h_2 = n^{-\frac{1}{3+s}}$ for the restricted model, and $h_3 = n^{-\frac{1}{4+d+s}}$ for the unrestricted model. The optimal bandwidths which minimize the mean squared errors from estimating f_1, f_2 and f are proportional to the values we have chosen. Table 1 provides a summary description of the estimated elasticity of scale[1].

Notice that the average scale elasticity for the unrestricted model is slightly higher than $0.965 = \sum_{i=1}^{5} \hat{\beta}_i$, the value predicted by the Cobb-Douglas form. The median values of the estimated scale elasticity for the

[1] Columns 4 and 5 list the mean and median values of the estimated elasticities after discarding estimates which are more than four standard deviations away from the mean. In our case this left us with 244 observations.

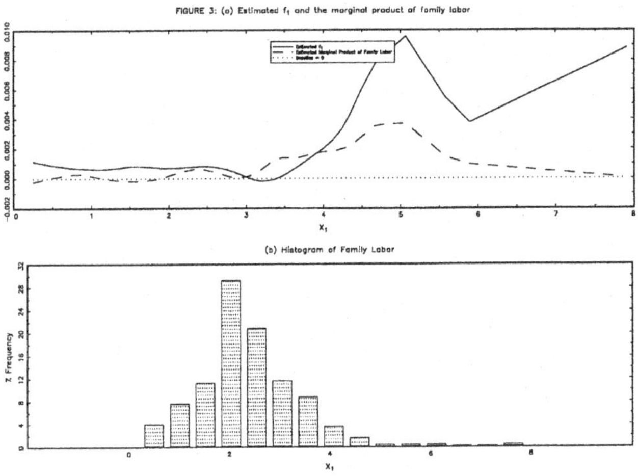

Fig. 3. Productivity of Family Labor:level(solid)and marginal(dash)

Table 1. Estimated $e(\tilde{x}, \tilde{z})$ for Wisconsin livestock data

Model	Estimated Scale Elasticity			
	Mean	Median	Mean	Median
	(full sample)		(excluding outliers)	
Restricted	1.067	1.018	1.060	1.016
Unrestricted	0.994	1.011	1.011	1.012

restricted and unrestricted models are very close. Moreover, a look at Figures 2(a) and 2(c) shows that, in the relevant range for Y, the point estimates of $e(\tilde{x}, \tilde{z})$ for the restricted and unrestricted models track one another. Although not a statistical test by any means, this is perhaps a good indication that our additive specification is a valid restriction on (7). The estimated $e(\tilde{x}_i, \tilde{z}_i)$'s seem to fluctuate around 1 with the median value being slightly greater than 1. Although it may not be possible to rule out constant returns to scale at the aggregate level, increasing returns, if present, are not very substantial. On the average this seems to indicate that larger farms enjoy economies of scale (because they tend to use more of $l_2, \ldots, l_5$ than smaller farms). This perhaps is not very surprising.

However, a feature which is not as easy to explain is the form of the estimated f_1 and the marginal product of labor. By comparing Figures 3(a) and 3(b) observe that in the relevant range for x_1 the estimated f_1 is relatively flat and then suddenly jumps up. Correspondingly, the marginal product is very close to zero (occasionally taking on negative values) and then increases rapidly. This is hard to explain since the neoclassical theory of production postulates that the production function has positive, but diminishing, marginal product. There may be two possible explanations for this effect: (*i*) Specification error; i.e. that we may have misspecified the additivity restriction in (8). However, since the elasticity estimates for the restricted and unrestricted models are very similar, perhaps this may not be as severe a problem. (*ii*) A second (more plausible) explanation for this effect may be the manner in which x_1 (family labor) enters the production process. So recall that in the data set family labor is reported in "dollar" units, and imagine a farm where some members of a family (say the children) are listed as being employed on the farm but in reality do not contribute substantially to the production process. If the price for employing family labor is calculated without taking into account the number of hours worked by each family member, more "wages" may get paid without more "work" being done. Loosely speaking, since family labor is measured in dollars, the "slack" in the number of family members employed is taken up by the price; i.e. in nominal terms the farm seems to be employing more family members which reduces the effect of adding a marginal worker. Clearly, this effect cannot persist. As the number of family members employed increases beyond a certain threshold, it will overwhelm the error caused by using the nominal wages and cause the marginal product to increase. In order to verify whether this is indeed the reason for the behavior of f_1, we would have to examine the manner in which the price for employing family labor was calculated in the data set. This, however, is beyond the scope of the present paper.

5 Conclusion

In this paper we show how to nonparametrically estimate an additive regression model when its components are homogeneous functions of known degree. The suggested procedure is easy to analyze and straightforward to implement. We use it to obtain some interesting results about livestock production in Wisconsin at the aggregate level: While there seem to be increasing returns to scale at the aggregate level, the economies of scale do not appear to be very large. The marginal product of family labor seems to be very close to zero up to a certain threshold and then increases (relatively) sharply. Possible explanations for such behavior are discussed above. Of course, a more careful empirical analysis needs to be performed if we want to claim any policy relevance for these results.

Appendix

Lemma 1. (Decomposition of Estimation Errors) *Assume that A.2 holds. Then,* $\widehat{\beta}_0(w) - \beta_0(w) = \frac{h^2}{2} BIAS_n + \widetilde{\tau}_n + o_p(h_1^2) + o_p(h_2^2)$.

Proof. First, observe that
$\widehat{\beta}_0(w) - \beta_0(w) = E^T Q^{-1} S_n^{-1}(w)\tau_n(w) + \left[E^T Q^{-1} S_n^{-1}(w) t_n^*(w) - \beta_0(w)\right]$,
where

$$\tau_n = \begin{bmatrix} \tau_{1n}(w) \\ \tau_{2n}(w) \end{bmatrix}, \; \tau_{jn}(w) = \begin{bmatrix} \tau_{jn}^0(w) \\ \tau_{jn}^1(w) \end{bmatrix},$$
$$t_n^* = \begin{bmatrix} t_1^*(w) \\ t_2^*(w) \end{bmatrix}, \; t_{jn}^*(w) = \begin{bmatrix} t^{*0}_{jn}(w) \\ t^{*1}_{jn}(w) \end{bmatrix},$$

$\tau_{jn}^l(w) = \frac{1}{n}\sum_{i=1}^n K_h\left(W_i - w\right)\left(\frac{W_{ji}-w_j}{h_j}\right)^l X_{di}^{\alpha_1(2-j)} Z_{si}^{\alpha_2(j-1)}\varepsilon_i$,
$t_{jn}^{*l}(w) = \frac{1}{n}\sum_{i=1}^n K_h\left(W_i - w\right)\left(\frac{W_{ji}-w_j}{h_j}\right)^l X_{di}^{\alpha_1(2-j)} Z_{si}^{\alpha_2(j-1)}[X_{di}^{\alpha_1}\beta_1\left(U_i\right)$
$+ Z_{si}^{\alpha_2}\beta_2\left(V_i\right)]$. Using Taylor Expansion, we can show that

$$\begin{aligned} t_n^* &= \frac{1}{n}\sum_{i=1}^n K_h\left(W_i - w\right)\left[X_{di}^{\alpha_1}\beta_1\left(U_i\right) + Z_{si}^{\alpha_2}\beta_2\left(V_i\right)\right] \\ &\quad \times \left[X_{di}^{\alpha_1}, X_{di}^{\alpha_1}(\frac{W_{1i}-w_1}{h_j})^T, Z_{di}^{\alpha_1}, Z_{si}^{\alpha_2}(\frac{W_{2i}-w_2}{h_j})^T\right]^T \\ &= S_n Q\beta\left(w\right) + B_n + o_p\left(h_1^2\right) + o_p(h_2^2), \end{aligned}$$

where

$$B_n = \frac{1}{n}\sum_{i=1}^n K_h\left(W_i - w\right)\left[X_{di}^{\alpha_1}, X_{di}^{\alpha_1}(\frac{W_{1i}-w_1}{h_1})^T, Z_{di}^{\alpha_1}, Z_{si}^{\alpha_2}(\frac{W_{2i}-w_2}{h_2})^T\right]^T$$
$$\left\{\sum_{j=1}^2 \frac{h_j^2}{2} X_{di}^{\alpha_1(2-j)} Z_{si}^{\alpha_2(j-1)}\left[\left(\frac{W_{ji}-w_j}{h_j}\right)^T D^2\beta_j(w_j)\left(\frac{W_{ji}-w_j}{h_j}\right)\right]\right\}.$$

The last equality comes from

$$\begin{aligned} &\sum_{j=1}^2 X_{di}^{\alpha_1(2-j)} Z_{si}^{\alpha_2(j-1)}\left[\beta_j(w_j) + h_j\left(\frac{W_{ji}-w_j}{h_j}\right)^T D\beta_j(w_j)\right] \\ &= \left[X_{di}^{\alpha_1}, X_{di}^{\alpha_1}\left(\frac{W_{1i}-w_1}{h_1}\right)^T, Z_{di}^{\alpha_1}, Z_{si}^{\alpha_2}\left(\frac{W_{2i}-w_2}{h_2}\right)^T\right] Q \times \\ &\quad \left[\beta_1(w_1), D\beta_1(w_1), \beta_2(w_2), D\beta_2(w_2)\right]^T, \end{aligned}$$

and

$$\frac{1}{n}\sum_{i=1}^{n} K_h(W_i - w)\left[X_{di}^{\alpha_1}, X_{di}^{\alpha_1}\left(\frac{W_{1i}-w_1}{h_1}\right)^T, Z_{di}^{\alpha_1}, Z_{si}^{\alpha_2}\left(\frac{W_{2i}-w_2}{h_2}\right)^T\right]^T$$

$$\sum_{j=1}^{2} X_{di}^{\alpha_1(2-j)} Z_{si}^{\alpha_2(j-1)}\left[\beta_j(w_j) + h_j\left(\frac{W_{ji}-w_j}{h_j}\right)^T D\beta_j(w_j)\right]$$

$$= S_n Q\left[\beta_1(w_1), D\beta_1(w_1), \beta_2(w_2), D\beta_2(w_2)\right]^T = S_n Q\beta(w).$$

Thus, $Q^{-1}S_n^{-1}(z)t_n^*(z) - \beta(w) = Q^{-1}S_n^{-1}(w)B_n + o_p(h_1^2) + o_p(h_2^2)$, which proves the lemma.

Let $E_{|w}(\cdot)$ denote $E_{|W=w}(\cdot)$.

Lemma 2. (Convergence of S_n, B_n, Bias) *Assume that A1–A6 hold. Then,*

(i) $S_n(w) \longrightarrow^p p_W(w)\begin{pmatrix} M_{1+d}E\left(X_d^{2\alpha_1}|W=w\right) & 0_{(1+d)\times(1+s)} \\ 0_{(1+s)\times(1+d)} & M_{1+s}E\left(Z_s^{2\alpha_2}|W=w\right)\end{pmatrix}$,

(ii) $B_n \longrightarrow^p \frac{h^2}{2}p_W(w)\times$

$$\begin{bmatrix} E_{|w}(X_d^{2\alpha_1})vech'\left(\mu_K^2 I_d\right) & E_{|w}\left(X_d^{\alpha_1}Z_s^{\alpha_2}\right)vech'\left(\mu_K^2 I_s\right) \\ E_{|w}(X_d^{2\alpha_1})\int K(s_1)\, s_1 vech'(s_1 s_1')ds_1 & 0 \\ E_{|w}\left(X_d^{\alpha_1}Z_s^{\alpha_2}\right)vech'\left(\mu_K^2 I_d\right) & E_{|w}(Z_s^{2\alpha_2})vech'\left(\mu_K^2 I_s\right) \\ 0 & E_{|w}(Z_s^{2\alpha_2})\int K(s_2)\, s_2 vech'(s_2 s_2')ds_2 \end{bmatrix}$$

$$\times\begin{bmatrix} vech\left(D^2\beta_1(w_1)\right) \\ vech\left(D^2\beta_2(w_2)\right)\end{bmatrix},$$

where $M_{1+d} = \begin{bmatrix} 1 & 0_d \\ 0_d & \mu_K^2 I_d\end{bmatrix}$.

(iii) $BIAS_n \longrightarrow^p \dfrac{h^2}{2}\mu_K^2$

$$\begin{bmatrix} tr\left(D^2\beta_1(w_1)\right) + tr\left(D^2\beta_2(w_2)\right)E_{|W=w}\left(X_d^{\alpha_1}Z_s^{\alpha_2}\right)/E_{|W=w}(X_d^{2\alpha_1}) \\ tr\left(D^2\beta_2(w_2)\right) + tr\left(D^2\beta_1(w_1)\right)E_{|W=w}\left(X_d^{\alpha_1}Z_s^{\alpha_2}\right)/E_{|W=w}(Z_s^{2\alpha_2})\end{bmatrix}$$

Proof. (i) Under A1–A5, applying a WLLN for i.i.d observations shows that $s_{jk}^{lm}(w) = \frac{1}{n}\sum_{i=1}^{n}\varphi_i - E\{\varphi_i\} = o_p(1)$, where

$$\varphi_i = K_h(W_i - w)\left(\frac{W_{ji}-w_j}{h}\right)^l\left(\left(\frac{W_{ki}-w_k}{h}\right)^m\right)^T X_{di}^{\alpha_1(4-j-k)} Z_{si}^{\alpha_2(j+k-2)}.$$

By the dominated convergence theorem, the expectation of φ_i converges to

$$\left(\int K(s)\, s_j^l\,(s_k^m)^T ds\right)p_W(w)\, E\left(X_{di}^{\alpha_1(4-j-k)}Z_{si}^{\alpha_2(j+k-2)}|W=w\right).$$

Thus, $S_n(w) \to^p p_W(w)\begin{pmatrix} M_{1+d}E\left(X_d^{2\alpha_1}|W=w\right) & 0_{(1+d)\times(1+s)} \\ 0_{(1+s)\times(1+d)} & M_{1+s}E\left(Z_s^{2\alpha_2}|W=w\right)\end{pmatrix}$,

where $M_{1+d} = \begin{bmatrix} 1 & 0_d \\ 0_d & \mu_K^2 I_d\end{bmatrix}$.

(ii) Using the similar argument, we can show that, when $h_1 = h_2 = h$, B_n converges in probability to
$\frac{h^2}{2} \int K(s) \left[r_1^{\alpha_1}, r_1^{\alpha_1} s_1^T, r_2^{\alpha_2}, r_2^{\alpha_2} s_2^T\right]^T \sum_{j=1}^2 r_1^{\alpha_1(2-j)} r_2^{\alpha_2(j-1)} s_j^T D^2\beta_j(w_j) s_j ds$
$\times\, p_{W,X_d,Z_s}(w, r_1, r_2)\, dr$. By straightforward algebra,

$$\int K(s)\, r_k^{\alpha_k} \left\{ \sum_{j=1}^{2} r_1^{\alpha_1(2-j)} r_2^{\alpha_2(j-1)} \left[s_j^T D^2\beta_j(w_j) s_j\right] \right\} ds$$

$$= r_k^{\alpha_k} \sum_{j=1}^{2} r_1^{\alpha_1(2-j)} r_2^{\alpha_2(j-1)} vech^T\left(\mu_K^2 I_{d_j}\right) vech\left(D^2\beta_j(w_j)\right).$$

Since $\int K(s)\, r_k^{\alpha_k} s_k^T r_1^{\alpha_1(2-j)} r_2^{\alpha_2(j-1)} \left[s_j^T D^2\beta_j(w_j) s_j\right] ds = 0, for j \neq k$, it follows that

$$\int K(s)\, r_k^{\alpha_k} s_k^T \left\{ \sum_{j=1}^{2} r_1^{\alpha_1(2-j)} r_2^{\alpha_2(j-1)} \left[s_j^T D^2\beta_j(w_j) s_j\right] \right\} ds$$

$$= r_k^{\alpha_k} r_1^{\alpha_1(2-k)} r_2^{\alpha_2(k-1)} \left[\int K_k(s_k)\, s_k^T vech^T(s_k s_k^T) ds_k\right] vech\left(D^2\beta_k(w_k)\right).$$

Therefore, for $k = 1, 2$,

$$B_{kn} = \begin{bmatrix} B_{kn}^0 \\ B_{kn}^1 \end{bmatrix} \longrightarrow^p \frac{h^2}{2} \begin{bmatrix} \sum_{j=1}^2 \psi_{kj} [vech^T\left(\mu_K^2 I_{d_j}\right) vech\left(D^2\beta_j(w_j)\right)] \\ \psi_{kk} \int K(s_k)\, s_k vech^T(s_k s_k^T) ds_k vech(D^2\beta_k(w_k)) \end{bmatrix},$$

where $\psi_{kj} = \int r_k^{\alpha_k} r_1^{\alpha_1(2-j)} r_2^{\alpha_2(j-1)} p_{W,X_d,Z_s}(w, r_1, r_2)\, dr$. That is,

$$B_{1n}^0 \rightarrow^p \frac{h^2}{2} p_W(w) \{E_{|w}\left(X_d^{2\alpha_2}\right) \left[vech^T\left(\mu_K^2 I_d\right) vech\left(D^2\beta_1(w_1)\right)\right]$$
$$+ E_{|w}\left(X_d^{\alpha_1} Z_s^{\alpha_2}\right) \left[vech^T\left(\mu_K^2 I_s\right) vech\left(D^2\beta_2(w_2)\right)\right]\},$$
$$B_{1n}^1 \rightarrow^p \frac{h^2}{2} p_W(w)\, E_{|w}(X_d^{2\alpha_2}) \int K_1(s_1)\, s_1 vech^T(s_1 s_1^T) ds_1 vech\left(D^2\beta_1(w_1)\right),$$

which proves (ii).

(iii) is straightforward from (i) and (ii).

Lemma 3. *Assume that A1–A6 hold. Then,*

(i) (Asymptotic Normality of $\sqrt{nh^{d+s-2}}\left[\tau_{1n}^0(w), \tau_{2n}^0(w)\right]^T$)
$\sqrt{nh^{d-1}}\tau_n(w) \longrightarrow^{\mathcal{L}} N\left(0,\ p_W(w)\, ||K||_2^2 \Sigma_\tau\right)$,
where

$$\Sigma_\tau = \begin{bmatrix} E_{|w}(X_d^{2\alpha_1} \sigma_1^2(W, X_d, Z_s)) & E_{|w}\left(X_d^{\alpha_1} Z_s^{\alpha_2} \sigma_1^2(W, X_d, Z_s)\right) \\ E_{|w}\left(X_d^{\alpha_1} Z_s^{\alpha_2} \sigma_1^2(W, X_d, Z_s)\right) & E_{|w}(Z_s^{2\alpha_2} \sigma_1^2(W, X_d, Z_s)) \end{bmatrix}.$$

(ii) (Asymptotic Normality of the main stochastic term $\widetilde{\tau}_n$)

$$Q\sqrt{nh^{d+s-2}}\widetilde{\tau}_n \longrightarrow^{\mathcal{L}} N\left(0,\ p_W^{-1}(w)\,||K||_2^2\Sigma_{\widetilde{\tau}}\right),$$

where

$$\Sigma_{\widetilde{\tau}} = \begin{bmatrix} \frac{E_{|w}(X_d^{2\alpha_1}\sigma_1^2(W,X_d,Z_s))}{E_{|w}^2(X_d^{2\alpha_1})} & \frac{E_{|w}(X_d^{\alpha_1}Z_s^{\alpha_2}\sigma_1^2(W,X_d,Z_s))}{E_{|w}(X_d^{2\alpha_1})E(Z_s^{2\alpha_2})} \\ \frac{E_{|w}(X_d^{\alpha_1}Z_s^{\alpha_2}\sigma_1^2(W,X_d,Z_s))}{E_{|w}(X_d^{2\alpha_1})E_{|w}(Z_s^{2\alpha_2})} & \frac{E_{|w}(Z_s^{2\alpha_2}\sigma_1^2(W,X_d,Z_s))}{E_{|w}^2(Z_s^{2\alpha_2})} \end{bmatrix}.$$

Proof. When deriving the asymptotic distribution of $E^TQ^{-1}S_n^{-1}(w)\tau_n(w)$ we only consider $\left[\tau_{1n}^0(w), \tau_{2n}^0(w)\right]$ from the result (Lemma 2) concerning the convergence of $E^TQ^{-1}S_n^{-1}(w)$, i.e.,

$$E^TQ^{-1}S_n^{-1}(w) \longrightarrow^p P_W^{-1}(w)\begin{pmatrix} E_{|w}(X_d^{2\alpha_1})^{-1} & 0_{1\times d} & 0 & 0_{1\times s} \\ 0 & 0_{1\times d} & E_{|w}(Z_s^{2\alpha_2})^{-1} & 0_{1\times s} \end{pmatrix}.$$

(i) To calculate the variance of $\left[\tau_{1n}^0(w), \tau_{2n}^0(w)\right]^T$, we use the iterative law of expectation with the argument of changing variables.

$$\begin{aligned} &Var\left(\sqrt{nh^{d+s-2}}\left[\tau_{1n}^0(w), \tau_{2n}^0(w)\right]'\right) \\ &= \frac{1}{h^{d+s-2}}E\left(K^2\left[(W-w)/h\right]\begin{bmatrix} X_d^{2\alpha_1} & X_d^{\alpha_1}Z_{si}^{\alpha_2} \\ X_d^{\alpha_1}Z_s^{\alpha_2} & Z_{di}^{2\alpha_2}\end{bmatrix} E_{|(W,X_d,Z_s)}(\varepsilon^2)\right) \\ &\simeq ||K||_2^2\int\begin{bmatrix} r_1^{2\alpha_1} & r_1^{\alpha_1}r_2^{\alpha_2} \\ r_1^{\alpha_1}r_2^{\alpha_2} & r_2^{2\alpha_2}\end{bmatrix}\sigma_1^2(W,r_1,r_2)\,p_{W,X_d,Z_s}(w,r_1,r_2)\,dr_1dr_2 \\ &= p_W(w)\,||K||_2^2\Sigma_\tau. \end{aligned}$$

Under A1–A5, the Lindeberg condition is satisfied when K has bounded support. Now, (i) follows from the Lindeberg CLT.

(ii) is clear from the Slutsky Theorem and the results in Lemma 2 and Lemma 3(i).

Proof (Theorem 1 and Corollary 2). The proof of Theorem 1 is obvious from Lemma 3. Corollary 2 is also a consequence of Lemma 3 upon noting that
$[x_d^{\alpha_1}, z_s^{\alpha_2}]\,[\widehat{\beta}_0(w) - \beta_0(w) - BIAS] = \widehat{f}(x) - f(x) - BIAS_f$.

Proof (Theorem 3). If we use the uniform convergence result proved in Lemma 4.2 of Yang, Härdle, and Nielsen (1999), the first part of Lemma 2 holds uniformly in w with an approximation error of $O_p(\ln n/\sqrt{nh_1^{(d-1)}h_2^{(s-1)}} + \max(h_1,h_2))$, under assumption A.7. Now, applying the same argument again in Lemma 4.3 of Yang, Härdle, and Nielsen (1999), we can show that

$$BIAS_n^*(u) = \frac{1}{n}\sum_{j=1}^n e_1^TS^{-1}(u,V_j)B_n(u,V_j)\left(1+o_p(1)\right),$$

$$\widetilde{\tau}_n^*(u) = \frac{1}{n}\sum_{j=1}^n e_1^TS^{-1}(u,V_j)\tau_n(u,V_j)(1+o_p(1)),$$

where S is given from Lemma 2 above.

(ia) Bias term:
Since $e_1^T S^{-1}(u, V_j) = p_W^{-1}(u, V_j) E_{|(u,V_j)}(X_d^{2\alpha_1})^{-1} e_1^T$, we only consider the probability limit of $(1/n)\sum_{j=1}^n p_W^{-1}(u, V_j) E_{|(u,V_j)}(X_d^{2\alpha_1})^{-1} e_1^T B_n(u, V_j)$ as the asymptotic bias, $BIAS^*(u)$. Using Lemma 1, we have

$$
\begin{aligned}
&(1/n)\sum_{j=1}^n p_W^{-1}(u, V_j) E_{|(u,V_j)}(X_d^{2\alpha_1})^{-1} e_1^T B_n(u, V_j) \\
&= \frac{h_1^2}{2}\frac{1}{n}\sum_{i=1}^n K_{h_1}(U_i - u) X_{di}^{\alpha_1}[\frac{1}{n}\sum_{j=1}^n p_W^{-1}(u, V_j) E_{|(u,V_j)}(X_d^{2\alpha_1})^{-1} K_{h_2}(V_i - V_j)] \\
&\times X_{di}^{\alpha_1}\left(\frac{U_i - u}{h_1}\right)^T D^2\beta_1(u)\left(\frac{U_i - u}{h_1}\right) + \frac{h_2^2}{2}\times \\
&\frac{1}{n}\sum_{i=1}^n K_{h_1}(U_i - u) X_{di}^{\alpha_1} Z_{si}^{\alpha_2}\{\frac{1}{n}\sum_{j=1}^n p_W^{-1}(u, V_j) E_{|(u,V_j)}(X_d^{2\alpha_1})^{-1} K_{h_2}(V_i - V_j) \\
&\times \left[\left(\frac{V_i - V_j}{h_2}\right)^T D^2\beta_2(V_j)\left(\frac{V_i - V_j}{h_2}\right)\right]\}.
\end{aligned}
$$

Since

$$
\begin{aligned}
&\frac{1}{n}\sum_{j=1}^n p_W^{-1}(u, V_j) E\left(X_d^{2\alpha_1}|W = (u, V_j)\right)^{-1} K_{h_2}(V_i - V_j) \\
&= p_V(V_i) p_W^{-1}(u, V_j) E\left(X_d^{2\alpha_1}|W = (u, V_j)\right)^{-1}(1 + o_p(1)),
\end{aligned}
$$

the first term of the bias converges in probability,

$$
\begin{aligned}
&\frac{1}{n}\sum_{i=1}^n K_{h_1}(U_i - u) X_{di}^{2\alpha_1}\frac{p_V(V_i)}{p_W(u, V_i) E_{|(u,V_i)}(X_d^{2\alpha_1})} \\
&\times \left(\frac{U_i - u}{h_1}\right)^T D^2\beta_1(u)\left(\frac{U_i - u}{h_1}\right) \\
&\to^p \int K_1(s_1) r_1^{2\alpha_1}\frac{p_V(s_2)}{p_W(u, s_2) E_{|(u,s_2)}(X_d^{2\alpha_1})}\left[s_1^T D^2\beta_1(u) s_1\right]\times \\
&\quad p_{W,X_d}(u, s_2, r_1)\, ds dr_1,
\end{aligned}
$$

which is simplified as

$$
\begin{aligned}
&vech^T\left(\mu_K^2 I_d\right) vech\left(D^2\beta_1(u)\right)\times \\
&\int \frac{p_V(s_2)}{E_{|(u,s_2)}(X_d^{2\alpha_1})}\left(\int r_1^{2\alpha_1} p_{X_d|W}(r_1|u, s_2,)\, dr_1\right) ds_2 \\
&= vech^T\left(\mu_K^2 I_d\right) vech\left(D^2\beta_1(u)\right).
\end{aligned}
$$

In a similar way, we can show that the second term converges to $\int \frac{E_{|(u,s_2)}(X_d^{\alpha_1} Z_s^{\alpha_2})}{E_{|(u,s_2)}(X_d^{2\alpha_1})} vech^T\left(\mu_K^2 I_s\right) vech\left(D^2\beta_2\left(s_2\right)\right)) p_V(s_2) ds_2$.
Thus, the bias term is

$$\mu_K^2\left[\frac{h_1^2}{2} tr\left(D^2\beta_1(u)\right) + \frac{h_2^2}{2}\int p_V\left(v\right)\frac{E_{|(u,v)}(X_d^{\alpha_1} Z_s^{\alpha_2})}{E_{|(u,v)}(X_d^{2\alpha_1})} tr\left(D^2\beta_2(v)\right) dv\right].$$

(ib) Asymptotic Normality of the Stochastic term:

From $e_1^T S^{-1}(u, V_j) = p_W^{-1}(u, V_j) E_{|(u,V_j)}^{-1}(X_d^{2\alpha_1}) e_1^T$, we have only to consider the asymptotic distribution of $(1/n)\sum_{j=1}^n \frac{e_1^T \tau_n(u,V_j)}{p_W(u,V_j) E_{|(u,V_j)}(X_d^{2\alpha_1})}$. Note that the above can be written as

$$\frac{1}{n}\sum_{j=1}^{n} p_W^{-1}(u, V_j) E_{|(u,V_j)}(X_d^{2\alpha_1})^{-1}\frac{1}{n}\sum_{i=1}^{n} K_{1h}\left(U_i - u\right) K_{2h}(V_i - V_j)\, X_{di}^{\alpha_1}\varepsilon_i$$
$$= \frac{1}{n}\sum_{i=1}^{n} K_{1h}(U_i - u) X_{di}^{\alpha_1}\frac{p_V(V_i)}{p_W(u, V_i) E_{|(u,V_i)}(X_d^{2\alpha_1})}\varepsilon_i\left(1 + o_p\left(1\right)\right).$$

The variance of this term is

$$Var\left(\sqrt{nh^{d-1}}\tau_n^*\right)$$
$$= \frac{1}{h^{d-1}} E\left(K_1^2\left[\left(U - u\right)/h\right] X_d^{2\alpha_1}\frac{p_V^2(V)}{p_W^2(u, V) E_{|(u,V)}^2(X_d^{2\alpha_1})}\sigma_2^2\left(W, X_d\right)\right)$$
$$\simeq ||K||_2^{2(d-1)}\int \frac{p_V^2(s_2)}{p_W(u, s_2)}\frac{E_{|(u,s_2)}(X_d^{2\alpha_1}\sigma_2^2\left(W, X_d\right))}{E_{|(u,s_2)}^2(X_d^{2\alpha_1})} ds_2,$$

where $\sigma_2^2\left(W, X_d\right) = E\left(\varepsilon^2 | W, X_d\right)$. Now, the standard argument of Lindeberg Central Limit Theorem gives the results. The proof of (ii) is immediate from (i).

References

1. Chavas, J.P., and M. Aliber (1993) An Analysis of economic Efficiency in Agriculture: A Nonparametric Approach. Journal of Agricultural and Resource Economics **18**, 1-16
2. Chen, R. (1997) Functional Coefficient Autoregressive Models: Estimation and Tests of Hypotheses. SFB 373, Humboldt University, Discussion Paper
3. Chen, R. and R. Tsay. (1993) Functional-Coefficient Autoregressive Models. Journal of the American Statistical Association **88**, 298-308

4. Deaton, A. and J. Muellbauer. (1980) Economics and Consumer Behavior. Cambridge. University Press, Cambridge
5. Fan, J. (1992) Design-adaptive nonparametric regression. J. Am. Statist Soc. **82**, 998-1004
6. Ghysels, E., E. Renault, O. Torres, and, V. Patilea. (1998) Non-parametic Methods and Option Pricing, in Statistics in Finance edited by D. Hand and S. Jacka, Arnold, Great Britain
7. Hastie, T. and Tibshirani, R. (1990) Generalized Additive Models. Chapman and Hall, London.
8. Hastie, T., and R. Tibshirani. (1993) Varying-Coefficient Models, J. R. Statist. Soc. B. **55**, No. 4, 757-796
9. Hildenbrand, W. (1994) Market Demand: Theory and Empirical Evidence. Princeton University Press
10. Linton, O. and W. Härdle (1996) Estimating additive regression models with known links. Biometrika **83**, 529-540.
11. Linton, O. and J. Nielsen. (1995) A kernel method of estimating structured nonparametric regression based on marginal integration. Biometrika **82**, 93-100.
12. Newey, W.K. (1994) Kernel estimation of partial means. Econometric Theory **10**, 233-253.
13. Severance-Lossin, E. (1994) Nonparametric Hypothesis Testing of Production Assertions Using data with Random Shocks. Ph.D. Thesis, dept. of Agricultural Economics, University of Wisconsin-Madison
14. Severance-Lossin, E., and S. Sperlich. (1997) Estimation of Derivatives for Additive Separable Models. Discussion paper #30. Quantification and Simulation Ökonomischer Prozesse, Humboldt-Universität zu Belrin
15. Stone, C.J. (1985) Additive regression and other nonparametric models. Ann. Statist. **13**, 685-705
16. Tjøstheim, D., and Auestad, B. (1994) Nonparametric identification of nonlinear time series: projections. J. Am. Stat. Assoc. **89**, 1398-1409
17. Tripathi G., and W. Kim. (2000). Nonparametric Estimation of Homogeneous Functions. SFB 373, Humboldt University, Discussion Paper
18. Varian, H.R. (1992) Microeconomic Analysis W. Norton and Company. 3rd edn
19. Yang, L., W. Härdle, and J. Nielsen. (1999) Nonparametric Autoregression with Multiplicative Volatility and Additive Mean. Journal of Time Series Analysis **20**(5), 579-604

A Reinforcement Procedure Leading to Correlated Equilibrium*

Sergiu Hart[1] and Andreu Mas-Colell[2]

[1] Center for Rationality and Interactive Decision Theory; Department of Mathematics; and Department of Economics, The Hebrew University of Jerusalem, Feldman Building, Givat-Ram, 91904 Jerusalem, Israel
[2] Department of Economics and Business and CREI, Universitat Pompeu Fabra, Ramon Trias Fargas 25-27, 08005 Barcelona, Spain

Abstract. We consider repeated games where at any period each player knows only his set of actions and the stream of payoffs that he has received in the past. He knows neither his own payoff function, nor the characteristics of the other players (how many there are, their strategies and payoffs). In this context, we present an adaptive procedure for play — called "modified-regret-matching" — which is interpretable as a stimulus-response or reinforcement procedure, and which has the property that any limit point of the empirical distribution of play is a correlated equilibrium of the stage game.

1 Introduction

Werner Hildenbrand has repeatedly emphasized the usefulness, conceptual and technical, of carrying out equilibrium analysis by means of distributional notions. For social situations modelled as N-person games, the concept of correlated equilibrium, an extension of Nash equilibrium introduced by Aumann, can be viewed in a most natural way as imposing equilibrium conditions on the distribution of action combinations of the different players. Correlated equilibrium will be the subject of the current paper, and the style of our analysis should not surprise anybody familiar with Hildenbrand's research.

This paper continues the study of Hart and Mas-Colell [2000], where the notion of correlated equilibrium and that of approachability by means of simple "rules of thumb" or "adaptive procedures" of play were linked. We showed there that if a game is repeatedly played and the players determine their stage probabilities of play according to a procedure called "regret-matching," then the empirical distribution of play converges with probability one to the set

* Dedicated with great admiration to Werner Hildenbrand on his 65th birthday. Previous versions of these results were included in the Center for Rationality Discussion Papers #126 (December 1996) and #166 (March 1998). We thank Dean Foster for suggesting the use of "modified regrets." The research is partially supported by grants of the Israel Academy of Sciences and Humanities; the Spanish Ministry of Education; the Generalitat de Catalunya; CREI; and the EU-TMR Research Network.

of correlated equilibria of the given game. *Regret-matching* means that if at period t player i has taken action j, then the probability of playing another action k at time $t+1$ will be proportional to the "regret for not having played k instead of j," which is defined simply as the increase, if any, in the average payoff that would result if all past plays of action j were replaced by action k (and everything else remained unaltered).

The implementation of regret-matching by a player requires that player to observe the actions taken by *all* players in the past. But that is not all. The player should also be able to carry out the thought experiment of computing what his payoffs would have been, had his actions in the past been different from what they really were. For this he needs to know what game he is playing (or, at the very least, his own payoff function).

In this paper we will show that this level of sophistication and knowledge is not really necessary to obtain correlated equilibria. We shall modify the regret-matching procedure in such a way that the play probabilities are determined from the *actual realizations only.* Specifically, each player only needs to know the payoffs he received in past periods. He need not know the game he is playing — neither his own payoff function nor the others players' payoffs; in fact, he may well be oblivious of the fact that there is a game at all. The procedure that we shall examine is a "stimulus-response" or "reinforcement" procedure, in the sense that a relatively high payoff at period t will tend to increase the probability of playing at period $t+1$ the same action that was played at t.

In Section 2 we present the basic model and state our results. Section 3 contains some further discussions, and the proofs are given in Section 4.

To summarize: We consider repeated games where each player knows only his set of available choices (but nothing about the other players), and observes only his own actually realized payoffs. We exhibit simple strategies of play whereby the long-run frequencies of the various action combinations being played are tantamount to a correlated equilibrium. Of course, this sophisticated "macro"-picture that emerges cannot be seen at the individual level. This is a conclusion, we trust, with which Werner Hildenbrand can truly sympathize.

2 Model and results

We consider finite N-person games in strategic (or "normal") form. The set of players is a finite set N, the action[1] set of each player $i \in N$ is a finite set S^i, and the payoff function of i is $u^i : S \to \mathbb{R}$, where[2] $S := \prod_{\ell \in N} S^\ell$. We will denote this game $\langle N, (S^i)_{i \in N}, (u^i)_{i \in N} \rangle$ by Γ.

[1] To avoid confusion, we will use the term "action" for the one-shot game, and "strategy" for the multi-stage game.

[2] $\mathbb{R}$ denotes the real line.

A correlated equilibrium — a concept introduced by Aumann [1974] — is nothing other than a Nash equilibrium where each player may receive a private signal before the game is played (the signals do not affect the payoffs; and the players may base their choices on the signals received). This may be equivalently described as follows: Assume that the signal of each player i is in fact a "play recommendation" $s^i \in S^i$, where the N-tuple $s = (s^i)_{i \in N}$ is selected (by a "device" or "mediator") according to a commonly known probability distribution. A correlated equilibrium results if each player realizes that the best he can do is to follow the recommendation, provided that all the other players do likewise.

Equivalently, a probability distribution ψ on the set S of action N-tuples (i.e., $\psi(s) \geq 0$ for all $s \in S$ and $\sum_{s \in S} \psi(s) = 1$) is a *correlated equilibrium* of the game Γ if, for every player $i \in N$ and every two actions $j, k \in S^i$ of i, we have

$$\sum_{s \in S : s^i = j} \psi(s) \left(u^i \left(k, s^{-i} \right) - u^i(s) \right) \leq 0, \tag{1}$$

where $s^{-i} \in S^{-i} := \prod_{\ell \neq i} S^{\ell}$ denotes the action combination of all players except i (thus $s = \left(s^i, s^{-i}\right)$). The inequality (1) (after dividing the expression there by $\sum_{s \in S : s^i = j} \psi(s)$) means that when the recommendation to player i is to choose action j, then choosing k instead of j cannot yield a higher expected payoff to i. Finally, a *correlated ε-equilibrium* obtains when 0 is replaced by ε on the right-hand side of (1).

Now assume that the game Γ is played repeatedly in discrete time $t = 1, 2, \ldots$. Denote by $s_t^i \in S^i$ the (realized) choice of player i at time t, and put $s_t = (s_t^i)_{i \in N} \in S$. The payoff of player i in period t is denoted $U_t^i := u^i(s_t)$.

The basic setup of this paper assumes that the information of each player i consists just of his set of available choices S^i. He does not know the game Γ; in fact, he does not know how many players there are besides himself,[3] what their choices are and what the payoff functions (his own as well as the others') are. The only thing player i observes is his own realized payoffs and actions. That is, in determining his play probabilities at time $t+1$, player i's information consists of his own realized payoffs $U_1^i, U_2^i, \ldots, U_t^i$ in the previous t periods, as well as his actual actions $s_1^i, s_2^i, \ldots, s_t^i$ there.

In Hart and Mas-Colell [2000] — henceforth [HM]— we introduced *regret-matching procedures*. These are simple adaptive strategies where the play probabilities are proportional to the "regrets" for not having played other actions. Specifically, for any two distinct actions $j \neq k$ in S^i and every time t, the *regret* of i at t from j to k is

$$R_t^i(j, k) := \left[D_t^i(j, k) \right]^+ \equiv \max \left\{ D_t^i(j, k), 0 \right\}, \tag{2}$$

[3] Perhaps none: it could be a game against Nature.

where

$$D_t^i(j,k) := \frac{1}{t} \sum_{\tau \le t: s_\tau^i = j} \left(u^i\left(k, s_\tau^{-i}\right) - u^i\left(s_\tau\right) \right). \tag{3}$$

This is the change in the average payoff of i that would have resulted if he had played action k every time in the past that he actually chose j. Rewriting this as

$$D_t^i(j,k) = \frac{1}{t} \sum_{\tau \le t: s_\tau^i = j} u^i\left(k, s_\tau^{-i}\right) - \frac{1}{t} \sum_{\tau \le t: s_\tau^i = j} u^i\left(s_\tau\right)$$

shows that player i can compute the second term: it is just $(1/t) \sum_{\tau \le t: s_\tau^i = j} U_\tau^i$. But i cannot compute the first term, since he knows neither his own payoff function u^i nor the choices s_τ^{-i} of the other players.

Therefore we replace the first term by an "estimate" that can be computed on the basis of the available information; namely, we define

$$C_t^i(j,k) := \frac{1}{t} \sum_{\tau \le t: s_\tau^i = k} \frac{p_\tau^i(j)}{p_\tau^i(k)} U_\tau^i - \frac{1}{t} \sum_{\tau \le t: s_\tau^i = j} U_\tau^i, \tag{4}$$

where p_τ^i denotes the play probabilities at time t (thus $p_\tau^i(j)$ is the probability that i chose j at period τ); these probabilities p_τ^i are defined below (they will indeed depend only on $U_1^i, ..., U_t^i$). As in (2), the *modified regrets* are then

$$Q_t^i(j,k) := \left[C_t^i(j,k)\right]^+ \equiv \max\left\{C_t^i(j,k), 0\right\}. \tag{5}$$

In words, the modified regret for not having used k instead of j measures the difference (strictly speaking, its positive part) of the average payoff over the periods when k was used and the periods when j was used. In addition, the payoffs of these periods are normalized in a manner that, intuitively speaking, makes the length of the respective periods comparable.[4]

Next we define the play probabilities, based on these modified regrets. Recall the regret-matching procedure of [HM]: If $j := s_t^i$ is the action chosen by i at time t, then the probability of switching at time $t+1$ to another action $k \neq j$ is proportional (with a fixed factor $1/\mu$) to the regret from j to k; with the remaining probability, the same action j is chosen again. Here we shall make two changes relative to [HM]. First, we need to guarantee that the sum of the proposed probabilities does not exceed one; multiplying the modified regrets by a factor $1/\mu$ (which we still do) does not suffice

[4] For instance, if the probability of k being chosen is always twice that of j, then in the long run k will be played twice as often as j. So, in order to compare the sum of the payoffs over those periods when j is played with the parallel sum when k is played, one needs to multiply the k-sum by $1/2$. When the probabilities change over time, Formula (4) uses the correct normalization: the difference between the regrets and the modified regrets has conditional expectation equal to 0 (see Step 10(i) and the Proof of Step 11(iii) in Section 4).

because the modified regrets are not bounded.[5] Second, we need every action to be played with some minimal frequency.[6] Thus we shall require that the transitions "tremble" over every action.

Let therefore $\mu > 0$ be a sufficiently large number; as in [HM], it suffices to take μ so that $\mu > 2M^i(m^i - 1)$ for all i, where $m^i := |S^i|$ is[7] the number of actions of i, and M^i is an upper bound on $|u^i(s)|$ for all $s \in S$. Let $0 < \delta < 1$, and define the play probabilities of player i at time $t+1$ by

$$\begin{aligned} p_{t+1}^i(k) &:= (1-\delta)\min\left\{\frac{1}{\mu}Q_t^i(j,k), \frac{1}{m^i - 1}\right\} + \delta\frac{1}{m^i}, \text{ for } k \neq j; \text{ and} \\ p_{t+1}^i(j) &:= 1 - \sum_{k \in S^i : k \neq j} p_{t+1}^i(k), \end{aligned} \tag{6}$$

where $j := s_t^i$ is the choice of i in (the previous) period t. As for the first period, the play probabilities at $t = 1$ are given by an arbitrary strictly positive vector $p_1^i \in \Delta(S^i)$; for simplicity, assume that $p_1^i(j) \geq \delta/m^i$ for all j in S^i.

Formula (6) says that p_{t+1}^i is a weighted average of two probability vectors (note that $p_{t+1}^i(j) = (1-\delta)\left(1 - \sum_{k \neq j}\min\left\{Q_t^i(j,k)/\mu, 1/(m^i - 1)\right\}\right) + \delta/m^i$). The first, with weight $1-\delta$, is given by the modified regrets in a manner similar to [HM, Formula (2.2)] (note that taking the minimum with $1/(m^i - 1)$ guarantees that the resulting sum does not exceed 1). The second term, with weight δ, is just the uniform distribution over S^i: each $k \in S^i$ has equal probability $1/m^i$. This "uniform tremble" guarantees that all probabilities at time $t+1$ are at least $\delta/m^i > 0$.

Putting (4), (5) and (6) together implies that p_{t+1}^i depends only on the previously realized payoffs $U_1^i, ..., U_t^i$ and play probabilities $p_1^i, ..., p_t^i$. Therefore, by recursion, p_{t+1}^i does indeed depend only on $U_1^i, ..., U_t^i$.

Let[8] $z_t \in \Delta(S)$ be the empirical distribution of play up to t; that is, for every $s \in S$,

$$z_t(s) := \frac{1}{t}\left|\{\tau \leq t : s_\tau = s\}\right|$$

is the relative frequency that the N-tuple of actions s has been played in the first t stages.

---

[5] Notice that there is no *a priori* lower bound on the probabilities appearing in the denominators.

[6] Roughly speaking, one needs this exogenous statistical "noise" to be able to estimate the contingent payoffs using only the realized payoffs (recall the first term in the modified regret). In fact, this is quite delicate, since the actions of the other players are never observed.

[7] We write $|A|$ for the number of elements of a finite set A.

[8] We write $\Delta(A) := \left\{p \in \mathbb{R}_+^A : \sum_{a \in A} p(a) = 1\right\}$ for the set of probability distributions over the finite set A.

Our first result is:

Theorem 1. *For every $\varepsilon > 0$ there is a $\delta_0 \equiv \delta_0(\varepsilon) > 0$ such that for all $\delta < \delta_0$, if every player i plays according to adaptive procedure (6), then the empirical distributions of play z_t converge almost surely as $t \to \infty$ to the set of correlated ε-equilibria of the game Γ.*

Thus: for almost every trajectory, z_t is close to a correlated ε-equilibrium for all large enough t; equivalently, z_t is a correlated 2ε-equilibrium from some time on (this time may depend on the trajectory; the theorem states that, with probability one, it is finite). As in the Main Theorem of [HM], note that the convergence is not to a *point*, but to a *set*; that is, the distance to the set goes to 0. Finally, we remark that both μ and δ can be taken to be different for different players.

To obtain in the limit correlated equilibria — rather than correlated *approximate* equilibria — we need δ to decrease to 0 as t increases. A simple way to do this is to replace δ in (6) by δ/t^γ, where γ is a number strictly between 0 and[9] 1/4. Thus, we now define

$$p_{t+1}^i(k) := \left(1 - \frac{\delta}{t^\gamma}\right) \min\left\{\frac{1}{\mu} Q_t^i(j,k), \frac{1}{m^i - 1}\right\} + \frac{\delta}{t^\gamma}\frac{1}{m^i}, \quad \text{for } k \neq j; \text{ and}$$

$$p_{t+1}^i(j) := 1 - \sum_{k \in S^i : k \neq j} p_{t+1}^i(k), \tag{7}$$

where, again, $j := s_t^i$ is the choice of i in period t. At $t = 1$, let p_1^i be an arbitrary vector in $\Delta(S^i)$ with $p_1^i(j) \geq \delta/m^i$ for all j in S^i. The second result is:

Theorem 2. *If every player i plays according to adaptive procedure (7), then the empirical distributions of play z_t converge almost surely as $t \to \infty$ to the set of correlated equilibria of the game Γ.*

We have chosen the particular type of sequence $\delta_t := \delta/t^\gamma$ for simplicity and convenience only. What matters is, first, that δ_t converge to 0, and second, that it do so sufficiently slowly (otherwise the modified regrets C_t^i may become too large; recall that the probabilities p_t^i, which are bounded from below by δ_{t-1}/m^i, appear in the denominators). This explains the need for an upper bound on γ (it turns out that $\gamma < 1/4$ suffices; see the proof in Section 4). Moreover, we note that one may well take different sequences δ_t^i for different players i (cf. the Remark at the end of Section 4).

[9] The reason for this restriction will be explained below.

3 Discussion

(a) Reinforcement and stimulus-response

The play procedures of this paper can be interpreted as "reinforcement" or "stimulus-response" procedures (see, for example, Bush and Mosteller [1955], Roth and Erev [1995], Borgers and Sarin [1995], Erev and Roth [1998], Fudenberg and Levine [1998, Section 4.8]). Indeed, the behavior of our players is very far from the ideal of a sophisticated decision-maker that makes optimal decisions given his (more or less well-formed) beliefs about the environment. The behavior we postulate is, in fact, much closer to the model of a reflex-oriented individual that, from a very limited conception of the world in which he lives, simply reacts to stimuli by reinforcing those behaviors with "pleasurable" consequences.

In order to be specific and to illustrate the above point further, let us assume that the payoffs are positive and focus on the limit case of our procedure where probabilities are chosen in exact proportion to the modified regrets (5). Suppose that player i has played action j at period t. We then have for every $k \neq j$:

- if $Q_t^i(j,k) > 0$ then $Q_{t+1}^i(j,k) < Q_t^i(j,k)$; and
- if $Q_t^i(j,k) = 0$ then $Q_{t+1}^i(j,k) = 0$.

Thus all the modified regrets decrease (or stay null) from t to $t+1$. Hence the probability of choosing j at $t+1$ gets "reinforced" (i.e., increases relative to the same probability at t) by the occurrence of j at t, while the probabilities of the other actions $k \neq j$ decrease. Moreover, as can easily be seen from Definitions (4) and (5), the higher the payoff obtained at time t (when j was played), the greater this reinforcement. Finally, all these effects decrease with time — since we average over t in (4).

(b) Related work

There is by now a substantive body of work on not fully optimal behavior in repeated games (see for instance the book of Fudenberg and Levine [1998]). In particular, strategies that lead to the set of correlated equilibria have been proposed by Foster and Vohra [1997] and by Fudenberg and Levine [1999]. There is also an older tradition, beginning with Hannan [1957], that focuses on another form of regrets (of an "unconditional" kind — see (c) below) and on strategies that asymptotically take them down to zero. Clearly, our work (here and in Hart and Mas-Colell [2000, 2001]) belongs to these lines of research. Since the main difference between [HM] and the current paper is that here the players do not know the game, we want to point out that this "unknown game case" has already been studied. Specifically, in the context of Hannan regrets, see Foster and Vohra [1993, 1998], Auer *et al.* [1995] and Fudenberg and Levine [1998, Section 4.8] (and also Baños [1968] and Megiddo [1980] for related work).

(c) Hannan-consistency

We say that a strategy of a player is *Hannan-consistent* if it guarantees that his long-run average payoff is as large as the highest payoff that can be obtained by playing a constant action; that is, it is no less than the one-shot best-reply payoff against the empirical distribution of play of the other players. Formally, the *Hannan regret* of player i at time t for action $k \in S^i$ is defined as

$$DH_t^i(k) := \frac{1}{t}\sum_{\tau=1}^{t} u^i(k, s_\tau^{-i}) - \frac{1}{t}\sum_{\tau=1}^{t} U_\tau^i = u^i(k, z_t^{-i}) - \frac{1}{t}\sum_{\tau=1}^{t} U_\tau^i,$$

where $z_t^{-i} \in \Delta(S^{-i})$ is the empirical distribution of the actions chosen by the other players in the past.[10,11] A strategy of player i is then called *Hannan-consistent* if, as t increases, all Hannan-regrets are guaranteed to become almost surely non-positive in the limit, no matter what the other players do; that is, with probability one, $\limsup_{t\to\infty} DH_t^i(k) \leq 0$ for all $k \in S^i$. The reader is referred to Hart and Mas-Colell [2001] for detailed discussions and results.

In the setup of the current paper, the "modified-regret-matching" approach leads to a simple reinforcement strategy that is Hannan-consistent (recall [HM, Theorem B]): For every $k \in S^i$ define

$$CH_t^i(k) := \frac{1}{t}\sum_{\tau \leq t : s_\tau^i = k} \frac{1}{p_\tau^i(k)} U_\tau^i - \frac{1}{t}\sum_{\tau=1}^{t} U_\tau^i,$$

and

$$p_{t+1}^i(k) := (1-\delta_t)\frac{\left[CH_t^i(k)\right]_+}{\sum_{j\in S^i}\left[CH_t^i(j)\right]_+} + \delta_t \frac{1}{m^i}. \tag{8}$$

Here $\delta_t = \delta/t^\gamma$ for some $\delta > 0$ and $0 < \gamma < 1/2$; we take $p_{t+1} \in \Delta(S^i)$ to be arbitrary for $t = 0$ and whenever the denominator vanishes. We have

Theorem 3. *The strategy (8) is Hannan-consistent.*

The proof of this theorem is parallel to, and simpler than, the proof of Theorem 2 below, and therefore omitted.

---

[10] I.e., $z_t^{-i}(s^{-i}) := \left|\{\tau \leq t : s_\tau^{-i} = s^{-i}\}\right| / t$ for each $s^{-i} \in S^{-i}$.

[11] Note that $DH_t^i(k) = \sum_{j \neq k} D_t^i(j,k)$; we can thus refer to $DH_t^i(k)$ as the "unconditional regret for k," and to $D_t^i(j,k)$ as the "regret for k, conditional on j."

4 Proof

In this section we will prove Theorems 1 and 2 of Section 2 together. Let

$$\delta_t := \frac{\delta}{t^\gamma}$$

where $\delta > 0$ and $0 \leq \gamma < 1/4$. For Theorem 1 take $\gamma = 0$, and for Theorem 2, $\gamma > 0$.

We introduce some notations, in addition to those of the previous sections. Fix player i in N; for simplicity, we drop reference to the index i whenever this does not create confusion (thus we write C_t instead of C_t^i, and so on). Recall that $m := \left|S^i\right|$ is the number of strategies of i, and M is an upper bound on the payoffs: $M \geq \left|u^i(s)\right|$ for all $s \in S$. Denote $L := \left\{(j,k) \in S^i \times S^i : j \neq k\right\}$; then $\mathbb{R}^L$ is the $m(m-1)$ Euclidean space with coordinates indexed by L.

For each $t = 1, 2, ...$ and each (j,k) in L, denote[12]

$$\begin{aligned} Z_t(j,k) &:= \frac{p_t^i(j)}{p_t^i(k)} \mathbf{1}_{\{s_t^i = k\}} - \mathbf{1}_{\{s_t^i = j\}}; \\ B_t(j,k) &:= Z_t(j,k)\, u^i(s_t); \\ A_t(j,k) &:= \mathbf{1}_{\{s_t^i = j\}} \left(u^i\left(k, s_t^{-i}\right) - u^i(s_t)\right). \end{aligned}$$

Thus, we have

$$C_t(j,k) = \frac{1}{t} \sum_{\tau \leq t} B_\tau(j,k) \text{ and}$$

$$D_t(j,k) = \frac{1}{t} \sum_{\tau \leq t} A_\tau(j,k).$$

We shall write B_t for the vector $(B_t(j,k))_{(j,k)\in L} \in \mathbb{R}^L$; and similarly for the other vectors A_t, C_t, and so on. Next, define

$$\Pi_t(j,k) := \begin{cases} (1-\delta_t)\min\left\{\frac{1}{\mu}C_t^+(j,k), \frac{1}{m-1}\right\} + \delta_t \frac{1}{m}, & \text{if } k \neq j, \\ (1-\delta_t)\left(1 - \sum\limits_{k' \neq j} \min\left\{\frac{1}{\mu}C_t^+(j,k'), \frac{1}{m-1}\right\}\right) + \delta_t \frac{1}{m}, & \text{if } k = j. \end{cases}$$

Note that $\Pi_t(j,\cdot) \in \Delta\left(S^i\right)$ for all $j \in S^i$; thus Π_t is a transition probability matrix on S^i. Both procedures (6) and (7) satisfy $p_{t+1}^i(k) = \Pi_t\left(s_t^i, k\right)$ for all k (where, again, $\gamma = 0$ corresponds to (6) and $\gamma > 0$ to (7)). Let

$$\rho_t := \left(\text{dist}\left(C_t, \mathbb{R}_-^L\right)\right)^2 \equiv \sum_{j \neq k} \left(C_t^+(j,k)\right)^2$$

[12] We write $\mathbf{1}_E$ for the *indicator* of the event E (i.e., $\mathbf{1}_E = 1$ if E occurs and $= 0$ otherwise).

be the squared Euclidean distance (in $\mathbb{R}^L$) of the vector C_t from the non-positive orthant $\mathbb{R}^L_-$.

We will use the standard "**O**" notation: For two real-valued functions $f(\cdot)$ and $g(\cdot)$ defined on a domain X, we take "$f(x) = \mathbf{O}(g(x))$" to mean that there exists a constant $K < \infty$ such that $|f(x)| \leq Kg(x)$ for all x in X. From now on, t, v, w will denote positive integers; $h_t = (s_\tau)_{\tau \leq t}$ will be histories of length t; j, k, and s^i will be strategies of i (i.e., elements of S^i); s and s^{-i} will be elements of S and S^{-i}, respectively. Unless stated otherwise, all statements should be understood to hold "for all t, v, h_t, j, k, etc."; where histories h_t are concerned, only those that occur with positive probability are considered. Finally, **P** stands for Probability, **E** for Expectation and **Var** for Variance.

The proof of Theorems 1 and 2 will be divided into 14 steps. Step 14 shows that the regrets are "small" in the limit; the Proposition of Section 3 of [HM] then implies that the empirical distributions are correlated approximate equilibria. We note that Steps 1–11 hold for *any* non-increasing sequence $\delta_t > 0$, whereas Steps 12–14 make use of the special form $\delta_t = \delta/t^\gamma$. A guide to the proof follows the statement of the steps.

- **Step 1:**

$$\text{(i)}\ \mathbf{E}\left[(t+v)^2 \rho_{t+v} \mid h_t\right] \leq t^2 \rho_t + 2t \sum_{w=1}^{v} C_t^+ \cdot \mathbf{E}\left[B_{t+w} \mid h_t\right] + \mathbf{O}\left(\frac{v^2}{\delta_{t+v}^2}\right).$$

$$\text{(ii)}\ (t+v)^2 \rho_{t+v} - t^2 \rho_t = \mathbf{O}\left(\frac{tv + v^2}{\delta_{t+v}^2}\right).$$

Define[13]

$$\beta_{t+w}(j) := \sum_{k \neq j} \frac{1}{\mu} C_t^+(k,j)\, p_{t+w}^i(k) - \sum_{k \neq j} \frac{1}{\mu} C_t^+(j,k)\, p_{t+w}^i(j).$$

- **Step 2:**

$$C_t^+ \cdot \mathbf{E}\left[B_{t+w} \mid h_t\right] = \mu \mathbf{E}\left[\sum_{j \in S^i} u^i\left(j, s_{t+w}^{-i}\right) \beta_{t+w}(j) \mid h_t\right].$$

- **Step 3:**

$$\text{(i)}\ C_{t+v}(j,k) - C_t(j,k) = \mathbf{O}\left(\frac{v}{t\delta_{t+v}}\right).$$

$$\text{(ii)}\ \Pi_{t+v}(j,k) - \Pi_t(j,k) = \mathbf{O}\left(\frac{v}{t\delta_{t+v}} + (\delta_t - \delta_{t+v})\right).$$

---

[13] Note that $\beta_{t+w}(j)$ is measurable with respect to h_{t+w} (actually, it depends only on h_{t+w-1} and s_{t+w}^{-i}, but not on s_{t+w}^i).

Define

$$\overline{Z}_t(j,k) := \frac{1}{t}\sum_{\tau=1}^{t} Z_\tau(j,k); \text{ and}$$

$$Y_t := \sum_{(j,k)\in L} \left|\overline{Z}_t(j,k)\right|.$$

- **Step 4:**

$$\Pi_t(j,k) - \frac{1}{\mu}C_t^+(j,k) = \mathbf{O}(\delta_t + Y_t) \text{ for all } j \neq k.$$

- **Step 5:**[14]

$$C_t^+ \cdot \mathbf{E}[B_{t+w} \mid h_t] = \mu\mathbf{E}\left[\sum_{j\in S^i} u^i(j, s_{t+w}^{-i})\left((\Pi_t)^2 - \Pi_t\right)(s_{t+w-1}^i, j) \mid h_t\right] + \mathbf{O}\left(\delta_t + Y_t + \frac{w}{t\delta_{t+w}}\right).$$

For each $t > 0$ and each history h_t, we define an auxiliary stochastic process $(\hat{s}_{t+w})_{w=0,1,2,\ldots}$ with values in S as follows: The initial state is $\hat{s}_t = s_t$, and the transition probabilities are[15]

$$\mathbf{P}[\hat{s}_{t+w} = s \mid \hat{s}_t, \ldots, \hat{s}_{t+w-1}] := \prod_{\ell\in N} \Pi_t^\ell(\hat{s}_{t+w-1}^\ell, s^\ell).$$

That is, the $\hat{s}$-process is stationary: It uses the transition probabilities of period t at each period $t+1, t+2, \ldots, t+w, \ldots$.

- **Step 6:**

$$\mathbf{P}[s_{t+w} = s \mid h_t] - \mathbf{P}[\hat{s}_{t+w} = s \mid h_t] = \mathbf{O}\left(\frac{w^2}{t\delta_{t+w}} + w(\delta_t - \delta_{t+w})\right).$$

- **Step 7:**

$$C_t^+ \cdot \mathbf{E}[B_{t+w} \mid h_t] = \mu\mathbf{E}\left[\sum_{j\in S^i} u^i(j, \hat{s}_{t+w}^{-i})\left((\Pi_t)^2 - \Pi_t\right)(\hat{s}_{t+w-1}^i, j) \mid h_t\right] + \mathbf{O}\left(\delta_t + Y_t + \frac{w^2}{t\delta_{t+w}} + w(\delta_t - \delta_{t+w})\right).$$

14 $(\Pi_t)^2$ is the second power of the matrix Π_t (i.e., $\Pi_t\Pi_t$), and $\left((\Pi_t)^2 - \Pi_t\right)(k,j)$ is the (k,j)-element of the matrix $(\Pi_t)^2 - \Pi_t$.

15 We write Π_t^ℓ for the transition probability matrix of player ℓ (thus Π_t is Π_t^i).

• **Step 8:**

$$\mathbf{E}\left[\sum_{j\in S^i} u^i\left(j,\hat{s}_{t+w}^{-i}\right)\left(\left(\Pi_t\right)^2-\Pi_t\right)\left(\hat{s}_{t+w-1}^i,j\right)\mid h_t\right]$$

$$=\sum_{s^{-i}\in S^{-i}} \mathbf{P}\left[\hat{s}_{t+w}^{-i}=s^{-i}\mid h_t\right]\left(\left(\Pi_t\right)^{w+1}-\left(\Pi_t\right)^{w}\right)\left(s_t^i,j\right)=\mathbf{O}\left(\frac{1}{\sqrt{w}}\right)$$

• **Step 9:**

$$\mathbf{E}\left[(t+v)^2\rho_{t+v}\mid h_t\right]\leq$$

$$t^2\rho_t+\mathbf{O}\left(tv\delta_t+tvY_t+\frac{v^3}{\delta_{t+v}}+tv^2\left(\delta_t-\delta_{t+v}\right)+t\sqrt{v}+\frac{v^2}{\delta_{t+v}^2}\right).$$

• **Step 10:**

$$\text{(i)}\quad \mathbf{E}\left[Z_t(j,k)\mid h_{t-1}\right]=0.$$
$$\text{(ii)}\quad \mathbf{Var}\left[Z_t(j,k)\right]=\mathbf{O}\left(\frac{1}{\delta_t}\right).$$

• **Step 11:**

$$\text{(i)}\quad \lim_{t\to\infty}\overline{Z}_t(j,k)=0 \text{ a.s.}$$
$$\text{(ii)}\quad \lim_{t\to\infty}Y_t=0 \text{ a.s.}$$
$$\text{(iii)}\quad \lim_{t\to\infty}\left(C_t(j,k)-D_t(j,k)\right)=0 \text{ a.s.}$$

Let ξ satisfy[16]

$$1<\xi<\min\left\{\frac{2}{1+\gamma},\frac{1}{4\gamma}\right\}; \tag{9}$$

such a ξ exists since $0\leq\gamma<1/4$. For each $n=1,2,...$, let $t_n:=\left\lfloor n^{\xi}\right\rfloor$ be the largest integer not exceeding n^{ξ}.

• **Step 12:** There exists $\eta<2\xi-1$ such that

$$\mathbf{E}\left[t_{n+1}^2\rho_{t_{n+1}}\mid h_{t_n}\right]\leq t_n^2\rho_{t_n}+\mathbf{O}\left(\delta n^{2\xi-\xi\gamma-1}+Y_{t_n}n^{2\xi-1}+n^{\eta}\right).$$

• **Step 13:**

$$\text{(i)}\quad \text{If } \gamma=0 \text{ then } \limsup_{n\to\infty}\rho_{t_n}=\mathbf{O}(\delta) \text{ a.s.}$$
$$\text{(ii)}\quad \text{If } \gamma>0 \text{ then } \lim_{n\to\infty}\rho_{t_n}=0 \text{ a.s.}$$

[16] When $\gamma=0$, (9) is $1<\xi<2$.

- **Step 14:**

$$\text{(i) If } \gamma = 0 \text{ then } \limsup_{t\to\infty} R_t(j,k) = \mathbf{O}\left(\sqrt{\delta}\right) \text{ a.s.}$$

$$\text{(ii) If } \gamma > 0 \text{ then } \lim_{t\to\infty} R_t(j,k) = 0 \text{ a.s.}$$

We now provide a short intuitive overview of the steps of the proof. The proof is based on the Proof of the Main Theorem of [HM] (see Steps M1–M11 in the Appendix there) — which in turn is inspired by the Approachability Theorem of Blackwell [1956] — with a number of additional steps needed to take care of the modifications. Most of the proof is devoted to showing that the modified regrets $Q_t \equiv C_t^+$ are small. From this one readily gets in Step 14 that the actual regrets $R_t \equiv D_t^+$ are also small, since the difference $C_t - D_t$ is a martingale converging almost surely to 0 (see Step 11(iii)). The main steps in the proof are as follows: We start with the basic recursion equation in Step 1(i) (similar to [HM, Step M1(i)]). Next, we estimate the "middle term" on the right-hand side of 1(i) by approximating the s-process with the $\hat{s}$-process, which is independent across players (Steps 2–7; parallel to [HM, Steps M2–M6]). This leads to a formula similar to [HM, Formula (3.4)], except that the invariant distribution q_λ in [HM, (3.4b)] is replaced here by the transitions after w and $w+1$ periods, which are close to one another (Step 8; compare with [HM, Step M7]). Finally, we obtain the recursion formula in Step 9. On comparing this formula with the parallel one in [HM, Step M8], we see that in Step 9 there are additional terms; one of them, which comes about because the modified regrets are not bounded, contains a random variable Y_t. Step 10, Step 11 and the Proof of Step 13 show that this term also goes to zero. Steps 12 and 13 complete the proof for the modified regrets, in a manner that is similar to [HM, Steps M9–M11] (though more complicated, partly because of the Y_t terms). As we have indicated above, Step 14 yields the needed result for the actual regrets.

We now proceed to the proofs of Steps 1–14.

- Proof of Step 1: Because $C_t^- \in \mathbb{R}_-^L$ we have

$$\rho_{t+v} \le \left\|C_{t+w} - C_t^-\right\|^2 = \left\|\frac{t}{t+v}C_t + \frac{1}{t+v}\sum_{w=1}^{v} B_{t+w} - C_t^-\right\|^2$$

$$= \frac{t^2}{(t+v)^2}\left\|C_t - C_t^-\right\|^2 + \frac{2t}{(t+v)^2}\sum_{w=1}^{v}\left(B_{t+w} - C_t^-\right)\cdot\left(C_t - C_t^-\right)$$

$$+ \frac{v^2}{(t+v)^2}\left\|\frac{1}{v}\sum_{w=1}^{v} B_{t+w} - C_t^-\right\|^2$$

$$\le \frac{t^2}{(t+v)^2}\rho_t + \frac{2t}{(t+v)^2}\sum_{w=1}^{v} B_{t+w}\cdot C_t^+ + \frac{v^2}{(t+v)^2}m(m-1)\frac{4M^2m^2}{\delta_{t+v}^2}.$$

Indeed: For the second term, note that $C_t^- \cdot (C_t - C_t^-) = C_t^- \cdot C_t^+ = 0$. As for the third term, we have $|u^i(s)| \leq M$ and $|Z_{t+w}(j,k)| \leq m/\delta_{t+w} \leq m/\delta_{t+v}$ for $w \leq v$ (since the sequence δ_t is non-increasing); therefore $B_{t+w}(j,k)$ and $C_t(j,k)$ are each bounded by $2Mm/\delta_{t+v}$. This yields (ii). To get (i), take the conditional expectation given h_t (thus ρ_t and C_t are fixed). □

• PROOF OF STEP 2: Note that $B_{t+w}(j,k)$ vanishes except when $s_{t+w}^i = j, k$. We condition on h_{t+w-1} and s_{t+w}^{-i} (i.e., on the whole history h_{t+w} *except* player i's choice at time $t+w$):

$$\begin{aligned}
&\mathbf{E}\left[B_{t+w}(j,k) \mid h_{t+w-1}, s_{t+w}^{-i} = s^{-i}\right] \\
&\quad = p_{t+w}^i(k) \frac{p_{t+w}^i(j)}{p_{t+w}^i(k)} u^i(k, s^{-i}) - p_{t+w}^i(j) u^i(j, s^{-i}) \\
&\quad = p_{t+w}^i(j) \left(u^i(k, s^{-i}) - u^i(j, s^{-i})\right)
\end{aligned}$$

Hence

$$\begin{aligned}
&C_t^+ \cdot \mathbf{E}\left[B_{t+w} \mid h_{t+w-1}, s_{t+w}^{-i} = s^{-i}\right] \\
&\quad = \sum_j \sum_{k \neq j} C_t^+(j,k) p_{t+w}^i(j) \left(u^i(k, s^{-i}) - u^i(j, s^{-i})\right) \\
&\quad = \sum_j u^i(j, s^{-i}) \left(\sum_{k \neq j} C_t^+(k,j) p_{t+w}^i(k) - \sum_{k \neq j} C_t^+(j,k) p_{t+w}^i(j)\right)
\end{aligned}$$

(we have collected together all terms containing $u^i(j, s^{-i})$). Conditioning now on h_t yields the result. □

• PROOF OF STEP 3: We have

$$(t+v)\left|C_{t+v}(j,k) - C_t(j,k)\right| \leq \sum_{w=1}^{v} \left|B_{t+w}(j,k) - C_t(j,k)\right|.$$

Since both $B_{t+w}(j,k)$ and $C_t(j,k)$ are $\mathbf{O}(1/\delta_{t+v})$, we get $C_{t+v}(j,k) - C_t(j,k) = \mathbf{O}(v/(t\delta_{t+v}))$. For $j \neq k$, the difference between $\Pi_{t+v}(j,k)$ and $\Pi_t(j,k)$ is therefore at most $(1-\delta_t)\mathbf{O}(v/(t\delta_{t+v})) + (\delta_t - \delta_{t+v})/(m-1)$. For $j = k$, it is at most $m-1$ times this amount. □

• PROOF OF STEP 4: We distinguish two cases. First, when $(1/\mu) C_t^+(j,k) \leq 1/(m-1)$, we have

$$\Pi_t(j,k) - \frac{1}{\mu} C_t^+(j,k) = \delta_t \left(\frac{1}{m} - \frac{1}{\mu} C_t^+(j,k)\right),$$

and this is $\mathbf{O}(\delta_t)$ (it lies between 0 and δ_t/m).

Second, when $(1/\mu)\, C_t^+(j,k) \geq 1/(m-1)$, we have

$$\Pi_t(j,k) = \frac{1-\delta_t}{m-1} + \frac{\delta_t}{m} \leq \frac{1}{m-1} \leq \frac{1}{\mu} C_t^+(j,k).$$

For the opposite inequality, note that $|Z_\tau(j,k)| \leq 2 + Z_\tau(j,k)$ (since the only possible negative value of $Z_\tau(j,k)$ is -1), thus

$$\begin{aligned}
\frac{1}{\mu} C_t^+(j,k) &\leq \frac{1}{\mu} |C_t(j,k)| \leq \frac{1}{\mu t} \sum_{\tau=1}^{t} |Z_\tau(j,k)| \left|u^i(s_\tau)\right| \\
&\leq \frac{2M}{\mu} + \frac{M}{\mu} \overline{Z}_t(j,k) < \frac{1}{m-1} + \frac{M}{\mu} \overline{Z}_t(j,k) \\
&= \Pi_t(j,k) + \frac{\delta_t}{m(m-1)} + \frac{M}{\mu} \overline{Z}_t(j,k)
\end{aligned}$$

(recall that $\mu > 2M(m-1)$). □

- Proof of Step 5: Denote s_{t+w-1}^i by r; then

$$\beta_{t+w}(j) = \sum_{k \neq j} \frac{1}{\mu} C_t^+(k,j)\, \Pi_{t+w-1}(r,k) - \sum_{k \neq j} \frac{1}{\mu} C_t^+(j,k)\, \Pi_{t+w-1}(r,j).$$

Also,

$$\begin{aligned}
\left((\Pi_t)^2 - \Pi_t\right)(r,j) &= (\Pi_t)^2(r,j) - \Pi_t(r,j) \\
&= \sum_{k \in S^i} \Pi_t(k,j)\, \Pi_t(r,k) - \Pi_t(r,j) \sum_{k \in S^i} \Pi_t(j,k) \\
&= \sum_{k \neq j} \Pi_t(k,j)\, \Pi_t(r,k) - \sum_{k \neq j} \Pi_t(j,k)\, \Pi_t(r,j)
\end{aligned}$$

(we have subtracted the j-term from both sums). Comparing the last expression with $\beta_{t+w}(j)$, we see that $\left((\Pi_t)^2 - \Pi_t\right)(r,j)$ is obtained by replacing each C_t^+/μ and each Π_{t+w-1} in $\beta_{t+w}(j)$ by Π_t. Thus

$$\begin{aligned}
\beta_{t+w}(j) - \left((\Pi_t)^2 - \Pi_t\right)(r,j) &= \sum_{k \neq j} \left(\frac{1}{\mu} C_t^+(k,j) - \Pi_t(k,j)\right) \Pi_{t+w-1}(r,k) \\
&\quad + \sum_{k \neq j} \Pi_t(k,j) \left(\Pi_{t+w-1}(r,k) - \Pi_t(r,k)\right) \\
&\quad - \sum_{k \neq j} \left(\frac{1}{\mu} C_t^+(j,k) - \Pi_t(j,k)\right) \times \\
&\quad \times \Pi_{t+w-1}(r,j) \\
&\quad - \sum_{k \neq j} \Pi_t(j,k) \left(\Pi_{t+w-1}(r,j) - \Pi_t(r,j)\right) \\
&= \mathbf{O}\left(\delta_t + Y_t + \frac{w}{t\delta_{t+w}}\right),
\end{aligned}$$

by the estimates of Steps 3(ii) and 4. It only remains to substitute this into the formula of Step 2. □

• PROOF OF STEP 6: We use the Lemma of [HM, Step M4], which implies that if the 1-step transition probabilities of two Markov processes on S differ by at most β, then the w-step transition probabilities differ by at most $|S|\, w\beta$. Applying this to the $\hat{s}$- and s-processes, with β given by Step 3(ii), yields the result. □

• PROOF OF STEP 7: Replacing $(s_{t+w})_w$ by $(\hat{s}_{t+w})_w$ in the formula of Step 5 gives an additional error that is estimated in Step 6 (note that the two processes $(s_{t+w})_w$ and $(\hat{s}_{t+w})_w$ start from the same history h_t). □

• PROOF OF STEP 8: Given h_t, the random variables $\hat{s}^{-i}_{t+w}$ and $\hat{s}^{i}_{t+w-1}$ are independent, since the transition probabilities of the $\hat{s}$-process are all determined at time t, and the players randomize independently. Hence:

$$\begin{aligned}
&\mathbf{E}\left[\sum_{j\in S^i} u^i\left(j, \hat{s}^{-i}_{t+w}\right)\left((\Pi_t)^2 - \Pi_t\right)\left(\hat{s}^i_{t+w-1}, j\right) \mid h_t\right] \\
&= \sum_{s^{-i}\in S^{-i}} \mathbf{P}\left[\hat{s}^{-i}_{t+w} = s^{-i} \mid h_t\right] \sum_{r\in S^i} \mathbf{P}\left[\hat{s}^i_{t+w-1} = r \mid h_t\right]\left((\Pi_t)^2 - \Pi_t\right)(r, j) \\
&= \sum_{s^{-i}} \mathbf{P}\left[\hat{s}^{-i}_{t+w} = s^{-i} \mid h_t\right] \sum_{r} (\Pi_t)^{w-1}\left(s^i_t, r\right)\left((\Pi_t)^2 - \Pi_t\right)(r, j) \\
&= \sum_{s^{-i}} \mathbf{P}\left[\hat{s}^{-i}_{t+w} = s^{-i} \mid h_t\right]\left((\Pi_t)^{w+1} - (\Pi_t)^{w}\right)\left(s^i_t, j\right).
\end{aligned}$$

The estimate of $\mathbf{O}\left(1/\sqrt{w}\right)$ is obtained by the Lemma of [HM, Step M7].[17] □

• PROOF OF STEP 9: Putting together the estimates of Steps 7 and 8 and recalling that $\sum_{w=1}^{v} w^{\lambda} = \mathbf{O}\left(v^{\lambda+1}\right)$ for $\lambda \neq -1$ yields

$$2t\sum_{w=1}^{v} C_t^+ \cdot \mathbf{E}\left[B_{t+w} \mid h_t\right] = \mathbf{O}\left(tv\delta_t + tvY_t + \frac{tv^3}{\delta_{t+v}} + tv^2\left(\delta_t - \delta_{t+v}\right) + t\sqrt{v}\right).$$

Recalling the formula of Step 1(i) completes the proof. □

[17] Which is based on a Central Limit Theorem estimate. Note that here (unlike the Main Theorem of [HM]) Π_t is a strictly positive stochastic matrix: all its entries are $\geq \delta_t/m > 0$. It can then be shown that $\left|(\Pi_t)^{w+1}(k,j) - (\Pi_t)^{w}(k,j)\right| \leq (1-\delta_t/m)^w$. This alternative estimate can be used instead of $O\left(w^{-1/2}\right)$ (but we then need $\gamma < 1/5$ rather than $\gamma < 1/4$).

• Proof of Step 10: Part (i) follows immediately from the definition of $Z_t(j,k)$:

$$\mathbf{E}\left[Z_t(j,k) \mid h_{t-1}\right] = \frac{p_t^i(j)}{p_t^i(k)} p_t^i(k) - p_t^i(j) = 0.$$

Therefore $\mathbf{E}\left[Z_t(j,k)\right] = 0$, and

$$\begin{aligned}\mathbf{Var}\left[Z_t(j,k)\right] &= \mathbf{E}\left[Z_t^2(j,k)\right] = \mathbf{E}\left[\mathbf{E}\left[Z_t^2(j,k) \mid h_{t-1}\right]\right] \\ &= \mathbf{E}\left[\frac{\left(p_t^i(j)\right)^2}{\left(p_t^i(k)\right)^2} p_t^i(k) + (-1)^2 p_t^i(j)\right] \leq \mathbf{E}\left[\frac{1}{p_t^i(k)}\right] \leq \frac{m}{\delta_t},\end{aligned}$$

which gives (ii). □

• Proof of Step 11: We will use the following Strong Law of Large Numbers for Dependent Random Variables; see Loève [1978, Theorem 32.1.E]:

Theorem 4. *Let $(X_n)_{n=1,2,\ldots}$ be a sequence of random variables and $(b_n)_{n=1,2,\ldots}$ a sequence of real numbers increasing to ∞, such that the series $\sum_{n=1}^{\infty} \mathbf{Var}(X_n)/b_n^2$ converges. Then*

$$\lim_{n\to\infty} \frac{1}{b_n} \sum_{\nu=1}^{n} \left(X_\nu - \mathbf{E}\left[X_\nu \mid X_1, \ldots, X_{\nu-1}\right]\right) = 0 \text{ a.s.}$$

In our case, we have by Step 10(ii)

$$\sum_{t=1}^{\infty} \frac{1}{t^2} \mathbf{Var}\left[Z_t(j,k)\right] \leq \sum_{t=1}^{\infty} \frac{m}{t^2 \delta_t} = \sum_{t=1}^{\infty} \frac{m}{\delta t^{2-\gamma}}.$$

This series converges, since $\gamma < 1/4 < 1$. Therefore

$$\frac{1}{t} \sum_{\tau \leq t} \left(Z_\tau(j,k) - \mathbf{E}\left[Z_\tau(j,k) \mid Z_1(j,k), \ldots, Z_{\tau-1}(j,k)\right]\right) \to 0 \text{ a.s.}$$

and thus, by Step 10(i), $\overline{Z}_t(j,k) \to 0$ a.s. This yields (i) and (ii).

To get (iii), note that $\mathbf{1}_{\{s_t^i=k\}} u^i(s_t) = \mathbf{1}_{\{s_t^i=k\}} u^i\left(k, s_t^{-i}\right)$, so

$$\begin{aligned}&B_t(j,k) - A_t(j,k) \\ &= \left(\frac{p_t^i(j)}{p_t^i(k)} \mathbf{1}_{\{s_t^i=k\}} - \mathbf{1}_{\{s_t^i=j\}}\right) u^i(s_t) - \mathbf{1}_{\{s_t^i=j\}} \left(u^i\left(k, s_t^{-i}\right) - u^i(s_t)\right) \\ &= \left(\frac{p_t^i(j)}{p_t^i(k)} \mathbf{1}_{\{s_t^i=k\}} - \mathbf{1}_{\{s_t^i=j\}}\right) u^i\left(k, s_t^{-i}\right) = Z_t(j,k)\, u^i\left(k, s_t^{-i}\right).\end{aligned}$$

But s_t^i and s_t^{-i} are independent given h_{t-1}, therefore

$$\mathbf{E}\left[B_t(j,k) - A_t(j,k) \mid h_{t-1}\right] = \mathbf{E}\left[Z_t(j,k) \mid h_{t-1}\right] \mathbf{E}\left[u^i\left(k, s_t^{-i}\right) \mid h_{t-1}\right] = 0,$$

since the first term is 0 by Step 10(i). Moreover,

$$\begin{aligned}\mathbf{Var}\left[B_t(j,k) - A_t(j,k)\right] &= \mathbf{E}\left[Z_t^2(j,k)\left(u^i\left(k, s_t^{-i}\right)\right)^2\right] \\ &\leq M^2 \mathbf{E}\left[Z_t^2(j,k)\right] = \mathbf{O}\left(\frac{1}{\delta_t}\right).\end{aligned}$$

It follows that the series $\sum_t \mathbf{Var}\left[B_t(j,k) - A_t(j,k)\right]/t^2$ converges, implying that[18] $C_t(j,k) - D_t(j,k) = (1/t)\sum_{\tau \leq t}\left(B_\tau(j,k) - A_\tau(j,k)\right) \to 0$ a.s. $t \to \infty$ (argument as in the proof of (i) above). □

• PROOF OF STEP 12: Apply the inequality of Step 9 with $t = t_n = \lfloor n^\xi \rfloor$ and $v = t_{n+1} - t_n$. Then: $v = \mathbf{O}\left(n^{\xi-1}\right)$; $\delta_t \approx \delta n^{-\xi\gamma}$; $\delta_{t+v} \approx \delta(n+1)^{-\xi\gamma} = \mathbf{O}\left(n^{-\xi\gamma}\right)$; and[19] $\delta_t - \delta_{t+v} = \mathbf{O}\left(n^{-\xi\gamma-1}\right)$. Therefore

$$\begin{aligned}\mathbf{E}\left[t_{n+1}^2 \rho_{t_{n+1}} \mid h_{t_n}\right] \leq t_n^2 \rho_{t_n} &+ \mathbf{O}\left(\delta n^{2\xi-\xi\gamma-1} + Y_{t_n} n^{2\xi-1}\right) \\ &+ \mathbf{O}\left(n^{3\xi+\xi\gamma-3} + n^{3\xi-\xi\gamma-3} + n^{(3\xi-1)/2} + n^{2\xi+2\xi\gamma-2}\right).\end{aligned}$$

To complete the proof, note that the definition (9) of ξ implies that: $3\xi - \xi\gamma - 3 \leq 3\xi + \xi\gamma - 3 < 2\xi - 1$ since $\xi < 2/(1+\gamma)$; $(3\xi - 1)/2 < 2\xi - 1$ since $\xi > 1$; and $2\xi + 2\xi\gamma - 2 < 2\xi - 1$ since $\xi < 1/(4\gamma) \leq 1/(2\gamma)$. Therefore we take $\eta := \max\{3\xi + \xi\gamma - 3, (3\xi - 1)/2, 2\xi + 2\xi\gamma - 2\} < 2\xi - 1$. □

• PROOF OF STEP 13: Let $b_n := t_n^2 \approx n^{2\xi}$ and $X_n := b_n \rho_{t_n} - b_{n-1}\rho_{t_{n-1}} = t_n^2 \rho_{t_n} - t_{n-1}^2 \rho_{t_{n-1}}$. By Step 1(ii) we have $X_n = \mathbf{O}\left(\left(t_n v_n + v_n^2\right)/\delta_{t_{n+1}}^2\right) = \mathbf{O}\left(n^{2\xi+2\xi\gamma-1}\right)$; thus $\sum_n \mathbf{Var}\left(X_n\right)/b_n^2 = \sum_n \mathbf{O}\left(n^{4\xi+4\xi\gamma-2}/n^{4\xi}\right) = \sum_n \mathbf{O}\left(n^{4\xi\gamma-2}\right)$ converges (since $4\xi\gamma < 1$ by the choice of ξ).

Next, consider $(1/b_n)\sum_{\nu \leq n} \mathbf{E}\left[X_\nu \mid X_1, \ldots, X_{\nu-1}\right]$. The inequality of Step 12 yields three terms: The first is $\mathbf{O}\left(n^{-2\xi}\delta \sum_{\nu \leq n} \nu^{2\xi-\xi\gamma-1}\right) = \mathbf{O}\left(\delta n^{-\xi\gamma}\right)$; the second one converges to 0 a.s. as $t \to \infty$, since $Y_{t_n} \to 0$ by Step 10(ii) and Lemma 1 below (with $y_n = Y_{t_n}$ and $a_n = n^{2\xi-1}$); and the third one is $\mathbf{O}\left(n^{\eta-(2\xi-1)}\right) \to 0$ since $\eta < 2\xi - 1$. Altogether, we get $\mathbf{O}(\delta)$ when $\gamma = 0$, and 0 when $\gamma > 0$.

---

[18] It is interesting to note that, while the regrets are invariant to a change of origin for the utility function (i.e., adding a constant to all payoffs), this is not so for the modified regrets. Nonetheless, Step 13 shows that the resulting difference is just a martingale converging a.s. to 0.

[19] When $\gamma = 0$ (and thus $\delta_t - \delta_{t+v} = 0$), this yields an (over)estimate of $O\left(n^{-1}\right)$, which will turn out however not to matter.

The proof is completed by applying again the Strong Law of Large Numbers for Dependent Random Variables (Theorem 4) and noting that $0 \leq \rho_{t_n} = (1/b_n) \sum_{\nu \leq n} X_\nu$. □

Lemma 1. *Assume: (i) $y_n \to 0$ as $n \to \infty$; (ii) $a_n > 0$ for all n; and (iii) $\sum_{n=1}^{\infty} a_n = \infty$. Then $c_n := \sum_{\nu=1}^{n} a_\nu y_\nu / \sum_{\nu=1}^{n} a_\nu \to 0$ as $n \to \infty$.*

Proof. Given $\varepsilon > 0$, let n_0 be such that $|y_n| < \varepsilon$ for all $n > n_0$. Then $c_n = \sum_{\nu \leq n_0} a_\nu y_\nu / \sum_{\nu \leq n} a_\nu + \sum_{n_0 < \nu \leq n} a_\nu y_\nu / \sum_{\nu \leq n} a_\nu$. The first term converges to 0 (since the numerator is fixed), and the second is bounded by ε. □

• PROOF OF STEP 14: When $t_n \leq t \leq t_{n+1}$, we have by Step 3(i): $C_t(j,k) - C_{t_n}(j,k) = \mathbf{O}(v_n / (t_n \delta_{n+1})) = \mathbf{O}\left(n^{\xi\gamma - 1}\right) \to 0$, for all $j \neq k$. Thus $\limsup_{t \to \infty} \rho_t$
$= \limsup_{n \to \infty} \rho_{t_n}$. Recalling Step 11(iii) completes the proof. □

Remark. For simplicity, we have assumed that all players use the same sequence $(\delta_t)_t$. In the case of different sequences $\left(\delta_t^\ell\right)_t$ for the different players $\ell \in N$, with $\delta_t^\ell = \delta^\ell / t^{\gamma^\ell}$ for some $\delta^\ell > 0$ and $0 \leq \gamma^\ell < 1/4$, it is straightforward to check that the estimate of Step 6 becomes now $\sum_{\ell \in N} \mathbf{O}\left(w^2 / \left(t\delta_{t+w}^\ell\right) + w\left(\delta_t^\ell - \delta_{t+w}^\ell\right)\right)$. Choosing ξ to satisfy $1 < \xi < \min\{2/(1+\overline{\gamma}), 1/(4\overline{\gamma})\}$, where $\overline{\gamma} := \max_{\ell \in N} \gamma^\ell$, yields, on the right-hand side of Step 12, $t_n^2 \rho_{t_n} + \mathbf{O}\left(\delta^i n^{2\xi - \xi\gamma^i - 1} + Y_{t_n} n^{2\xi - 1}\right) + \mathbf{O}\left(n^{2\xi - 1}\right)$, and Steps 13 and 14 go through with δ^i and γ^i instead of δ and γ, respectively. The final result in Step 14 becomes:

(i) If $\delta_t^i = \delta^i$ for all t, then $\limsup_t R_t^i(j,k) = \mathbf{O}\left(\sqrt{\delta^i}\right)$ a.s.
(ii) If $\delta_t^i \to 0$ (i.e. if $\gamma(i) > 0$, then $\lim_t R_t^i(j,k) = 0$ a.s.

References

1. Auer P., N. Cesa-Bianchi, Y. Freund and R. E. Schapire [1995], Gambling in a Rigged Casino: The Adversarial Multi-Armed Bandit Problem, *Proceedings of the 36th Annual Symposium on Foundations of Computer Science*, 322–331.
2. Aumann, R. J. [1974], Subjectivity and Correlation in Randomized Strategies, *Journal of Mathematical Economics* 1, 67–96.
3. Baños, A. [1968], On Pseudo-Games, *The Annals of Mathematical Statistics* 39, 1932–1945.
4. Blackwell, D. [1956], An Analog of the Minmax Theorem for Vector Payoffs, *Pacific Journal of Mathematics* 6, 1–8.
5. Borgers, T. and R. Sarin [1995], Naive Reinforcement Learning with Endogenous Aspirations, University College London (mimeo).
6. Bush, R. and F. Mosteller [1955], *Stochastic Models for Learning*, Wiley.

7. Erev, I. and A. E. Roth [1998], Predicting How People Play Games: Reinforcement Learning in Experimental Games with Unique, Mixed Strategies, *American Economic Review* 88, 848–881.
8. Foster, D. and R. V. Vohra [1993], A Randomized Rule for Selecting Forecasts, *Operations Research* 41, 704–709.
9. Foster, D. and R. V. Vohra [1997], Calibrated Learning and Correlated Equilibrium, *Games and Economic Behavior* 21, 40–55.
10. Foster, D. and R. V. Vohra [1998], Asymptotic Calibration, *Biometrika* 85, 379–390.
11. Fudenberg, D. and D. K. Levine [1998], *Theory of Learning in Games*, MIT Press.
12. Fudenberg, D. and D. K. Levine [1999], Conditional Universal Consistency, *Games and Economic Behavior* 29, 104–130.
13. Hannan, J. [1957], Approximation to Bayes Risk in Repeated Play, in *Contributions to the Theory of Games*, Vol. III (*Annals of Mathematics Studies* 39), M. Dresher, A. W. Tucker and P. Wolfe (eds.), Princeton University Press, 97–139.
14. Hart, S. and A. Mas-Colell [2000], A Simple Adaptive Procedure Leading to Correlated Equilibrium, *Econometrica.*
15. Hart, S. and A. Mas-Colell [2001], A General Class of Adaptive Strategies, *Journal of Economic Theory.*
16. Loève, M. [1978], *Probability Theory*, Vol. II, 4th Edition, Springer-Verlag.
17. Megiddo, N. [1980], On Repeated Games with Incomplete Information Played by Non-Bayesian Players, *International Journal of Game Theory* 9, 157–167.
18. Roth, A. E. and I. Erev [1995], Learning in Extensive-Form Games: Experimental Data and Simple Dynamic Models in the Intermediate Term, *Games and Economic Behavior* 8, 164–212.

A Theoretical Analysis of the Mean Slutsky-Income Effect in the CAPM

Thorsten Hens*

Institute for Empirical Economic Research, University of Zurich,
Blümlisalpstrasse 10, CH-8006 Zurich, Switzerland

Abstract. The purpose of this paper is to demonstrate that in the Capital Asset Pricing Model (CAPM) the mean Slutsky-income effect is positive if on average investors have non-increasing absolute risk aversion. Together with some lower bounds on the degree to which absolute risk aversion decreases with income this result will be shown to be sufficient for the uniqueness of CAPM-equilibria.

1 Introduction

In his excellent book *Market Demand* Werner Hildenbrand (1994) gives a rigorous empirical analysis of the mean Slutsky-income effect. Based on some thorough theoretical modeling he shows that the mean Slutsky-income effect for commodity aggregates like food, housing, transport, fuel etc. is positive semi-definite. Hence this property contributes to the *Law of Demand* which is a sufficient condition for the uniqueness of competitive equilibria.

The purpose of this paper is to demonstrate that the mean Slutsky-income effect in the Capital Asset Pricing Model (CAPM) is positive if on average investors have non-increasing absolute risk aversion. Together with some lower bounds on the degree to which absolute risk aversion decreases with income this result will be shown to be sufficient for the uniqueness of CAPM-equilibria.

The CAPM is a cornerstone of finance. Based on Markovitz's (1952) assumption of mean-variance preferences, this model is a rich source of intuition and the basis for many practical decisions. Ever since Sharpe (1964), Lintner (1965) and Mossin (1966), the CAPM has been known to be an equilibrium model. The competitive equilibria of the CAPM provide us with quite simple and useful asset pricing rules which are summarized in the so-called *security market line theorem.* According to this theorem the price of any asset has to be equal to its expected payoff minus some risk premium which is measured by the covariance of the assets' return and the market portfolio.

* I am grateful to Andras Löffler for a fruitful collaboration on the theoretical foundations of the CAPM. This collaboration has resulted in two related papers in which the foundations of some aspects of this paper have been laid. Moreover I would like to thank Anke Gerber and Marc Oliver Bettzüge for a critical reading of this paper. All remaining errors are mine.

Werner Hildenbrand has always emphasized that the usefulness of any equilibrium model crucially depends on the number of its equilibria. In a recent paper Bottazzi, Hens and Löffler (1998) demonstrate that the CAPM can in general have any number of equilibria. Across the multiple equilibria risk premia differ substantially and in effect any asset prices are shown to be compatible with the CAPM. Hence as in any other model of competitive equilibria conditions guaranteeing the uniqueness of equilibria are warranted.

To derive plausible hypotheses guaranteeing the uniqueness of CAPM-equilibria we will first show that the CAPM can be interpreted as a certain equilibrium model with two commodities: mean and variance. Although the mean-variance economy has some disturbing non-standard properties (the one commodity (variance) is not desired, the other commodity (mean) is not bounded from below, income can become negative, and indifference curves typically intersect with the boundary of the consumption sets), we demonstrate that the standard Slutsky-decomposition can still be quite useful to derive conditions for the uniqueness of competitive equilibria. In particular, we show that the mean Slutsky-income effect is positive if on average investors have non-increasing absolute risk aversion. Hence given this plausible (Varian (1992)) assumption in the CAPM the mean Slutsky-income effect naturally contributes toward the uniqueness of equilibria. Indeed, in an economy in which all investors are endowed only with first period income, which they seek to invest in a given set of assets, CAPM-equilibria are unique. This fairly standard case of an asset market economy is known as a *distribution economy* (Malinvaud (1972)). Moreover in asset market economies in which investors seek to mutually insure their endowment risks (*re-insurance market*) an additional assumption has to be made. If on average there exist some appropriate lower bounds on the degree with which absolute risk aversion decreases then together with the positivity of the mean Slutsky-income effect CAPM-equilibria are shown to be unique. This additional condition is always satisfied in the case of distribution economies. It balances the sum of the Slutsky-substitution effect and the wealth effect in favor of the former.

Various other conditions for the uniqueness of CAPM-equilibria can be found in the literature. Based on the expected utility hypothesis, the assumptions of quadratic or exponential von Neumann-Morgenstern utility functions are well known to be sufficient conditions for the uniqueness of CAPM-equilibria. In the first case, however, absolute risk aversion is increasing while in the second case absolute risk aversion is constant. Moreover, based directly on mean-variance preferences Dana (1999) has recently shown that some reasoning analogous to that of Mitjushin and Polterovich (1978) can also be applied to derive the uniqueness of CAPM-equilibria. But in her reasoning, again absolute risk aversion is increasing. Among the sufficient conditions provided in the literature the conditions given in Hens, Löffler and Laitenberger (2000) are most similar to the ones used here. These authors assume that every investor has non-increasing absolute risk aversion and that no investor has strictly decreasing absolute risk aversion for mean-variance combinations smaller than the mean-variance of his endowments.

The rest of this paper is organized as follows. In the next section we will outline the standard CAPM-model as it is for example also presented in Duffie (1988). Then following Dana (1999) we show how this model can be transformed to the mean-variance economy and finally in section 4 we derive our results on the uniqueness of CAPM-equilibria.

2 The model

The description of the model follows Duffie (1988, section I.11). Let $(M, \mathcal{M}, \eta)$ be a probability space. Consider $\mathcal{L}$, the space of real–valued measurable functions on $(M, \mathcal{M}, \eta)$. We endow $\mathcal{L}$ with the scalar product $x \cdot y := \int_M x(m) y(m) d\eta$ and with the norm $\|x\| = \sqrt{(x \cdot x)}$. The consumption set will be the subset of $\mathcal{L}$ with finite norm, $L^2(\eta) = \{x \in \mathcal{L} \mid \|x\|^2 < \infty\}$. The price space is also $L^2(\eta)$. Denote the expectation of a portfolio x by $\mu(x) := \int_M x(m)\eta(dm)$ and the covariance of $x, y \in L^2(\eta)$ by $cov(x, y) = \mu(xy) - \mu(x)\mu(y)$. The standard deviation of x is accordingly $\sigma(x) := \sqrt{cov(x, x)}$.

Let X denote the marketed subspace of the consumption space $L^2(\eta)$. We assume that X is a closed vector space. The space X can be interpreted as the set of linear combinations of an underlying set of securities in $L^2(\eta)$. Security markets are called complete if $X = L^2(\eta)$; otherwise they are incomplete.

Let $\mathbb{I} \in \mathrm{L}^2(\eta)$ be a riskless asset, in the sense that $\mathbb{I}(\mathrm{m}) = 1$ for all m in M. We assume that $\mathbb{I} \in \mathrm{X}$. This assumption is essential for our reasoning. It is convenient to decompose every $x \in L^2(\eta)$ as the sum of a riskless asset with the same mean as x and a vector with mean 0, $x \equiv \mu(x)\mathbb{I} + \tilde{\mathrm{x}}$, where $\mu(\tilde{x}) = \tilde{x} \cdot \mathbb{I} = 0$.

An agent $i = 1, \ldots, I$ is described by his endowments ω^i and his utility function $u^i : X \to \mathbb{R}$. We assume 'spanning', i.e. $\omega^i \in X$, $i = 1, \ldots, I$. The agent's decision problem is

$$\max_{x \in X} u^i(x)$$

$$s.t. \; p \cdot x \leq p \cdot \omega^i$$

The essential assumption that makes the model a CAPM, is the

Assumption 1 *(mean–variance preferences)*
Every agent $i = 1, \ldots, I$ has a mean–variance preference, i.e. there exist functions $v^i : \mathbb{R} \times \mathbb{R}_+ \to \mathbb{R}$, $(\mu, \sigma) \mapsto v^i(\mu, \sigma)$ increasing in μ and decreasing in σ such that $u^i(x) = v^i(\mu(x), \sigma(x))$ for all $x \in X$.

In addition, for demand to be a well defined function, we introduce the following assumption which goes back to Sharpe (1964).

Assumption 2 *(strict quasi–concavity)*
For every agent $i = 1, \ldots, I$, the utility function v^i is continuously differentiable and strictly quasi–concave.

We normalize prices such that $\mu(p) = 1$. This normalization is possible since by the no-arbitrage condition in the CAPM all prices must have positive mean (Bottazzi, Hens and Löffler (1998)). To complete the description of the model, we state an assumption on the distribution of the agents' endowments $(\omega^i)_{i \in I}$.

Assumption 3 *For every agent $i = 1, ..., I, \mu(\omega^i) \geq 0$ and $\mu(\omega) = \sigma^2(\omega) = 1$ where $\omega = \sum_{i=1}^{I} \omega^i$, is the market portfolio.*

Given the Assumptions 1 and 2, Dana (1999) has demonstrated that Assumption 3 is sufficient to show existence of CAPM-equilibria, which are defined in

Definition 1 *A CAPM-equilibrium consists of a price vector $\overset{*}{p} \in L^2(\eta)$ and an allocation $\overset{*}{x}{}^i \in L^2(\eta)$, $i = 1, ..., I$, such that (i) $\overset{*}{x}{}^i$ maximizes $u^i(x)$ subject to $x \in X$ and $\overset{*}{p} \cdot x \leq \overset{*}{p} \cdot \omega^i$, $i = 1, ..., I$, and (ii) $\sum_{i=1}^{I} \overset{*}{x}{}^i = \sum_{i=1}^{I} \omega^i$.*

The following proposition recalls an important characterization of CAPM equilibria.

Proposition 1 *(Mutual Fund Theorem)*
Let $(\overset{*}{p}, \overset{*}{x})$ with $\overset{*}{x} = (\overset{*}{x}{}^1, ..., \overset{*}{x}{}^I)$ be a CAPM equilibrium. Then there exist non-negative scalars $\phi^i \in \mathbb{R}_+$, $i = 0, 1, ..., I$, and scalars $\psi^i \in \mathbb{R}$, $i = 0, 1, ..., I$ such that $\overset{*}{p} = \psi^0 \mathbb{1} - \phi^0 \omega$ and $\overset{*}{x}{}^i = \psi^i \mathbb{1} + \phi^i \omega$ for every $i = 1, ..., I$.

Proof
Let $x^i \in \arg\max_{x \in X} u^i(x)$ s.t. $p \cdot x \leq p \cdot \omega^i$. Then by Assumption 1, $p \cdot x^i = p \cdot \omega^i$. We first show that x^i is in the span of $\mathbb{1}$ and p, or - equivalently - $\mathbb{1}$ and $\tilde{p}$. Decompose $x^i = y^i + z^i$ where z^i is perpendicular to $\mathbb{1}$ and $\tilde{p}$. From the decomposition it follows that $p \cdot z^i = 0$ so that y^i is also budget feasible. But from z^i being perpendicular to $\mathbb{1}$ it is obtained that $\mu(x^i) = \mu(y^i)$. Furthermore for $z^i \neq 0$

$$\sigma^2(\tilde{x}^i) = \|\tilde{x}^i\|^2 = \|\tilde{y}^i + \tilde{z}^i\|^2 = \|\tilde{y}^i\|^2 + \|\tilde{z}^i\|^2 > \|\tilde{y}^i\| = \sigma^2(\tilde{y}^i)$$

because $\tilde{z}^i$ is perpendicular to $\tilde{y}^i$. Hence $z^i = 0$ is the agent's best choice.

Given this insight, supposing $\tilde{p} \neq 0$, write x^i in the form $x^i = \psi^i \mathbb{1} - \phi^i \frac{\tilde{p}}{\|\tilde{p}\|^2}$, for some scalars ψ^i and ϕ^i. Using the budget restriction $p \cdot y^i = p \cdot \omega^i$ one can deduce $\psi^i = p \cdot \omega^i + \phi^i \|\tilde{p}\|^2$. To show that ϕ^i is non-negative, note that

$\mu(x^i) = p \cdot \omega^i + \phi^i \|\tilde{p}\|^2$ and $\sigma(x^i) = \phi^i$. Thus, since higher mean is preferred, $(p \cdot \omega^i + |\phi^i| \|\tilde{p}\|^2)\mathbb{1} - |\phi^i| \frac{\tilde{p}}{\|\tilde{p}\|^2})$ is preferred to $(p \cdot \omega^i - |\phi^i| \|\tilde{p}\|^2)\mathbb{1} + |\phi^i| \frac{\tilde{p}}{\|\tilde{p}\|^2})$ unless $\phi^i = 0$, where $|\phi^i|$ denotes the absolute value of ϕ^i. This implies that ϕ^i is non-negative. Furthermore, $\phi^i = 0$ if $\tilde{p} = 0$.
Strict quasi-concavity implies the uniqueness of the optimal portfolio.
Thus for any p, $x^i(p) = \psi^i(p)\mathbb{1} - \phi^i(p)\frac{\tilde{p}}{\|\tilde{p}\|^2}$, $i = 1, ..., I$.

Let $\overset{*}{p}$ be an equilibrium price, i.e. $\sum_{i=1}^{I} x^i(\overset{*}{p}) = \omega$.

If $\overset{*}{\tilde{p}} = 0$ then $\overset{*}{x^i} = \psi^i \mathbb{1}$, i = 1, ..., I and $\overset{*}{p} = \psi^0 \mathbb{1}$, where $\psi^0 = \sum_i \psi^i$.

Otherwise $\frac{\overset{*}{\tilde{p}}}{\|\overset{*}{\tilde{p}}\|} = -\phi^0 \omega + \psi^0 \mathbb{1}$ where $\phi^0 = \frac{1}{\sum_i \phi^i} \geq 0$, and $\psi^0 = \frac{\sum_i \psi^i}{\sum_i \phi^i}$, so that

$\overset{*}{x}{}^i = \psi^i(1 - \psi^0)\mathbb{1} + \phi^i \phi^0 \omega$, i = 1, ..., I.

Hence redefining the coefficients of $\mathbb{1}$ and ω finishes the proof of proposition 1. □

3 The mean-variance economy

In this section we recall from Dana (1999) how the Mutual Fund Theorem can be used to reduce the CAPM economy to an economy with two artificial commodities, *mean* and *variance*. This economy has the same number of equilibria as the original CAPM economy. The excess demand, however, will be different to that in the CAPM economy. Thus studying the excess demand in terms of the new 'commodities' does not give any insight into questions like the stability of CAPM-equilibria.

First we define an auxiliary economy which is in terms of two commodities, the riskless asset $\mathbb{1}$ and the market portfolio ω. The mean variance economy is then obtained from the auxiliary economy by a change of coordinates.

To begin with, let H denote the span of the riskless asset $\mathbb{1}$ and the market portfolio ω. Let an upper bar denote expressions in the auxiliary economy. Then we define the auxiliary consumption sets, $\bar{X}$, the auxiliary utility functions, $\bar{u}^i$, and the auxiliary endowments, $\bar{\omega}^i$, $i = 1, ..., I$, by

$\bar{X} = X \cap H = \{\phi\omega + \psi\mathbb{1}, \phi \in \mathbb{R}_+, \psi \in \mathbb{R}\}$

$\bar{u}^i(\phi\omega + \psi\mathbb{1}) = v^i(\phi + \psi, \phi)$

$\bar{\omega}^i$ is the projection of ω^i on H, i.e.

$\bar{\omega}^i = (\bar{\phi}^i)\omega + \bar{\psi}^i\mathbb{1}$, with $\bar{\phi}^i = \sqrt{cov(\omega, \omega^i)}$, $\bar{\psi}^i = \mu(\omega^i) - \bar{\phi}^i$.

Thus in this economy, we have two commodities, the riskless asset $\mathbb{1}$ and the market portfolio ω. Let r denote the price of ω. Due to the price normalization $\mu(p) = 1$, in the auxiliary economy the price of $\mathbb{1}$ will be 1.

Definition 2 *An equilibrium in the auxiliary economy is a triple* $(\overset{*}{\phi}, \overset{*}{\psi}, \overset{*}{r}) \in \mathbb{R}_+^I \times \mathbb{R}^I \times \mathbb{R}$ *with* $\overset{*}{\phi} = (\overset{*}{\phi}{}^1, ..., \overset{*}{\phi}{}^I), \overset{*}{\psi}, = (\overset{*}{\psi}{}^1, ..., \overset{*}{\psi}{}^I)$, *such that*

(i) $(\overset{*}{\phi}{}^i, \overset{*}{\psi}{}^i)$ *maximizes* $v^i(\phi + \psi, \phi)$
subject to $\overset{*}{r}\, \phi + \psi \leq \overset{*}{r}\, \bar{\phi}^i + \bar{\psi}^i$ *for every* $i = 1, ..., I$, *and*
(ii) $\sum_{i=1}^{I} \overset{*}{\phi}{}^i = \sum_{i=1}^{I} \bar{\phi}^i$, $\sum_{i=1}^{I} \overset{*}{\psi}{}^i = \sum_{i=1}^{I} \bar{\psi}^i$.

It is more intuitive to work in the space of mean and standard deviations. Let us therefore make the change of coordinates $\mu = \phi + \psi$, $\sigma = \phi$, $q = 1 - r$. Let $\bar{\mu}^i = \mu(\omega^i)$, $\bar{\sigma}^i = \sqrt{cov(\omega, \omega^i)}$.

Consequently, we define

Definition 3 *An equilibrium of the mean-variance economy is a triple* $(\overset{*}{q}, \overset{*}{\mu}, \overset{*}{\sigma}) \in \mathbb{R} \times \mathbb{R}_+^I \times \mathbb{R}$ *with* $\overset{*}{\mu} = (\overset{*}{\mu}{}^1, ..., \overset{*}{\mu}{}^I), \overset{*}{\sigma} = (\overset{*}{\sigma}{}^1, ..., \overset{*}{\sigma}{}^I)$ *such that*

(i) $(\overset{*}{\mu}{}^i, \overset{*}{\sigma}{}^i)$ *maximizes* $v^i(\mu, \sigma)$ *subject to* $\mu - \overset{*}{q}\, \sigma \leq \bar{\mu}^i - \overset{*}{q}\, \bar{\sigma}^i$, $i = 1, ..., I$,
(ii) $\sum_{i=1}^{I} \overset{*}{\mu}{}^i = \sum_{i=1}^{I} \bar{\mu}^i$, $\sum_{i=1}^{I} \overset{*}{\sigma}{}^i = \sum_{i=1}^{I} \bar{\sigma}^i$.

Having reduced the CAPM economy to the mean-variance economy, it is important to observe that the sets of equilibria of the two economies correspond to each other[1].

Proposition 2 *(Dana (1999))*
Let $(\overset{*}{p}, \overset{*}{x})$ *be an equilibrium of the CAPM economy. Then* $(\overset{*}{q}, \overset{*}{\mu}, \overset{*}{\sigma})$ *with* $\overset{*}{q} = 1 - \overset{*}{p} \cdot \omega$, $\overset{*}{\mu}{}^i = \mu(\overset{*}{x}{}^i)$, $\overset{*}{\sigma}{}^i = \sigma(\overset{*}{x}{}^i)$, $i = 1, ..., I$, *is an equilibrium of the mean-variance economy. Conversely, let* $(\overset{*}{q}, \overset{*}{\mu}, \overset{*}{\sigma})$ *be an equilibrium of the mean-variance economy. Then there exists* $(\overset{*}{p}, \overset{*}{x}{}^1, ..., \overset{*}{x}{}^I)$ *with* $1 - \overset{*}{p} \cdot \omega = \overset{*}{q}$, $\mu(\overset{*}{x}{}^i) = \overset{*}{\mu}{}^i$, $\sigma(\overset{*}{x}{}^i) = \overset{*}{\sigma}{}^i$, $i = 1, ..., I$ *such that* $(\overset{*}{p}, \overset{*}{x})$ *is an equilibrium of the CAPM economy.*

Proof
Let $(\overset{*}{p}, \overset{*}{x})$ be an equilibrium in the CAPM economy. Then by Proposition 1 there exist scalars $(\phi^i, \psi^i) \in \mathbb{R}_+ \times \mathbb{R}$, $i = 0, 1, ..., I$ such that

$$\overset{*}{p} = -\phi^0 \omega + \psi^0 \mathbb{1} \quad \text{and}$$
$$\overset{*}{x}{}^i = \phi^i \omega + \psi^i \mathbb{1} \quad \text{for every } i = 1, \ldots, I.$$

[1] This observation has first been used by Dana (1999).

From the market clearing conditions it follows that $\sum_i \phi^i = 1$ and $\sum_i \psi^i = 0$. Let $\bar{\phi}^i = \sqrt{cov(\omega, \omega^i)}$ and $\bar{\psi}^i = \mu(\omega^i) - \bar{\phi}^i$, $i = 1, ..., I$. By Assumption 3, $\sum_i \bar{\phi}^i = 1$ and $\sum_i \bar{\psi}^i = 0$ thus the scalars (ϕ^i, ψ^i), $i = 1, ..., I$ fulfill the market clearing conditions in the auxiliary economy. Note that $\mu(\overset{*}{x}^i) = \phi^i \mu(\omega) + \psi^i \mu(\mathbb{1})$ and that $\sigma^2(\overset{*}{x}^i) = (\phi^i)^2 \sigma^2(\omega)$, so that by Assumption 3 $\mu(\overset{*}{x}^i) = \phi^i + \psi^i$ and $\sigma^2(\overset{*}{x}^i) = (\phi^i)^2$, $i = 1, ..., I$. Since by Assumption 1 the CAPM agent was only interested in mean and variance, he has chosen $\overset{*}{x}^i$ so as to maximize v^i subject to $p \cdot x \leq p \cdot \omega^i$, which implies that (ϕ^i, ψ^i) maximizes $v^i(\phi + \psi, \phi)$ subject to $\overset{*}{r}\, \phi + \psi \leq \overset{*}{r}\, \bar{\phi}^i + \bar{\psi}^i$, $i = 1, ..., I$, where $\overset{*}{r} = \overset{*}{p} \cdot \omega$. Hence $\overset{*}{r}$ and $(\phi^1, ..., \phi^I), (\psi^1, ..., \psi^I)$ constitute an equilibrium in the auxiliary economy. And by a change of coordinates, $\mu^i = \phi^i + \psi^i$, $\sigma^i = \phi^i$, $i = 1, ..., I$ and $q = 1 - \overset{*}{r}$ is an equilibrium of the mean variance economy.

Conversely, let $(\overset{*}{q}, \overset{*}{\mu}, \overset{*}{\sigma})$ be an equilibrium of the mean-variance economy, then by a change of coordinates, $\overset{*}{r} = 1 - \overset{*}{q}$, $\overset{*}{\phi}^i = \overset{*}{\sigma}^i$, $\overset{*}{\psi}^i = \overset{*}{\mu}^i - \overset{*}{\phi}^i$, $i = 1, ...I$ is an equilibrium of the auxiliary economy. Consider $\overset{*}{p} = -(\overset{*}{r} - 1)\omega + (2 - \overset{*}{r})\mathbb{1}$, and $\overset{*}{x}^i = \overset{*}{\phi}^i\, \omega + \overset{*}{\psi}^i\, \mathbb{1}$, $i = 1, ..., I$. Thus $\overset{*}{p} \cdot \omega = \overset{*}{r}$, markets clear and by the proof of Proposition 1 $\overset{*}{x}^i$ is the agent's best choice given $\overset{*}{p}$. □

This finishes the description of the mean variance economy.

4 The results

In this section we discuss sufficient conditions for the uniqueness of CAPM-equilibria. From the general equilibrium model it is well known that the monotonicity of demand and the gross substitution property are two such conditions (Mas-Colell, Whinston and Green (1995)). While in general these conditions are different (Kehoe (1992)), in a two commodity economy they coincide. Given the price normalization chosen above and given that variance is a non-desired commodity, both conditions are satisfied if the demand for variance is an *increasing* function in its price. The demand for variance is derived from the following maximization problem:

$$\max_{(\mu^i, \sigma^i) \in \mathbb{R} \times R_+} \quad v^i(\mu^i, \sigma^i)$$

$$\text{s.t. } \mu^i - q\sigma^i \leq \bar{\mu}^i - q\bar{\sigma}^i$$

where $\bar{\mu}^i = E(\omega^i)$ and $\bar{\sigma}^i = \sqrt{\text{cov}(\omega^i, \omega)}$. The following figure shows a typical situation for this solution.

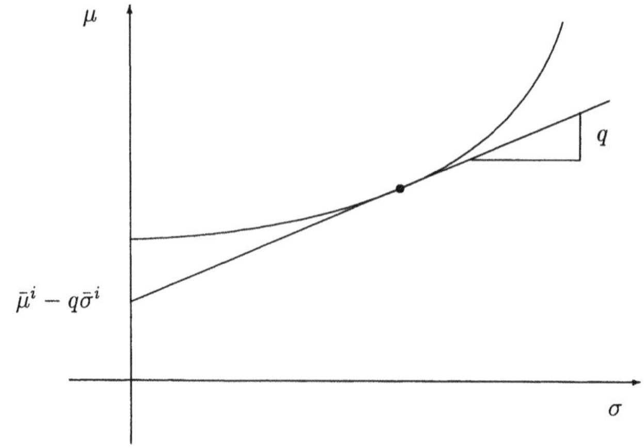

The discussion of the various conditions for uniqueness will be in terms of the slope of the indifference curves in the (μ, σ)- diagram,

$$R^i(\mu, \sigma) := -\frac{\partial_\sigma v^i(\mu, \sigma)}{\partial_\mu v^i(\mu, \sigma)}.$$

This slope is a measure of the investor's absolute risk aversion; for a detailed discussion of this measure see Nielsen (1988) and Lajari and Nielsen (1994). Moreover, as we will show, how $R^i(\mu, \sigma)$ changes with μ is the key determinant for the monotonicity of the agent's optimal choice σ^i as a function of q. The following terminology is quite useful.

Definition 4 *A mean-variance utility function exhibits non-increasing (non-decreasing) risk aversion if for all $\sigma \geq 0$ the slope of its indifference curves are non-increasing (non-decreasing) functions in mean, i.e. $\partial_\mu R^i(\mu, \sigma) \leq 0$ for all (μ, σ). It exhibits constant absolute risk aversion if this slope is constant.*

Define a simple portfolio problem as a decision problem where an investor maximizes utility over portfolios formed by one riskless and one risky asset. As Lajari and Nielsen (1994) have shown, non-increasing risk aversion is equivalent to the property that in every simple decision problem the demand of the risky asset is non-increasing in income.

The following proposition provides a decomposition of the price induced change on demand for variance into the Slutsky-substitution effect, the Slutsky-income effect and the wealth effect.

Proposition 3 *For any investor $i = 1, ..., I$, and for all prices $q > 0$ we get:*

$$\partial_q \sigma^i(q) = \frac{\partial_{\mu^i} v^i(\mu^i, \sigma^i)}{-d^i(\mu^i, \sigma^i)} + \frac{\partial_{\mu^i} R^i(\mu^i, \sigma^i)\partial_{\mu^i} v^i(\mu^i, \sigma^i)(\sigma^i - \bar{\sigma}^i)}{d^i(\mu^i, \sigma^i)}$$

where $d^i(\mu^i, \sigma^i) = \partial^2_{\mu^i} v^i(\mu^i, \sigma^i) q^2 + 2\partial_{\mu^i}\partial_{\sigma^i} v^i(\mu^i, \sigma^i) q + \partial^2_{\sigma^i} v^i(\mu^i, \sigma^i) < 0.$

At a no-trade allocation, i.e. at $\sigma^i = \bar{\sigma}^i$, the derivative of σ^i with respect to q is equal to the Slutsky-substitution effect, which then is

$$\partial_q \sigma^i(q) = \frac{\partial_{\mu^i} v^i(\mu^i, \sigma^i)}{-d^i(\mu^i, \sigma^i)} > 0.$$

Moreover, splitting the difference $(\sigma^i - \bar{\sigma}^i)$ into two parts results in the Slutsky-income effect

$$\frac{\partial_{\mu^i} R^i(\mu^i, \sigma^i)\partial_{\mu^i} v^i(\mu^i, \sigma^i)\sigma^i}{d^i(\mu^i, \sigma^i)}$$

and the wealth effect

$$\frac{\partial_{\mu^i} R^i(\mu^i, \sigma^i)\partial_{\mu^i} v^i(\mu^i, \sigma^i)\bar{\sigma}^i}{-d^i(\mu^i, \sigma^i)}.$$

Proof of Proposition 3
To solve the maximization problem

$$\max_{(\mu^i, \sigma^i)\in \mathbb{R}\times R_+} \quad v^i(\mu^i, \sigma^i)$$

$$\text{s.t. } \mu^i - q\sigma^i \leq \bar{\mu}^i - q\bar{\sigma}^i$$

note that since v^i is increasing in μ the budget restriction must hold with equality. Thus supposing positivity of σ^i the first order condition is

$$\partial_{\mu^i} v^i(\bar{\mu}^i + q(\sigma^i - \bar{\sigma}^i), \sigma^i)q + \partial_{\sigma^i} v^i(\bar{\mu}^i + q(\sigma^i - \bar{\sigma}^i), \sigma^i) = 0.$$

By strict quasi-concavity of $v^i(\mu^i, \sigma^i)$ the solution to the first order condition is necessary and sufficient for a solution of the mean-variance maximization problem.

Application of the implicit function theorem leads to[2]

$$\partial_q \sigma^i = \frac{[(\partial_{\mu^i} v^i) + (\partial^2_{\mu^i} v^i)q(\sigma^i - \bar{\sigma}^i) + (\partial_{\mu^i}\partial_{\sigma^i} v^i)(\sigma^i - \bar{\sigma}^i)]}{-[((\partial_{\sigma^i}\partial_{\mu^i} v^i) + \partial^2_{\mu^i} v^i q)q + (\partial_{\mu^i}\partial_{\sigma^i} v^i)q + (\partial^2_{\sigma^i} v^i)]}.$$

Using the definition of d^i, the identity $q = -\frac{\partial_{\sigma^i} v^i}{\partial_{\mu^i} v^i}$ and the formula

$$\partial_{\mu^i} R^i(\mu^i, \sigma^i) = -\frac{[(\partial_{\mu^i}\partial_{\sigma^i} v^i)(\partial_{\mu^i} v^i) - (\partial^2_{\mu^i} v^i)(\partial_{\sigma^i} v^i)]}{(\partial_{\mu^i} v^i)^2}$$

proves our claim. Note that by strict quasi-concavity of v^i, d^i is negative. □

[2] For brevity of this expression we have omitted the arguments μ^i and σ^i from the function v^i.

The Jacobian of market demand $S(q) := \sum_{i=1}^{n} \sigma^i(q)$ can most conveniently be written as a certain average of the individual investors' derivative terms. To this end, for all $i = 1, ..., I$, we define $\rho^i := \frac{\delta^i}{\sum_j \delta^j}$ where $\delta^i := \frac{\partial_{\mu^i} v^i(\mu^i, \sigma^i)}{-d^i(\mu^i, \sigma^i)} > 0$ and $\gamma^i := \frac{\delta^i \sigma^i}{\sum_j \delta^j \sigma^j}$. Using these definitions we get:

$$\partial_q S(q) = (\sum_{i=1}^{I} \delta^i) \sum_{i=1}^{I} \rho^i (1 + \partial_{\mu^i} R^i(\mu^i, \sigma^i)\, \bar{\sigma}^i) - (\sum_{i=1}^{I} \delta^i \sigma^i) \sum_{i=1}^{I} \gamma^i \partial_{\mu^i} R^i(\mu^i, \sigma^i)$$

where the first term is the average of the sum of investors' Slutsky-substitution and wealth effects and the second term is the average Slutsky-income effect.

Note that $\rho := (\rho^1, ..., \rho^I)$ and $\gamma := (\gamma^1, ..., \gamma^I)$ are probability measures on the set of agents. Hence, the average Slutsky-income effect is non-negative iff the γ-average of the investors' absolute risk aversion is non-increasing. This decomposition of the derivative of market demand then allows us to state the following results.

Result 1 *CAPM-equilibria are unique if investors have constant absolute risk aversion.*

In fact in this case $\partial_{\mu^i} R^i(\mu^i, \sigma^i) = 0$ for all $i = 1, ..., I$ and hence the derivative defined above is positive.

Moreover, consider a CAPM-economy in which one set of investors is only endowed with riskless asset while the other set of investors has risky endowments. Assume that the latter ones are only interested in riskless consumption and hence inelastically supply all risky assets. Such an exchange economy is formally equivalent to the distribution economy mentioned in the introduction. Then for the second set of investors the derivative of their market demand with respect to q is zero while for the first set of investors, $\bar{\sigma}^i = 0$, and hence the derivative of market demand is positive provided that on average their absolute risk aversion is not increasing.

Result 2 *In distribution economies CAPM-equilibria are unique if the γ-average of investors' absolute risk aversion is non-increasing.*

Uniqueness of CAPM-equilibria can also be derived in economies where all investors have risky endowments provided that in addition to the just mentioned assumption on average the degree of reduction in an investors' absolute risk aversion $\partial_{\mu^i} R^i(\mu^i, \sigma^i)$, is bounded below by minus the reciprocal of the variance of his endowments. That is to say, provided that the first term in the above stated decomposition of the derivative of market demand is positive.

Result 3 *CAPM-equilibria are unique if the γ-average of investors' absolute risk aversion is non-increasing and if the ρ-average of the degree of reduction* *in their risk aversion is bounded by minus the reciprocal of the variance of their endowments.*

5 Conclusion

Our theoretical analysis shows that in the CAPM the mean Slutsky-income effect is positive if on average the plausible assumption of non-increasing absolute risk aversion is satisfied.

The simplicity of this observation is the result of a careful transformation of the CAPM into a specific two-commodities equilibrium model. Application of standard techniques from microeconomic theory then allows to identify the mean Slutsky-income effect with a term which is a certain average of the degree with which investors' risk aversions change with income. Hence given that decreasing absolute risk aversion is a plausible assumption in the CAPM the mean Slutsky-income effect is "naturally" positive. Our line of arguments shows that this important result draws mainly on the ingenious construction of the CAPM rather than on the depth of our reasoning. The importance of this result can therefore only be appreciated by recalling how much statistical effort and clever reasoning one needs in order to justify the positivity of the mean Slutsky-income effect in the *general equilibrium model* - even if one restricts attention to only two commodities. Hence the celebrated CAPM turns out to be a very well behaved *special equilibrium model.*

References

1. J.M. Bottazzi, Th. Hens and A. Löffler (1998): Market Demand Functions in the CAPM, *Journal of Economic Theory* 79,192-206.
2. R.A. Dana (1999): Existence, Uniqueness and Determinacy of Equilibrium in C.A.P.M. with a riskless Asset, J. Math. Econ.,32(2),167-75.
3. D. Duffie (1988): Security Markets: Stochastic Models, Academic Press.
4. Th. Hens, A. Löffler and J. Laitenberger(2000): Existence and Uniqueness of Equilibria in the CAPM with a Riskless Asset, University of Zürich IEW-Working Paper No. 36.
5. W.Hildenbrand (1994): Market Demand, Princeton University Press.
6. T.Kehoe(1992): Gross Substitutability and the Weak Axiom of Revealed Preferences, J. Math.Econ.,21(1),37-50.
7. F. Lajari and L.T. Nielsen (1994): Risk Aversion and Prudence: The Case of Mean-Variance Preferences, mimeo INSEAD.
8. J. Lintner (1965): The Valuation of Risky Assets and the Selection of Risky Investment in Stock Portfolios and Capital Budgets, *Review of Economics and Statistics* 47 , 13–37.
9. Malinvaud, E. (1972): Microeconomic Theory, North Holland.
10. H.M. Markowitz (1953): Portfolio Selection, *Journal of Finance* 7, 77-91.
11. A. Mas-Colell, M.D. Whinston and J.R. Green (1995): Microeconomic Theory, Oxford University Press.

12. L.G. Mitjushin, L.G. and V. Polterovich (1978): Criteria for Monotonicity of Demand Functions. (In Russian), *Ekonomika i Matematicheskie Metody* 14 122-128.
13. J. Mossin (1966): Equilibrium in a Capital Asset Market, *Econometrica* 22, 265-290.
14. L.T. Nielsen (1988): Uniqueness of equilibrium in the classical capital asset pricing model, *J. Finan. Quant. Anal.* 23,329-336.
15. W. Sharpe (1964): Capital Asset Prices: A Theory of Market Equilibrium Under Conditions of Risk, *Journal of Finance* 19, 425-442.
16. J. Tobin (1958): Liquidity Preference as Behavior Towards Risk, *Rev. Econ. Stud.* 25, 65–86.
17. H. Varian (1992): Microeconomic Theory, Norton.

Demand Dispersion, Metonymy and Ideal Panel Data

Michael Jerison

Department of Economics, SUNY, Albany, NY 12222, USA

Abstract. In a generic competitive distribution economy with "increasing dispersion," market demand satisfies the weak axiom of revealed preference and equilibrium is unique. Increasing dispersion requires, roughly, that when the households' incomes rise slightly their demand vectors move apart. We show how to test for it using panel data with fixed relative prices under a "structural stability" hypothesis [10]. We also show how to test for it using cross section data if the households' demand functions and incomes are independently distributed, or under a much weaker assumption that is implied by "metonymy." Metonymy, introduced in [6], relates the demand distribution of households with income x to the demand distribution that slightly poorer households would have if their incomes rose to x. We show that metonymy for a single population is untestable—even with ideal panel data that allow a direct test of increasing dispersion. Thus, cross section tests of increasing dispersion rely on an assumption that is not potentially falsifiable.

1 Introduction

In a generic competitive production economy, equilibrium is unique if mean consumer demand satisfies the weak axiom of revealed preference. Moreover, the weak axiom is the weakest demand-side restriction that ensures uniqueness of equilibrium. In a distribution economy (in which household incomes do not vary with prices) mean consumer demand satisfies the weak axiom if the consumption sector has *increasing dispersion*, which means, roughly, that a slight increase in the households' incomes makes their demand vectors move apart on average. Considering the importance of the weak axiom for mean consumer demand, it is natural to ask whether the hypothesis of increasing dispersion is consistent with demand data. This question is addressed by Werner Hildenbrand in [8]. In the present paper we review the implications of increasing dispersion in a unified framework, following the approach of [12,13]. We present new tests of increasing dispersion based on panel and cross section data. The tests depend on auxiliary hypotheses that are commonly assumed in demand analysis. We will show that these auxiliary hypotheses are too weak to be testable.

The main hypotheses examined below, increasing dispersion and a weak form of individual consistency, which together imply the weak axiom in the aggregate, are satisfied in consumption sectors with sufficient heterogeneity in the sense of Grandmont [5] and Kneip [18]. The hypotheses do not restrict the parametric forms for the households' demand functions. They also do not require that the households demands have the consistency implied by competitive optimizing behavior. This contrasts with the approach in [20–22].

Increasing dispersion is a restriction on the effect of raising the households' incomes. With ideal panel data it can be tested directly. The test can be performed if the households' incomes rise in fixed proportion while relative prices remain fixed. Data for such a test are, in principle, obtainable from consumption experiments, as discussed below. Alternatively, an approximate version of the test can be performed using panel demand data from a period of nearly contant relative prices and nearly constant relative income distribution. The latter requirement is not compatible with the equal income changes used in [8]. In addition, since preferences and circumstances change over time, it is necessary to make a supplementary "structural stability" assumption similar to one introduced by Hildenbrand and Kneip [10]. However, the structural stability hypothesis itself is not testable.

In practice, it is difficult to obtain data required for a direct test of increasing dispersion—data showing changes in the distribution of household demands during periods of unchanging relative prices and relative income distribution. This was the motivation for the cross section tests of increasing dispersion in [8,13]. The idea there is to treat a measure of the dispersion of the demand vectors of households with income x as an estimate of the dispersion that slightly poorer households would have if their incomes rose to x. If the estimation errors are uncorrelated with income, the effects of increasing household incomes can be estimated using the method of average derivatives from nonparametric statistics. In cross section tests in [8], increasing dispersion is accepted and its negation is rejected. However the tests are potentially sensitive to the treatment of the tails of the income distribution. We present a simpler cross section test based on [13] that might have more stable statistical properties.

Cross section tests of increasing dispersion require a supplementary hypothesis that relates the income effects to cross section data. The supplementary hypothesis is satisfied if the households' demand functions and their incomes are independently distributed. But this is a very special case. The supplementary hypothesis is also satisfied under the *metonymy* hypothesis introduced in [6]. The main contribution of the present paper is to show that metonymy itself is untestable, even using ideal panel data that make it possible to test for increasing dispersion directly. Thus, cross section tests of increasing dispersion depend on a hypothesis that is not potentially falsifiable. This extends a theorem in [4].

In the next section we present the model of a consumption sector in a distribution economy. In section 3, we review the definition of increasing dispersion and show that it implies the weak axiom in the aggregate. In section 4, we show how increasing dispersion can be tested directly using panel data under a modified version of structural stability. In section 5 we show how to test for increasing dispersion using a single cross section, under a weakened version of metonymy. In section 6, we show that metonymy for a single population is not falsifiable, even using ideal panel data. In section 7 we discuss open questions raised by these results.

2 Notation

We consider economies with many heterogeneous households. The consuming units are called "households" because it is usually not possible to obtain data on the division of consumption within real households. We consider only "distribution economies" in which the households' incomes do not vary with prices and are treated as exogenous. A distribution economy can be viewed as a special case of a private ownership economy in which there is a good (income) that each household offers in fixed supply. The households' demands in the distribution economy are their excess demands for goods other than "income" in the corresponding private ownership economy. It can be shown that the results presented below apply with only slight modification to general private ownership economies.

The consumption side of a distribution economy is represented by a joint distribution of household demand types and incomes. Let $\mathbf{R}^n_+$ and $\mathbf{R}^n_{++}$ be the nonnegative and strictly positive orthants of $\mathbf{R}^n$ respectively. We consider a measurable space $(A, \mathcal{A})$ of demand types, and, for each type $a \in A$ and each good $j = 1, \ldots, n$, a nonnegative C^1 demand function $f_j(a, \cdot, \cdot)$ that is homogeneous of degree zero. The vector-valued demand function $f = (f_j)_{j=1}^n$ is assumed to satisfy the budget identity $p \cdot f(a, p, x) = x$ for every price vector $p \in \mathbf{R}^n_{++}$ and income level $x \geq 0$. A *consumption sector* is a triple (η, λ, f) with the following properties: η is a probability measure on $\mathbf{R}$ representing the income distribution (with $\eta(X) = 0$ for every measurable $X \subset (-\infty, 0)$); $\lambda(x, \cdot)$ is the conditional distribution of demand types for the households with income x; $\lambda(\cdot, B)$ is Lebesgue measurable for each $B \in \mathcal{A}$; and $f(\cdot, p, x)$ is measurable on $(A, \mathcal{A})$ for each price and income vector (p, x). We let μ be the corresponding joint distribution of demand types and incomes, the product of η and λ on $A \times \mathbf{R}$.

In the consumption sector (η, λ, f), the *marginal propensity to consume function* is $m = (m_j)_{j=1}^n$, where $m(a, p, x) \equiv \partial_x f(a, p, x)$ is the vector of income derivatives for demand type a. The *Slutsky (substitution) matrix* of type a at (p, x) is $S(a, p, x) \equiv [\partial_p f(a, p, x)] + m(a, p, x) f(a, p, x)^T$, where $\partial_p f(a, p, x)$ is the Jacobian matrix of $f(a, \cdot, x)$ at p. (Vectors in Euclidean space are treated as columns, and superscript T denotes the transpose.) The Slutsky matrix is a matrix of derivatives of the demands with respect to the prices when the income is adjusted so that the initial demand vector remains barely affordable, [19].

We restrict attention to consumption sectors in which the *mean income*, $\bar{x} \equiv \int x\eta(dx)$, is well defined, and in which, for every p, the functions $m(\cdot, p, \cdot)$ and $\partial_p f(\cdot, p, \cdot)$ are integrable with respect to μ. Then the *mean demand function*

$$F(p, y) \equiv \int f(a, p, yx/\bar{x})\mu(da, dx) \tag{1}$$

is also well-defined. The income argument of f in (1) is chosen so that F satisfies the budget identity. F is also homogeneous of degree 0 since $f(a, \cdot, \cdot)$ is.

We will consider hypotheses under which the mean demand function satisfies the weak axiom of revealed preference. A demand function $\hat{F} : \mathbf{R}^n_{++} \times \mathbf{R}_+ \to \mathbf{R}^n_+$ satisfies the *weak axiom* if $p \cdot \hat{F}(q, z) \leq x$ and $q \cdot \hat{F}(p, x) \leq z$ imply $\hat{F}(p, x) = \hat{F}(q, z)$. The demand function $\hat{F}$ satisfies the *weak weak axiom* if $p \cdot \hat{F}(q, z) \leq x$ implies $q \cdot \hat{F}(p, x) \geq z$. The weak axioms are consistency requirements. They are satisfied if the demand function is generated by utility maximization; but they do not imply that the demand function is generated that way. The weak weak axiom has a simple differential characterization that will be used below. A C^1 demand function satisfies the weak weak axiom if and only if at each element of its domain its Slutsky matrix is negative semidefinite, [16]. If at each (p, x) the Slutsky matrix is negative definite on the set $\{v : v \cdot p = 0\}$ then the demand function satisfies the weak axiom. (An $n \times n$ matrix M (not necessarily symmetric) is *positive semidefinite* [respectively, *negative semidefinite*] if $x^T M x \geq [\leq] 0$ for every n-vector x. M is *positive definite* [resp., *negative definite*] on a set U if $x^T M x > [<] 0$ for every nonzero $x \in U$.)

Mean excess demand does not generally satisfy the weak axiom even if all the individual households do. In fact, if there are at least as many household types as goods, then utility maximizing behavior by the households does not imply any useful structure for mean demand beyond homogeneity and the budget identity [3,23].

3 Increasing dispersion and the aggregate weak axiom

We now introduce hypotheses leading to the weak axiom in the aggregate. The main hypothesis, increasing dispersion, requires that a small proportional increase in all the households' incomes increases the dispersion of their "normalized" demand vectors. The normalized demand vectors are the demand vectors rescaled so as to lie in the frontier of the budget set determined by the mean income. With the subsidy, this budget set expands, so there is more room for the normalized demand vectors to spread out—more possibility for diversity in the households' demands. The hypothesis is especially plausible at the lower end of the income distribution. With additional income, poorer households might be less restricted to buying a limited number of necessities. But increasing dispersion can hold even if the rise in income does not lead any households to change the set of goods that they buy. For example, a sufficient condition for increasing dispersion is that the households have homothetic preferences (not necessarily identical). On the other hand, increasing dispersion is a much weaker requirement than homotheticity. It places no restrictions on the forms of the households' demand functions; it only restricts the way in which the demand functions are related to each other.

In order to define increasing dispersion, we let $\bar{x}$ be the mean income and we consider the *normalized demand vector* $(\bar{x}/x)f(a,p,\kappa x)$ of a household of demand type a and initial income $x > 0$ when the income is multiplied by κ. Note that the value of this vector at the prices p is $\kappa\bar{x}$. Increasing dispersion requires that for each price vector p, the variance of the households' normalized demand vectors increases in all directions orthogonal to p when the households are weighted by their shares of aggregate income. If v is a unit n-vector, the orthogonal projection of a vector u onto the line spanned by v has length $u \cdot v$. When the households' incomes are multiplied by κ, the mean of their normalized demand vectors is $\int (x/\bar{x})[(\bar{x}/x)f(a,p,\kappa x)]\mu(dx,da) = F(p,\kappa\bar{x})$. The variance of their normalized demand vectors in the direction v is

$$\begin{aligned} V^{\mu}(\kappa,p,v) &\equiv Var\{v \cdot (\bar{x}/x)f(a,p,\kappa x)\} \\ &\equiv \int (x/\bar{x})\{v \cdot [(\bar{x}/x)f(a,p,\kappa x) - F(p,\kappa\bar{x})]\}^2 \mu(da,dx), \end{aligned} \tag{2}$$

where the integration with respect to x is over $\mathbf{R}_{++}$. The consumption sector has *ID: Increasing Dispersion at* p if for each nonzero v with $v \cdot p = 0$

$$V_1^{\mu}(1,p,v) = \partial_{\kappa} Var\{v \cdot (\bar{x}/x)f(a,p,\kappa x)\}|_{\kappa=1} > 0, \tag{3}$$

where the subscript on V^{μ} denotes the partial derivative with respect to the first argument. The consumption sector has *increasing dispersion* (*ID*) if it has ID at every $p \in \mathbf{R}^n_{++}$.

Define $\alpha(a,p,x) \equiv f(a,p,x)/x$, the *average propensity to consume vector* of a household of demand type a and income $x > 0$. When the households are weighted by their shares of aggregate income, the mean of their average propensities to consume is $\bar{\alpha} \equiv \int (x/\bar{x})\alpha(a,p,x)\mu(da,dx)$, and the mean of their marginal propensities is $\bar{m} \equiv \int (x/\bar{x})m(a,p,x)\mu(da,dx)$.

It is easy to verify that the derivative in (3) equals $2\bar{x}^2 v^T C v$, where

$$\begin{aligned} C &\equiv \int_{\mathbf{R}_{++}} \int_A (x/\bar{x})(m(a,p,x) - \bar{m})(\alpha(a,p,x) - \bar{\alpha})^T \lambda(x,da)\eta(dx) \\ &= \frac{1}{\bar{x}} \int [m(a,p,x)f(a,p,x)^T - (x/\bar{x})m(a,p,x)F(p,\bar{x})^T]\mu(da,dx) \end{aligned} \tag{4}$$

is the covariance matrix of the households' marginal and average propensities to consume. Increasing dispersion is equivalent to positive definiteness of this covariance matrix on the space orthogonal to p. When it holds, households with higher than average budget shares for any good tend to have higher than average marginal propensities to consume that good. If the households' demands are generated by homothetic preferences then the marginal and average propensity to consume vectors are equal and C is the positive semidefinite variance-covariance matrix of the households' average propensities to consume. It follows from theorems of Kneip [18] that NAS and ID are satisfied if the households' demands are sufficiently heterogeneous in the sense of Grandmont [5] or Kneip [17].

"Increasing dispersion" is defined in [8] as requiring

$$\partial_\delta \int [v \cdot f(a,p,x+\delta) - F(p,\bar{x}+\delta)]^2 \mu(da,dx)|_{\delta=0} \geq 0 \tag{5}$$

whenever $v \cdot F(p,\bar{x}) = 0$. It can be shown that this requirement is equivalent to positive semidefiniteness of C and also to (3), with the strict inequality replaced by a weak inequality, cf. [14].

In order for mean demand to satisfy the weak axiom it is neither necessary nor sufficient that the households satisfy the axiom. It helps if the households do satisfy the axiom, but a weaker restriction is sufficient when ID holds. We say that the consumption sector has

NAS: Nonpositive Average Substitution at p if the mean of the households' Slutsky matrices, $\int S(a,p,x)\mu(da,dx)$, is negative semidefinite.

We omit reference to p if the sector has NAS at every $p \in \mathbf{R}^n_{++}$.

The sector has NAS if all the households satisfy the weak weak axiom. It follows that the sector has NAS if the households are competitive utility maximizers. However, there is evidence suggesting that consumers often violate even the weak weak axiom, cf. [2,24]. NAS allows for such violations. The households' Slutsky matrices do not have to be negative semidefinite. If some households have positive substitution effects for price changes in a particular direction, the negative substitution effects of other households can make up for it.

Proposition 1. *In a consumption sector with NAS and ID, the mean demand function satisfies the weak axiom.*

Proof. It is sufficient to show that for each $p \in \mathbf{R}^n_{++}$ the Slutsky matrix of the mean demand function $S^*(p,\bar{x})$ is negative definite on the set of v orthogonal to p.

$$\begin{aligned} S^*(p,\bar{x}) &= [\partial_p F(p,\bar{x})] + [\partial_y F(p,y)|_{y=\bar{x}}]F(p,\bar{x})^T \\ &= \int [\partial_p f(a,p,x)\mu(da,dx) + \int (x/\bar{x}) m(a,p,x)\mu(da,dx) F(p,\bar{x})^T \\ &= \int S(a,p,x)\mu(da,dx) - \int m(a,p,x) f(a,p,x)^T \mu(da,dx) \end{aligned}$$

$$+ \int (x/\bar{x}) m(a, p, x) \mu(da, dx) F(p, \bar{x})^T$$

$$= \int S(a, p, x) \mu(da, dx) - \bar{x} C \tag{6}$$

where C is defined in (4). NAS implies that $\int S(a, p, x)\mu(da, dx)$ is negative semidefinite, and ID implies that C is positive definite on $\{v : v \cdot p = 0\}$. Together they imply that $S^*(p, \bar{x})$ is negative definite on $\{v : v \cdot p = 0\}$, hence that mean demand satisfies the weak axiom. ◇

It is clear from the decomposition in (6) that increasing dispersion is not necessary in order for mean demand to satisfy the weak weak axiom. Violations of increasing dispersion can be compensated for by sufficient negativity of the quadratic form of the mean of the households' Slutsky matrices.

4 A direct test of increasing dispersion using panel data

Increasing dispersion can be tested directly if the households' demands can be observed when their incomes rise proportionally with no change in relative prices. The comparison can also be made under more general conditions described in the next proposition. It is not necessary for the households' shares of aggregate income to remain fixed. Some households can move up while others move down in the relative income distribution. We assume, however, that there is no change in the distribution of characteristics of the households with a given set of observable attributes and a given income share in that attribute class. The fraction of the population with a particular set of attributes can change over time.

The direct test of increasing dispersion will be formalized as a comparison of different consumption sectors even though the goal is to test for increasing dispersion in a single sector. The sectors to be compared are interpreted as belonging to the same economy at different dates. Other interpretations are possible and will be discussed below. If the households' demand functions change over time, then only in special cases can we use information about the distribution of demands in one period to draw conclusions about effects of income changes in another period. The main hypothesis that allows such conclusions to be drawn is a modification of the "structural stability" hypothesis introduced in [10]. Structural stability places no restrictions on the evolution of any particular household's characteristics. It restricts only the evolution of the *distribution* of household characteristics.

In order to formulate our version of the structural stability hypothesis we need new notation representing information about observable household attributes. We consider a population of households consisting of a finite number of attribute classes observed over a number of periods. The households in each attribute class c and period $t \in \mathcal{T}$ form their own consumption sector

$\mathcal{D}_t^c \equiv (\eta_t^c, \lambda_t^c, f)$ with probability distribution of demand types and incomes μ_t^c. The consumption sector for the whole population at date t is the aggregate of all the consumption sectors for the different attribute classes. It is denoted by $(\mathcal{D}_t^c, \pi_t^c)_{c,t}$, where $\pi_t^c > 0$ is the fraction of the population in attribute class c in period t. The mean income of attribute class c in period t is $x_t^c \equiv \int x\eta_t^c(dx)$, and the mean demand function is

$$F_t^c(p, y) \equiv \int f(a, p, yx/x_t^c)\lambda_t^c(x, da)\eta_t^c(dx).$$

The mean income and mean demand for the entire population are respectively $x_t = \sum_c \pi_t^c x_t^c$ and $\sum_c \pi_t^c F_t^c(p, x_t^c)$.

Our structural stability hypothesis requires that for households with the same observable attributes who stay in the same percentile in the income distribution of their attribute class, the conditional distribution of demand types remains the same over time. Formally, the population has *structural stability for attributes* over $\mathcal{T}$ if $\eta_t^c((-\infty, \xi_t]) = \eta_s^c((-\infty, \xi_s])$ implies $\lambda_t^c(\xi_t, \cdot) = \lambda_s^c(\xi_s, \cdot)$ for each attribute class c and all periods t and s in $\mathcal{T}$. Hildenbrand and Kneip [10] use a slightly different version of this hypothesis to derive a simple formula for changes in the ratio of aggregate consumption to aggregate income. Our version of the hypothesis holds under the standard assumption that the households' budget shares are functions of prices, household income or total expenditure and observable household attributes, plus a random variable with a distribution that does not change over time. Since structural stability for attributes is a hypothesis about unobservables it cannot be tested directly.

Structural stability for attributes is not strong enough to permit time series testing of increasing dispersion. We will assume in addition that (a) each attribute class has *fixed relative income* (relative to the mean income of the whole population), so that x_t^c/x_t is constant in $t \in \mathcal{T}$, and (b) each attribute class c has *invariant relative income distribution*, so that for each $\kappa \in \mathbf{R}_+$ and t and s in $\mathcal{T}$, $\eta_t^c((-\infty, \kappa x_t^c]) = \eta_s^c((-\infty, \kappa x_s^c])$. Under (b), in each attribute class the distribution of income *as a fraction of the total income of that class* is constant over time. Hypotheses (a) and (b) can be tested using time series data. If all of the above hypotheses are satisfied during a period of constant relative prices, then it is possible to test for increasing dispersion using time series data. The next proposition shows how.

For each pair of periods t and s, define $x_{ts} \equiv \sum_c \pi_s^c x_t^c$ and $F_{ts}(p) \equiv \sum_c \pi_s^c F_t^c(p, x_t^c)$. These are respectively what the mean income and mean demand for the entire population would be in period t if the sizes of the attribute classes remained the same as in period s. The variance-covariance matrix of the households' normalized demands would then be

$$V_{ts} \equiv \sum_c \pi_s^c \int \frac{x}{x_{ts}} [\frac{x_{ts}}{x} f(a, p_t, x) - F_{ts}(p_t)][\frac{x_{ts}}{x} f(a, p_t, x) - F_{ts}(p_t)]^T \mu_t^c(da, dx). \quad (7)$$

Proposition 2. *In the notation above, suppose that the consumption sectors* $(\mathcal{D}_t^c, \pi_t^c)_{c,t}$ *have structural stability for attributes, and that each attribute class* c *has a fixed relative income and invariant relative income distribution over* $\mathcal{T}$.

If ID holds in period $s \in \mathcal{T}$ *then* $V_{ts} - V_{ss}$ *is positive [resp. negative] definite on* $\{v \neq 0 : p_s \cdot v = 0\}$ *whenever* $p_t = \zeta p_s$, *with* $x_t > [<] \zeta x_s$.

In order to test for ID, we need to compare the variance-covariance matrix of the households' normalized demands in period s with what the variance-covariance matrix would be in period t if the sizes of the attribute classes were the same as in period s. The latter matrix, V_{ts}, can be estimated by replacing the terms on the right side of (7) by their values in samples of households in class c from periods t and s.

Proof. Under the hypotheses, $F_t^c = F_s^c$ for each attribute class c and each t and s in $\mathcal{T}$. To see this, note that invariance of the relative income distribution implies that for each $x \in \mathbf{R}_+$, $\eta_s^c((-\infty, x]) = \eta_t^c((-\infty, x_t^c x / x_s^c])$. Therefore, by structural stability for attributes, for each $p \in \mathbf{R}^n_{++}$,

$$\begin{aligned} F_s^c(p, x_s^c) &= \int f(a,p,x)\lambda_s^c(x, da)\eta_s^c(dx) \\ &= \int (x_t^c/x_s^c) f(a,p,x)\lambda_t^c(x_t^c x/x_s^c, da)\eta_t^c((x_t^c/x_s^c)dx) \\ &= \int f(a,p,(x_s^c/x_t^c)z)\lambda_t^c(z, da)\eta_t^c(dz) \\ &= F_t^c(p, x_s^c). \end{aligned} \tag{8}$$

Let $V^s(\kappa, p, v)$ be the variance defined in (2) when μ is replaced by μ_s, the joint distribution of demand types and incomes in the whole population in period s. The homogeneity of $f(a,\cdot,\cdot)$ implies that $V^s(\cdot,\cdot,v)$ is homogeneous of degree zero, and that its partial derivative with respect to the first argument, $V_1^s(\cdot,\cdot,v)$ is homogeneous of degree -1. Suppose that the consumption sector for the entire population in period s has ID. If $v \cdot p = 0$ and $v \neq 0$ then for every $\zeta > 0$ we have $V_1^s(1, \zeta p, v) > 0$ and $V_1^s(1/\zeta, p, v) = \zeta V_1^s(1, \zeta p, v) > 0$. Therefore, $V^s(\kappa, p, v) > V^s(1, p, v)$ when $\kappa > 1$.

Define $F_{ts} \equiv \sum_c \pi_s^c F_t^c(p_t, x_t^c)$. Under the hypotheses, $x_{ts} = \sum_c \pi_s^c x_t^c = \sum \pi_s^c x_s^c x_t / x_s = x_t$. Let

$$G(a,p,x,b) \equiv (b/x) f(a,p,x) - F_{ts}.$$

In the notation above, using (7) and the change of variables $z = x_s^c x / x_t^c = x_s x / x_t$,

$$\begin{aligned} V_{ts} &= \sum_c \int \frac{x}{x_t} G(a,p_t,x,x_t) G(a,p_t,x,x_t)^T \lambda_t^c(x, da)\eta_t^c(dx) \\ &= \sum_c \int \frac{z}{x_s} G(a,p_t,x_t z/x_s, x_t) G(a,p_t,x_t z/x_s,x_t)^T \lambda_s^c(z, da)\eta_s^c(dz). \end{aligned} \tag{9}$$

It follows that if $p_t = \zeta p_s$ then $v^T V_{ts} v = V^s(x_t/\zeta, p_s, v)$. Also, $v^T V_{ss} v = V^s(1, p_s, v)$, so ID implies that $v^T[V_{ts} - V_{ss}]v > 0$ when $x_t/\zeta > x_s$. ◇

Ideal panel data cannot be used to test the alternative definition of increasing dispersion in (5) nonparametrically. The problem is that the space orthogonal to the mean demand vector $F(p, \bar{x})$ typically changes when $\bar{x}$ changes. Another test, relying on a weak version of metonymy, will be described in the next section.

5 A test of increasing dispersion using cross section data

In this section we show how increasing dispersion can be tested using a single cross section. We will need a hypothesis, called *dispersion metonymy* that links the effects of increasing the households' incomes to the effects of moving up the income distribution in the cross section. We will use a measure of the dispersion of the demands of households with income x as an estimate of the dispersion that slightly poorer households would have if their incomes rose to x. Dispersion metonymy is essentially the hypothesis that the estimation error is uncorrelated with household income. The estimation error is zero if the households' demand functions and incomes are independently distributed. Dispersion metonymy is a substantially weaker hypothesis. It is similar to, but different from "average covariance metonymy" in [8]. We will show in the appendix that dispersion metonymy is weaker than the metonymy hypothesis introduced in [6] and examined in the next section. This implies that, like metonymy, dispersion metonymy is not refutable with ideal panel data.

Let (η, λ, f) be a consumption sector with mean income $\bar{x} \equiv \int x\eta(dx)$ and mean demand vector $F \equiv \int f(a,p,x)\lambda(x,da)\eta(dx)$ at the price vector p. We focus on a single cross section so that p is fixed and will be supressed as an argument of the functions f and m.

If the households' demand functions and incomes are independently distributed, then $\lambda(x, \cdot)$, the distribution of demand types with income x does not depend on x. In that case,

$$\begin{aligned} &\partial_x \int_A (f(a,x) - (x/\bar{x})F)(f(a,x) - (x/\bar{x})F)^T \lambda(x, da) \\ &= \int_A [(m - (1/\bar{x})F)(f - (x/\bar{x})F)^T + (f - (x/\bar{x})F)(m - (1/\bar{x})F)^T]\lambda(x, da) \\ &= \int_A \left[mf^T - \frac{x}{\bar{x}}mF^T + fm^T - \frac{x}{\bar{x}}Fm^T\right]\lambda(x, da), \qquad (10) \end{aligned}$$

where the omitted argument of m and f is (a, x).

We will only require (10) to hold "on average." This means that we require (10) to hold when all the terms are integrated with respect to income, x. We say that the consumption sector has *dispersion metonymy* at p if

$$\int_{\mathbf{R}} \left[\partial_x \int_A (f(a,x) - \frac{x}{\bar{x}}F)(f(a,x) - \frac{x}{\bar{x}}F)^T \lambda(x, da) \right] \eta(dx) = \bar{x}(C + C^T). \quad (11)$$

Increasing dispersion is equivalent to positive definiteness of C on the space orthogonal to p. It can be tested under dispersion metonymy by estimating the left side of (11) and testing whether it is positive semidefinite. The left side of (11) is the average derivative of a regression function, the regression of the matrix of household demand dispersions, $(f(a,x) - (x/\bar{x})F)(f(a,x) - (x/\bar{x})F)^T$ on x. The average derivative matrix can be estimated nonparametrically using a random sample of observations of the household demand vectors $f(a,x)$ from the cross section, as in [9]. The distribution of these average derivatives can be estimated by bootstrap methods to obtain a statistical test of the hypothesis that the left side of (11) is positive definite on the space orthogonal to p. Under dispersion metonymy, this is a test of increasing dispersion.

In principle, it should be possible to obtain ideal panel data from experiments using the experimental design due to Sippel [24]. Subjects are asked to choose consumption vectors in a number of different budget sets, then one of the sets is chosen at random and the subjects consume the vector that they chose for that set. In this way the subjects have the incentive to report accurately what they would buy, and several demand choices from a single period are observed.

6 Unfalsifiable metonymy

In this section we show that the metonymy hypothesis introduced in [6], which is stronger than dispersion metonymy, is still too weak to be testable using ideal panel data. This result extends the main theorem in [4].

Metonymy was introduced so that the mean of the households' symmetrized income effects matrices $(m_i f_j + m_j f_i)$ could be estimated using cross section data. Here, m_i is the marginal propensity to consume function for good i. As in the previous section, the price vector is fixed and suppressed as an argument of all functions. Metonymy relates averages of income effects $\int_A \partial_x [f_i(a,x) f_j(a,x)^T] \lambda(x, da)$ to slopes of cross section regression functions: $\partial_x \int_A f_i(a,x) f_j(a,x) \lambda(x, da)$. These derivatives are equal if the households' demand functions and incomes are independently distributed. Under metonymy, they need not be equal, but their averages over the income distribution are equal. The average derivatives of the regression functions can be estimated from cross section data.

It might seem that the income effects could be estimated using ideal panel data in which the households' incomes rise without changes in relative prices. Then metonymy could be tested by comparing the estimated income effects to the cross sectional average derivatives. We will show that this intuition is incorrect. Metonymy is a local, differential condition, and it cannot be tested using data from a finite number shifts in household incomes.

Without loss of generality we let every price equal 1. We also assume that *demands are positive*, i.e., that each household with a positive income demands a positive quantity of every one of the n goods. This simplifies the proof considerably and does not seem unduly restrictive since the demands are allowed to be arbitrarily close to zero.

We will need to consider variations in the measurable space of household demand types, so we include that space in the notation for a consumption sector. The consumption sector $\Lambda \equiv (A, \mathcal{A}, \eta, \lambda, f)$ satisfies *metonymy* (or is *metonymic*) if for each $i, j = 1, \ldots, n$,

$$\int_{\mathbf{R}} \int_{A} \{\partial_x [f_i(a,x) f_j(a,x)]\} \lambda(x, da) \eta(dx) \\ = \int_{\mathbf{R}} [\partial_x \int_{A} f_i(a,x) f_j(a,x) \lambda(x, da)] \eta(dx). \tag{12}$$

Our definition of a consumption sector implies that the integral on the left side of (12) exists. We say that the consumption sector has a *smooth cross section* if the integral on the right side of (12) exists. In that case, the integral can be estimated as an average derivative of the regression function $\int_A f_i(a,\cdot) f_j(a,\cdot) \lambda(\cdot, da)$ using cross section data, treating the observed demand vectors as random draws from the distribution on $\mathbf{R}^n_+$ induced by f.

Metonymy is a restriction on the effects of giving every household the same small income subsidy δ. Suppose that we can give the households such a subsidy and observe the effects. Starting with a consumption sector $\Lambda = (A, \mathcal{A}, \eta, \lambda, f)$ we obtain a new consumption sector called an *income translation* or δ*-translation*) of Λ. The δ*-translation* of Λ is the sector $\Lambda_\delta \equiv (A, \mathcal{A}, \eta_\delta, \lambda_\delta, f)$, where $\eta_\delta(X) \equiv \eta(X - \delta)$ for measurable $X \subset \mathbf{R}$, and where $\lambda_\delta(x, A') \equiv \lambda(x - \delta, A')$ for each $x \in \mathbf{R}$ and $A' \in \mathcal{A}$.

Given the consumption sector $\Lambda \equiv (A, \mathcal{A}, \eta, \lambda, f)$ and $\Delta \subset \mathbf{R}$, define $f^\Delta(a,x) \equiv \{f(a, x+\delta)\}_{\delta \in \Delta}$. A measurable function $G : (A, \mathcal{A}) \to \mathbf{R}^k$ determines a measure $G(\cdot) \circ \lambda(x, \cdot)$, which takes the value $\lambda(x, U)$ at Q, where $U \equiv \{a \in A | G(a) \in Q\}$. The income translations $\{\Lambda_\delta\}_{\delta \in \Delta}$ and $\{\Gamma_\delta\}_{\delta \in \Delta}$ of the consumption sectors Λ and $\Gamma = (B, \mathcal{B}, \eta, \gamma, g)$ are *observationally equivalent* if $f^\Delta(\cdot, x) \circ \lambda(x, \cdot) = g^\Delta(\cdot, x) \circ \gamma(x, \cdot)$ for every $x \in \mathbf{R}$. The last equation states that for each x the two consumption sectors have the same distribution of *Engel curves* $f(a, \cdot)$ restricted to $\{x + \delta\}_{\delta \in \Delta}$ for households with initial income x. In addition the consumption sectors Λ and Γ have the same income distribution η. Note that observational equivalence is stronger than the requirement that $f(\cdot, x) \circ \lambda_\delta(x, \cdot) = g(\cdot, x) \circ \gamma_\delta(x, \cdot)$ for all x and all $\delta \in \Delta$. The latter condition restricts the distributions of households' demand vectors in Λ_δ and Γ_δ for each $\delta \in \Delta$. But observational equivalence restricts the distribution of household *Engel curves* at finite sets of income levels for households at each initial income level x.

The following result shows that metonymy for a single population cannot be tested with panel data on a finite number of income translations, even if we have a continuum of data from each cross section.

Proposition 3. *For every finite set of income translations of an arbitrary consumption sector with positive demands and smooth cross section there is an observationally equivalent set of metonymic income translations.*

Proof. Consider the consumption sector $\Lambda = (A, \mathcal{A}, \eta, \lambda, f)$ and δ-translations $\Lambda_\delta = (A, \mathcal{A}, \eta_\delta, \lambda_\delta, f)$ for δ in a finite set Δ. Without loss of generality we can let $\Delta \subset \mathbf{R}_+$. Let L^2_δ be the Hilbert space of real valued functions on $A \times \mathbf{R}_+$ that are square-integrable with respect to the measure μ_δ, the product of eta_δ and λ_δ. For ϕ and ψ in L^2_δ define $\langle \phi, \psi \rangle_\delta \equiv \int \phi(a,x)\psi(a,x)\mu_\delta(dx, da)$. Let

$$\Phi^{ij}_\delta \equiv \int_{\mathbf{R}} [\partial_x \int_A f_i(a,x) f_j(a,x) \lambda_\delta(x, da)] \eta_\delta(dx).$$

The consumption sector Λ_δ satisfies metonymy if for each $i, j = 1, \ldots, n$,

$$\Phi^{ij}_\delta = \langle f_i, m_j \rangle_\delta + \langle f_j, m_i \rangle_\delta, \tag{13}$$

where m is the marginal propensity to consume function. The proof of Proposition 1 in [4] implies that for each $\delta \in \Delta$ there exist functions $\psi_{\delta i} \in L^2_\delta$, $i = 1, \ldots, n$, satisfying $\sum_i \psi_{\delta i} = 1$ and $\Phi^{ij}_\delta = \langle f_i, \psi_{\delta j} \rangle_\delta + \langle f_j, \psi_{\delta i} \rangle_\delta$ for $i, j = 1, \ldots, n$. We will use these functions $\psi_{\delta i}$ to construct a consumption sector and its income translations, which are metonymic and observationally equivalent to the Λ_δ sectors.

Let $B \equiv A \times \mathbf{R}$ and let $\mathcal{B}$ be the product measure of $\mathcal{A}$ and Lebesgue measure on $\mathbf{R}$. Define $\gamma(x, \cdot) = \beta_x \circ \lambda(x, \cdot)$, where $\beta_x : a \in A \mapsto (a, x)$ for each $x \in \mathbf{R}$. The measure $\gamma(x, \cdot)$ is concentrated on the set $B_x = \{(a, y) \in B | y = x\}$, with the same stucture on that set as the measure $\lambda(x, \cdot)$ on A.

Let $\Delta = \{\delta_1, \delta_2, \ldots, \delta_k\}$ with $\delta_j < \delta_{j+1}$ for $j = 1, \ldots, k-1$. Fix $(a, y) \in B$ and define $x_j \equiv y + \delta_j$ and $f_{ij} \equiv f_i(a, x_j)$ for each $i, j = 1, \ldots, k$. For each $i = 1, \ldots, n$, consider the piecewise linear function ϕ_i on $[x_1, x_k]$ satisfying $\phi_i(z) = f_{ij} + [(z - x_j)(f_{i,j+1} - f_{ij})/(x_{j+1} - x_j)]$ when $z \in [x_j, x_{j+1}]$, $j = 1, \ldots, k-1$. Then ϕ_i is affine on each segment $[x_j, x_{j+1}]$ and $\phi_i(x_j) = f_{ij}$ for each j. By construction, for $0 < z \in [x_1, x_k]$, $\phi_i(z) > 0$ and $\sum_i \phi_i(z) = z$. For each $i = 1, \ldots, n-1$, let $g_i(a, y, \cdot)$ be a C^1 nonnegative real valued function on $\mathbf{R}$ such that $g_i(a, y, 0) = 0$ and $g_i(a, y, x) > 0$ for $x > 0$, and such that $g_i(a, y, x) = f_i(a, x)$ and $\partial_x g_i(a, y, x) = \psi_{\delta i}(a, x)$ whenever $x = y + \delta$ for some $\delta \in \Delta$. The function $g_i(a, y, \cdot)$ restricted to $[x_1, x_k]$ is a smoothed approximation to ϕ_i, and can be chosen close enough in the sup norm to ϕ_i so that $\sum_{i=1}^{n-1} g_i(a, y, x) < x$ for each $x > 0$. Since $f_i(\cdot, x)$ and $\psi_{\delta i}(\cdot, x)$ are measurable, $g_i(\cdot, x)$ can be chosen to be measurable for each x. Define $g_n(a, y, x) \equiv x - \sum_{i=1}^{n-1} g_i(a, y, x)$. Since $\sum_{i=1}^{n} f_i(a, x) = x$ for $x \geq 0$, and $\sum_{i=1}^{n} \psi_{\delta i}(a, x) = 1$, we have $g_n(a, y, x) = f_n(a, x)$ and $\partial_x g_n(a, y, x) = \psi_{\delta n}(a, x)$ when $x = y + \delta$ for $\delta \in \Delta$.

By construction $g = (g_i)_{i=1}^n$ satisfies $g(a,y,x) = f(a,x)$ and $\partial_x g_i(a,y,x) = \psi_{\delta i}(a,x)$ for every $a \in A$, $y,x \in \mathbf{R}_+$ with $x = y + \delta$ for some $\delta \in \Delta$. In addition, $g(\cdot,x)$ is measurable in B for each $x \in \mathbf{R}$. It follows from the definition of γ that $g^{\Delta}(\cdot,x)\circ\gamma(x,\cdot) = f^{\Delta}(\cdot,x)\circ\lambda(x,\cdot)$. Thus letting $\gamma_\delta(x,\cdot) = \gamma(x-\delta,\cdot)$, the income translations $\Gamma_\delta = (B,\mathcal{B},\eta_\delta,\gamma_\delta,g)$ are observationally equivalent to the Λ_δ sectors.

By construction, for each $\delta \in \Delta$ and each nonnegative $x \geq \delta$, we have $\int_B g_i(b,x)[\partial_x g_j(b,x)]\gamma_\delta(x,db) = \int_A f_i(a,x)\psi_{\delta j}(a,x)\lambda_\delta(x,da)$ and therefore

$$\int_{\mathbf{R}_+\times B} \{\partial_x[g_i(b,x)g_j(b,x)]\}\gamma_\delta(x,db)\eta_\delta(dx) = \langle f_i,\psi_{\delta j}\rangle_\delta + \langle f_j,\psi_{\delta i}\rangle_\delta = \Phi_\delta^{ij},$$

so $\Gamma_\delta \equiv (B,\mathcal{B},\eta_\delta,\gamma_\delta,g)$ satisfies metonymy. This completes the proof. ◇

Metonymy is also unfalsifiable if one observes consumption sectors obtained by multiplying the incomes of all the households in one sector by a common factor. Given $X \subset \mathbf{R}$, let $\kappa X \equiv \{\kappa x : x \in X\}$ for $\kappa \in \mathbf{R}$. Given $\kappa > 0$, we define the *κ-multiple* of a consumption sector $\Lambda = (A,\mathcal{A},\eta,\lambda,f)$ to be the sector $\Lambda^\kappa \equiv (A,\mathcal{A},\eta^\kappa,\lambda^\kappa,f)$ obtained by multiplying every household's income by κ, where $\eta^\kappa(X) \equiv \eta((1/\kappa)X)$ for measurable $X \subset \mathbf{R}$, and where $\lambda^\kappa(x,A') \equiv \lambda(x/\kappa,A')$ for each $x \in \mathbf{R}$ and $A' \in \mathcal{A}$.

Given $\mathcal{K} \subset \mathbf{R}_{++}$, define $f^{\mathcal{K}}(a,x) \equiv \{f(a,\kappa x)\}_{\kappa\in\mathcal{K}}$. Sectors $\{\Lambda^\kappa\}_{\kappa\in\mathcal{K}}$ and $\{\Gamma^\kappa\}_{\kappa\in\mathcal{K}}$, κ-multiples of $\Lambda = (A,\mathcal{A},\eta,\lambda,f)$ and $\Gamma = (B,\mathcal{B},\eta,\gamma,g)$ are *observationally equivalent* if $f^{\mathcal{K}}(\cdot,x)\circ\lambda(x,\cdot) = g^{\mathcal{K}}(\cdot,x)\circ\gamma(x,\cdot)$ for every $x \in \mathbf{R}$.

A slight modification of the proof of Proposition 3 yields the following.

Proposition 4. *For every finite set of κ-multiples of an arbitrary consumption sector with positive demands and smooth cross section there is an observationally equivalent set of κ-multiples of another sector that satisfy metonymy.*

We showed in section 4 how to test for increasing dispersion in a single consumption sector using data on a finite set of κ-multiples of that sector. But according to Proposition 4, data on the κ-multiples are not enough to test whether a sector Γ is metonymic. Whether it is or not, there is another sector with metonymic κ-multiples that are observationally equivalent to the κ-multiples of Γ.

7 Conclusion

In a competitive distribution economy with increasing dispersion, mean demand satisfies the weak axiom and there is a unique equilibrium allocation. We have described new ways to test for increasing dispersion using suitable data from periods with constant relative prices and a form of structural stability, or using data from a single cross section under metonymy (or dispersion metonymy). However, the structural stability used above and metonymy and dispersion metonymy cannot be tested using ideal panel data.

Other sources of information might offer hints about the plausibility of the auxiliary hyptheses. It might be reasonable to apply the structural stability hypothesis to periods in which the consumers report that their preferences and other circumstances did not change significantly. Metonymy seems plausible when applied to narrow attribute classes, defined by characteristics that are the most important determinants of demand. The proof of Proposition 3 suggests another way to judge the metonymy hypothesis. The construction of the metonymic consumption sectors in that proof will not necessarily work if there are bounds on the households' marginal propensities to consume. If there are known bounds on the marginal propensities, then metonymy is potentially refutable using data from income translations or income multiples.

We have not considered tests of the nonpositive average substitution (NAS) assumption in Proposition 1. Experimental evidence suggests that although consumers often violate the weak axiom, the violations are not large in the sense of Afriat [1,2,24]. The connection between the sizes of violations of the weak axioms and violations of Slutsky negative semidefiniteness is described in [11] for the case of deterministic smooth demand functions.

Most of the results in the present paper can be modified to apply to general private ownership economies, following the approach in [15]. But many questions remain concerning the relationship between the models and data. For example, how do we allow for discreteness of purchases? At what levels of commodity aggregation is increasing dispersion likely to hold? With finely defined commodities, there are likely to be inferior goods that violate increasing dispersion. When the households' incomes rise enough, the variance of their demands for such goods falls as the demands approach zero.

The treatment of time is also problematic. Consumption data typically come from surveys in which households report their expenditures during a two to four week period. But the duration of applied models is typically longer. This means that part of the demand vector in the models is not observed. However, in that case, the propositions and empirical tests discussed above can be interpreted as applying to models with suitable time separability of consumer demands. For those models, the empirical dispersion analyses based on the Slutsky decomposition carried out by Werner Hildenbrand and his collaborators have led to a deeper understanding of the structure of market demand and the stability of price adjustment.

Appendix

Proof that metonymy implies dispersion metonymy:
Consider a metonymic consumption sector. Using the notation of section 7,

$$\int [\partial_x \int f(a,x) f(a,x)^T \lambda(x,da)]\eta(dx) = \int (mf^T + fm^T)\mu(da,dx), \quad (14)$$

where the omitted argument for m and f is (a, x). Post multiplying both sides of (14) by the price vector p, we obtain

$$\int [\partial_x \int x f(a,x)\lambda(x,da)]\eta(dx) = \int (xm + f)\mu(da,dx) \tag{15}$$

Therefore,

$$\begin{aligned}
&\int [\partial_x \int (f(a,x) - (x/\bar{x})F)(f(a,x) - (x/\bar{x})F)^T \lambda(x,da)]\eta(dx) \\
&= \int [\partial_x \int (ff^T - \frac{x}{\bar{x}} fF^T - \frac{x}{\bar{x}} Ff^T + (x^2/\bar{x}^2)FF^T)\lambda(x,da)]\eta(dx) \\
&= \int [mf^T + fm^T - \frac{1}{\bar{x}}(xm + f)F^T - \frac{1}{\bar{x}}F(xm+f)^T + \frac{2x}{\bar{x}^2}FF^T]\mu(da,dx) \\
&= \int (mf^T + fm^T - \frac{x}{\bar{x}}mF^T - \frac{x}{\bar{x}}Fm^T)\mu(da,dx) - \frac{2}{\bar{x}}FF^T + \frac{2}{\bar{x}}FF^T \\
&= \bar{x}(C + C^T),
\end{aligned} \tag{16}$$

where the missing argument of m and f is (a, x), and where C is defined in (4). Thus the consumption sector has dispersion metonymy. ◊

Acknowledgments

I thank Werner Hildenbrand for inviting me to spend three years at the University of Bonn. The environment was especially stimulating because of his efforts to promote empirical investigation and collaboration among economists and statisticians. He has made lasting contributions to demand analysis with his classic result on the impact of the income distribution [7], his search for properties created (not merely preserved) by aggregation and his insistence on relaxing parametric and "rationality" assumptions. I learned a great deal about demand aggregation from him and from his students, colleagues and other visitors: J. Arns, C. Blackorby, R. Blundell, E. Dierker, H. Dierker, J. Engel, I. Evstigneev, P. Funk, J.-M. Grandmont, B. Grodal, W. Härdle, H. Hennig-Schmidt, T. Hens, K. Hildenbrand, I. Jang, R. John, K. Koch, A. Kneip, M. Lehmann-Waffenschmidt, A. Lewbel, A. Mas-Colell, R. Matzkin, W. Neuefeind, J.-U. Scheer, U. Schweizer, W. Shafer, R. Sippel, T. Stoker, K. Utikal, K. Vind.

References

1. Afriat, S.N. (1973) On a system of inequalities in demand analysis. International Economic Review **14**, 460–472
2. Battalio, R.C., et. al. (1973) A test of consumer demand theory using observations of individual consumer purchases. Western Economic Journal **11**, 411-428

3. Chiappori, P.-A., Ekeland, I. (1999) Aggregation and market demand: an exterior differential calculus viewpoint. Econometrica **67**, 1435–1457
4. Evstigneev, I.V., Hildenbrand, W., Jerison, M. (1997) Metonymy and cross-section demand. J. Mathematical Econ. **28**, 397–414
5. Grandmont, J.-M. (1992) Transformation of the commodity space, behavioral heterogeneity and the aggregation problem, J. Economic Theory **57**, 1–35
6. Härdle, W., Hildenbrand, W., Jerison, M. (1991) Empirical evidence on the law of demand, Econometrica **59**, 1525–1549
7. Hildenbrand, W. (1983) On the law of demand. Econometrica **51**, 997–1019
8. Hildenbrand, W. (1994) Market Demand. Princeton University Press, Princeton
9. Hildenbrand, W., Kneip, A. (1993) Family expenditure data, heteroscedasticity and the law of demand. Ricerche Economiche **47**, 137–165
10. Hildenbrand, W., Kneip, A. (1999) Demand aggregation under structural stability. J. Mathematical Econ. **31**, 81–109
11. Jerison, D., Jerison, M. (1993) Approximately Rational Consumer Demand. Economic Theory **3**, 217–241
12. Jerison, M. (1982) The representative consumer and the weak axiom when the distribution of income is fixed. SUNY Albany Discussion Paper 150
13. Jerison, M. (1987) Testing hypotheses concerning mean demand and uniqueness of competitive equilibrium. Manuscript, U. Bonn
14. Jerison, M. (1994) Optimal income distribution rules and representative consumers. Review of Economic Studies. **61**, 739–771
15. Jerison, M. (1999) Dispersed excess demands, the weak axiom and uniqueness of equilibrium. J. Mathematical Econ. **31**, 15–48
16. Kihlstrom, R., Mas-Colell, A., Sonnenschein, H. (1976) The demand theory of the weak axiom of revealed preference. Econometrica **44**, 971–978
17. Kneip, A. (1993) Heterogeneity of Demand Behavior and the Space of Engel Curves. Universität Bonn Habilitation.
18. Kneip, A. (1999) Behavioral heterogeneity and structural properties of aggregate demand. J. Mathematical Econ. **31**, 49–79
19. Mas-Colell, A., Whinston, M., Green, J. (1995) Microeconomic Theory. Oxford U. Press, Oxford
20. Mas-Colell, A. (1991) On the uniqueness of equilibrium once again, in Barnett, W.A. et. al., eds., Equilibrium Theory and Applications. Cambridge U. Press, Cambridge
21. Quah, J.K.H. (1999) The weak axiom and comparative statics, Oxford University Working Paper 1999-W15
22. Quah, J.K.H. (2000) The monotonicity of individual and market demand. Econometrica **68**, 911–930
23. Shafer, W., Sonnenschein, H. (1984) Market and excess demand, ch. 14 in Handbook of Mathematical Economics. Elsevier, Amsterdam
24. Sippel, R. (1997) An experiment on the pure theory of consumer's behavior. Economic J. **107**, 1431–1444

Some Problems and Perspectives in Economic Theory

Alan Kirman

GREQAM, 2 rue de la Charitè, 13002 Marseille

1 Introduction

Economists are interested in the "states of the economy." They wish to characterise certain states, which are "efficient" or "social optimal" in some sense. They are particularly interested in "equilibria" of the economy, "states" from which the individuals in the economy have no incentive to deviate. Furthermore, they are concerned with the relationship between the notions of efficiency and equilibria. More ambitiously they may be interested in the passage from one state, or perhaps equilibrium to the other, that is, in the dynamics of the economy. What I have just described somewhat simplistically, corresponds to the programme of theoretical or mathematical economics over the last century.

When I first met Werner Hildenbrand some thirty years ago he was in the forefront of this programme. The "General Equilibrium" project was being pushed forward irresistibly, and the only protests were of an ideological nature. Solid and rigorous foundations were being established for a theory of economic behaviour, or so we thought. The relationship between cooperative game theory and General Equilibrium was being neatly tied up, after the pioneering contributions of Shubik (1959) and Debreu and Scarf (1963) and this was largely due to Werner Hildenbrand. With the contributions of Aumann (1964 and 1966) the notion of perfect competition was given a rigorous basis and the problem of how to incorporate an unlimited time horizon for individuals was also dealt with and incorporated into the model. Hildenbrand's numerous contributions during the seventies bear witness to the optimism of the period. Yet if one reads the preface to *Market Demand* (Hildenbrand (1994)), one gets a very different impression. When he says, referring to the results of Sonnenschein (1973), Mantel (1976) and Debreu (1974),

> Up to that time I had the naive illusion that the microeconomic foundations of the General Equilibrium model which I admired so much, does not only allow us to prove that the model and the concept of equilibrium are logically consistent (existence of equilibrium) but also allows us to show that the equilibrium is well determined. This illusion, or should I say this hope, was destroyed, once and for all.

It is clear that he has come to the conclusion that the basic approach to which he contributed so much is fundamentally flawed. He is thus a counterexample to Max Planck's observation that scientists are incapable of changing their paradigm. The object of this paper is to examine some of the difficulties that have emerged with the standard approach and to suggest some alternative ways of examining some of the basic problems that should be central to any economist's interests. In particular, two aspects merit particular attention. Firstly, apart from the Sonnenschein-Mantel-Debreu results, the role of information in the General Equilibrium model suggests why that model contained the seeds of its own destruction. Secondly, I think that we have to explain how aggregate behaviour of systems may arise from the very process of aggregation. Thus, what we need are models for which, unlike the standard General Equilibrium Model, aggregation adds structure. This I believe is the central theme of Werner Hildenbrand's current work, and suggests why we have to look at assumptions on behaviour very different from those that we habitually use as to the preferences and objectives of individual agents.

Some economists will, at this point, ask why this preoccupation with General Equilibrium theory which, in any event, has fallen from favour? The answer is simple, the General Equilibrium model, often in drastically reduced or simplified form, is the basis for almost any modern paper in economics, particularly in macroeconomics. There is something paradoxical about the current attitude which is to use the General Equilibrium framework, in particular in macroeconomic models, whilst denying its intrinsic intellectual interest, or, more importantly, the interest of its fundamental limitations. Furthermore, an examination of the problems with the General Equilibrium model sheds light on possible ways forward.

2 Understanding economic phenomena

My first assertion will not necessarily meet with general approval but I claim that any economist should be interested in explaining empirical economic phenomena. This does not mean that he will not wish to simplify and make abstractions in order to be able to build models which he can analyse but does mean that he should always have an answer to the question, on which economic phenomena will my analysis shed some light. Without this anchor an intellectual ship can continue to sail under its own momentum and never see land. This has been the case for General Equilibrium, although a careful look at Hildenbrand's contributions reveals that he never lost sight of the importance of a more empirical approach even though the contributions in question (see e.g. Hildenbrand (1983), Hildenbrand and Hildenbrand (1986), Hildenbrand (1989), Härdle, Hildenbrand and Jerison (1991), and Hildenbrand and Kneip (1993)) were regarded by his colleagues as marginal with respect to his purely theoretical work.

Whilst most of his collaborators were pursuing the goal of refining and generalising the underlying model Hildenbrand was posing a number of questions which were to prove of real importance and which suggested why the General Equilibrium model was not the appropriate vehicle for analysing real economic phenomena. He was caught in the middle between those economists, particularly the macroeconomists who were happy to use the General Equilibrium model in a basic and oversimplified form without questioning the legitimacy of doing so, and those General Equilibrium theorists for whom the pursuit of greater generality was a worthwhile exercise in itself.

I started this paper by asserting that economists were interested in the "states of an economy" without specifying what I mean by this term. Depending on the particular problem at hand the economist may be interested in a detailed description of some part of the economy or may simply wish to examine some highly aggregate variables. At the most general level we might be interested in specifying everything about the allocation and activity of every agent in the economy. This was the lofty ambition of General Equilibrium theory. At the other end of the spectrum we might simply be interested in the number of people "out of work" or the "inflation rate." Theoretical microeconomists have typically been interested in the first problem and have been preoccupied since the early 1900's with, for example, the existence and efficiency of the competitive equilibrium of a fully specified economy. No "organization" or specification of interpersonal relationships is assumed. The consistency of allocations in the sense that what individuals receive is just what they desire is achieved by an anonymous price system which all agents take to be given. Thus there is no need for any specification of the relationships within the economy, the only way in which agents communicate is through the price system. Indeed, in order to pursue their analysis economists have stripped away all the institutional details and structures which were still very much present in the work of both Walras and Pareto and even more so in the work of Marshall. In particular, economists have focused on the assumptions about individual characteristics and resultant behaviour which will ensure achieving an "equilibrium outcome."

This is, of course, a very static view of economics but even when looking at economic dynamics economists have concentrated on looking at "steady states" or equilibrium growth paths. One might well enquire as to how economists have reached this position. A neat and clear explanation of the development of economic theory in this century would be that it was essentially dominated by the analytical methods of classical mechanics and that physics triumphed as a model for economics and this is indeed the view advanced by Ingrao and Israel (1990).

In this view, each agent in an economy maximises some concave or quasi-concave objective function over a convex set defined by parameters over which he has no control. The natural way to analyse such a system is to look for an equilibrium state, that is values of the parameters determining the constraints of the individuals and choices of those individuals such that none of them has any incentive to modify his action. The passage from micro to macro behaviour is simply additive. Furthermore, no explanation is given as to how the equilibrium comes about. This is the subject of stability analysis which has usually been reduced to examining the convergence of artificial price adjustment processes.

It is here that the Sonnenschein-Mantel-Debreu result reveals its full force. The standard and restrictive assumptions on the preferences of individuals do not guarantee stability. Without this the intrinsic interest of economic analysis based on the General Equilibrium model is extremely limited as Hildenbrand has pointed out on many occasions.

Before proceeding with the basic argument, it is worth mentioning that an avenue to restore structure has been opened to overcome these difficulties and that this stems from ideas advanced already by Cournot. This approach suggests that, if the economy consists of a large number of sufficiently heterogeneous agents, properties like uniquenes and stability of equilibrium may be restored (see Grandmont (1987, 1992) and Hildenbrand (1983, 1994)). Thus structure may be introduced into aggregate behaviour by the presence of enough differences between the characteristics of the agents. This approach has not led far for the present, as recent work by Billette de Villemeure (1999) and Kurt Hildenbrand (1998) have shown. The problem is with the definition of heterogeneity. What has been shown so far by Hildenbrand is that heterogeneity of behaviour imposes structure, the "Law of Demand," on aggregate behaviour. What has not been shown, as yet, is how to make assumptions on the distribution of the underlying preferences in the standard model that will guarantee the dispersion of behaviour. However, my basic argument here is that the difficulties with the basic model are too fundamental to be solved by such assumptions on the distribution of characteristics.

It is of little interest to insist on the basic defects of a model without explaining what the consequences of those defects are and without suggesting any alternative form of analysis. My aim here is to examine four aspects of the problems posed. Firstly, the role of information in economic models (section 3); secondly, the role of direct interactions between the agents in the economy, and the notion of equilibrium (sections 4 and 5); thirdly, the type of rationality that should be assumed for individuals (section 6); and lastly, the influence of the way in which the network that governs interactions organises itself (section 7). In each case the relation between collective and individual behaviour is posed.

3 The role of information

One of the major achievements of General Equilibrium theory has been to demonstrate that the competitive mechanism is remarkably parsimonious in terms of the amount of information that it uses. The standard theorem, due, in its most general form, to Jordan (1982) says that the competitive mechanism needs a "message space" with dimension $n(l-1)$, where n is the number of agents and l the number of goods. This is quite remarkable. To see why it is so consider a simple exchange economy. At equilibrium, every agent except one needs to transmit his vector of excess demands for $l-1$ goods because of Walras' Law) and thanks to the homogeneity of degree 0 of excess demand functions a vector of $l-1$ prices is needed. This result seems, at first sight, to reinforce the efficiency of the competitive market mechanism, since one can show that no other mechanism which achieves Pareto efficiency uses less information. Indeed, it can be extended to show how, in general, such informational efficiency may be achieved.

Consider the problem in which one is interested in mechanisms which will achieve, not only Pareto efficiency, but will also be "fair" in the sense that no individual prefers someone else's allocation to his own. This would seem to be a very demanding requirement in terms of information since every individual must be able to compare his allocation with that of all the other agents. Nevertheless, one can show that a mechanism which uses a message space of only nl dimensions can achieve this result (see Calsamiglia and Kirman (1993)). The secret of this result is to use the competitive mechanism to form an equal division of resources. Thus the Walrasian mechanism allows an enormous economy of information. Surely such results should strengthen the position of those who defend General Equilibrium analysis? The answer is negative and to see why, one has to recall that so little information is needed for the economy to function *at equilibrium*.

What interests us is not only how informationally demanding the mechanism is at equilibrium but also how much information it requires to get there. This is the problem of stability. Equilibria are of interest if they can be attained through a reasonable adjustment process. It is often claimed that the "tâtonnement" process is reasonable, yet, as we know from the results of Sonnenschein, Mantel and Debreu, the equilibria of economies are not necessarily stable. It has then been argued that the problem lies with the adjustment process rather than with the General Equilibrium model. If a more general adjustment rule were to be specified, perhaps the equilibria of the economy could be shown to be stable. Yet, what became immediately clear after the innovative work of Smale (1976) was that stability could only be achieved at the price of an enormous increase in the amount of information.[1]

Smale's Global Newton Method is an extension of standard methods which allow one to find a fixed point of a mapping, such as an aggregate excess demand function, if one starts sufficiently near the boundary of definition. It has two major drawbacks. Firstly, it does not behave well in the interior of the domain which, in the case under consideration, is the space of all strictly positive prices. Secondly, as already mentioned, it uses a great deal of information. What is needed is a knowledge of all the partial derivatives and this increases the size of the message space without guaranteeing convergence from any arbitrary starting point. An additional problem is with the economic content of the process. While the original tâtonnement process has

[1] For a full account of the problems outlined here see Flaschel (1991).

a very natural interpretation this is not the case for the Newton Methods, despite the efforts of Varian (1977).

Is the informational content of the Newton Method a necessary evil? Saari and Simon (1978) asked the following question. Can one find what they called "Locally Effective Price Mechanisms," that is ones which turn all economic equilibria into sinks, which use less information than the Newton Methods? They proved, unfortunately, that this cannot be done. This is disappointing since the Generalised Newton Method has the undesirable property that it reduces excess demands monotonically. One might have hoped that, by relaxing these features one could have found less informationally demanding mechanisms.

As Jordan (1986) pointed out, all the alternative adjustment processes that had been constructed when he wrote had no economic interpretation. There have been many efforts to construct globally and universally stable price adjustment processes since and, in a certain sense, Kamiya (1990), Flaschel (1991) and Herings (1995) succeeded. Yet if one looks closely at these results there is always some feature which is open to objection. In Kamiya's case the excess demand function is artificially defined outside the original price domain. In Flaschel's case the adjustment process depends on a parameter which varies with the economy and indeed, he says that it is too much to hope that one would find a process that would work for all economies. Hering's mechanism has the curious feature that prices are adjusted according to the relation between current price and the starting price.

All of this seems, to me at least, to suggest that there is no hope of finding an economically interpretable adjustment process which will converge from any price vector independent of the economy. In fact the Saari and Simon result might be thought of as saying that such a process would require an infinite amount of information.[2]

Where does all this leave us? The informational requirements of adjustment processes seem to be so extreme that only economy specific processes would seem to be plausible. This is hardly reassuring for those who argue for the plausibility of the equilibrium notion. Any change in the parameters of an economy would entail a change in the price adjustment mechanism that would keep the economy stable. Alternatively, one could argue that economies are not, in general, stable in this sense. If one accepts this point of view then one has to focus on the disequilibrium dynamics of economies as a certain number of authors have done.

However, the real issue is deeper and the difficulties with stability that I have outlined are symptomatic of conceptual problems. Almost all of the literature to which I have referred considers the evolution of a price vector, the dimension of which corresponds to the number of commodities, over time.

[2] Some suthors have quarrelled with Saari and Simon's definition of an adjustment mechanism, and Flaschel's mechanism, for example, does not satisfy their definition.

In the Arrow-Debreu model such time is undefined. Adjustment must be instantaneous. Yet, this well known problem simply reflects the unrealistic nature of the basic model. More disturbing are the obvious questions, what are prices at any moment in time and who sets them?

In almost any market one can think of, there is no vector of prices of commodities at any one time. Different prices coexist for the same commodity unless one takes absolutely literally the definition of a commodity in Debreu's *Theory of Value* (1959). These prices are set by individuals and the latter modify them according to what is happening on the market. Rare are the markets in which some central clearing mechanism exists which matches demand and supply. Consider financial markets which function on a double auction basis. At any point in time a bid is matched with an offer and a transaction takes place. The price at which this transaction takes place is in no sense an equilibrium price. All those who might have wished to transact at this price would not necessarily have been satisfied, yet it is this price that appears in the high frequency stock price series which are more and more frequently used. What happens at the next point in time? The other traders observe the price and the transaction and now decide on what to bid or to offer. Thus new bids and offers are made which may replace those which were made in the previous period. What is important here is that the trades taking place at each point in time reveal information. Why did that trader purchase that share at a price which I was not willing to pay? Perhaps he had information that I do not have? Such inferences may have important consequences for the evolution of prices. Where is the difference with the standard model?

Firstly, transactions take place sequentially and at each point agents observe what other agents are doing. They then obtain information and this influences their subsequent conduct. Thus there is interaction among the agents other than through a price system which everyone accepts as given. Such interaction is an essential feature of the real economy but is largely absent from economic models, and this is particularly true for most standard macroeconomic models.

4 Interaction and information

As I have suggested the failure to take direct interaction between agents into account is partly due to the basic paradigm in economic theory, namely that individuals take decisions in isolation, using only the information received through some general market signals such as prices. Communication and interaction other than through the price system are ignored altogether. Yet, while coordination through prices is undoubtedly important, can we afford to ignore the influence of other coordination and interaction mechanisms?

These difficulties can be sidestepped, as is frequently done in macroeconomics, by assuming that a sector of the economy can be described by a "representative individual."[3] This idea of representing a society by one exemplar denies the fact that the organisational features of the economy play a crucial role in explaining what happens at the aggregate level. The way in which markets are organised is assumed to have no influence on aggregate outcomes. Thus aggregate behaviour, unlike that of biological or physical systems, can be reduced to that of a glorified individual. Such an idea has, as a corollary, the notion that collective and individual rationality are similar. This is the antithesis of the way forward as I see it.[4] Indeed, what I would like to suggest is that collective outcomes be thought of as the result of the interaction between agents who may have rather simple rules of behaviour and who may adapt rather than optimise.

Once one allows for direct interaction among agents, macro behaviour cannot, in general, be thought of as reflecting the behaviour of a "typical" or "average" individual. There is no simple, direct, correspondence between individual and aggregate regularity. It may be that, in some cases, aggregate choices correspond to those that could be generated by an individual. However, even in such exceptional cases, the individual in question cannot be thought of as maximising anything meaningful from the point of view of society's welfare. Indeed the basic idea that I will develop is exactly the opposite from the representative individual approach. Instead of trying to impose restrictions on aggregate behaviour, by using the first order conditions obtained from the maximisation programme of the representative individual, the claim is that the structure of aggregate behaviour actually emerges from the interaction between the agents. In other words, complex patterns of interacting individual behaviour may generate a certain regularity at the aggregate level. Before arguing this, it is worth seeing how simple interaction between agents can undermine standard results.

Let me come back to the problem of the information conveyed by the unfolding of individual decisions in a market. An important consequence of the interaction between agents that I have mentioned is the sort of "herd behaviour" that may arise as agents are influenced by what other agents do, and, indeed, a number of phenomena corresponding to Keynes' "beauty queen" contest can arise.[5] To see how this can happen, recall that one of the most important features of most real world markets is that the actions taken by individuals reveal something about the information they possess. This feature of markets is poorly incorporated in most economic models and yet is characteristic of many financial markets. The reason for this is easy to see if one considers the extension of the standard theory to financial markets which is the so-called "efficient markets" framework. Within the latter, at

[3] For a detailed examination of the theoretical foundations of this approach see Stoker (1995) and the important contribution of Jerison (1982).

[4] Further reasons to reject this appraoch are discussed in Kirman (1993).

[5] See, for example, Banerjee (1992), Froot et al. (1992), Kirman (1993), and Sharfstein and Stein (1990).

each point in time, the private information of individuals is immediately transmitted into the central price signal. However, there are many situations in which this does not happen. Indeed one of the main problems in analysing financial markets has been to explain why the movement of stock prices is so much more volatile than that of the dividend process on which those prices are supposed, according to the standard theory, to be based (see e.g. Shiller (1981)). In seeking to explain this "excess volatility," economists have been led to the idea that individuals are influenced by each others' behaviour (see e.g Shiller (1989)), and may, for example, be led to modify their choices in the light of the choices or experience of others. This may lead to self fulfilling situations in which agents all "herd" on some particular choice or forecast which may not reflect any underlying "fundamental." A series of such events might explain the volatility of stock prices.

Consider a very simple stylised example, due to Banerjee (1992). Agents receive private signals, but also observe the choices made by others. There are two restaurants, A and B and one is, in fact "better" than the other. Individuals receive two sorts of signals as to which of the two is better. They receive a public signal which is not very reliable and which, say, has 55% probability of being right and a private, independently drawn signal which has a 95% probability of being correct. Suppose that restaurant A is actually better, and that 95 out of the 100 potential clients of the two restaurants receive a signal to that effect, and 5 get a signal indicating restaurant B as being superior. However the public signal recommends B. Now, suppose that one of the 5 who received a signal indicating B chooses first. The second client, observing the first, realises that the latter must have received a B signal. He is aware that all private signals are equally reliable and that his own signal, if it indicated A, is cancelled out. He will, therefore, have to follow the public signal and enter restaurant B. Thus, whatever the private signal of the second agent, he will enter restaurant B. The third client is now in the same situation as the second and will enter restaurant B. Thus all the clients will end up in B, and this is an inferior outcome. There is only a 5 percent probability of this happening but such a result will always occur with positive probability.

A criticism that is frequently made of such models is that they depend, in an essential way, on the sequential nature of the decision making process. This, it is argued, is not a common feature of actual markets. Yet in financial markets, for example as I have mentioned, in addition to any information acquired from a private source, a trader observes what other participants are doing or at least proposing to do. Consider the market for foreign exchange, for example. Traders try to anticipate the direction of the move of market prices, and they gain a great deal of information from various sources including other traders. Each such piece of information modifies their individual information set. However, since there is no central equilibrium price, this information cannot be incorporated and become public through the price. It can only be inferred from the observable actions of the individuals. Thus the action of one individual based on some private piece of information may give rise to a whole sequence of actions by others, and may, as a result, lead to significant moves in prices. When agents change their actions, in the light of the information they obtain from observing others, a so-called "information cascade" may arise. In such a situation individuals progressively attach more importance to the information they infer from the actions of others. They gradually abandon their private information.[6] Thus, as the number of people involved grows, the cascade reinforces itself. Whilst quite fragile to start with, cascades later become almost immune to relevant private information. Hence, as more and more individuals act in this way, a trader would have to have almost unbounded confidence in his own information not to conform, particularly if such cascades lead to self-fulfilling outcomes. There is a significant loss of efficiency here. The private information acquired by all the early agents would be of use to their later counterparts but if they choose to follow what others do, this information is not made available. In this way possibly relevant private information about fundamentals, for example, may never be used and prices might no longer be related to these fundamentals. Thus the conclusion to be drawn from this work is that the information obtained by observing the actions of others can outweigh the information obtained by the individuals themselves and lead to inefficient outcomes. Although all the information necessary to arrive at a socially efficient outcome was available at the outset of the process, some of it was lost as individuals followed the actions of others rather than rely on their own source. Thus interaction generates a result other than that which would have been obtained had individuals only observed signals and not behaviour.

5 Imitation

A second source of herd behaviour is the tendency to imitate those who are successful. This in itself might merely imply a learning process which would lead less successful participants to improve their performance. However, two things can happen. Firstly, if individuals follow simple imitative rules rather than behaving strategically, the outcome may be different from, and possibly more efficient than, the game theoretic outcome. For example, Vega-Redondo (1997) has shown that imitative behaviour in an oligopoly game can lead to a Walrasian equilibrium. Secondly, an individual may become successful as a result of some chance event, or series of chance events. The fact that he is then imitated may lead to the market moving in the direction he predicts or may end in a collapse of what will become apparent was a bubble. It is possible, indeed, that imitation of success will lead to perpetually changing patterns of behaviour in the market.[7]

[6] See Bikhchandani et al. (1992, 1998), and Welch (1992).
[7] See Ellison and Fudenberg (1993).

As another example of the consequences of sequential interaction between individuals, consider a very simple economic model developed in Kirman (1991). The underlying theory for the stochastic process involved, which was originally intended to explain experimental evidence about the behaviour of ants[8], was developed with Hans Föllmer.

Agents are faced with a price process p_t for a financial asset and form expectations about tomorrow's prices. There are two different ways[9] of forming expectations and each agent uses one of them. However, the expectations of the individual agents are influenced by random meetings with other agents. Call the two methods of forming expectations the two "opinions" in the model and then if there are N agents define the state of the system by the number k of agents holding opinion one, i.e. $k \epsilon \{0, 1, \ldots, n\}$.

One agent meets another at random and is converted to the other's view with probability $(1 - \delta)$. The underlying idea is that meeting another individual is like drawing a sample from the population and since the majority opinion is closer to the outcome one is likely to adopt the opinion of the person encountered.[10] There is also a small probability ϵ that the first agent will change her opinion independently of whom she meets. This is a technical necessity to prevent the process from being "absorbed" into one of the two states 0 or N, but can be allowed to go to zero as N becomes large.[11] Indeed, it is important, in what follows, that ϵ be small.

The process then evolves as follows:

$$k \to \begin{cases} k+1 & \text{with probability} \quad p(K, K+1) = (1 - \frac{k}{n})[\epsilon + (1-\delta)\frac{K}{N-1}], \\ k & \text{with probability} \quad p(K, K) = 1 - p(K, K+1) - p(K, K-1), \\ k-1 & \text{with probability} \quad p(K, K-1) = \frac{k}{n}[\epsilon + (1-\delta)\frac{N-K}{N-1}]. \end{cases}$$

The first problem is to look at the equilibrium distribution, $\mu(k)$, of the Markov Chain defined above. This is important in the economic model since it describes the proportion of time that the system will spend in each state in the long run. Now the form of $\mu(k)$ will depend, naturally, on the values of ϵ and δ. The case of particular interest here is that in which $\mu(k)$ has the form indicated in Figure 1. It is easy to see that if $\epsilon < 1 - \delta/(N-1)$, then $\mu(k)$ will indeed be convex. Thus this case in which the process spends most of its time in the extremes, corresponds to the case in which the probability ϵ

[8] See Kirman (1993).

[9] There could be any finite number of ways of forming expectations and this would not change the nature of the results.

[10] The model can be refined to make the probability of conversion dependent on the size of the majority but the simple version given here is sufficient to illustrate the point.

[11] This ϵ can be thought of as the replacement of some old agents in each new period by agents who may hold either opinion (see for example, the evolutionary model of Young and Foster (1991)), or by some external shock which influences some people's expectations.

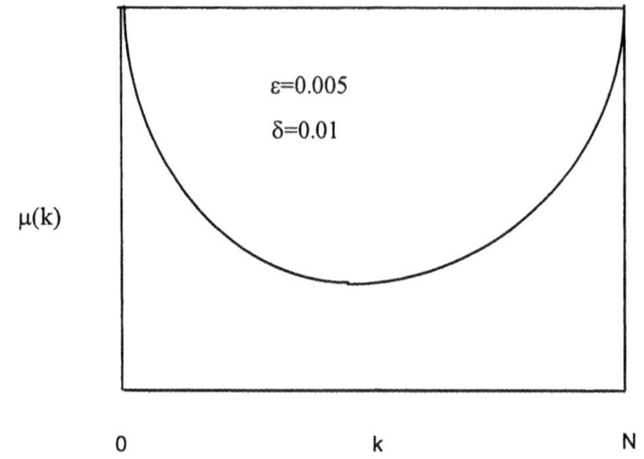

Fig. 1. Equilibrium Distribution

of "self conversion" is small relative to the probability of being converted by the person one meets. The ϵ, as mentioned, can be considered as a technical artefact which has been added to ensure that the market does not get stuck in a situation in which all agents hold the same beliefs. Thus, one would like ϵ to be as small as possible, in which case the previous condition will be satisfied. Indeed, Föllmer proved that, when N becomes large and ϵ goes to zero, the limit distribution, which we can call f, is the density of a symmetric Beta distribution i.e. $f(x) = \text{constant} \cdot x^{a-1}(1-x)^{a-1}$. Thus for $a < 1$, the distribution has the form illustrated in Figure 1.

Although the probability of conversion is independent of the numbers in each group, which type will actually meet which type depends on the relative numbers in each type at any moment, i.e. on the state of the system. Thus when one type is in the minority, conversion of any individual is much less likely than when the numbers of the two types are fairly equal.

This stochastic model of shifts of opinion is related to the urn models of Arthur et al. (1983) and also to models which have been developed for shifts in voter opinion (see the examples given by Weidlich cited in Haken (1977), where a similar bimodal distribution is derived). The latter model could also have been taken as the basis for the conversion from one opinion to another. One can use the interaction model just developed to examine shifts in expectations in a financial market, for example Kirman (1991).

What conclusions can we draw so far? If information is available from other sources than through the price system and the market does not have one price vector announced at each period, then aggregate outcomes need not be efficient. Furthermore, there may be no equilibrium state in the standard sense. There may be some sort of limit behaviour in the system but this may well be characterised by continual movement from one state to another. A different notion of equilibrium, such as the limit distribution of the stochastic process is required.

There has been a burst of activity in modelling the consequences of direct interaction between agents. Starting with the pioneering work of Föllmer (1974) who was first interested in this problem by Hildenbrand, efforts have been made to analyse the impact of the type of interaction and the network through which it is mediated. The idea that social interaction as, for example, modelled through Markov Random Fields, is an important determinant of the aggregate state of the economy is well on the way to wide acceptance, (see Durlauf (2000)) for a recent survey.

Suppose now that we take the idea of interaction seriously. It is no longer enough to specify the anonymous constraints with which an individual is faced but also the state in which those with whom he is linked find themselves. How should agents react? One answer is that agents will behave in a fully game theoretic way and will reflect on the reaction of their neighbours to their own behaviour and will take into account the fact that the other agents are doing the same thing. Such "eductive" reasoning, to use Binmore's (1990) term, is not only difficult to imagine for ordinary economic individuals but also presents logical problems.

However, evolutionary game theory proposes an answer that does away with this difficulty. The idea is that successful strategies will spread and wipe out less successful strategies. One way of phrasing this is to envisage agents as converting to those strategies that have had more success in the past. Thus agents do not optimise from the outset but adapt. Such a justification may be used to justify the imitative behaviour mentioned previously. To argue in this way is to move far from the tight optimising reasoning of the individuals in the General Equilibrium model. Why, however, are we so attached to that reasoning? As Hildenbrand (1994) says when discussing the characteristics of individual demand,[12]

> Do empirical studies of household demand behaviour establish or at least suggest some general properties of the individual expected demand functions? By properties I naturally think of qualitative predictions about how a household reacts to changes in prices and income. Given the hypothetical nature of the demand function f^i, I am afraid the answer is negative.

If we are to abandon the rigorous optimisation that we inherited from classical mechanics then I would suggest that we replace our introspective assumptions by considering adaptive behaviour and thus shifting to a more biological paradigm. This seems particularly important when significant externalities are present which undermines the sort of independence assumptions which are made for much aggregate analysis.

[12] Hildenbrand, op.cit. has a long and complete discussion on the appropriate assumptions to make about rational behaviour.

6 Adaptation and evolution or optimisation?

At least since Marshall there has been an effort to replace mechanical optimisation by more biological notions of learning and adaptation. The use of arguments based on natural selection has been present in economic analysis over a long period although such arguments have, in general, not been regarded as central. Hayek[13], for example, systematically used evolutionary arguments to justify the emergence of social and economic order. He maintained that the emergence of the market system was a result of evolutionary forces operating not only on individuals' behaviour but also on rules and social structure. His view of the result as optimal would, of course, be contestable from a strictly evolutionary standpoint, but his view of economic organisation itself as evolving endogenously was far from being widely accepted.

Indeed, for the most part, evolutionary arguments have been used by economists in the mainstream to suggest that optimising behaviour can been justified in economics as the result of adaptive behaviour or of natural selection. Friedman's (1953) remarks are so well known that it is not worth repeating them here. Though the logical objections to his position are clear, they reflect a widely held view. Alchian developed this reasoning and argued that natural selection would engender optimising behaviour. If this is the case, many economists have argued that one might as well take the short-cut of assuming complete rationality and studying the equilibria that would arise. Thus, Harry Johnson (1968) states without qualification:

> it has been shown ... that whether firms consciously seek to maximize profits and minimize costs or not, competition will eliminate the inefficient firms; and that whether consumer behaviour is rational or purely random, the demand curves for a product will tend to slope downwards as in the Marshallian analysis. In consequence, it is possible for economists to treat the economy as an interdependent system responding to change according to certain general principles of a rational kind, with considerably more confidence than appeared justifiable thirty years ago.

What Johnson is saying is that the system has properties which are not dependent on the specific behaviour of individuals. He is arguing that the aggregate structure that Hildenbrand derives from the dispersion of behaviour may result from natural selection. The basic argument is not formal but it leads, as does Hildenbrand's work, to an important observation. Johnson is arguing that the system as a whole has a certain rationality. This rationality emerges at the aggregate level and is of the same order as that which economists *assume* for individuals. As a result the system as a whole behaves like a large optimising individual. This is rather far from the idea of self

[13] See Hayek (1989) for example.

organisation used in biological or physical systems which is rather that the behaviour of the system may be qualitatively different from the behaviour of an individual. Thus, without imposing any specific rationality on individuals, some sort of collective rationality may emerge. Indeed, this is one way of interpreting Hildenbrand's work on market demand.

Johnson's argument is extremely simple and is close to the position held by Friedman since he argues that the role of selection eliminates the inefficient or unfit individuals. Thus for Johnson, selection takes place at the level of the individual and order emerges as a result of this. This is related to the position adopted by Lucas (1988) when he says,

> In general we view or model an individual as a collection of decision rules (rules that dictate the action to be taken in given situations) and a set of preferences used to evaluate the outcomes arising from particular situation-action combinations. These decision rules are continuously under review and revision: new decisions are tried and tested against experience, and rules that produce desirable outcomes supplant those that do not. I use the term "adaptive" to refer to this trial-and-error process through which our modes of behaviour are determined.

However, Lucas then goes on to argue that we can safely ignore the dynamics of this process since,

> Technically, I think of economics as studying decision rules that are steady states of some adaptive process, decision rules that are found to work over a range of situations and hence are no longer revised appreciably as more experience accumulates.

Thus the difference between the approach of many economists who rely on standard theory and those who argue for a biological style of analysis, is one concerning the stability of the adjustment to equilibrium and the speed of that adjustment. The basic tenet of those who concentrate on equilibrium is that the individuals in an economy learn or are selected relatively rapidly to behave optimally and that the economic environment changes sufficiently slowly so that in the resulting situation they have no need to continue to learn. This contrasts with the contention of authors who, like myself, hold the view that the economy is a complex adaptive system and that the very process of learning and adaptation and the feedback from the consequences of that adaptation generate highly complicated dynamics which may well not converge to any standard economic equilibrium. However what is clear is that adaptation and selection have not been absent from economic theory except in the most rigorous General Equilibrium models. They were used as a means of justifying the assumption of complex optimisation by economic agents rather than as an alternative to that optimisation.

It is also true that such a position was not left unchallenged even in its earlier stages. Winter (1962) took issue with Friedman and said:

> There is then a basic difficulty in the existing statements of the selection argument, a difficulty which is rooted in the fact that the relative deviations from profit maximization of different firms may change through time. Since there has been no careful treatment of the dynamic process by which some patterns of behaviour are shown to be viable and others nonviable, it has escaped notice that firms cannot in general be unambiguously ranked in terms of their closeness to maximising behaviour. Such a ranking must, in general, presume a particular state of the environment, but the environment is changed by the dynamic process itself.

This brings us face to face with the most difficult problem with the evolutionary approach. Fitness, or utility, or the capacity to survive and reproduce are measured with respect to the environment. Yet the environment consists, in economics, of the behaviour of the other agents and the organisational set-up. If one agent is adapting or learning then so probably are the others. Thus in simple game theoretic terms, we cannot assume that a change is profitable just because it would be so if other agents do not modify their behaviour. Agents who adopt strategies which were better in the past may make them less beneficial in the future. This, in turn, will lead them to change again and there is no guarantee that this process will converge. Thus one cannot hope, in general, to use adaptive behaviour to rationalise the equilibria that would have been achieved by fully optimising agents. This does not mean that one should abandon the assumption of adaptive behaviour but rather casts some doubt on the value of the equilibrium notion and suggests that we should be more interested in the dynamics of disequilibrium.

Having severed so many links with the General Equilibrium model, let me come to a last quarrel with that model. As I have suggested, the way in which economic activity is organised has an impact on aggregate outcomes. Nevertheless, considerations of organisational structure are largely absent from most economic models.

7 Market organisation

What I have in mind here is not organisation in its most general sense but rather the way in which the interaction between agents develops and influences market outcomes. The idea that market organisation, in this sense, has an important impact on economic outcomes is, of course, far from new (see the contributions of North (1990) and Greif (1993, 1994)). Historians have spent a great deal of time discussing the emergence of economic organisation and it would be remarkable if this had had no effect on the nature of aggregate economic activity. Certainly, in early economies direct interpersonal links played an important role. Finley (1973) suggests there was no market in the modern sense, in which interaction is anonymous and through prices, in the classical world. Medieval markets in England were characterised by personal and hierarchical relationships. As McLean and Padgett (1996) point out, markets in Renaissance Florence were strongly influenced by networks of family relationships and, as these were modified, market outcomes changed. Thompson (1971) describes how markets in 18th century England displayed a pattern of relationships and implicit rules governing those relationships.

This concern with the influence of market arrangements did not, as is sometimes suggested, disappear with the "marginal revolution." As Walker (1996) clearly explains, Walras was preoccupied with the way in which exchanges and communication in markets are organised. Although the standard paradigm referred to as "Walrasian" is normally taken to be one in which individuals receive prices from some unspecified source such as an auctioneer, in fact, Walras never specified such an auctioneer and indeed, each of his models specifies carefully how individuals meet and change prices. Marshall (1890) is also at pains to point out the importance of the way in which markets are organised for economic outcomes. Hayek (1989) suggested that organisation or "order" is an emergent phenomenon and argued that what is known as the market, in modern terms, was but one form of spontaneous order. He maintained that this form of organisation was superior to others, thereby making explicitly the point that the efficiency of outcomes is intimately linked to the way in which the economy is organised. There has been a tradition in Sweden of treating the economy as a network (see Johanson and Mattsson (1987)), and the adherents to this approach argue strongly that the type of network that develops in the economy has an important influence on the kind of allocation of resources that will occur.

Recently, Kelly and Ó Gráda (2000) have shown how the social network linking individuals influenced their behaviour in various financial crises, individuals being much more likely to panic and withdraw their deposits if those to whom they were linked did so. We come back to the idea that individuals infer information from those to whom they are linked or they have a tendency to conform to the behaviour of the group to which they belong. However, two questions arise. How is the structure of the network of relationships linked to aggregate outcomes and how do the networks evolve?

The first question has many ramifications. Much of the literature specifying an interaction structure has taken as a basis a two dimensional lattice or some sort of locational arrangement on the unit interval as in the original Hotelling model or on a circle as in the work of Ellison (1993). The latter shows that the evolution of the states of a population which interact in a game theoretic way will be very different depending on whether all the agents interact with each other or whether they only interact locally. It is clear however that one should be interested in more general graph structures and in this case, for the moment, there has been a tendency to focus on the connectivity of the graph representing the social or economic links. This can be used, in a cooperative setting, to limit the number of coalitions that can form, (see

Kirman et al. (1986)) or to study the speed with which information diffuses (see Allen (1982) and Durlauf (2000)). There are many properties of graphs, in particular of stochastic graphs which can be exploited to explain particular economic phenomena. Stochastic graphs seem particularly appropriate since many of the links which one can use are physically present but are only used intermittently, if at all. One only has to consider the internet to see this. Recent work by Watts (1999) shows how the connectivity of a network may change abruptly with the addition of new links, and he also emphasises the tendency for stochastic graphs to be characterised by "clusters" or dense local networks.

Even if we understand the influence of the network structure on the aggregate outcome, one would still like to explain how the network came about. We can either model this process as one in which individuals reflect on the consequences of forming links with others and the reactions of other agents to their formation. This is in the spirit of the literature on coalition formation (see Greenberg (1995)). Alternatively one can think of agents as reinforcing those links that have been profitable in the past. Such an assumption may lead to networks in which some links are used systematically whilst others are used only occasionally. The particular structure that emerges will depend on the distribution of the characteristics of the agents.

Why is all this important and how is it related to the problems with the General Equilibrium model? In many cases economists use the following argument. We know that agents will be subject to idiosyncratic shocks or that they may have characteristics which are drawn from a given distribution. However, if there are enough agents the randomness will be eliminated and one can safely reason in the mean as Hildenbrand (1994) points out. This appeal to the law of large numbers depends crucially on the independence of the random terms. If there is too much dependence, as Föllmer (1974) pointed out, one cannot ignore the stochastic nature of the problem. This is true even if all agents interact with each other. However, the problem is aggravated if interaction is local. In this case the influence of random terms may not disappear even when externalities are relatively weak. This will depend crucially on the structure of the network and the neighbourhoods within it. Thus one of the standard routes from individual to aggregate behaviour is no longer legitimate.

8 Conclusion

Theoretical economists have watched with fascination the change in status of the General Equilibrium model. Once thought of as the central element of economic modelling on which all rigorous work in economics should ultimately be based, it has come to be recognised as empty of empirical content. What is interesting is that this change came from within. General Equilibrium withstood many uninformed attacks in the past but was unable to resist the force of the Sonnenschein-Mantel-Debreu results. The reactions to this situation have been very different. Macroeconomists have continued to utilise the underlying individual assumptions as if only these confer legitimacy on economic models. The problems of aggregation and lack of structure are avoided by resorting to such devices as the "representative individual."

More thoughtful economists have come to recognise that the basic structure of the model was flawed. This is the position of Werner Hildenbrand when he argues against the automatic resort to assumptions on individual behaviour which are due to introspection and are not empirically testable.

I have tried to outline what I consider to be among the major difficulties that make it so difficult to use the General Equilibrium model as a basis for empirical economics. The first of these is the problem of information. The parsimony of the information required by the Walrasian mechanism is illusory. If the mechanism is to be able to adjust from disequilibrium positions then it requires an arbitrarily large amount of information. This is symptomatic of the inappropriateness of the mechanism as a basis for the analysis of real economic phenomena. Furthermore when one considers the way in which markets actually function, the prices observed are not equilibrium prices in the standard sense. Yet the transactions that occur at these prices are observed and information is inferred from them. This may lead to price dynamics which do not converge to an equilibrium state. Information is not transmitted fully through prices and bubbles may occur. This inferring of information is but one example of the direct interaction that takes place between agents. Yet we cannot exclude considerations of such interaction on the grounds that it constitutes a mere imperfection of the standard model. Such interaction is a fundamental and not a marginal feature of economic behaviour. Taking such interaction into account should lead us to less demanding and less introspective assumptions about individual behaviour. Although Werner Hildenbrand would probably consider this nothing more than a loose metaphor, we need a more biological and less mechanical approach to the analysis of behaviour. Lastly, the network which governs interaction has to be taken into account if we wish to be able to analyse aggregate empirical phenomena.

All of this constitutes an ambitious programme which is far from being achieved. I am not at all sure that this is the sort of intellectual route that Werner Hildenbrand had in mind when he left the General Equilibrium highway but the aim is the same, to understand and analyse real economic phenomena.

References

1. Allen B. (1982), Some stochastic processes of interdependent demand and technological diffusion of an innovation exhibiting externalities among adopters, International Economic Review, Vol. 23, n. 3, October, pp. 595-608.
2. Arthur W.B., Y. Ermoliev and Y. Kaniovski (1983), Generalised urn-problem and its applications, Kibernetika, vol. 1, pp. 49-56.

3. Aumann R.J. (1964), Markets with a continuum of traders, Econometrica 32, pp. 39-50.
4. Aumann R.J. (1966), Existence of competitive equilibria in markets with a continuum of traders, Econometrica 34, pp. 1-17.
5. Banerjee A. (1992), A simple model of herd behaviour, Quarterly Journal of Economics, vol. 108, pp. 797-817.
6. Bikhchandani S., D. Hirschleifer and I. Welch (1992), A theory of fads, fashion, custom and cultural change as informational cascades, Journal of Political Economy, vol. 100. pp. 992-1026.
7. Bikhchandani S., D. Hirschleifer and I. Welch (1998), Learning from the behavior of others: conformity, fads and informational cascades, Journal of Economic Perspectives, vol. 12, pp. 151-170.
8. Billette de Villemeure E. (1999), Aggregation of demand and distribution of characteristics: A difficulty in modelling behavioural complementarity. Document de travail no.99/38, Universit de Cergy-Pontoise, Cergy-Pontoise.
9. Binmore K. (1990), Essays on the Foundations of Game Theory, Basil Blackwell, Oxford.
10. Calsamiglia X. and A. Kirman (1993), A unique informationally efficient and decentralized mechanism with fair outcomes, Econometrica, vol. 61, 1147-72.
11. Debreu G. (1959), Theory of Value, Yale University Press, New Haven, Connecticut.
12. Debreu G. (1974), Excess demand functions, Journal of Mathematical Economics, vol. 1, pp. 15-23.
13. Debreu G. and H. Scarf (1963), A limit theorem on the core of an economy, International Economic Review, vol.4, pp. 235-246.
14. Durlauf S. (2000), A framework for the study of individual behavior and social interactions, mimeo, Department of Economics, University of Wisconsin.
15. Ellison G. (1993), Learning, local interaction and coordination, Econometrica, vol. 61, September, pp. 1047-1072.
16. Ellison G. and D. Fudenberg (1993), Rules of thumb for social learning, Journal of Political Economy, 101, 41, pp. 612-43.
17. Föllmer H. (1974), Random economies with many interacting agents, Journal of Mathematical Economics, vol. 1, 1, March, pp. 51-62.
18. Finley M. (1973), The Ancient Economy, University of California Press, Berkeley, California.
19. Flaschel P. (1991), Stability independent of economic structure?, Structural Change and Economic Dynamics, Vol. 2, No. 1, pp. 9-35.
20. Friedman M. (1953), The methodology of modern economics, in: Essays in Positive Economics, University of Chicago Press, Chicago.
21. Froot K.A., Scharfstein D.S. and J.C. Stein (1992), Herd on the street: informational inefficiencies in a market with short-term speculation, Journal of Finance, XLVII, 4, pp. 1461-1484.
22. Grandmont J-M. (1987), Distributions of preferences and the 'Law of Demand', Econometrica, vol. 55, 1, pp. 155-61.
23. Grandmont J-M. (1992), Transformations of the commodity space, behavioural heterogeneity, and the aggregation problem, Journal of Economic Theory, vol. 57, pp. 1-35.
24. Greenberg J. (1995), Coalition structures, in R. Aumann and S. Hart (eds), Handbook of Game Theory with Applications, North Holland, Amsterdam, pp. 1305-1337.

25. Greif A. (1993), Contract enforcebility and economic institutions in early trade: the Maghribi trader's coalition. American Economic Review vol.83, pp. 525-548.
26. Greif, A. (1994), Cultural beliefs and the organization of society: A historical and theoretical reflection on collectivist and individualist societies, Journal of Political Economy, vol. 102, pp. 912-950
27. Härdle W., W. Hildenbrand and M. Jerison (1991), Empirical evidence on the law of demand, Econometrica, vol. 59, pp.1525-1549.
28. Haken H. (1977), Synergetics, Springer Verlag, Berlin.
29. Herings P. (1995), A globlaly and universally stable price adjustment process, CentER Discussion Paper no. 9432, Tilburg, University of Tilburg.
30. Hildenbrand K. (1998) On J.M. Grandmont's modelling of behavioral heterogeneity, Discussion Paper No. A-580, University of Bonn, Bonn.
31. Hildenbrand K. and W. Hildenbrand (1986), On the mean income effect: a data analysis of the U.K. family expenditure survey, in W. Hildenbrand and A. Mas-Colell (eds), Contributions to Mathematical Economics in Honor of Gerard Debreu, North Holland, Amsterdam, pp. 247-268.
32. Hildenbrand W. (1983), On the law of demand, Econometrica, vol. 51, pp. 997-1019.
33. Hildenbrand W. (1989), Facts and ideas in microeconomic theory, European Economic Review, vol. 33, pp. 251-76.
34. Hildenbrand W. (1994), Market Demand: Theory and Empirical Evidence, Princeton, Princeton University Press.
35. Hildenbrand W. and A. Kneip (1993), Family expenditure data, heteroscedacity and the law of demand, Ricerche Economiche, vol. 47, pp.137-165.
36. Ingrao B. and G. Israel (1990), The Invisible Hand, M.I.T. Press, Cambridge.
37. Jerison M. (1982), The representative consumer and the weak axiom of revealed preference when the distribution of income is fixed, Discussion Paper no. 150, State University of New York, Albany.
38. Johanson J. and L-G. Mattson (1991), Interorganizational relations in industrial systems: a network approach compared with the transactions cost approach, in: G. Thompson, J. Frances, R. Levacic and J. Mitchell (eds), Markets, Hierarchies and Networks, Sage Publications, London.
39. Johnson H. (1968), The economic approach to social questions, Economica, vol. 35, pp. 1-21.
40. Jordan J.S. (1982), The competitive allocation process is informationally efficient uniquely, Journal of Economic Theory, vol. 28, pp. 1-18.
41. Jordan J.S. (1986), Instability in the implementation of Walrasian allocations, Journal of Economic Theory, vol. 28, pp. 1-18.
42. Kamiya K. (1990), A globally stable price adjustment process, Econometrica, vol. 58, pp. 1481-1485.
43. Kelly M. and C. Ó Gráda (2000), Market contagion: evidence from the panics of 1854 and 1857, American Economic Review, vol 90, pp. 1110-1125.
44. Kirman A.P. (1991), Epidemics of opinion and speculative bubbles in financial markets, in: M. Taylor (ed.), Money and Financial Markets, Macmillan, London, pp. 354-68
45. Kirman A.P. (1993), Ants, rationality and recruitment, The Quarterly Journal of Economics, vol. 108, February, pp. 137-156.
46. Kirman A.P., C. Oddou and S. Weber (1986), Stochastic communication and coalition formation, Econometrica, vol. 54, January, pp. 129-138.

47. Lucas R. (1988), Adaptive behaviour and economic theory, Journal of Business, vol. 59, pp. 401-426.
48. Mantel R.R. (1976), Homothetic preferences and community excess demand functions, Journal of Economic Theory, vol. 12, pp. 197-201.
49. Marshall A. (1890), Principles of Economics, Macmillan, London.
50. McLean P.D. and J.F. Padgett (1996), Was Florence a perfectly competitive market?: transactional evidence from the Renaissance, Theory and Society (forthcoming).
51. North, D. (1990), Institutions, Institutional Change and Economic Performance, Cambridge University Press, Cambridge, UK.
52. Saari D. and C.P. Simon (1978), Effective price mechanisms, Econometrica, 46, pp. 1097-1125.
53. Sharfstein D.S. and J.C. Stein (1990), Herd behavior and investment, American Economic Review, vol. 80, pp. 465-79.
54. Shiller R.J. (1981), Do stock prices move by too much to be justified by subsequent changes in dividends?, American Economic Review, 71, pp. 421-36.
55. Shiller R.J. (1989), Market Volatility, M.I.T. Press, Cambridge, Mass.
56. Shubik M. (1959), Edgeworth market games, in Contributions to the Theory of Games lV, R.D. Luce and A.W. Tucker (eds.) Annals of Mathematical Studies 40, Princeton, Princeton University, pp. 267-278.
57. Smale S. (1976), Exchange processes with price adjustment, Journal of Mathematical Economics, 3, pp. 211-226.
58. Sonnenschein H. (1973), Do Walras' Identity and continuity characterise the class of community excess demand functions? Journal of Economic Theory, vol. 6, pp. 345-354.
59. Stoker T. (1995), Empirical approaches to the problem of aggregation over individuals, Journal of Economic Literature, vol. XXXl, pp. 1827-1874.
60. Thompson E. P. (1971), The moral economy of the English crowd in the eighteenth century, Past and Present, vol. 50, pp. 78-98.
61. Varian H. R. (1977), A remark on boundary restrictions in the global Newton method, Journal of Mathematical Economics, 4, pp. 127-130.
62. Vega-Redondo F. (1997), The evolution of Walrasian behavior, Econometrica, vol. 65, pp. 375-384 .
63. von Hayek, F. (1989), Spontaneous ('grown') order and organized ('made') order, in N. Modlovsky (ed.) Order - With or Without Design? London: Centre for Research into Communist Economies, pp. 101-23.
64. Walker. D.A. (1996), Walras' Market Models, Cambridge University Press, Cambridge.
65. Watts D. (1999), Small Worlds, Princeton University Press, Princeton, N.J.
66. Welch I. (1992), Sequential sales, learning and cascades, Journal of Finance, vol. 47.
67. Winter S. (1962), Economic natural selection and the theory of the firm. Yale Economic Essays, vol. 4, pp. 225-72.
68. Young H.P. and D. Foster (1991), Cooperation in the short and in the long run, Games and Economic Behavior, vol. 3, pp. 145-56.

Time Trends in the Joint Distributions of Income and Age

Alois Kneip and Klaus J. Utikal

Lehrstuhl für Statistik und Mathematik, Department of Economics, FB 03, University of Mainz, 55099 Mainz, Germany

Abstract. We propose a method of analyzing time changes of joint income-age densities. Change is decomposed into time invariant components which act on the densities as deformations with time varying strength. The functional form of these components is estimated non parametrically from cross sectional data. The method is applied to analyze British household data on income and age for the years 1968-95. It is learned that for the young and middle aged there is a trend towards increasing inequality, while during the early eighties there seems to occur a reversal in the evolution of the income distribution for the old.

1 Introduction and summary

Governmental institutions in many countries perform ongoing studies which aim to obtain information about socioeconomic characteristics of households[1]. Examples are the British Family Expenditure Survey (FES), the French Enquête Budget de Famille (EBF), or the Consumer Expenditure Survey (CEX) in the US. These surveys collect cross-sectional data about variables like income, age, household size, occupation, etc. They are conducted regularly, and many of them provide samples of several thousand HHs every year. They thus provide huge databases on the distributions of important economic variables, as well as on the *changes* of these distributions over time. Hence there is a growing need for advanced statistical and econometric methods which, non parametric and computer intensive, exploit data to the point of gaining detailed insight into basic structural properties that play a role in applied economics and economic model building.

In this paper we present a new method to study distributional change on related socioeconomic variables. It is intended to provide a flexible statistical tool which is able to capture unforeseen features. The procedure is fully non parametric; no assumptions are made concerning the structure of underlying distributions, their kind of dependence, or the nature of change.

We concentrate on the variables income and age. The structure of income distributions and the relation between income and age are of considerable importance in economics. For example, in consumption analysis the interdependence between income and age is essential in the context of the life cycle

[1] For convenience we abbreviate household by HH and HHhead by HHH

model (see for example Atanasio, 1999). However, in economic analysis not only the structure of the distributions of income and age in a fixed year is of interest. A major issue is an appropriate understanding of the development of such distributions over time. There is an increasing literature which addresses this problem. Most work concerns the analysis of time trends characterizing the income distribution, see e.g. Goodman and Webb (1994), and some papers also use age as an explanatory variable, see Jenkins (1995). The classical approach is to compare certain characteristics of the different distributions over time. Time trends are studied via the evolution of coefficients which are designed to quantify important features of the distributions. For example, the Gini coefficient is often used to measure the amount of inequality in the income distribution.

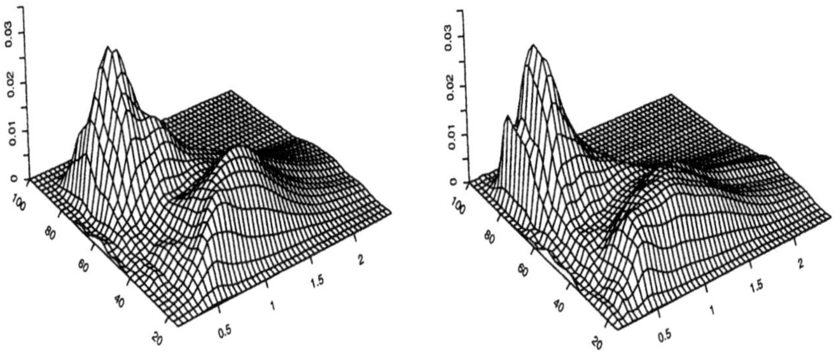

Fig.1.1: relative income-age densities, 1984 [left] and 1990 [right]

Our approach is different in that we focus on the joint densities characterizing the distributions of income and age in different years. Change is expressed in terms of the changing structure of these densities. The reader will be reminded that a density e.g. of HHs at some income level corresponds to the frequency of occurrence of HHs with this income in the total population. Classical parametric models of income densities include the lognormal and Pareto, see e.g. Atkinson(1983). During the last decades non parametric density estimation as described for example in Silverman (1986) has become a standard tool to discover previously unknown features of the underlying distribution. For example, it is shown by nonparmetric methods (see Cowell et al (1996)) that income distributions tend to be multimodal. Similarly, in the study of the joint distribution of income *and* age we obtain bivariate non parametric density estimates such as those displayed in Fig.1.1. Such density estimates provide insight into the local as well as global structure of the distribution. They yield a wealth of information that cannot be obtained by common global measures of spread or inequality.

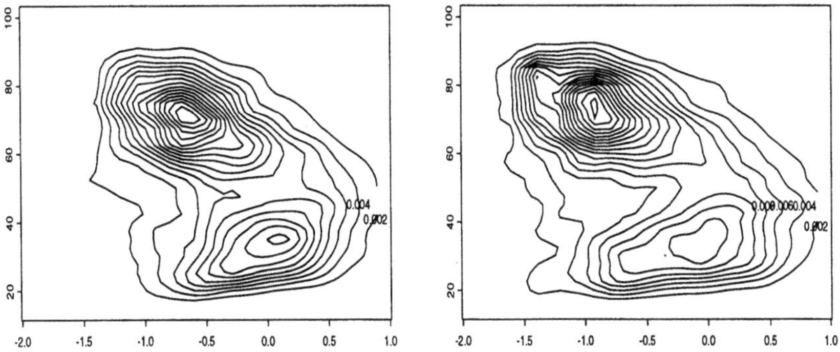

Fig.1.2: contours of relative income-age densities, plotted on the **log-income**-scale (for higher resolution at small incomes) 1984 [left] 1990 [right]

Since we are mainly interested in the redistribution of income and age over time we find it convenient to work with "relative HH income". This is determined by dividing (disposable, net) HH income by its mean over all HHs for each respective year[2]. Hence, in Figure 1.1 households at income level "1" are those of mean income. Other specifications of income and age variables are possible and could be used similarly in the analysis.

Not surprisingly, eventual changes take place gradually, and the figures show that distributions maintain their basic structure over time. They all remain roughly bimodal, concentrating low incomes among the old while spreading it around the mean (=1) around midlife. However, it is clear from comparing the densities with help of the contour plots that they differ over time, see Fig.1.2. This has also been observed in Hildenbrand et al (1999) by plotting estimated age densities over income strata for different years. We also note that these differences over many years cannot be sufficiently well understood by simply looking at a collection of estimated densities.

A method for analyzing such developments has been elaborated by Kneip and Utikal (2001) in the univariate case. It is based on concepts of so-called functional principal component analysis (FPCA). The idea is to describe change among densities in terms of the same components over several years which are transforming some base line density each time with varying strength. This way one year's density is approximately transformed into the future and the main tendencies in the changing frequencies can be estimated and predicted globally as well as locally. To apply it in the study of the changing interplay of income and age a generalization of the method to the

[2] For a precise definition of income and age variables analyzed we refer to the beginning of Section 3

bivariate case is required. This generalized method is applied to study the evolution of the joint density of income and age in the UK from 1968-1995.

Our analysis reveals the following facts about the time evolution of these differences[3]

1) For the period from 1968 up to the early nineties a basic trend is identified characterizing the redistribution of income for young and middle aged households. This trend consists of a continuous increase in frequency of households with small and high incomes at the expense of those with incomes around the mean. We may interpret this effect as a trend towards "increasing inequality"
2) There seems to be a reversal in the evolution of income distributions for old households.
   - *During a first period from 1968 until approximately 1981* the old are on the rise at all income levels, though frequencies of incomes above average remain small in absolute terms. There is a marked decrease of very poor and an increase of moderate income.
   - *In a second period from 1982-1995* this trend is partly reversed. A sharp increase of poor and very poor at the expense of those just slightly better off is noted. This development has its climax in 1990 and tapers off thereafter.

These results, to be discussed in detail in Section 3, are consistent and shed new light on previous findings in Kneip and Utikal (2001) based on separate analyses of income and age distributions.

Our methodological approach is described in Section 2. It consists of a two-dimensional generalization of the method of Kneip and Utikal (2001). This is preceded by an introductory motivation which also shows its relation to the familiar classical principal component analysis. The mathematical groundwork is laid in the appendix.

2 Methods

Our general objective is to characterize and study change in the joint distribution of two socio-economic variables (X, Y) over T different time periods. The problem is how to measure change and how to estimate it from cross-sectional samples of observations. Our major concern is the joint distribution of income and age but our methodology readily applies to other variables.

The method we apply is based on functional principal component analysis (FPCA). It can be motivated to some extend by traditional principal component analysis (PCA) taught in most introductory courses on multivariate

[3] We will call "very old" everybody above 85, "old" above 65, "young" below 30, "very poor" are incomes less than 0.25 the mean, "poor" less than 0.50, "medium" between 0.50 and 1.50, "rich" above 1.50 times the mean

statistics, and we thus start with a brief reminder of the basic concepts of PCA.

Given a sample $Y_1, Y_2, ..., Y_p$ of q measurements on each of p experimental units such as HHs these observations can be considered as q-dimensional (column) vectors and represented by a cloud of p points in q-space. Denote by $\langle \cdot, \cdot \rangle$ the Euclidean scalar product, and let $\bar{Y}$ be the average of the p measurements.

Principal component analysis determines the best linear projections of the q-dimensional space onto lower dimensional linear spaces. The first "principal component" yields a best possible approximation by a one-dimensional space. One searches for the vector P_1, $\langle P_1, P_1 \rangle = 1$ with the property that the empirical variance of the projections $\theta_{i1} = \left\langle Y_i - \bar{Y}, P_1 \right\rangle$ is maximal. This means that $var(\theta_{i1}) = \frac{1}{p} \sum_i \theta_{i1}^2$ has to be as close as possible to the total sample variance $\frac{1}{p} \sum_i (Y_i - \bar{Y})'(Y_i - \bar{Y})$. If the difference between these two variances is small we may approximate $Y_i - \bar{Y} \approx \theta_{i1} P_1$.

Usually, exact equality cannot be reached, and the remaining differences can be approximated by higher order principal components. The r-th principal component P_r is an orthonormal vector with the property that the variance of $\theta_{ir} = \left\langle Y_i - \bar{Y}, P_r \right\rangle$ is maximal subject to $\langle P_r, P_j \rangle = 0, j = 1, \ldots, r-1$. Frequently the θ_{ir} are called "scores".

It is well known that principal components correspond to the eigenvectors obtained from a spectral decomposition of the $q \times q$ matrix of empirical covariance (respectively, of correlations). We have

$$M := \sum_i (Y_i - \bar{Y})(Y_i - \bar{Y})' = P \Lambda P' \tag{2.1}$$

Here, $\Lambda = diag(\lambda_1, ..., \lambda_q)$ is the diagonal matrix of ordered eigenvalues, $\lambda_1 \geq \lambda_2 \geq \cdots \geq \lambda_q$ and $P = [P_1, ..., P_q]$ is the matrix of corresponding eigenvectors. It is easily seen that necessarily

$$Y_i - \bar{Y} = \sum_{j=1}^{q} \theta_{ij} P_j$$

Since $\lambda_r = \sum_i \theta_{ir}^2$ and $\sum_r \lambda_r = \sum_i (Y_i - \bar{Y})'(Y_i - \bar{Y})$, the relative importance of a component can be judged by using the percentage of explained variation $\lambda_r / \sum_s \lambda_s$. It is common experience that for a vast majority of applications the importance of high order principal components tends to be very small. In this case the space of observations can be well approximated by its projection on a much smaller subspace of dimension $L < q$, and

$$Y^{(i)} - \bar{Y} \approx \sum_{j=1}^{L} \theta_{ij} P_j \tag{2.2}$$

As a first approximation it may often be found that a substantial variation can already by captured by choosing $L = 1$ or $L = 2$.

Let us now return to our original problem to characterize and study change in the joint distribution of two socioeconomic variables (X, Y) over T different time periods. The distribution in any period is characterized by its density and we thus have to study a family of T bivariate densities $f_1, f_2, ..., f_T$. All densities are supposed to be square integrable i.e. belonging to the space $\mathcal{L}^2$ with scalar product between two functions $\langle \, , \, \rangle$ defined as integral over their product. Let $f_\mu = \frac{1}{T}\sum_t f_t$ denote the common mean.

Generalizing the ideas of traditional PCA, we are interested in projections of the density family onto low dimensional linear **function** spaces. Similar to (2.2) we thus consider approximations of the form

$$f_t - f_\mu \approx \sum_{r=1}^{L} \theta_{tr} g_r \tag{2.3}$$

for some small $L < T$. The "principal component functions" $g_1, \ldots, g_L$ now form a system of orthonormal functions such that $\langle g_r, g_r \rangle = 1$ and $\langle g_r, g_s \rangle = 0$, $r \neq s$.

The first principal component is given by the function g_1 with the property that the empirical variance of the projections $\theta_{i1} = \langle f_t - f_\mu, g_1 \rangle$ is maximal, and hence $\sum_i \theta_{i1}^2$ is as close as possible to the total variation $\sum_t \langle f_t - f_\mu, f_t - f_\mu \rangle$ of the density family. Generally, the r-th principal component g_r is an orthonormal function with the property that $\sum_t \theta_{tr}^2 = \sum_t \langle f_t - f_\mu, g_r \rangle^2$ is maximal subject to $\langle g_r, g_j \rangle = 0$, $j = 1, \ldots, r-1$.

In analogy to ordinary PCA calculation of the functions g_r and scores θ_{tr} is based on empirical covariances. However, the f_t are functions, and the covariance matrix is replaced by a covariance operator. Fortunately, there is a simpler approach which consists in considering a dual problem by interpreting the density family as an infinite dimensional collection of T vectors $(f_1(x), \ldots, f_T(x))'$, $x \in \mathbb{R}^2$. The elements of the $T \times T$ covariance matrix M of these vectors are defined by

$$M_{ts} = \langle f_t - f_\mu \, , \, f_s - f_\mu \rangle = \int (f_t(x,y) - f_\mu(x,y))(f_s(x,y) - f_\mu(x,y))dxdy \tag{2.4}$$

A spectral decomposition of M then leads to principal components and scores:

$$M = P \Lambda P' \tag{2.5}$$

where, similarly to (2.1), Λ is the diagonal matrix of eigenvalues $\lambda_1 \geq \cdots \geq \lambda_T$ of M and $P = [P_1, ..., P_L]$ is a $T \times L$ matrix of eigenvectors. Some algebra shows that

$$\theta_{tj} = \sqrt{\lambda_j} p_{tj} \tag{2.6}$$

and

$$g_j = \frac{1}{\sqrt{\lambda_j}} \sum_{t=1}^{T} p_{tj} f_t \tag{2.7}$$

for $j = 1, \ldots, L$ where p_{tj} is the tth entry of P_j, i.e. $P_j = [p_{1j}, ..., p_{Tj}]'$. The relative importance of a component can again be measured by the percentage of explained variation

$$\frac{\lambda_r}{\sum_s \lambda_s} = \frac{\sum_t \theta_{tr}^2}{\sum_t \langle f_t - f_\mu, f_t - f_\mu \rangle}$$

Often a few principal components will suffice to achieve a good approximation in terms of model (2.3). They can therefore be used as a tool for economic analysis. Changes in the densities for different t are captured by changes in the scores, while the functions g_r provide information about the structure of such changes.

By definition the first principal component plays a particularly important role. In Section 3 we will concentrate on this component to describe the main features of the development of joint income-age densities over time. Basic time trends can be assessed by analyzing the one-dimensional time series of scores $\theta_{11}, \ldots, \theta_{T1}$. The structure of the function g_1 then allows us to study how these trends affect the frequencies of HHs at any given income and age level.

The analogy between PCA in q-dimensional spaces and in $\mathcal{L}^2$ is best not be carried any further. Different from traditional PCA, the matrix decompositions (2.4)-(2.7) do not yet constitute a practically applicable procedure for determining principal components. The crucial point is that the true densities $f_1, \ldots, f_T$ are unknown. Hence, any application of the concepts discussed above additionally requires an efficient procedure for estimating principal components and scores from **cross-sectional data**.

Estimation

We assume bivariate samples $(X_{1t}, Y_{1t}), ..., (X_{n_t t}, Y_{n_t t})$, $t = 1, \ldots, T$, from T distributions with underlying densities $f_1, \ldots, f_T$. To apply the above machinery we first need to estimate the different densities f_t.

Sometimes the density is approximated by the pervasive histogram. By increasing the sample size and the granulation of the histogram at a certain rate this estimator converges to the underlying density in most cases. A superior estimate is given by the well-known kernel density estimator which can be considered a refinement of the histogram estimator.

Based on a give sample $(X_1, Y_1), ..., (X_n, Y_n)$ a bivariate kernel estimators of the underlying density is defined as

$$\hat{f}(x, y) = \frac{1}{nh_1h_2} \sum_{i}^{n} K\left(\frac{x - X_i}{h_1}, \frac{y - Y_i}{h_2}\right) \tag{2.8}$$

where K is a bivariate kernel with (double) integral equal to one. Similar to the univariate case the bandwidth parameters h_1 and h_2 determine the degree of smoothness of the estimate. As an example we consider the estimates displayed as a two-dimensional surface in see Fig.1.1 and Fig.1.2.

Using this estimator we proceed as follows:

(0) Estimate the family $\{f_t\}$ by $\{\hat{f}_t\}$

(1) Estimate the matrix M by $\widehat{M}$ whose entries are defined by

$$\widehat{M}_{t_1,t_2} = \langle \hat{f}_{t_1} - \hat{f}_\mu, \hat{f}_{t_2} - \hat{f}_\mu \rangle$$

where $\hat{f}_\mu$ is the arithmetic mean of $\{\hat{f}_1, \dots, \hat{f}_T\}$

(2) Compute $\hat{\lambda}_j$, $\widehat{P}_j$ from $\widehat{M}$.

(3) Estimate θ_{tj} and g_j by plugging these estimates into formulas (2.6) respectively (2.7).

The asymptotic behavior of our estimates is studied in the appendix. Our theory shows that in steps (0)-(3) the following data transformation and fine tuning of bandwidth parameters is necessary to obtain reliable estimates.

to (0): log transforming the income scale. More reliable estimates of the joint income-age density can be obtained by applying a two-stage procedure instead of ordinary kernel smoothing: all observed incomes are transformed by taking logarithms and kernel estimation is used to determine an estimate of the joint density of log income and age; back transformation then leads to an estimate of the income-age density . It is easy to see that this is equivalent to estimation in the direction of income with a variable bandwidth proportional at each income level to its reciprocal (see Simonoff (1996), p.61). We therefore achieve a substantial reduction of bias in the estimates for small incomes.
This procedure has been used to determine individual density estimates for various years as presented in the introduction and in Section 3. We have chosen K as a product of two Gaussian kernels with bandwidths equal to 2 in the age direction and 0.30 in the log income direction.

to (1): extreme under smoothing. Bandwidth selection requires quite some care. Different bandwidths have to be applied in different steps of our procedure. Note that the integrals $\left\langle \hat{f}_t, \hat{f}_s \right\rangle$ are estimated by $\left\langle \hat{f}_t, \hat{f}_s \right\rangle$ $= \frac{1}{n_t n_s h_1 h_2} \sum_i^{n_t} \sum_j^{n_s} \int K\left(\frac{x-X_{it}}{h_1}, \frac{y-Y_{it}}{h_2}\right) K\left(\frac{x-X_{js}}{h_1}, \frac{y-Y_{js}}{h_2}\right) dxdy$
In this case it is essential for reasons of efficiency of the estimate that we under smooth extremely, i.e. h_1, h_2 have to be much smaller than optimal bandwidths for best estimation of individual joint densities in given years. We have chosen $h_1 = 0.025$ in the income and $h_2 = 1$ in the age direction. By choosing the bandwidth this small the arguments given above concerning the necessary log transform of income no longer apply.

to (1): bias correction. It is further noted that for $t = s$ the diagonal contains the term $\delta + o(1/n_t h_1 h_2)$ where

$$\delta = \frac{1}{n_t h_1 h_2} \int\int K(u,v)^2 \, du \, dv$$

which produces unnecessary bias. We therefore correct the diagonal by subtracting δ from $\langle f_t, f_t \rangle$. In other words, define $\langle f_s, f_t \rangle_c := \langle f_t, f_t \rangle - \delta$ if $s = t$ and equal to $\langle f_s, f_t \rangle$ else. This way we estimate the entries of M by

$$\widehat{M}_{s,t} = \langle \hat{f}_s, \hat{f}_t \rangle_c - \frac{2}{T}\left(\sum_t \langle \hat{f}_s, \hat{f}_t \rangle_c + \sum_s \langle \hat{f}_s, \hat{f}_t \rangle_c\right) + \frac{1}{T^2}\sum_{s,t} \langle \hat{f}_s, \hat{f}_t \rangle_c$$

to (3): moderate under smoothing. Plugging estimators into (2.7) we obtain an estimator of g_r as

$$\hat{g}_r = \frac{1}{\sqrt{\hat{\lambda}_r}} \sum_t^T \widehat{p_{tr}} \, \hat{f}_{t,b_1 b_2} \tag{2.9}$$

where $\hat{f}_{t,b_1 b_2}$ denote kernel estimators with bandwidths b_1, b_2 not necessarily equal to h_1, h_2 in steps (0) or (1). It is recommended to slightly under smooth. We used $b_1 = 0.25$ (on log income) and $b_2 = 1$ years.

For some additional conceptual discussion of our procedure in the univariate case we refer to Kneip and Utikal (2001). Most of their arguments also apply to the multivariate situation. They also propose a method for determining a "best" dimension L in the context of model (2.3). In view of Theorem 1 in the appendix, their procedure can easily be generalized to the multivariate case.

3 Income-age-dynamics of British households

We now use the method presented in Section 2 to study the time evolution of the joint distributions of relative HH income and HHH age. We use data from the Family Expenditure Survey (FES) which provides independent cross sectional samples of more than seven thousand households each year. For a description of the sampling design we refer to Kemsley et. al. (1985), for a precise definition of variables we refer to the respective ESCR manuals. We analyze data for the years 1968-1995, except for 1978, where, unfortunately, our income variable could not be constructed consistently from the data.

As income variable we use aggregated, current income of all household members, i.e. those who live under the same roof and share a common meal.

Included is income from employment, self-employment, social security benefits, private pensions, investments and all other sources. Net taxes such as income tax, National Insurance contributions, and local taxes have been deduced. In order to obtain consistent variables which are comparable over time, consumption and income were defined by adding relevant items from the elementary database. As mentioned in the introduction we rescale the income variable to *relative* HH income. The HHH for married couples is the husband, the chief economic supporter in all other cases.

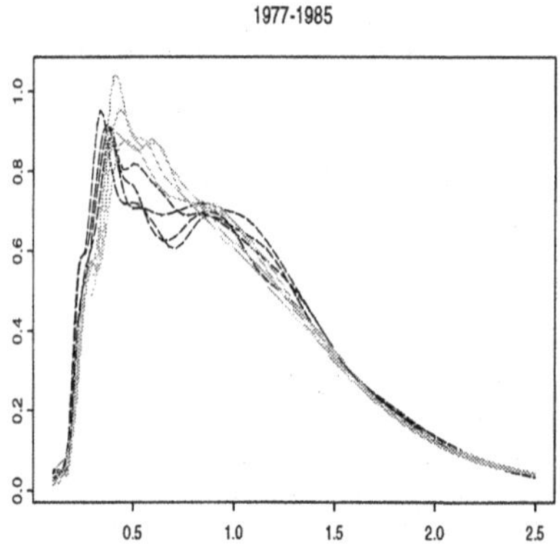

Fig.3.1: relative income densities 1977-81 (broken), 1982-85 (gray)

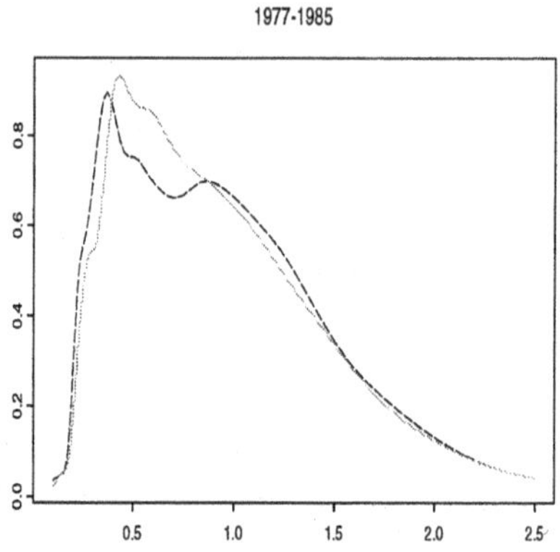

Fig.3.2: time average densities 1968-81 (broken), 1982-95 (gray)

Before starting the joint income-age analysis we scan data and densities separately in each variable. In particular, the relative income densities are estimated for each year and plotted over successive five year periods. From this a marked change in the shape of the densities is seen. A transition from a multimodal to a unimodal, heavily right skewed shape in the period of 1981-1982 seems likely to be the case, see[4] Fig.3.1. Splitting the total period into two sub periods and averaging over each we see in Fig.3.2 that the mean over the first and second are very clearly of different distributional form. We therefore consider this time point as marking a rupture in the family of income densities suggesting separate analyses over each subinterval.

Our method described in Section 2 has been applied separately for each of the two periods. By inspecting the average joint income-age density over the period 1968-1981 we see in Fig.3.4 that income and age are highly dependent. The density is bimodal with a sharp peak of 1/2 the mean income at age 70. The second peak is flatter at the overall mean income around age 30. The higher incomes, i.e. at least 1.5 times the mean, are found between 30 and 60 but mainly within 40-50 years.

[4] for color plots see *http://wiwi.uni-mainz.de/vwl/kneip/knpu.htm*

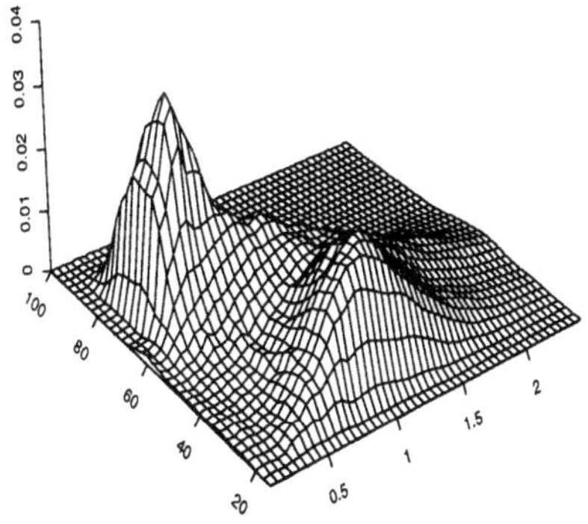

Fig.3.3: time average of joint income-age densities, 1968-1981

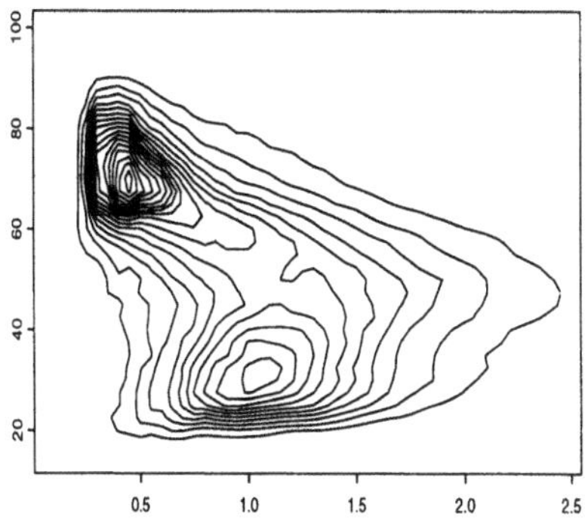

Fig.3.4: contours of joint income-age densities, 1968-1981

From the spectrum of eigenvalues (not displayed) for the first period it can be seen that the first principal component explains about 50% of the family's total variation and a second and third component seem to be relevant by increasing the explained variation by another 10%-20% each.

The first component has been decomposed for ease of exposition into its positive and negative parts in Fig.3.5 and Fig. 3.6. The corresponding scores displayed in Fig.3.7 show a clear tendency to increase all through the seventies. Combining Fig.3.6 and Fig. 3.7 we conclude that the frequencies of HHs over 65 years with an income close to 1/2 the mean are on the rise.

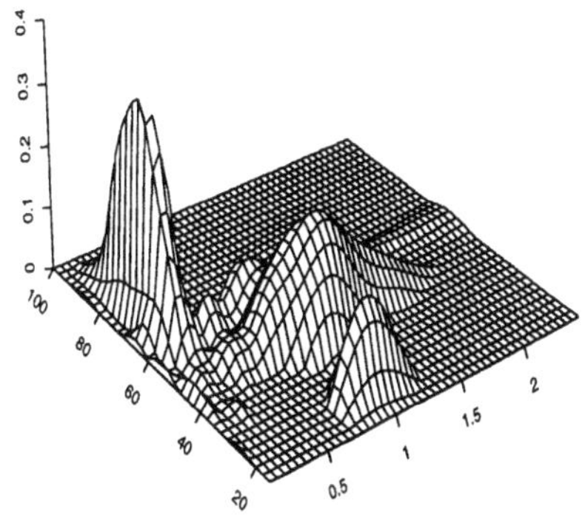

Fig.3.5: 1. component, negative part

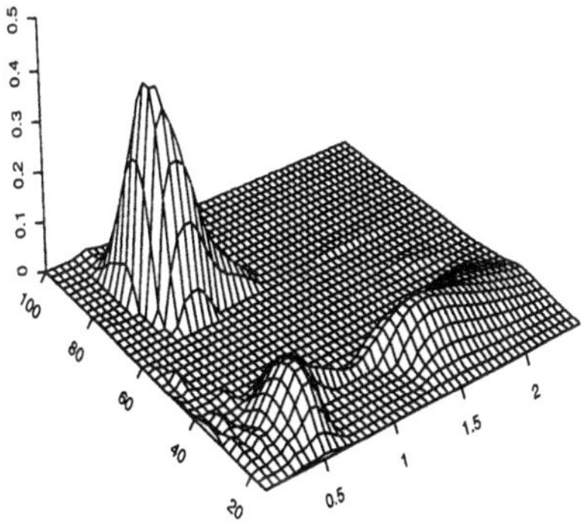

Fig.3.6: 1. component, positive part

In addition, we see a substantial rise in the frequency of rich HHs which are exclusively of ages below 40. This age group, moreover, is mostly affected by a dramatic erosion of their average income group. Noting an additional buildup of this age group at levels close to poverty we tend to conclude that increasing inequality is mainly driven by those around 30.

From Fig.3.5 we see that the very poor above 65 are decreasing sharply in frequency and so are the average incomes around 50 years and the young of mean income.

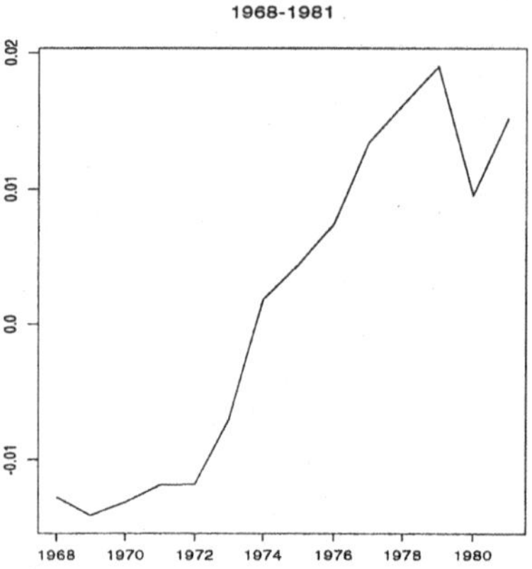

Fig.3.7: scores of the 1. component

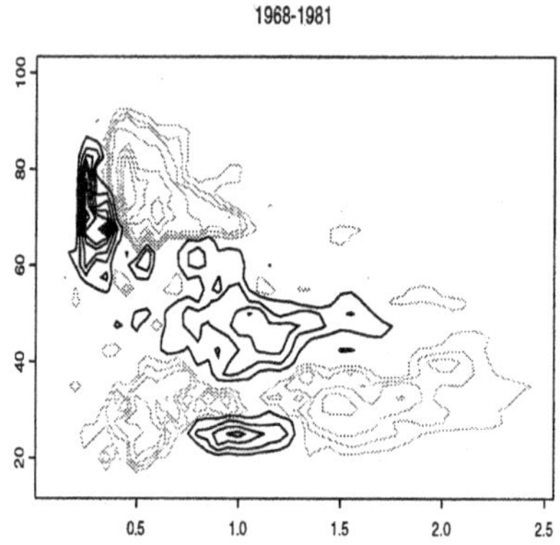

Fig.3.8: contours of 1. component values< 0 (black), values> 0 (gray)

The limits of increase, decrease, and immobility can be drawn more clearly by inspecting the contour plot of the first component displayed in Fig.3.8. Again we see a redistribution from a center around 1/4 of mean income and 70 years of age to a new location at around 1/2 of mean income. The age group of 40-60 is decreasing on the range of 1/2 to 3/2 of the income mean.

These findings are in accordance with the more limited type of analysis obtained by running a one-dimensional FPCA on the family of income distributions as in Kneip and Utikal (2001) for the period 1968-1988. From a one-dimensional analysis carried out on our first sub period we display the first component and its scores in Fig.3.9 and Fig.3.10. By combining component and score plots we see that very low income HHs are decreasing in frequency and moving in the direction to moderately low income HHs during 1968-1981. Also on the rise are a second group corresponding to a second local maximum of the first component slightly above 1/2 the mean income, see Fig.3.9. These can be identified as being of ages 30-40. The pronounced decrease of the middle income group is accompanied by a strong decrease of middle aged households. This is also reflected by a one dimensional FPCA by Kneip and Utikal (2001) on the distributions of ages without clues on the corresponding income structure.

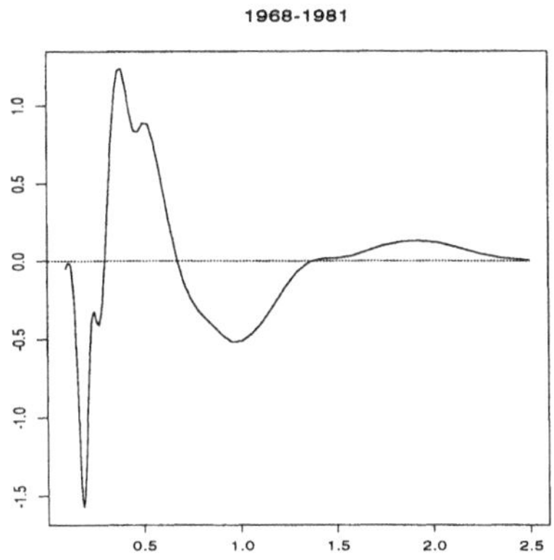

Fig.3.9: first component

Fig.3.10: scores of first component

It is interesting to see that for certain ages the mobilities found in the period of 1968-1981 are reversed in the second period from 1982 to 1995 which will be discussed next.

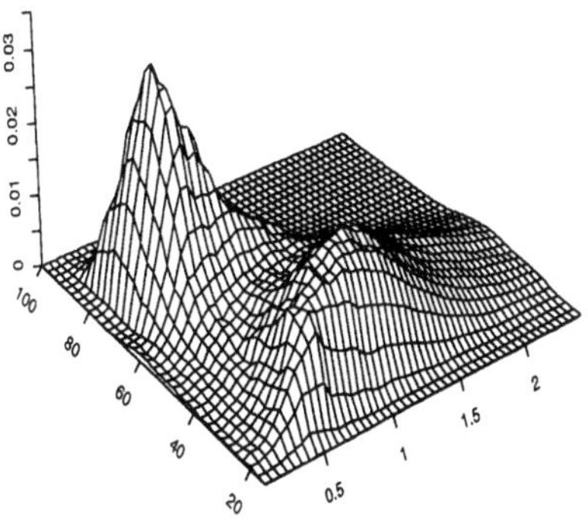

Fig.3.11: time average of income-age densities over period 1982-95

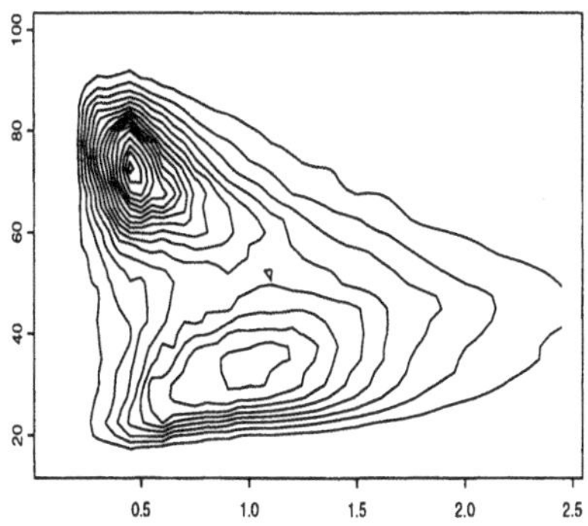

Fig.3.12: contours of income-age family over period 1982-95

Mean densities and spectrum (not shown) for the second period do not differ drastically from those of the first period. Note, however, that the richest segment of the population is around 40 and has on the average slightly increased its income.

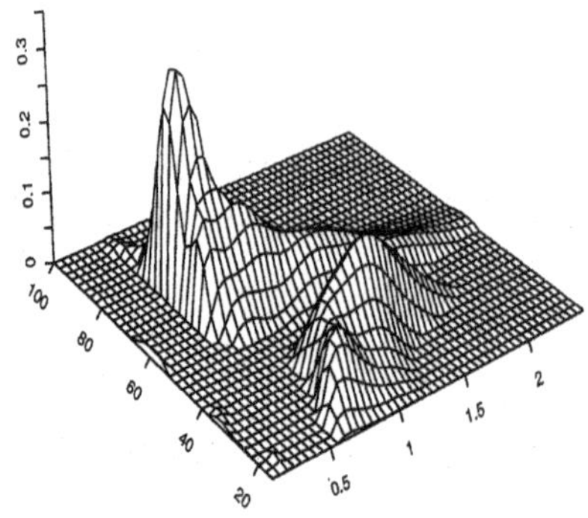

Fig.3.13: 1. component, negative part

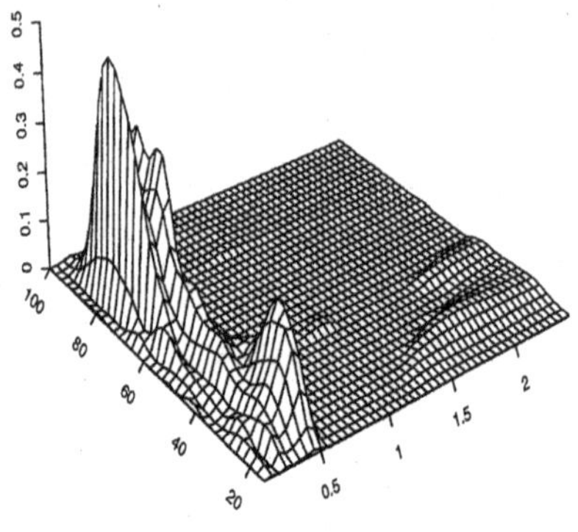

Fig.3.14: 1. component, positive part

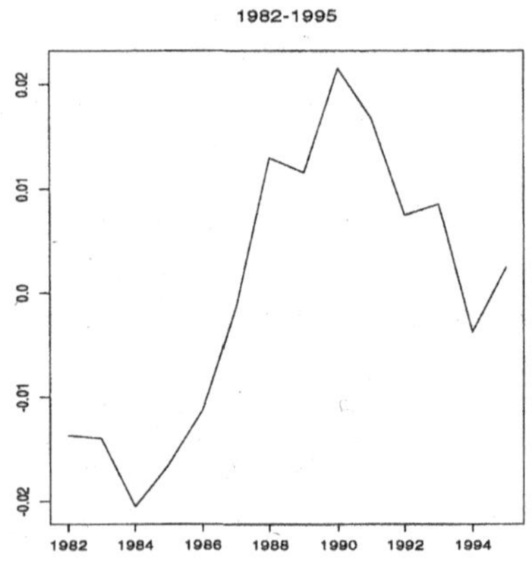

Fig.3.15: scores of 1. component

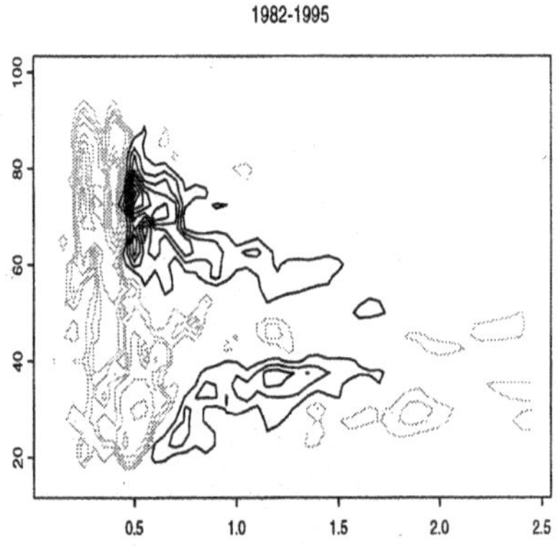

Fig.3.16: contours of 1. component values< 0 (black), values> 0 (gray)

Considering the resulting first principal component displayed in Fig.3.13 and Fig.3.14 in combination with the scores of Fig.3.15 we see that there is a buildup of poor HHs throughout the eighties. This affects HHs of all ages but most strongly the very old, i.e. around 80, and to a lesser degree those around thirty. This increase in the low income range frequencies is accompanied by a drastic decrease of elderly with moderate incomes, i.e. more than half the average income, also of the 30-40 years old who earn slightly above the average, and of the 20-30 years old slightly below average income. Furthermore, we note a slight increase in the fraction of higher incomes of age 20-30 and those of incomes twice the average and of ages around 40. These trends reach their peak in 1990 and taper off in the nineties.

Some further aspects can be discerned from the contours of the first component displayed in Fig.3.16. For the old we conjecture a pronounced skid of incomes slightly above 1/2 the mean towards two new peaks at lower income, one located at 1/4. This is paralleled by similar movements for the 30-40 years old though to less degree. Relatively unaffected remain the average earners and the slightly better off in the 40-60 years age group.

Another interesting feature to note is that in comparison to the first period the rise of young HHs on the side of high income has significantly slowed down. The vanishing of medium income HHs is no longer sharply located at the young but rather affecting HHs up to 40. Since these effects are loosing their momentum during the nineties we conjecture that effects of inequality are less pronounced and stabilize during the nineties. This seems to be in agreement with findings concerning the personal income distribution, see Jenkins (1995).

A comparison of the evolution of joint income-age and multivariate income densities during 1982-1995 is complicated by the fact that, for ease of interpretation of the bivariate evolution, we had reversed signs of both scores and components. Though this does not affect their product and the yearly deformations exerted, nevertheless it has to be kept in mind when reinterpreting the univariate components with help of the bivariate evolution just analyzed.

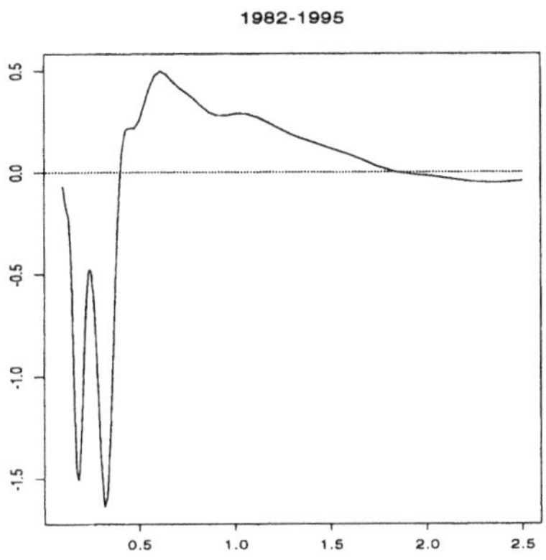

Fig.3.17: 1. component

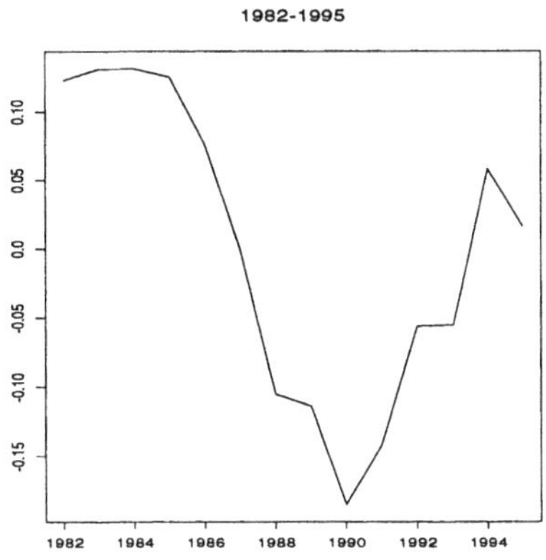

Fig.3.18: scores of the 1. component

Comparing Fig.3.18 with Fig.3.15 we see that the scores of the two-dimensional and one-dimensional components have similar trajectories. Moreover, can it be seen that the univariate component in Fig.3.17 which points at a growth of below average income HHs goes through all ages but is most pronounced at the very old, which accounts for the first minimum of the component, as well as the age group of 20-40 years which is reflected in the second minimum.

In summary it can be said that trends in redistribution of income found by an analysis of one dimensional income densities are also to be seen when the two dimensional income-age family is analyzed. In addition, we are able to characterize some of the prominent features of income movements by their age structure. The older generations are subjected to the most pronounced shifts of income. Also, the young are found to play a special role. Trends of income redistribution established during the seventies are found to be reversed in the eighties and loosing significance during the first half of the nineties.

An analysis focussing on the nineties remains to be done once data on the second half of the decade have become available to us. Another point the reader might have noted is that our analysis has relatively little to say about changes in the upper most part of the income distribution. We should like to point out that this can be altered by the introduction of weight functions as in Kneip and Utikal (2001) for the one-dimensional case, giving higher weight to cases in the upper tail. This however would be beyond the scope of this paper.

Finally, we note that a more detailed analysis needs to take into account higher order components and trends in their respective scores. It is known from one-dimensional FPCAs that some of the tendencies captured by the most important component are dampened by smaller and rather unsystematic movements of higher order. This can be expected also to be the case for the two-dimensional families where it can be seen from the spectrum that higher order components seem to play an even more important role. These would have to be taken into account by a more complete analysis of income-age dynamics.

4 Methodological appendix

As outlined before, our aim is to analyze a family $\{f_t\}$ of multivariate densities on the basis of the method discussed in Section 2. Since, the basic approach characterized by relations (2.3)-(2.7) applies to any dimension, we will not only consider the two-dimensional case, but generally analyze densities for d-dimensional data, $d \geq 1$. The goal of this section is to give some theoretical results on the asymptotic properties of our estimators of the eigenvalues of M, the scores θ_{tr}, and the principal components g_r. All results discussed in this appendix have to be seen as multivariate generalizations of the approach presented in Kneip and Utikal (2001).

We thus assume multivariate data $\{X_{it}\}$ where the observations $X_{1t}, \ldots, X_{n_t t} \in \mathbb{R}^d$, $d \geq 1$ are an i.i.d. sample with underlying density f_t for every $t = 1, \ldots, T$. For every $x = (x_1, \ldots, x_d)^T$ we estimate f_t by a d-dimensional kernel estimator which can be written in the form

$$\hat{f}_t(x) = \frac{1}{n_t h_1 \ldots h_d} \sum_i K\left(H^{-1} \cdot (x - X_{it})\right),$$

where $h_1, \dots, h_d$ are possibly different bandwidth that allow smoothing in the d directions, and H is a $d \times d$ diagonal matrix with $diag(h) = (h_1, \dots, h_d)$. The kernel function K is assumed to be a symmetric d-variate density satisfying $\int K(x) x_j dx = 0$ as well as $\int K(x)|x_j|^k dx < \infty$ for all $j = 1, \dots, d$ and $k > 0$.

With $< \hat{f}_t, \hat{f}_s >_c := < \hat{f}_t, \hat{f}_s >$ for $t \neq s$, and $< \hat{f}_t, \hat{f}_s >_c := < \hat{f}_t, \hat{f}_s > - \frac{1}{n_t h_1 \dots h_d} \int K(u)^2 du$ for $t = s$, our estimators of $M_{t,s}$ are given by

$$\widehat{M}_{ts} = < \hat{f}_t, \hat{f}_s >_c - \frac{1}{T}\left(\sum_r < \hat{f}_t, \hat{f}_r >_c + \sum_r < \hat{f}_r, \hat{f}_s >_c\right) + \frac{1}{T^2} \sum_{q,r} < \hat{f}_q, \hat{f}_r >_c$$

After calculating the eigenvalues $\hat{\lambda}_j$ and eigenvectors $\hat{\mathbf{p}}_j$ of $\widehat{M}$ for $j = 1, 2, \dots$,, estimate θ_{tj} and g_j in analogy to the defining relations by $\hat{\theta}_{tj} = \hat{\lambda}_j^{1/2} \hat{p}_{tj}$ and

$$\hat{g}_j = \frac{\sum_t^T \hat{\theta}_{tj} \hat{\hat{f}}_{t,b}}{\sum_{t=1}^T \hat{\theta}_{tr}^2} = \hat{\lambda}_j^{-1/2} \sum_t^T \hat{p}_{tj} \hat{\hat{f}}_{t,b}$$

Here $\hat{f}_{t,b} = \frac{1}{n_t b_1 \dots b_d} \sum_i K\left(B^{-1} \cdot (x - X_{it})\right)$ denote kernel estimators with bandwidths $b_1, \dots, b_d$ not necessarily equal to $h_1, \dots, h_d$. In fact, an appropriate choice of bandwidths is quite important for the performance of the method. This point will be discussed in the context of the asymptotic results below.

Asymptotics is based on sampling more and more observations per population such that $n = \min\{n_1, \dots, n_T\} \to \infty$. As $n \to \infty$ the number T of different densities as well the corresponding dimension $L \leq T - 1$ of our model may remain fixed, but we will also allow that T and L increase with n. Formally, we thus consider non decreasing sequences $\{T_n\}$ and $\{L_n\}$ as $n \to \infty$. Note that principal components $g_r \equiv g_{r,T}$ may change with T. This will go without saying.

We will need some additional assumptions:

A1 The densities f_t are twice continuously differentiable, and there exist constants $C_1, C_2 < \infty$ such that $\int |\partial^\alpha_{x_j} f_t(x))^\beta| dx \leq C_1$ as well as $\sup_j \sup_x |\partial^\alpha_{x_j} f_t(x)| \leq C_2$ hold for all n, T, $t = 1, \dots, T$, $\alpha \in \{0, 1, 2\}$ and $\beta \in \{1, 2, 3, 4\}$.

A2 For all n, T and any fixed $r \in \{1, \dots, L\}$ there exist constants $0 < C_{3,r} < \infty$ as well as $0 < C_{4,r} \leq C_{5,r} < \infty$ such that

$$\min_{s=1,\dots,T; s \neq r} |\lambda_r - \lambda_s| \geq T C_{3,r} \quad \text{and} \quad T C_{4,r} \leq \lambda_r \leq T C_{5,r}$$

Obviously, assumption (A1) postulates a common degree of smoothness characterizing all densities. Assumption (A2) is a natural condition in the context of our approach. Note that $\lambda_r = \sum_{i=1}^T \theta_{ri}^2$, which motivates to assume that λ_r be proportional to T.

The following proposition provides results on the asymptotic properties of our estimators $< \hat{f}_t, \hat{f}_s >_c$ of $< f_t, f_s >$. We introduce the notation

$$\tau_{ts} =< \hat{f}_t - f_t \, , \, \hat{f}_s - f_s > - \frac{\delta_{ts}}{n_t h_1 \dots h_d} \int K(u)^2 du$$

where $\delta_{ts} = 1$ if $t = s$ and zero otherwise.

Proposition 1. *Let* $n = \min\{n_1, \dots, n_T\} \to \infty$ *and suppose that* $\max_j h_j \to 0$ *as well as* $\frac{1}{nh_1 \dots h_d} \to 0$. *Then*

$$< \hat{f}_t, \hat{f}_s >_c - < f_t, f_s >=< \hat{f}_t - f_t, f_s > + < f_t, \hat{f}_s - f_s > +\tau_{ts} \tag{4.1}$$

where for some constants $C_1, C_2, C_3 < \infty$

$$|\mathbb{E} < \hat{f}_t - f_t, f_s > | \leq C_1 \max_j h_j^2 \tag{4.2}$$

$$\mathbb{V} < \hat{f}_t - f_t, f_s >= \frac{1}{n_t} \left(\int f_t(x) f_s(x)^2 dx - < f_t, f_s >^2 \right) (1 + o(1)) \tag{4.3}$$

as well as

$$|\mathbb{E}\tau_{ts}| \leq C_2 \max_j h_j^4, \quad |\mathbb{E}(\tau_{ts}\tau_{uv})| \leq C_3 \max_j h_j^4 \quad \text{if } (t,s) \neq (u,v) \tag{4.4}$$

$$\mathbb{V}\tau_{ts} = \frac{2^{\delta_{ts}} < f_t, f_s >}{n_t n_s h_1 \dots h_d} \left(\int \left(\int K(u) K(u+v) du \right)^2 dv \right) \tag{4.5}$$

$$+ O(\frac{\max_j h_j^4}{n}) + o(\frac{1}{n^2 h_1 \dots h_d})$$

Moreover, the distributions of all terms $< \hat{f}_t - f_t, f_s >$ *and* τ_{ts} *are asymptotically normal.*

Proof. Relation (4.2) is an immediate consequence of the definition of $< \hat{f}_t, \hat{f}_s >_c$. We obtain

$$< \hat{f}_t - f_t, f_s >$$

$$= \frac{1}{n_t h_1 \dots h_d} \sum_i \int K(H^{-1}(x - X_{it})) f_s(x) dx - < f_t, f_s > \tag{4.6}$$

$$= \frac{1}{n_t} \sum_i \int K(u) f_s(H \cdot u + X_{it}) du - < f_t, f_s > \tag{4.7}$$

Obviously, $\mathbb{E}(f_s(X_{it}) =< f_t, f_s >$. Using assumptions (A1) and (A2), Taylor expansions lead to

$$\left| E(\int K(u) f_s(Hu + X_{it}) du) - E(f_s(X_{it}) \right| = C_1 \max_j h_j^2$$

for some $C_1 > 0$. This proves (4.2). Relation (4.3) follows from

$$\mathbb{V}(\frac{1}{n_t} \sum_i \int K(u) f_s(Hu + X_{it}) du) = \mathbb{V}(\frac{1}{n_t} \sum_i f_s(X_{it})) + o(\frac{1}{n})$$

$$= \frac{1}{n_t}(E(f_s(X_{it})^2) - < f_t, f_s >^2)$$

Since by (4.7) $< \hat{f}_{t,h} - f_t, f_s >$ can be represented as a sum of independent random variables with bounded variances, asymptotic normality is immediately obtained from standard arguments. This also applies to asymptotic normality of linear combinations of the type $\sum_t \sum_s \beta_{ts} < \hat{f}_t - f_t, f_s >$.

Relation (4.4) can be shown by calculations similar to those used to derive (4.2). Let $K_h(x, y) = \frac{1}{h_1 \ldots h_d} K(H^{-1}(x - y))$, and note that

$$\begin{aligned}
\mathbb{V}\tau_{tt} &= \mathbb{V}(\frac{1}{n_t^2} \sum_i \sum_{i \neq j} \int (K_h(x, X_{it}) - \mathbb{E}K_h(x, X_{it})) \\
&\qquad (K_h(x, X_{jt}) - \mathbb{E}K_h(x, X_{jt}))\, dx) \\
&= \frac{2}{n_t^4} \sum_i \sum_{i \neq j} \mathbb{E}(\int (K_h(x, X_{it}) - \mathbb{E}K_h(x, X_{it})) \\
&\qquad (K_h(x, X_{jt}) - \mathbb{E}K_h(x, X_{jt})) dx\,)^2 \\
&= \frac{2}{n_t^2 h_1^2 \ldots h_d^2} \int (\int K(u) K(u + H^{-1}(x - y)) du\,)^2 f_t(x) f_t(y) dx dy + O(\frac{2}{n_t^2}) \\
&= \frac{2}{n_t^2 h_1 \ldots h_d} \int (\int K(u) K(u + v) du\,)^2 f_t(H^{-1}v + y) f_t(y) dv dy + O(\frac{2}{n_t^2})
\end{aligned}$$

Relation (4.5) for $t = s$ then follows from a straightforward Taylor expansion. A proof for the case $t \neq s$ is analogous. Asymptotic normality of the terms τ_{ts} can be shown by arguments similar to Hall (1984). □

By the construction of $\widehat{M}$ from $< \hat{f}_t, \hat{f}_s >_c$ one can conclude that under the conditions of the proposition we have

$$|\mathbb{E}\widehat{M}_{ts} - M_{ts}| = O(\max_j h_j^2) \quad \text{and} \quad \mathbb{V}\widehat{M}_{ts} = O(\frac{1}{n} + \frac{1}{n^2 h_1 \ldots h_d})$$

These results show that the bandwidths h_j for estimating the elements of M should be small. For $d = 2$ bandwidths in the range between $n^{-1/2}$ and $n^{-1/4}$ lead to

$$\mathbb{E}\left((\widehat{M}_{ts} - M_{ts})^2\right) = O(\frac{1}{n})$$

To achieve the same rate of convergence of the mean squared error for $d = 3$, an h in the range between $n^{-1/3}$ and $n^{-1/4}$ is necessary, while for $d = 4$ the h_j must be proportional to $n^{-1/4}$. For $d \geq 5$ the "parametric" rate of convergence $\frac{1}{n}$ is no longer possible, and the optimal h_j is proportional to $n^{-2/(d+4)}$. Then

$$\mathbb{E}\left((\widehat{M}_{ts} - M_{ts})^2\right) = O(n^{-\frac{8}{d+4}})$$

Note that the distance between two neighboring points X_{it}, X_{jt} in $\mathbb{R}^d$ is of order $n^{-1/d}$. Hence, for $d = 1, 2, 3, 4$ the optimal rate of convergence can be achieved by choosing $h_1, \ldots, H_d$ to be the smallest possible bandwidths with the property that for all x in the center of the distribution there are four of five observations, say, in a neighborhood of size h.

For the case $d = 1$, asymptotic properties of our estimates of eigenvalues, scores and basis functions can be obtained from Theorems 3.1 and 3.2 of Kneip and Utikal (2001). Multivariate generalization are given in Theorems 1 and 2 below. Proofs are omitted, since they follow from immediate generalizations of the arguments used in Kneip and Utikal (2001) for the one dimensional situation. The only modification to be applied in dependence of d consists in plugging in the appropriate expressions for biases and variances of $< \hat{f}_t - f_t, f_s >$ and τ_{ts}.

Let us first introduce some notation. Denote the eigenvalues of $\widehat{M}$ by $\hat{\lambda}_1 \geq \hat{\lambda}_2 \geq \ldots$, and let $\hat{\mathbf{p}}_1, \hat{\mathbf{p}}_2, \ldots, \hat{\mathbf{p}}_T$ be a complete orthonormal system of corresponding eigenvectors. For a sequence of random variables $\{Z_n\}$ we will say that "Z_n is $AN(a_n, b_n)$" if $(Z_n - a_n)/b_n^{1/2}$ converges in distribution to $N(0,1)$. Furthermore, $\|\cdot\|_2$ will denote the Euclidean norm on R^T.

Theorem 1. *Let $h_j \sim n^{-\delta}$ for all $j = 1, \ldots, d$, where $\frac{1}{4} \leq \delta < 1$ for $d = 1$, $\frac{1}{4} \leq \delta \leq \frac{1}{2}$ for $d = 2$, $\frac{1}{4} \leq \delta \leq \frac{1}{3}$ for $d = 3$, and $\delta = 2/(d+4)$ for $d \geq 4$. If $T/n \to 0$ as $n = \min\{n_1, \ldots, n_T\} \to \infty$, then*

(a) For any fixed $r \in \{1, \ldots, L\}$

$$\hat{\lambda}_r - \lambda_r = \mathbf{p}_r'(\hat{M} - M)\mathbf{p}_r + O_P(Tn^{-1}) = O_P(\frac{T^{1/2}}{n^{1/2}} + \frac{T^{1/2}}{n^{4/(d+4)}}) \quad (4.8)$$

(b) For any fixed $r \in \{1, \ldots, L\}$

$$\|\hat{\mathbf{p}}_r - \mathbf{p}_r - S_r\mathbf{q}_r\|_2 = O_P(T^{-1/2}n^{-1}(\min_j h_j)^{-1/2} + n^{-1} + n^{-8/(d+4)}), \quad (4.9)$$

where $S_r = \sum_{s=1,s\neq r}^{T} \frac{1}{\lambda_s - \lambda_r}\mathbf{p}_s\mathbf{p}_s'$, and the elements of the vector $\mathbf{q}_r$ are given by

$$q_{tr} = \sum_{s=1}^{T} p_{rs}\left(\langle \hat{f}_{t,h} - f_t, f_s\rangle - \langle \hat{f}_\mu - f_\mu, f_s\rangle + \langle \hat{f}_{s,h} - f_s, f_t - f_\mu\rangle\right) \quad (4.10)$$

Moreover, we have $|\hat{\theta}_{tr} - \theta_{tr}| = O_P(n^{-1/2} + n^{-4/(d+4)})$, *and* $\|\hat{\mathbf{p}}_r - \mathbf{p}_r\|_2 = O_p(n^{-1/2} + n^{-4/(d+4)})$.

(c) *If* $T^2/n \to 0$ *and if* $\lambda_{L+1} = 0$ *for some fixed* $L \in \{0, 1, 2, \dots\}$, $L < T - 1$, *then* $\sum_{r=L+1}^{T} \hat{\lambda}_r$ *is* $AN(0, V_{n,T,L})$, *where*

$$V_{n,T,L} := \sum_{t=1}^{T}\sum_{s=1}^{T}\left(\delta_{ts} - \frac{1}{T} - \sum_{r=1}^{L} p_{tr}p_{sr}\right)^2 \mathbb{V}\tau_{ts} = O(\frac{T}{n^2 h_1 \dots h_d})$$

The second theorem concerns asymptotic properties of $\hat{g}_r$. We introduce the notation $d_K := \int K^2(v)\,dv$, and $\theta^*_{tr} := \theta_{tr}/\sum_{i=1}^{T}\theta^2_{ir}$. Moreover, $\mathbb{B}\hat{g}_r(x)$ and $\mathbb{B}\hat{f}_{t,b}$ will be used to denote the biases of $\hat{g}_r(x)$ and $\hat{f}_{t,b}$.

Theorem 2 *In addition to the assumptions of Theorem 1 let* $\max_j b_j \to 0$ *and* $h_j/b_j \to 0$ *for all* j. *We then obtain that for all* $r = 1, \dots, L$ *and all* x

$$\hat{g}_r(x) - g_r(x) \text{ is } AN(\mathbb{B}\hat{g}_r(x)\,,\,\mathbb{V}\hat{g}_r(x)) \tag{4.11}$$

with

$$\mathbb{B}\hat{g}_r(x) = O(\max_j b_j^2)$$

$$\mathbb{V}\hat{g}_r(x) = \sum_{t=1}^{T}(\theta^*_{tr})^2\left(\frac{d_K}{n_t b_1 \dots b_d} f_t(x)\right)(1 + o(1)) = O(\frac{1}{Tnb_1 \dots b_d})$$

We can conclude from the theorem that in a first order approximation the mean integrated squares error is of order of magnitude

$$\text{AMISE}(\hat{g}_r) = O(\max_j b_j^4 + \frac{1}{Tnb_1 \dots b_d})$$

This implies that optimal bandwidths $b_{opt,j}$ are of order of magnitude $(nT)^{-1/(d+4)}$ which leads to

$$\text{AMISE}(\hat{g}_r) = O\left((nT)^{-4/(d+4)}\right)$$

It is well known that when estimating an individual density by kernel estimation, the rate of convergence of the mean squared error of an optimal estimator is $n^{-4/(d+4)}$. In contrast, the accuracy of our estimator of g_r also improves as $T \to \infty$. If a small dimension L is sufficient, this carries over to our modified estimator $\hat{\hat{f}}_t$. Since there we simultaneously use information from all T samples, we obtain more efficient estimates of the original densities. Nevertheless. it is also seen that the general quality of estimation deteriorates with increasing dimension d. This is to be attributed to the well known "curse of dimensionality". Hence, though for the sake of completeness we have presented a theory for all dimensions d, we do not recommend to use our method to analyze really high dimensional density families. In addition to estimation problems, the lack of a graphical representation of the resulting components will usually not allow to obtain well interpretable results.

Acknowledgement: Material from the Family Expenditure Survey made available by the CSO through the ESRC data archive has been used by permission of the Controller Her Majesty's Stationery Office. The CSO and the ESRC data archive bear no responsibility for the analysis or interpretation of the data reported here. Any errors are entirely the authors'. We thank J. Arns for carefully building from these data the income variables used in this analysis. Guidelines for this were kindly provided by the Institute for Fiscal Studies, London.

References

1. Atanasio, O.P. (1999). *Consumption.* In: J.B. Taylor and M. Woodford eds., Handbook of Macroeconomics, Vol. 1B, North-Holland, 742-812 Taylor
2. Atkinson, A.B. (1983). *The Economics of Inequality.* Clarendon Press, Oxford.
3. Cowell, F.A., Jenkins, S.P.,and Litchfield, J.A. (1996). The changing shape of the UK income distribution: kernel density estimates. In J. Hills (Ed.) *New Inequalities.* (pp. 49-75), Cambridge University Press.
4. ESCR Data Archive at the University of Essex, Family Expenditure Survey, Annual Tapes 1968-1995, Department of Employment, Statistics Division, Her Majesty's Stationery Office, London.
5. Goodmann, A. and Webb, S. (1994). For Richer, For Poorer: the Changing Distribution of Income in the U.K., 1961-91. Commentary 42, London. Inst. for Fiscal Studies.
6. Hall, P. (1984). Central limit theorem for integrated square error of multivariate non parametric density estimators. *Journal of Multivariate Analysis* **14**, 1-16.
7. Hildenbrand, W., Kneip, A, Utikal, K.J. (1999). Une analyse non paramé-trique des distributions du revenu et des caractéristiques des ménages. *Revue de statistique appliquée.* in print
8. Jenkins, S.P. (1995). Accounting for inequality trends: decomposition analyses for the UK 1971-86, *Economica* **62**, 29-63.
9. Kemsley, W.F., Redpath, R.D., and Holmes, M. (1980). *Family Expenditure Survey Handbook* Her Majesty's Stationery Office, London.
10. Kneip, A, Utikal, K.J. (2001). Inference for density families using functional principal component analysis. (with discussion) *Journal of the American Statistical Association* to appear.
11. Silverman, B.W. (1986). *Density Estimation for Statistics and Data Analysis.* Chapman and Hall, London.
12. Simonoff, J.S. (1996). *Smoothing Methods in Statistics.* Springer Verlag, New York.

The Economics of Network Industries

Günter Knieps

Albert-Ludwigs-Universität Freiburg i. Br., Germany

Abstract. In this paper a disaggregated approach to network regulation is provided. The question is analyzed to what extent interconnection/access problems can be solved by voluntary market contracts of the parties involved and to what extent government interventions should be implemented. The key concept is the identification of monopolistic bottlenecks where market power can be identified ex ante. In all other parts of networks regulatory interventions are detrimental. Possible fallacies with respect to the regulation of monopolistic bottlenecks (inadequate price-setting rules, extending the regulatory basis) are pointed out.

1 Introduction

As a consequence of the recent developments toward deregulation and subsequent vertical disintegration of networks, problems of network access as well as network interconnection are gaining increasing importance.[1] The purpose of this paper is to approach the increasing vertical and horizontal interconnection problems within networks in a conceptual way.[2] In particular, the question will be analyzed to what extent interconnection/access problems can be solved by voluntary market contracts of the parties involved and to what extent government interventions (e.g., harmonization and integration policies by the Council of the European Union) should be implemented. The basic idea behind this disaggregated approach to network regulation is to identify those parts of networks where market power remains, which may be abused in the interconnection process. The key concept is the identification of monopolistic bottlenecks and the application of the Essential Facilities Doctrine, which is well known from the US Antitrust law. In the context of networks, this principle, which is traditionally applied case by case, can be generalized and applied to a class of cases, where the localization of market power is based on the same reasons.

As it turns out, government regulation of interconnection/access conditions (tariffs, quality of access, etc.) is only justified in those parts of networks where market power can be identified ex ante. In all other parts of networks, government regulations of interconnection/access conditions are not only superfluous but hamper efficient negotiations of the parties involved. Finally,

[1] For the problem of standard setting the reader is referred to Blankart, Knieps (1993, 1995); Holler, Knieps, Niskanen (1997).

[2] Case studies focussing on railway systems and airlines are provided in Knieps (1996); for the telecommunications sector, see Albach, Knieps (1997); Engel, Knieps (1998); Knieps (1997).

possible fallacies with respect to remaining regulatory interventions (e.g., prescribing inadequate price-setting rules, extending the regulatory basis) are pointed out. The paper is organized as follows: In section 2 the disaggregated approach is developed, localizing the monopolistic bottlenecks. In section 3 the necessity of a symmetric regulatory approach is pointed out. The regulation of market power is only justified in monopolistic bottleneck areas. As an example, in section 4 the disaggregated approach is applied to telecommunicatons. In section 5 the role of efficient private bargaining of interconnection/access conditions is shown, as long as monopolistic bottlenecks are absent. In section 6 the regulation of interconnection to monopolistic bottlenecks is analyzed, in particular the role of the Essential Facilities Doctrine. In section 7 unbundling and the proper role of the Essential Facilities Doctrine in the telecommunications sector are discussed. Finally, in section 8 costing and pricing issues of interconnection services are discussed for the case of telecommunications.

2 Localization of monopolistic bottlenecks

It is important to note that the characteristics of network structures are not a sufficient reason to guarantee market power. The markets for network services are far from the ideal picture of perfect atomistic markets. For example, an essential characteristic with respect to the supply of train services is its network structure. Incentives may exist for train companies to bundle traffic either on a given line (economies of scale) or serve several lines jointly (economies of scope). However, a possible lack of competition between active firms in the market in a particular area with low population density could be replaced by efficient potential competition. The same argumentation also holds for other network service providers, for example airline companies, bus companies, telecommunications and postal service providers. If the incumbent companies produce inefficiently or make excessive profits, entry by newcomers will occur.

The pressure of potential competition can create incentives for the active supplier to improve the quality and variety of services as well as to produce more efficiently. These networks are, therefore, called contestable (e.g., Baumol, Panzar, Willig, 1982). An essential condition for the functioning of potential competition in order to discipline firms already providing network services is that the incumbent firms do not have asymmetric cost advantages in comparison with potential entrants. In fact, trains, like planes or buses, are not considered as sunk costs. They can be used to serve other networks in different locations once demand in the former network has dropped too far to keep up a profitable train service. Another example for contestable networks are the markets for telecommunications services (see section 4).

An important condition for the effectiveness of potential competition is, however, that all (active and potential) suppliers of service networks have equal (symmetric) access to the complementary infrastructures. As long as a train company has preferred access to rails and stations (e.g., if there is congestion) or has advantages with respect to scheduling procedures, it possesses competitive advantages with respect to potential entrants and active competitors. The same holds for airline companies having preferred access to landing rights or telecommunication service providers having preferred access to local telephone networks.

When economies of scale arise (due to indivisibilities) in combination with sunk costs so that entry and in particular exit are not free, we can expect network specific market power to emerge (e.g. Knieps, Vogelsang, 1982). Sunk costs are no longer decision relevant for the incumbent monopoly, whereas a potential entrant is confronted with the decision whether to build network infrastructure and thereby incur the irreversible costs. The incumbent firm, therefore, has lower decision relevant costs than the potential entrants. This creates scope for strategic behavior of the incumbent firm in such a way that inefficient production or excessive profits do not automatically result in market entry. Economies of scale together with irreversible costs are characteristic for the construction of transportation infrastructures such as railroads and airports. Consider for example a domestic railroad operator supplying rail capacities and simultaneously rail transport services as all national railroad companies do. The railroad operator may exploit its monopoly position vis-à-vis a foreign rail transport company and restrict access to its own market. Non-contestable networks can also be observed in local infrastructures for gas, water and electricity.

Network infrastructure, however, need not always create network-specific market power. In the first place, economies of scale may become exhausted, as for example in long-distance telecommunications transmission. Secondly, technological change may provide alternative network infrastructures, such that monopolistic bottlenecks are losing importance. Examples are the increasing relevance of cableless local mobile communications and the increasing relevance of cable television networks for telecommunication purposes (e.g. Knieps, 1997). A clear-cut distinction between network infrastructure as monopolistic bottlenecks and contestable networks is therefore not always easy to find. Careful sector studies seem unavoidable.

3 The necessity of a symmetric regulatory approach

Symmetric regulatory conditions should neither advantage nor disadvantage the former network monopolist. On the one hand, all monopoly privileges must be abandoned, on the other hand, all one-sided regulatory obligations (e.g. to cross-subsidize universal services) must end. In general terms symmetric regulation means "providing all suppliers, incumbents and new entrants alike, a level playing field on which to compete: the same price signals, the same restrictions, and the same obligations. ... But all forms of asymmetric regulation contain an intrinsic bias toward some firms or technologies ... " (see Shankerman, 1996, p. 5f).

Even if one accepts criteria like relative market share, financial strength, access to input and service markets etc. as a starting point in order to evaluate the existence of market power, nevertheless the development of an ex ante regulatory criterion creates a need for a more clear-cut definition of market power. This is even more important, because "Vermutungskriterien" on the basis of market shares can lead to wrong criteria for government intervention in network industries.

Therefore it is important to develop and apply a disaggregated approach of market power regulation. It is necessary to differentiate between those areas in which active and potential competition can work and other areas, so-called monopolistic bottleneck areas, where a natural monopoly situation (due to economies of bundling), in combination with irreversible costs, exists. The regulation of market power is only justified in monopolistic bottleneck areas. In all other cases, the existence of active and potential competition will lead to efficient market results.

The pressure of potential competition is sufficient to create an incentive for the active supplier to improve the quality and variety of services as well as to produce more efficiently (see section 4). An essential condition for the functioning of potential competition in order to discipline firms already providing network services is that the incumbent firms do not have asymmetric cost advantages in comparison with potential entrants.

An interesting question is the relation between "pure economic" analysis and real life networks (and the services that use them). What about the reality of "contestable networks"? It seems obvious that the behavior of markets for network services, as soon as competition works, becomes more complex than assumed in the "simple" models of the theory of contestable markets. Examples may be strategies of product differentiation, price differentiation, goodwill etc. However, even strategic behavior on competitive markets for network services should not lead to the opposite conclusion to re-regulate these markets again. In contrast, the very point of the disaggregated approach is the development of the preconditions for competition on the markets for network services. The only purpose of the theory of contestable markets is therefore to localize the stable network specific market power, which systematically hampers the development of competition on the markets for network services. Whereas strategic behavior and informational problems do not lead to stable market power on the markets for network services, monopolistic bottlenecks - due to sunk costs - do create stable market power even if all market participants are well informed. The development of a set of rules to deal with transactions across the boundary between contestable networks and (non-contestable) monopolistic bottlenecks is therefore important in order to guarantee the preconditions for competition on the markets for network services (see section 6).

4 Example: The case of telecommunications

An important example for contestable networks are the markets for telecommunications services, which are often provided via service networks. Even the market for public telephone services is contestable, because suppliers of value added services are also prepared to offer telephone services (after legal entry barriers disappear). An important condition, however, is the guarantee of number portability. The term "number portability" means the ability of users of telecommunications services to retain, at the same location, existing telecommunications numbers without impairment of quality, reliability or convenience when switching from one telecommunications carrier to another. Even if market shares of incumbent firms are large, inefficient suppliers would then be immediately confronted with rapidly decreasing market shares (see Knieps, 1997). But contestable subareas can also be localized in the area of telecommunications infrastructure. The pressure of potential competition in wireless networks, for example satellite, microwave systems, mobile communication, is guaranteed as long as symmetric access to complementary inputs, for example right of way, radio spectrum etc., is ensured. More generally, an important condition for the effectiveness of actual and potential competition is that all (active and potential) suppliers have equal (symmetric) access to the complementary monopolistic bottleneck.

In contrast, in local cable-based networks, where sunk costs are relevant, consumers, who would intrinsically be willing to switch immediately to less costly firms, cannot do this. Market entry therefore cannot be expected easily, if sunk costs are sufficiently high and very relevant. Therefore we can conclude that sector specific ex ante regulatory intervention in order to discipline market power can only be justified in non-contestable networks (monopolistic bottleneck areas), i.e. where bundling in combination with irreversible costs is relevant. Sunk costs are no longer decision relevant for the incumbent monopoly, whereas the potential entrant is confronted with the decision whether to build network infrastructure and thus spend the irreversible costs. The incumbent firms therefore have lower decision relevant costs than the potential entrants. This creates scope for strategic behaviour of the incumbent firms, so that inefficient production and monopoly profits will not necessarily result in market entry.

The aim of future regulatory policy should, however, not be the global regulation of markets. Instead, only a disaggregated regulation of non-contestable networks is justified. The aim is then to localize the market power in monopolistic bottleneck areas and discipline this market power by regulatory intervention. Asymmetry of market power due to monopolistic bottleneck facilities, however, does not by itself require asymmetric regulation. Instead, the symmetry principle requires that all firms have access to local telecommunications networks on terms identical to those of the incumbent (nondiscriminatory access). The symmetry principle demands that only bottleneck facilities are regulated, irrespective of whether the owner is the incumbent or a newcomer.

5 Unregulated interconnection among contestable networks

Consider the case where interconnection/access requirements arise among contestable networks. One may think of a local community operating a mobile radio network and considering one or various opportunities for establishing a long distance connection by microwaves, or of two specialized satellite networks to be connected. Other examples are the horizontal interconnection among different specialized value added service networks of telecommunications or the (vertical) interconnection of a value added service network into a microwave long distance network.

5.1 Efficient private bargaining of interconnection/access conditions

Potential competition fulfills the function of mitigating market power. It can be expected that private bargaining of interconnection/access conditions between the different network owners will lead to economically efficient solutions. Strategic behavior can be excluded, because every bargaining partner can easily be substituted by an alternative (potential) network carrier (due to the contestability of networks).

Private bargaining solutions on interconnection conditions among contestable network carriers are not only beneficial for the carriers themselves but in particular improve the market performance of the network services provided to the customers. Independent of the market size of the carriers involved, inefficient suppliers of interconnection services are rapidly confronted with strongly decreasing market shares due to the strong pressure of alternative (potential) network service providers. The rapidly changing computer and telecommunications equipment market during the 60s and 70s in the U.S. already indicates the enormous switching potential of the consumers (e.g. Fisher et al., 1983). Government regulation of such private bargaining processes would artificially disturb the bargaining process and automatically lead to inferior solutions.

5.2 Unregulated interconnection/access tariffs

Carriers of contestable networks do not possess market power due to the (potential) competition of alternative network carriers. Excessive interconnection/access charges which allow monopoly rents or insufficient network service quality would immediately initiate switching to an alternative network carrier. There is no need for government interventions aiming to discipline the market power of active network carriers if the underlying networks are contestable.

The question arises whether interconnection tariffs resulting from private bargaining can guarantee the viability of efficient providers of network capacities. Price regulations with the aim of achieving interconnection tariffs according to long-run incremental costs (including fixed costs of capacity) would either be superfluous or would violate the viability of the incumbent carrier. In case of long-run incremental costs for private interconnection capacity being equal to stand-alone costs of interconnection facilities, cost-covering interconnection tariffs would be the result of private bargaining.[3] If common costs (overhead costs) between the interconnecting networks play a significant role, the problem arises of how to cover the difference between stand-alone costs and incremental costs, because the sum of the incremental costs does not cover total costs. As a consequence, the network providers must have flexibility to raise interconnection tariffs such that the total cost covering constraint (viability condition) is fulfilled. In particular, they must be free to allocate common costs depending on the price elasticities of the relevant demand schedules. Ex ante allocations of overhead costs according to fully allocated cost principles, however, would be detrimental (e.g., Owen, Braeutigam, 1978, pp. 212-220). They would neither be based on economically justified cost-causality nor taking into account demand side considerations. As a consequence, regulators who set interconnection rates on the basis of fully allocated costs may promote inefficient bypass activities, even when efficient (viable) market solutions exist.

Pricing rules enforced by regulatory agencies in order to allocate overhead costs cannot solve the problem. The most popular methods of pricing access are according to the principle of fully distributed costs. For example, a proportional sharing rule distributing the common costs (among the complementary networks) in proportion to the incremental costs, such that the relative markup is equal (e.g., Tye, 1993, pp. 46) may create incentives for inefficient bypass of interconnection facilities. If, for example, the stand-alone costs of a specialized entrant for building a separate network are lower than the incremental costs of interconnection capacities plus the symmetrically allocated common costs, private bargaining would result in lower markup requirements for the entrant. Nevertheless, the bargaining result would be efficient, because the competitor also contributes to cover common costs. In contrast, a proportional sharing rule induces inefficient cost duplications because it creates incentives for inefficient bypass on the part of the entrant. In

[3] Since the focus of this paper is on analyzing regulatory problems of remaining market power after legal entry barriers within networks are abolished we ignore the problem of cream-skimming (unsustainability) and the related discussion on the re-establishing of legal entry barriers (e.g., Faulhaber, 1975; Holler, 1990).

a similar way it can be shown that the many other possible fully distributed cost principles may induce inefficient bypass activities as well.

In the context of the unbundling of networks, Baumol has proposed an access pricing rule, called the "efficient component pricing rule" (see Baumol, 1983; Baumol, Sidak, 1994). Suppose that entrants supply a component in competition with the incumbent, for which, however, they need access to the incumbent's facility. Then this rule states that the efficient interconnection/access charges to the single-supplier's component covers the incremental costs of this component plus the opportunity costs, which include any foregone revenues from a concomitant reduction in the single-supplier's sales of the complementary component. The basic idea behind this rule is that an entrant on the competitive segment should only enter if he is more efficient. However, in the case of contestable networks an enforcement of the "efficient component pricing rule" is superfluous. Since excessive profits on the competitive part of the network do not exist, "opportunity costs" in the sense of foregone profits are zero, and subsequently interconnection/access tariffs automatically reflect real opportunity costs of network access, including congestion costs to use the single-supplier's component (irrespective of the question by whom this facility is used). In case that common costs between different networks must also be covered, the "efficient component pricing rule" may be interpreted as arguing in favor of pre-entry allocation of common costs. As a consequence, incentives for inefficient bypass might be created, especially in situations where stand-alone costs of a specialized entrant would be below the sum of incremental costs and the portion of common costs attributed by the "efficient component pricing rule". In contrast, under such circumstances, private bargaining would result in lower markup requirements for the entrant. Again, the bargaining result would be efficient, because the competitor also contributes to cover common costs without incentives for inefficient bypass.

6 Regulation of interconnection to monopolistic bottlenecks

6.1 The impact of market power on the bargaining of interconnection/access conditions

Interconnection among contestable networks may play an increasing role in the future, especially in the telecommunications sector. Nevertheless, there still remains the problem that non-contestable network infrastructures may be involved. An illustrative example are railway systems, where competitive suppliers of transportation services still need access to the tracks and railway stations. In contrast to rail services, railway tracks must be regarded as sunk costs, which cannot be shifted to another market. Therefore, if a potential competitor plans an entry with a parallel track, the incumbent railway owner could reasonably claim to reduce his tariffs to short-run variable costs. As soon as a railway network is completed, one therefore cannot expect further entries with additional tracks. The decision relevant costs of entry include the costs of tracks, which could not be covered by tariffs based on short-run variable costs. In contrast to the supplier of rail services, the track owner in question has obtained market power (see Fremdling, Knieps, 1993, pp. 148-152). A similar situation holds (at least for the present technology) for cable based local telecommunications networks as well as for airports, electricity and gas networks.

In contrast to interconnection among contestable networks, the market power involved in non-contestable network infrastructures fundamentally disturbs such bargaining processes. One extreme alternative could be (vertical) foreclosure of competitors on a complementary service market. Such a tying can be used as a method of price discrimination, enabling a monopolist to earn higher profits.[4] Another way of abusing market power within the bargaining process on interconnection/access conditions is to provide insufficient network access quality or excessive interconnection charges. Examples of insufficient interconnection/access quality may vary within the network sectors under consideration. An example of inferior access conditions is lower quality access to local telephone networks offered to competitive long distance carriers. A central argument in favor of the Antitrust Divesture Case in the US has been to guarantee non-discriminatory equal access conditions (equal quality and tariffs) for all interstate long distance competitors (see CC Docket 78-72, Phase III, May 31, 1983). Monopolistic interconnection/access charges are another danger when market power due to non-contestable networks is involved.

A consequence of these different obstacles of interconnection processes due to non-contestable network infrastructures may be to argue in favor of the traditional vertically integrated networks. Interconnection and access problems could again be solved internally without creating problems of strategic behavior among the different parties involved. This paper, however, recommends an opposite course of action for several reasons. In the first place, the avoidance of strategic interaction among different bargaining partners would not solve the problem of disciplining the market power of vertically integrated networks due to the fact that subparts of the infrastructure networks are non-contestable. Secondly, vertically integrated systems are less capable of exhausting the advantage of the horizontal integration of specific functions within networks. For example, traffic control systems possess an intrinsic potential for Europe-wide coordination and cooperation. This advantage of horizontal integration cannot only be illustrated by the case of air traffic control in Europe but also for the case of an integrated Europe-wide train traffic control system, involving the harmonization of train schedules and the coordination of train movements on a Europe-wide scale (e.g. Knieps, 1993, pp.

[4] See Posner (1976), pp. 171-184; for the case of railroads, see Fremdling, Knieps (1993), pp. 150-152.

204-205). It seems obvious that such a process of horizontal integration can be implemented more easily after vertical disintegration. Thirdly, the benefits of competition among different suppliers of network services can only be derived after vertical disintegration. Instead of arguing for a reversal of the development towards vertical integration, we shall analyze the role of regulatory interventions in order to restrict the degree of disturbance of private bargaining when non-contestable network infrastructures are involved.

6.2 Regulatory instruments to discipline market power

An adequate starting point for government interventions when market power is involved in interconnection/access processes seems to be the Essential Facilities Doctrine. Well known and often applied in the US antitrust law, the Essential Facilities Doctrine gains increasing importance also in the European competition law (e.g., Glasl, 1994). The focus is on access on equal terms for all competitors to what is sometimes referred to as a "monopolistic bottleneck". It is through the application of the Sherman Act 1890 that the Essential Facilities Doctrine has developed in the US.[5]

Liability under the Essential Facilities Doctrine is based on the following criteria:[6]

1. control of an "Essential Facility" by a monopolist (endowing monopoly power);
2. a competitor's inability practically or reasonably to duplicate the facility;
3. the denial of the use of the facility to a competitor; and
4. the feasibility of providing the facility.

It is obvious that the preconditions of the Essential Facilities Doctrine are not fulfilled in the case of interconnection/access among contestable networks, because competitors always possess access to alternative (potential) networks. There simply is no case of market power. If an incumbent carrier were to foreclose access or behave in other aspects in a non-competitive way, new network providers would arise automatically (independent of the market share of the incumbent carrier). The application of the Essential Facilities Doctrine to

[5] The Act has two major provisions:

- Section 1. Every contract, combination in the form of a trust or otherwise, or conspiracy, in restraint of trade or commerce among the several States, or with foreign nations, is hereby declared to be illegal ...
- Section 2. Every person who shall monopolize, or attempt to monopolize, or combine or conspire with any other person or persons to monopolize any part of the trade or commerce among the several States, or with foreign nations, shall be guilty of a misdemeanor ...

[6] City of Anaheim v. Southern California Edison Co., 995 F. 2d 1373, 1380 (9th Cir. 1992).

interconnection/access among contestable networks would even be detrimental, because it would artificially restrict degrees of freedom in the search for Pareto-optimal bargaining solutions among the market participants.

As a consequence, the "Essential Facility" concept should be applied in a restrictive manner only to those interconnection/access cases where market power (at least on one side) is involved. In the US antitrust law the Essential Facilities Doctrine has been applied in a case-by-case procedure to specific infrastructures (e.g. terminal railroads, local electricity networks of a municipality). In spite of the purpose of the "Essential Facility" concept to restrict monopoly power, interpretations of this doctrine by different US courts varied over time. One controversial issue was, whether the feasibility of providing the facility to a competitor would be an absolute criterion or whether "valid business reasons" would be a rationale for a refusal to deal with a direct competitor. This quite elusive interpretation can easily be criticized because, obviously, the fact that granting access would reduce the profit of the owner of the facility cannot by itself constitute a "valid business reason" (e.g., Tye, 1987, p. 346).

The enforcement of the Essential Facilities Doctrine cannot be seen independently from the terms of access provided to the competitors. It is obvious that the effect of a total denial of access by refusing to offer a bundled and an unbundled rate can also be achieved if access is offered on such burdensome terms that the foreclosure of competition would have the same effect (e.g., Tye, 1987, p. 359). An effective application of the Essential Facilities Doctrine must therefore be combined with an adequate regulation of access conditions (quality and tariffs). Partly, this requirement has been included in the criteria of the Essential Facilities Doctrine itself. Not only the denial of the use of the facility but also the imposition of restrictive terms for the use of the facility with the consequence of substantial harm to competition has been considered in earlier case law as a criterion for the Essential Facilities Doctrine (e.g., Tye, 1987, p. 346). Nevertheless, a significant scope for interpretation remains, especially given the historical fact, that antitrust lawyers are typically not specialized in dealing with complex matters of access conditions.

As a consequence, enforcement of the Essential Facilities Doctrine should be combined with the application of regulatory instruments focussing on access conditions (especially regulation of interconnection/access charges). Another advantage of the explicit combination of regulatory concepts with the antitrust concept of the Essential Facilities Doctrine is the shift from case-to-case applications towards the definition of a class of cases characterized by non-contestable network infrastructures. In contrast, the rather global concept of the abuse of market power by dominant firms requires that the relevant market be established (in a narrow sense) and that the meaning of dominance be clarified (e.g., George, Jacquemin, 1990, p. 228). Nevertheless, a generalization of the concept of the Essential Facilities Doctrine seems possible focussing on the class of cases where market power is based on the same reasons. Within networks, this leads to the non-contestable network infrastructures.

Similar to the case of interconnection among contestable networks, access charges must not only cover long-run incremental costs but also total costs of the monopolistic bottlenecks. Common costs to provide contestable and non-contestable networks must be covered by access/interconnection charges, without the owner of an "Essential Facility" being accused of the abuse of market power. If, however, the "efficient component pricing rule" was applied in such a manner that the monopolist's "opportunity costs" of providing access also included monopoly profits as part of its foregone opportunities in the contestable segment, market power of the non-contestable network carrier would be cemented. The application of the "efficient component pricing rule" in this context would be anticompetitive because (potential) entrants in the complementary contestable networks would have to reimburse incumbents for their foregone monopoly rents. Such artificial "opportunity" costs should not be confused with real opportunity costs for the usage of scarce capacities of bottleneck facilities (e.g., Economides, White, 1995).

The reference point for regulatory rules concerning interconnection/access charges should be the coverage of the full costs of the monopolistic bottleneck (in order to guarantee the viability of the facility). In particular, when alternatives to bypass "Essential Facilities" are absent, the cost-covering constraint may not be sufficient to forestall excessive profits. Therefore the instrument of price-cap regulation should be introduced (e.g., Beesley, Littlechild, 1989). Its major purpose is to regulate the level of prices, taking into account the inflation rate (consumer price index) minus a percentage for expected productivity increase. It seems important to restrict such price-cap regulation to the non-contestable parts of networks, where market power due to monopolistic bottlenecks is really creating a regulatory problem. In other subparts of networks price-setting should be left to the competitive markets.

The question remains whether regulators should also be allowed to prescribe pricing rules focussing on tariff structures within monopolistic bottlenecks. There are serious arguments for regulators to refrain from detailed tariff regulation. In the first place, firms should have the flexibility to design (Pareto-superior) optional tariff schemes (e.g., Willig, 1978). Pricing rules prescribed by the regulator could induce inefficient bypass activities. For example, a first pricing rule could be access tariffs according to long run average costs of the "Essential Facility". Since in such a case a differentiation among different user groups according to different price-elasticities is not possible, incentives for inefficient bypass of the bottleneck facility may be created for certain user groups. A second pricing rule would be access pricing according to the Ramsey pricing principle (e.g., Baumol, Bradford, 1970). Mark-ups on the marginal costs of access to the monopolistic bottlenecks are chosen according to the elasticities of demand for network access in order to maximize social welfare given the cost-covering constraint. However, Ramsey prices could become unsustainable, even if strictly applied to monopolistic bottlenecks. The technological trend towards the unbundling of monopolistic bottleneck components increases the possibilities for inefficient bypass. Secondly, the danger arises that regulators extend the regulatory basis including the contestable subparts of networks. From the point of view of increasing static (short-run) efficiency such behavior could even be justified by welfare theory. It is well known that efficiency distortions applying Ramsey pricing can be reduced by extending the regulatory basis (e.g., Laffont, Tirole, 1994). Nevertheless, such an endeavour would in fact mean a return to fully regulated networks, including price- and entry-regulation of the contestable subparts. As such, this would not be a suitable response to deregulation (e.g., Damus, 1984).

In any case, regulators should not be allowed to intervene in the competitive price-setting process within the contestable subparts of networks. Otherwise the competition process within the contestable networks would be severely hampered. Regulation of interconnection/access conditions should be strictly limited to those parts of networks where market power has been localized. The design of pricing rules should be within the decision making process of the firms.

7 Unbundling and the proper role of the Essential Facilities Doctrine

The Essential Facilities Doctrine is the tailor-made answer to a specific competition problem: the vertical integration between a competitive market and a complementary, monopolistic bottleneck area. The provision has two elements: Localization of the monopolistic bottleneck as a factual finding and the right to access as a legal consequence.

As has been shown in section 4, from the point of view of competition in the long-distance network, the local networks still have to be considered as monopolistic bottlenecks. This is because in order for a long-distance network operator to conduct his own business, he needs to have access not just to a few local networks, but to all local networks. The Essential Facilities Doctrine can, in principle, be applied to substantiate a claim made by long-distance network competitors to be allowed to have access to the local networks of the established carrier.

The purpose of the Essential Facilities Doctrine is to overcome the structural market entry barrier caused by vertical integration with a monopolistic bottleneck. A claim to access merely to elements of the monopolistic bottleneck ("demand-oriented" unbundling) can therefore not be derived from the Essential Facilities Doctrine. Moreover long-distance competitors must accept the established carrier's local network as it is, including the disadvantages and problems that have evolved historically. They cannot bypass this by simply selecting elements from the local networks that a network set up today would ideally contain.[7]

8 Costing and pricing of interconnection services: The case of telecommunications[8]

8.1 The role of long-run incremental costs (LRIC) in determining interconnection prices

It is well-known that even after complete entry deregulation economies of scale and economies of scope create common costs which cannot be directly attributed to the individual network services. Although activity-based costing can help to identify the directly attributable costs to specific products it is still not possible to declare all costs incremental costs without applying economically unjustified allocation of common costs. Provided the established network carrier is determining incremental costs based on decision-oriented accounting methods it becomes immediately clear that the sum of the incremental costs does not allow survival. In fact the established firm must also cover its product-group specific costs as well as the firm-specific overhead costs by means of mark-ups on the LRIC. In order to avoid inefficient bypass activities of entrants, market-driven mark-ups should be raised by the established carriers. An obligation to provide the services according to LRIC, however, would disturb the symmetric treatment of infrastructure owner and service provider. Incentives to be the owner of infrastructure for interconnection and network access would disappear, because it would be cheaper to use the infrastructure of the competitors and avoid a contribution to the common costs. Symmetric treatment of owners and users of infrastructure therefore requires that the stand-alone costs of network infrastructure must be covered.

8.2 Management accounting versus pseudo data models

The obsoleteness of historical cost accounting

In competitive industries the value of the firms's productive assets is equal to the discounted (present) value of the anticipated net cash flows earned by the assets over their remaining useful life. These net cash flows are determined by competitive market forces and the firm's actions, but are not influenced by book asset value. In regulated industries, however, the value of the firm's assets in place, the rate base has been strongly influenced by regulated depreciation charges. Since the regulatory agencies were under political pressure

[7] A detailed analysis of these topical issues with special emphasis on the German Telecommunications Act is provided in Engel, Knieps (1998).

[8] For a more extensive analysis the reader is referred to Knieps (1998).

to keep down the local rates, and therefore also the capital costs of local networks, artificially low depreciation charges and a too long life time were prescribed (not sufficiently taking into account technical progress, changed substitution possibilities etc.).

Although it is true that historical cost accounting is obsolete, the reform towards decision relevant costing should still be based on management and financial accounting data. Management accounting approaches are based on real costing data, observing the relationship between input-prices, outputs and the costs of production. In contrast, engineering-economic models (process analysis approaches) develop pseudo cost data. After describing the production function from engineering data, the cost-output relationship is then derived as a result of assumed global optimization behavior. It shall be shown in the following section that instead of engineering-economic models, an adequate reform of management accounting is needed, based on forward-looking cost accounting methods. Moreover, it should become clear that the concept of an efficient network needs much further elaboration. Whereas current-cost accounting methods take into account, by their very nature, the path-dependency of network evolution (as long as it is efficient from a forward-looking perspective) engineering-economic models usually ignore the strategy of successive upgrading of networks.

The fallacies of pseudo data models in determining long-run incremental costs

In the following we shall argue that engineering-economic models are inadequate for determining the long-run incremental interconnection costs of the interconnection services of established carriers. Process analysis is based on simulating the production function from engineering data. After describing the production function, the cost-output relationship is then derived as a result of assumed opimization behavior. Instead of real accounting data, the cost-data developed by engineering-economic models are simulated (pseudo) data, their informational value strongly dependent on the quality and the characteristics of the underlying process model. Although the process analysis approach was not very popular for a long time (see Griffin, 1972, p. 47), it has also been applied in the field of telecommunications (see Gabel, Kennet, 1991). Gabel and Kennet developed the so-called LECOM (Local Exchange Cost Optimization Model) in order to generate data to address the issue of economies of scope in local telephone networks. With LECOM it became possible to solve the problem of selecting the combination and location of facilities that minimized the costs of satisfying varying levels of demand (see Gabel, Kennet, 1994, pp. 386 ff.). The three types of facilities within the local exchange carrier's network are the local loop, switching and trunking. The local loop is composed of facilities that provide signalling and voice transmission path between a central office and the customer's station. The central office houses the switching computer that connects a customer's line to either another customer who is served by the same switch, or to an interoffice trunk. Calls between central offices are carried on trunks. The model takes as data a city's dimensions and customer usage level. LECOM then searches for the technological mix, capacity and location of switches that minimize the annual cost of production. The location of the switches is optimized by the non-linear optimization model. In principle, there are an infinite number of possible configurations to be considered. For each economically and technically feasible combination of switches, a certain number of possible iterations are allowed. An iteration involves the calculation of the cost of service at one or more alternative locations for the switches. For each market, and a given level of demand, LECOM evaluates a number of different switch combinations. In other words, LECOM has been designed to develop a green-field approach. Gabel, Kennet (1994, pp. 390 ff.) already pointed out important limitations of engineering optimization models. In the first place, optimization models typically are not designed to quantify the less tangible costs of providing service (administrative costs). Secondly, LECOM is limited by bounded rationality. Since global optimization is not feasible, only a reasonable number of possible solutions are examined. It is obvious that a great degree of freedom exists in the search for "plausible" solutions. Thirdly, the value of the pseudo-data approach ultimately rests on the quality and completeness of the underlying process models. Measurement errors and behavioral errors still persist, even in the best model (see Griffin, 1977, p. 125).

Beyond this immanent critique of engineering-economic models the most important point is that they are simply the wrong tool for deriving the LRIC of established carriers. Even if the analysis is based on a "scorched node" assumption, which implies that the incremental cost estimate reflects the current network topology, engineering-economic models - by their very nature - are not able to derive the LRIC of the efficient network of the established carrier. The reason is the path-dependency of networks. This means that the gradual upgrading is efficient (given the network history), if the additional costs of upgrading are lower than the costs of building new network facilities. This implies that the economically efficient incremental costs must be calculated on the basis of the factual costs of the incumbent's network in place (including its history of upgrading). As long as the incremental costs of upgrading of the established carrier are lower than the stand-alone costs of a hypothetical new network of an entrant, the required network capacity should be provided by the historically grown network of the established carrier. This is true because entry would replace the service of the incumbent firm over its existing network, not the service of a hypothetical efficient provider. Path-dependent costs of gradual upgrading are then economically efficient and are also relevant from a foreward-looking costing perspective.[9] They should there-

[9] As long as upgrading is an efficient strategy its costs should not be confused with phantom costs due to overvaluation of installed investment (based on differences between economic and historical depreciation patterns (see next section c)).

fore also not be confused with sunk costs, because the upgrading strategy is then incentive-compatible, even if all investments could easily be shifted to another market (perfect "second-hand" market). Under efficient upgrading strategies the economic value of the existing network components is the only decision basis. It is simply not in the spirit of the engineering-economic models to take into consideration this network history. Even under the scorched node assumption engineering-economic models use the high degree of freedom of simulation models to find cost-minimizing solutions by ignoring the historically grown network infrastructure that is already in existence.

Beyond this fundamental critique of the usefulness of engineering-economic models for determining the LRIC of the established carriers, other points of criticism have already been indicated in NERA's studies for OFTEL.[10] In particular, the insufficient determination of the factual usage of network capacities, and of the factual routing patterns have been stated.

The necessity of reforming management accounting: From historical cost accounting to current cost accounting

It is often argued, that the necessary and overdue departure from historical cost accounting (HCA) in a competitive environment can only be accomplished by introducing engineering-economic models. This is, however, particularly misleading because the necessary reform should still be based on management accounting. In the following we shall argue that a transition from historical cost accounting to forward looking current cost accounting (CCA) is unavoidable. Under competitive conditions the valuation of the assets and the depreciation-charges must reflect their economic values. The true economic value of any productive asset is the discounted present value of the anticipated stream of net earnings it is capable of producing. Thus the economic depreciation of a productive asset during a time period is the decrease in its economic value during this period. It should be noted that historical book values and historical depreciation patterns typically reflect neither capital market valuation of assets in place nor economic depreciation. A transition from historical cost accounting to current cost accounting thus necessarily poses the problem of phantom costs ("Altlastenproblem") due to an overvaluation of existing network equipment (see Albach, Knieps, 1997, p. 31). However, phantom costs should not be confused with economically efficient foreward looking costs of upgrading existing network (path-dependency). A periodical reevaluation of the assets as well as an adaptation of economic depreciation rates seems unavoidable, especially in such dynamic markets as telecommunications.

[10] The reader is referred to a series of studies NERA provided to OFTEL: The Methodology to Calculate Long-Run Incremental Costs, March 1996; Reconciliation and Integration of Top Down and Bottom Up Models of Incremental Costs, June 1996; Reconciliation and Integration of Top Down and Bottom Up Models of Incremental Costs, Final Report, December 1996.

References

1. Albach, H., Knieps, G. (1997): Kosten und Preise in wettbewerblichen Ortsnetzen, Nomos, Baden-Baden
2. Baumol, W. J. (1983): Some subtle issues in railroad regulation. International Journal of Transport Economics 10/1-2, 341-355
3. Baumol, W. J., Bradford, D. F. (1970): Optimal Departures from Marginal Cost Pricing. American Economic Review 60, 265-283
4. Baumol, W. J., Panzar, J. C., Willig, R. D. (1982): Contestable Markets and the Theory of Industry Structure. Harcourt Brace Jovanovich, New York
5. Baumol, W. J., Sidak, J. C. (1994): Toward Competition in Local Telephony, MIT Press and the American Enterprise Institute
6. Beesley, M. E., Littlechild, S. C. (1989): The regulation of privatized monopolies in the United Kingdom. Rand Journal of Economics 20/3, 454-472
7. Blankart, Ch. B., Knieps, G. (1993): State and Standards. Public Choice 77, 39-52
8. Blankart, Ch. B., Knieps, G. (1995): Market-Oriented Open Network Provision. Information Economics and Policy 7, 283-296
9. Damus, S. (1984): Ramsey pricing by U.S. railroads - Can it exist? Journal of Transport Economics and Policy 18, 51-61
10. Economides, N., White, N. E. (1995): Access and Interconnection Pricing: How Efficient is the 'Efficient Component Pricing Rule'? Antitrust Bulletin 40/3, 557-580
11. Engel, C., Knieps, G. (1998): Die Vorschriften des Telekommunikationsgesetzes über den Zugang zu wesentlichen Leistungen: Eine juristisch-ökonomische Untersuchung. Nomos, Baden-Baden
12. Faulhaber, G. R. (1975): Cross-Subsidization: Pricing in Public Enterprises. American Economic Review 65, 966-977
13. Fisher, F. M, McGowan, J. J., Greenwood, J. E. (1983): Folded, Spindled and Multilated - Economic Analysis and U.S. v IBM, A Charles River Associates Study (Massachusetts Institute of Technology)
14. Fremdling, R., Knieps, G. (1993): Competition, Regulation and Nationalization: The Prussian Railway System in the Nineteenth Century. The Scandinavian Economic History Review XLI / 2, 129-154
15. Gabel, D., Kennet, D. M. (1991): Estimating the Cost Structure of Local Telephone Exchange Network. Columbus, OH: National Regulatory Research Institute at Ohio State University
16. Gabel, D., Kennet, D. M. (1994): Economies of Scope in the Local Telephone Exchange Market. Journal of Regulatory Economics 6, 381-398
17. Glasl, D. (1994): Essential Facilities Doctrine in EC Antitrust Law: A Contribution to the Current Debate. ECLR 6, 306-314
18. George, K., Jacquemin, H. (1990): Competition Policy in the European Community, in: Comanor, W. (Ed.): Competition Policy in Europe and North America. Harmwood Academic Press, Chur, 206-245
19. Griffin, J. M. (1972): The Process Analysis Alternative to Statistical Cost Functions: An Application to Petroleum Refining. American Economic Review 62, 46-56
20. Griffin, J. M. (1977): Long-run production modeling with pseudo-data: electric power generation. Bell Journal of Economics 8, 112-127

21. Holler, M. J. (1990): Umstrittene Märkte und die Theorie der reinen Kosten, in: Graf von der Schulenburg, J.-M., Sinn, H.-W. (Eds.): Theorie der Wirtschaftspolitik - Festschrift zum fünfundsiebzigsten Geburtstag von Hans Möller. Mohr (Siebeck), Tübingen, 146-161
22. Holler, M. J., Knieps, G., Niskanen E. (1997): Standardization in Transportation Markets: A European Perspective. EURAS Yearbook of Standardization 1, 371-390
23. Knieps, G. (1993): Competition, coordination and cooperation - A disaggregated approach to transportation regulation. Utilities Policy 3, 201-207
24. Knieps, G. (1996): Wettbewerb in Netzen - Reformpotentiale in den Sektoren Eisenbahn und Luftverkehr. Mohr (Siebeck), Tübingen
25. Knieps, G. (1997): Phasing out Sector-Specific Regulation in Competitive Telecommunications. Kyklos. 50/3, 325-339
26. Knieps, G. (1998): Costing and Pricing of Interconnection Services in a Liberalized European Telecommunications Market, American Institute for Contemporary German Studies (Ed.): Telecommunications Reform in Germany: Lessons and Priorities. Washington D.C., 51-73
27. Knieps, G., Vogelsang, I. (1982): The Sustainability Concept under Alternative Behavioral Assumptions. Bell Journal of Economics 13/1, 234-241
28. Laffont, J.-J., Tirole, J. (1994): Access pricing and competition. European Economic Review 38, 1673-1710
29. Owen, B. M., Braeutigam, R. (1978): The regulation game - Strategic use of the administrative process. Ballinger Publishing Company, Cambridge, Ma.
30. Posner, R. A. (1976): Antitrust Law. An Economic Perspective. The University of Chicago Press, Chicago
31. Shankerman, M.(1996): Symmetric regulation for competitive telecommunications. Information Economics and Policy 8, 3-23
32. Tye, W. B. (1987): Competitive access: a comparative industry approach to the essential facility doctrine. Energy Law Journal 8/2, 337-379
33. Tye, W. B. (1993): Pricing Market Access for Regulated Firms. Logistics and Transportation Review 29/1, 39-67
34. Willig, R. D (1978): Pareto-superior Nonlinear Outlay Schedules. Bell Journal of Economics 9/1, 56-69

On Price Competition with Heterogeneous Consumers

Martin Peitz

University of Alicante, Dpto. Fundamentos Analisis Economico, 03071 Alicante, Spain

Abstract. Address models of product differentiation form an important class of models of imperfect competition. Recent work has focused on distributions of consumer characteristics which guarantee the existence of Nash equilibrium where price is a pure strategy. Here, I present results in the case of unit-elastic demand which concentrate on the heterogeneity of budget shares among consumers. Also, I provide existence results on an extended model of discrete choice among goods provided in perfectly and imperfectly competitive markets.

1 Introduction

The foundation of imperfect competition in partial equilibrium analysis has seen a steady flow of contributions over the last decades. In this paper, I follow the strand of literature which has looked at models of price competition with a heterogeneous population of consumers. In particular, I consider address models of product differentiation according to which goods are described by addresses in some characteristics space (see Hotelling, 1929, Gorman, 1980, Lancaster, 1966, among others). Consumers then are characterized by preferences over these characteristics, and it is the heterogeneity of consumer tastes which gives rise to aggregate demand being less elastic than individual demand. Aggregate demand has to satisfy certain concavity conditions in order to show that profit functions are quasi-concave. The property of quasi-concavity has turned out to be central in the work on models of price competition because existence of price equilibrium is usually shown invoking Kakutani's fixed point theorem.

Unfortunately, seemingly innocent examples suffer from a violation of the quasi-concavity of profit functions and from the nonexistence of price equilibrium (in pure strategies). The perhaps most famous example is Hotelling's linear city as analyzed in d'Aspremont, Gabszewicz and Thisse (1979). Consequently, one can never hope for a general model but only for a class of models in which profit functions satisfy the property of quasi-concavity at least on a compact set of prices (see also Roberts and Sonnenschein, 1977).

The first contributions to the theory of imperfect competition making use of aggregation results by Prékopa (1971, 1973) and Borell (1975) on log-concave densities are the papers by Caplin and Nalebuff (1991b) and Dierker (1991). Both show that profits are quasiconcave in price (or logarithmic price) for a class of models. Caplin and Nalebuff focus on address models of product differentiation in which consumers have unit demand. They impose joint restrictions on utility functions which have to be linear in the characteristics of the consumers – these characteristics relate to product differentiation – and on the distribution of characteristics which has to satisfy some generalized notion of concavity.[1] Dierker associates switching parameters to price ratios at which a consumer switches from one to another good. He postulates that expenditure in the market does not depend on demand and requires that the density of the distribution of switching parameters is log-concave. Under the hypothesis that consumers have heterogeneous individual demand functions, which make total expenditure in the market less price sensitive than individual expenditure, the analysis can be extended to individual demand functions which give rise to variable individual expenditure (see Peitz, 2000)..

In Peitz (1998b) a framework has been presented which allows for an analogous treatment of the unit-elastic case compared to the unit demand case as presented by Caplin and Nalebuff (1991b). Unit demand models suffer from some theoretical limitations which are avoided when replaced by unit elastic demand. Repeating the argument in Peitz (1998b), a model with multiple imperfectly competitive markets, in each of which consumers buy one unit, has the property that the ability to pay in one market depends upon the prices in the other markets which makes the model intractable.[2] With total market expenditure independent of the prices extensions to multiple imperfectly competitive markets are straightforward. The second and to my mind more severe theoretical limitation is that the introduction of sufficiently heterogeneous income leads to nonexistence problems of price equilibrium in the framework of unit demand, as shown in Peitz (1999). A model which does not allow for income heterogeneity in a to some extent general way can only be seen as rather restrictive, with respect to the specification of consumer behavior. Clearly, when looking at real world markets unit-elastic demand modeling is complementary rather than a substitute to unit demand modeling.

In this paper, I first review one result derived in Peitz (1998b) where tastes for the differentiated goods and income are the relevant sources of consumer heterogeneity. I then set out to provide additional results with respect to the expenditure pattern of consumers. Namely, it is postulated that consumers have different expenditure shares in the market and that, from the viewpoint

[1] In earlier work Caplin and Nalebuff (1986) and Neven (1986) require a concave density and the latter a one-dimensional characteristics space. Bester (1992) requires a one-dimensional characteristics space and a distribution which is "close" to the uniform. – Dierker and Podczeck (1992) address the question which algebraic structure on consumers' tastes should be chosen.

[2] This is due to the fact that in models of unit demand the budget constraint is violated for high prices when consuming one unit of the good. Hence prices in other markets have an effect on the critical price in one market at which the budget becomes binding.

of the consumers, these affect the relative attractiveness of the differentiated goods in the market. This third source of heterogeneity is incorporated into the analysis.

Furthermore, I introduce the possibility that consumers can choose not to participate in the imperfectly competitive market at all introducing outside options into the model with variable individual demand. Such outside options are modeled as perfectly competitive submarkets. In particular, I allow for decreasing returns to scale in the competitive submarkets. This model can be seen as an attempt to incorporate a competitive fringe in a differentiated product market. This makes it possible to address the interaction between a perfectly competitive part of the economy and an imperfectly competitive one.

In the final two sections I discuss the possibility that expenditure shares are income dependent or dependent on the tastes which concern the attractiveness of the brands.

One issue not addressed in this paper is the uniqueness of equilibrium. As is well-known, conditions are rather restrictive (see Milgrom and Roberts, 1990, Peitz, 1998b, Dierker and Dierker, 1999). Also, I did not elaborate on examples in the style of those used in the industrial organization literature where tractability rather than generality is the main concern. For this I refer to Peitz (1997, 1998a).

2 Price equilibrium with constant expenditure shares: summary and discussion

Following Peitz (1998b), in a differentiated market n single-product firms are located at l_i, $i \in N = \{1, \ldots, n\}$ in a k-dimensional space of product characteristics $L \subset \Re^k$. Each differentiated product is called a brand which is fully described by its brand characteristics l_i; characteristics shared by all brands can be eliminated. The collection of brands in the differentiated market is denoted by $l \equiv (l_1, \ldots, l_n)$.

Each firm i sets its price $p_i \in \Re_+$ in order to maximize profits, and product characteristics are given. Profits are $\pi_i(p; l) = (p_i - c_i(l_i))X_i(p; l)$ where $c_i(l_i)$ denotes the constant marginal cost of production of firm i and $X_i(p; l)$ is the mean demand of firm i. The production cost may depend on the good's characteristics. Such a dependence is likely if the brands are of a different quality, which is reflected by different variable inputs. A price equilibrium consists of a price vector p^* such that $\pi_i(p^*; l) \geq \pi_i(p_i, p^*_{-i}; l)$ for all p_i and $i = 1, \ldots, n$ and the corresponding allocation. To determine whether a price equilibrium exists, consumer behavior has to be specified and aggregate demand functions for each good have to be derived from the set of individual demand functions.

Consumers can buy quantities x_i, $i = 1, \ldots, n$, and they may spend some part of their income (or budget) on the Hicksian composite commodity with index 0. The price of good 0 is normalized to 1. Hence prices p_i, $i = 1, \ldots, n$, and income y are measured in units of the composite commodity. $p \in \Re^n_+$ denotes the vector of prices p_i, $i = 1, \ldots, n$, and $x \in \Re^n_+$ the corresponding vector of quantities. The budget constraint reads $x_0 + p \cdot x \leq y$ where $y \in Y$ is a consumer's income. Income is an element of a convex set $Y \subseteq \Re_+$. Consumers are postulated to buy one brand in the differentiated market and spend a fixed income share in it.

With $\Omega \subseteq \Re^m$ I denote the space of consumers' taste parameters, which determine the relative evaluation of the brands. These taste parameters are an important component in describing the heterogeneity of consumers. There are two additional sources of heterogeneity: income $y \in Y \subseteq \Re_+$ and an additional taste parameter $\alpha \in A \subseteq [0, 1]$ which determines the relative evaluation of any brand relative to the composite commodity. Essentially, there are two types of assumptions about consumers. First, all consumers are assumed to belong to a particular class specified by a particular functional form of utility functions. In the following sections this assumption is modified in order to accommodate different types of consumer behavior. Second, distributional assumptions are made specifying in which sense consumers are heterogeneous.

- **Assumption (U.1).** The utility function of a consumer with taste parameters

$$(\omega, \alpha, y) \in \Omega \times A \times Y$$

is defined as

$$u^{(\omega,\alpha,y)}(x_0, x, l) = \left(\sum_{i=1}^{n} \tilde{u}_i^{(\omega,y)}(x_i, l_i) \right)^{\alpha} x_0^{1-\alpha}$$

where $\tilde{u}_i^{(\omega,y)}(x_i, l_i)$ denotes the utility which a consumer with type (ω, y) derives from the consumption of brand i.

$$\tilde{u}_i^{(\omega,y)}(x_i, l_i) = x_i \exp \left\{ t_1(l_i) + \sum_{j=1}^{m} \omega_j t_{j+1}(l_i) + \log y \, t_{m+2}(l_i) \right\}.$$

Since $\tilde{u}_i$ is linear and thus convex in x_i, consumers consume only one of the brands. Consumers spend αy in the differentiated product market and $(1-\alpha)y$ on the Hicksian composite commodity; this individual expenditure is not affected by preference parameters ω. The function $t : \Re^k \longrightarrow \Re^{m+2}$ translates the brands' characteristics into vectors which relate them to preference parameters ω and logarithmic income.

In the present model a consumer type is fully described by a triple of consumer characteristics $(\omega, \alpha, y) \in \Omega \times A \times Y$. The attractiveness of a brand is characterized by an exponential function which depends on (ω, y). In my specification the brand utility depends linearly on the consumer characteristics with respect to the different brands ω and logarithmic income (considering logarithmic utilities). The attractiveness of a brand is modeled similarly to that in Caplin and Nalebuff (1991b) for unit demand models. Particular exponential functions have been used in the literature on international trade and economic geography where firms are modeled as engaging in quantity competition (for details, see Peitz, 1998b).

Income is allowed to affect the discrete choice behavior; this seems to be a desirable property when income is related to parameters such as ability or education level, and when these affect consumption decisions.

In the following, I consider a particular monotone transformation of conditional indirect utility, where (x_0, x_i) are chosen optimally,

$$v_i(p_i, l_i; \omega, \alpha, y) \equiv \log y - \alpha \log p_i + \alpha t_1(l_i) + \alpha \sum_{j=1}^{m} \omega_j t_{j+1}(l_i)$$
$$+\alpha \log y\, t_{m+2}(l_i) + (\alpha \log \alpha + (1-\alpha)\log(1-\alpha)).$$

A consumer buys brand i if she derives a higher utility from its consumption (together with the composite commodity) than from the consumption of others. Consequently, individual demand can be written as $\xi_i^{(\omega,\alpha,y)}(p,l) = \psi_i(p,l,\omega,y)\alpha y/p_i$ where $\psi_i(p,l,\omega,y)$ denotes the value of an indicator function taking value 1 if the consumer buys brand i; otherwise it will take value 0. It takes value 1 if

$$-\log p_i + t_1(l_i) + \sum_{k=1}^{m} \omega_k t_{k+1}(l_i) + \log y\, t_{m+2}(l_i)$$
$$\geq -\log p_j + t_1(l_j) + \sum_{k=1}^{m} \omega_k t_{k+1}(l_j) + \log y\, t_{m+2}(l_j) \text{ for all } j \neq i. \quad (1)$$

Since mass points will be excluded when aggregating, the consumption decision in case of equality is arbitrary. Mean demand is derived by taking the average over the population. The space of taste parameters Ω is constructed such that it constitutes the smallest convex and closed subset of $\Re^m$, containing a set of full measure of consumers. Without loss of generality I consider only a set of consumer characteristics ω_j, $j = 1, \ldots, m$, where consumers do not have the same ω so that they value the goods' characteristics differently and the population is heterogeneous. Moreover, consumer characteristics which can be expressed as linear combinations of other consumer characteristics are replaced. Then the interior of Ω relative to $\Re^m$, denoted by int Ω, is nonempty.

Each consumer is represented by an element of the product space $\Omega \times A \times Y \subset \Re^{m+2}$, which is assumed to be measurable. Weights are attached to groups of consumers by the probability measure μ. Hence one has $\mu(\Omega \times A \times Y) = 1$. Mean demand for brand i is written as

$$X_i(p,l) = \int_{\Omega \times A \times Y} \xi_i^{(\omega,\alpha,y)}(p,l)\, d\mu(\omega,\alpha,y)$$

Since a consumer (ω, α, y) spends αy in the differentiated market and buys exactly one brand there, mean demand can be rewritten as

$$X_i(p,l) = \int_{\Omega \times A \times Y} \psi_i(p,l,\omega,y)\frac{\alpha y}{p_i} d\mu(\omega,\alpha,y)$$

In order to separate the different dimensions of heterogeneity, we assume throughout that the variables ω, α, y, which describe consumer behavior, are stochastically independent. For results in the absence of stochastic independence, refer to Peitz (1998b).

- **Assumption (I.1).** The variables ω, α, y are stochastically independent.

As stated above, income may be related to parameters such as ability or education level, and these parameters affect the critical price ratios at which a consumer switches from one brand to another. Under A.1 parameters ω are unrelated to income. Hence A.1 is satisfied if parameters such as ability are stochastically independent of parameters (ω, α), and if the heterogeneity with respect to ability can be replaced by income heterogeneity (income as a perfect proxy of ability in the mean of each group of consumers (ω, α)).

It will be useful to rewrite demand and to replace logarithmic income by the variable z, i.e. $z \equiv \log y$. Denote $Z \equiv \{z | e^z \in Y\}$. The set of consumers belonging to the turf of firm i is denoted by $M_i(p,l)$.

$$X_i(p,l) = \frac{1}{p_i}\int_{M_i(p,l)} \alpha e^z f(z) g(\omega) h(\alpha) d(\alpha,\omega,z) \tag{2}$$
$$\text{where } M_i(p,l) \equiv \{(\alpha,\omega,z) \in A \times \Omega \times Z |$$
$$v_i(p_i, l_i; \omega, \alpha, e^z) \geq v_j(p_j, l_j; \omega, \alpha, e^z), \text{ for all } j \in N\}.$$

Under (I.1) demand for brand i can be rewritten, assuming that logarithmic income $\log y$, ω, and α have distribution functions F, G, H with densities f, g, and h, respectively. Because of (U.1), the discrete choice of consumers is independent of the realization of α. Consequently, in the present specification the set M_i is independent of it, and only the population mean $\bar{\alpha} = \int_A \alpha h(\alpha) d\alpha$ needs to be considered (only for convenience, I implicitly assume that the distribution of α has a density). Demand for brand i can then be written as

$$X_i(p,l) = \frac{\bar{\alpha}}{p_i}\int_{M_i(p,l)} e^z f(z) g(\omega) d(\omega,z)$$

Clearly, to establish properties of mean demand, aggregation results are needed for a heterogeneous population. The importance of a generalized Brunn-Minkowski inequality as developed by Prékopa (1971, 1973) and Borell

(1975) for models of imperfect competition, has been discovered by Dierker (1991) and Caplin and Nalebuff (1991b). For accessible proofs of the Prekopa-Borell result see Das Gupta (1980). The result stated here refers to log-concave functions, where a function ϕ is called *log-concave* if $\log \circ \phi$ is concave, that is, $\phi(\lambda\nu + (1-\lambda)\nu') \geq \phi(\nu)^{\lambda}\phi(\nu')^{1-\lambda}$ for any $\lambda \in [0,1]$. The *Minkowski average* A_λ of two sets A_0 and A_1 is defined as the set of all points of the form $x_\lambda = (1-\lambda)x_0 + \lambda x_1$, with $x_0 \in A_0$, $x_1 \in A_1$, and $0 \leq \lambda \leq 1$.

Proposition 1 *Let ϕ be a function on $\Re^n$ with convex support B. Take any measurable subsets A_0 and A_1 of B. For $0 \leq \lambda \leq 1$, define $A_\lambda = (1-\lambda)A_0 + \lambda A_1$ the Minkowski average of the two sets. If ϕ is a log-concave function, then*

$$\int_{A_\lambda} \phi(\nu)d\nu \geq \left(\int_{A_0} \phi(\nu)d\nu\right)^{1-\lambda} \left(\int_{A_1} g(\nu)d\nu\right)^{\lambda}$$

The proposition states that log-concavity of ϕ translates into log-concavity of the cumulative integral. Note also that the product of log-concave functions is log-concave. I will apply this property throughout the paper. Taste parameters ω are the first source of heterogeneity.

- **Assumption (D.1).** The parameter ω is distributed according to the distribution function G with density $g : \Omega \to \Re_+$ which is positive and log-concave on int Ω.

The assumption of a log-concave density of taste parameters is discussed in detail in Caplin and Nalebuff (1991a). I only want to point out that several classes of density functions are log-concave. For instance, the normal and, under some parameter restrictions, the beta distribution have log-concave densities. However, the lognormal distribution does *not* have a log-concave density.

Special case: The density g is *unimodal* if all upper contour sets are convex. As a special case, consider that $\omega_1, ..., \omega_m$ are independently and identically distributed with densities $g_1 = ... = g_m$. As shown by Marshall and Olkin (1974), if $g = g_1 \cdot ... \cdot g_m$ is unimodal, continuously differentiable and positive, then all g_i are log-concave.

The second important source of heterogeneity is income heterogeneity. In order to allow for income distributions which are empirically well-founded, I make the following assumption about the distribution of income:

- **Assumption (D.2).** Logarithmic income $z = \log y$ is distributed according to the distribution function F with density $f : Z \to \Re_+$, which is positive and log-concave in z on int Z; average income $\int_Y yf(\log y)d(\log y)$ is finite.

The assumption of a log-concave income distribution would seem to be a major limitation because in emprical work, for instance, the lognormal distribution or the Pareto distribution seem to fit rather well, but do not have log-concave densities. These two densities are log-concave in logarithmic income. In the case of a lognormal density this is obvious: logarithmic income is normally distributed, and a normal distribution has a log-concave density. When allowing for multi-parameter densities, again densities which are log-concave in logarithmic income seem to be very successful in providing a good fit.

Example: McDonald (1984) introduced the following class of densities which he called generalized beta of the second kind. It has four parameters a, b, c, d and includes many known distributions used in the analysis of income distributions as special or limiting cases. In particular, it includes the Singh-Maddala distribution (Singh and Maddala, 1976). The density is defined for $y \geq 0$ as

$$f(y) = \frac{ay^{ac-1}}{b^{ac}B(c,d)(1+(y/b)^a)^{c+d}}$$

where B is the Beta function. Namely, $B(c,d) = \Gamma(c)\Gamma(d)/\Gamma(c+d)$ and Γ is the Gamma function, $\Gamma(q) = \int_0^\infty x^{q-1}e^{-x}dx$. As pointed out in McDonald (1984), density f has a decreasing elasticity $\partial \log f(y)/\partial \log y$ and is consequently log-concave in logarithmic income.

My proof of equilibrium existence is based on the following observations: First, following from (D.1) and (D.2) the function with values $e^z f(z)g(\omega)$ is log-concave in (ω, z) because e^z is also log-concave in z. Second, to show that sales $p_i X_i(p,l)$ are log-concave in $\log p_i$, it is sufficient to show that the Minkowski average describes the set of consumers who buy given a convex combination of logarithmic prices. Note that a firm i has an *effectively differentiated brand* if for any $j \neq i$ some $k \in \{2, \ldots, m+2\}$ with $t_k(l_i) \neq t_k(l_j)$ can be found.

Proposition 2 (Peitz, 1998b) *Assume (U.1), (I.1), (D.1), and (D.2). For any firm i with an effectively differentiated brand, sales $p_i X_i(p,l)$ are log-concave, where positive, in logarithmic price* $\log p_i$.

This result, together with some rather technical arguments which guarantee that prices are always chosen from compact sets, establishes the existence of equilibrium. This is stated as Theorem 1. Here, I do not rule out the possibility that some (or all) brands are not differentiated. Clearly, non-differentiated brands are of less interest because they compete as in a possibly asymmetric Bertrand model with homogeneous goods. This competition among a group of non-differentiated goods with $t_k(l_i) \neq t_k(l_j)$ for all possible pairs i, j in such a group then provides an upper bound for prices set by this group of non-differentiated brands. If this upper bound is sufficiently low, these non-differentiated brands anchor the price in one segment of the market and increase the competitive pressure in the market. Note also that demand is not necessarily differentiable everywhere. When prices are such that a marginal consumer reaches the boundary of the support, demand is possibly kinked since densities are possibly non-vanishing on their support. Proposition 2 and Theorem 1 are proved in Peitz (1998b).

Theorem 1 (Peitz, 1998b) *Assume (U.1), (I.1), (D.1), and (D.2). Then there exists a price equilibrium.*

3 The dependence of discrete choice on expenditure shares

Assumption (U.1) implies that the evaluation of a brand only depends on characteristics ω and income. Discrete choice was assumed to be separated from the realization of the expenditure share a consumer has in the differentiated market. I will now allow for such a dependence and modify (U.1) accordingly.

- **Assumption (U.2)**. The utility function of a consumer with taste parameters

$$(\omega, \alpha, y) \in \Omega \times A \times Y$$

is defined as

$$u^{(\omega,\alpha,y)}(x_0, x, l) = (\sum_{i=1}^{n} \tilde{u}_i^{(\omega,\alpha,y)}(x_i, l_i))^{\alpha} x_0^{1-\alpha}$$

where $\tilde{u}_i^{(\omega,\alpha,y)}$ denotes the utility which a consumer of type (ω, α, y) derives from the consumption of brand i,

$$\tilde{u}_i^{(\omega,\alpha,y)}(x_i, l_i)$$

$$= x_i \exp\left\{ t_1(l_i) + \sum_{j=1}^{m} \omega_j t_{j+1}(l_i) + \log y \, t_{m+2}(l_i) + \alpha t_{m+3}(l_i) \right\}.$$

Consequently, the discrete choice is allowed to depend on the budget share. For instance, consumers with a high budget share might on average be more concerned with quality or the reverse. The more general specification of the consumers' utility functions comes at a cost: I will need a stronger distributional assumption. Aggregate demand can still be written as in equation

(2), the difference being that indirect utilities are derived from (U.2), which is

$$v_i(p_i, l_i; \omega, \alpha, y) \equiv \log y + \alpha(t_1(l_i) - \log p_i + \sum_{j=1}^{m} \omega_j t_{j+1}(l_i) + \log y \, t_{m+2}(l_i))$$
$$+\alpha^2 \, t_{m+3}(l_i) + (\alpha \log \alpha + (1 - \alpha)\log(1 - \alpha)).$$

Hence a consumer of type (ω, α, y) buys brand i if

$$- \log p_i + t_1(l_i) + \sum_{k=1}^{m} \omega_k t_{k+1}(l_i) + \log y \, t_{m+2}(l_i) + \alpha t_{m+3}(l_i)$$
$$\geq - \log p_j + t_1(l_j) + \sum_{k=1}^{m} \omega_k t_{k+1}(l_j) + \log y \, t_{m+2}(l_j) + \alpha t_{m+3}(l_j) \quad (3)$$

for all $j \neq i$. One obtains a set of consumers who buy from firm i. Denoting this set by $M_i(p, l)$ demand for firm i is

$$X_i(p, l) = \frac{1}{p_i} \int_{M_i(p,l)} \alpha e^z f(z) g(\omega) h(\alpha) d(\alpha, \omega, z)$$
$$\text{where } M_i(p, l) \equiv \{(\alpha, \omega, z) \in A \times \Omega \times Z |$$
$$v_i(p_i, l_i; \omega, \alpha, e^z) \geq v_j(p_j, l_j; \omega, \alpha, e^z), \text{ for all } j \in N\}.$$

In order to show that sales are log-concave, it is sufficient to make an additional distributional assumption about the distribution of consumer characteristics α.

- **Assumption (D.3).** The parameter α is distributed according to the distribution function H with density $h : A \to \Re_+$ which is positive and log-concave on int$A$.

Note that, by definition, α has a compact support which is a subset of $[0, 1]$. Since any truncation of a log-concave density is log-concave, it is easy to construct examples for densities of H which are log-concave. Alternatively, one might consider densities such that the likelihood of a consumer spending almost nothing or all of his income in the differentiated market is vanishing as α turns towards 0 or 1, respectively. For this the Beta-distribution (under some parameter restrictions) provides a nice example.

Proposition 3 *Assume (U.2), (I.1), (D.1), (D.2), and (D.3). For any firm i with an effectively differentiated brand, sales $p_i X_i(p, l)$ are log-concave, where positive, in logarithmic price* $\log p_i$.

Proof. Denote $q_i \equiv \log p_i$. Denote $(\omega^0, \alpha^1, z^0)$ a consumer buying brand i at q_i^0 given q_{-i} and denote $(\omega^1, \alpha^1, z^1)$ a consumer buying brand i at q_i^1 given

q_{-i}. Then, for all $j \neq i$, the following inequalities are satisfied:

$$-q_i^0 + t_1(l_i) + \sum_{k=1}^{m} \omega_k^0 t_{k+1}(l_i) + z^0\, t_{m+2}(l_i) + \alpha^0 t_{m+3}(l_i)$$
$$\geq -q_j + t_1(l_j) + \sum_{k=1}^{m} \omega_k^0 t_{k+1}(l_j) + z^0\, t_{m+2}(l_j) + \alpha^0 t_{m+3}(l_j)$$

$$-q_i^1 + t_1(l_i) + \sum_{k=1}^{m} \omega_k^1 t_{k+1}(l_i) + z^1\, t_{m+2}(l_i) + \alpha^1 t_{m+3}(l_i)$$
$$\geq -q_j + t_1(l_j) + \sum_{k=1}^{m} \omega_k^1 t_{k+1}(l_j) + z^1\, t_{m+2}(l_j) + \alpha^1 t_{m+3}(l_j)$$

In order to apply Proposition 1, it only remains to be shown that the consumer type which is a convex combination of the two consumer types above buys brand i at the convex combination of logarithmic prices, that is, type $(\omega^\lambda, \alpha^\lambda, z^\lambda)$ buys brand i at q_i^λ given q_{-i}, where ω^λ for any $\lambda \in [0,1]$ is defined as $\omega^\lambda = (1-\lambda)\omega^0 + \lambda\omega^1$. Similarly, α^λ and z^λ are defined. For a given j multiplying the first of the two inequalities above with $1-\lambda$ and the second with λ gives the sum

$$-q_i^\lambda + t_1(l_i) + \sum_{k=1}^{m} \omega_k^\lambda t_{k+1}(l_i) + z^\lambda\, t_{m+1}(l_i) + t_{m+3}(l_i)$$

$$\geq -q_j + \sum_{k=1}^{m} \omega_k^\lambda t_{k+1}(l_j) + z^\lambda\, t_{m+1}(l_j) + t_{m+2}(l_j). \qquad \square$$

Similar to the proof of Theorem 1, the result of Proposition 2 can then be used to establish the existence of equilibrium in the present setup. Without proof I state the existence of equilibrium in Theorem 2.

Theorem 2 *Assume (U.2), (I.1), (D.1), (D,2), and (D.3). Then there exists a price equilibrium.*

4 The possibility of nonparticipation of consumers

If consumers do not participate in the imperfectly competitive part of the differentiated market, they might alternatively resort to a competitive market which offers a substitute. For example, one might think of a set of n patented goods plus one or several goods, the patent of which expired so that it or they are in competitive supply. The simplest case is one in which the perfectly competitive submarkets operate with constant marginal costs of production.

Consider that there are $\widetilde{n}$ such submarkets. Utility functions are written as in (U.1) or (U.2), the only difference being that

$$u^{(\omega,\alpha,y)}(x_0,x,l) = (\sum_{i=1}^{n+\widetilde{n}} \widetilde{u}_i^{(\omega,\alpha,y)}(x_i,l_i))^{\alpha} x_0^{1-\alpha}$$

so that consumers can pick a good $i = n+1,...,n+\widetilde{n}$ in competitive supply instead of any of the brands $i = 1,...,n$. The goods in competitive supply are sold at their marginal cost $c_i(l_i)$, $i = n+1,...,n+\widetilde{n}$, and the other firms take this price as given. Denote $\widetilde{p} = (p_{n+1},...,p_{n+\widetilde{n}})$. A price equilibrium $(p^*,\widetilde{p}^*)$ in this extended model satisfies that $\pi_i(p^*,\widetilde{p}^*) \geq \pi_i(p_i,p^*_{-i},\widetilde{p}^*)$ for all p_i, $i = 1,...,n$, and all submarkets $i = n+1,...,n+\widetilde{n}$ clear, that is, on these submarkets there is zero excess demand. All previous results generalize to this extension.

It is perhaps more interesting to consider the more general case, in which the perfectly competitive submarkets do not operate with constant but increasing marginal costs of production. As a special case, each submarket may be thought of as a collection of many small firms producing at different but constant marginal costs under a capacity constraint. The resulting supply curve is a nondecreasing correspondence. Considering these firms to be small and heterogeneous, jumps in the aggregate supply curve can be excluded, and the supply curve becomes a function. The supply curve of a competitive submarket is derived from the marginal cost functions of the firms in a submarket. I will make assumptions about the "aggregate" marginal cost function of each competitive submarket which takes the value of the lowest marginal cost at which the last unit in the competitive submarket can be produced, denoted by $c_i(x_i,l_i)$, $i = n+1,...,n+\widetilde{n}$. When this marginal cost function is increasing and continuously differentiable on some interval, the supply curve is also increasing and continuously differentiable on the image set of this interval.

Consider for a moment the case of a single competitive submarket. Suppose that the inverse supply curve (which is the marginal costs curve of the submarket) is continuously differentiable and increasing. The demand function X_{n+1} is continuous in $(p_1,...,p_{n+1})$ and decreasing in p_{n+1} with finite slope, and has an inverse demand function P^X_{n+1}, so that the inverse excess demand function, which takes values $P^X_{n+1}(p,x_{n+1}) - P^S_{n+1}(x_{n+1})$, is decreasing in x_{n+1} and continuous in (p,x_{n+1}). For any given prices $p_1,...,p_n$, there exists a unique equilibrium in the competitive submarket. For given prices $p_1,...,p_n$, the price p_{n+1} which clears the competitive submarket is called the reaction of the competitive segment r_{n+1} which takes values $r_{n+1}(p)$.

Inverse excess demand $P^X_{n+1} - P^S_{n+1}$ is continuously differentiable in p_1,..., p_n, x_{n+1} on any set of prices such that the set of active imperfectly competitive firms does not change. In order to obtain continuously differentiable inverse excess demand for all prices, the distributional assumption is strengthened to the extent that densities f,g are vanishing on their support in the framework of Section 2, and f, g, h are vanishing on their support in the framework of Section 3, respectively. Denote ∂B the boundary of a set B.

- **Assumption (V.1).** Densities f, g are vanishing on their support, that is,
$$\lim_{y \to \partial Y} f(\log y) = 0, \ \lim_{\omega \to \partial \Omega} g(\omega) = 0.$$
- **Assumption (V.2).** Density h is vanishing on its support, that is,
$$\lim_{\alpha \to \partial A} h(\alpha) = 0.$$

Under these assumptions, the reaction of the competitive segment r_{n+1} is a continuous function in $p_1, ..., p_n$ (by the implicit function theorem). It is then easy to show equilibrium existence because an equilibrium price vector $(p_1, ..., p_{n+1})$ is a fixed point of the best responses of the $i = 1, ..., n$ firms, r_i, and the reaction of the competitive segment, r_{n+1},

$$(p_1, ..., p_{n+1}) \in (r_1(p_{-1}, p_{n+1}), ..., r_n(p_{-n,n+1}), r_{n+1}(p))$$

where $r_i(p_{-i}, p_{n+1}) \equiv \arg\max_{p_i} \pi_i(p, p_{n+1})$, $i = 1, ..., n$.

The argument for equilibrium existence can be extended to consider any finite number of $\widetilde{n}$ competitive submarkets. In this more general setup of more than one competitive segment, it needs to be shown that there exists a unique reaction of the group of competitive submarkets and that this reaction $(r_{n+1}, ..., r_{n+\widetilde{n}})$ is continuous in $p_1, ..., p_n$. For this, first note that the Jacobian of excess demand has a negative dominant diagonal, as will be shown below. The excess demand function of the competitive segments is written as $Z : \Re_+^{n+\widetilde{n}} \longrightarrow \Re_+^{\widetilde{n}}$ where $Z_i(p, \widetilde{p}) = (X_i(p, \widetilde{p}) - S_i(p_i))$, $i = n+1, ..., n+\widetilde{n}$. For the moment, I consider prices $p_1, ..., p_n$ as parameters so that the Jacobian collects all derivatives with respect to $p_{n+1}, ..., p_{n+\widetilde{n}}$. This Jacobian is well-defined for all prices $p_i \in [P_i^S(0), P_i^S(\infty)]$, for which a given set of submarkets (including imperfectly competitive ones) is active. If densities f, g, h are 0 at the boundary of their support, then the Jacobian is well-defined for all prices $p_i \in [P_i^S(0), P_i^S(\infty)]$. Note that the Jacobian satisfies the gross substitute property for all prices such that demand is positive for all competitively supplied goods, that is,

$$\partial Z_i(p, \widetilde{p})/\partial p_j = \partial X_i(p, \widetilde{p})/\partial p_j > 0,$$

$i, j = n+1, ..., n+\widetilde{n}$ and $j \neq i$. (Abusing notation, I suppress l as an argument of the demand function in this section so that demand only depends on $p_1, ..., p_{n+\widetilde{n}}$.)

Lemma 1 *Assume either that the assumptions of Theorem 1 and (V.1) hold or that the assumptions of Theorem 2, (V.1), and (V.2) hold. The Jacobian of demand X has a negative dominant diagonal, that is,*

$$\frac{\partial X_i(p, \widetilde{p})}{\partial p_i} + \sum_{j=n+1, j \neq i}^{n+\widetilde{n}} \frac{\partial X_i(p, \widetilde{p})}{\partial p_j} < 0$$

for all $i = n+1, ..., n+\widetilde{n}$ *on the set of prices*

$$[c_1(l_1), \infty) \times ... \times [c_n(l_n), \infty) \times [0, \infty)^{\widetilde{n}} \cap \{(p, \widetilde{p}) | X_i(p, \widetilde{p}) > 0\}.$$

Proof. On this set of prices excess demand is continuously differentiable in $\widetilde{p}$. Note that the cross- derivative captures the demand of consumers who switch to the competitive submarket when $\widetilde{p}_{-i}$ is marginally increased. Since goods are (weak) gross substitutes, all cross derivatives are positive. This equals demand of those consumers that leave submarket i when p_i is marginally increased. Hence, if the remaining effect on excess demand is negative when p_i is marginally increased, X has a negative dominant diagonal. This effect concerns the individual demand effect of those consumers who stay. Since consumers spend a fixed share out of their income, this effect is unambiguously negative. □

If supply is a continuously differentiable increasing function, excess demand is continuous in prices on $[c_1(l_1), \infty) \times ... \times [c_n(l_n), \infty) \times [0, \infty)^{\widetilde{n}}$, and the dominant diagonal condition holds for excess demand Z with the additional restriction on prices that $p_i \geq P_i^S(0)$ and that demand is positive.

Given these properties, it is easy to show that, for given prices $p_1, ..., p_n$, a unique equilibrium of the competitive submarkets exists.

Lemma 2 *In the model with* $\widetilde{n}$ *competitive submarkets assume that the marginal cost functions* c_i *of the competitive submarkets are increasing and continuously differentiable in quantity* x_i. *In addition, suppose either that the assumptions of Theorem 1 and (V.1) or that the assumptions of Theorem 2, (V.1), and (V.2) hold. Then there exists a price equilibrium for the* $n+\widetilde{n}$ *submarkets. Furthermore, for any prices* p *there exists a unique reaction of the competitive submarkets. This reaction is continuous in* p.

Proof. The proof consists of two steps.

i) The Jacobian of excess demand has a negative dominant diagonal and satisfies the gross substitute property on a compact set of prices. Any equilibrium with positive trade lies within a set of prices greater than or equal to $P_i^S(0)$. Clearly, if all consumers buy in submarket i there exists a price $\overline{p}_i$ which clears the market and any equilibrium has the property that $p_i \leq \overline{p}_i$. Prices $\widetilde{p}$ are in $[P_{n+1}^S(0), \overline{p}_{n+1}] \times ... \times [P_{n+\widetilde{n}}^S(0), \overline{p}_{n+\widetilde{n}}]$. In any equilibrium with positive trade in all competitive submarkets, prices are in the interior of the intersection of this set and the set of prices such that the demand for all goods is positive if marginal costs are increasing. Such equilibria will be considered first.

It has been assumed that marginal costs are increasing. Since excess demand functions are continuously differentiable and the Jacobian satisfies the gross substitute property on the subset of prices such that demand is positive, there exists a parameter $k > 0$ such that $\gamma_i(\widetilde{p}; p) \equiv kZ_i(p, \widetilde{p}) + p_i$ is increasing in $\widetilde{p}$, $i = n+1, ..., n+\widetilde{n}$. An equilibrium for the competitive submarkets is a fixed point of the mapping $\gamma(\cdot; p) \equiv (\gamma_{n+1}(\cdot; p), ..., \gamma_{n+\widetilde{n}}(\cdot; p)))_i$, i.e. $\gamma(\widetilde{p}; p) = \widetilde{p}$. Applying Tarski's fixed point theorem an equilibrium exists, and the equilibrium set has a largest and a smallest element denoted by $\widetilde{p}^a$ and $\widetilde{p}^a$ respectively, $\widetilde{p}^a = (p^a_{n+1}, ..., p^a_{n+\widetilde{n}})$ and correspondingly for $\widetilde{p}^b$. Suppose $\widetilde{p}^a > \widetilde{p}^b$ exist. One has

$$Z_i(p, \widetilde{p}^1) - Z_i(p, \widetilde{p}^0) = 0$$

by the definition of an equilibrium, $i = n+1, ..., n+\widetilde{n}$. However, take the submarket j where $p^a_i - p^b_i$ is largest, i.e., j satisfies $p^a_j - p^b_j \geq p^a_i - p^b_i$, $i = n+1, ..., n+\widetilde{n}$, and one obtains

$$\begin{aligned} Z_j(p, \widetilde{p}^a) - Z_j(p, \widetilde{p}^b) &= \int_0^1 \left(\sum_{i=n+1}^{n+\widetilde{n}} (p^a_i - p^b_i) \frac{\partial Z_j(p, \lambda \widetilde{p}^a + (1-\lambda)\widetilde{p}^b)}{\partial p_i} \right) d\lambda \\ &= \int_0^1 \left((p^a_j - p^b_j) \frac{\partial Z_j(p, \lambda \widetilde{p}^a + (1-\lambda)\widetilde{p}^b)}{\partial p_j} \right. \\ &\quad \left. + \sum_{i=n+1, i\neq j}^{n+\widetilde{n}} (p^a_i - p^b_i) \frac{\partial Z_j(p, \lambda \widetilde{p}^a + (1-\lambda)\widetilde{p}^b)}{\partial p_i} \right) d\lambda. \end{aligned}$$

By the choice of j and the dominant diagonal established in Lemma 1 the integrand is negative, contradicting that $\widetilde{p}^a > \widetilde{p}^b$. Hence, for any prices $p_1, ..., p_n$ an equilibrium for the competitive submarkets exists which uniquely defines prices (and quantities) when all competitive submarkets are active and marginal costs are increasing.

Now I will allow for submarkets to be nonactive. For given prices $(p, \widetilde{p}_{-i})$ with $p_j \in [P^S_j(0), \overline{p}_j]$, $j = n+1, ..., n+\widetilde{n}$, $j \neq i$, if submarket i is nonactive, the market clears at any price $p_i \leq P^S_i(0)$ because demand and supply are equal to 0 for good i. Hence, for such a market which is not active for given prices $(p, \widetilde{p}_{-i})$, the price can be set equal to $P^S_i(0)$, this is $\gamma_i(\widetilde{p}; p) = P^S_i(0)$. With the above construction, $\gamma_i(\widetilde{p}; p)$ is nondecreasing and there exists a unique price equilibrium in the competitive segment.

Under assumptions (V.1) (and (V.2)), demand functions are continuously differentiable on the boundary of the support of the relevant densities. Thus, excess demand functions are continuously differentiable. Because of its dominant diagonal, the Jacobian is non-singular, and the implicit function theorem can be applied. Consequently, equilibrium prices of the competitive submarkets are continuous in the prices $p_1, ..., p_n$. One can define this reaction of the competitive submarkets as a continuous function $\widetilde{r} : \Re^n_+ \longrightarrow \Re^{\widetilde{n}}_+$.

ii) The quasiconcavity of the profit function of the imperfectly competitive firms also holds in this extended model. Hence the best response correspondence of the imperfectly competitive firms are convex-valued. Profits are continuous if brands are differentiated. Otherwise, the dimensionality of the problem can be reduced following Peitz (1998b) for instance. Also, following the arguments in Lemma 3 in Peitz (1998b), it can be shown that imperfectly competitive firms choose prices from compact strategy spaces. As demonstrated above, the reaction of the competitive submarkets is continuous. Consequently, one can apply Kakutani's fixed point theorem to show the existence of equilibrium. □

Note that the existence result of the theorem is much easier to prove: since demand is continuously differentiable in $(p, \widetilde{p})$, then, whenever prices $\widetilde{p} \in [S_{n+1}^{-1}(0), \overline{p}_{n+1}] \times ... \times [S_{n+\widetilde{n}}^{-1}(0), \overline{p}_{n+\widetilde{n}}]$ and the supply curve continuously differentiable in p_i on $[S_i^{-1}(0), \overline{p}_i]$, the reaction of each single competitive submarket is continuous in $(p, \widetilde{p}_{-i})$ on the relevant set of prices, with the result following immediately.

Note also that, based on results by Nikaido (1968) (or based on results on supermodular functions), it can be shown that the reaction of the competitive sector, $\widetilde{p}^c$, is nondecreasing in $p_1, ..., p_n$. If all competitive submarkets are active, the reaction is increasing.

In Lemma 2 marginal costs were assumed to be increasing. I now extend the existence result to a class of nondecreasing marginal cost functions for the perfectly competitive submarkets. Note that in this case excess demand no longer necessarily constitutes a function, and the mapping γ becomes an upper-hemicontinuous correspondence. If one considers a function by taking a selection from this correspondence such that the absolute value of excess demand is minimized at prices with $p_i = P_i^S(0)$ (or more generally such that a submarket is balanced whenever possible), then one cannot necessarily find a parameter value k such that the function is nondecreasing. Consequently, Tarski's fixed point theorem cannot always be applied. For equilibrium existence it is possible to apply Kakutani's fixed point theorem considering reactions of each competitive submarket separately. A more general result than Lemma 2 can be shown:

Proposition 4 *In the model with $\widetilde{n}$ competitive submarkets assume that marginal cost functions c_i, $i = n+1, ..., n+\widetilde{n}$ are continuous in x_i on $[0, \infty)$, constant in x_i on $[0, \widehat{x}_i)$, where $\widehat{x}_i \geq 0$, and continuously differentiable and increasing in x_i on $(\widehat{x}_i, \infty)$. In addition, suppose either that the assumptions of Theorem 1 and (V.1) or that the assumptions of Theorem 2, (V.1), and (V.2) hold. Then there exists a price equilibrium for the $n + \widetilde{n}$ submarkets. Furthermore, for any price vector p there exists a unique reaction of the competitive submarkets. This reaction is continuous in p.*

Sketch of Proof. Consider the following procedure for finding an equilibrium for the competitive submarkets. If marginal costs are constant on some range of quantities for some submarkets, then one can fix the price at $P_i^S(0)$ for these submarkets and establish an equilibrium $\widetilde{p}^0$ according to step (i) in the proof of Lemma 2 where only the prices of the other competitive submarkets are varied. Any submarket which violates the supply condition is then subsequently eliminated from this set, and equilibrium existence is shown resulting in a sequence $\widetilde{p}^0, \widetilde{p}^1, ..., \widetilde{p}^t$, as above. Since each reaction of a single submarket is nondecreasing in the prices of all other submarkets (gross substitutes), this sequence has to converge in the sense that at some point supply conditions are met for all submarkets in which prices are still fixed. By construction, a unique reaction of the competitive submarkets to $p_1, ..., p_n$ is selected. Consider the set of competitive submarkets for which $P_i^X(X_i(p, p_i + \varepsilon, \widetilde{p}_{-i})) - P_i^S(0) > 0$ for all $\varepsilon > 0$ in equilibrium. To this set of submarkets one can apply the implicit function theorem to show that the reaction is continuous in prices $p_1, ..., p_n$. The remaining set of competitive submarkets (locally) has a constant reaction $P_i^S(0)$. Equilibrium existence for all markets then holds as shown in step (ii) of the proof of Lemma 2.

It remains to be shown that the reaction of the competitive submarkets is unique. Note that X_i is a nonincreasing function in p_i for all prices such that $p_i \geq P_i^S(0)$. Excess demand Z_i constitutes a correspondence because it may take a whole range of values at price $P_i^S(0)$. Consider now the function Z_i^0 which takes values $Z_i^0(p, \widetilde{p})$ where $|Z_i^0(p, \widetilde{p})| = \min\{|Z_i(p, \widetilde{p})|\}$ is satisfied, that is, excess demand is chosen such that it comes as close as possible to balancing the market. Also consider the function Z_i^+ which takes values $Z_i^+(p, \widetilde{p}) = X_i(p, \widetilde{p}) - \max\{S_i(p_i)\}$. An increase of p_i at $P_i^S(0)$ then leads to a possible jump from $Z_i^0(p, \widetilde{p})$ down to $Z_i^+(p, \widetilde{p})$ plus the accumulated marginal changes of Z_i^+, both changes being of negative sign.

Suppose two equilibria $\widetilde{p}^a \neq \widetilde{p}^b$ exist. Take the submarket j where $|p_i^a - p_i^b|$ is largest, that is, j satisfies $|p_j^a - p_j^b| \geq |p_i^a - p_i^b|$, $i = n+1, ..., n+\widetilde{n}$. Without loss of generality, one can consider $p_j^a > p_j^b$. Then $Z_j^0(p, \widetilde{p}^a) = Z_j^+(p, \widetilde{p}^a)$. One obtains

$$\begin{aligned} Z_j^0(p, \widetilde{p}^a) - Z_j^0(p, \widetilde{p}^b) &\leq Z_j^+(p, \widetilde{p}^a) - Z_j^+(p, \widetilde{p}^b) \\ &\leq \int_0^1 \Bigg((p_j^a - p_j^b) \frac{\partial Z_j^+(p, \lambda\widetilde{p}^a + (1-\lambda)\widetilde{p}^b)}{\partial p_j} \\ &\quad + \sum_{i=n+1, i\neq j}^{n+\widetilde{n}} |p_i^a - p_i^b| \frac{\partial Z_j^+(p, \lambda\widetilde{p}^a + (1-\lambda)\widetilde{p}^b)}{\partial p_i} \Bigg) d\lambda. \end{aligned}$$

The integrand is negative because of the gross substitute property and the dominant diagonal from Lemma 1. This contradicts the fact that two equilibria $\widetilde{p}^a \neq \widetilde{p}^b$ exist and that the equilibrium is unique. □

Note that the above results can also be shown in the two modifications presented below.

5 Income-dependent expenditure shares

In a market in which rich consumers tend to spend a smaller or larger budget share than poor consumers these budget shares are income-dependent. I formalize this by postulating that there exists a reference income level which implies that consumers spend a share α in the differentiated market. For other income levels the budget share is lower than α.

- **Assumption (U.3).** The utility function of a consumer with taste parameters
$$(\omega, \alpha, y) \in \Omega \times A \times Y$$
is defined as
$$u^{(\omega,\alpha,y)}(x_0, x, l) = (\sum_{i=1}^{n} \tilde{u}_i^{(\omega,\alpha,y)}(x_i, l_i))^{\eta(\alpha,y)} x_0^{1-\eta(\alpha,y)}$$
where η is a function mapping into $[0, 1]$ which is log-concave in (α, y) and where $\tilde{u}_i^{(\omega,\alpha,y)}(x_i, l_i)$ denotes the utility from (U.2).

By the above assumption, the set of consumers buying from firm i is the set M_i, as defined in Section 3. Demand for brand i can then be written as

$$X_i(p, l) = \frac{1}{p_i} \int_{M_i(p,l)} \eta(\alpha, e^z) e^z f(z) g(\omega) h(\alpha) d(\alpha, \omega, z).$$

Consequently, if η is log-concave in (α, z), one obtains the required properties to show existence of equilibrium.

Example: $\eta(\alpha, e^z) = s(z)\alpha$ where s maps into $[0, 1]$ and is log-concave. The multiplicative interaction works because I again rely on the fact that log-concavity is preserved under multiplication. Reference consumers satisfy $s(z) = 1$, and consumers with different income z spend a smaller budget share in the market. In this example $s(z)$ is a scaling factor. Since log-concavity implies single-peakedness, one can say that, if the reference consumers have a finite income, very rich consumers tend to spend less in terms of budget shares in the differentiated market.

Proposition 5 *Assume (U.3), (I.1), (D.1), (D.2), and (D.3). For any firm i with an effectively differentiated brand, sales $p_i X_i(p, l)$ are log-concave, where positive, in logarithmic price* $\log p_i$.

6 Taste-dependent expenditure shares

Up to now I have assumed that the conditional distribution of consumers' budget shares α is independent of the parameters ω which reflect the tastes of consumers concerning differentiated brands. From Section 3 on, I allowed for the budget share to affect the discrete choice of the consumers in the market. Now I will also make budget shares dependent on ω. For this consider a budget share $\widetilde{\eta}(\alpha,\omega) \in [0,1]$. A reference consumer with parameters ω has the property that $\widetilde{\eta}(\alpha,\omega) = \alpha$. Other consumers with different parameters ω may spend more (or less) than α in the differentiated market.

- **Assumption (U.4).** The utility function of a consumer with taste parameters
$$(\omega, \alpha, y) \in \Omega \times A \times Y$$
is defined as
$$u^{(\omega,\alpha,y)}(x_0, x, l) = (\sum_{i=1}^{n} \widetilde{u}_i^{(\omega,\alpha,y)}(x_i, l_i))^{\widetilde{\eta}(\alpha,\omega)} x_0^{1-\widetilde{\eta}(\alpha,\omega)}$$
where $\widetilde{\eta}$ is a function mapping into $[0,1]$ which is log-concave in (α,ω) and where $\widetilde{u}_i^{(\omega,\alpha,y)}(x_i, l_i)$ denotes the utility from (U.2).

As in the previous section, the set of consumers buying from firm i is the set M_i as defined in Section 3. Demand for brand i can then be written as
$$X_i(p,l) = \frac{1}{p_i} \int_{M_i(p,l)} \widetilde{\eta}(\alpha,\omega) e^z f(z) g(\omega) h(\alpha) d(\alpha,\omega,z).$$

If η is log-concave in (α,ω) one can show existence of equilibrium. I modify the example of the previous section: $\widetilde{\eta}(\alpha,\omega) = s(\omega)\alpha$ where s maps into $[0,1]$ and is log-concave. Reference consumers satisfy $s(\omega) = 1$, and consumers with other types ω spend a smaller budget share in the market.

Proposition 6 *Assume (U.4), (I.1), (D.1), (D.2), and (D.3). For any firm i with an effectively differentiated brand, sales $p_i X_i(p,l)$ are log-concave, where positive, in logarithmic price* $\log p_i$.

References

1. Anderson S.P., de Palma A., Thisse J.-F. (1992) Discrete Choice Theory of Product Differentiation, MIT Press, Cambridge, Mass
2. Bester H. (1992) Bertrand Equilibrium in Differentiated Duopoly, International Economic Review 33:433–448
3. Borell C. (1975) Convex Set Functions in d-Space, Periodica Mathematica Hungarica 6:111–136
4. Caplin A., Nalebuff B. (1986) Multi-Dimensional Product Differentiation and Price Competition, Oxford Economic Papers 38(Suppl.):129–145
5. Caplin A., Nalebuff B. (1991a) Aggregation and Social Choice: A Mean Voter Theorem, Econometrica 59:1–23
6. Caplin A., Nalebuff B. (1991b) Aggregation and Imperfect Competition: on the Existence of Equilibrium, Econometrica 59:25–59

7. Das Gupta S. (1980) Brunn-Minkowski Inequality and its Aftermath, Journal of Multivariate Analysis 10:296–318
8. D'Aspremont C., Gabszewicz J.J., Thisse J.-F. (1979) On Hotelling's 'Stability in Competition', Econometrica 47:1145–1150
9. Dierker E. (1991) Competition for Customers, In: Barnett W., Cornet B., d'Aspremont C., Gabszewicz J.J., Mas-Colell A. (Eds.), Equilibrium Theory and Applications, Cambridge University Press, Cambridge, UK
10. Dierker E., Dierker H. (1999) Product Differentiation and Market Power, Advances in Mathematical Economics 1:39–67
11. Dierker E., Podczeck K. (1992) The Distribution of Consumers' Tastes and the Quasiconcavity of the Profit Function, University of Vienna, Working Paper No. 9208
12. Gorman W.M. (1980) A Possible Procedure for Analyzing Quality Differentials in the Egg Market, Review of Economic Studies 47:843–856
13. Hotelling H. (1929) Stability in Competition, Economic Journal 39:41–57
14. Lancaster K. (1966) A New Approach to Consumer Theory, Journal of Political Economy 74:132–157
15. Marshall A., Olkin I. (1974) Majorization in Multivariate Distributions, The Annals of Statistics 2:1189–1200
16. McDonald J. (1984) Some Generalized Functions for the Size Distribution of Income, Econometrica 52:647–663
17. Milgrom P., Roberts J. (1990) Rationalizability, Learning and Equilibrium in Games with Strategic Complementarities, Econometrica 58:1255–1277
18. Neven D. (1986) On Hotelling's Competition with Non-Uniform Customer Distribution, Economics Letters 21:121–126
19. Nikaido H. (1968) Convex Structures and Economic Theory, Academic Press, New York
20. Peitz M. (1997) Differentiated Bertrand Duopoly with Variable Demand, Research in Economics 51:85–100
21. Peitz M. (1998a) Two-Stage Models of Product Differentiation with Unit-Elastic Demand, IVIE working paper AD 98-18
22. Peitz M. (1998b) Price Competition in Address Models of Product Differentiation: Unit-Elastic Demand, mimeo, University of Alicante
23. Peitz M. (1999) A Difficulty with the Address Models of Product Differentiation, Economic Theory 9:717–727
24. Peitz M. (2000) Aggregation in a Model of Price Competition, Journal of Economic Theory 90:1–38
25. Prékopa A. (1971) Logarithmic Concave Measures with Applications to Stochastic Programming, Acta Sci. Math. 32:301–315
26. Prékopa A. (1973) On Logarithmic Concave Measures and Functions, Acta Sci. Math. 34:335–343
27. Roberts J., Sonnenschein H. (1977) On the Foundation of the Theory of Monopolistic Competition, Econometrica 45:101–113
28. Singh S.K., Maddala G.S. (1976) A Function for the Size Distribution of Income, Econometrica 44:963–970

On the Core of a Cartel

Roy Radner

Stern School of Business, NYU, New York, NY 10012

Abstract. Consider an industry with a given set of firms producing a homogeneous product, in which all the firms have the same constant cost per unit output, but possibly different capacities. Each firm chooses a level of output, and the market price is determined by the total industry output and the industry demand function (the "Cournot model"). I show that the core of the corresponding game, in which the firms are the players, is not empty, and includes the allocation in which the firms' outputs and profits are proportional to their respective capacities. The core is characterized by a convex "Lorenz curve" that limits the inequality in the distribution among firms of profit per unit capacity; this curve can be calculated explicitly, given the cost parameter and the industry demand function. I also consider a two-stage game in which, in the first stage, the firms choose their capacities noncooperatively, at a constant cost per unit capacity, and in the second stage they receive the proportional allocation described above. In the limit, as the number of firms increases without bound, total industry capacity and output are positive, but net profit is zero; price and output are in fact what would be optimal for the cartel if capacity were costless.

1 Introduction

Suppose that the firms in an industry form a cartel to fix total industry output so as to maximize total industry profit. What is a "rational" way to divide industry output and profit among the several firms? One answer to this question is provided by the game-theoretic concept of the *core*. An allocation of output and profit is said to be in the core if it yields to each subset of firms at least as much profit as that subset could guarantee itself by acting on its own. Thus the core is a *set* of allocations, possibly empty (the definition of a subset's guaranteed profit will be made precise in Section 2).

In his influential monograph, *Core and Equilibria of a Large Economy* (1974), Werner Hildenbrand provided a thorough study of the core of an exchange economy, in which the players were the consumers. He also introduced the idea of the core of an economy with production, again with the consumers as the players, who could also form coalitions for the purpose of production. The present paper complements Hildenbrand's study with a preliminary investigation of the core of an industry in which the active players are the *firms*, and the consumers are passive "demanders."

In this note I shall consider a very simple model of an industry in which the firms produce a homogeneous good, have the same unit cost, but have possibly different capacities. The guaranteed profit of a subset of firms can then be reasonably defined as the maximum profit that the subset can earn if all the other firms produce at capacity (Sec. 2). I first consider the case in which the number of firms and their capacities are fixed. Under some regularity conditions on demand, I show that the core is not empty, and in particular contains the allocation in which each firm produces a share of the total cartel output proportional to its capacity, and receives the corresponding profit; call this the *proportional allocation* (Sec. 3). In other words, the proportional allocation equalizes profit per unit of capacity across firms. Note that if capital investment is proportional to capacity, then this core allocation also equalizes the rate of return on investment across firms.

Under some further regularity conditions, I can fully characterize the core (Sec. 4). If the total industry capacity does not exceed the optimal cartel output (namely, the output that would maximize the cartel profit in the absence of any capacity constraint), then the proportional allocation is the only one in the core. On the other hand, if industry capacity exceeds the optimal cartel output, then there will be many allocations in the core. In fact, the core will consist of all allocations such that the Lorenz curve of the distribution across firms of profit-per-unit-capacity lies on or above a given function, which I denote by G. Thus the function G bounds the inequality in the distribution of profit-per-unit-capacity for allocations in the core. The function G can, in principle, be calculated explicitly from the demand function, the unit cost, and the industry capacity, and does not depend on the number of firms. More detailed information about G is also derived, depending on whether industry capacity is less than or greater than the industry output at which price equals unit cost. Section 5 describes an example.

I next consider the noncooperative game in which the firms simultaneously choose their respective capacities in the expectation that thereafter they will receive the proportional allocation (Sec. 6). In this model, I assume that the cost of capacity is proportional to capacity, and that this unit cost is the same for all firms. The Nash equilibrium of this game is easy to calculate, and has the property that the industry output exceeds the output that would be optimal for the cartel if capacity were costless (i.e., the optimal cartel output of Section 2). In fact, as the number of firms increases without bound (which is a way of describing free entry), then in equilibrium,

1. individual firm capacity tends to zero;
2. total industry capacity approaches a positive limit;
3. total industry profit (net of the cost of capacity) tends to zero, and hence so does individual firm profit;
4. total industry output equals that which would be optimal for the cartel if capacity were costless.

I conclude the discussion with some remarks on (1) an alternative definition of the core, (2) an extension of the analysis (by A. Postlewaite) to the case in which firms have different unit costs, and (3) possible extensions to models of sequential actions by the firms (Sec. 7).

Acknowledgments

Andrew Postlewaite worked out an extension of Section3 to the case in which firms may differ in their unit costs (Section 7.2). Martin Osborne, Richard Steinberg, Wilhelm Neuefeind, and Walter Trockel provided useful comments on earlier drafts. Martin Osborne also called my attention to two papers (Osborne and Pitchik, 1983, 1987), in which the Nash Bargaining Solution is used to predict the behavior of a cartel.

2 The Model with fixed capacity constraints

Consider an industry producing a single product, with a demand function

$$P = \phi(Q), \tag{1}$$

where P is the price at which the total quantity Q will be demanded. There are n firms, all with the same linear cost function, so that if firm j produces Q_j, its corresponding cost is γQ_j. Therefore, if the firms' respective outputs are $Q_1, ..., Q_n$, then the total output is $Q = \sum_j Q_j$ and firm j's profit is

$$\pi_j = Q_j\phi(Q) - \gamma Q_j = Q_j[\phi(Q) - \gamma]. \tag{2}$$

Finally, each firm j has a capacity K_j, so that

$$0 \leq Q_j \leq K_j, \; j = 1, ..., n. \tag{3}$$

By an *allocation* I shall mean an n-tuple of feasible outputs, $Q_1, ..., Q_n$, together with the n-tuple or corresponding profits, $\pi_1, ..., \pi_n$. The *core* is the set of all the allocations such that no subset of firms receives less total profit than it could *guarantee* to itself, acting on its own. To make the notion of guaranteed profit precise, let J denote any (nonempty) subset of firms, let x denote its total output, and let y denote the total output of all firms not in J. The total profit of subset J is, from (2),

$$f(x, y) \equiv x[\phi(x + y) - \gamma]. \tag{4}$$

Define the *guaranteed profit* of subset J by

$$g_J \equiv \max_x \min_y f(x, y), \tag{5}$$

subject to

$$0 \leq x \leq \sum_{j \in J} K_j \equiv K', \text{ and } 0 \leq y \leq \sum_{i \notin J} K_i \equiv K''. \tag{6}$$

The core is defined as the set of allocations $(\pi_1, \cdots, \pi_n)$ such that

$$\sum_{j \in J} \pi_j \geq g_J, \text{ for all } J. \tag{7}$$

In particular, taking J to be the set of all firms, g_J is the monopoly (cartel) profit, and the inequality in (7) must be an equality.

I shall assume in what follows that ϕ is continuous and strictly decreasing except where $\phi(Q) = 0$, that $\phi(Q)$ converges to zero as Q increases without limit, and that $\phi(0) > \gamma$.

First observe that, for any group of firms, the least favorable situation is the one in which all other firms produce at capacity; this follows from the assumption that the demand function is decreasing, and therefore the profit function (4) is decreasing in y or every x. From this it follows that the guaranteed profit levels g_J are given by:

$$g_J = \max_x f(x, K'') \text{ subject to } 0 \leq x \leq K'. \tag{8}$$

Let K denote the total industry capacity, i.e.,

$$K \equiv \sum_{j=1}^{n} K_j,$$

and for any subset J let r_J denote the ratio of J's capacity to total industry capacity, i.e.,

$$r_J \equiv \frac{1}{K} \sum_{j \in J} K_j. \tag{9}$$

If J's total output is x and all other firms produce at capacity, then J's total profit is

$$f(x, (1 - r_J)K);$$

this motivates the following definition:

$$G_K(r) \equiv \max_x f(x, (1 - r)K) \text{ subject to } 0 \leq x \leq rK. \tag{10}$$

We can now rewrite (8) as

$$g_J = G_K(r_J). \tag{11}$$

The study of the core thus reduces to the study of the function G_K.

3 The proportional outcome is in the core

Let $\hat{\pi}$ denote the maximum total industry profit and let $\hat{Q}$ be the corresponding optimal cartel output. Define the *proportional allocation* as the one for which each firm produces a share of the optimal cartel output proportional to its capacity, and receives a corresponding share of the total industry profit, i.e.,

$$Q_j = (K_j/K)\,\hat{Q}, \text{ and } \pi_j = (K_j/K)\,\hat{\pi}, \quad j = 1, ..., n. \tag{12}$$

Proposition 1. *The proportional allocation is in the core.*

Proof. Recall that, for any subset J, r_J is the ratio of J's capacity to the total capacity. Let

$$K' \equiv r_J K, \; K'' \equiv (1 - r_J)K.$$

If J produces a total output x $(0 \leq x \leq K')$ and all other firms produce at capacity, then J's profit is, from (4)

$$\begin{aligned} f(x, K'') &= x[\phi(x + K'') - \gamma] \\ &= \frac{x}{x + K''}(x + K'')[\phi(x + K'') - \gamma]. \end{aligned} \tag{13}$$

However,

$$\frac{x}{x + K''} \leq \frac{K'}{K' + K''} = r_J, \text{ and } (x + K'')[\phi(x + K'') - \gamma] \leq \hat{\pi}.$$

Hence, from (13),

$$f(x, K'') \leq r_J \hat{\pi}. \tag{14}$$

Since this is true for every x $(0 \leq x \leq K')$,

$$g_J = G_K(r_J) \leq r_J \hat{\pi},$$

which completes the proof.

4 Further characterization of the core

As noted at the end of Section 2, the study of the core reduces to the study of the properties of the function G_K. Recall that

$$f(x, y) \equiv x[\phi(x + y) - \gamma], \text{ and} \tag{15}$$

$$G_K(r) \equiv \max_x f(x, (1-r)K) \text{ subject to } 0 \leq x \leq rK, \tag{16}$$

where $K > 0$ and $0 \leq r \leq 1$. Recall also that $f(x, y)$ is the profit of a subset producing output x when the remaining firms produce a total of y, and $G_K(r)$ is the guaranteed profit of a subset that has a fraction r of the total capacity K. It is immediate that

$$G_K(r) \geq 0, \quad G_K(0) = 0, \quad G_K(1) = \hat{\pi}, \tag{17}$$

where $\hat{\pi}$ is the maximum total industry profit. I shall show below that, with an additional assumption about demand, for each K the function G_K is nondecreasing and convex in r. Further details about G_K depend upon the magnitude of total industry capacity, K.

Before stating and proving these results in detail, I want first to show how the function G_K provides a bound for core allocations on the distribution across firms of profit per unit of capacity. To lighten the notation, I shall henceforth suppress the subscript K, i.e., I shall write $G(r)$ for $G_K(r)$.

For a given core allocation, let π_j be the profit of firm j. Let the firms be ranked in increasing order of the ratio of profit to capacity, with the firm with the lowest ratio numbered 1, etc. For any number r, define $J(r)$ to be the set of firms for which $(\pi_j/K_j) \leq r$, let $\pi(r)$ be the sum of their profits, and let $\rho(r)$ be the ratio of their total capacity to industry capacity, i.e.,

$$\pi(r) \equiv \sum_{j \in J(r)} \pi_j, \text{ and } \rho(r) \equiv r_{J(r)}. \tag{18}$$

Since the allocation is in the core,

$$\pi(r) \geq G(\rho(r)), \quad \text{for all } r. \tag{19}$$

There are, of course, only n different (nonempty) sets $J(r)$, where n is the number of firms. If we plot the n points with coordinates $(\rho(r), \pi(r))$, corresponding to the n different sets $J(r)$, in the size-profit plane, all of these points must lie on or above the graph of G, by (19). In particular the last point will have the coordinates $(1, \hat{\pi})$.

Let L be the "curve" obtained by connecting successive points by straight-line segments, and by connecting as well the origin and the first point. (See Fig. 1.) The curve L is in a sense the "Lorenz curve" for the *distribution of profits per unit capacity*. It is easy to see that: (1) the curve is convex, and lies on or below the line joining the origin with $(1, \hat{\pi})$; (2) the curve L lies above (or touches) the graph of G; (3) from (17) and the conclusion that the function G is convex and nondecreasing (see below), for any ordering of the firms there is a corresponding allocation in the core for which all of the

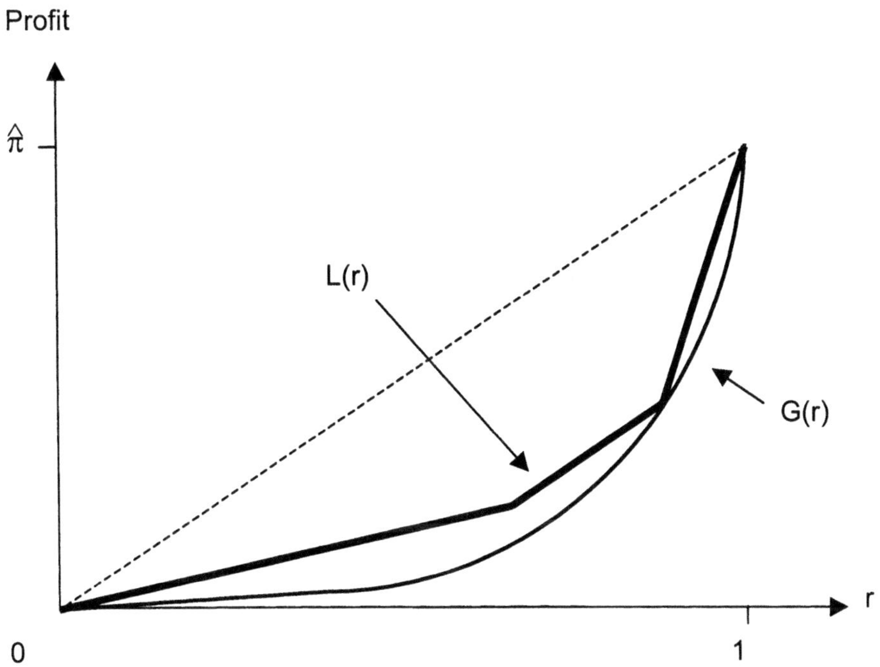

Fig.1. A Lorenz curve for the distribution of profits per unit capacity for a cartel with 3 firms.

points $(\rho(r), \pi(r))$ actually lie on the graph of G (maximal inequality); (4) as the number of firms increases, and if the distribution of shares of capacity approaches a continuous distribution on the interval [0,1], then the lower envelope of all L-curves approaches the graph of G.

I turn now to the properties of G. Henceforth, I shall assume that the following condition is satisfied.

Condition U: For each $y \geq 0$, the function $f(x, y)$ has a unique global maximum in $x \geq 0$.

For Condition U to be satisfied it is sufficient, but not at all necessary, that the demand function ϕ be concave where $\phi(x)$ is positive.

Two output levels are important for determining the properties of G, and hence of the core. Let Q^M denote the smallest industry output that would maximize total industry profit *in the absence of any capacity constraint*, and let Q^* denote the total (industry) output for which price equals marginal cost, i.e., $\phi(Q^*) = \gamma$. As is well known,

$$0 < Q^M < Q^*.$$

(For this, one uses only the assumptions about demand stated in Section 2.) It is useful to distinguish three cases, according as (1) K does not exceed Q^M, (2) K lies between Q^M and Q^*, or (3) K exceeds Q^*. Propositions 2-4 characterize the function G, and hence the core, in each of the three cases, respectively. Figures 2-4 illustrate the propositions.

Proposition 2. *If* $K \leq Q^M$, *then* $G(r) = r\hat{\pi} = rK[\phi(K) - \gamma]$. *(See Fig. 2.)*

Corollary 1. *If* $K \leq Q^M$, *then the proportional allocation is the only one in the core.*

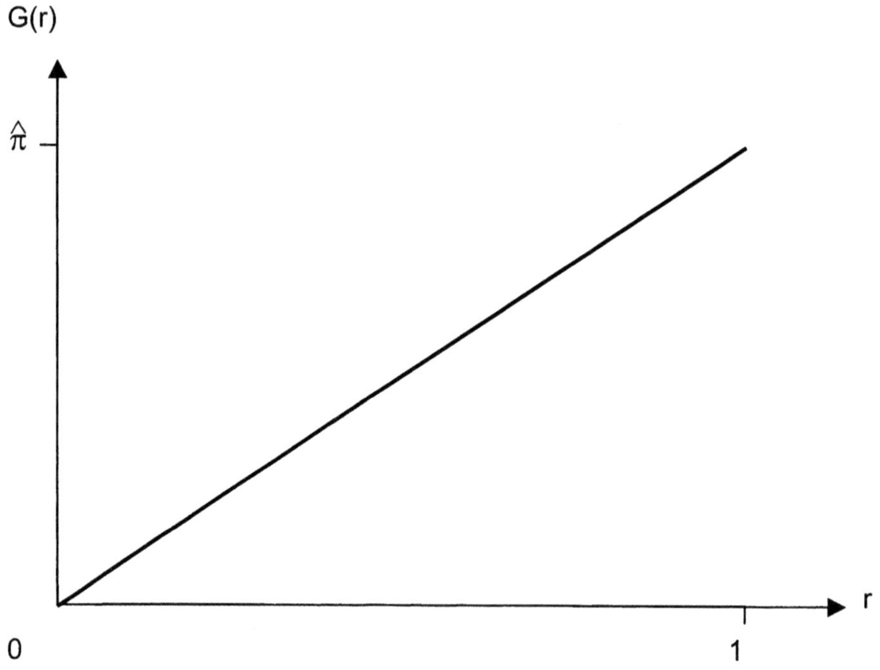

Fig. 2. G(r) for K < QM .

Proof. From Condition U it follows that total industry profit is maximized at capacity, so that,

$$\hat{Q} = K, \quad \text{and } \hat{\pi} = K[\phi(K) - \gamma].$$

From (14), for $0 \le r \le 1$ and $0 \le x \le rK$,

$$f(x, (1-r)K) \le r\hat{\pi} = f(rK, (1-r)K),$$

which proves the proposition. On the other hand, in the proportional allocation each subset J receives exactly $G(r_J)$, and since it is producing at capacity it cannot make a higher profit in the core, which proves the corollary.

Proposition 3. *If $Q^M < K < Q^*$, then G is convex and strictly increasing. Furthermore, there exists $r^M > 0$ (depending on K) such that, for $0 \le r \le r^M$, the function G is linear in r,*

$$G(r) = rK[\phi(K) - \gamma], \tag{20}$$

with positive slope less than $\hat{\pi}$, and for a subset of firms of total capacity r its guaranteed profit is attained by producing at capacity. (See Fig. 3.)

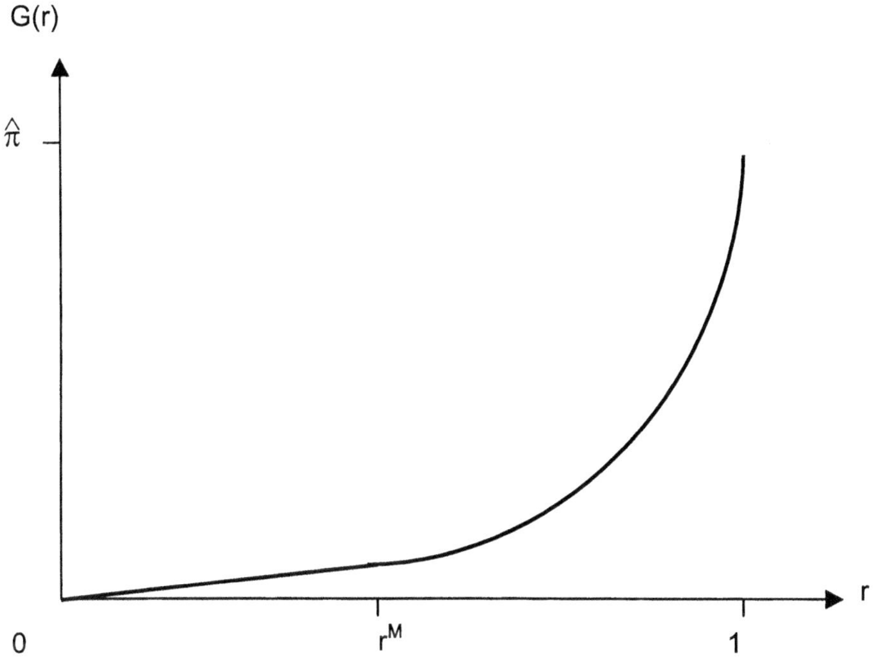

Fig. 3. G(r) for QM < K < Q*.

The proof is based on the following lemma, which is proved at the end of this section. For any r $(0 \le r \le 1)$ let $\xi(r)$ denote the unique value of x that maximizes $f(x, (1-r)K)$ subject to $0 \le x \le rK$.

Lemma 1. *For any r and r_0 in $[0,1]$,*

$$G(r) \geq G(r_0) + (r - r_0)K[\phi(q_0) - \gamma], \tag{21}$$

where $q_0 \equiv \xi(r_0) + (1 - r_0)K$.

To see that the lemma implies that G is strictly increasing, note that $K < Q^*$ implies that $\phi(q_0) - \gamma > 0$, so that, from (21), if $r > r_0$ then $G(r) > G(r_0)$.

The convexity of G also follows immediately from the lemma, since if $r_1 < r_0 < r_2$ then

$$\frac{G(r_2) - G(r_0)}{r_2 - r_0} \geq K[\phi(q_0) - \gamma] \geq \frac{G(r_0) - G(r_1)}{r_0 - r_1}.$$

To prove the rest of the proposition's conclusion, for each r in [0,1] let $\xi_0(r)$ denote the unique x that maximizes $f(x, (1 - r)K)$ subject only to $x \geq 0$. By the Theorem of Maximum, ξ_0 is continuous. Furthermore, $f(x, K)$ is zero at $x = 0$ but strictly positive for $x > 0$ and sufficiently small; hence $\xi_0(0) > 0$. Therefore, for some $r' > 0$ and sufficiently small,

$$\xi_0(r) \geq rK \text{ for } 0 \leq r \leq r';$$

Let r^M be the largest such r'. Condition U now implies that

$$G(r) = rK[\phi(K) - \gamma] \; for \; 0 \leq r \leq r^M,$$

which is (20), since (21) implies that $f(x, (1 - r)K)$ is nondecreasing on the interval $[0, rK]$. Finally, $K > Q^M$ implies that $K[\phi(K) - \gamma] < \hat{\pi}$, the maximum cartel profit. Hence, from (20) the slope of G on the interval $(0, r^M)$ is strictly less than $\hat{\pi}$.

Proposition 4. *Let $r^* \equiv 1 - (Q^*/K)$. If $K \geq Q^*$, then, for $0 \leq r \leq r^*$, $G(r) = 0$, and G is convex and strictly increasing for $r > r^*$. (See Fig. 4.)*

Proof. For $0 \leq r \leq r^*$ we have $(1 - r)K \geq Q^*$, and hence for $x \geq 0$,

$$\begin{aligned} \phi[x + (1 - r)K] &\leq \gamma, \\ f(x, (1 - r)K) &\leq 0, \\ G(r) &= 0. \end{aligned}$$

For $r > r^*$ we are in a situation like that of Proposition 3, and a corresponding analysis yields the desired conclusion that G is convex and strictly increasing. I omit the details.

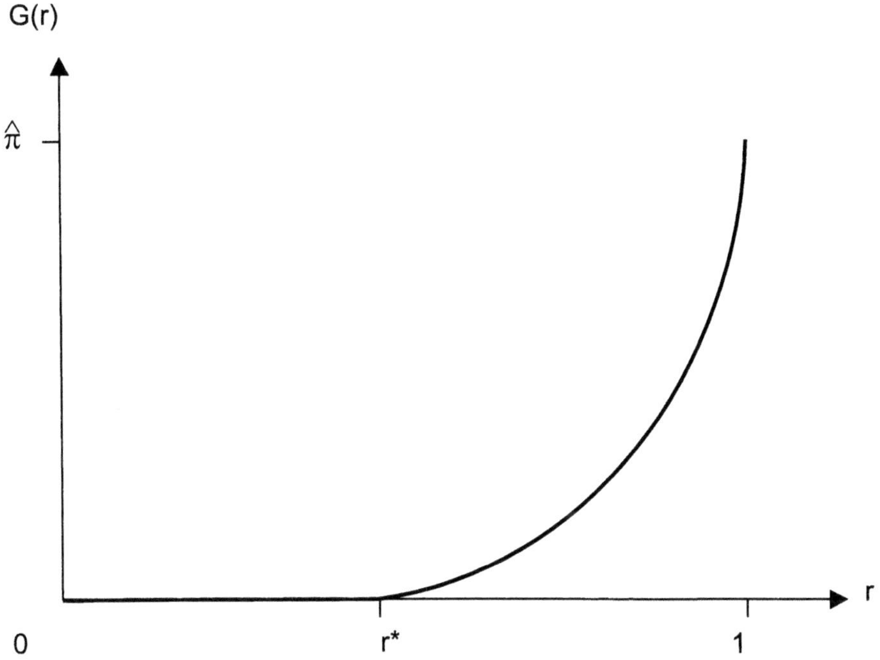

Fig. 4. G(r) for Q* < K.

To prove the lemma, define

$$\begin{aligned} x_0 &\equiv \xi(r_0), \\ x &\equiv x_0 + (r - r_0)K. \end{aligned} \tag{22}$$

Let H denote the right-hand side of (21). Then

$$\begin{aligned} H &= x_0[\phi(q_0) - \gamma] + (r - r_0)K[\phi(q_0) - \gamma] \\ &= x[\phi(q_0) - \gamma]. \end{aligned}$$

Further

$$\begin{aligned} x + (1 - r)K &= q_0, \text{ and} \\ x - rK &= x_0 - r_0 K \leq 0. \end{aligned}$$

If $x \geq 0$, then the last inequality implies that x is feasible for r, and $H = f(x, (1-r)K) \leq G(r)$. If $x < 0$, then $H < 0$, and again $H \leq G(r)$, which completes the proof.

5 An example

Suppose that the demand function, ϕ, is linear where positive, so that

$$\phi(x) = \begin{cases} \alpha - \beta x & \text{for} \quad 0 \le x \le \frac{\alpha}{\beta}, \\ 0 & \text{for} \quad \ge \frac{\alpha}{\beta}, \end{cases} \tag{23}$$

where α and β are strictly positive parameters. To avoid trivialities, assume that $\phi(0) = \alpha > \gamma > 0$; we can then make the convention that

$$\alpha = 1, \ 0 < \gamma < 1. \tag{24}$$

If the cartel's total output is Q, its total profit is

$$(1 - \gamma)Q - \beta Q^2. \tag{25}$$

One immediately verifies that

$$Q^M = \frac{1-\gamma}{2\beta}, \ Q^* = \frac{1-\gamma}{\beta} \tag{26}$$

(recall that Q^M maximizes (25) and that $\phi(Q^*) = \gamma$; see Sec. 4). One easily verifies that

$$\begin{aligned} \xi_0(r) &= \frac{1 - \beta K - \gamma + \beta r K}{2\beta} \\ &= Q^M - \frac{(1-r)K}{2} \\ &= \frac{1}{2}(Q^* - (1-r)K), \end{aligned} \tag{27}$$

so that

$$0 < \xi_0(r) < Q^M, \text{ and} \tag{28}$$

$$\xi_0'(r) = \frac{K}{2}. \tag{29}$$

Hence

$$\begin{aligned} f(\xi_0(r), (1-r)K) &= \frac{1 - \gamma - \beta(1-r)K^2}{4\beta} \\ &\equiv \pi_0(r), \end{aligned}$$

$$\begin{aligned} \hat{\pi} = \pi_0(1) &= \frac{(1-\gamma)^2}{2\beta}, \\ \pi_0'(r) &= \xi_0(r)\beta K > 0, \\ \pi_0''(r) &= \frac{\beta K^2}{2} > 0. \end{aligned}$$

If $Q^M < K < Q^*$, then

$$r^M = \frac{2Q^M}{K} - 1 = \frac{Q^*}{K} - 1,$$

$$0 < r^M < 1, \text{ and}$$

$$G(r) = \begin{cases} rK[1 - \beta K - \gamma] & \text{for} \quad 0 \leq r \leq r^M, \\ \pi_0(r) & \text{for} \quad r^M \leq r \leq 1. \end{cases}$$

It is straightforward to verify that G is differentiable at r^M.

On the other hand, if $K \geq Q^*$, then

$$r^* = 1 - \frac{Q^*}{K}, \text{ and}$$

$$G(r) = \begin{cases} 0 & \text{for} \quad 0 \leq r \leq r^*, \\ \pi_0(r) & \text{for} \quad r^* \leq r \leq 1. \end{cases}$$

Again, one can verify that G is differentiable at r^*.

6 Noncooperative choice of capacities

Imagine now that each of the n firms chooses its capacity at time zero, anticipating that thereafter it will obtain an allocation in the core of the "output game." Of course, if the core allocation is not unique, then each firm's anticipation will not be well-determined. Suppose then that each firm anticipates that it will obtain the corresponding proportional allocation in the core (see Sec.3). This assumption is, of course, somewhat *ad hoc*, but the proportional allocation has in its favor a certain fairness property, namely, that it equalizes across firms the ratio of profit per unit capacity, and hence, in the model described below, it *equalizes the rate of return on capital.*

Suppose, for the moment, that the number, n, of firms is given exogenously, and that at time zero the firms choose their respective capacities, K_i, simultaneously and noncooperatively. After that; each firm receives in every period its corresponding proportional allocation in the core. I assume that all firms discount future profits with the same discount factor. If Γ is the unit cost of capital for each firm, K is the total capacity of the industry, $\hat{\pi}(K)$ is the industry cartel profit, and δ is the (common) discount factor, then firm i's total discounted profit, $\Pi_i(K_1, ..., K_n)$, will be

$$\begin{aligned} \Pi_i(K_1, ..., K_n) &= -\Gamma K_i + \sum_{t=1}^{\infty} \delta^t \frac{K_i}{K} \hat{\pi}(K) \\ &= \frac{\delta}{1-\delta} \frac{K_i}{K} \hat{\pi}(K) - \Gamma K_i, \end{aligned} \tag{30}$$

where $K \equiv K_1 + ... + K_n$. Recall from Sec. 4 that

$$\hat{\pi}(K) = \begin{cases} K[\phi(K) - \gamma] & \text{for} \quad K \leq Q^M \\ Q^M[\phi(Q^M) - \gamma] & \text{for} \quad K \geq Q^M . \end{cases} \tag{31}$$

where Q^M denotes the optimal cartel output without a capacity constraint. Equations (30) and (31) define an n-person simultaneous-move game in which player (firm) i's action is $K_i (\geq 0)$.

Let $\pi^M \equiv \hat{\pi}(Q^M)$. I shall show that if

$$\frac{\delta \pi^M}{1-\delta} - \Gamma Q^M > 0, \tag{32}$$

then for sufficiently large n the Nash equilibrium of this game is given by

$$K_i = k(n) \equiv \frac{(n-1)\delta\pi^M}{n^2(1-\delta)\Gamma}, \tag{33}$$

$$K = nk(n) = \frac{(n-1)\delta\pi^m}{n(1-\delta)\Gamma} > Q^M, \tag{34}$$

and the corresponding individual firm and industry profits are

$$p(n) = \frac{\delta\pi^M}{n^2(1-\delta)}, \tag{35}$$

$$np(n) = \frac{\delta\pi^n}{n(1-\delta)}. \tag{36}$$

Note that these profits are independent of Γ!

If free entry were possible at time zero, then – since the individual firm profit (35) is strictly positive – the number of participating firms would be unbounded. I shall not attempt a serious analysis of entry here, but (35) and (36) suggest that unlimited entry would drive both individual firm and industry profits to zero. This would come about, of course, entirely through the acquisition of excess capacity, since the market price and output would remain at their monopoly levels.

To derive (33)-(36), first suppose that $K < Q^M$. Firm $i's$ profit function is

$$\Pi_i(K_1, ..., K_n) = \frac{\delta}{1-\delta} K_i[\phi(K) - \gamma] - K_i\Gamma,$$

and its partial derivative with respect to its own capacity is

$$\frac{\partial \Pi_i}{\partial K_i} = \frac{\delta}{1-\delta}[\phi(K) - \gamma] - \Gamma + \frac{\delta}{1-\delta} K_i \phi'(K).$$

One can show that an equilibrium must be symmetric, so that in equilibrium, $K_i = K/n$, and

$$\begin{aligned}\frac{\partial \Pi_i}{\partial K_i} &= \frac{\delta}{1-\delta}[\phi(K)-\gamma] - \Gamma + \frac{1}{n}\frac{\delta}{1-\delta}K\phi'(K) \\ &= \frac{n-1}{n}\frac{\delta}{1-\delta}[\phi(K)-\gamma] - \Gamma \\ &\quad + \frac{1}{n}\frac{\delta}{1-\delta}[\phi(K)-\gamma+K\phi'(K)] \\ &= \frac{n-1}{n}\frac{\delta}{1-\delta}[\phi(K)-\gamma] - \Gamma \\ &\quad + \frac{1}{n}\frac{\delta}{1-\delta}\hat{\pi}'(K).\end{aligned}$$

Since $K < Q^M$, it follows that $\hat{\pi}'(K) > 0$. Furthermore, assumption (32) implies that

$$\frac{\delta}{1-\delta}[\phi(K)-\gamma] - \Gamma > 0.$$

Hence, for n sufficiently large,

$$\frac{n-1}{n}\frac{\delta}{1-\delta}[\phi(K)-\gamma] - \Gamma > 0,$$

which, together with $\pi'(K) > 0$, implies that

$$\frac{\partial \Pi_i}{\partial K_i} > 0 \text{ for } K_i = \frac{K}{n}, K < Q^M.$$

Hence there is no equilibrium with $K < Q^M$.

To complete the calculation, suppose that $K \geq Q^M$; then

$$\Pi_i(K_1, ..., K_n) = \frac{\delta}{1-\delta}\frac{K_i}{K}\pi^M - \Gamma K_i,$$

and a routine calculation leads to (33)-(36).

7 Further remarks

7.1 An alternative definition of guaranteed profit

In the definition of the core (Sec. 2), the guaranteed profit of a subset of firms was defined to be the maximum profit the subset can earn if all of the other firms produce at capacity. Recall that Q^* is the industry output at which price equals unit cost. Consider a subset J, and let J' denote the complementary subset. If the industry capacity exceeds Q^*, then if J is small enough, the capacity of J' will exceed Q^*; in this case the firms in J' would make a loss if they produced at capacity. However, if we changed the definition of the core so that J' produces at its capacity or Q^*, whichever is smaller, then the guaranteed profit of J would be unchanged, since the maximum profit of J would be zero in either case. Thus the core would be unchanged, as well.

7.2 An extension

Andrew Postlewaite (in a private communication) has extended the analysis of Section 3 to cover the case in which different firms may have different unit costs. He shows that the following analogue of the proportional allocation is in the core. Given the capacities of the firms, there will be an optimal cartel output; to attain this output some firms may not produce anything. Let I denote the set of all the firms that actually participate in producing the optimal cartel output, and let L denote the largest unit cost of firms in I. Now consider a hypothetical industry in which all the firms have the unit cost L, but the same capacities as before, and let P be the maximum industry profit for this second (hypothetical) industry. One can show that there is a core allocation with the following allocation of profit: (1) a firm not in I receives a share of P proportional to its capacity; (2) a firm in I receives its proportionate share of P, plus a premium. For a firm in I, its premium equals its capacity times the difference between L and its own (true) unit cost. *Note that a firm not in I receives a positive share of the cartel profit, although it produces no output.*

7.3 Sequential games

A more thorough theoretical treatment of collusion would consider a model in which the firms make a sequence (possibly infinite) of decisions regarding their *capacities* and *outputs*. In addition to characterizing the core of such a game, one might also like to know under what conditions (if any) a collusive allocation can be sustained as a sequential noncooperative equilibrium. I know of no such treatment in the literature. Note that this situation is not a repeated game, since the capacities of the firms may change.

One could envisage a more limited sequential model in which the capacities of the firms are given in advance, but the firms are free to change their outputs from one period to the next. This would be a repeated game in the strict sense of the term. According to a theorem of Aumann, in a repeated game with no discounting (the payoff to a player is the long-run average of his one-period payoffs) the set of strong-Nash equilibrium payoffs of the repeated game is the same as the set of core payoffs of the one-period game. (Recall that a strong-Nash equilibrium is a profile of strategies such that no subset of players can increase its total payoff by jointly changing the members' strategies.) Of course, strong Nash-equilibrium is not exactly a noncooperative game concept.

Elsewhere, I studied the (noncooperative) epsilon-equilibria in such a model (Radner, 1980). Recall that in an epsilon-equilibrium each firm is satisfied to be close (within epsilon in profit, where epsilon is a "small" number) to its optimal response to the other firms' sequential strategies. I considered a game with a finite number of repetitions, and a fixed number of firms, and focused on the proportional allocation as the target for collusive behavior.

I showed that: (1) If the lifetime of the industry is large compared to the number of firms, then collusion can be sustained in equilibrium for "most" of the lifetime of the industry; (2) if the number of firms is large compared to the industry's lifetime, then all equilibria will be close (in some sense) to the competitive equilibrium.

References

1. Hildenbrand, Werner (1974), *Core and Equilibria of a Large Economy*, Princeton University Press, Princeton.
2. Osborne, Martin J., and Carolyn Pitchik (1983), "Profit-Sharing in a Collusive Industry," *European Economic Review*, 22, 59-74.
3. Osborne, Martin J., and Carolyn Pitchik (1987), "Cartels, Profits, and Excess Capacity," *International Economic Review*, 28, 413-428.
4. Radner, Roy (1980), "Collusive Behavior in Noncooperative Epsilon-Equilibria of Oligopolies with Long but Finite Lives," *Journal of Economic Theory*, 22, 136-154.

Blame Avoidance as Motivating Force in the First Price Sealed Bid Private Value Auction

Reinhard Selten

Zentrum für interdisziplinäre Forschung, Universität Bielefeld, Bielefeld, and Universität Bonn, Bonn, Germany

Abstract. The author's consulting experience suggests that blame avoidance is a strong motivating force in practical bidding behavior. The reasons for this are discussed and the consequences for the sealed bid private value auction are explored.

1 Introduction

Recently the author repeatedly became involved in giving advice to bidders in radio frequency auctions. One of the most striking experiences gained from these contracts is the definite impression that the bidders are not primarily concerned about expected profits or expected utility of profits but rather about the blame which may fall on them after the auction. They want to avoid to be blamed for not bidding enough or for bidding too much in the light of the hindsight available to critics when the final outcome is known.

Blame avoidance is by no means irrational. Usually the persons actually bidding in the auction are in a high but still subordinate position. They have to fear the criticism of superiors. Top management itself has to face the reaction of the stock holders. This is a good reason for blame avoidance.

Consider the case of an auction in which only one object is sold. Usually top management specifies a "budget", an upper limit for the bid. The bidding team has the task to acquire the object for a price not above this limit as cheaply as possible. There are two sources of blame. One is the "lost opportunity". The object is sold to somebody else at a price within the reach of one's budget. The other one is "overpayment". The bidding team succeeds in buying the object, but at an unnecessarily high price. Blame is modelled as a fixed disutility in the case of the lost opportunity and as proportional to the amount paid too much in the case of overpayment.

Blame avoidance means that the bidding team wants to minimize expected blame. The consequences of this assumption will be explored for the symmetric first price sealed bid private value auction with values uniformly and independently distributed over an interval. An equilibrium bid function is determined. For low values the optimal bid is equal to the budget. From a certain critical value on the optimal bid function becomes strictly concave.

The last part of the paper contains some remarks on blame avoidance and auction design. It is argued that the popularity of the English auction is due to its blame avoidance properties.

2 Rules of the game

The rules of the sealed bid first price private value auction examined here are as follows:

1. The players are n *bidders* $1, \ldots, n$ with $n = 2, 3, \ldots$.
2. For each bidder i, independently a *budget* x_i is randomly drawn from the uniform distribution over the interval [0,1].
3. Each bidder is informed about her budget, but not about the budgets of the others.
4. Each bidder independently makes a *bid* p_i with $0 \leq p_i \leq x_i$.
5. The *price* p is the maximum of the bids $p_1, \ldots, p_n$.
6. The *winner* is randomly selected from the set W of all i with $p_i = p$. Each $i \epsilon W$ has the same probability of becoming the winner. For each i we define a variable w_i, the *winning index:* We have $w_i = 1$ for the winner, and $w_i = 0$ for everybody else.
7. The object is sold to the winner at price p.
8. After the end of the auction, all bids become publicly known.

If i is the winner, i's profit is $P_i = x_i - p_i$. Otherwise i's profit is zero. Suppose that the bidders maximize expected profit. It is well known in the literature that under this assumption,

$$p_i = \frac{n-1}{n} x_i \quad \text{for} \quad i = 1, \ldots, n$$

is the uniquely determined symmetric equilibrium strategy for the game defined by 1 to 7 together with expected profits as the payoff function (Cox, Robertson and Smith 1982; Cox, Smith and Walker 1983; Cox, Smith and Walker 1988).

Here we will combine the rules 1 to 8 with a different payoff function based on the idea of blame avoidance. Let N be the set $\{1, \ldots, n\}$ and for every $i \in N$ let

$$q_i = \max_{j \in N \setminus \{i\}} p_j$$

be the maximum of all bids of other bidders. The blame b_i of player i is a function of p_i, q_i, x_i, and w_i:

$$b_i(p_i, q_i, x_i, w_i) = \begin{cases} 0 & \text{for} \quad q_i \geq x_i \quad \text{and} \quad w_i = 0, \\ F & \text{for} \quad q_i < x_i \quad \text{and} \quad w_i = 0, \\ p_i - q_i & \text{for} \quad w_i = 1. \end{cases}$$

Here F is a positive constant. In the first case $q_i \geq x_i$ and $w_i = 0$, the bidding team could not have outbid the auction winner within its budget constraint. It cannot be blamed for not getting the object. In the second case $q_i < x_i$ and $w_i = 0$, the bidding team is blamed for not getting the object in spite of the fact that the winning bid could have been overbid. The blame for missing the opportunity is modelled as a constant F. This reflects the idea that it should be the goal of the bidding team to obtain the object no matter what has to be paid up to the budget limit. The blame for not reaching this goal if it could have been reached is independent of the price which would have had to be paid. The third case $w_i = 1$ arises if the bidding team succeeds in buying the object. Here the blame is modelled as proportional to the amount $p_i - q_i$ paid too much. Without loss of generality the proportionality factor can be normalized to 1. In this way a unit of measurement for blame is fixed.

The payoff h_i of player i is negative blame

$$h_i = -b_i(p_i, q_i, x_i, w_i).$$

The assumption of blame avoidance means that expected negative blame is maximized.

The game has the structure of an extensive game starting with a random move, the selection of $(x_1, \ldots, x_n)$. Then each player i, knowing only x_i, chooses p_i with $0 \leq p_i \leq x_i$. After the bid choices the game ends. A *strategy* of player i is a function φ_i which assigns a bid $\varphi_i(x_i)$ with $0 \leq \varphi_i(x_i) \leq x_i$ to every x_i with $0 \leq x_i \leq 1$. More precisely, such bid functions are *pure* strategies, but since no other strategies are considered in this paper we simply speak of strategies.

We permit only piecewise continuous strategies with finitely many points of discontinuity. Such strategies are called *permissible*. In view of the symmetry of the game all players have the same strategy space. The set of all permissible strategies is denoted by Φ.

A *permissible strategy combination*

$$s = (\varphi_1, \ldots, \varphi_n)$$

is an n-tuple of permissible strategies $\varphi_i \in \Phi$ for the players $i = 1, \ldots, n$. The set of all permissible strategy combinations is denoted by S.

Suppose that a player i faces a budget x_i and makes the bid p_i while the other players play their strategies in a permissible strategy combination $s = (\varphi_1, \ldots, \varphi_n)$. Player i's *expected blame* $B_i(p_i, x_i, s_i)$ in this situation is the conditional expectation of $b_i(p_i, q_i, x_i, w_i)$, given p_i, x_i, and s.

$$H_i(p_i, x_i, s) = -B_i(p_i, x_i, s)$$

is player i's *local payoff* for p_i at the information set determined by x_i as a function of the strategy combination s. Of course, $B_i(p_i, x_i, s)$ does not depend on player i's own strategy φ_i in s, but it is convenient not to express this explicitly in our notation.

Since only piecewise continuous strategies with finitely many points of discontinuity are permissible, no difficulties can arise with respect to the existence of expected values.

3 Regular symmetric equilibrium

The game described in section 2 will be analyzed non-cooperatively. However, attention will be restricted to special Nash equilibria.

An *equilibrium* $s = (\varphi_1, \ldots, \varphi_n)$ is a permissible strategy combination such that for $i = 1, \ldots, n$ the inequality

$$H_i(p_i, x_i, s) \leq H_i(\varphi_i(x_i), x_i, s)$$

holds for every x_i with $0 \leq x_i \leq 1$ and every p_i with $0 \leq p_i \leq x_i$.

We define equilibrium by local payoff maximization rather than global payoff maximization. An optimal choice must be taken at every information set. A global payoff maximization requirement would be weaker since finitely many deviations from local payoff maximization would not matter. Local payoff maximization implies global payoff maximization.

A permissible strategy combination $s = (\varphi_1, \ldots, \varphi_n)$ is *symmetric* if we have

$$\varphi_i = \varphi \quad \text{for} \quad i = 1, \ldots, n.$$

Every player uses the same strategy φ.

A strategy $\varphi \in S$ is called *regular* if it is continuously differentiable and monotonically increasing everywhere for $0 \leq x_i \leq 1$. A *regular symmetric equilibrium* is an equilibrium

$$s = (\varphi, \ldots, \varphi)$$

in which every player uses the same regular strategy $\varphi \in S$.

We will restrict our attention to regular symmetric equilibria. No attempt will be made to answer the question whether there are other equilibria. Symmetry and regularity must be looked upon as plausible equilibrium selection criteria.

4 Existence and uniqueness of regular symmetric equilibrium

It is our intention to prove that the game described in section 2 has one and only one regular symmetric equilibrium. This will be the content of a theorem preceded by two lemmata. The first lemma concerns properties of expected blame in a symmetric strategy combination with a regular symmetric equilibrium. Finally, the theorem is proved by showing that there is no other regular symmetric equilibrium.

Since we always deal with symmetric strategy combinations in a symmetric game, we can focus on the situation of one of the players, say player 1. It will be convenient to drop the index 1 where it refers to player 1. Thus p and x stand for player 1's bid and budget, respectively, and q denotes the maximal price of the others. $B(x, p, s)$ is player 1's expected blame in $s = (\varphi, \ldots, \varphi)$ if players $2, \ldots, n$ play φ.

We will only look at regular symmetric strategy combinations $s = (\varphi, \ldots, \varphi)$ with a regular common strategy φ. A regular strategy φ is monotonically increasing and therefore invertible. ψ will denote the inverse of φ.

In equilibrium the bid p must minimize the expected blame $B(p, x, s)$. Therefore the derivative of expected blame with respect to p is important.

Lemma 1. *Let φ be a regular strategy and let*

$$s = (\varphi, \ldots, \varphi)$$

be the symmetric strategy combination with φ as the common strategy of all players. Let ψ be the inverse of φ. The following equation holds for the partial derivative $B_p(p, x, s)$ of $B(p, x, s)$ with respect to p:

$$B_p(p, x, s) = [\psi(p)]^{n-2}[\psi(p) - (n-1)F\psi'(p)]$$

where ψ' is the derivative of ψ.

Proof. The bid p_j of a player j with $j \neq 1$ is below p if and only if j's budget x_j is below $\psi(p)$. Let $W(p)$ be the probability that the bids of all players $2, \ldots, n$ are below p. We have

$$W(p) = (\psi(p))^{n-1}.$$

Obviously, $W(p)$ can also be interpreted as the probability that q is below p. Therefore the density $w(q)$ of q is the derivative of $W(p)$ at $p = q$:

$$w(q) = (n-1)(\psi(p))^{n-2}\psi'(p).$$

The expected blame $B(p, x, s)$ for the bid p at the budget x can now be described as follows:

$$B(p, x, s) = F[W(x) - W(p)] + \int_0^p (p - q)w(q)dq.$$

The expression $W(x) - W(p)$ is the probability of missing the opportunity to overbid the maximal bid of the others, if it is between p and x. Under the integral we find the overpayment weighted by its density, if q is below p. The integral is the contribution to the expected blame due to winning the object but paying more than necessary. We now can determine $B_p(p, x, s)$. The derivative of the first term is $-Fw(p)$. The second term depends on p in two ways. p is the upper limit of integration and it is a parameter under the integral. We have to form the sum of the two partial derivatives with respect to the upper limit and the term under the integral. The derivative with respect to the upper limit is the value of the integrand at the upper limit. In our case this value is zero. Therefore we obtain

$$B_p(p,x,s) = -Fw(p) + \int_0^p w(q)dq$$

or equivalently

$$B_p(p,x,s) = W(p) - Fw(p).$$

We can make use of our equations for W and w. This yields

$$B_p(p,x,s) = [\psi(p)]^{n-1} - (n-1)F[\psi(p)]^{n-2}\psi'(p)$$

or equivalently

$$B_p(p,x,s) = [\psi(p)]^{n-2}[\psi(p) - (n-1)F\psi'(p)].$$

This completes the proof of the lemma. □

Lemma 2. *Let φ be the strategy with*

$$\varphi(x) = \begin{cases} x & \text{for} \quad x < (n-1)F, \\ (n-1)F[1 - \ln(n-1)F + \ln x] & \text{for} \quad x \geq (n-1)F \end{cases}$$

for $0 \leq x \leq 1$. Then the symmetric strategy combination

$$s = (\varphi, \dots, \varphi)$$

is a regular symmetric equilibrium.

Proof. At $x = (n-1)F$ both lines in the definition of φ yield the same value $(n-1)F$. The derivatives of both lines at $x = (n-1)F$ are 1. Obviously φ is continuously differentiable in the interval $0 \leq x \leq 1$. It is also clear that φ is monotonically increasing. φ is regular.

It remains to be shown that $s = (\varphi, \dots, \varphi)$ is an equilibrium. Easy algebraic transformations show that the inverse ψ of φ is as follows:

$$\psi(p) = \begin{cases} p & \text{for} \quad p < (n-1)F, \\ (n-1)Fe^{\frac{p}{(n-1)F} - 1} & \text{for} \quad p \geq (n-1)F. \end{cases}$$

This yields

$$\psi'(p) = \begin{cases} 1 & \text{for} \quad p < (n-1)F, \\ e^{\frac{p}{(n-1)F} - 1} & \text{for} \quad p \geq (n-1)F. \end{cases}$$

It follows by Lemma 1 that we have

$$B_p(p,x,s) = \begin{cases} p^{n-2}[p - (n-1)F] & \text{for} \quad p < (n-1)F, \\ 0 & \text{for} \quad p \geq (n-1)F. \end{cases}$$

Interestingly, $B_p(p,x,s)$ does not depend on x, not only for the special φ considered here, but in general, as can be seen by Lemma 1. With the help of the last equation for $B_p(p,x,s)$ we now show that $p = \varphi(x)$ minimizes $B(p,x,s)$ for all x in the interval $0 \leq x \leq 1$. This is trivially true for $x = 0$ in view of $0 \leq p \leq x$. For $0 < x < (n-1)F$ we have $p < (n-1)F$ and therefore $B_p(p,x,s) < 0$. Therefore for $0 < x < (n-1)F$ the bid p must be chosen as high as possible in order to minimize $B(p,x,s)$. This is achieved by $\varphi(x) = x$.

Now consider the case $x \geq (n-1)F$. In order to minimize $B(p,x,s)$ the bid must be chosen not smaller than $(n-1)F$ since expected blame as a function of p falls up to $p = (n-1)F$ and remains constant from then on. Since $\varphi(x)$ is monotonically increasing and equal to $(n-1)F$ at $x = (n-1)F$, it is greater for higher budgets x. Therefore, the choice of $p = \varphi(x)$ minimizes the blame $B(p,x,s)$ there, too. We can conclude that $s = (\varphi,\ldots,\varphi)$ is a regular symmetric equilibrium. □

Remark: The proof of Lemma 2 has shown that the regular symmetric equilibrium $s = (\varphi,\ldots,\varphi)$ described there is weak in the sense that a player has many alternative best replies to the equilibrium behavior of the others. The situation is similar to that in mixed strategy equilibria of finite games. The behavior of the other players has the effect that a player becomes indifferent between many best replies.

Theorem. *For $n = 2,3,\ldots$ and every $F > 0$ the game described in section 2 has one and only one regular symmetric equilibrium*

$$s = (\varphi,\ldots,\varphi)$$

with the common strategy

$$\varphi(x) = \begin{cases} x & \text{for } \; x < (n-1)F, \\ (n-1)F[1 - \ln(n-1)F + \ln x] & \text{for } \; x \geq (n-1)F. \end{cases}$$

Proof. Lemma 2 shows that s is a regular symmetric equilibrium. It remains to be shown that s is the only regular symmetric equilibrium. We will assume that $s = (\varphi,\ldots,\varphi)$ is a regular symmetric equilibrium, not necessarily the one described by the Theorem, and we will show that φ must have the asserted form.

We must have $\varphi(0) = 0$ in view of $0 \leq \varphi(x) \leq x$. Therefore the proof that the formula for φ must hold can restrict itself to $x > 0$. Since φ is monotonically increasing we must have $\varphi(x) > 0$ for $x > 0$ and therefore $\psi(p) > 0$ for $p > 0$.

For $p = \varphi(x)$ we can write

$$\psi'(p) = \frac{1}{\varphi'(x)}.$$

For $x > 0$, Lemma 1 yields the following conclusion:

$$B_p(\varphi(x), x, s) < 0 \quad \text{if and only if} \quad \varphi'(x) > \tfrac{(n-1)F}{x},$$

$$B_p(\varphi(x), x, s) = 0 \quad \text{if and only if} \quad \varphi'(x) = \tfrac{(n-1)F}{x},$$

$$B_p(\varphi(x), x, s) > 0 \quad \text{if and only if} \quad \varphi'(x) < \tfrac{(n-1)F}{x}.$$

For every $x > 0$ we have $0 < \varphi(x)$ in view of the fact that φ is monotonically increasing. If $\varphi(x) < x$, the derivative $B_p(\varphi(x), x, s)$ must vanish for such x, since otherwise expected blame could be decreased by a transition from $\varphi(x)$ to a higher or lower bid.

We now show

$$\varphi(x) = x \quad \text{for} \quad 0 \leq x < (n-1)F.$$

We must have $\varphi(0) = 0$. Suppose that for some x_0 with $0 \leq x_0 < (n-1)F$ we have $\varphi(x_0) < x_0$. In view of the fact that φ is increasing, $0 \leq \varphi(x_0) < x_0$ holds. Since φ is regular, the existence of an x_0 of this kind implies the existence of an open interval $x_1 < x < x_2$ with $x_2 > x_1$ and $\varphi(x) < (x)$. Within this interval $B_p(\varphi(x), x, s)$ vanishes and

$$\varphi'(x) = \frac{(n-1)F}{x} > 1$$

holds. The same inequality holds for every x with $\varphi(x) < x < (n-1)F$. For $\varphi(x) = x$ we have $\varphi'(x) = 1$, since the 45°-line is a tangent of φ at x. This has the consequence

$$\int_0^{(n-1)F} \varphi'(x)dx = \varphi((n-1)F) > (n-1)F$$

contrary to $\varphi(x) \leq x$. Therefore $\varphi(x) = x$ holds for $0 \leq x < (n-1)F$ and by the continuity of φ also for $x = (n-1)F$. Of course, $(n-1)F$ may be greater than or equal to 1. In this case $\varphi(x) = x$ holds for $0 \leq x \leq 1$.

Assume $(n-1)F < 1$. Suppose that for some x_0 with $(n-1)F < x_0 \leq 1$ we have $\varphi(x_0) = x_0$. Then $\varphi'(x_0) = 1$ holds. In view of $x_0 > (n-1)F$, this has the consequence

$$\varphi'(x_0) > \frac{(n-1)F}{x_0}.$$

Therefore the inequality

$$B_p(\varphi(x_0), x_0, s) < 0$$

holds and $B(\varphi(x_0), x_0, s)$ can be decreased by a transition from $\varphi(x_0)$ to a smaller bid. Therefore we have

$$0 < \varphi(x) < x \quad \text{for} \quad (n-1)F < x \leq 1.$$

The lower bound zero is due to the monotonicity of φ. This has the consequence that $B_p(\varphi(x), x, s)$ vanishes for $(n-1)F < x \leq 1$. Therefore the following is true:

$$\varphi'(x) = \frac{(n-1)F}{x} \quad \text{for} \quad (n-1)F < x \leq 1.$$

The solution of this differential equation is

$$\varphi(x) = C + (n-1)F \ln x \quad \text{for} \quad (n-1)F < x \leq 1$$

where C is an integration constant. We can determine C by the requirement that for $x = (n-1)F$ we have $\varphi(x) = x$. In this way one obtains

$$\varphi(x) = (n-1)F[1 - \ln(n-1)F + \ln x] \quad \text{for} \quad (n-1)F \leq x \leq 1.$$

This completes the proof of the theorem. □

5 Comparison with the equilibrium for the case of expected profit maximization

If the bidders are risk neutral and motivated by profits, the equilibrium bid function is

$$\pi(x) = \tfrac{n-1}{n}x \quad \text{for} \quad 0 \leq x \leq 1$$

(see section 2). The bid function $\varphi(x)$ in the regular symmetric equilibrium obtained for the case of expected blame minimization is more aggressive for small x, since $\varphi(x) = x$ holds for $0 \leq x < (n-1)F$, but for $x \geq (n-1)F$ the bid function $\varphi(x)$ is concave and smaller than x. There may be a point x_0 with $(n-1)F < x_0 < 1$ where $\varphi(x)$ intersects $\pi(x)$. In this case we have

$$\pi(x) > \varphi(x) \quad \text{for} \quad x_0 < x \leq 1.$$

There is such an x_0 if we have $\pi(1) > \varphi(1)$. This is the case for

$$\tfrac{n-1}{n} > (n-1)F(1 - \ln(n-1)F)$$

or equivalently for

$$1 > nF(1 - \ln(n-1)F).$$

This inequality requires that F is sufficiently small.

Admittedly, the comparison of $\varphi(x)$ and $\pi(x)$ neglects the difference between the meaning of x in both cases. In the theory of risk neutral expected profit maximization, x is the private value of the object, whereas in the case of blame orientation, x is a budget fixed by the superiors of the bidder.

6 The influence of the parameter F

The parameter F is the fixed blame for not getting the object if its price could have been overbid within the budget constraint. How does an increase of F influence the bid function φ? Clearly the region where $\varphi(x) = x$ holds is expanded, because $(n-1)F$ is increased. Consider a point $x > (n-1)F$. At such a point we have $\varphi(x) < x$ and

$$\frac{\partial \varphi(x)}{\partial F} = (n-1)[1 - \ln(n-1)F + \ln x] - 1$$

or equivalently

$$\frac{\partial \varphi(x)}{\partial F} = n - 2 + (n-1)\ln\frac{x}{(n-1)F}.$$

In view of $x > (n-1)F$ the second term is positive. The first term is zero for $n = 2$ and positive for $n = 3, 4, \ldots$. We have

$$\frac{\partial \varphi(x)}{\partial F} > 0 \quad \text{for} \quad x > (n-1)F.$$

Clearly, the bidding function becomes more aggressive if F is increased. Wherever $\varphi(x)$ is changed, it is increased.

7 Informal remarks on blame avoidance and auction design

The formal developments of sections 2 to 7 concern the simple case of the first price sealed bid private value auction. Of course, this is only an example which highlights the differences between expected profit maximization and the minimization of expected blame.

The rules of real radio frequency auctions tend to be much more complicated. The formal analysis of these auctions often meets serious difficulties which usually cannot be overcome in the available time from the publication of the rules to the beginning of the auctions unless one is willing to make unrealistic simplifying assumptions. Nevertheless, it is possible to say something about the consequences of blame orientation for problems of auction design.

Suppose that the government wants to sell m objects (e. g. radio frequency bands). Assume that the objects are equal for all practical purposes, such that for a buyer only the number of objects bought matters, but not which of the objects she gets. Auction designs for this situation may always lead to the same price for all objects sold or they may permit different prices. In the first case we speak of a "uniform price auction" and in the second one of a "discriminatory auction".

The distinction between discriminatory and uniform price auctions can be illustrated by a simple example. Suppose that m objects are to be sold in a sealed bid auction in which each of the bidders $1, \ldots, n$ makes just one bid. Assume $n > m$. The m objects are sold to the m highest bidders. This means that the bidders are ranked according to the size of the bids, and those with ranks $1, \ldots, m$ receive the object. If there are ties, then one of the rankings respecting the size order is picked at random. We are looking at two different auctions which have these features in common.

In the uniform price version the price for all objects is the bid of the m-th bidder. In the discriminatory version each of the m highest bidders pays what he has bid.

Buyers usually prefer a uniform price auction, since there the blame of paying more than somebody else for the same thing is avoided. However, in the above example, an auction designer would prefer the discriminatory version, since in the uniform price auction there is a risk of being blamed for selling much below the willingness to pay. If for example 2 objects are sold and the highest bidder has bid 1 million and the second highest one has bid only 1000, both objects are sold at the price 1000. In this case the auction designer will be blamed for wasting money by taking only 1000 from somebody who was willing to pay a million.

Public officials are maybe even more blame oriented than private bidders. In our example the interests of blame oriented buyers and sellers in the pricing rules are opposed to each other. However, there is a simple auction design which does not lead to such a conflict. This design is a generalization of the ordinary English auction which may be called the multi-object English auction.

The multi-object English auction proceeds by potentially many successive bidding rounds. In each round each bidder bids for each of the m objects, but a new bid for an object must be higher by a fixed increment than the highest bid for the same object in the preceding round. In the first period bids must be at least as high as a fixed minimum price. After each round one of the highest bidders for an object is randomly selected as the "holder". The bids within one bidding round are made simultaneously and independently. The auction ends as soon as in a round no bids are made. If this happens, all objects are sold to their holders.

The multi-object English auction does not have uniform prices by design, but competition leads to almost equal prices for all objects. Great price differences can occur only if at least one bidder makes a serious mistake. In this sense the multi-object English auction has almost uniform prices. It makes it possible to avoid the risk of having to pay substantially more for the same thing than somebody else. There is also no need to face a risk of not getting an object, if it would have been possible to overbid the last holder within one's budget constraint.

The willingness to pay is not revealed in the English auction. Nobody knows how much more a buyer might have bid, if the auction did go on longer. Therefore the auction designer does not face any risk of being blamed for not having exhausted the willingness to pay of a buyer. The virtual absence of a risk of blame on both sides is also a feature of the ordinary English auction of only one object. This is maybe the reason for the great popularity of the English auction.

References

1. Cox, James C., Robertson, Bruce, and Smith, Vernon L. (1982), Theory and Behavior of Single Object Auctions. In: Smith, Vernon L. (Ed.), Research in Experimental Economics, Vol. 2, Greenwich, CT: JAI Press, 1-43.
2. Cox, James C., Smith, Vernon L., and Walker, James N. (1983), Test of a Heterogenous Bidders Theory of First Price Auctions. Economic Letters 12, 207-212.
3. Cox, James C., Smith, Vernon L., and Walker, James N. (1988), Theory and Individual Behavior of First-Price Auctions. Journal of Risk and Uncertainty 1, 61-99.

Evasion of Tax on Interest Income in a Two-Country Model

Georg Tillmann

Faculty of Economics, University of Mainz

Abstract. t We consider a model where agents can invest money at home and abroad. Their total income comprises interest income from these investments and labor income. Tax on interest income can be evaded - at the risk of being detected and fined. We analyze the optimal portfolio and tax evading decisions of agents with different incomes. In a second step, we scrutinize the optimal government policy. Using different instruments government tries to maximize total tax receipts and to prevent flight of capital as far as possible.

1 Introduction

Tax evasion has become an important problem, not only in the Third World but also in many western countries. Theory has also taken this into account. Since the classical paper of Allingham/Sandmo (1972) there has been a steadily growing body of literature analyzing the behavior of a tax payer facing the tax authorities. Although, as Sandmo (1981) already mentioned, some years ago most people "tended to associate tax evasion with income from capital and Swiss bank accounts", theoretical papers nearly always deal with the evasion of labor income only (which, of course, is a major problem, as the "black market economy" keeps growing). However, for most employed agents who have one "official" job only, evasion of tax on labor income is very difficult, as in some countries such an income is directly taxed at source. Although this is also valid for capital or interest income, there is a big difference in tax rates: labor is mostly taxed at source with the definite rate, interest income at a lower rate. This does, of course, not imply that this kind of income is taxed less heavily: at the end of the year people have to file a return stating their *total* income; nevertheless, in such a combination of taxation at source and declaration of one's income, some evasion is possible, though at the risk of being detected and fined. This risk can, however, be diminished, by investing abroad. As capital is very mobile, it can be transferred to foreign countries without problems. That has at least two advantages for an individual agent: first, an investment abroad and income from it can hardly ever be detected (think of a Swiss bank account) and, second, the tax rates at home and in all foreign countries normally differ substantially such that a consumer can pick out the most advantageous form of investment. We therefore have the following problem: an agent has labor income w, directly taxed at source at the definite rate, and capital income S which he can split up and invest at home and abroad (i.e. foreign countries). In both places there is a tax at source at a lower rate than the definite one with respect to interest income; therefore evasion may be lucrative. How such a (w, S) agent splits up his S and how he evades has already been scrutinized in Tillmann (1998), together with the optimal behavior of a tax maximizing government which has different instruments available, namely a fine parameter α, the probability of detection p and the tax at source for interest income b. In the following we generalize this model. First, we no longer consider an individual agent only (section 1.3), but assume that there is a distribution of labor and interest income (section 1.4). Second, we compare two different cases: a) "direct control" of every taxpayer by the tax authorities without and with (section 1.5I) tax exemption up to a certain amount, which is the case, for example, in the Netherlands and the US; b) the "usual case", where tax evaders are investigated with a certain probability p, as already mentioned above. The instruments α, p, b and tax exemption are dealt with in section 1.5II. All proofs are presented in section 1.6.

2 The model

There is only one good called money. All consumers in the *economy* have identical preferences, but differ with respect to their wage income w and their wealth S. Therefore, we can parametrize agents by $(w, S) \in R_+^2$. The distribution of (w, S) on R_+^2 is described by a probability measure μ with $B(R_+^2)$ being the Borel σ-algebra. Wealth S can be invested in two different ways: everybody can buy assets at home and abroad. The interest rates are given by r_1 (at home) and r_2 (abroad). When an agent invests s_1 units of money at home and $s_2 = S - s_1$ units abroad the interest income will be $r_1 s_1 + r_2 s_2$ and total gross income will be equal to $w + r_1 s_1 + r_2 s_2$. There is a linear income tax τ such that the net income will be $(1-\tau)(w+r_1 s_1+r_2 s_2)$ if his declaration was "honest". Although tax evasion is also possible for labor, we assume that the agent is an employee who is directly taxed at source, implying that it is impossible for him to evade taxes; he gets net $w(1-\tau)$ only. On the contrary, tax on interest income may be evaded; to restrict tax evasion the government may raise taxes at source on those incomes, however, normally at rates lower than τ such that evasion may be profitable. We denote the taxation rate at source for interest income at home and abroad by b_1 and b_2 respectively, where $b_i < \tau$. Every agent may now choose two strategies: to declare his income correctly or to underreport an amount of his interest income. If he chooses the latter, his total pay-off will depend on whether or not he is investigated by the tax authorities. We will assume that he is (not) investigated with probability of p_1 $(q_1 = 1 - p_1)$ at home and $p_2(q_2)$ abroad. If he has made an incorrect declaration and is audited, he will be detected and fined. Therefore, his decision involves a degree of uncertainty. We assume that every agent behaves as a von Neumann-Morgenstern utility maximizer, with money as the only argument of the utility function.

Assumption 1 *$u : R_+ \to R$ is C^3, bounded, strictly increasing and strictly concave.*

Risk aversion is measured by $R_A(c)$, the absolute risk aversion, and $R_R(c)$, the relative risk aversion. What are the total amounts of income after taxes for an agent in the two different cases?

Case 1) Not investigated

As wage income is directly taxed at source at a rate of τ, the interest income at rates b_i, the agent's income before declaration is $w(1-\tau)+(1-b_1)r_1s_1+(1-b_2)r_2s_2$. The agent gets written confirmation that he has already paid $b_ir_is_i$; these amounts can in principle be deducted when he makes his declaration. Assume now that at home the agent evades H_1, equivalently he declares $r_1s_1 - H_1$ only. Officially, he had to pay for this $\tau(r_1s_1 - H_1)$; however, he has already paid $b_1r_1s_1$. Of course, he cannot declare the total amount, as it would be obvious that he is underreporting. Therefore, only $b_1(r_1s_1-H_1)$ can be specified and as a result he has to pay $(\tau - b_1)(r_1s_1 - H_1)$. Analogously, for assets of the foreign country he has to pay $(\tau - b_2)(r_2s_2 - H_2)$ when he evades H_2. The total amount of money available to him after declaration is $Q = S + (1-\tau)(w + r_1s_1 + r_2s_2) + (\tau - b_1)H_1 + (\tau - b_2)H_2$. This result is as expected: it is the sum of money he would obtain if he had made a correct declaration plus the net amounts after evading H_i.

Case 2) Investigated

Let us assume the following: If the agent has evaded taxes, only the evasion at home can be detected, but not the evasion abroad, implying $p_2 = 0$ and $q_2 = 1$. This is rather realistic if you think, for example, of bank accounts in Switzerland or other countries where only in extreme cases banks give information about their customers - maybe the main reason why bank accounts abroad are sought after. Therefore, it is trivial that $H_2 = r_2s_2$, all interest income abroad is evaded. For the evasion at home let us assume: the net evaded amount $(\tau - b_1)H_1$ has to be paid back plus a fine depending on the gravity of the offense. The fine is a multiple of the amount, resulting from tax evasion $\alpha(\tau - b_1)H_1, \alpha \geq 0$. Having paid the liabilities, the following amount of money remains: $Q - (\tau - b_1)H_1 - \alpha(\tau - b_1)H_1 =: P$. Every agent maximizes his expected utility $q_1u(Q) + p_1u(P)$. In the following, we omit index 1. We can split this maximization into two steps: in a first one, the agent determines the optimal evasion at home, $H_1(s_1, s_2)$ and abroad, $H_2(s_1, s_2)$ for given (s_1, s_2). In a second step the optimal portfolio is chosen. Therefore, the problem is given by: $\max_{s_i} \max_{H_i} qu(Q) + pu(P)$ where $s_i \geq 0, s_1 + s_2 = S$, and $0 \leq H_i \leq r_i s_i$. In the next part, we will present our results. In abbreviated form we set $R_i := r_i(1-b_i), i = 1,2, x = R_1 - R_2, y = (\alpha+1)r_1(\tau - b_1)$ and $ER_1 = x - py$.

3 The portfolio decision of a typical (w,S) agent

We have already looked at the individual portfolio decision in Tillmann (1998). In this section, we generalize our former results, considering tax exemptions F. This is one of the governmental instruments dealt with later. All interest income $r_1 s_1 \leq F = r_1 \bar{s}_1$ is exempt from taxation, taxes have to be paid on $r_1(s_1 - \bar{s}_1)$ only. Such an instrument $\bar{s}_1$ changes the portfolio decision in the following way if we vary R_2:

Lemma 1 *If there are tax exemptions $F = r_1\bar{s}_1$, the portfolio decision looks as follows: All money is invested abroad if $R_2 > r_1$. For $R_2 = r_1$ the amount of monetary holding is indefinite, $s_1 \in [0, min(S, \bar{s}_1)]$ and for $R_2 \in [R_1 - py, r_1)$ we have $s_1 = \min(S, \bar{s}_1)$. If $R_2 < r_1(1-\tau)$ always $s_1 = S$. On $[r_1(1-\tau), R_1 - py)$ we obtain $s_1 = S$ if $S \leq \bar{s}_1$ and $S \geq s_1 > \bar{s}_1$ otherwise. Whether we have $s_1 = S$ or $s_1 \in [\tilde{s}_1, S], \tilde{s}_1 < S$ in $r_1(1-\tau)$, with $s_1 = S(s_1 < S)$ in a right neighborhood of $r_1(1-\tau)$ depends on (α, p_1, b_1), but also on the relation between w and S. s_1 is a continuous function or a compact-valued upper hemi-continuous correspondence.*

In comparison to $\bar{s}_1 = 0$ we see that $\bar{s}_1$ has a positive effect on the monetary holding at home, if $R_2 \in [R_1 - py, r_1)$. Anybody who obtained foreign assets only shifts $\bar{s}_1$ of his total wealth back to his home country. Does such a $\bar{s}_1$ also have positive effects for all situations where $S > s_1 > \bar{s}_1$? An answer is given in:

Proposition 1 *$s_{1,\bar{s}_1} > 0$ for $b_1 = 0$ or, if $b_1 > 0$, for $R_A' \leq 0$. Moreover, as $s_{1,\bar{s}_1} = 1 + (r_1 - R_2)s_{1,\delta}$ we obtain: $s_{1,\bar{s}_1} \gtreqless 1$ if $R_A' \lesseqgtr 0$.*

For most utility functions ($R_A' \leq 0$) our intuition is confirmed, for $b_1 = 0$ it is even valid for every utility function. Our result can be considerably strengthened, however. We see that effect $s_{1,\bar{s}_1}$ is much stronger than "the income effect" $s_{1,\delta}$ where $\delta = w(1-\tau) + S(1+R_2)$ is the total (secure) money income an agent has available if he invests his total capital abroad. As $s_{1,\delta}$ depends on the absolute risk aversion only, we get $s_{1,\bar{s}_1} = 1$ for $R_A' = 0$ as in such a situation $s_{1,\delta} = 0$, for every additional dollar tax exemption the agent will reinvest one dollar at home. The effect is even stronger with $R_A' < 0$, as then also $s_{1,\delta} > 0$. Therefore, a tax exemption seems to be a suitable tool if the government wants to keep as much capital as possible in the country.

4 The portfolio decision of different (w, S) agents

Having looked at the individual portfolio decision, we want to consider the behavior of different agents. How do higher wage w or capital S influence the portfolio (s_1, s_2)? Who holds all his money in the form of inland assets, who invests abroad? Do rich people rather than poor ones invest money abroad? A first answer is given in:

Proposition 2 *For all (w, S) with $w(1-\tau) + S(1+R_2) = \delta$ the monetary holding at home is constant and therefore equal to $s_1(\delta)$ as long as $s_1 < S$. $s_{1,\delta} \gtreqless 0 \Leftrightarrow R_A' \lesseqgtr 0$. $s_{1,\delta}\delta/s_1 \gtreqless 1$ if $R_R' \lesseqgtr 0$. For wage w and capital S taken separately we obtain: a) $(s_{1,s}, s_{1,w}) \gtreqless 0 \Leftrightarrow R_A' \lesseqgtr 0$. b) $s_{1,s}.\ S/s_1 \gtreqless S(1+R_2)/\delta$ if $R_R' \lesseqgtr 0$ implying that always $s_{1,s} < 1$ if $R_R' \geq 0$. c) $(s_1/S)_S < 0$ if $R_R' \geq 0$.*

For given δ we see that monetary holding at home is constant, as long as $s_1 < S$, that is, for all those (w, S) with S being sufficiently large. The sign of $s_{1,\delta}$ depends on R_A'. R_R' is responsible for the elasticity of s_1 with respect to δ. Considering w and S, we see that agents with higher w or S hold more (less) assets at home, if the absolute risk aversion decreases (increases), for $R_A' = 0$ the effect is nil. It is also self-evident that the wage effect is much smaller than the wealth effect, as always $s_{1,w} = (1-\tau)(1+R_2)^{-1}s_{1,s}$. The wealth elasticity $s_{1,s}.S/s_1$ for $R_R' \geq 0$ is always smaller than one and decreases if R_R becomes bigger: this is also in accordance with intuition, as the agent becomes more cautious in such a situation. c) goes into the same direction: the relation s_1/S decreases, the richer an agent, the more money absolutely (for $R_A' < 0$) and relatively (for $R_R' \geq 0$)) he holds abroad.

Up to now we considered how s_1 changes for different wage and capital amounts (w, S). In the following, it will be very interesting to know when an agent invests at home only, what will be the case for $R_2 < r_1(1-\tau)$, but not for $R_2 > r_1(1-\tau)$. (Lemma 1). When R_2 is attractive, more and more money will be invested abroad. How do the agents differ with respect to flight of capital? Can we place them in groups such that "the rich" always invest (partially) abroad, but the "the poor" remain at home? We hold α, p, b_1, R_2 and $\bar{s}_1$ fix with $r_1(1-\tau) < R_2 < R_1 - py.W.l.o.g.\bar{s}_1 = 0$. If we define $A := qx(p(y-x))^{-1}$ and $REV := (1+R_1)(1+R_1-y)^{-1}$ we obtain:

Proposition 3 *1. For every $w > 0$ there is a $\tilde{S}_0(w)$ such that $s_1 = S$ for all $S \leq \tilde{S}_0(w)$.*

2. Assume that $y \geq 1 + R_1$ or $\lim_{t\to\infty} R_R(t) = \infty$. Then for every w there is a $S_0(w)$ such that for all $S > S_0$ we have $s_1(w, S) < S$.

3. Assume $\lim_{t\to\infty} R_R(t) = R < \infty$. If $R > (\ln A)(\ln REV)^{-1}$ the result of 2. remains valid, otherwise $s_1(w, S) = S$ for all (w, S), at least if $R_R' \geq 0$.

4. *Moreover, if $y \geq 1 + R_1$ or $R_R'(t) \geq 0$ or if $R_R' \geq 0$ up to $t = t_0$ and $R_R' \leq 0$ for $t > t_0$ then $\tilde{S}_0(w) = S_0(w)$, i.e. there is a function $S_0(w)$ such that $s_1 = S$ for all $S \leq S_0(w)$ and $s_1 < S$ for all $S > S_0(w)$.*

For $R_A' \geq 0$ we always have $R_R(\infty) = \infty$, therefore for $R_A' \geq 0$ there is always flight of capital. The same is true for a large class of functions with $R_A' < 0$. Write for this $R_A(t) = 1/f(t)$ with $f'(t) > 0$. Then $R_R(t) = t(f(t))^{-1}$ and $R_R(\infty) = \infty$ if $f(t)$ remains bounded what is equivalent to $R_A(\infty) > 0$ or, using l'Hospital's rule, if $f'(\infty) = 0$. Only if for very large t, too, the absolute risk aversion diminishes "very fast", R_R remains bounded, and only in this case is it possible that **all** agents hold assets at home only. Proposition 3 is an existence and a uniqueness result. We see that agents with small S invest at home only - and take the full risk of being fined provided their wage income is not too small. The reason is that their possible loss is not too high in comparison to their (secure) wage income. On the other hand, agents with considerable capital S become cautious and invest always partially abroad if $y \geq 1 + R_1$ or $R_R(\infty) = \infty$. The reason is as follows: if $y \geq 1 + R_1$ the fine parameter α must be rather large. This will induce the agents to diminish their monetary holding at home if S becomes large. For small α the threat is rather negligible and a condition concerning risk behavior is needed. If the relative risk aversion is high for large amounts of money, agents with considerable capital S will invest abroad. $s_1 = S$ for all S is possible only if (α, R_R, R_2) are small, whereby R_2 must be in the neighborhood of $r_1(1-\tau)$.

Under the conditions given in 4., there is a unique transition from agents who invest at home only, to those who also invest abroad. Such a unique separation occurs if α is very large, or if the relative risk aversion is monotone (constant or increasing). As $R_R' < 0$ is impossible because, according to Arrow, $R_R(0) < 1 < R_R(\infty)$ the uniqueness result remains valid if R_R increases up to a certain point and decreases later on. This is also a sort of monotonicity. We have to exclude fluctuations of R_R. In a further step, we look at the qualitative behavior of the separating function $S_0(w)$.

Proposition 4 *$S_0(w)$ is at least C^2. We obtain: $S_0'(w) \gtreqless 0 \Leftrightarrow R_A' \lesseqgtr 0$ and for $R_A' > 0$: $S_0''(w) > 0$ if $R_A'' \leq 0$. For $R_A' < 0$ we get, writing $R_A(t) = (f(t))^{-1}$: $S_0''(w) \gtreqless 0 \Leftrightarrow f'' \gtreqless 0$. The boundary behavior can be described as follows: For $w = 0$ we obtain: $S_0(0) > 0 (= 0)$ if $R_R(0) < (\geq)(\ln A)(\ln REV)^{-1}$. If $R_A(\infty) = 0$ we get $S_0(\infty) = \infty$, if $R_A(\infty) > 0$, $S_0(w)$ remains bounded.*

We see that S_0 is decreasing, remains constant or increasing, depending on the absolute risk aversion. If $R_A' < 0$ the function S_0 increases in accordance with intuition. For $f'' < 0$, that is "going slowly to $R_A = 0$ (if at all)" $S_0(w)$ is a concave function reflecting the situation that there is a high level of precaution. This effect is also partially reflected in $S_0(\infty) < \infty$. On the other hand, if $f'' = 0$, we get a straight line and, as long as $f'' > 0$ even a convex function reflecting more risk-taking. Considering the boundary behavior in $w = 0$, we see that $S_0(0) = 0$ if $y \geq 1 + R_1$ or $R_R(0) >> 0$; agents with a small wage are more cautious and invest a part abroad. On the other hand, if the expected fine is not very high such that $y < 1 + R_1$ and if, in addition, the relative risk aversion $R_R(0)$ is low or even zero, $S_0(0) > 0$, even agents with no wage income risk the maximal sanction when their S is small. For later use, we define the set of all (w, S) with $S \geq S_0$ as SA, with $S_0 \geq S \geq \bar{s}_1$ as $SB1$ and with $\bar{s}_1 \geq S \geq 0$ as SBO, where $SB := SB1 \cup SBO$ and $SA1 := SB1 \cup SA$. It will be interesting to know how S_0, which is a differentiable function of $(w, \alpha, p, b_1, R_2, \bar{s}_1)$, will alter when one of the parameters is changed.

Lemma 2 *$S_{0,v} < 0$ for $v = \alpha, p, R_2$. For $R_A^{'} \leq 0$ we have $S_{0,\bar{s}_1} > 0$. Concerning b_1 we get: $S_{0,b_1} > 0$ if b_1 is small and $S_{0,b_1} < 0$ for rather large b_1.*

For α, p the result is as expected: increasing α or p means that it becomes more risky to evade taxes, therefore the agents invest more abroad and S_0 goes down; the same is valid if R_2 increases as then the foreign asset becomes more attractive. On the other hand, with a higher tax exemption $r_1\bar{s}_1$ the agents hold more assets at home and therefore S_0 increases. Only with b_1 the sign of the derivative is not unequivocal. If b_1 is small, such that the effect to buy more s_1 to compensate for higher taxation by evading more is stronger than the price effect, S_0 increases. More and more agents hold all their money at home. However, if b_1 is rather large, the inland asset becomes less attractive - that is, the price effect dominates. In this case, a further increase of b_1 leads to more flight of capital, expressed by a decreasing S_0.

5 The maximization problem of the government

Let us consider the targets of the government. There are a lot of possible welfare functions. We assume that the government has two objectives: to maximize tax receipts $T = \int T(w, S, .)\, d\mu(w, S)$ and to keep - as far as possible - capital at home $\Sigma = \int s_1(w, S, .)\, d\mu(w, S)$. Looking at the public discussion, this seems to be a good approximation of the governmental objectives; in Germany, for example, the huge flight of capital was one of the reasons to abolish the "small capital tax" in 1989. For the above reasons, the government tries to maximize (Σ, T) by using the instruments it has available, namely (α, p, b_1, F). There is an additional tool, applied in the Netherlands and the US, namely direct control. This means that banks have to inform the tax authorities immediately about the interest income of their customers. Thus, in principle the tax authorities are perfectly informed. In practice, however, tax evasion cannot be totally excluded, but it is extremely risky. Likewise, the probability of being detected is very high. Although our results will not change if we consider $q < \alpha p$, we will assume that direct control implies $p = 1$. We therefore have two possibilities: $(\alpha, p, b_1, F) = (0, 1, 0, F)$ (direct control without ($F = 0$) and with ($F > 0$) tax exemption); and (α, p, b_1, F) (indirect control and again $F = 0$ or $F > 0$). Although $R_2 > r_1(1-\tau)$ is the most interesting case, we start with $R_2 < r_1(1-\tau)$, that is, the net return of the foreign asset is very small.

Proposition 5 *If $R_2 < r_1(1-\tau)$ all capital is invested at home, therefore Σ is maximal. For optimal tax receipts there should be* no *tax exemptions. Each of the instruments direct control, α, p, b_1, yields* maximal *tax receipts if $\alpha \geq q/p, p \geq 1/(\alpha+1), b_1 = \tau$.*

The government is in an excellent position: as the net return of the foreign asset is small, all the money is invested at home and none of the instruments has any influence on the portfolio decision. Each of them can be used to eliminate tax evasion totally. Agents cannot escape, as even for an honest person the inland net return is higher than the return of assets abroad. We move to $R_2 > r_1(1-\tau)$ below. In such a situation it may be very lucrative to invest money abroad. Moreover, as was shown in Tillmann (1998), agents totally evade tax on their interest income, $H_1 = r_1 s_1$ if $q > \alpha p$. We will start with:

I. Direct control with and without exemption

In this section we assume that $R_2 < r_1$, as for $R_2 > r_1$ nobody would invest money at home. If the maximal amount free of tax is given by $F = r_1 \bar{s}_1$, we obtain:

Proposition 6 $(\Sigma(F), T(F)) = (\int \min(S, \bar{s}_1) d\mu, 0)$.

Tax receipts are always zero and also, the holding of money at home is very limited: nobody will invest more than $\bar{s}_1$ at home. Moreover, Σ will decrease if exemptions are reduced. If exemptions are completely canceled inland investment will also be zero! In short, direct control is a weak instrument, even in the case of exemptions. Because agents fear to be detected, there is a huge flight of capital to foreign countries; and inland capital is free of tax. Therefore we move to indirect control.

II. Indirect control - the instruments α, p, b_1 and $\bar{s}_1$

First, we will determine possible tax receipts. A typical (w, S) agent, who is not audited, pays $w\tau + b_1 r_1(s_1 - \bar{s}_1)$ at home, as long as $s_1 > \bar{s}_1$; if he is audited and fined he has to pay $w\tau + b_1 r_1(s_1 - \bar{s}_1) + y(s_1 - \bar{s}_1)$. If there are sufficiently many agents of the (w, S) type, p% of them are fined such that total tax receipts from the (w, S) type are $T(w, S) = w\tau + (b_1 r_1 + py)(s_1 - \bar{s}_1)$. Therefore, total tax receipts are equal to $T = \int_{SA1}(w\tau + (b_1 r_1 + py)(s_1(., w, S) - \bar{s}_1) d\mu(w, S)$. In abbreviated form we define $AR := (\ln A)(\ln REV)^{-1}$ for the following section.

II.a The instruments α and p

It is known (Tillmann 1998) that at an individual level decreasing α or p encourages the holding of assets at home. The same is also true for the total economy. But are α or p also suitable tools to regain *all* the capital $\Sigma = \int S d\mu(w, S)$? At least for α, this will not always be true:

Proposition 7 *$\Sigma_\alpha(\alpha) < 0$, a smaller fine increases the total money held. Consider $AR_0 = AR(\alpha = 0)$. If $R_R(\infty) > AR_0$, the wealthy will invest only partially at home, therefore $\Sigma(0) < \Sigma_{\max}$.*

By decreasing α, more agents will invest at home only: as $S_0(w)$ increases, for every w those with a small S will return their holding first; but all others will increase s_1. However, those with a large S will carry on investing partially abroad when R_R is large. Only if $AR_0 > R_R(\infty)$ will there be a $\alpha_0 > 0$, such that for all $\alpha \leq \alpha_0 : \Sigma(\alpha) = \Sigma_{\max}$. Concerning p, the situation is much more favorable. As $\lim_{p \to 0} AR = \infty$, we directly obtain:

Proposition 8 *Assume $R_R(\infty) < \infty$. Then there is a $p_0(R_R) > 0$ such that for all $p \leq p_0 : \Sigma(p) = \Sigma_{\max}$. For $p > p_0$, always $\Sigma_p < 0$.*

Decreasing p increases the money held at home. As long as R_R remains bounded, we can always find a p_0 such that there is no more flight of capital. It is clear, of course, that $p_0(R_R)$ is a decreasing function: if R_R increases, we have to decrease p further to prevent flight of capital of the wealthiest who will again be the agents investing abroad first, as can be directly seen from the changes of $S_0(w, p)$. The situation is more favorable than with α: For *all* situations with $R_R < \infty$, we can prevent any flight of capital. Only for $R_R(\infty) = \infty$, we have to dispense with the detection factor if we want to keep all the capital at home. What about tax receipts T?

Proposition 9 *If $AR_0 > R_R(\infty)$ the optimal α^* is positive. As long as $R_R(\infty) < \infty$, we also should have a positive probability of detection p^* for maximal tax receipts.*

In the cases considered above, we should use the indirect system with a positive α or p also in the future. Moreover, there is no direct conflict between maximizing Σ and T: as a (maybe) small, but positive (α, p) leads to a situation where all the capital remains at home we can expect rather large amounts of tax receipts, too (although in most cases, the optimal (α, p) for T will be larger than for Σ). A conflict arises when it is not possible to make Σ maximal with $(\alpha, p) > 0$. To illustrate this, consider $T = \int_{SB1}(r_1 b_1 + py)S d\mu + \int_{SA}(r_1 b_1 + py)s_1(\alpha, p, w, S)d\mu$. Let us start with $b_1 = 0$. As tax on total interest income is evaded, the only tax receipts are from investigated (and fined) agents. But then we have two countervailing effects: If α or p decrease, fewer agents are fined or less severely fined, implying smaller receipts if Σ were constant. However, with smaller α or p, Σ increases; although fewer agents are investigated, those who are caught are possibly more fined than their additional investment Δs_1. It is not clear which effect of the two dominates the other. The elasticity $(\partial s_1/\partial v).v/s_1$ with $v = \alpha, p$ and the distribution of (w, S) play a dominant role.

II.b The taxation at source b_1

Consider $b_1 = 0$ and $R_2 = r_1(1-\tau)+\epsilon$, ϵ small. According to proposition 3, there is $S_0(w, 0, r_1(1-\tau)+\epsilon)$ with $s_1 = S$ for $S \leq S_0(w)$ and $s_1 < S$ for $S > S_0(w)$ if R_R is sufficiently large. It has been shown in Tillmann (1998) that, using some additional assumptions, for $S > S_0(w)$ there is always a function $b_1 = F_0(R_2, w, S)$ with $s_{1,b_1}(b_1, R_2) = 0$. We can show the following:

Proposition 10 *If $R_A(t) = (at+b)^{-1}$, the function $F_0(R_2)$ is independent of (w, S). The function is defined on $[r_1(1-\tau), \bar{R}_2]$ with $F_0(r_1(1-\tau)) = \tau$, $F_0(\bar{R}_2) = 0$. F_0 is monotonely decreasing.*

It has already been shown that for $b_1 \lesseqgtr F_0(R_2)$ we have $s_{1,b_1} \gtreqless 0$. Agents with $S < S_0(w)$ hold all their money at home, independently of b_1.

Proposition 11 *If $R_A(t) = (at+b)^{-1}$, Σ will be maximal for $b_1 = F_0(R_2) > 0$ as long as $R_2 < \bar{R}_2$. For T the optimal b_1 must be greater than $F_0(R_2)$.*

We see that for linear $R_A(t)^{-1}$ we should increase b_1 up to $F_0(R_2)$ to make Σ maximal. As all agents increase their s_1 exactly up to this point the money held becomes maximal. For maximal tax receipts we should increase b_1 even more, thereby accepting some flight of capital abroad. For $R_2 \geq \bar{R}_2$ we should dispense with b_1 if we are interested in Σ. The same will be true for T if $R_2 > \bar{R}_2 + \epsilon$, as then the cutback of s_1 is so strong for a positive b_1 that receipts will fall. For $R_A = (f)^{-1}$ with f concave, implying $R_R^{'} > 0$, we know that the individual behavior depends on α. If $\alpha \geq 1$, normally $F_0(R_2)$ will fall when S increases. This means that, if we increase b_1, agents with small S will still be increasing their s_1, whereas the wealthy (those with large S) will reduce their inland holding. It will then essentially depend on the distribution of (w, S) what the "average b_1" will be, to maximize Σ or T. Roughly speaking the less wealthy agents pay their taxes whereas the wealthy can again escape. If only b_1 is available as an instrument, it is not very effective in most situations. We therefore move to the last instrument available, $\bar{s}_1$.

II.c The tax exemption $\bar{s}_1$

It was shown in proposition 1 that $\bar{s}_1$ has a positive effect on the money holding at home if $R_A^{'} \leq 0$. For every additional unit tax exemption s_1 increases by one unit ($R_A' = 0$) or even more ($R_A' < 0$). Therefore, to maximize Σ an exemption is a very suitable tool. Will the same be true for maximizing T? For this, consider a typical (w, S) agent.

Proposition 12 *For every* (w, S) *agent with* $\bar{s}_1 < s_1 < S$ *we get* $T_{\bar{s}_1}(w, S) \gtreqless 0 \Leftrightarrow R_A' \lesseqgtr 0$. *For an agent with* $s_1 = S$ *tax receipts decrease,* $T_{\bar{s}_1} < 0$.

We see that only for $R_A' < 0$ the receipts increase, for $R_A' = 0$ they are nil, or even negative for $R_A' > 0$. For the economy we obtain:

Proposition 13 *For* Σ *we get:* $\Sigma_{\bar{s}_1} > 0$ *if* $R_A' \leq 0$. *For the tax receipts* T *an exemption should be dispensed with for* $R_A' \geq 0$. *Only for* $R_A' < 0$ *is a positive exemption possible.* $\bar{s}_1$ *should be positive if* $\int_{SA} s_{1,\bar{s}_1}(., w, S) d\mu > 1$.

As already mentioned s_1 strongly encourages a money holding at home. This is always true for $R_A' \leq 0$, but also for $R_A' > 0$, as long as $s_{1,\delta}$ is greater than - $(r_1 - R_2)^{-1}$, which is fulfilled for most preferences with $R_A' > 0$. Considering T, however, we do not have such a positive result. Those who invest also abroad, pay more taxes on a net basis only if $R_A' < 0$; those who invest at home only pay less as $\bar{s}_1$ has no effect on their money holding S, which is already maximal, but the amount of money subject to tax $S - \bar{s}_1$ diminishes. Therefore, we have again two countervailing effects and two groups separated by $S_0(w, \bar{s}_1)$. It is obvious that the distribution of (w, S), but also all other parameters including risk aversion, are very important to determine the net effect for the whole economy. If $R_A(z) = (az + b)^{-1}$, we know that $s_{1,\bar{s}_1}$ is independent of (w, S), therefore our condition concerning $\bar{s}_1 > 0$ becomes simplified to $\int_{SA} d\mu > (s_{1,\bar{s}_1})^{-1} < 1$. Also, if μ has a density with compact support CS, we may obtain a similar condition. $\min_{CS} s_{1,\bar{s}_1} = s^m_{1,\bar{s}_1}$ exists and our condition for a positive $\bar{s}_1$ is given by $\int_{CS} d\mu > (s^m_{1,\bar{s}_1})^{-1} < 1$.

If there is enough weight on SA, an exemption should always be introduced. This is equivalent to saying that only few agents have already invested all their money at home. If we assume - which is rather realistic - that there is a positive correlation between w and S, demonstrated by a strip between the two straight lines A and B with a positive slope, and if this strip lies for the most part above $S_0(w)$, a tax exemption is desirable. F should *always*, and for all possible preferences, be introduced if it lies totally above $S_0(w, 0)$. If one of the other parameters α, p or R_2 decreases, there are two countervailing effects. We know that $S_0(w)$ increases; more agents invest at home only, and $\int_{SA} d\mu$ becomes smaller. On the other hand, for smaller α, p the agents become less cautious and invest more at home. But then the effect $s_{1,\bar{s}_1}$ also becomes larger; the instruments α, p and $\bar{s}_1$ are "no complements but substitutes" which impairs their total effect when they are used together. In any case, it is not clear which of the two effects dominates the other. However, if we have a compact support if p is decreased sufficiently we should dispense with $\bar{s}_1$. The same is true for α or R_2 if the effect is large enough. This, of course, will again depend on all parameters, but also on $R_R(t)$.

Up to now we have considered all the instruments separately. All have shown a lot of disadvantages; in any case, p seems to be the most effective one. Therefore, in a last step we consider all instruments together.

Proposition 14 *Assume that all instruments are available. Then Σ and T become maximal if $(\alpha, p, b_1, \bar{s}_1) = (0, 0, 1 - R_2 r_1^{-1}, 0)$, whereas $\Sigma = \Sigma_{\max}$, tax receipts $T < T_{\max}$. The larger R_2, the smaller T.*

We see that there should be no more investigation and fining. As there is no longer any risk for the consumers they will keep all their money at home, thereby evading tax on all interest income. The government should then try to maximize its receipts by raising b_1 up to a point where the foreign asset and the inland asset are equally attractive. Obviously the per unit return of the foreign asset R_2 is very important for b_1. If R_2 is rather large, the government has only a limited range for varying b_1, and thus also small tax receipts. Therefore, it might be in the interest of the government to enter into negotiations with the government of another country about the taxation at source in the two countries concerned. This could be an interesting extension, a further one, to introduce transaction costs. To invest abroad is costly, and some groups of agents may not be prepared to pay those costs. These points should be the subject of further research.

6 Proofs

We will use the following additional abbreviations: $\rho := r_1(1-\tau) - R_2, \gamma := S + w(1-\tau), \delta := \gamma + R_2 S$.

Lemma 1 Assume there is a tax exemption $F = r_1\bar{s}_1$. If $s_1 \leq \bar{s}_1$ it is not necessary to evade anything and we have $Q = P = \delta + s_1(r_1 - R_2)$. If $s_1 > \bar{s}_1$ he gets $r_1\bar{s}_1$ for sure. The decision how much to evade - abroad he evades everything - is then taken with respect to $\tilde{s}_1 = s_1 - \bar{s}_1$ whereby $H_1 \leq r_1\tilde{s}_1$. Then $Q = \delta + s_1\rho + (\tau - b_1)H_1 + \tau r_1\bar{s}_1$. For P we obtain $P = Q - (\alpha+1)(\tau - b_1)H_1$. As long as $q - \alpha p > 0$ we have $H_1 > 0$. We can directly demonstrate that for $\rho < 0$ always $H_1 = r_1\tilde{s}_1$; for $\rho \geq 0$ we get $H_1 = H_1^* \leq r_1\tilde{s}_1$. On the other hand, as long as $\rho > 0$ we have $s_1 = S$ with $H_1^* \leq r_1(S - \bar{s}_1)$, in $\rho = 0$ we obtain $s_1 \in [s_1^*, S]$ with $s_1^* \leq S$ and $H_1^* = r_1(s_1^* - \bar{s}_1)$. For $\rho < 0$ everything is evaded. Then $\bar{Q} = \delta + s_1 x + r_1\bar{s}_1 b_1, \bar{P} = \bar{Q} - y\tilde{s}_1 = \delta + s_1(x-y) + (y + r_1 b_1)\bar{s}_1$. To determine the optimal s_1, we have to consider $G(s_1)$ which is equal to $u(\delta + s_1(r_1 - R_2))$ for $s_1 \leq \bar{s}_1$ and equal to $qu(\bar{Q}) + pu(\bar{P})$ for $s_1 > \bar{s}_1$, where $\bar{Q}, \bar{P}$ are defined above. G is differentiable, with the exception of $s_1 = \bar{s}_1$, where $\lim_{s_1 \downarrow \bar{s}_1} G'(s_1) = (x - py)u'(\delta + \bar{s}_1(r_1 - R_2))$ and $\lim_{s_1 \uparrow \bar{s}_1} G'(s_1) = (r_1 - R_2)u'(\delta + \bar{s}_1(r_1 - R_2))$. As $r_1 - R_2 > x - py$ the left side derivative is larger than the right side one. Both functions which define G are concave. We directly see that $s_1 = 0$ if $r_1 < R_2$ and $s_1 \geq \bar{s}_1$ for $r_1 > R_2$. For $r_1 = R_2$ the agent is indifferent between all values $[0, \bar{s}_1]$. On the other hand, as long as $x - py > 0 \Leftrightarrow ER_1 > 0$ we have $s_1 > \bar{s}_1$ and $s_1 = \bar{s}_1$ for $x - py \leq 0$. Only for $R_2 \in (r_1(1-\tau), R_1 - py)$ we have to look whether we get an interior solution $s_1 < S$ or $s_1 = S$. This is valid iff $G'(S) = qxu'(\gamma + SR_1 + r_1 b_1 \bar{s}_1) + p(x - y)u'(\gamma + S(R_1 - y) + (y + r_1 b_1)\bar{s}_1) < 0 (\geq 0)$. To see which condition is fulfilled we vary S. The case $S \leq \bar{s}_1$ was already dealt with. Assume therefore $S > \bar{s}_1$ and $x > py$, as otherwise always $s_1 \leq \bar{s}_1$. We have $\lim_{S \downarrow s_1} G'(S) = G'(\bar{s}_1) = (x - py)u'(\gamma + \bar{s}_1 r_1) > 0$, implying that also in a (right) neighborhood of $\bar{s}_1$ we obtain a boundary solution as $G'(S) > 0$. Increase S now. It will depend on R_A, R_R, but also on the (R_2, b_1) combination whether we get $s_1 < S$ or not. In any case if R_2 is sufficiently large we obtain $s_1 < S$, as always $G'(S) < (x - py)u'(P) = 0$ for $x = py$. In an interior solution we have $G'(s_1) = 0 = qxu'(\delta + s_1 x + b_1 r_1 \bar{s}_1) + p(x - y)u'(\delta + s_1(x - y) + (r_1 b_1 + y)\bar{s}_1)$. $N := G'_{s_1}(s_1) = qx^2 u''(Q) + p(x - y)^2 u''(P) = -qxu'(Q)(R_A(Q)x + (y - x)R_A(P)) < 0$. Using the implicit function theorem s_1 will be a function of all relevant variables, $s_1(\delta, x, r_1, b_1, y, q, \bar{s}_1)$.

Proposition 1 The derivative $s_{1,\bar{s}_1}$ is given by $-N^{-1}(qxu''(Q)$ $r_1 b_1 + p(x-y)u''(P)(r_1 b_1 + y)) = [b_1 r_1 Z + yR_A(P)]H^{-1} = 1 + (r_1 - R_2)ZH^{-1}$ with $Z := R_A(P) - R_A(Q)$ and $H := xR_A(Q) + (y - x)R_A(P) > 0$. Therefore $s_{1,\bar{s}_1} \gtreqless 1 \Leftrightarrow R'_A \lesseqgtr 0$. Even for $R'_A > 0$ the derivative is positive for $b_1 = 0$. Consider again $G'(s_1) = 0$, with $\bar{s}_1 = 0$, such that $qxu'(\delta + s_1 x) + p(x - y)u'(\delta + s_1(x - y)) = 0$. For every variable $z \neq p$ we have $s_{1,z} = -N^{-1}(qxu''(Q)Q_z + p(x - y)u''(P)P_z + qu'(Q)x_z + pu'(P)(x - y)_z) = [(y - x)x_z + x(x - y)_z + x(y - x)(R_A(P)P_z - R_A(Q)Q_z)][x(y - x)H^{-1}]$. As the nominator is always positive the sign of $s_{1,z}$is always identical to that of the denominator.

Proposition 2 For $z = \delta$ we obtain $x_z = (x - y)_z = 0$, $Q_z = P_z = 1$, therefore $s_{1,\delta} = ZH^{-1} \gtreqless 0 \Leftrightarrow R'_A \lesseqgtr 0$. $s_{1,\delta}\delta s_1^{-1} \gtreqless 1 \Leftrightarrow Z\delta \gtreqless R_A(Q)s_1 x - R_A(P)s_1(x - y) \Leftrightarrow R'_R \lesseqgtr 0$. As $\delta = w(1 - \tau) + S(1 + R_2)$ we have $s_{1,S} = (1 + R_2)s_{1,\delta}$ and $s_{1,w} = (1 - \tau)s_{1,\delta}$, the sign of both derivatives is the same as sign $s_{1,\delta}$. If $R'_R \geq 0$ we have $s_{1,\delta} \leq s_1\delta^{-1}$ or $s_{1,S} \leq s_1(1 + R_2)\delta^{-1} < S(1 + R_2)\delta^{-1} < 1.(s_1/S)_S = (s_{1,S}S - s_1)S^{-2}$. The bracket is equal to $(\delta - w(1 - \tau))s_{1,\delta} - s_1 < s_1(-w(1 - \tau)\delta^{-1}) < 0$ if $R'_R \geq 0$.

Proposition 3 Write the derivative $u'(t)$ in another way. Start with $R_A(t) = -u''(t)/u'(t)$. Integrating this equation and applying the exponential function we get $u'(t) = u'(t_0)exp(-J(t_0, t))$ with $J(t_0, t) = \int_{t_0}^{t} R_A(z)dz$ and $0 < t_0 < t$. We see: $\lim_{t_0 \to 0} u'(t_0) = \infty$ is equivalent with $\int_{t_0}^{t} R_A(z)dz \to \infty$ for $t_0 \to 0$

as $u'(t)$ remains bounded. Consider next $G'(S) = qxu'(Q) + p(x-y)u'(P)$ with $Q = w(1-\tau)+S(1+R_1)$ and $P = Q - Sy$. We already know: as long as $G'(S) \geq 0$ we have $s_1 = S$, for $G'(S) < 0$ we obtain $s_1 < S$. For $w > 0$ and S small we always have $s_1 = S$ as $G'(0) = (x-py)u'(w(1-\tau)) > 0$ and the same must be valid for small S because of continuity. What will happen in $w = 0$ or S large? $G'(S) \lesseqgtr 0 \Leftrightarrow A = A(p,x,y) = qx[p(y-x)]^{-1} \lesseqgtr F_0(S)$ with $F_0(S) = (u'(P)(u'(Q))^{-1} = exp(J(P,Q))$ using our formula from above. For $w > 0$ but $S = 0$ we have $P = Q > 0$ therefore $J(P,Q) = 0$ and $F_0(0) = 1 < A$, implying $s_1 = S$ in a suitable neighborhood of $S = 0$. To determine s_1 for large S consider $\lim_{S\to\infty} F_0(S) = exp(\lim J(P,Q))$. Start with $y \geq 1 + R_1$. This implies $P = w(1-\tau)$ or $P \to 0$ for S becoming bigger, $Q \to \infty$ for $S \to \infty$. As $u'(w(1-\tau)) > 0$ and also $u'(0) > 0$, but $u'(\infty) = 0$ we have $F_0(S) \to \infty$ for $S \to \infty$. Therefore always $s_1 < S$ for large S. Assume next $y < 1 + R_1$. For $R_A' \geq 0$ we have $J(P,Q) \geq (Q-P)R_A(P) = SyP^{-1}R_R(P) \to_{S\to\infty} \infty$ as $SyP^{-1} \to y(1+R_1-y)^{-1} > 0$ and $R_R \to \infty$ because of $R_A' \geq 0$. If $R_A' < 0$ we obtain: For $[P,Q]$, R_R is a continuous function, therefore $\max R_R$ and $\min R_R$ exist for $[P,Q]$. Denote them by $R^{\max}(P,Q)$ and $R^{\min}(P,Q)$. Then $R^{\max}(P,Q)t^{-1} \geq R_R(t)t^{-1} = R_A(t) \geq R^{\min}(P,Q)t^{-1}$ for all $t \in [P,Q]$, implying that $R^{\max}(P,Q)\ln(QP^{-1}) \geq J(P,Q) \geq R^{\min}(P,Q)\ln(QP^{-1})$. For $S \to \infty \lim QP^{-1} = REV$; on the other hand also $(P,Q) \to \infty$. If $R_R(t) \to \infty$ for $t \to \infty$ then also $R^{\min}(P,Q) \to \infty$ and $J(P,Q) \to \infty$. If $R_R(\infty) = K < \infty$ we obtain $(R^{\min}, R^{\max}) \to K$ and therefore $K\ln(REV) = \lim J(P,Q)$. If $R_R(\infty) = \infty$ we always have $s_1 < S$ for large S as $A(p,x,y)$ is always finite as long as $p > 0$ and $R_2 > r_1(1-\tau)$. If $R_R(\infty) = R^\infty < \infty$ we obtain $G'(S) < 0$ if $\ln A < R^\infty \ln(REV)$ or $R^\infty > \ln A[\ln(REV)]^{-1}$. Differentiating $F_0(S)$, we obtain $F_0'(S) = F_0(S)(R_A(Q)(1+R_1) - R_A(P)(1+R_1-y))$. For every $w > 0$ we get $Q = P$ for $S = 0$ and therefore $F_0'(0) = R_A(w(1-\tau))y > 0$, F is always increasing in a neighborhood of 0. More generally, F_0 is strictly increasing over the whole range if $y \geq 1 + R_1$ or $R_R' \geq 0$. The first is clear at once, for the second rewrite the bracket in $F_0'(S)$ as $R_R(Q)(1+R_1)Q^{-1} - R_R(P)P^{-1}(1+R_1-y) \geq R_R(P)P^{-1}Q^{-1}yw(1-\tau) > 0$. To deal with the case $R_R' < 0$ we write w.l.o.g. $R_A(z) = (f(z))^{-1}$ with $f'(z) > 0$. If F_0 is still increasing all the time we are ready, so assume that for a given w_0 there is a S_0 such that $F_0'(S_0) = 0 \Leftrightarrow R_A(Q)(1+R_1) = R_A(P)(1+R_1-y)$. The second derivative of F is equal to $F_0''(S) = F_0'(S)(R_A(Q)(1+R_1) - R_A(P)(1+R_1-y)) + F_0(S)(R_A'(Q)(1+R_1)^2 - R_A'(P)(1+R_1-y)^2)$ with $F_0''(S_0) = F_0(S_0)(1+R_1)^2(f(Q))^{-2}(f'(P) - f'(Q))$ where we have used $F_0'(S_0) = 0$ and $R_A'(z) = -f'(z)(f(z))^{-2}$. As $R_R'(z) = (f(z) - zf'(z))(f(z))^{-2}$ we know: If f is concave, i.e. $f'' < 0$, $f(z)z^{-1}$ decreases, therefore $R_R' > 0$ what was already dealt with; we can restrict ourselves to functions with $f'' \geq 0$. If $f'' > 0$, we obtain $F_0''(S_0) < 0$, F must be concave in S_0, i.e. S_0 is local maximum. As this must be valid for every other zero point of F', there can be at most one such point S_0. This implies that F_0 is strictly increasing up to S_0 and then strictly decreasing. As $F_0(0) = 1 < A < F_0(\infty)$ we have that $F_0(S_0) > A$ and using the intermediate value theorem there is one point $\tilde{S}$ with $F_0(\tilde{S}) = A$ which must be unique because $F_0'(\tilde{S}) > 0$ on $[0, S_0]$. Consider at last $f'' = 0 \Leftrightarrow f(z) = az + b; b \in R, a \in R_+$. If $b \geq 0$ we have $R_R' \geq 0$, therefore assume $b < 0$. (This implies, of course, that always $z > |b|a^{-1}$, otherwise R_A is not defined.) Assume that there is a point S_0 with $F_0'(S_0) = 0 \Leftrightarrow (1 + R_1)(aP + b) = (1 + R_1 - y)(aQ + b) \Leftrightarrow Q - w(1-\tau))(aP+b) = (P - w(1-\tau))(aQ+b) \Leftrightarrow (Q-P)b = w(1-\tau)a(P-Q)$ or $w_0(1 - \tau) = |b|a^{-1}$. Therefore, for all $w > w_0$ we always have $F_0' > 0$. In w_0 we get $F_0'(S) \equiv 0$ for all S and as always $F_0(0) = 1$ we get that in w_0 always $s_1 = S$. If for utilities with $R_A' < 0$ and $R_R' \geq 0$ we have that $A(p, x, y) \geq \lim_{S \to \infty} F_0(S)$ for all w, (what is only possible for $R_A' < 0$, as otherwise $F_0(\infty) = \infty$) then always $s_1(w, S) = S$ as in such a case $G'(S) \geq 0$ for all S because $F_0(S)$ is increasing in S. The condition for this result is equivalent to $\ln A \geq J(P, Q) = \int_P^Q R_R(t)t^{-1}dt$. But we have already shown above that for $R_A' < 0$ and $R_R' \geq 0$ we get $R_R(Q)\ln(QP^{-1}) \geq J(P, Q) \geq R_R(P)\ln(QP^{-1})$. For $S \to \infty$ we have $\lim R_R(Q) = \lim R_R(P) = R < \infty$ and $\lim(QP^{-1}) = REV$. Therefore $\lim J(P, Q) = R\ln(REV)$ and our condition can be written as $A \geq (REV)^R$. We have already demonstrated: $F_0(S)$ is strictly increasing (at least in the relevant range) if $y \geq 1 + R_1$ or $R_A' \geq 0$ or if $R_A' < 0$ and $R_A(z) = (f(z))^{-1}$, when f' is monotone, i.e. for $f'' \gtreqless 0$. In all these cases there can be at most one solution, i.e. at most one $S_0(w)$ with $A = F_0(S_0(S_0(w))$ where also $F_{0,S}(S) = F_0'(S) > 0$. Therefore if also $R > (\ln A)(\ln REV)^{-1}$ we get a function $S_0(w)$ such that for all $S < S_0(w)$ we have $s_1 = S$ and for all $S > S_0(w)$ we obtain $s_1 < S$. Because $F_0'(S) > 0$ we can apply the implicit function theorem. Then $S_0(w)$ is a differentiable function with separates total from partial evaders.

Proposition 4 The derivative of $S_0(w)$ is given by: $S_0'(w) = -F_{0,w}(S)/F_{0,S}(S) = (1 - \tau)Z(R_A(Q)(1 + R_1) - R_A(P)(1 + R_1 - y))^{-1}$. We directly see: $S_0'(w) \gtreqless 0 \Leftrightarrow R_A' \lesseqgtr 0$. Some tedious computation shows that $sign S_0''(w) = sign(R_A'(P)R_A^2(Q) - R_A'(Q)R_A^2(P))$. Using again $R_A(z) = (f(z))^{-1}$ for $R_A' \leq 0$ we see: $S_0''(w) \gtreqless 0 \Leftrightarrow f'' \gtreqless 0$. Consider next the boundary behavior of $S_0(w)$. As $\ln A = J(P, Q)$ this integral must be constant if only w (and then $S_0(w)$) change. Consider $R_A' < 0$ only (as only here $S_0'(w) > 0$). It is obvious that $R_A(P)S_0(w)y > J(P, Q) > R_A(Q)S_0(w)y$. If $w \to \infty$ then in any case, independently of $S_0(w)$, $P \to \infty$ and $Q \to \infty$, too. But this implies that $R_A(\infty) = 0 \Leftrightarrow S_0(\infty) = \infty$ and $R_A(\infty) > 0 \Leftrightarrow S_0(\infty) < \infty$ as $0 < J(P, Q) = K < \infty$. Consider the behavior for $w = 0$ next. As R_R is continuous for every interval $[P, Q]$ the maximum and the minimum of R_R exist, denote them by $R_R^{\max} R(P, Q)$ and $R_R^{\min}(P, Q)$. Then $R_R^{\max}(P, Q)t^{-1} \geq R_R(t)t^{-1} = R_A(t) \geq R_R^{\min}(P, Q)t^{-1}$ for all $t \in [P, Q]$ implying that $R_R^{\max}\ln(QP^{-1}) \geq J(P, Q) \geq R_R^{\min}\ln(QP^{-1})$. Assume that $(w, S) \to 0$. Then $(P, Q) \to 0$, as always $R_R \geq 0$ and, according to Arrow, $R_R(\epsilon) < 1$ for small ϵ, $\lim_{z\to 0} R_R(z)$ must exist and $\lim R_R(P) = \lim R_R(Q) = R_R(0) \geq 0$. The limes of QP^{-1} does not exist, consider for this $S = \lambda w, 0 \leq \lambda \leq \infty$. Then $QP^{-1} = ((1-\tau) + \lambda(1+R_1))((1-\tau) + \lambda(1+R_1-y))^{-1} = \lim QP^{-1}$ for $S = \lambda w$ and $w \to 0$). It can directly be seen that $(QP^{-1})'(\lambda) > 0$; if λ increases QP^{-1} increases. $QP^{-1}(0) = 1, QP^{-1}(\infty) = REV$. Therefore QP^{-1} which is continuous on $R^2_+ - \{0\}$ is a correspondence in the zero-point with values contained in $[1, REV]$. We therefore have to distinguish two cases: If $R_R(0) = 0$ then $\lim R_R \ln(QP^{-1})$ exists again and is equal to zero, therefore $\lim F_0(S) = e^0 = 1$ for any sequence $(w, S) \to 0$. As $A > 1$ we see that $s_1 = S$ for small S, even for $w = 0$, implying that $S_0(0) > 0$. For $R_R(0) > 0$ we obtain for $w = 0$ that $F_0(0) \in [1, (REV)^{R_R(0)}]$ Again, if $REV^{R_R(0)} < A \Leftrightarrow R_R(0) < (\ln A)(\ln REV)^{-1}$ we obtain $S_0(0) > 0$, if $1 < A \leq REV^{R_R(0)}$ we get $S_0(0) = 0$.

Lemma 2 $s_1(w, S_0(.), .) - S_0(.) = 0$ defines S_0 implicitly. We obtain for any variable v: $s_{1,S}S_{0,v} + s_{1,v} = S_{0,v}$ or $S_{0,v} = s_{1,v}(1 - s_{1,S})^{-1}$. S_0 exists if $y \geq 1 + R_1$ or $R_R' \geq 0$. These conditions also assure that $s_{1,S} < 1$, therefore sign $S_{0,v}$ equal sign $s_{1,v}$. It was shown in Tillmann (1998), that $s_{1,\alpha}$, $s_{1,p} < 0$, also $s_{1,R_2}|s_1 = S < 0$, on the other hand $s_{1,b_1} = s_{1,b_1}|s_1 = S \gtrless 0$, depending upon whether b_1 is small ($s_{1,b_1} > 0$) or b_1 is large ($s_{1,b_1} < 0$). For $\bar{s}_1$ we have $s_{1,\bar{s}_1} > 0$ if $R_A' \leq 0$ as was already demonstrated in proposition 2.

Proposition 5 This proof is omitted, compare Tillmann (1998).

Proposition 6 If we have a tax exemption $F = r_1\bar{s}_1$ we need to consider $S > \bar{s}_1$ only. As long as $s_1 \geq \bar{s}_1$ we have $Q = \delta + s_1\rho + \tau r_1\bar{s}_1 + (\tau - b_1)H_1$ and $P = Q - (\alpha+1)(\tau - b_1)H_1$ with $H_1 \leq r_1(s_1 - \bar{s}_1)$. Instead of considering $p = 1$ only we take the more general case of $q - \alpha p < 0$. Maximizing $qu(Q) + pu(P)$ with respect to H_1 we see that the derivative in $H_1 = 0$ is negative. As $qu(Q) + pu(P)$ is concave $H_1 = 0$ is optimal, therefore $P = Q = \delta + s_1\varrho + \tau r_1\bar{s}_1$. For $\rho < 0$ we obtain $s_1 = \bar{s}_1$. For $s_1 \leq \bar{s}_1$ there is no uncertainty any longer and $Q = \delta + s_1(r_1 - R_1)$, implying that $s_1 = 0$ for $R_2 > r_1$ and $s_1 = \bar{s}_1$ for $r_1 > R_2$. As for $R_2 > r_1(1-\tau)$ any agent holds at most $\bar{s}_1$ in the inland the tax receipts are zero. That $\Sigma = \Sigma_F$ is also trivial.

For the following propositions we must determine, how Σ and T change when one parameter is altered. We know that $\Sigma(\alpha, p, b_1, \bar{s}_1) = \int s_1(., w, S)d\mu(w, S) = \int_{SB} S d\mu + \int_{SA} s_1(.)d\mu$. If we differentiate Σ with respect to v, where v is one of the four instruments, the two expressions resulting from differentiating with respect to the upper bound of the first integral and the lower bound of the second integral cancel as $s_1(., S_0) = S_0$ and we obtain $\Sigma_v = \int_{SA} s_{1,v}(.)d\mu(w, S)$. The total tax receipts are given by $T(\alpha, p, b_1, \bar{s}_1) = \tau \int w d\mu(w, S) + (b_1 r_1 + py)[\int_{SB1}(S - \bar{s}_1)d\mu(w, S) + \int_{SA}(s_1(.) - \bar{s}_1)d\mu(w, S)]$. The first integral does not depend on any instrument; analogously to Σ the two terms from differentiation with respect to the upper and lower bound of the second and third integral cancel. There remains: $T_v = (b_1 r_1 + py)_v[.] + (b_1 r_1 + py)[\int_{SB1}(S - \bar{s}_1)_v d\mu + \int_{SA}(s_1(.) - \bar{s}_1)_v d\mu]$.

Proposition 7 For $v = \alpha$ we have $\Sigma_\alpha = \int_{SA} s_{1,\alpha}(.)d\mu$. We know that $s_{1,\alpha} < 0$ for all s_1, therefore, as long as $S_0(\alpha, w)$ still exists, $\Sigma_\alpha < 0$. If $R_R(\infty) > AR_0$ we know from proposition 3 that there are always agents with $s_1 < S$, therefore $\Sigma(0) < \Sigma_{\max}$.

Proposition 8 A and also $AR \to \infty$ for $p \to 0$. If $R_R(\infty)$ is finite there must be $p_0 > 0$ such that $AR(p_0) = R_R(\infty)$ and, applying proposition 3, everybody invests in the inland only. The same is true for all $p \leq p_0$. For $p > p_0$ at least for the richest agents $s_1 < S$. As for all those agents $s_{1,p} < 0$ the result follows.

Proposition 9 Setting $v = \alpha$ we obtain $T_\alpha = pr_1(\tau - b_1)\int_{SA1}(s_1(.) - \bar{s}_1)d\mu + (b_1 r_1 + py)\int_{SA} s_{1,\alpha}(.)d\mu$. If $AR_0 > R_R(\infty)$ there is $\alpha_0 > 0$ such that for $\alpha \leq \alpha_0 S_0(\alpha, w) = \infty$. Then even $T_\alpha(\alpha_0) > 0$ and there should always be a positive fine. $T_p = y\int_{SA1}(s_1(.) - \bar{s}_1)d\mu + (b_1 r_1 + py)\int_{SA} s_{1,p}d\mu$. If $R_R(\infty) < \infty$ there is a $p_0 > 0$, such that $S_0(p, w)$ does no longer exist for all $p \leq p_0$. Therefore $T_p > 0$ for all $p < p_0$ and the optimal $p^* \geq p_0$.

Proposition 10 We know that $s_{1,b_1} = 0 \Leftrightarrow B(b_1, R_2, \delta) = (\alpha+1)x - y + x(y - x)s_1(R_A(Q) + \alpha R_A(P))) = 0$. Fixing R_2 we obtain $b_{1,\delta} = -B_\delta(B_{b_1})^{-1}$. We have shown elsewhere (Tillmann 1998) that all points which fulfill $s_{1,b_1} = 0$ must be maxima, therefore $B_{b_1} < 0$ and the sign of $b_{1,\delta}$ equals the sign of $B_\delta = (y - x)x[s_{1,\delta}(R_A(Q) + \alpha R_A(P)) + s_1(R_A'(Q)Q_\delta + \alpha R_A'(P)P_\delta)]$. We already know that $s_{1,\delta} = ZH^{-1}$, therefore $Q_\delta = 1 + x s_{1,\delta} = yR_A(P)H^{-1}$ and $P_\delta = 1 + (x - y)s_{1,\delta} = yR_A(Q)H^{-1}$. Filling in into the square bracket of B_δ we get $Z(R_A(Q) + \alpha R_A(P)) + ys_1(R'_A(Q)R_A(P) + \alpha R_A'(P)R_A(Q))$ where we have omitted the denominator $H > 0$. If $R_A(t) = c$ this expression is zero as $Z = 0 = R_A'$. Consider $R_A' < 0$ with $R_A(t) = f(t))^{-1}$. The expression above is equivalent (considering again the nominator only) to $(*)(f(Q) - f(P))(f(P) + \alpha f(Q)) - (Q - P)(f'(Q)f(P) + \alpha f'(P)f(Q))$. If $f(t) = at + b$, $f'(t) = a$ again this expression is zero whereby $R_A' = 0$ is a special case with $a = 0$. For $b = 0$ the function f describes precisely all functions with $R_R'(t) = 0$.

Proposition 11 We get $\Sigma_{b_1} = \int_{SA} s_{1,b_1}()d\mu$ and $T_{b_1} = r_1(q - \alpha p)\int_{SA1} s_1()d\mu + (b_1 r_1 + py)\int_{SA} s_{1,b_1}()d\mu$. Set $\bar{s}_1 = 0$. If $R_A(t) = (at + b)^{-1}$, we know that $F_0(R_2)$ is independent of δ (and therefore (w, S), too. Therefore Σ becomes maximal in $F_0(R_2)$ and for T we get $b_1^* > F_0(R_2)$.

Proposition 12 We already know that $T(w, S) = w\tau + (b_1 r_1 + py)(s_1 - \bar{s}_1)$. Therefore $T_{\bar{s}_1}(w, S) = (b_1 r_1 + py)(s_{1,\bar{s}_1} - 1)$. Use proposition 1.

Proposition 13 Using Σ_v with $v = \bar{s}_1$ we obtain $\Sigma_{\bar{s}_1} = \int_{SA} s_{1,\bar{s}_1} d\mu > 0$, as $s_{1,\bar{s}_1} > 0$ for $R_A^{'} \leq 0$. For $R_A^{'} \geq 0$ $T_{\bar{s}_1}(w, S) \leq 0$, therefore the same is valid for $T_{\bar{s}_1}$. We obtain $T_{\bar{s}_1} = (b_1 r_1 + py). \left[- \int_{SB1} d\mu + \int_{SA}(s_{1,\bar{s}_1} - 1) d\mu\right] = (b_1 r_1 + py)(- \int_{SA_1} d\mu + \int_{SA} s_{1,\bar{s}_1} d\mu)$. For $\bar{s}_1 = 0$ the first integral is equal to one and the result follows.

Proposition 14 For $p > 0$ we know from lemma 1 that $S \geq s_1 > \bar{s}_1$ if $R_2 < R_1 - py \Leftrightarrow r_1 b_1 + py < r_1 - R_2$. Therefore $T(\alpha, p, b_1, \bar{s}_1) < \tau \int w d\mu + (r_1 - R_2) \int (s_1(.) - \bar{s}_1) d\mu < \tau \int w d\mu + (r_1 - R_2) \int S d\mu$. For $p = 0$ we have to maximize $Q = \delta + s_1 x + \bar{s}_1 r_1 b_1$ only. If $x > 0$ we always obtain $s_1 = S$. (We will assume the same for $x = 0$ where the agents are indifferent.) This implies for T if $\bar{s}_1 = 0$, that $T = \tau \int w d\mu + b_1 r_1 \int S d\mu$. Because of $x \geq 0 \Leftrightarrow r_1(1 - b_1) \geq R_2 \Leftrightarrow r_1 - R_2 \geq r_1 b_1$, $T_{\max}$ will be equal to $\tau \int w d\mu + (r_1 - R_2) \int S d\mu$. But this is also the supremum if $p > 0$. Therefore we should always set $p = 0$ (and then $\alpha = 0$, as a positive α does no longer make any sense economically) and $\bar{s}_1 = 0$, as otherwise we would lose tax receipts. b_1 should be increased as far as possible, namely up to $r_1 - R_2$.

References

1. Allingham, M.G. and A. Sandmo (1972), Income tax evasion: A theoretical analysis, Journal of Public Economics 1, pp. 323-338.
2. Arrow, K.J. (1970), Essays in the theory of risk bearing (North-Holland, Amsterdam), pp. 90-120.
3. Christiansen, V. (1980), Two comments on tax evasion, Journal of Public Economics 14, pp. 389-401.
4. Cowell, F.A. (1981a), Taxation and labour supply with risky activities, Economica 48, pp. 365-379.
5. Cowell, F.A. (1985), Tax evasion with labour income, Journal of Public Economics 26, pp. 19-34.
6. Cowell, F.A. (1987), The economic analysis of tax evasion, in: Hey, J. and P. Lambert (eds.): Surveys in the Economics of uncertainty, London, pp. 173-203.
7. Hagedorn, R. (1989), Die Quellensteuer auf ZinsertrŠge und die Hinterziehung von Einkommensteuern, Finanzarchiv N.F. 47, pp. 24-45.
8. Kolm, S.-C. (1973), A note on optimum tax evasion, Journal of Public Economics 2, pp. 265-270.
9. Sandmo, A. (1981), Income tax evasion, labour supply and the equity-efficiency trade-off, Journal of Public Economics 16, pp. 265-288.
10. Tillmann, G. (1989), Zur Belastungswirkung von Quellensteuer und Kontrollmitteilungen auf unterschiedliche Einkommensgruppen, Finanzarchiv N.F. 47, pp. 428-459.
11. Tillmann, G. (1998), Tax evasion in an open economy, University of Mainz, mimeo
12. Tillmann, G. (1999), Interest income evasion in a two country model, University of Mainz, mimeo

13. Yaniv, G. (1988), Withholding and not-withheld tax evasion, Journal of Public Economics 35, pp. 183-204.
14. Yaniv, G. (1990), Tax evasion under differential taxation, Journal of Public Economics 43, pp. 327-337.
15. Yitzhaki, S. (1974), A note on income tax evasion: A theoretical analysis, Journal of Public Economics 3, pp. 201-202.

GPSR Compliance

The European Union's (EU) General Product Safety Regulation (GPSR) is a set of rules that requires consumer products to be safe and our obligations to ensure this.

If you have any concerns about our products, you can contact us on ProductSafety@springernature.com

In case Publisher is established outside the EU, the EU authorized representative is:

Springer Nature Customer Service Center GmbH
Europaplatz 3
69115 Heidelberg, Germany

Batch number: 10682207

Printed by Printforce, the Netherlands